Stockport County

Stockport County

A Complete Record

PETER FREEMAN
with assistance from
RICHARD HARNWELL

Breedon Books
Publishing Company
Derby

First published in Great Britain by
The Breedon Books Publishing Company Limited
44 Friar Gate, Derby, DE1 1DA
1994

ISBN 1 873626 72 X

Printed and bound by Butler & Tanner, Frome, Somerset
Covers printed by BDC Printing Services Limited of Derby

– Contents –

Introduction

WHEN I first undertook the task of writing this book, although I was under no illusions as to the likelihood that a tremendous amount of work would be involved, I had no conception of the problems with which I would be confronted. From previous experience, I was used to library work but gathering the material for *Stockport County: A Complete Record* was a totally unpredicted ordeal. That is not to say that the thousands of hours spent have been painful, for much of the research has been fascinating and thoroughly enjoyable, but simply that the range of problems was immense. One major difficulty has been that none of the many sources used could be relied upon with total confidence; this has resulted in having to accept that the best I could do was to adopt a consistent approach, note discrepancies and, at times, provide my own solution.

Unlike the majority of authors in Breedon's Complete Record series, I have been neither a football statistician nor a football historian; for some 30 years I have been, and remain, quite simply, a County supporter. I cannot boast that I have been visiting Edgeley Park since I first took an interest in football. Although born in Manchester, I spent the first 11 years of my supporting career following West Bromwich Albion. Looking back, I suspect that there are only two possible reasons for this: either I was so bloody-minded that I refused to support either City or United or, more likely, because the first game I saw was an end-of-season match at Old Trafford between Manchester United and West Brom. As an impressionable seven-year-old, I probably felt sorry for the team that had little support and, within the first 45 minutes and almost before I knew it, I became a Baggies fan. The next 12 years saw me following my adopted team whenever they were in the North-West but it was not until my family moved all of a mile and a half over the Manchester border into Stockport that I became aware of the Fourth Division team down the road.

In November 1964, and at a loose end, a friend and I went to Edgeley Park for a laugh to see a team which was bottom of the League and experiencing their worst-ever start to a season. A 1-1 draw and, incomprehensibly, that was it - I was smitten. In the event, I was fortunate as County were in the process of embarking upon their last great FA Cup run. As one of the 19,654 who saw the third-round game against Bristol Rovers in January 1965, I would defy anyone to fail to have been affected by the hysteria of that evening. Nonetheless, the twin loves of County and West Brom lived in reasonable harmony for another six or seven years until, in the early 1970s, I realised that trips to The Hawthorns were becoming fewer and fewer. By this time, visits to Edgeley Park involved a round-trip of 70 miles and, despite the sterility of much of the football I saw, I realised all too late that I had become addicted and that there was no cure.

As the research for this book developed, I became aware that the suffering involved in watching my team, whose poverty (in every way) was remarkably consistent for 20 years, was similar to that which generations of County followers had endured. For a comparatively select number of clubs, their history is steeped in tradition; some have enjoyed success in modern times whilst others look back longingly to a golden era. However, whilst these clubs have provided some wonderful teams and great players, they cannot match County's achievement: survival against the odds in a way which almost defies credibility. County have never had a golden era; there is no history of success, no nostalgic looking back at glory years. They can point to the occasional success, be it promotion years, the very infrequent exciting Cup run and, recently, undreamed of appearances at Wembley, but County's continued existence is their greatest achievement, the fact that, with the exception of one season, they have retained their Football League status since 1900.

A comprehensive study of County's 103 years of competitive football demonstrates that, from the earliest days, the club has struggled for survival. It has moved from one financial crisis to another, appeals to the Stockport public to help the club maintain its existence repeated in every decade since 1900. It has never enjoyed a period when it could compete in the transfer market or hold on to the talented players it had developed or acquired; selling to survive has existed since Tommy Brittleton's departure to Sheffield Wednesday in 1905. Whilst many other clubs would argue that they have experienced precisely the same problems, virtually none have survived so long. Of the 26 clubs who have played more League games than County, only one other has failed to achieve First Division status, namely Lincoln City. The fact that this book is published is a testament to all those who, in the face of adversity, have somehow managed to keep the club afloat. It is in this context that the successes of the last five years should be viewed, County's recent achievements verging on the extraordinary.

The season-by-season records cover every competitive League match played by County's First XI since 1891, the year in which the club first played League football by being accepted into The Combination. In addition to the period prior to County being elected to the Football League (1891-1900), Lancashire Combination results are included for the single season (1904-05) between failure to gain re-election in May 1904 and subsequent election in May 1905. Details of every FA Cup, Football League Cup and Divisional competitions are also included.

One of the consequences of the devastating fire which destroyed the grandstand in July 1935 was that all records were lost. As a result, statistical information has been gleaned from various sources, in particular contemporary newspapers and Football League records. Dates of matches, opponents, results and goalscorers have been, at the very least, triple-checked, but it is acknowledged that goalscorers cited must occasionally be accepted as open to question. The principle followed has been to use the Stockport-based *Cheshire Daily Echo* as the primary source for all matches played until the end of 1939 (the year in which that newspaper ceased publication), supplemented by the *Stockport Chronicle* published from 1891-1906 and the *Cheshire County News*, published from 1876-1912. Up to ten other newspapers have been consulted in cases where there appears to be any discrepancy but even this cannot guarantee that every piece of information is 100 per cent accurate. Players' names are taken from official Football League records but, in the case of individuals who played in the early part of this century, the spelling of such names may be inconsistent with newspaper versions.

Official League attendances are given from 1925-26, this being the first season that the Football League kept such records. All Football League and League Cup attendances stated are those recorded by the Football League even where they conflict with well-publicised published figures, the most notable discrepancy concerning the record League attendance at Edgeley Park on 1 May 1937. FA Cup attendances are given for almost every match since County's first entry in 1892-93, although those given for pre-World War One games are estimated and clearly not official.

As far as factual information is concerned, it would be hugely satisfying to state that every piece of information included is guaranteed error-free, but this is not the case. Since this is the first comprehensive record of County matches, some mistakes are inevitable; all I can promise is that I have made every effort to ensure accuracy. Should the publishers be sufficiently generous to produce a second edition, in addition to mistakes which I discover, I have little doubt that readers will have communicated errors which could then be corrected. With regard to non-factual material, any views expressed are personal, made as a supporter of Stockport County and which, presumably, include certain prejudices which are inherent in any supporter. For that, I make no excuse.

Peter Freeman
July 1994

Acknowledgements

It appears to be common practice for acknowledgements to be somewhat brief but, whilst accepting that it is impossible to mention every person who has provided me with some help, I make no apology for giving a comprehensive thank you to a relatively large number of people.

Had County historian Richard Harnwell not been in a position to supply me with some match details for the early 1900s, I would, in all probability, never have embarked upon this project. Richard has spent considerable time interviewing players, both past and present, collecting details for many post-war biographies and borrowing a number of photographs used within the Complete Record. He has provided photographs from his own collection and, additionally, collated details of some of the memorable matches which are incorporated into the text.

The following former players have provided invaluable assistance in terms of providing detail and lending photographs from their personal collections: Arthur Burrows, Jack Connor, Tony Coyle, Ted Critchley, Ray Drake, Jabez Foulkes, Fred Goodwin, Tony Hancock, David Herd, Ken Hodder, Bill Holden, Andy Kilner, Sammy McMillan, Eddie Moran, Bob Murray, Trevor Porteous, Johnny Price, Hugh Ryden, Ken Shaw, Arthur Woodcock, Ray Weigh, Gordon Wilmott and Gene Wilson. The current squad at County have been very helpful as have many other former players who have furnished details about their careers. Families of former players have also been generous in giving up time to search their lofts for old photographs and memorabilia and personal thanks go to Steven Johnston, Sheila Paterson and Elizabeth Stevenson. At Edgeley Park, Steve Bellis has been consistently helpful and is deserving of credit.

Valuable support has been given in a variety of ways by John Bourne, Stephen Byrne, Alec Calvert, Bill Green, Marcus Heap, Howard Jones, Bob Jeffries, Dave Johnson, Dave McPherson, Ray Simpson, Roy Smith and John Snellgrove. Particular thanks are owed to Allan Jones who has made available his enormous collection of photographs, programmes and other material. The reproduction of old photographs has been highly important and I am especially grateful to Carol Longford at Stoke-on-Trent and Paul Sidebotham of Oasis Photographics, Stockport.

The friendly and efficient help given by the staff of Stockport Local Studies Library has been quite superb, as has the support of the British Newspaper Library at Colindale. The Football League have readily made available all their relevant volumes of information, and done so in the most hospitable way possible. Specific mention of members of staff at Lytham St. Annes is necessary, namely Lorna Parnell, Chris Pickford and Nicola Deluce.

It is easy to forget the incalculable help provided by those around you. Whilst Richard Harnwell has been ably supported by his wife Nicola, I have enjoyed the support, both direct and indirect, of my family: my younger daughter Simone, who has saved me hours of time by accompanying me to the Football League, my older daughter Reva and my wife Teresa. The nightmare task of proof-reading has been made almost tolerable by Simone, Teresa and close friends Geoff Hawley and Stephen Pratt. Acknowledging indirect assistance enables me to express my gratitude to Dr Geryl Rees who has probably been unaware that her professional and sensitive care has helped to provide me with the resolve to complete this book.

I have come to realise why other titles in this series direct specific thanks to Anton Rippon and others at Breedon Books. As a result of various obstacles, it has not been the easiest task to get this book published and, throughout, Breedon have been long-suffering and patient. I can only hope that all at Breedon Books find the completed exercise proves to be worthwhile.

Identifying all the people who have helped in other ways would make an already enormous list unmanageable, but, for those who have given me a lead or provided the odd snippet of information, many, many thanks, together with apologies for not naming you all.

Peter Freeman
July 1994

Photographs

As the vast majority of photographs have been borrowed and bear no identifiable source, acknowledgement is not possible. Others have been used courtesy of Freelance Pictures, Stockport County FC and the *Stockport Express*. The EMPICS Agency of Nottingham supplied the colour picture of Kevin Francis used on the front cover as well as some of the photographs from County's various Wembley appearances.

Dedication

This book is dedicated to the 1,039 supporters who watched
County's worst attended home League game on 15 February 1985.

From Wycliffe to Wembley
A History of Stockport County

ppp 'The story of . . .the existence of Stockport County is not one of notable triumphs, and of success followed by success. It is a story of a club always fighting against adversity, of heroic efforts to keep going despite discouragement and ill-luck, and yet I doubt whether any of the stalwarts who all along have backed up the club would have the story different, for the real test of loyalty is steadfastness in the face of misfortune.'

Cheshire Daily Echo 8 August 1933

STOCKPORT County have never been one of the big or famous clubs and, as a result, their early history is far from well-documented. Little corroborative evidence remains of their earliest days; that which did exist was destroyed in the Edgeley Park fire of July 1935. The origins of the club are found in reflections of former players many years after the event and, by their nature, are impossible to verify. If the passing of time dimmed the memory of those who first brought together the team that would become Stockport County, there is no way of authenticating what has since become acknowledged as accepted fact.

There is no doubt that Heaton Norris Rovers were the team which later became Stockport County, but the development of the original club is, to say the least, blurred. Those players who, as young men, had formed the club, explained that in the autumn of 1883, whilst members of Wycliffe Congregational Church, they decided to 'get an association football team together', rugby being by far the major sport in the town at that time. Subsequently, a group met at McLaughlin's Temperance Bar and Restaurant, a well known cafe close to the town centre, and established a 'junior' club. Whether they adopted the name of Heaton Norris Rovers at the outset is not known, for there are no newspaper reports of such a team's existence until approximately a year later. One possible reference to the club might be found in a brief piece in *The Advertiser* in January 1884, reporting a football match in which Wycliffe CC defeated Belmont 3-1 at the Heaton Norris Recreation Ground, an area which has remained virtually unchanged. As this parkland is supposedly where Heaton Norris Rovers began their football, it is possible that Wycliffe CC was the original Heaton Norris Rovers. However, whilst the fire of 1935 destroyed such

In this 1905 photograph of Wellington Road South, on the right of the tram is McLaughlin's Cafe (actually 'Temperance and Restaurant Bar') where the young members of the Wycliffe Congregational Church held a meeting in 1883 to form Heaton Norris Rovers, the County club's original name. The bar was well-known as a 'favourite haunt of footballers and young men of the town'.

confirmation, according to an article in the *Cheshire Daily Echo* in the Jubilee season of 1933-34, 'there is evidence that the Rovers were in existence before [the autumn of 1884], for in the Boardroom of the County the balance sheet and fixtures for the season 1883-84 are framed for all to see.'

By the beginning of 1884-85, it appears that the Norrisites, as they became known, had moved to Lomas's field on the site of the Heaton Norris Wanderers Cricket Ground, adjacent to Ring Avenue, Brinksway. The ground became the site for the Ring Spinning Mill No.1, which was built in 1892, and lies near to the well-known 'pyramid' alongside the M63. The first newspaper reference to the club came in an exceptionally curt 'report' in the *Cheshire County News and Chronicle* referring to a game played on 11 October 1884 and which read: 'Heaton Norris Rovers v Stalybridge (second team). Played on Saturday at Heaton Norris, and resulted in a victory for the visitors, who scored three goals to nil for Heaton Norris'. There was a further report the following week of a match between Heaton Norris Christ Church v Heaton Norris Rovers which the former won 1-0 but 'the game was an unpleasant one and the Christ Church captain has cancelled the return fixture'.

Subsequent weeks saw further fixtures against Tame Valley, Gorton (second team), Old St George's (Stalybridge) – which provided Rovers with their first victory – Hurst Park Road and Stalybridge. In the last mentioned game, Rovers were described as putting up an excellent fight in their 4-1 defeat, having arrived at Stalybridge without their goalkeeper and with only eight players. During the first game of 1885, Rovers played a home game against St Francis's (West Gorton) which, it was reported, 'resulted in a draw in favour of Heaton Norris by two goals and one disputed goal to St Francis's two'. The 'disputed' goal was disallowed for handball, but the report provides an interesting concept of how a draw can be a winning draw! One factor which is difficult to understand is that many of these games, which took place between November and March, did not kick off until 3.45 or 4.00pm. How the games were completed is difficult to see, both metaphorically and literally.

Rovers opened the 1885-86 season on 26 September with a trial match behind 'Chorlton's Farm, off Didsbury Road', a site which has not been possible to locate. By the time they began playing 'proper' fixtures at the beginning of October, it is clear that they had both a first team and an 'A' team. Meanwhile, during the summer of 1885, the Heaton Norris Cricket Club had formed a football team called, simply, 'Heaton Norris' and, on 17 October, whilst Rovers were playing at Manchester Clifford, Heaton Norris were playing their first match 'since formation of the club', losing 6-0 at Whaley Bridge. This club played at the Cricket Ground next to the Ash Inn on Manchester Road, a ground where 12 months later, the Rovers would play. (Reuben Street, which ran alongside the cricket ground still remains, but Kingsley Avenue, Horace Grove, Bournville Avenue and Selby Street now exist where the ground used to be). The two Heaton Norris teams played each other home and away on 24 October and 26 December 1885, the Rovers team winning 1-0 on both occasions.

In the first game of the 1886-87 season, Heaton Norris Rovers beat Crewe Villa 4-2 at the Heaton Norris Cricket

Club ground, the *Cheshire County News and Chronicle* reporting that 'the Heaton Norris Cricket Club have kindly placed their ground on the Manchester Old Road, at the disposal of the Rovers and the latter commenced their attractive list of fixtures with the runners-up of the Crewe Steam Shed Cup.' Perhaps because of the move to the cricket ground, it has always been assumed that Heaton Norris FC merged with Heaton Norris Rovers, but there is no firm evidence of this. It might have been that Heaton Norris folded, as they did not have the playing resources to continue. Further conjecture might lead to the conclusion that, by allowing Rovers to play at the Cricket Ground, those who wished to see the association game take place could do so. It is unclear what the exact colours of the Rovers team were during this period but, in a report of the game against Bradford (Manchester) on 30 October 1886, reference is made to 'the dark blues'.

By the time Rovers began the 1887-88 season, the club had moved once again, to a site which has been referred to variously as 'Belmont Street' and 'Wilkes's Field'. It is probable that this refers to Carr's Field, owned by William Wilks, and that Lloyd Street and All Saints Primary School now stand where the club played. The 'Rovers' element of the team's name appeared to have been dropped that season, although occasional newspaper reports refer to the original name.

Heaton Norris's first fixture at its new ground was almost an 'accidental' one against Crewe Excelsior on 24 September 1887. This fixture was not 'on the card' although Heaton Norris's secretary had written to Crewe earlier in the week, inviting them for a match. No reply having been received, it was assumed that there was no game. Crewe arrived to find no opposition whereupon Heaton Norris quickly put a team together, kicked-off at 3.30pm, and provided the very small group of spectators with a highly entertaining match which they won 8-6. By early 1888, it was clear that there were a number of 'Heaton Norris' teams in the area, including Heaton Norris Olympic and Heaton Norris Villa, which may have provided another reason for the eventual change of name in 1890. Although all its games were at least notional 'friendlies', attendances were generally acceptable, frequently around the 2,000 figure.

At the beginning of 1888-89, yet another move saw Heaton Norris playing at Green Lane, where the club would remain for the next 14 years. When they first moved to Green Lane, the 'ground' was simply an open field, but with 12 months, it was properly enclosed and a small wooden stand was built. Soon afterwards, the Nursery Inn effectively became the 'home' of the club, the teams changing in an adjacent barn before walking around the bowling green (which still remains behind the Nursery Inn) to the enclosure which has since been built upon. From then until 1890, Heaton Norris continued to play friendlies but had expanded their fixture list considerably.

Although unaware of it at the time, on 10 May 1890, Heaton Norris played their final game under that name when they played Taunton at Green Lane, winning 3-1 through goals by Smith (2) and Billy Riley. The club had enjoyed a successful year, with a record of Played 34, Won 18, Drawn 4, Lost 12, scoring 88 goals and conceding 48. Shortly after the Taunton game, it was announced that the club's expenses for the season had

The first known photograph of Stockport County, taken in 1890 in front of the Nursery Inn, where the players changed before matches at the Green Lane ground. Players only (back row, left to right): Urmston, Gaskell, Ferguson. Middle row: Pixton, Dr Blades, Jepson, Simpson, Roberts. Front row: Smith, Upton, Perry.

been £166 2s 3d, whilst their income had been £171 12s 7d, thus making a profit of £5 8s 4d (£5.42). On 24 May the *Cheshire Daily Echo* announced: 'The Stockport County AFC – a rather ambitious title, certainly – is to be the new designation of the Heaton Norris Club.'

It has always been assumed, no doubt correctly, that the club's change of name came about as a result of Stockport becoming a County Borough on 1 April 1889, although the precise reason for the change is unclear. The newspaper reference to an 'ambitious title' may well have reflected the motivation for the alteration: that the club had begun to see itself as more than a small local team, aspiring for recognition at a higher level.

On 6 September 1890, the club played its first game under the name of Stockport County, losing 5-3 at Hurst before winning their first game, 5-2 at Gorton Villa, on 8 September. After six years of friendly matches, County entered the Manchester Senior Cup for the first time, fortunately receiving a 'bye' in the first round. County's first senior competitive match was, therefore, their second round tie against Heaton Park which was even more farcical than was their first FA Cup-tie two years later. Heaton Park had the choice of venue and decided to play the tie at Green Lane.

County's team for this historic introduction to senior competitive football was Heyes; Ferguson, Bearon; Pixton, Gaskell, Jepson; Gabbutt, Simpson, Smith, Upton and Wright. On 17 January 1891, Heaton Park arrived at

Green Lane with a weakened team and, prior to the start of the game, complained to the referee about the state of the pitch. Although it was acknowledged both that the pitch was in a very poor state following incessant rain and that Heaton Park's protest was likely to be upheld, the game still took place. County led 4-0 at half-time and 'after a short break to indulge in lemon-sucking', proceeded to score another ten goals in the second half. The scorers in this absurd 14-0 'contest' were Upton (4), Gabbutt (3), Simpson, Wright (2), Smith, Jepson (2) and Gaskell. As expected, Heaton Park's objection was upheld and a 'replay' was scheduled for 31 January. On this occasion, as opposed to bringing a weak team to Green Lane, Heaton Park brought only six players. They therefore 'scratched' and agreed to play an 'exhibition' match after persuading five spectators to join them. A somewhat disinterested County won 2-0 in front of a small and rather unimpressed group of spectators.

Through to the third round by default, County were drawn at home to Royton who, earlier in the season, had beaten them comprehensively 9-2. On 14 February, County finally made their official introduction to the Cup, the team being the same as that which had played four weeks earlier, with the exception of Gabbutt who was replaced by Roberts. Over 2,000 spectators saw Royton go into a 2-0 lead before Jepson scored to bring County back into the game. Two goals from centre-forward Smith climaxed a wonderful comeback, giving County a 3-2 victory to the delight of their supporters. County were through to the semi-final in their first year of competing and were drawn to play Newton Heath (Manchester United) at Ardwick. Although 5,500 saw County lose 3-1, their consolation goal coming from Smith, the Stockport team's performance was excellent, particularly as Newton Heath were to be elected to the First Division of the Football League a little over a year later.

It was ironic that, even in the latter stages of the previous season, the 'old' County, Heaton Norris, frequently complained about games being cancelled due to their opponents' involvement in Cup competitions but now, having tasted the excitement of competitive football, they were keen to expand their participation in organised competitions.

On 16 May 1891, County's application to join The Combination was successful and, on 5 September, they played their first League match, a home game against Macclesfield. The eagerly awaited event proved to be a disappointing anticlimax as County were easily beaten 3-0 by their more experienced opponents. The Green Lane club quickly discovered that this standard of football was considerably harder than that which they had encountered in friendly matches. They lost their opening six matches, Upton scoring their first League goal in a 3-1 defeat at Wrexham, before gaining their first success, a 2-0 victory at home to Chirk on 17 October.

Although County struggled in their first League season, finishing second from the foot of the League, they were ten points clear of bottom-placed Denton – against whom they had recorded their biggest win, 7-2 – and only three points behind Chirk, who were four places above them. Additionally, the crowds, for the time, were good, attendances of between 2,000 and 4,000 being the norm. County's most impressive performance came towards the end of the season with a 2-0 victory at Green Lane against runners-up Northwich Victoria who were elected to the Football League in May 1892. In the Manchester Senior Cup, County were drawn against a Bolton Wanderers team which was to finish third in the First Division of the Football League. On 13 February, an estimated Green Lane crowd of 4,500 saw Jack Wallwork equalise an early Bolton goal but, despite a spirited display against genuinely first class opponents, County eventually lost 2-1.

The following season, 1892-93, saw Dresden United and Nantwich replace Northwich Victoria and Denton in The Combination. Now rather more accustomed to the standards of the League, County showed a significant improvement when compared to their first season, ending in 6th place, winning as many games as they lost and enjoying an excellent 1-0 victory at runners-up, Stoke Swifts, in the final game. For the first time, County entered the English (FA) Cup, beating Helliwell Rovers 4-2 after extra-time in the first qualifying round. This victory was the second over Helliwell, who County had defeated 4-0 in a tie ten days earlier, but which the FA ordered to be replayed after upholding Rovers's protest about the state of the Green Lane pitch. In the second qualifying round, County were brought down to earth, demolished 8-1 on 29 October 1892 in front of 6,000 at Bury who, two years later, were elected to the Football League. In the Manchester Senior Cup, County beat Gorton Villa 3-0 on 12 November before, for the second

year running, losing to Bolton Wanderers in the first round proper, on this occasion defeated 4-1 on 27 February 1893. Nonetheless, whilst they were not enjoying immediate success, County were gradually adapting to the required standards of League and Cup football.

In what was to be County's last season in The Combination, 1893-94 provided the club with some historic moments and undreamed of success in the FA Cup. Although only ten clubs completed their fixtures in The Combination – Gorton Villa having resigned early in the season – County's final position of fourth place demonstrated how much the team had developed, especially as they finished only one point behind runners-up, Stoke Swifts. In the League, apart from a seven match unbeaten run between Christmas Day 1893 and late March 1894, their most impressive result was against Everton Reserve. On 11 November, in front of a crowd of 4,500 at Green Lane, County beat the Liverpool team 4-0, thereby inflicting upon the champions their only defeat of the season.

Although County were eliminated in the first round of the Manchester Senior Cup, beaten 3-2 by Heywood on 3 February 1894, they made history that season by becoming the first Combination club to reach the first round proper of the FA Cup. After a walk-over against Bootle in the first qualifying round, they defeated Tranmere Rovers 2-1 and Wrexham 7-0 (in a 'replay' following a first game in which the Welsh side protested about the state of the pitch after losing 3-2), before being drawn against Crewe Alexandra in the last qualifying round. When County only managed a 0-0 draw in a tight encounter at Green Lane, most supporters believed their FA Cup run to be over, but goals from Billy McCombie and Smith gave County an excellent 2-1 victory in the replayed tie at Crewe. Remarkably, County were through to the first round proper (the equivalent of the current fourth round) where they had another home tie, this time against the strong Burton Wanderers, who were to join the Football League the following season. Green Lane's largest crowd of over 4,500 witnessed a tense game which resulted in a narrow 1-0 win for the Staffordshire club who were defeated 2-0 in the next round by eventual Cup winners, Notts County. The most likely reason for County's improved form was that they did not succumb to constant changes in the team, using only 15 players during the season, of whom six were ever-present in both League and Cup games.

In June 1894, the club held its Annual General Meeting, during which discussion took place regarding County's future in The Combination. As the wage-bill had virtually doubled at the same time as the number of League games had decreased, considerable concern was voiced about the club being able to pay its way. Attention was drawn to the fact that the Lancashire League, which enjoyed a higher standard of football, was extending its membership to 14 clubs. The committee decided that County should apply for one of the vacant positions and their application was successful.

In order to cope with the demands of their first season in the new League, County introduced 15 players who had not played during the previous season. It is questionable whether such a shake-up was beneficial as there was considerable disappointment with County's performance in 1894-95. Following a 5-0 away defeat at former founder members of the Football League, the original Accrington FC, the *Cheshire Daily Echo* was moved to comment that 'Stockport County have been beautifully consistent in the manner in which they have consistently played second fiddle.' This was an excessively harsh indictment of the team for, over the season as a whole, County performed well, more than holding their own against stronger opposition than they had met in their Combination days. In a League of 14 teams, their final position of ninth was highly respectable as was gaining 25 points from 26 games. However, there were to be no heroics in the Cup competitions, County beaten 3-2 by Lancashire League winners Fairfield in the FA Cup and 3-1 by Bury in the first round of the Manchester Senior Cup.

In 1895-96, the League was further extended to 16 teams, Halliwell Rovers (County's first FA Cup 'scalp'), Liverpool South End, Stalybridge Rovers and Ashton North End joining the League whilst Accrington and Heywood Central withdrew. A final position of 12th place appeared disappointing in a season which had three distinct parts: five wins in the first nine games; seven defeats in the next eight games; eight victories in the last 13 games. Their best League performance was reserved for the home game against runaway leaders Nelson, County beating the Lancashire club 4-0 at Green Lane with inside-right Smith scoring a hat-trick. In the FA Cup, County had a good 2-0 win against Liverpool South End before losing 5-1 away to the consistently strong Fairfield club. The Manchester Senior Cup brought two 5-1 victories in the first two qualifying rounds against Hurst Ramblers on 28 September and Stalybridge Rovers on 25 October. On 31 January 1896, in the first round proper, County were comprehensively beaten 7-2 at Bury.

Prior to the start of the 1896-97 season, County made some useful signings, the most significant being goalkeeper Joe Lee and outside-left Arthur Lee, both from Earlestown, and half-back Tommy Hall from Macclesfield. The season began with the same number of clubs in the Lancashire League, although Oldham County had replaced Blackpool who were elected to the Football League somewhat surprisingly, having ended the past season one place lower than County. The fact that Blackpool had become a limited company in May 1896 was probably a significant factor in their elevation, as it helped to demonstrate the financial commitment of an ambitious club. For the first time, County ended the season having won more games than they lost, finishing ninth out of 15, Liverpool South End having resigned from the League in February 1897. Once again, whilst enjoying some excellent performances, they were unable to achieve consistency over the whole season, failing to recover fully from a poor start which saw them lose six of the first eight games. The first qualifying round of the FA Cup had paired County against the lightweight Barnton Rovers who were summarily beaten 6-0 in front of a poor crowd at Green Lane. The second tie took County to Ruabon where they were defeated 3-2 by Welsh Druids. In the Manchester Senior Cup, County had been eliminated in the first qualifying round, beaten 1-0 at Middleton on 3 October 1896.

The Lancashire League changed dramatically in 1897-98, Fleetwood Rangers, Rossendale and West Manchester dropping out whilst five new teams entered the League.

Horwich, Middleton, Rochdale and Wigan County were new entrants but the most significant addition was that of the well-known but short-lived New Brighton Tower. The New Brighton team had not developed as had most clubs, from a local football team gradually working their way up; it had been established by the New Brighton Tower and Recreation Company strictly as a commercial enterprise, wealthy and with the avowed intention of being a top Football League team. Refused admission to the Lancashire FA, they were allowed to join the Lancashire League, thereby adding more than a little spice to that League. As for County, the signing of two forwards, Worrall from Nelson and Joe Foster from Coppenhall, was to play an important part in helping the club to its most successful season thus far.

Although County won their first two matches, interest was centred upon their first clash with New Brighton Tower. A remarkable 7,000 crowd filled Green Lane to see the team of former internationals and League players beaten 1-0 by County. This victory was followed by an excellent 4-0 win at home to Ashton North End, a game in which Joe Foster scored his first hat-trick for the club. For those who yearn for bygone days of innocence and sportsmanship, the report of this game in the *Cheshire Daily Echo* included the comment that 'it shall be recorded that Ashton played a fair and gentlemanly game and in these days of referee mobbing and field fighting, such a fact is worth noting.' New Brighton Tower reversed their 1-0 scoreline against County shortly before the Green Lane club transferred centre-half Charlie Wilson to Bolton Wanderers, replacing him by signing Billy Bolton from Macclesfield. In the New Year, County enjoyed a magnificent run of seven consecutive League wins, during which they scored 28 goals and conceded only six.

A disappointing decline in form at the end of the season resulted in them losing four of their last six matches and they had to settle for a best ever third place in what had become a 14 team League, Bacup, Fairfield and Oldham County all withdrawing from the League. The powerful Towerites inevitably ended as champions, shortly after which they were elected to the Football League, only one year after their formation.

Whilst County could be well pleased with their League form, their major achievements were reserved for the Cup competitions. The FA Cup saw County win through the first four qualifying rounds, beating Chester 2-1, Oswestry 2-1, Rock Ferry 2-1 and Aberystwyth 5-0 before meeting New Brighton Tower in the final qualifying round. The tie was watched by another 7,000 crowd at Green Lane but, to the disappointment of County fans, Tower won by a single goal. The Manchester Senior Cup provided County with undreamed of success. On 5 February 1898, they defeated Bolton Wanderers 2-1 with goals from Arthur Lee and Bob Mann to give them a semi-final place against the powerful Glossop North End who, like New Brighton Tower, would be elected to the Football League at the end of the season. On 5 March, the teams drew 1-1 before, in the replay two weeks later, a Tommy Hall penalty sent County through to the Final. In between these two games, Arthur Lee was transferred to Bolton who 'lent' him back to County for the Manchester Senior Cup Final. County's opponents were Manchester City, the match taking place at Fallowfield where the 1893

The County team which won the 1899 Ashton Charity Cup and Stockport & District Cup. Players only (back row, left to right): Lyons, Morrow, Hill. Middle row: Spooner, Hulme, Davies, Seed. Front row: H.Henshaw, T.Henshaw, Kellock, Axon.

FA Cup Final between Wolves and Everton had been played. A large crowd of 15,000 saw City beat County 4-0 but County lodged an appeal, arguing that City's outside-left Dougal was ineligible. The Manchester FA ruled that Dougal was not officially registered to play and over-ruled City's appeal that County's Arthur Lee was not qualified to play. A much smaller crowd of 4,000 attended the replay at Newton Heath's ground and, to the amazement of many, especially Stockport fans and players, two Joe Foster goals gave County a 2-1 victory and their first trophy.

Crewe Alexandra and Haydock joined the Lancashire League in 1898 whilst Clitheroe dropped out and New Brighton Tower were elected to the Football League. After their excellent previous season, County's performances were disappointing as they could only finish in sixth place. Significant signings made during the season included Betteley and Chesworth from Nantwich, and Moores from Rock Ferry (who resigned from the League in February 1899). County's best form, once again, came in the Cup competitions. In the FA Cup, they disposed of fellow Lancashire League clubs Ashton North End and Middleton before being defeated in the final qualifying round by eventual Second Division runners-up, Glossop North End.

The Manchester Senior Cup gave County the opportunity to repeat their remarkable success of the previous year. Once again, County's progress was subject to controversy, but on this occasion in the semi-final rather than the Final. On Good Friday, 30 March 1899, County met old rivals Ashton North End in the semi-final

at Fallowfield. Goddard and Harvey gave County a 2-1 win but Ashton protested, both about the ground and the fact there was 'something wrong with the goalposts and crossbars.' Their protest was upheld and the game was replayed on 8 April, a twice-taken penalty by Tommy Hall and a goal by Axon giving County a 2-0 win. In the Final, they met First Division Bury at Ardwick. On 12 April, a crowd of over 6,000 saw County come from 2-0 down, with only 15 minutes left, to score two goals through Artie Goddard and Frank Chesworth, so earning a replay. The replayed Final, on 29 April, was watched by 5,000 at Newton Heath's ground in Clayton, County retaining the Cup in a 2-1 win, their goals coming from Chesworth and Billy Betteley.

Despite County's average display in the Lancashire League, their second successive Manchester Senior Cup win encouraged them to apply for election to the Football League. On 20 May 1899, County's election hopes were dashed as Loughborough Town (28 votes), Chesterfield (27) and Middlesbrough (17) were elected to the Football League whilst Blackpool (15), County (11), Chorley (Lancashire League winners, 7), Wigan County (7), Coventry City (0) and Ashton North End (0) all failed to be elected. Although there was bitter disappointment at Green Lane, this failure helped the club to maintain a steely determination to redress the situation the following year.

County kept faith with the majority of the previous seasons's team for 1899-1900, their two important captures, Andrew Limond from Wigan County and Percy Pickford from Macclesfield, arriving after the season had started. The Lancashire League had a number of changes, Blackpool, Darwen, Earlestown, South Liverpool and Liverpool White Star entering the League whilst Ashton North End and Halliwell Rovers withdrew. From the outset, it was clear that whatever glory County had enjoyed in previous Cup competitions, their prime target was the League. Although they enjoyed a magnificent FA Cup win against First Division Glossop (who were to knock them out of the Manchester Senior Cup), their fourth round qualifying defeat to Lancashire League rivals, Stalybridge Rovers was no more than 'disappointing'. County won the first four games of the season and, despite two defeats in the next five games, enjoyed a wonderful 11-game unbeaten run to take them to the top of the League. A defeat at Blackpool on 10 March was followed by six consecutive wins, during which a 2-1 win at South Liverpool guaranteed County as champions. A tight defence and a free-scoring attack, in which Chesworth (18 goals), Foster (14), Betteley (13) and Patterson (11) made weighty contributions, were the major factors in County's success. They were considerably more confident when they applied for the second year running for election to the Football League and, in May 1900, that confidence was proved to be justified. Barnsley (29 votes), County (28) and Blackpool (24) were elected to the Football League. The club enjoyed a state of euphoria, unaware that their elevation to League status was the beginning of an unending struggle for survival.

In 1919, nearly 20 years after election to the Football League, the *Cheshire Daily Echo* commented that 'It is no secret that the County cannot afford to pay heavy transfer fees for the polished player. They have to find the diamond in the rough and apply the polishing business themselves.' This brief comment was appropriate from the time that County first competed in League football and has been equally valid ever since. County's first ever Football League fixture on 1 September 1900 gave no hint as to the problems which would confront them. For 1900-01, County kept faith with eight of the team which had won the Lancashire League, adding only the former Sheffield Wednesday captain, amateur Jack Earp, inside-right Billy Smith and outside-right Harry Stansfield who they had signed from Preston North End for the princely sum of £12 10s (£12.50). Some 7,000 attended the Leicester Fosse ground to see the first game of the season, County, according to the *Leicester Daily Mercury,* 'appearing in rather pretty cerise and white shirts'! Much to the amusement of the crowd, when Swift and Earp, the two captains, met in the centre of the field, there was no coin to toss and a somewhat embarrassed Swift ran to borrow a coin from a spectator, quickly returning it as the 'observant multitude laughed delightedly.' The young newcomers to the League put up a tremendous display, twice coming from behind to equalise through goals from Billy Betteley and Billy Smith. 'What go! What devilment they have!' a spectator was heard to comment. The *Cheshire Daily Echo* concluded their report by stating that 'the players on both sides were cheered as they left the ground, and it was generally agreed that Stockport had 'made a good start." This 'good start' seemed highly appropriate when, two days later, County visited Hanley to play Burslem Port Vale and won 1-0 through a Billy Smith penalty. However, when the wealthy New Brighton

Tower visited Green Lane on 8 September for Stockport's first home game, the crowd were stunned as the Hatters were comprehensively beaten 5-0. ('The Hatters' nickname developed as a result of Stockport being a well-known centre of the felt-hat trade in the 18th and 19th centuries.) County won their first League game at Green Lane a fortnight later, beating Walsall 4-1 with Joe Foster scoring all four goals (although some reports credit him with only three and give the other scorer as Billy Parker).

On 25 November, County officials met with Wilsons, the Newton Heath brewers, who had just bought the land, with a view to leasing Edgeley Park which, in the past, had been occupied by Stockport Rugby Club. The *Cheshire Daily Echo* reported that 'the result of these negotiations is watched with keen anxiety by the rugby supporters in the town.' These negotiations were, to say the least, protracted, County not leaving Green Lane until the beginning of the 1902-03 season.

In the FA Cup, County beat Wrexham 6-2 before losing 3-1 at home to former Lancashire League rivals Crewe Alexandra. Meanwhile, in the League, County were slipping down, eventually finishing next to the bottom. This was a little harsh, for the newcomers had won 11 games, as many as Port Vale who finished eight places above them. However, County had lost too many games, 20 in all, and had to face the embarrassment of re-election in their first season. Whilst they were successfully re-elected, the wealthy New Brighton Tower (who had completed the double over County), resigned immediately prior to the start of the following season, much to the anger of the Football League. Although Tower had finished fourth, such a position was not good enough for a company that demanded First Division football.

Following their disappointing first season of Second Division football, County made a considerable number of changes to their playing staff for 1901-02. New forwards Joe Davies and former player Frank Chesworth came into the team and County achieved a coup in persuading former international Smart Arridge to join the Green Lane club. There was, unfortunately, little change in results, as County never recovered from losing their first three matches. They had won only four games by the middle of March although they had drawn seven, frequently gaining a point where their play merited none as a result of the consistently outstanding performances of goalkeeper Joe Butler. During the match at Leicester Fosse on 23 November, County managed to hold out for a 1-1 draw, a Leicester spectator commenting that 'they'll never beat him till they hold him down.'

Nine defeats in ten games appeared to have condemned County to bottom place, but a surprising run of three wins in the last four games saw them finish next to the bottom, a relative success considering what had passed. Their sole loss in those last four games was the 8-1 defeat at Chesterfield when County played with only seven players, the remainder having missed the train. The FA Cup provided unconvincing victories against Buxton and Crewe Alexandra before they were defeated by local rivals Glossop in the final qualifying round.

At a special meeting on 6 May, serious consideration was given as to whether County should apply for readmission to the Second Division. It was argued that the expense was too great and that it might well be better and, more importantly, cheaper to return to the Lancashire

League. Against this, it was submitted that, should County leave the Second Division, they would never get back in. It was decided that they would apply if the £60 required for admission was obtained. Supporters and members were summoned to another special meeting on 12 May. A poor response led to only £17 5s (£17.25) being raised although five members then each donated £1. A resolution in favour of seeking admission to the Second Division was rescinded and it was decided that the matter be left to the committee who, in the event, did apply and County were re-elected.

The season was, to say the least, best forgotten and it was hoped that County's move from Green Lane to the more impressive Edgeley Park would coincide with improved results. It was not to be, 1902-03 proving to be even less successful than the previous season. By New Year's Day, County had been eliminated from the FA Cup in a second qualifying round at home to non-League Stalybridge Rovers but, more importantly, had won only one League match and that against newly named Manchester United. The introduction of Tommy Brittleton helped to improve County's record (although it was scarcely possible to make it worse), County winning a further six of their last 17 games. The bottom two places were being contested by County and Burnley, the teams meeting twice in three days in the final week of the season. Although losing the away game 3-2, a 3-0 home win for County and a point at home to Preston North End on the last Saturday enabled County to finish ahead of Burnley on goal average. A third application for re-election followed in May – and a third reprieve.

There was to be no miraculous change in fortune in 1903-04, the team suffering another disastrous season. By the end of February 1904, County had only won four games and yet another bottom place beckoned. On 12 March, Mr Axon, County's chairman, made an impassioned plea to the County supporters, who, he trusted 'will turn up in large numbers at the remaining matches, firstly because the committee are needing support to enable them to pay their way, and secondly to ensure a good enclosure and good games in the future. The members might pay for admission from now to the end of the season and I think they would if they knew how matters stood: several accounts ought to have been settled long ago and rents must be paid. Regular and increased attendances will enable us to satisfy all claims and ensure better games.'

Attendances did improve a little whilst County's form improved immeasurably as April saw them draw once and win three games, the last a fine 1-0 victory at Burnden Park against Bolton Wanderers. A 'great escape' was on the cards as County prepared for the last match of the season, a home fixture against fifth place Burnley. The re-election zone at this time was the bottom three places and Leicester Fosse were already condemned to the bottom position. The other re-election places were contested by Blackpool (25 points), County (26) and Glossop (26). With Blackpool away to mid-table Bradford City, and Glossop at home to seventh from the bottom Gainsborough Trinity, it appeared that Blackpool were unlikely to win and that, for County to escape, they would have to win and rely on the 'unlikely event of Glossop failing to win against Gainsborough'. On 23 April, an expectant and nervous Edgeley Park crowd were visibly relieved when Jimmy Pass put County in front after only 15 minutes. Burnley were then reduced to ten men when outside-right Tommy Aspden was injured but, far from losing heart in a match in which they had nothing tangible to play for, the visitors fought back. An increasingly anxious Edgeley Park crowd were not surprised when Dugald McFarlane equalised for Burnley shortly after half-time. Mid-way through the second-half, a Burnley attack led to Tommy Hall scoring an own-goal and, unbelievably, County were behind to the ten man team.

A late rally saw Bob Suart level the score but County were unable to get a winning goal, having to be content with a 2-2 draw. When the supporters discovered the other results, they were stunned: Gainsborough had done all that County could have wished by beating Glossop 2-0 at North Road but Blackpool had somehow managed to win 2-0 at Bradford City to go above County on goal-average.

Although County had only finished third from the bottom on goal-average (their highest position in their four years in the Second Division), the *Sheffield Telegraph* observed that 'this is by no means the first time that the Cheshire club have been in that position and it is quite within the bounds of possibility that this time they will not be re-selected.' At the annual meeting of the Football League on 30 May 1904, voting for membership of Second Division was: Leicester Fosse 33, Glossop 27, Doncaster Rovers 21, County 11 and Crewe Alexandra 10. After four years of almost unrelenting struggle, County were out of the Football League and back where they started.

For the 1904-05 season, County applied for entry to the Lancashire Combination and, notwithstanding their four years of struggle, embarked upon a determined fight to gain re-entry to the Football League. They began the season with four straight wins, the players doing their utmost to remain unaffected by financial crises. On 1 October 1904, it was announced that there was 'no wages for players' as the crowds were not big enough to pay their wages. At a supporters' meeting, Mr Axon, County's chairman, suggested a rise in the entrance charge from 4d (slightly under 2p) to 6d (2½p) but this was considered to be too much. After seven wins in their first eight games, on 29 October County were presented with a dilemma: they were required to fulfil a Lancashire Combination fixture on the same day that they had a third round qualifying FA Cup match against Stalybridge Rovers. Although winning the League was a priority, the committee were aware that a good FA Cup run could bring in much needed revenue. After due consideration, County fielded their first team in the FA Cup match which they won 2-0 whilst playing 11 completely different players in their Lancashire Combination fixture against Bolton Wanderers Reserves and only losing 3-1. County won through two more qualifying rounds, which included wins against Wrexham and Second Division Glossop, before being knocked out at Chesterfield in the last qualifying round.

Considering the circumstances, it was quite staggering that from the start of 1905 until the end of the season, County only lost two of their last 19 matches. On 7 January, the highly talented and popular inside-right Tommy Brittleton was transferred to Sheffield Wednesday for £300, a move which so incensed supporters that an 'indignation meeting' was called to protest. However, the financial position of the club left the committee with little choice and, within a little over a month, on 11 February, further risked the wrath of the supporters by transferring centre-forward Tommy Green to Middlesbrough for £300. This coincided with County's inspirational left-back, Arthur Waters, being taken critically ill, suffering from pneumonia and not expected to survive. At this time, County lay in second place, a point behind Liverpool but with three games in hand. Waters not only recovered but returned to the team within a little over six weeks. In spite of all these factors seemingly conspiring to prevent success, a spirited County went on to

Stockport County, 1905-06. Back row (left to right): S.Hoole (trainer), Suart, Heywood, Butler, S.Dodd, Butterworth. Front row: White, Waters, Pass, Crump, G.Dodd, Robinson.

clinch the Lancashire Combination with two games to play. On 23 May, a landau carried the champions round Stockport, transferred favourites, Tommy Brittleton and Tommy Green, accompanying the other County players.

In May 1905, the Football League had taken the decision to enlarge both the First and Second Divisions from 18 to 20 clubs. Thus, in addition to three Second Division clubs seeking re-election, another four places were created. On 29 May 1905, whilst Burslem Port Vale and Burton United were re-elected, Doncaster United were not which left five positions to be filled. These were taken by Hull City, Leeds City, Chelsea, Clapton Orient and County. It was generally accepted that, had the Football League not been extended that year, County would not have been elected before the other contenders and, in this respect, the club were most fortunate.

Prior to the start of the season, both Joe Butler and Roland Codling went to Orient, whilst County brought in Eddie Cresser from Birmingham, Tommy Butterworth (Bury), Joe Schofield (Manchester United), Bob Manson (Bryn Central), Fred Crump (Stalybridge Rovers), and George Dodd (Birkenhead).

County's first game back in the Second Division was against another elected club, Chelsea. New to the League Chelsea might have been but they were 'well known throughout the kingdom'. The *Cheshire Daily Echo* explained that 'Chelsea's life has been started on such a big scale that it has attracted the attention of all interested in the doings of big clubs. Between £20,000 and £30,000 has been spent on ground and team before a match has been played.' Considering County's very humble beginnings and their lack of financial resources, it was very much a 'David and Goliath' contest and, in front of over 7,000 spectators at Edgeley Park, 'David' won again with a goal by Bob Manson who 'was enthusiastically hugged for his achievement.'

At the end of October, County signed Sammy Dodd from Sheffield Wednesday, and the inaptly named 6ft tall and 14½ stones goalkeeper Frail from Middlesbrough. Although County were hardly setting the Second Division alight, they were performing respectably, obtaining 12 points from their first 14 games. Whether expectations

were too high was hard to say but the supporters seemed to have expected more. A letter to the *Cheshire Daily Echo* published on 9 December lamented the fact that 'If some of the clubs in the Second Division had a team playing such games as ours do at home, they would go mad with delight but our men must not make a mistake. They must seize every opportunity, make good use of every opening and altogether play a faultless game else what a storm of abuse they have to stand.'

In relative terms, this was to be County's best season since their acceptance into the Football League in 1900. After beating Walsall, they reached the first round proper of the FA Cup for only the second time in 14 attempts before falling to Lincoln City whilst, in the League, three victories in the final four games saw them finish in a best ever tenth place.

A number of useful signings were made for 1906-07, including Tommy White and Billy Kennedy from Brighton. However, the most popular signing by far saw the return of Joe Butler from Clapton Orient. County enjoyed their best League start, gaining 17 points from their first 13 games whilst conceding only 11 goals. However, an article in the *Cheshire Daily Echo* on 1 December enthusing about County's 'wonderful defence', provided a classic example of tempting providence, County losing 5-0 to Port Vale that day and 6-1 to Leeds City two weeks later. Subsequent to the highly complimentary report, County won only five of their remaining 21 games, ending in 12th place which, though at first sight was acceptable, was, in fact, very disappointing after their excellent start.

Following their highest League position the previous season, 1906-07 saw County exempt from the qualifying rounds of the FA Cup for the first time. In the first round, they were drawn at home to Southern League Fulham but, despite the objections of supporters, County could not resist the offer of a guaranteed £600 to hold the game at Craven Cottage. The players trained at Hastings prior to the tie on 12 January when 30,000 saw the teams battle out a goalless draw. The team went back to Hastings before returning to Fulham four days later when they lost the replay 2-1, Jimmy Pass scoring County's goal. On 11

Action from the drawn FA Cup tie between Stockport County and Fulham at Craven Cottage in January 1907, when County 'sold' their home advantage for a guaranteed £600.

Below: *County in 1907-08. Back row (left to right, players only): Green, Craig, Dodd, Butler, Suart, Whittle, Smith, Molyneux. Front row: Carter, Galloway, Crump, Waters, Mitchell, Butterworth, Abrams. (In front of captain Waters is reputedly the smallest man in the world, Harold Pigott, who at 21 stood less than 24ins tall).*

February 1907, supporters were shocked to hear that their former player Frank Chesworth had died in a tragic accident after falling from the top of a tram.

In March, the postponement of matches led, once again, to financial problems and a resultant plea from the directors to the Stockport public, stating that the club needed 'at least 8,000 from all remaining home games'. It came as no surprise when, in April, Jimmy Heywood, a former junior with the club, was transferred to Blackburn 'for a big transfer fee'. In the same month, former 'star' player Tommy Brittleton won a Cup winners' medal for Sheffield Wednesday.

In 1907-08, County began an 'association' with the amateur team, Northern Nomads, in the hope that they could act as a 'feeder' team for the professional club. Tommy Galloway was transferred from Ayr and former favourite, Tommy Green, re-signed from Queen's Park Rangers. For the second year running, County were drawn at home in the first round of the FA Cup and the protests were even more vehement when the club agreed to play Aston Villa at Villa Park on the basis of a guaranteed £450 and 50 per cent of any gross receipts exceeding £900. However, the dilemma facing the board was one which they had been confronted by before and would be regularly confronted by again; with attendances of approximately 4,000, receipts averaging £112-£120 and a wage bill of 'nearly £50 per match', there were reports of

committee members contributing to the club's running expenses out of their own pockets. There was, therefore, a depressing inevitability about the Committee's decision with the result that County's diehard supporters were let down by the fickleness of the Stockport public. Those supporters might have been more forgiving had County managed to progress to the second round but, as in the previous season, they were knocked out convincingly, 3-0.

Towards the end of the season, a series of transfers took place which involved Ralph Goodwin arriving from Stalybridge to start a 13 season spell and 'Cobbler' Hodgkinson returning to County. The departures included Joe Butler, who moved to Glossop with County 'declining to publish the transfer fee' (but which was believed to be approximately £150), and Bob Suart and Bob Carter, who were involved in a double transfer to Fulham for £550. Carter, son of Raich Carter, was an excellent outside-right who had come to County from Port Vale and who scored regularly with all his four clubs, averaging a goal every three games, dying in his early 40s in 1927.

Although individual players such as Crump and Porter had successful seasons, County again were unable to find any consistency, ending the season in 13th place. Considering the strength of the Second Division at time, such a final position was highly respectable, but its mediocrity resulted in an inability to attract large crowds to Edgeley Park, prolonging the seemingly never ending cycle of financial problems.

One of the consequences of County's inability to compete in the transfer market with the resultant lack of support had led to the board's decision to announce the floatation of the club. During the early part of 1908-09, a prospectus for 'Stockport County FC Limited' was issued and, in October, the club was at last confirmed as a Limited Liability Company. County had made a number of useful signings, including Fred Burden from Walsall, Peter Proudfoot and Ben Whitehouse from Chelsea and Jimmy Settle from Everton. Immediately before embarking upon their worst ever record of consecutive defeats, County were enjoying one of their best spells since joining the League. After beating Bolton in early December 1908, County had played 16 games and were third from the top, three points behind the leaders, West Brom, with a game in hand. An appalling run of nine consecutive defeats saw them slide alarmingly down the table, with the result that the season ended with their worst position, 18th, since their return to the Football League. In the FA Cup, County reached the second round (equivalent to the current fourth round) after an excellent 2-0 win at Grimsby. This was especially creditable as it was a 'replay' of the tie which had been abandoned four days earlier when County were leading 2-0 and, with the Hatters in the middle of their disastrous League run, many believed that their chance had gone. Ben Whitehouse and Jimmy Lomax scored the goals which set up a second round tie with arch-rivals Glossop, a game that attracted a 13,000 attendance at Edgeley Park. A Whitehouse penalty was only enough to give County a draw and they lost the replay at North Road by a single goal during extra-time. (Glossop went on to record their best ever FA Cup run, beating Sheffield Wednesday before losing to Bristol City in a replayed quarter-final.)

There were a considerable number of new arrivals in 1909-10, including Frank Kelly from Watford, Ernie Newman (Walsall), Tommy Charlton (Darlington), Jimmy Kennedy (Leeds City), Eddie Gettins (Glossop), and Willie Fotheringham Bauchop (Carlisle) who had played for Hearts in the 1907 Scottish Cup Final. At the beginning of December, Bert Elkin was sold to Spurs for £500 and, a week later, Chris Porter, who had moved to Glossop, scored the goal that beat County at North Road.

Despite selling both Lawrence Abrams and Fred Burden to Hearts for the regulation 'undisclosed but handsome fee', County were experiencing yet more financial problems. The smallest ever New Year's Day attendance saw them trounce Barnsley 5-0 and, two weeks later, only 8,000 saw them have an exceptional 4-1 first round FA Cup win against First Division Bolton Wanderers. Commenting on County's crowds, the *Athletic News* were 'at a loss to account for the wretched support which is accorded Stockport County, except it is that football is on the wane in that town. They have several players whose services most clubs would be pleased to enlist and they play football good enough to keep the club at any rate in a decent financial position.' Any potential for an improvement in attendances was all but destroyed when, with their best ever chance of reaching the last 16 of the FA Cup, County were humbled by non-League Leyton at Edgeley Park, losing 2-0. Once more County were forced to rely upon selling players, this time Jimmy

Kennedy and Ernie Newman to Spurs, for the now commonly labelled 'substantial fees'. County finished a mediocre 12th and managed to reach the Final of the Manchester Senior Cup only to lose 2-0 to Manchester United on 20 April 1910 before a crowd of only 800 at United's new Old Trafford ground.

Prior to the start of 1910-11, goalkeeper Jimmy Molyneux left for Chelsea and Jimmy Kenyon moved to Bradford. Additions to the County playing-staff included Richard Prout from Fulham, Jimmy Hindmarsh from Plymouth Argyle, and local amateurs Jimmy Rourke and Norman Rodgers. Although in many ways, this was another dismal season for County, having won only four of their first 24 games, their escape from the dreaded re-election area was an excellent achievement. This was accomplished only on the last day of the season when they beat Leicester by a single goal whilst Barnsley crashed 5-1 at Derby to leave the Yorkshire club next to the bottom.

On 7 January 1911, County had suffered their first, and unfortunately not their last, crowd problem which resulted in a ground suspension. Having suffered a run of bad results, eight games without a win, they faced Blackpool at Edgeley Park on 7 January 1911. Although losing 3-0 at half-time, after Prout had reduced the lead, County laid siege to the Blackpool goal. On two occasions, referee Garner of Barnsley rejected vociferous appeals for a penalty following challenges on Prout and Whitehouse and, when sections of the crowd responded with considerable hostility by descending to stone-throwing, Mr Garner was twice forced to halt the game. The *Athletic News* reported that 'there was clearly some excuse for the crowd to complain of the fates but no excuse for such unruly incident.' Whatever, 'the conduct of the hooligan element', as the *Cheshire Daily Echo* described it, resulted in a two-week ground suspension which, in the event, required County to move only one game, from Saturday, 11 February to Monday, 13 February, together with the associated loss of gate-money.

On the more positive side, County had now acquired two good wingers in Bauchop and Charlton and, at last, discovered a genuine goalscorer in Richard Prout who scored a then record 17 League goals. In May 1911, shortly after the end of the season, long-serving manager, Fred Stewart, at first declined and then accepted the job as manager of Cardiff City. By August, County had appointed Harry Lewis as his replacement.

There were few major changes before the start of the 1911-12 season, goalkeeper Billy McIver being signed from Brentford and the useful outside-left Richard O'Brien from Leith Athletic, Willie Bauchop having moved on to Leicester Fosse. The first half of the season was disastrous, County winning only two League games before the turn of the year. For the second time that year, the home match against Blackpool ended in defeat accompanied by further hostile reactions from the crowd. The *Cheshire Daily Echo* were 'sorry to hear large sections of the crowd using language that was far from gentlemanly to certain players. It is evident that certain spectators do not yet know how to conduct themselves.'

Fortunately, County's form improved in the New Year, four consecutive wins during February a significant factor in helping them to end in 16th place. The most encouraging aspects for County were the successful performances of December signing Fred Smith from

Hearts and the emergence of young amateur Norman Rodgers, the two forwards both scoring ten goals in their first season. The highlights of the season were undoubtedly County's New Year's Day 4-0 routing of eventual champions, Derby County, and the acceptance of professional terms by the extremely promising Norman Rodgers. County won through two qualifying rounds of the FA Cup before falling in the first round proper to their old adversaries Lincoln City, who had failed to gain re-election at the end of the previous season.

It was ironic that, whilst 1912-13 saw County's worst season since their return to League football, accompanied by the need to apply for re-election, the club made what would turn out to be their best signings for many years. Steven Fagan arrived from Bristol City, Fred Garrett from Notts County, Jimmy Mitton from Glossop, the talented Scottish inside-forward Jimmy Blair from Bradford City and outside-right Harold Crossthwaite from Heywood. However, County did not get the benefit from the majority of these players during this season which, in almost every conceivable way, was totally disastrous.

Although Rodgers scored four goals in the first four games, County were still without a win in five games when, on 27 September 1912, the club suspended goalkeeper McIver, full-back Graham, and forwards Prout, Smith and O'Brien for one week on the grounds of 'insubordination and breach of training rules'. Without these five players, County managed a fighting 1-1 draw at Birmingham, which was especially noteworthy as goalkeeper, Joe Birds, was carried off whilst playing his first game for 18 months, leaving a weakened County to play with ten men. The following week, a 7,000 attendance at Edgeley Park saw County gain their first win of the season, 12½ stone Lol Cook, signed from Chester, scoring a hat-trick on his home debut in a 3-1 win against Huddersfield Town. Only three weeks after the multiple suspension of players, on 17 October the County management sensationally gave Richard Prout '14 days notice to terminate his engagement with the club' on the grounds of 'palpable and gross misconduct'. If these decisions were intended to produce a positive response from the players, results hardly provided any evidence of this, County winning only four of their first 20 League games.

At the end of November, County set up a 'Shilling Fund' to try to help the beleaguered club and, following an early exit in the qualifying round of the Manchester Senior Cup at home to Glossop, they managed to record their biggest away win in the FA Cup, 7-2 at non-League King's Lynn, before suffering three successive League defeats. County were then eliminated from the FA Cup by Everton at Goodison Park on 15 January, before losing their next two League matches. On 1 February, during an unpleasantly physical 2-2 draw at local rivals Glossop, the colourful Tommy Charlton was sent off together with the Derbyshire club's Stapley, who allegedly attacked Charlton after the game. Three weeks later, Charlton was suspended 'until further notice', an FA decision which provoked the *Cheshire Daily Echo* to comment caustically that 'because Stockport County are not one of the leading lights in the football firmament, any sort of a judgement will do for [the FA].' Clearly, complaints that 'smaller' clubs receive less than justice were as common in 1913 as in more recent times. Charlton's suspension

had a further sting in its tail. Whilst still banned, County transferred the wayward winger to Burnley on 14 March for £650, the former County player surprisingly restored to League football seven days later. The fans were not impressed by Charlton's departure and, within days, two County directors resigned.

As if all these events were not enough, a week before Charlton's move to Burnley, County's most creative player, Jimmy Blair, was omitted from the team following a 7-0 defeat by Fulham at Craven Cottage. Suffering from illness and depression, the 28-year-old Blair returned to his native Dumfries over the Easter period and, on Bank Holiday Monday, committed suicide. Although Norman Rodgers succeeded in equalling the sacked Richard Prout's record of 17 League goal and became the first County player to score in five successive matches, the season ended as gloomily as it had started, County sharing bottom place with Blackpool and forced to apply for re-election for the first time since their return to the League in 1905. On 26 May 1913, County fans awaited a potentially fateful decision, one which was to become all too common-place some 60 years later, before heaving a sigh of relief as they (and Blackpool) were convincingly re-elected to Division Two.

The beginning of 1913-14 saw extensive 're-modelling of the ground' taking place, resulting in Edgeley Park's capacity increased to approximately 25,000. The 'popular' side was moved to its present location (now known as 'The Barlow Stand') with a capacity of 10,000, the playing pitch being moved six yards nearer to the 'pop' side, with a new grandstand replacing the so-called 'cowshed' on Hardcastle Road (the site of the present Main Stand). On the playing side, County made three important signings, Ernie Gault from Everton, Albert Waterall from Notts County and Norman Wood from Chelsea.

All three new signings helped County to an acceptable 12th position, despite the season starting badly with two successive defeats. Dame Fortune was somewhat unkind early in the season when, during a 5-0 defeat at Bristol City, goalkeeping captain Tommy Lunn received a sufficiently serious leg injury to end his career. On 4 October, County's bad luck seemed to be summed up by the experience of their new inside-left, 23-year-old Norman Wood. Playing at Edgeley Park against Fulham, the unfortunate Wood scored an own-goal before both conceding and missing a penalty as County went down to a 3-1 defeat. However, results improved, at least away from Edgeley Park, and a week after the Fulham game, County obtained an excellent 2-0 win at Bradford. A second home defeat preceded what was probably their best away win to date against second-placed Leicester. With the Fosse having taken maximum points from their first four home games, it was no surprise when County found themselves 2-0 down after 38 minutes. An Albert Waterall penalty reduced the arrears before half-time and when the same player scored a second penalty in the first minute of the second half, the Leicester fans were unimpressed, the referee 'vigorously hooted' and policemen called to quell disturbances behind the goal. After Fred Garrett had put County ahead, Wood scored a fourth with a shot that was so ferocious that it broke the net, before Gault sealed a magnificent 5-2 win with a last-minute goal. Some Filbert Street fans were so incensed

Stockport County, 1913-14. Players only (middle row, left to right): Goodwin, Fagan, Garrett, Gault, Rodgers. Front row: Bluer, Proctor, Lunn, Wood, Chivers, O'Brien.

that, at the final whistle, the referee had to be escorted from the pitch by police in what was described, euphemistically, as a 'lively scene' in which County goalkeeper Tommy Evans was kicked on the thigh by a spectator. Leicester's season collapsed to the extent that they escaped re-election only on goal-average.

County's home form continued to be quite abysmal, winning only once in nine games at Edgeley Park before, playing their third game in three days over the Christmas period, they demolished Bristol City 5-1 with Norman Rodgers scoring his first and only League hat-trick. Thereafter, County's home form improved immeasurably, winning eight of their last ten games at Edgeley whilst, almost inevitably, seeing a previously respectable away record become as dismal as their early home record. For the fourth year in succession, County had been drawn away in the FA Cup and were beaten 3-2 by non-League Gainsborough Trinity. Shortly before the end of the season, manager Harry Lewis left to take over at Barnsley and, on 1 May 1914, David Ashworth replaced him after surprisingly leaving Oldham Athletic, who he had just guided to fourth position in the First Division.

Although County began 1914-15 with a fairly settled side, there was anything but a settled atmosphere, war on Germany having already been declared on 4 August 1914. It was more than a little surprising that not only did the Football League commence a 'normal' League season, but that the season was completed without suspension. As for the FA Cup, on 7 December, the Council of the FA met to decide whether the English Cup should be abandoned but concluded that it should go ahead. For many people, the continuation of League football was unacceptable, even bearing in mind the popular media-inspired belief that the war would be 'over by Christmas'.

For County, this last season of League football for four years was another satisfactory one, the club now having their most productive inside-forwards since their entry to League football. Rodgers, Gault and Wood scored 42 League goals between them, Rodgers becoming the first County player to score 50 League goals, this being achieved in County's best win of the season against future champions, Derby County, in a 3-2 victory at Edgeley Park on 30 January 1915. The unassuming Rodgers also enjoyed the distinction of becoming the first County player to score 20 League goals in a season, but sadly, his inside-forward colleague, Norman Wood, who joined up in February 1915, was killed in action.

County had the misfortune to be drawn away to Liverpool in the first round proper of the FA Cup and, predictably, lost 3-0 at Anfield. By the early part of March, County had climbed to sixth place following a good run of results from the turn of the year. However, only one victory in the last eight League games put paid to hopes of a best ever final position as they slipped to 14th place. County's major success came in the Manchester Senior Cup when, after beating Manchester United in the semi-final, they overcame Rochdale in the Final on 1 May. With the score 1-1 at the end of normal time, Gault having scored County's goal, an exiting period of extra-time saw Stockport win 4-3 through goals by Albert Waterall 2 (1 penalty) and Norman Rodgers in front of an excellent attendance of over 10,000 at Hyde Road, then home of Manchester City. By 19 April, the Football League had decided that no matches would be played the following season should the war continue.

In the summer of 1915, the Football League was indeed suspended and the majority of clubs continued to play wartime football on a regional basis. In 1915-16, County participated in the Lancashire Section, which attracted many games of local interest against the bigger clubs, including Liverpool, Everton and the two Manchester neighbours. For the duration of the war, the payment of players was not allowed, a practice which made some concession to the view that all organised football should have been suspended.

Whereas a number of other clubs were quickly deprived of many of their best players, some indeed being unable to continue in the localised League football, Stockport were relatively fortunate in being able to rely on many of the players who had ended the previous season; Crossthwaite, Gault, Goodwin, Graham, Mitton, Robson, Rodgers and Waterall all continued to play and they were supported by former County favourites, goalkeeper Jimmy Molyneux from Chelsea and Bob Suart from Port Vale. In addition, Albert Waterall's brother, the experienced Tommy Waterall from Watford, played in all but five games and 'Tiny' Fayers, the Huddersfield Town centre-half, was to miss only four games throughout the wartime period. When Rodgers was injured in the spring of 1916, whilst on leave, Jack Mitton, Jimmy Mitton's brother, made four appearances at centre-forward and scored three times. Whilst accepting that the quality of the Lancashire Section was diminished by the absence of many players who were engaged in active service, County fared well in the first season of wartime football, finishing in fifth place in the Principal Tournament and enjoying two excellent victories against fourth place Everton, their 5-2 win at Goodison in November 1915 being their best result. Ernie Gault ended the season as top scorer with 18 goals, whilst this first wartime season was the only one in which Norman Rodgers failed to score 20 goals, ending with ten in only 18 games.

The second season of wartime football, 1916-17, saw an expansion of the Lancashire Section to 16 teams, Port Vale and Blackburn Rovers joining the League. Blackburn had been one of the clubs hardest hit by the loss of players and had not competed in the League the previous season, those players who were left combining with Blackpool. County lost Jimmy Mitton and Joe Graham to the services and, in October 1916, Jimmy Molyneux was called up although he did not leave for the front until the following April. At the end of October 1916, with County already having their former goalkeeper as a regular, the fans were even more delighted to welcome the return of, perhaps their greatest ever goalkeeper, Joe Butler, with the result that some ten years after he and Molyneux had shared goalkeeping responsibilities, history repeated itself.

Butler and the Waterall brothers worked as coalminers and, being engaged in essential work, were not at that time called up. Although the season has to be put into perspective in that those clubs who competed in the League did not include all their pre-war 'stars', in terms of opposition, 1916-17 saw County's best-ever season, the

club finishing as runners-up to Liverpool in the Principal Tournament, losing only five games out of 30. Their final position was achieved by a superb seven wins and a draw from their last eight games, which included a 6-0 win against Blackpool with Ernie Gault scoring a hat-trick in his last game before being loaned to Everton for the remainder of the war.

With three matches left and Liverpool virtually assured of first place, the runners-up position was contested by County, Stoke, Everton and Manchester City. County enjoyed victories against all the other contenders, beating Stoke 2-0, Manchester City 3-1 in front of 18,000 at Maine Road and Everton 5-1. The end of season run saw Norman Rodgers score 12 goals in eight games, completing the season as top-scorer with 20 goals, a feat which he repeated in the following two seasons. For the second year running, Harold Crossthwaite was an ever-present as County succeeded in being able to play a fairly settled side, ten players making at least 20 appearances.

The penultimate wartime season, 1917-18, saw the practice develop of players playing under assumed names. Thus, newspaper reports in the early part of the season referred to County's goalkeeper as 'Stewart' and their inside-left as 'Castor' who were in fact Causer and Doncaster respectively. Although real names were sent to the Football League, in October 1917, the League ordered that the practice had to stop. The season saw the introduction of playing each team home and away on successive weeks, a practice which continued following the resumption of League football in 1919. From an attendance point of view, opening fixtures against Manchester City were good news, 12,000 seeing the game at Maine Road whilst 7,000 attended the return fixture at Edgeley Park. However, County lost both fixtures by the odd goal before they enjoyed a double demolition of the unfortunate Blackburn Rovers who had lost virtually all their team to the services and who lost 32 of their 36 games that season.

A good season ended with County finishing in sixth position, Rodgers again scoring 20 goals, ably supported by Jimmy Kenyon with ten, the two forwards helping the club to continue its remarkable run of success at Goodison Park as they completed a hat-trick of victories there.

On 24 November 1917, after making 84 consecutive wartime appearances, Harold Crossthwaite missed his first game in order to play in a charity match at Port Vale in aid of North Staffordshire troops in the trenches. Goalkeeping duties fell mainly upon Joe Butler, with Jimmy Molyneux making three appearances following his being sent back to England in October suffering from shrapnel wounds. The first of these appearances came within days of him being discharged from hospital. Mid-February saw the Waterall brothers called up and, as the season drew to a close, County found themselves struggling to field an experienced team, made worse by ending the season with double fixtures against heavyweights, Everton and Liverpool. Their final fixture, away at Anfield, was notable for County being unable to field 11 players and having to play two Liverpool reserves, Hewitt and Metcalf, both of whom scored in County's 4-2 defeat.

In what was the last wartime season, 1918-19, County had an average record, finishing in eighth place, although this was their lowest position in the four seasons of regionalised football. Additionally, this was the only season when County conceded more than they scored. Their best spell came with four successive wins immediately following Armistice Day in November 1918, although the 'doubles' performed over Blackburn Rovers and Oldham Athletic involved the two sides who ended the season occupying the bottom positions of the Lancashire Section.

Former County player Bob Suart was killed in action shortly before the end of hostilities as were 'Cobbler' Hodgkinson, who had had two spells at Edgeley Park, and Fred Houghton, killed in Mesopotamia in the last month of the war, who had spent the last four peacetime seasons with County. With the end of the war and the gradual return of the surviving armed services, the regionalised football season fizzled out, County suffering from disappointing attendances as the resumption of the Football League was eagerly awaited. For the second successive season, County used a minimum of 40 players, only Fred Garrett being an ever-present. Rodgers scored his now standard 20 goals and, fittingly, in the last wartime fixture played against eventual Lancashire Cup winners, Liverpool, County's magnificent goalkeeper, Joe Butler, made his one and final appearance at Edgeley Park.

For the first post-war League game, County fielded a team which consisted of six players who had appeared prior to the suspension of the Football League, namely Harold Crossthwaite, Fred Garrett, Jimmy Mitton, Tommy Robson, Norman Rodgers and Albert Waterall. It was County who scored the first post-war Football League goal in their game at Grimsby on 30 August. Although not officially timed, County's opening goal was scored 'in under ten seconds'. From the kick-off, new signing George Dingwall passed the ball to Crossthwaite who ran down the wing before crossing for Dingwall to score. Further goals from Arthur Metcalf and Norman Rodgers gave County an emphatic 3-0 win. The same three players scored in County's second game, a 4-1 home victory over Rotherham County, a win which gave cause for optimism.

Although County lost their initial momentum, the season settled down to another moderate one for the club and, in a strong Second Division, they did well to be in tenth position by the beginning of February. For the sixth consecutive season, they were drawn away in the FA Cup, beaten 3-1 by First Division Preston North End, Rodgers scoring County's goal. However, within little over a week, at the end of February 1920, Rodgers was transferred to a desperate First Division Blackburn Rovers for £2,500 and Crossthwaite sold to Stoke for £2,000. The sale of Rodgers was hardly a popular decision, justified by the board as a 'result of poor response to the request that 3,000 shares be taken up by the public'. As they would continue to do for the next 70 years, although County received considerable fees for their talented home-grown players, they paid dearly for their loss on the pitch. Following the departure of their two best forwards, Stockport's form slumped alarmingly, as they won only two of their last 13 games, seven of these being goalless, eventually finishing in 16th position. For County, the writing was on the wall.

Prior to the start of 1920-21, additions were made to the County squad which would, in time, become highly

A Notts County defender clears the danger in the goalless draw at Edgeley Park on 7 April 1920.

beneficial but, unfortunately, such benefits would not come immediately. County brought full-back Joe Reid from Manchester City, and signed two local players, Jimmy Walsh and Harry Hardy but failed to find adequate replacements for either Crossthwaite or Rodgers. A disastrous 5-2 defeat at Edgeley Park to a rampant Cardiff City on the opening day of the season was the beginning of a quite appalling five-month run. By the fourth game of the season, County were playing their third centre-forward, half-back Albert Waterall. A remarkable 6-0 victory over Clapton Orient, with Waterall scoring the only hat-trick of his career, proved to be illusory, Orient gaining ample revenge seven days later with a 5-0 win.

By the time the experienced Ernie Gault was re-signed in December 1920, seven players had been tried at centre-forward, none of them capable of scoring with anything like the frequency of Rodgers. They were not helped by

County at the end of 1921-22 with the Third Division Northern Section championship shield. Players only (back row, left to right): Walmsley, Hardy, Reid, Richardson, Critchley. Middle row: Gault, Layton, Woodcock, Jones. Front row: Crossthwaite, Heath, Waterall, Griffiths.

weaknesses in other areas, the talented young Jimmy Walsh finding the tough Second Division play a demoralising initiation. By the beginning of February 1921, County's position was seemingly hopeless, marooned at the bottom of Division Two with only three victories from 26 games, and knocked out of the FA Cup by Everton, after being drawn away yet again. A spirited run which resulted in four wins in five games gave them a glimmer of hope, providing they could maintain their momentum. Further hope was created by the League decision to relegate only one club as the Third Division South would provide a promoted replacement.

With ten games left, County were level on points with Coventry City and single-goal defeats at Stoke and Sheffield Wednesday were partly compensated by a win and a draw against Nottingham Forest. A critical meeting with Wednesday on 2 April at Edgeley Park was marred by serious crowd trouble when referee Mason of Newcastle rejected County claims for a penalty. With Stockport losing 1-0, sections of the crowd demonstrated against the referee and smashed windows of his dressing-room. As a result, a month later, County suffered their second ground suspension, one which would remain in force until 12 September.

Their fate was sealed by a fighting late run by Coventry, who won six of their last ten games, and although the Hatters did not lose any of their last five games, the last four were drawn, two against Blackpool followed by two goalless draws against Leicester City. The last of these games was a drab encounter, made famous only because of the 'alleged' attendance of 13. With Edgeley Park suspended, and County already doomed to bottom place their last 'home' game was played at Old Trafford on 7 May 1921. With Manchester United at home to Derby County that afternoon, County's game, for some inexplicable reason, did not kick-off until 6.30, almost two hours after the United match had ended, and it was reported that only 13 spectators paid to get in to Old Trafford to see the Stockport game. What many patronising reports failed to mention is that, although the crowd was indeed sparse, County's match was watched by between one and two thousand spectators, the majority having arrived earlier to watch United's game against

Derby before staying to see County's last rites in Division Two.

The weaknesses County had demonstrated at the end of the previous season had never been remedied and the fact that Albert Waterall had finished top scorer with eight goals provided firm evidence of their paucity in attack. Although their luck seemed to have finally run out, County's future was assisted by a Football League decision on 7 March 1921, when it was decided, unanimously, to establish a Northern Section of the Third Division. Relegated they were, but as founder members of the new Northern Section, League football was not to be lost.

During the close season, a complete upheaval took place, resulting in the old board of directors retiring and a new, 'enterprising', and 'energetic' board taking its place. The changes were, without doubt, significant, in that there had been genuine fears as to whether County would 'enter on the voyage of another season'. By the beginning of 1921-22, although the club was experiencing severe financial difficulties, they were not regarded as insurmountable and a renewed optimism accompanied County's entry into the newly created first Third Division North. Two new signings were to play an important part that season, inside-left Charlie Jones from Cardiff City and right-back Billy Richardson from Wallsend. However, County fans were unable to see the new players in pre-season trials as the ground suspension was still in force and the trials took place 'behind closed doors'.

After County began their League campaign with two excellent away victories, Edgeley Park was opened to the public the day after the ground suspension expired. On Tuesday 13 September 1921, neighbours Manchester City visited Edgeley Park to play a friendly, the whole of the proceeds in aid of the County club funds. An attendance of 7,000 saw City win 4-1, Gault scoring County's consolation goal, but the game had produced over £300, no little help at that time. September also saw the return of Harold Crossthwaite from Stoke and the arrival of two young Scottish players, Gilbert Steele from Glenburn Rovers and David Young from Auchlecke. After winning five of their first six games, County finally suffered their first defeat, 2-1 at old rivals Southport, before reversing the scoreline seven days later at Edgeley Park, with Ernie Gault scoring his sixth goal in eight games. Following Grimsby Town getting 'the double' against them in early November, County enjoyed a run in which they lost only one of 19 League matches. In the game after the second Grimsby defeat, Joe O'Kane became the first County player to score a hat-trick on his debut in a 3-1 win against Walsall at Edgeley Park. O'Kane had joined County the

With the Leeds United defence in disarray, a youthful Eddie Critchley (second from left) watches as County fail to convert a scoring opportunity in September 1922.

previous season but had not succeeded in breaking into the first team; his success in the Third Division was a major factor in the club's promotion fight although he disappeared from the Edgeley scene at the end of the season.

An ignominious defeat in an FA Cup qualifying round match at non-League Lancaster was County's low spot in a season which saw them reach the semi-finals of the Manchester Senior Cup before losing a replay to Bolton Wanderers after the two sides had fought out a pulsating 4-4 draw on 1 May 1922, O'Kane, Westby Heath (two penalties) and Wilf Woodcock scoring for County. However, the various Cup competitions were of secondary importance when compared to County's fight to regain their Second Division status.

From New Year's Eve 1921 until the Easter weekend, County enjoyed a run of 15 games without defeat and, with six games of the season remaining, the championship looked theirs. A stutter on both Good Friday and the following day saw County lose two games, one to promotion rivals, Darlington, before they struggled to a 3-2 win against Ashington on Easter Monday. With three games left, County were three points ahead of both Darlington and Grimsby and, on 22 April, Stockport were due to play Darlington at Edgeley Park whilst Grimsby travelled to fourth-placed Accrington Stanley. Edgeley Park had a record crowd of approximately 18,500 for Darlington's visit, the fans well aware that the result of this match could determine the destination of the championship.

The game got off to a sensational start, Charlie Jones scoring from Wilf Woodcock's cross to give County a 1-0 lead in the first half-minute. Darlington came back strongly and, when half-time came, it was accepted that they were unlucky to be losing. The second-half began almost as dramatically as the first, the referee pointing to the spot to award a penalty for handball against a home defender. The County players protested vehemently, persuading Mr Josephs, the Durham referee, to consult his linesman. Following the consultation, to the relief of the County players and the crowd, the referee awarded a free-kick to the home team and, although there were chances to add to the one goal lead, Darlington fought skilfully and determinedly to the final whistle. Malcolm, the Darlington captain, was the first to congratulate Arthur Layton, the County skipper, demonstrating the sportsmanship shown by the Quakers. In truth, Darlington, with a number of reserves in their team, had been the better side, County failing to show the form they had demonstrated throughout most of the season, but it was County's day, made by the news that Grimsby had

been defeated at Accrington and so, with two games left, the Edgeley Park club had become the first champions of the Northern Section. The championship was presented to County seven days later when Lincoln City visited Edgeley Park and County wound up their season with a 1-0 win in the return match at Sincil Bank. Thus began the remarkable coincidence which has occurred in each of County's three championship seasons: that of Lincoln City being the opponents in the last game of each of those three seasons. County could hardly have been described as 'free-scoring', their solid defence, 23 'clean-sheets' in 38 League games, providing the backbone to the club's championship-winning team.

Prior to the start of the 1922-23 season, hopes were perhaps unrealistically high as to County's prospects on their return to the Second Division. County had released their two top goalscorers, Ernie Gault moving to New Brighton and Joe O'Kane to Stalybridge Celtic. Gilbert Steel was transferred to Crewe Alexandra and the talented Jimmy Walsh, who had arguably been overplayed in County's relegation season and under-utilised in the promotion season, was signed by Liverpool. The new players brought in were mainly from the Third Division, centre-forward Tommy Green who had scored 23 goals for Accrington Stanley, inside-right Harry Cousins who had scored 17 goals for Durham City and outside-right Alf Dolphin who had figured in Darlington's fight with County for Third Division honours. Inside-left John Wilson, who was brought from Newcastle United, was one of the few players who joined County in the summer of 1922 to have enjoyed First Division experience. The promising but inexperienced Duggie Humphrey was added to the squad from Bradford City.

Although County had kept faith with the defence that had been the bulwark of their Northern Section success, the changes in the forward line resulted in them being an unknown quantity in a very strong Second Division. With regular encouragingly increased attendances, the future was promising and, although knocked out of the FA Cup at the first hurdle, by mid-January, County were in a comfortable mid-table position. 12 matches without a win saw a disastrous fall into the relegation area. Completing the double over Derby County during the middle of April 1923 gave County a lifeline, but they entered the last Saturday of the season knowing that they would be relegated if they were defeated by Southampton. A crowd of 15,000 saw two goals from Woodcock and one from Humphrey give them a handsome win over mid-table Southampton, thus escaping the ignominy of immediate relegation.

County, 1924-25. Back row (players only, left to right): Swan, Bocking, Meads, Goodwin. Middle row: Critchley, Simms, Richardson, Molyneux, Hardy, J.Reid, Wilson, Morrison. Front row: Newman, Craven, Waterall, G.H.Reid, Mitchell, White.

The brightest spot was the winning of the Manchester Senior Cup, County achieving excellent wins against Bolton Wanderers by 2-0 (Cousins 2), Manchester City by 4-1 (Cousins, Woodcock 2, Wilson) and Stalybridge Celtic by 2-0 (Humphrey, Cousins) in the Final at Hyde Road. Although, overall, it had been a disappointing season, County could be well-pleased with the performances of Tommy Green who had netted 16 League goals in 31 matches, four of these coming in a 5-1 victory over Coventry City, the increasingly mature and reliable performances of goalkeeper Harry Hardy, and the introduction of young outside-right, Eddie Critchley.

Shortly after the start of the 1923-24 season, Ernest Barlow was elected chairman of the club, a position which he was to hold for some 30 years but overall, it was a quiet season for County, the team finishing in a reasonable but somewhat frustrating 13th place. County suffered fewer defeats than during any other season in the Second Division, but their record tally of 16 draws was to last for exactly 50 years and impeded their quest for a top ten placing. Goals were in short supply as, although young Critchley was developing into a fine outside-right and the arrival of 33-year-old Harold Edgley from Queen's Park Rangers provided experience on the left flank, County were unable to find the forwards who could finish off the work of these two wingers. The arrival of former international Ernie Simms from South Shields, at the beginning of January 1924, appeared, initially, to have solved the problem but, after scoring six goals in his first three games, Simms failed to score in the next 17 games.

In the FA Cup, County beat Cheshire rivals Crewe Alexandra in the fifth qualifying round but the final qualifying round resulted in elimination at Norwich. There was little doubt that County's most memorable match was against local rivals Manchester United at the end of October. A record attendance of 18,643, which also provided record gate receipts of just over £1,103, saw County gain revenge for a 3-0 defeat at Old Trafford seven days earlier. United dominated the first half, and led 2-0 through goals by Lockhead and Barber. This second goal inspired an immediate County fight back and, following two goal-bound headers being cleared away, Critchley centred for Waterall to reduce the arrears. In the second-half, County's persistence was rewarded after 70 minutes when Waterall's pass provided Purcell with the opportunity to equalise. Both sides created further chances until, after 81 minutes, Woodcock was brought down as he ran into the penalty area. The centre-forward picked himself up to convert the penalty and, though United fought to the end, County finished unlikely but ecstatic winners having come from 2-0 down. The same season saw Harry Hardy become the first County player to make 150 consecutive League appearances, the achievement coming in a 1-0 victory against Sheffield Wednesday on 8 March. Within a month, Hardy asked to go on the transfer list but, within days, asked to come off it.

On the face of it, 1924-25 was a disappointing season for County as one point gained from the last four games saw the team slide to 19th place but, whilst the results left a lot to be desired, a number of interesting and important signings were made. Prior to the start of the season,

Tommy Mitchell, a promising 19-year-old from Hartlepools United was signed for the relatively huge fee of £1,000 whilst Jimmy Molyneux, an old favourite, returned to Edgeley Park after spending 14 years with Chelsea. The redoubtable goalkeeper was re-signed to help the youngsters at County, but found himself playing in the last seven games of the season when Harry Hardy was unavailable. Ben Boardman and Billy Bocking, two young players who were to make their mark during subsequent years, made their debuts and, in an attempt to shore up their attack, Billy Johnston, Huddersfield Town's talented inside-forward, was signed as was Bob Blood from West Brom, who, in his stay at Port Vale, had scored four goals against County in a 6-1 defeat four years earlier. The blend of youth and experience gave a hint of possible success with County winning their opening two games against Stoke City and, eventual runners-up, Manchester United but this was soon followed by nine games without a win. Although County stumbled through most of the season, they deserved credit for escaping from the bottom of the League where they had sunk in late December. Manager Albert Williams was 'asked' to resign in November and was replaced by Bolton Wanderers's assistant secretary, Fred Scotchbrook. Notwithstanding County's alarming slide during the autumn, fans and officials were delighted when Harry Hardy was selected to play for the Football League against the Irish League on 11 October. Hardy's appearance in a 5-0 victory halted his remarkable run of 171 consecutive League games but eight weeks later he received the highest honour when he became County's only ever international, representing England in a 4-0 victory against Belgium on 8 December at The Hawthorns.

The 'double' over Barnsley during the Christmas period gave County hope for the New Year and three successive draws were followed by three good home wins as they pulled away from the relegation zone. County were safe but their continuing failure to score with any consistency remained a problem, evidenced by Tommy Meads ending the season as top scorer with ten goals, despite playing at half-back for nearly half the season. The FA Cup brought some respite for County, coming away from the capital with an excellent 3-1 victory at Queen's Park Rangers to progress to the second round proper for only the third time in their history. For an extraordinary 13th time in 14 FA Cup-ties, County were drawn away, this time at First Division Birmingham. A crowd of 36,000 saw a first-rate performance from County and, although Birmingham edged through 1-0, the result was in doubt until the final whistle. Both Hardy and Ernie Simms were selected to tour Australia with a Football League representative side and County lost the services of both players for the final seven games of the season, Billy Johnston replacing Simms and 39-year-old Jimmy Molyneux taking over in goal. County's best-ever servant, Albert Waterall, became their first player to be granted a second benefit match but, unlike the first, which he shared with Jimmy Mitton and Fred Garrett, this was for Waterall alone, an honour that was thoroughly justified.

The failure of what, on the surface, was a team which was more than capable of holding its own in the Second Division was of considerable concern when County

embarked upon the 1925-26 season. They had a goalkeeper who had been 'capped'; an excellent pair of full-backs in Bocking and Richardson; half-backs John Wilson, who at the end of the season would move to Old Trafford, and the old war-horse Albert Waterall, and forwards of the calibre of Critchley, Johnston, Meads, Simms and Mitchell. By the end of what was to be a thoroughly depressing season, the only explanation for County's relegation was that the team was not sufficiently invested with the necessary team spirit. On form and reputation, the players mentioned looked superior to the majority of other clubs in the division but, time after time, they were beaten by inferior teams. It was more than a little ironic that, following Hardy's successful tour of Australia with the League Representative side, on his return the goalkeeper suffered his worst spell before Everton signed him on 29 October.

County went through the season without an away win and, whilst beginning the season playing some excellent football, they became incapable of translating such play into victories. Only four wins before the turn of the year left County in an even worse position than in the previous year and, although a crowd of over 33,000 saw them put up a spirited performance in yet another away FA Cup-tie at First Division Sheffield United, from the end of January they won only once in 16 attempts. What turned out to be the last straw was an away game at Oldham which came between successive home wins over Stoke City and Clapton Orient. With County drawing 2-2 against the strong Latics side, the game was abandoned ten minutes before the end as fog engulfed Boundary Park. From the day the re-arranged game took place a fortnight later, County's season fell apart. The Oldham match degenerated into a brawl with Bocking sent off and, following an FA hearing on 22 February, Waterall was suspended for a month and Wilson for a fortnight. On 10 February, outside-left Tommy Mitchell, County's leading goalscorer, was transferred to Blackburn Rovers for an undisclosed 'big' fee, and, on 26 February, the directors suspended John Blunt, Billy Morton and John Whitelaw for a 'breach of training regulations'. The same month saw Fred Scotchbrook sacked, surprisingly taking over at Wolves shortly afterwards.

By early April, relegation looked inevitable, confirmed by four successive defeats. County reserved their most comprehensive win for their last game, defeating runners-up Derby County 3-0 in front of Edgeley Park's lowest attendance of the season. Although Derby's promotion was assured, as was County's relegation, the Stockport team frustratingly demonstrated what most supporters believed, that the players were indeed good enough. If nothing else, the emphatic win was an appropriate finale for Albert Waterall who, after 13 seasons, finally left County.

As events transpired, County were condemned to Third Division football for 11 seasons following their relegation in 1926. Although it was often a case of the frustrating 'nearly but not quite', this period in County's history was probably the most exciting to watch, with only one truly forgettable season. During this 11-year spell, County scored a mammoth 984 League goals, third highest behind the powerful Arsenal (997) and Aston Villa (988). It may be that, generally, supporters put success before goals but, after over 20 years of neither, Stockport's high-scoring teams, which almost succeeded, became a pleasant consolation.

In June 1926, a month after the end of the relegation season, former player Lincoln Hyde was appointed as manager, supported by Fred Westgarth who was to manage County eight years later. The nucleus of the team remained but Reid, Richardson and Waterall were freed and John Wilson was transferred to Manchester United. Former amateurs Harry Burgess and Tommy Scurr signed professional terms, and new signings included full-back Len Williams from The Wednesday, Harry Catterick from Chilton Colliery and Harold Odenrode from Aston Villa. County retained the promising Boardman, Bocking, Critchley and Johnston, together with Tommy Meads, but the club was aware that supporters' expectations could be too high, assuming that 'history would repeat itself' and County would bounce back into the Second Division as they had in 1921-22. There had been a distinct improvement in the quality of football in the Northern Section and it was evident that a number of clubs would provide stiff opposition to County's challenge for promotion. It should also be remembered that when there were two sections of the Third Division, only the champions were promoted.

A 4-1 defeat at Halifax on the opening day of the 1926-27 season put County's task into perspective: there would be no running away with the League. Following this sobering start, Harry Burgess came into the team and County embarked upon an eight-match unbeaten run, with both Burgess and Billy Johnston figuring regularly on the score-sheet, as they would do for the rest of the season. A 2-1 defeat by Wrexham was followed by three wins which included a fine 1-0 victory over promotion favourites Stoke at the Victoria Ground. November 1926 was a forgettable month for County who suffered two League defeats and a 4-1 hammering by a very strong Nelson team in the first round of the FA Cup. Stockport came back from this disappointment to record six successive victories at the end of the year, this despite the fact that, on 22 December, the highly gifted Eddie Critchley was transferred to Everton where he was to enjoy great success.

With half the season gone, County were lying in second place, four points behind leaders Stoke, but with a game in hand. County's surge up the table had followed the FA Cup defeat at Nelson and when they returned to Seedhill on 8 January for a League match, they were thrashed 6-1. A home defeat by Halifax the following week left County in a position where they could hardly afford to drop another point and, although they won three of their next four games, the remainder of the season was marked by the kind of inconsistency which was to hinder them for many years to come.

However, the fact that, by the end of February, the prospect of an immediate return to the Second Division looked highly improbable, did not mean that the remainder of the season was uneventful. On 10 March, Tommy Meads, who had been converted successfully from inside-forward to half-back, was transferred to First Division Huddersfield Town, who were looking well-placed to win their fourth consecutive championship. In the event, Meads's arrival at Leeds Road coincided with a disappointing run-in, Huddersfield's hold on the championship being wrested away by Newcastle United.

Meads's departure from Edgeley Park led to one of County's most famous 'big name' signings. Although Meads was a half-back and County had two goalscoring forwards in Burgess and Johnston, on 17 March, transfer-deadline day, the club quite sensationally brought Joe Smith, the famous Bolton captain and former England international, to Edgeley Park. County had managed to capture Smith by agreeing to pay Bolton Wanderers his benefit money, which amounted to £650. Considerable publicity accompanied the signing, particularly as Smith's debut was to be at home to League leaders Stoke. With the Potteries club bringing a considerable following, and County fans eager to see if one of the country's best-known players could help lift the club to an unlikely charge to the championship, a record crowd of 22,622 gathered at Edgeley Park. Shortly before the kick-off, County's chairman, Ernest Barlow, received a telegram from the Football League which stated curtly: 'don't play Smith – registration not in order'. Not surprisingly, Barlow was reluctant to risk the wrath of the huge number of County fans by withdrawing Smith at the last minute. Barlow told no one of the telegram and the crowd were treated to an exciting 2-2 draw after County had trailed 2-0 at half-time. Goals by Albert Pearson and Tommy Scurr brought County level and within two minutes of County's equalising goal, they were awarded a penalty. Despite his immense experience, Joe Smith contrived to miss the penalty and County had to be content with a draw. County's failure to make up ground on Stoke was made much worse as a result of Smith's appearance, the club being charged with a breach of League rules; County had two points deducted for fielding an 'unregistered player'.

The problem which had emerged was quite simple: County had dispatched Smith's transfer documents in the belief that the dated postmark was sufficient proof of date of registration. The League deemed this to be inadequate and, in addition to the penalty imposed, further ruled that Smith could only play in those games which could have no bearing on promotion or re-election. (Interestingly, the League records give Smith's date of registration as 17 March, two days before the Stoke game. An additional point of note was that County's misfortune led to a change of League rules which determined that 'proof of posting a transfer is proof of signing'.) Although the two points lost made promotion an impossibility and left County to finish the season with nothing to play for, there was no lack of interest during the final ten games.

For the first time ever, County ended the season with two players, Burgess and Johnston, scoring more than 20 goals and the heavy defeats suffered at Nelson were partially avenged by a 4-1 victory at Edgeley Park, one of the matches in which Joe Smith was barred but in which Harry Burgess became only the second County player to score all four goals; in so doing, Burgess broke Norman Rodgers's goalscoring record of 1914-15, finishing the season with 28 goals, seven more than Rodgers. The penultimate home match of the season on Easter Monday saw a remarkable game against Hartlepools United; leading 3-0 through Smith and Burgess (2), County somehow managed to concede three goals in the last 11 minutes, the match ending in a 3-3 draw. Although in some ways a disappointing season, it had, nonetheless, been an eventful one. In the light of what was to follow during subsequent years, perhaps the biggest disappointment came at the end of the season when the League failed to support a proposal by the Northern Section, that four clubs be relegated from Division Two and replaced by two promoted clubs from both the Northern and Southern Sections. A forward-looking proposal it was, but one that was 30 years ahead of its time.

When County kicked-off the 1927-28 season, the club was justifiably confident of its prospects. Whilst it had still not succeeded in finding a goalkeeper of Hardy's consistency, it had excellent full-backs in Bocking and the newly acquired Billy Wilson from Manchester City. With Billy Newton and Jack Jobson in the half-back line and a forward-line which included Ben Boardman, Harry Burgess, Billy Johnston and Joe Smith, County had a potentially outstanding team. In their penultimate practice match (which comprised their 22 most senior players), they had the unique distinction of having the opposing captains in the Wembley Cup Final of 1923, George Kay and Joe Smith, captaining 'The Whites' and 'The Blues'. With this kind of experience supporting the younger talent at Edgeley Park, on paper the team looked too good for the Northern Section but, as is so often the case, what looks good on paper does not necessarily translate to performances on the field. When Billy Johnston and Joe Smith gave County a 2-0 win in the first game of the season against Rotherham United, early confident predictions appeared well-founded – but they did not last long. Although he was to beat Harry Burgess's goalscoring record set the previous season, on 24 September, Joe Smith was sensationally dropped having scored only once in the first six League games. Within three weeks, Billy Johnston, Stockport's clever high-scoring inside-forward, was transferred to Manchester United and County's season was collapsing almost before it had started. From the first match of the season until after Christmas Day 1927, County won only six of their 16 League games and were knocked out of the FA Cup in the second round when they lost 2-0 at Crewe.

From late November, there were signs of improvement when three successive home games resulted in two wins and a 3-3 draw against Accrington Stanley in which Joe Smith scored a hat-trick. Although at Hartlepools, Smith scored in his fourth consecutive game, County continued their dismal away record, losing for the sixth time and without a win away from Edgeley Park. However, Boxing Day witnessed County begin an eight-match winning run, which included four victories away from home and Joe Smith in irresistible form. A hat-trick in a 4-0 home win against Barrow was followed by another hat-trick on 2 January 1928 against Rochdale in the next game at Edgeley Park. Five days later, Smith became the first County player to score five goals in a match as Southport were beaten 6-3. Before the end of the season, Smith was to score four against Tranmere Rovers and two on four occasions, one in an 8-0 thrashing of Nelson, whose poor form was in marked contrast to that of the previous year. Although County won 16 of their last 25 League games and finished in third place, their poor start to the season resulted in promotion never realistically being within their grasp as they finished nine points behind promoted champions Bradford. Contrary to his goalscoring success of the previous season, Harry Burgess, ended with a disappointing 12 goals from 35 games whilst, at the age of

38, Joe Smith had amassed a remarkable tally of 38 goals, and this after being dropped for two games!

It would be inappropriate to describe 1928-29 as anything other than a wonderfully exciting and entertaining season, in spite of the fact that County ended up without anything tangible to show for their exhilarating football. As ever, the *Cheshire Daily Echo* provided optimistic prospects prior to the start of the season, but the comments made were both thoughtful and incisive. Whilst believing that it was reasonable to assume that, of the half-dozen young players on the books, 'two or three of these will make good', it was recognised that there should be no surprise if any of 'the tried veterans fail before the end of the season'. County made a number of summer signings, including two outside-lefts, Billy Tompkinson from Rochdale and Alf Townsend from Nottingham Forest, goalkeeper George Crowther and centre-forward John Everest, both from York City (who had not yet joined the Football League), whilst Jimmy Scullion left Edgeley Park to join Crewe. In the event, it was generally not the new signings who were responsible for County's improved form but rather the maturing of younger players, supported by 'veterans' such as Smith.

The season began with two difficult games against highly rated teams; first, at home to Tranmere and then away to Chesterfield. When both these games were won, County fans sensed that this might be their year although a 2-0 defeat at local rivals Crewe, where Jimmy Scullion starred against his former colleagues, was a little deflating. Whilst County's away form was only average, their home record was staggering. By the turn of the year, County had played 11 League games at Edgeley Park, winning ten, drawing one and averaging almost five goals a game. A 4-1 victory in their first game against Tranmere was followed by scores of 4-0 (v Ashington), 7-3 (v Lincoln City), 6-1 (v Accrington Stanley), 2-2 (v Carlisle United), 6-2 (v Wrexham), 4-0 (v Rochdale), 7-3 (v Darlington), 7-1 (v South Shields), 4-1 (v Doncaster Rovers) and 1-0 (v Rotherham United). The goals were coming from all the forwards, particularly Smith, a revitalised Harry Burgess and County's most recent find, Frank 'Bonzo' Newton. As the season unravelled, a titanic struggle developed between County and Bradford City. After home victories against Halifax Town and Southport in the FA Cup, County were drawn away to Bradford City in the third round. On 12 January 1929, a little over 30,000 saw City win 2-0 at Valley Parade which left County to 'concentrate on the League'. This was clearly the view of the club who, within days of their FA Cup exit, brought the former Newcastle United captain Frank Hudspeth and his Tynecastle colleague Tom Curry to Edgeley Park.

It would be unfair to say that the struggle for the championship was a 'two-horse' race; Wrexham and Wigan Borough both had their best ever seasons whilst the newest team in the League, Carlisle United, were threatening to become champions at the first attempt. However, both County and Bradford City seemed to be the sides most likely to maintain their momentum, reflected by a record Edgeley Park crowd of 24,311 for the visit of Bradford on 2 February. Goals from Harry Burgess and Ben Boardman led County to a thrilling 2-1 victory which put them five points clear at the top, although this was followed, seven days later, by a surprising 2-0 flop at Peel Park against Accrington. When

County visited Brunton Park on 23 February second-place Carlisle were undefeated at home and the top of the table read: County 39 points from 28 games, Carlisle 36 from 30, Bradford City and Wrexham both with 35 from 28 games. County ran away to a remarkable 5-0 victory, a win which so demoralised the Cumbrian team that they slipped out of the title race. County's four point lead over Wrexham was halved the following Saturday when they lost 2-1 to the Welsh side, but three successive wins put County back on course as they entered the Easter programme, still top but now with Bradford City in hot pursuit.

The Easter programme has long been recognised as one which is highly significant in determining the destiny of championships and relegation and 1928-29 provided no exception. Over 13,000 attended Edgeley Park on Good Friday for the visit of Cheshire rivals, Crewe, when events that day should have forewarned County fans that it would not be their year. The loss of a point in a 2-2 draw was bad enough but County had thrown away their chance of victory with two missed penalties. The first was taken by Frank Hudspeth, who shot straight at Crewe's goalkeeper, and County fans could hardly believe it when, following a second award, Harry Burgess, who was on a hat-trick, shot wide of the post. Although Burgess partly redeemed himself on Easter Saturday with another two goals in a 3-2 win at Darlington, in front of an increasingly strong Wigan Borough side on Easter Monday, County fell apart, beaten 4-0 in front of a crowd of over 15,000 fans at Springfield Park. The following day, 2 April, Bradford City beat Hartlepools United 4-1 to go top on goal average and with County having three away games in their last five, Bradford looked firm favourites for the title.

However, four days later, whilst Bradford surprisingly dropped a home point to lowly Rochdale, County had an easy 3-0 win over Nelson and moved back to the top. With County's three successive away games to come and Bradford still having a precious game in hand, the odds still favoured City. County deserved enormous credit for continuing to battle as they won all three away games without conceding a goal. Unfortunately for them, Bradford also won three successive games and as the League season entered its last week, County remained one point in front of Bradford who, on Tuesday 30 April, were

to play their game in hand at Rochdale, the team who had helped to give County hope some three weeks earlier. Rochdale's previous home game had attracted a mere 2,894 but, in what was virtually the deciding game of the season, 20,945 packed into Spotland the majority making the short trip from Bradford, and no small number arriving from Stockport. In what was virtually a home game for City, they ran out comfortable 3-1 winners. Now a point ahead of Stockport and with a vastly superior goal average, Bradford needed only a point at Valley Parade against South Shields to clinch the championship. The fact that, barring a major upset, the title was decided, was reflected in the attendances on the final Saturday of the season: 35,000 at Valley Parade to see a predictable Bradford victory over South Shields whilst only a little over 7,000 attended Edgeley Park to see a Billy Tompkinson hat-trick help County to a 3-2 win against Barrow in what was a depressing anti-climax to a remarkable season.

Even though County had amassed a magnificent 62 points and won nine of their last 11 games, it had still not been enough. They had scored over 100 League goals for the first time and, in addition to Burgess's 31 League goals, County had five other players reaching double-figures: Boardman (12), Fielding (10), Frank Newton (16), Smith (19) and Tompkinson (14). Their attendance had also averaged over 10,000 for the first time. A memorable season it had been, but one that, in the end, was frustratingly disappointing.

Despite the magnificent showing of the previous season, changes were made before 1929-30 began. Now almost 40, the veteran Joe Smith was freed whilst the immense goalscoring talent of Harry Burgess was lost to Sheffield Wednesday, a club with whom he would gain international honours, although County were well-compensated for their loss, to the tune of £3,000. Little money was spent on replacements, only two newcomers making an impact in the coming season. The well-travelled Andy Lincoln arrived at Edgeley Park with little pedigree, yet was to be County's only ever-present, whilst a local Reddish youngster, Charlie Gee, was to have an outstanding season at centre-half.

Notwithstanding the fact that County's record in 1929-30 was even better than in the previous season, their 63 points were still not enough to bring the championship to Edgeley Park. In 1928-29, County finished ten points ahead of third placed Wrexham; in 1929-30, they finished 13 points ahead of third placed Darlington but, more importantly, concluded the season four points behind champions, Port Vale. This was despite the fact that County completed a magnificent double over Vale, more than 14,000 seeing Port Vale defeated 2-1 at Hanley on Christmas Day whilst nearly 23,000 saw County win 4-2 with goals from Billy Newton, Frank Newton and Andy Lincoln (2) in the return fixture at Edgeley Park on Boxing Day.

County, 1929-30. Back row (left to right): W.Newton, Helliwell, Crowther, Gee, Lincoln. Front row: Tompkinson, Boardman, Bocking, Wilson, F.Newton, Fielding.

Blackpool goalkeeper Wolfe drops on the ball to bring a Stockport attack to a halt in the FA Cup third-round tie at Bloomfield Road in January 1930. Tommy Browell's two goals gave the Seasiders victory.

On 21 September, Frank Newton had become only the second County player to score five goals in a match during a 6-1 victory over Nelson. The feat was made more sensational as he scored a hat-trick in a six-minute spell before half-time. A fortnight later on 5 October, Newton suffered a more sobering experience as County's record-breaking unbeaten home run came to an end when they were beaten 3-2 by their bogey team, Crewe Alexandra, former County player Jimmy Scullion again doing the damage by scoring a hat-trick. In this first home defeat for two and a half years, Frank Newton missed a penalty which, had it been converted, would not only have given him a hat-trick but would have preserved County's record. In the FA Cup, after beating Wellington 4-1 and Barrow 4-0, County again reached the third round only to lose, a little unfortunately, 2-1, to eventual Second Division champions, Blackpool, at Bloomfield Road.

Following County's 'double' over Port Vale, they dropped three points at home in successive games and promptly dropped leading goalscorer Frank Newton who had scored 22 goals in 22 League and Cup matches. His replacement, John Everest, scored in a 1-0 win at Wigan Borough and then four times in a 7-1 victory over Carlisle United at Edgeley Park. The latter victory gave a comprehensive double over the Cumbrian side, as earlier, County had scored five at Brunton Park for the second season running, a game in which elements of the 10,000 crowd vented their anger on the referee who was stoned by some of the Carlisle fans. Andy Lincoln's winning goal at Seedhill against Nelson began a record-breaking sequence for the former Northampton player in which he scored in nine consecutive matches. County's 4-0 win against third-placed Darlington at the beginning of April 1930 gave the Edgeley fans some hope that their side could gain promotion, a view strengthened by County's

win at Hartlepools whilst Vale dropped a point at Chesterfield. However, County's successive away defeats at New Brighton and Lincoln City put the Potteries club in a virtually impregnable position as they obtained a record-breaking 67 points to leave County runners-up for the second year running. County's 106 League goals had still not been enough, although Andy Lincoln's 26 goals had been a surprise to everyone, more so than the prolific 'Bonzo' Newton who had netted 36 times in 35 League games. It was, yet again, a case of what might have been and County supporters could not help but wonder whether their team could mount another serious challenge for the Northern Section championship.

'Hope deferred maketh the heart sick' wrote the football journalist in the *Cheshire Daily Echo's* review of County's prospects for 1930-31. 'Stockport County's unfortunate experience in the last three seasons, when they have narrowly missed gaining promotion, makes one reluctant to prophecy that they will gain promotion in the coming season'. It was genuinely believed that, in 1929-30, County had been the best team in the Northern Section but, when such a team failed both to get the bit of luck needed and to avoid unnecessary slips, any reluctance to even cautious optimism was understandable. There were changes at Edgeley Park with the highly rated Charlie Gee moving to Everton and wingers Billy Tompkinson and Horace Fielding replaced by Cyril Matthews from Lincoln City and 21-year-old Billy Webster from Unsworth Colliery.

The season started with two home victories which were followed by two heavy defeats, 6-1 at Lincoln and 5-1 at Carlisle. Another two home victories preceded a 2-1 defeat at Wigan where Borough's close-season signing from Crewe, Jimmy Scullion, continued his rich vein of scoring against his former colleagues as he netted both of Wigan's

New signings Alf Lythgoe, Jimmy Stevenson, Jack Hallam, Llewellyn Purcell and Percy Downes pose in the summer of 1932 with Fred Westgarth, who was then trainer at Stockport County.

goals. County then found some consistency in an excellent run which saw them win 11 of the next 16 League games, the last of these resulting in a 4-2 home victory over promotion rivals Lincoln City, with Frank Newton scoring his second successive hat-trick at Edgeley Park. Although County had been knocked out of the FA Cup by Bristol Rovers in the second round, there was a genuine sense of anticipation at Edgeley Park that it was to be third time lucky in the League. When County beat Wigan Borough 4-2 on 24 January 1931 in their 1,000th Football League game, they were second in the League, three points behind leaders Lincoln City. However, quite inexplicably, County's season then fell apart as they won only three of their last 16 games to end the season in seventh place. Ironically, champions Chesterfield won the title with 58 points, which was at least four fewer than County had acquired in their seasons as runners-up.

Shortly before the end of April, manager Lincoln Hyde took over at Preston North End and long-serving club captain, Billy Bocking, was transferred to Second Division champions, Everton, for a 'four-figure transfer fee'. In the circumstances, it was perhaps not surprising that the team which had changed only slightly during the previous four 'nearly' seasons, was now almost completely broken up. Of County's forwards, Frank Newton, who had enjoyed yet another excellent season, scoring 37 goals in 41 League and Cup games, was transferred to Fulham for an 'undisclosed figure', Andy Lincoln, who had not reproduced the scoring feats of his first season, moved, quite appropriately, to Lincoln, Ben Boardman was transferred to Manchester City and Cyril Matthews to Chester. In addition, Billy Newton was transferred to Hull City and other players were given free transfers. Of the incoming players, goalkeeper Tommy Gale from Barnsley was the best known, whilst Jimmy Scullion returned to County after haunting them whilst at both Crewe and Wigan. The most significant signing would prove to be that of Fred Jenkinson but his talents were to take more than a season to come to the fore.

By making a 'clean sweep', the County management had acted in a way that the supporters desired but, the complete change of players resulted in the club having a

team which was very much an unknown quantity. 'The County will rely on youth for the knockabout of the Third Division' was the verdict of the *Cheshire Daily Echo* but, even before the season began, it was arguable whether such reliance was advisable. The introduction of 'new brooms' was self-evident when County began the 1931-32 campaign with only Eddie Vincent and Billy Webster having played in the last match of the previous season. As it transpired, the season was disastrous, County's worst by far in the Northern Section. They finished in 12th place, scored a meagre 55 goals and played in front of increasingly smaller crowds at Edgeley Park. They suffered a humiliating first round FA Cup defeat at non-League Crook Town and there was little in the season that was admirable, memorable or which gave any grounds for optimism. One of the few points of interest was when, on 21 January 1932, County's highly promising 18-year-old George Farrow was involved in a direct exchange for the Wolves centre-forward Joe Griffiths who, two days later, provided a 5,500 Edgeley Park crowd with a notable hat-trick on his debut. Although Griffiths only played the last 15 games, he still ended the season as top scorer with 11 goals, which was five more than the next highest scorer. However, pessimism was not confined to Edgeley Park as, in the latter part of the season, there were rumours of the Northern Section folding up because of financial difficulties. The general economic situation was reflected in smaller crowds throughout the League and clubs other than County had to find ways of ensuring survival during the economic depression of the 1930s.

During the close season, four new directors were co-opted to the board and, having spent the previous season without a manager, Andrew Wilson was appointed to fill the position. As County's problems the previous season had revolved around the making and scoring of goals, it was hardly surprising that the majority of the summer signings were forwards. A talented 18-year-old outside-right, Jabez Foulkes, was signed from Huddersfield Town, inside-left Jimmy Stevenson, who had acquired considerable experience with Bradford City, arrived from Aldershot, outside-left Percy Downes, who had played in the First Division with Blackpool, was transferred from Hull City and Alf Lythgoe, an unknown 'live-wire of the Cheshire League', was signed from Ashton National.

The prognosis for 1932-33 was much improved, the signing of players of the quality and experience of Downes and Stevenson generating considerable enthusiasm in the town. Two days before the start of the season, County signed centre-half George Carr from Leicester City and, on 27 August, kicked-off with some optimism against Darlington at Edgeley Park. A hat-trick from Joe Griffiths and debut goals for Downes and Stevenson helped County to a 5-1 win but, although County lost only two of their first ten games, they drew four. Over the season, the number of draws in which County were involved, 12 in all, would prove costly, although during the period from early October to early December, even a final placing in the top half of the League looked unrealistically optimistic. A disastrous spell saw County gain only two points from seven League games. The FA Cup provided County with their only victory during this time, defeating Rochdale in the first round before being beaten 3-2 at home to Luton Town in the second round. The inexperienced Lythgoe had played twice during this period in place of the injured Griffiths, but had failed to score. On Griffiths' return, County gained their first League victory for over two months, winning 3-0 at Barrow, before returning to Edgeley Park to lose to Carlisle United.

For the Boxing Day visit of Walsall, Griffiths was 'absent without leave' and Lythgoe replaced him, scoring twice in a 5-0 win. Two wins and two draws were followed by a visit to Anlaby Road on 21 January 1933, League leaders Hull City comfortably beating the improving County 3-0. Remarkably, this was County's last defeat of the season as the team put together an unbeaten run which consisted of 12 wins and four draws in the last 16 games, and saw County surge into third place. It began on 28 January with a thrilling 5-4 victory over Barnsley at Edgeley Park when, for the first time, Alf Lythgoe played at centre-forward alongside Joe Griffiths, helping to establish the former Ashton player as County's principal forward. Two days after the Barnsley victory, the *Cheshire Daily Echo* published an 'open letter' from the County board appealing for support from the Stockport public after less than 3,500 had attended the nine-goal encounter. Attendances did improve as County's run gathered momentum but not to a degree which their play warranted. It was hardly surprising that, with such poor support, County were prepared to sell Lythgoe whose goalscoring feats had not gone unnoticed in the First Division. A transfer deal which involved both Lythgoe and Fred Jenkinson going to Wolves, who were fighting grimly against relegation from the First Division, fell through, much to the relief of County fans. 'At the last moment' reported the *Cheshire Daily Echo* on 17 March, 'the negotiations broke down between Wolverhampton Wanderers and Stockport, owing to the terms not being satisfactory, with the result that Lythgoe is still a Stockport player.' Whether the unsatisfactory terms related to the players' terms or to the club's was not clear but, from the supporters' point of view, the only issue of significance was that Lythgoe was 'still a Stockport player'.

County's final game of this uneven season was at home to Chester on 6 May. Although the two clubs were level on points, thanks to their 15 match unbeaten run, County were in third place on goal average which meant that Chester needed to win to take third spot. Following County's fine 1-0 victory over championship aspirants Wrexham seven days earlier, it was disappointing that there were only 4,255 spectators present to witness County's most remarkable match to date. The appalling weather did not help for, although it was the first week in

May, torrential rain drove across Edgeley Park before kick-off. Within half a minute of the start, Humpish centred for Percy Downes to head County in front, only for the rain to come down so heavily that the referee led the players off the pitch. After three or four minutes, the rain eased slightly and referee Caswell of Blackburn led the teams back on to the Park to an accompanying flash of lightning and a heavy peal of thunder. With the wind behind them, County made a number of chances but after 12 minutes and with the home team appealing for offside, Kelly ran through to equalise for Chester. Three minutes later, Lythgoe fed Percy Downes who sent in a shot which goalkeeper Burke got his hands to, but could not stop. Despite, or perhaps because of, the appalling weather, the match was played at a frantic pace, the treacherous conditions leading to mistakes at both ends. After 30 minutes, a delightful move ended with 'Jabber' Foulkes striking the ball past Burke for County's third goal. Five minutes later, Bert Humpish, who was having an outstanding game, made a brilliant run before slipping the ball to Lythgoe to score County's fourth. The celebrations had hardly died down when Downes back-heeled the ball to Jimmy Stevenson who passed for Foulkes to score the fifth goal. After 39 minutes, Kelly broke away and, with the County defenders once again claiming offside, clinically drove the ball past McGann to make the score 5-2.

The second half began in an almost identical way to the first half, County scoring in the first minute when Humpish followed up after a Foulkes shot was charged down. After 52 minutes, Humpish's pass put Lythgoe through to beat Burke with an excellent shot. Although County continued to press, Burke made important saves before Chester broke away after 65 minutes and outside-right Armes was brought down by Taylor in the penalty area. Kelly coolly converted the penalty to complete his hat-trick and make the score 7-3. Remarkably, although four goals behind, Chester took control, Kelly shooting just over the bar and Armes having a goal disallowed for offside before, following a free-kick, Cresswell headed Chester's fourth goal after 72 minutes. Some six minutes later, Downes made an excellent run down the left wing, beating the Chester right-back before crossing for Lythgoe to head the ball against the bar from where it rebounded to County's player of the match, Humpish, who drove it in the net for County's eighth goal, their 99th of the season. Chester still threatened as County strove for their 100th goal in the final ten minutes, and it was the away side who should have had another penalty when Lloyd handled in the area, and it was Chester who scored the last goal of the match, Kelly taking Armes's cross from another breakaway to score his fourth goal of the game. For County, a record-breaking 8-5 victory and for Chester a remarkable fighting performance in which Kelly achieved the notable distinction of scoring four times whilst ending on the losing side!

There was no doubt that County had found a formidable forward line and, despite conceding five goals in their final match, the basis of an excellent defence. Although Lythgoe's goalscoring exploits naturally drew the acclaim, centre-half John Stevens was almost as important a discovery. Morpeth-born Stevens had arrived on 1 October 1932 on a month's trial from Manchester City. Having failed to impress in the reserves as a left-half, County were prepared to part company with him when both the first and second choice centre-halves were injured. Stevens came into the team for the away trip to Barrow where County ended their dismal early winter run and showed such fine form that he became a permanent fixture for the rest of the season.

From a playing point of view, County seemed to be very much 'on course', the team that ended the season strengthened by the former Welsh amateur international full-back, Len Jones, from Rhyl and Joe Hill, a talented Sheffield-born inside-forward, signed from Queen's Park Rangers. Financially, the position was far less encouraging. County had made a loss of £1,700 in 1932-33 and, with the need to pay players' wages over the summer, the club appealed to supporters to get season tickets in advance to ensure payment of wages. It was reported that the club had turned down a 'four-figure fee for one of their players in the hope that the public would rally round them'. County also implemented a scheme whereby the unemployed could gain free admission. Two hundred 'books' were issued at a cost of one guinea (£1.05), sponsored by various townspeople in order that the unemployed could use them on a rota basis, different names chosen each week from Social Centres and the Labour Exchange. Efforts were also being made to raise £2,000 new share capital by supporters buying shares at a shilling (5p) a week. With 1933-34 being County's Jubilee season, there was little doubt that the whole club was making every endeavour for the season to be an historic one and historic it was.

It began with County extending their unbeaten run to 18 games as they defeated Accrington Stanley 3-0 and Doncaster Rovers 4-3 at Edgeley Park, Lythgoe scoring twice in both games. Their first away match took them to The Shay where their unbeaten run was destroyed well before half-time. Within 27 minutes, Halifax had demolished County, racing into a 4-0 lead, all four goals (including one penalty) scored by outside-left Freddie Tunstall. A record defeat was a distinct possibility but, as Halifax relaxed, County fought back, Lythgoe and Humpish scoring, to give the final 4-2 scoreline an air of respectability. Two days later, County returned to Yorkshire to complete the 'double' over a strong Doncaster Rovers team.

County were playing some good football and, despite losing away games at New Brighton and Walsall, were well placed at the end of October. Their first game in November was at Edgeley Park against Southport and, in front of a crowd of only 5,242, County recorded their highest score to date as they crushed the Sandgrounders 9-2, Lythgoe scoring four goals which included a hat-trick between the 37th and 40th minute. An excellent 1-0 win at Wrexham with Lythgoe inevitably the scorer, was followed by a 5-2 win at home to Hartlepools United, Lythgoe's two goals bringing his season's tally to

17 in 15 games. Following the Hartlepools game, the *News Chronicle* reported that 'on present form, no team in the Northern Section is their better – and I have seen Chesterfield [who were top]. Powerful, young and confident from goal forward; methods that vary from close passing and quick dribbling to well-directed big kicking – that is Stockport County'. In the circumstances, it was surprising that County only just scraped through the first round of the FA Cup by a single goal at non-League Lancaster.

December was a month of mixed fortunes for County as they were knocked out of the FA Cup 2-1 by Crystal Palace at Edgeley Park and defeated by a single goal at leaders, Chesterfield. However, three wins and two draws left them as serious promotion contenders as they entered the New Year. The background to County's remarkable match against Halifax is important, putting the result in a context which made it all the more astounding. With exactly half the season completed, the top positions saw Chesterfield with 34 points from 22 games, County 30 from 21, Walsall 28 from 21, Halifax 26 from 21 and Barnsley 25 from 21 games. Regarding the visit of Halifax, the *Cheshire Daily Echo* reported that the Shaymen 'occupy a good position in the League and have the distinction of having scored more goals against the County than any other club this term'. Halifax's only misfortune was that their first-choice goalkeeper, 'Watty' Shirlaw, was injured during a 5-0 defeat at Hartlepools on New Year's Day and Stanley Milton stepped in for his debut at Edgeley Park on 6 January 1934.

A crowd of 7,807 witnessed 'County Stagger the Football World', their 13-0 win still a League record (since shared by Newcastle United who, in very different circumstances, defeated bottom club Newport County by the same score on 5 October 1946). Playing with a strong wind in the first half, Joe Hill, who was making his home debut, put County 2-0 up with goals after eight and 14 minutes and, although more chances came their way, they were unable to add to the scoreline before half-time. The strong wind had tempted County to play the ball in the air but the second half saw them playing the ball on the ground and, when Lythgoe scored a brilliant individual goal after 50 minutes, the floodgates opened and, within another 16 minutes, County were ten up. During an incredible 15-minute spell, goals came from Hill (51), who completed his hat-trick, Eddie Vincent from a penalty (53), 'Jabber' Foulkes (57), a Percy Downes hat-trick (59, 65, 66) and Jimmy Stevenson (61). After a lull of 14 minutes, Lythgoe (80), Stevenson (86) and Downes (88) completed the rout.

The County team which beat Halifax Town 13-0 on 6 January 1934. Back row (left to right, players only): Vincent, McGann, Jenkinson, Stevenson. Middle row: Foulkes, Hill, Stevens, Lythgoe, Downes. Front row: Robinson, L.Jones.

County's chairman, Ernest Barlow, did not share others' amazement with the scoreline, believing that the quality and 'machine-like precision' of County's play that season should not have caused surprise when it resulted in such a huge score. With a classic example of stating the obvious, Mr Barlow added that 'it just happened to be one of those days when everything came off for our side.' Apart from the scoreline, notable individual achievements included Joe Hill's hat-trick on his Edgeley Park debut, Alf Lythgoe's brilliant play, which saw him involved in seven of County's goals, and Percy Downes's four goals. Downes had not only emulated Halifax's outside-left Freddie Tunstall's achievement earlier in the season, but had done so without the aid of a penalty and remains the only winger ever to score four goals in one game for County.

As for Halifax, the only criticism levelled at them was that they should have concentrated on defence! More positively, they were congratulated for continuing to play football throughout the 90 minutes with neither their play nor their attitude degenerating. Few reports blamed Halifax's young goalkeeper, Stanley Milton who, contrary to some references, did make further appearances for the Shaymen. To their utmost credit, having suffered the most demoralising defeat imaginable, in their next League match a fortnight later, Halifax entertained leaders Chesterfield at The Shay and proceeded to thrash the Spireites 5-0.

Stockport's victory over Halifax was the fourth game in a run of 16 undefeated matches, County winning 12 and drawing four whilst scoring 65 goals and conceding 18. However, after six consecutive wins, two defeats over the Easter weekend and a third a fortnight later against a rampant Barnsley side, left County's nerves frayed, and the championship, which had seemed to be theirs for the taking, began to slip away. Three successive wins in the last three games would have guaranteed promotion but consecutive 1-1 draws against Tranmere Rovers and bottom club Rochdale left County in the weakest position of the three contenders on the last Saturday of the season. Barnsley, who were unbeaten in their previous 20 matches, and Chesterfield both had 60 points, whilst County were two points behind on 58. Barnsley were to play away at New Brighton, who were in the bottom half of the table whilst County were to entertain Chesterfield at Edgeley Park. Any of the three teams could win promotion, but Chesterfield had a sightly better goal-average than Barnsley and a win at Edgeley Park would probably take them up. For their part, County not only had to beat Chesterfield but rely on New Brighton ending Barnsley's long unbeaten run. An Edgeley Park crowd of over 21,000 saw a nervous battle between two of the potential champions, but tension so inhibited both teams, neither could break the deadlock. Whilst this 0-0 draw was being fought out, a single goal for Barnsley saw the Yorkshire club champions, leaving both County and Chesterfield supporters numb with disappointment.

County had scored a record 115 goals, but only eight of these came in the final eight games, costing them promotion in their Jubilee season. A further disappointment had been suffered four days before the Chesterfield game when County, having fought their way through to the inaugural Northern Section Cup Final, lost 4-3 to Darlington at Old Trafford, having led 3-2 with only two minutes remaining. A magnificent season, which had seen a variety of records created, ended in anguish. However much there was to remember, not least Alf Lythgoe's 46 League goals in only 39 appearances, the ultimate prize of promotion had eluded County once more.

Financially, the club was in a much healthier position, having made a profit of £1,775 during the previous season. Summer transfers involved the departure of Eddie Vincent to Grimsby Town, Bert Humpish to Rochdale, Jimmy McGann to Reading and Percy Downes to Burnley whilst there were no significant pre-season arrivals. The 1934-35 season began with a 6-1 victory over Southport at Edgeley Park on 25 August. The game was marked by Alf Lythgoe scoring five goals in a game for the first time and by the appearance of outside-left Dr George McKenzie, a former Scottish amateur international, the first doctor to play for County since Dr Blades some 50 years earlier. Six days later, one of County's favourite 'sons' returned, Billy Bocking transferred back from Everton for a mere £150. County won nine of their first 13 games but of greater significance to the supporters was the departure of Alf Lythgoe to First Division Huddersfield Town on 23 October. Lythgoe had already scored 15 goals in only ten League games and, with his remarkable record of 86 goals in 75 appearances, his departure was inevitable. County immediately signed a direct replacement, Billy McNaughton, a proven goalscorer, from Hull City. Although McNaughton scored in his first three games, injuries restricted him to only 15 League appearances. Goalkeeper Frank McDonough was signed from Blackpool as County went through the first of a number of bad spells. Inconsistency yet again cost County the chance of promotion as they ended the season in seventh place, ten points behind champions Doncaster Rovers.

However, 1934-35 was made memorable by County's best ever FA Cup run. After scraping a 1-1 draw through an equaliser by Foulkes at non-League Blyth Spartans, County won the replay 4-1. Over 12,000 saw the second round tie against Darlington at Edgeley Park when, with the score at 2-2, County were awarded a penalty in the last minute. Bob Green scored from the spot to give County a third round tie at West Ham. An Upton Park crowd of 26,400 saw an heroic performance from County goalkeeper Frank McDonough help keep the score down to 1-0 before, to everyone's surprise, a deflected shot by 'Jabber' Foulkes gave the Hatters a 1-1 draw. Almost 18,000 attended the replay at Edgeley Park where a single Joe Hill goal was sufficient to put County into the 'modern' fourth round for the first time where they were drawn to meet old rivals, Bradford City.

More than 30,000 at Valley Parade watched Second Division Bradford control the majority of the match without being able to break down County's determined defence, the game finishing in a 0-0 draw. On 31 January 1935, the replayed tie brought a record mid-week attendance of 22,096 to Edgeley Park where one of County's most exciting games was played out. Shortly after Joe Urwin had agonisingly missed what was virtually an open goal, a free-kick from Bocking was sent into the Bradford penalty area for Bob Green to score from close range. Although County dominated the half, further chances went begging and, two minutes before

County in 1934-35 with the Northern Divisional Cup. Back row (players only, left to right): Robinson, L.Jones, McDonough, Jenkinson, Still. Front row: Foulkes, Hill, Bocking, McNaughton, Green, Scott.

Over 30,000 spectators pack Valley Parade to see County hold Bradford City to a goalless draw in the fourth round of the FA Cup on 26 January 1935. County won the replay to reach the fifth round for the first time.

employed in the process just a maximum of vigour and robustness, I give Stockport full credit.'

Such a testimony probably guaranteed that West Brom would come to Edgeley Park with some caution but, in the event, the fifth round tie was a terrible anticlimax for the Hatters. A new record crowd of 24,604 packed into Edgeley Park on 16 February, despite the most appalling conditions. Torrential rain and a gale-force wind blowing down the pitch meant that each side would have to fight the elements as well as their opponents. When County's captain, Bill Bocking, won the toss, he made what proved to be a fateful decision to play against the wind in the first half. Bocking was never allowed to forget that decision as, by half-time, County were out of the game, 5-0 down courtesy of a combination of the gale and the quality of West Brom's play.

The famous Cup run over and effectively out of contention for promotion, County took some consolation by again reaching the Final of the Northern Section Cup after beating Hartlepools United 6-2 in the semi-final. On this occasion, County made no mistake, beating Walsall 2-0 at Maine Road, the goals coming from Billy McNaughton and Bennett (own-goal).

The club was able to announce a profit of £2,196, due mainly to the FA Cup run but this was over-shadowed by a devastating fire at Edgeley Park shortly after mid-day on 23 July 1935. The grandstand was gutted and 12 houses and an adjoining printing works were seriously damaged in the biggest blaze seen in Stockport for many years. The terrific heat generated by the fire melted the telephone wires, thankfully after the fire brigade had been called, and although there were no serious casualties, at least 50 people were made homeless. All County's records were lost which included fixture lists of the original Heaton Norris Rovers amongst other valuable memorabilia.

The start of the 1935-36 season began brightly with two 4-0 victories, away at York City and at home to Rochdale but, for the rest of the season, County were unable to put together a sufficiently good run to mount a serious promotion challenge. Four wins in the last five games lifted them to fifth place but the season was notable for their inability to score as freely as in previous seasons. Joe Hill was the leading scorer with 19 goals, closely followed by Billy McNaughton with 17 (which included five in one match against Mansfield Town), but the team failed to score on ten occasions. In the FA Cup, County were exempt until the third round, a reward for their exploits during the previous season. Immediately before the Cup-tie against Plymouth Argyle, the *Cheshire Daily Echo* revealed that 'the site of the grandstand which was destroyed by fire has been banked up with cinders and will add greatly to the holding capacity of the ground.' By far County's highest crowd of the season, almost 17,000, saw the Hatters lose 3-2 somewhat unluckily to their Second Division opponents.

half-time, Bocking slipped as he went into a tackle and Hallows ran through to equalise for Bradford. In the second-half, the tension mounted as both sides had chances before, 15 minutes from time, Bob Still beat a number of Bradford defenders to get in a shot which was parried out to Joe Hill who put County back in front. The wild celebrations had hardly died down when Jenkinson failed to make a successful tackle on Bradford's Spence who cleverly lobbed the ball over McDonough to bring the scores level again. No further scoring led to extra-time and County dominated the first period without being able to beat goalkeeper Swindin. Soon after the start of the second period, Joe Hill scored from a Bert Hales corner and when Joe Urwin was carried off, County supporters bayed for the final whistle as Bradford strove desperately for a third equaliser. It was not to be and, County were in the fifth round for the first time where they could look forward to a home tie against First Division West Brom.

The *Yorkshire Observer* paid the following glowing tribute: 'The County, in a few words, commanded the inspiration and zeal almost of fanatics – of men who were prepared to work until they dropped in a common cause, and had this been the Cup Final itself, they could not have been more full of fight. For that reason, and the fact they

Third Division Northern Section champions 1936-37. Back row (left to right): Jenkinson, McDonough, G.Jones, L.Jones. Middle row: Stevens, Oxley, Reid, Rice, Smailes. Front row: Titterington, Still. Insets: Hill, R.Kelly (manager), Bocking.

After two seasons of making excellent profits, County made a loss of £3,000 which, in the light of having to finance the building of a new grandstand, was less than encouraging. The close season saw a number of signings which were to reap rich rewards; these included Tommy Leach, a former England international centre-half from Newcastle United, outside-left Jimmy Smailes from Grimsby Town, centre-forward Leo Stevens from Southend United and outside-right Bernard Oxley from Plymouth Argyle.

For County's opening game of 1936-37, the majority of the new stand was operational as a crowd of over 11,000 saw County draw 3-3 against Darlington with both Smailes and Stevens scoring on their debuts. This was the first of three consecutive draws which were followed by four straight wins. Two days before the second of these wins, on 10 September, County supporters were shocked to learn that manager Fred Westgarth had resigned, but it was not uncommon for the club to continue for some time without an official manager. On 24 October, the new stand was officially opened by C.E.Sutcliffe, the president of the Football League, during the half-time interval of County's match against York City. The Football League president witnessed County's biggest win of the season, a 6-0 victory which included a Joe Hill hat-trick. The following week, County were beaten 1-0 by Carlisle United in what was to be their last defeat before a 16 match unbeaten run. Less than two weeks after this defeat, Carlisle's manager, Bob Kelly, was appointed manager of County on 13 November. Coincidences multiplied when first, County met Carlisle in the first round of the FA Cup on 28 November, losing again at Brunton Park, and secondly when, on 17 December, County's manager at the

beginning of the season, Fred Westgarth, became manager of Carlisle United!

As far as the League was concerned, following the defeat at Carlisle at the end of October, County were virtually unbeatable as they lost only two of the next 28 games, one of them, predictably, a home defeat to Carlisle United. County's major problem was that they were involved in more draws than was desirable and their play was far less exciting than in some of the previous seasons. Considerable criticism was levelled at the team but the absence of defeats resulted in County maintaining touch with the leaders, first Chester and then Lincoln City. On 3 February 1937, the Carlisle connection emerged once more when an exchange deal was arranged which brought Joe Mantle and Joe Taylor to Edgeley Park whilst Tommy Leach, Bill Smith and Alec Scott moved North to Brunton Park. Mantle had scored the winning goal for Carlisle which knocked County out of the Cup and the only goal of the game in their League meeting earlier in the season. Both Taylor and Mantle scored on their debuts in a fine 2-1 win at Oldham in front of a crowd of 23,142. When Billy Bocking was injured in March, County signed Gwyn Jones from Rochdale and the newcomer fitted into the role admirably. Two wins during the Easter programme kept County firmly in contention with Lincoln City as the championship developed into a contest between these two clubs. With four games left, Lincoln held a two point advantage over County but, when County achieved the double over Crewe in mid-April, Carlisle United, of all teams, came to County's rescue as they beat Lincoln 3-1, leaving both clubs on 57 points. On the penultimate Saturday of the season, it was Hartlepools United's turn to do County a favour when they defeated Lincoln 3-1 whilst

County scrambled to a draw at Chester with an 82nd-minute equaliser from Jimmy Smailes.

As fortune would have it, the last match of the season brought the two promotion contenders together at Edgeley Park and with County one point ahead of Lincoln, the onus was on the Imps to win; anything less than that would give the championship to County. County surprisingly brought in Billy Harker, for only his second match of the season, and Joe Hill, omitting both Duggie Reid and Arthur Rice. A record attendance was assured, 'officially' recorded by the Football League as 26,135 but which the club's figures assessed as 27,304. Captain Frank McDonough led County out amid noisy enthusiasm and they soon gained the ascendancy whilst remaining wary of Lincoln breaking away. Early in the match, Jimmy Smailes was brought down heavily with the result that he was a virtual passenger for most of the game but, despite County's supremacy, the sides went in at half-time on level terms. The deadlock was finally broken in the 64th minute when Joe Hill lobbed the ball into the angle between the bar and the post. Lincoln's goalkeeper, McPhail, and County forwards, Smailes and Stevens, all charged towards the ball and in the resultant scramble, the ball ended up in the Lincoln net. Although most reports credited the injured Jimmy Smailes with the goal, the general consensus was that it was Joe Hill's. With the exception of the significant Lincoln contingent, the crowd rose in vociferous triumph. Two minutes later, Hill threaded the ball through to Stevens who raced into the penalty area before being tripped by two Lincoln defenders. The Repton referee, Dr Barton, instantly awarded a penalty despite the furious but futile protests of the Lincoln defenders. Stevens picked himself up and calmly placed the ball into the bottom left-hand corner of McPhail's goal. The supporters' excitement bordered on the frenzied and it was only after this second goal that Lincoln took the game to County, missing a number of chances before the final whistle signalled a pitch invasion as, after so many near misses, County returned to Division Two.

Although somewhat hard on the Imps after a splendid season in which they scored 103 goals, and had been at the top of the League for some time, County's success was based on a sound midfield and strong defence, evidenced by the remarkable record of having lost only five games during the League campaign. It was undoubtedly true that other County teams during the previous ten years had played more attractive and exciting football but this team, unlike those before them, had kept their nerve and, for this reason alone, deserved their success.

County's return to the Second Division began brightly, beating Luton Town 2-1 in front of over 19,000 at Edgeley Park, before gaining a 2-0 victory at Nottingham Forest where Joe Mantle scored both County goals. Another Joe Mantle goal in a 1-0 home win against Manchester United, watched by a crowd of 24,386, gave County their fourth win in seven games. Now playing in front of large attendances (in only six games, home and away, were County watched by less than 10,000), County appeared to be capable of enjoying a season of consolidation at the higher level. However, on 19 November, leading scorer Joe Mantle was transferred to Hearts where, within three weeks, he broke his leg. Even at the end of a dismal December, when County failed to

win, they were in 14th place, seven points above bottom club Plymouth Argyle. On New Year's Day 1938, County were involved in a high-scoring game at Luton Town, going down 6-4. Their confidence seemed to have ebbed away as they completed both December and January without a League victory and were knocked out of the FA Cup by First Division Middlesbrough in front of a 34,757 crowd at Ayresome Park. As County dropped down the League, on 4 March 1938, they re-signed Alf Lythgoe and, on transfer-deadline day, brought Charlie Sargeant from Chester, Walter Lumby from Grimsby Town and goalkeeper Walter Rigby from Shrewsbury Town. It was, however, too little too late and, in spite of successive wins in the middle of April, four successive defeats condemned County to relegation in their first season back in Division Two.

Twelve months after the euphoria of May 1937, a somewhat chastened County released over half of its team, Billy Brown, John Daniels, Dick Fuller, Joe Hill, Sammy Hunt, Gwyn Jones, Frank McDonough, Bernard Oxley, Arthur Rice, Jimmy Smailes, Leo Stevens, Billy Sullivan and Joe Taylor all leaving Edgeley Park during the close season. In July 1938, manager Bob Kelly declared his intention to resign at the end of the month and Bill Bocking announced his retirement. New arrivals at County included Tommy Bagley from Bradford City, Jack Bowles from Accrington Stanley, John Essex from Crewe Alexandra and Billy Smith from Portsmouth.

Although County's return to the Northern Section began with a 0-0 draw at New Brighton, this game was one of only four in which they failed to score in 1938-39, all the forwards finding the net regularly. County returned to the attractive style they had displayed in the years prior to their promotion but, as in previous seasons, they were unable to put together a run of victories upon which to base a serious challenge for promotion. Nonetheless, County's attacking football gave their supporters a number of games to remember and exciting players to watch. Whilst County's defence could hardly be described as frugal, their young goalkeeper Jack Bowles quickly made himself a favourite at Edgeley Park, making his name in two marvellous victories at runaway champions Barnsley. When County played at Oakwell in early April 1939, Barnsley were already champions and unbeaten at home. Bowles played a major part in ensuring Barnsley's first home defeat of the season after Duggie Reid had given County the lead. Reid, the 'gentle giant', had developed into a magnificent player with an explosive shot and his transfer to a First Division club was frequently rumoured.

County reserved their best performances for the FA Cup where they reached the third round after disposing of two non-League clubs, North Shields and, after a replay, Walthamstow Avenue. In the third round, they had an excellent 2-1 win at Barnsley before being comprehensively beaten 5-1 by Liverpool at Anfield.

However, the major talking point around the turn of the year was the meeting of a Joint FA and Football League Commission with regard to County. For a number of weeks, reference was made to the Commission sitting in Manchester, but no explanation was given as to the subject matter of the hearing. Finally, on 3 January 1939, the Joint Commission made public its findings which were both sensational and disturbing. It transpired that the

Commission had been appointed to inquire into alleged breaches of FA and Football League rules by Ernest Barlow, County's chairman, Carlisle United's manager, Fred Westgarth, and the players of both Carlisle United and Hartlepools United during the latter stages of the 1936-37 season.

Both the allegations and decision of the enquiry can be better understood by looking back at the last month of County's promotion season. On 10 April 1937, with three weeks of the season left, Lincoln City were top of the Northern Section with 55 points and County were second with 53 points, both clubs having played 38 games. Lincoln had lost only one of their previous 16 games but then lost three of the last four, beaten by Carlisle United, Hartlepools United and County. On 15 April, Carlisle beat Lincoln 3-1, Lincoln winning the return game two days later. On 24 April, Lincoln lost 3-1 at Hartlepools and, with County drawing at Chester, The Hatters were one point ahead with the final match against Lincoln to come.

On 21 November 1938, George Worsley, a County director, made and signed a statement prior to the first hearing of the Joint Commission. Mr Worsley did not attend the second hearing three weeks later, having informed the Commission that he had tendered his resignation as a director of Stockport County.

The Commission found the following admitted or proved: (i) that Mr Worsley offered a sum of money to then Carlisle player Tommy Leach (the former County player who had been transferred to Carlisle in February 1937) for distribution amongst the Carlisle players at the end of their match against Lincoln City on 15 April 1937; (ii) that Leach accepted the sum offered and distributed it amongst the Carlisle players; (iii) that Mr Worsley went to Lincoln on 17 April 'for the purpose of attempting to affect the result of a match by illegal payments' to the Carlisle players provided they beat Lincoln that day.

The Commission agreed that there was no evidence to support George Worsley's allegations (i) that he had acted under the instructions of County's chairman or that Carlisle United's manager, Fred Westgarth, or the club knew of his actions; (ii) that Fred Westgarth had attempted 'by improper means' to affect the result of the Hartlepools United v Lincoln City match on 24 April; (iii) that sums of money to make the illegal payments were received by him from the secretary and chairman of Stockport County. However, the Commission agreed that 'a degree of responsibility' rested with the Stockport club.

The Joint Commission's decision was (i) to suspend Mr George Worsley *sine die* from all football and football management and fine him £50; (ii) that Tommy Leach (by this time, ironically, a Lincoln player) be fined £20 and suspended for four weeks; (iii) that those players who had received illegal payments be fined between £15 and £20; (iv) that Stockport County should pay the costs of the enquiry and (v) that, other than the recipients of the illegal payments, the officials and other players of Carlisle United had no knowledge of these events.

Although the findings of the Joint Commission were damning, it was a great relief that they did not accept the numerous allegations made by County's former director, as the consequences could have been quite catastrophic. It is, of course, open to debate, but had County not been relegated in 1938, it would have been within the bounds of possibility for the Commission to order the club's

Some ten years after leaving County for Sheffield Wednesday, Harry Burgess guested at Edgeley Park in a wartime fixture against Chester on 14 September 1940. Burgess and Harry Catterick (second from left) both scored twice in a 4-0 win.

demotion. By the end of 1938-39, the events described were either forgotten or rarely referred to and County's new manager, Bobby Marshall, was pre-occupied by assessing the strengths of the squad he had inherited when he took control on 22 March 1939. Somewhat surprisingly, long-serving Fred Jenkinson and Bob Still were transfer-listed as was Alf Lythgoe who, though 32 years old, had still ended as County's top goalscorer with 20 League goals. In the event, these decisions proved academic for, within a week of the start of the 1939-40 season, World War Two broke out and, on 4 September, the Football League was suspended.

A wartime regional League was established and County were allocated to the Western Section which comprised Chester, Crewe, Everton, Liverpool, Manchester City, Manchester United, New Brighton, Port Vale, Stoke City, Tranmere Rovers and Wrexham. The League began seven weeks after the final Football League match and, although most clubs were affected by the loss of players to the armed forces, County found it difficult to compete with the strong teams in the Western Section. As a result of the relaxation of the rules governing players' registration with the Football League, a major facet of wartime football was the use of 'guest' players which meant that players could play for a number of club during any particular season. It also gave reserve players at some of the bigger clubs the opportunity to play regular first-team football at some of the smaller clubs. County's most successful and regular guest player was Harry Catterick (Jnr) of Everton who made 122 appearances and scored 98 goals for the Hatters in wartime competitions in addition to playing over 70 games for his primary club.

The most interesting period for County in this first (or, indeed, any) wartime season was between 25 November and 9 December 1939. In this two-week spell, a hat-trick was scored by a County player in three successive games, of which only one was won. A 5-0 victory over Tranmere Rovers, with Duggie Reid scoring four goals, was followed by a remarkable match at Maine Road. After going in at half-time with the score at 1-1, after 69 minutes County found themselves losing 5-2 to Manchester City before a remarkable recovery saw them bring the scores level. After 87 minutes, City made the score 6-5 and then, in the last minute, County were awarded a penalty. Fred Howe (the Grimsby Town 'guest') stepped up to record his fourth goal of the game and make the final score 6-6. One week later, County entertained Manchester United and, in spite of a Duggie Reid hat-trick, went down 7-4.

Whereas County had performed with some success in

The County team which beat Rochdale 4-0 on 21 September 1940. Back row (left to right): Percival, Howe, Topping, Fielding, Neilson, Butler. Front row: Toseland, Taylor, Catterick, Burgess, Burrows.

wartime football during World War One, this was not repeated during the seven seasons between 1939 and 1946. Most games were poorly attended, although the inclusion of famous guests maintained interest amongst the spectators. It was not unusual for clubs to find themselves short of players and, in such circumstances, in addition to quickly registering an opposition's 'surplus' player, a spectator was occasionally used to make up the numbers. This was the case with L.Fallows who played in goal against Stoke City in 1941, and Michael Murphy, who played outside-right against Everton at Goodison Park in 1944. Infrequently, such an unexpected appearance could lead to a more permanent signing-on, as was the case with Ken Shaw in December 1941. All of these factors led to large numbers of players representing County during the war years, 1944-45 providing a record 58 players donning the County kit in competitive first-team matches.

Although World War Two ended in 1945, the Football League did not resume until the following year. However, the FA Cup did resume and, for the first and last time, was run on a home and away basis up to the semi-final stage. This latter factor hardly affected County who lost 3-2 on aggregate to Rochdale in the first round. The last season of regionalised football gave clubs the opportunity to prepare for the resumption of League football and it was during this season that County made history as participants in 'the longest game'. Whereas the first 18 games of 1945-46 were played within the Division Three Northern Section (Western Region) League, the next ten games constituted the first part of a Northern Cup. Both Western and Eastern Regions had a 'mini' League of ten teams, the top eight in each region qualifying for a knock-out competition which was to be played over two legs. County finished top of the Western Region and were unluckily drawn against the winners of the Eastern Region, Doncaster Rovers.

The first leg at Belle Vue on 23 March 1946 ended 2-2, County somewhat fortunate to draw after being outplayed for long periods of the game. On 30 March, Doncaster arrived at Edgeley Park for the second leg which was played on an unusually warm afternoon. County's only change from the first meeting was that of Les Cocker who replaced Eddie Steele. An excellent crowd of 12,730 saw County take an early lead through a Ken Shaw penalty after Arthur Burrows had been brought down. Although seemingly well in control, County were first shocked by an equaliser from Rovers's outside-left Maddison after 22 minutes, and then stunned when, a minute later, inside-left Todd fired Doncaster in front. County fought tenaciously in the second-half and were finally rewarded after 72 minutes when Ken Shaw scored his second goal to bring the sides level. The score remained level at full-time, and 30 minutes of extra-time began. County completely dominated this period but were unable to penetrate the Doncaster defence and, at the end of extra-time, the score was still 2-2.

Whilst frantic telephone calls were made to find out what was to happen next, the County players walked wearily off the pitch and, still in their kit, stood under the

On 9 March 1946, the day of the Burnden Park disaster, Ken Shaw places a penalty beyond the reach of Crewe Alexandra's goalkeeper in County's 4-1 win. The victory ensured that County finished top of the Third Division (Northern Section) Western Region Cup Qualifying competition, which led to the famous tie against Doncaster Rovers.

showers beneath the stand. In fact, the rules for the competition were that, if the scores were still level at the end of extra-time, the game should continue until one side scored. Referee A.Baker of Crewe restarted the game which went on . . .and on. Hardwick, the Doncaster goalkeeper, performed heroically, saving his team on countless occasions. As time wore on, the players wore out, many suffering from cramp, an affliction which also affected Mr Baker who, following treatment, managed to continue. There were further opportunities for County to score: Sam Weaver ran on to a loose ball before shooting it

Only 131 minutes to go. On 30 March 1946, in front of over 12,500 spectators at Edgeley Park, Ken Shaw equalises against Doncaster Rovers to make the score 2-2 in the second leg of the Third Division North wartime cup competition. This was the last goal of the 'longest match', the aggregate being 4-4 after 90 minutes and another 113 minutes being played before the game was finally abandoned.

over the bar; Ken Shaw failed to convert the easiest of chances when he was left with only Hardwick to beat and then, after 173 minutes, Les Cocker controlled Arthur Woodcock's pass before dispatching the ball into the Doncaster net. Jubilation! To the dismay of the fans and the players (which probably included some of the Doncaster players), the remarkably zealous Mr Baker disallowed the goal for hand-ball. Although on the defensive for virtually the whole of the 'extra' extra-time, Doncaster almost won the game when Marriott's shot flew past County's Jack Bowles only to hit the upright before rebounding against the opposite post.

With conditions becoming extremely gloomy, made worse by the proximity of smoke from the adjacent Edgeley railway shed, and with many of the players suffering from exhaustion, shortly before 7.00pm. Mr Baker blew his whistle to signal the end of the game, a full 203 minutes after it had started. There were numerous amusing tales of spectators leaving the ground and going home for tea before returning to Edgeley Park. It was rather less amusing for some of the families of the majority of spectators who remained at the ground. The failure of some to return home at an expected time caused considerable anxiety, which was hardly surprising bearing in mind that the tragedy at Burnden Park, Bolton, in

which 33 people lost their lives and 400 suffered injuries, had occurred only three weeks earlier.

As a brief epilogue, a coin was tossed to decide where the replay would take place; Doncaster won the toss and the game in a convincing 4-0 victory before a crowd of 13,500 at Belle Vue, some of whom probably came out of curiosity to see if this remarkable tie could ever be settled.

On the resumption of League football in August 1946, County had only two players, Jack Bowles and Jimmy Morris, who had played prior to the outbreak of war. County favourite Duggie Reid had eventually made a move to the First Division, signing for Portsmouth in March 1946 for a fee of £7,000. However, the nucleus of the team revolved around those players who had spent time at Edgeley Park the previous season and there was, therefore, no lack of experience. County's first game was at home to Halifax Town, as it had been in the suspended season seven years earlier. A comfortable 4-1 victory was followed by an away draw at Carlisle and then a 3-1 home defeat by Doncaster Rovers. Seven days later, County reversed the Doncaster scoreline at Belle Vue which, in the light of Rovers's runaway championship success, was an excellent result. Although County enjoyed some commendable victories and were to finish in fourth place, they simply lost too many games, 16 in all, whilst drawing

The County team which beat Accrington Stanley 2-1 on 14 September 1946. Back row (left to right): Burrows, Brown, Bowles, Buckley, Chapman, Redfern. Front row: McCulloch, Walker, Morris, Earl, Brinton.

only two. As he had done in the last season of regionalised football, Ken Shaw finished as top scorer with 16 goals, whilst one of County's most industrious and inspirational players, Billy McCulloch, was the only ever-present. The FA Cup was restored to its single game format, County beating Southport 2-0 in the first round at Edgeley Park and then defeating Halifax Town 2-1 after a replay. The third round paired County with Bolton Wanderers, coincidentally the last First Division club County had beaten, almost 40 years earlier. However, in front of a crowd of 30,240 at Burnden Park, history was not to repeat itself as County were soundly beaten 5-1, Vic Walker scoring County's consolation goal.

To describe 1947-48 as a season of mixed fortunes would be a gross understatement for, at the same time as County were enjoying an excellent Cup run, they were also in danger of ending in the re-election area. The League season had started brightly enough with successive wins in the first two games, their 4-0 away victory at Southport especially noteworthy. This was followed by 13 games without a win before County enjoyed a 2-0 home success against Tranmere Rovers in early November. An excellent draw at Boundary Park against Oldham was followed by two home wins, a Tommy Barkas hat-trick helping County to a 4-2 victory over York City, the same player sharing four goals with George Glaister as Chester were beaten 4-1. Three successive home victories appeared to have halted County's slide but another disastrous run of nine games without a win left them struggling near the bottom of the Third Division.

Although signing two players in January, Ken Finney and Fred Kenny, who would become excellent servants of the club, it was the crisis signing of the vastly experienced 36-year-old Alex Herd from Manchester City on 16 March 1948 which was the single most important factor in County's revival. Herd's arrival, together with the signing of centre-forward Tommy Swinscoe from Chesterfield and half-back Alex Paterson from New Brighton, helped them to win seven of the last 11 games, inspiring County to vastly improved performances. Swinscoe's nine goals in his 14 appearances were of particular value, prompted by the craft and experience of Herd. However, even with this impressive end of season run, County still finished in 17th place, their lowest-ever position in the Northern Section.

County's major excitement that season came in the FA Cup. In the first round, they defeated Accrington Stanley 3-1 at Edgeley Park before being drawn against (then) non-League Shrewsbury Town. A crowd of 18,000 saw County held 1-1 after extra-time, this being a season in which the FA required extra-time to be played at the end of the initial tie. In fact, the game at Edgeley Park was abandoned eight minutes before the end of extra-time but the FA ruled that the tie be replayed at Gay Meadow. The teams fought out an exciting 2-2 draw, again after extra-time, thus necessitating a further replay. The second replay at Maine Road, Manchester, went to extra-time yet again, before a brave Billy McCulloch header gave County a 3-2 win over their tenacious non-League opponents. McCulloch's winning goal was both brave and

McGann, Glover, McCulloch and Paterson watch as Jack Bowles punches clear during County's 2-0 FA Cup second-round win over Nottingham Forest at the City Ground on 10 December 1949.

costly, causing him a severe head injury which put him out of the side for the remainder of the season. A third home tie brought Torquay United to Edgeley Park for the first time, County enjoying a comfortable 3-0 win through goals by Jimmy Morris and Tommy Barkas (2). The fourth round draw took County to The Valley to play the Cup holders, Charlton Athletic. Fractionally under 40,000 saw County put up a brave fight before succumbing 3-0 to Charlton, who were then beaten by eventual Cup winners, Manchester United.

Stockport's first victory of the 1948-49 season did not arrive until their sixth game, away at New Brighton, and another inconsistent and somewhat unsatisfactory season followed. On 28 August, County showed great spirit in coming from 3-0 down at Crewe to earn a draw, Len Barker scoring a hat-trick on his debut, thereby becoming the only player to achieve this feat away from Edgeley Park. Three weeks later, on 18 September, County were beating Carlisle United 1-0 with four minutes left but somehow managed to lose 2-1. Whilst there was little doubt that there were some talented players at Edgeley Park, there were also sufficient weaknesses for the team to fail to gel. They had the ability to beat any team in the Division whilst retaining the inconsistency to lose to far less talented teams. In Ron Staniforth, they had one of the most promising full-backs in the country and in September, County had persuaded the prodigious goalscoring 15-year-old Bryan Brennan to sign amateur forms. Having won only six League games by the end of the year, at least five players had asked for transfers, providing little evidence of a happy and settled team which was prepared to battle it out.

New Year's Day signalled a revival when County

enjoyed a comprehensive 4-0 victory over Crewe Alexandra at Edgeley Park. This was followed by six wins in the next eight games, including, at last, County's first away victory since early September, which came at highly-placed Gateshead on 19 February. Midway through this run, County manager Bobby Marshall resigned to take control of Second Division Chesterfield. This burst of consistency was quickly replaced by the erratic form of earlier in the season as County won only three of their last 11 games. Andy Beattie became manager on 30 April, which coincided with their visit to League leaders, Hull City, where they crumbled 6-1 in front of 38,192, the highest attendance of any League match in which County have played. The season ended with typical perversity when County thrashed runners-up Doncaster Rovers 5-1. Although they had shown a considerable improvement in their League position, finishing in eighth place compared to the previous season's 17th, they had acquired only five more points than in 1947-48.

In the FA Cup, County again progressed to the third found following away victories at Workington with goals from Alex Herd (2) and George Glaister, who scored the only goal of the second round tie at (then) non-League Scunthorpe United. County's third away tie found them facing eventual First Division champions Portsmouth, where their Cup interest was ended comprehensively in a 7-0 defeat at Fratton Park.

In 1949-50, although County's League form showed no significant improvement, on this occasion at least, it was perhaps forgivable in the light of them equalling their record-breaking FA Cup run of 1934-35.

A 3-0 victory over non-League Billingham Synthonia

was followed by a 2-0 win at then Third Division South Nottingham Forest. Les Cocker (2), Tommy Swinscoe and a Jimmy McGuigan penalty provided the goals in a fine 4-2 third round home tie against Second Division Barnsley in front of 23,847. Another Second Division side, promotion-seeking Hull City, were County's fourth round opponents, the clubs meeting at Edgeley Park in front of 26,600 on 28 February 1950. The tie was full of suspense but short of action until the last 20 minutes produced a flurry of activity, Swinscoe shooting wide in front of an open goal and Hull goalkeeper Bly defying Cocker with a brilliant save. A goalless draw left County very much as the underdogs for the replay but, on the following Thursday, County gained a quite magnificent victory at Boothferry Park. A crowd of 24,566 witnessed not simply a win for the Third Division side, but one in which the visitors were superior in almost every department of the game. County had already missed a number of chances when, after 33 minutes, Alex Herd controlled a loose ball and scored. Hull enjoyed a period of ascendancy shortly after escaping from a two-goal deficit when a Herd 'goal' was disallowed for offside. However, after 70 minutes, Les Cocker received a pass from Frank Reid and sent in a wickedly swerving shot which beat Bly to make the score 2-0. County held out easily to take themselves into the fifth round for only the second time, where they were drawn to play First Division leaders Liverpool at Edgeley Park.

Record receipts of £4,300 and a record crowd of 27,833 saw County play some wonderful football, controlling the majority of the game without having any luck whatsoever. In addition to the headline 'Stockport Had Reds On Defence For Most Of The First Half', the *Liverpool Echo* reporter admitted to being 'impressed by the calibre of the County's football. This was no Third Division stuff . . .in fact it was good class stuff.' The tragedy for County was that no matter what the quality of their football was like, they were short of the one essential – not good luck, but an absence of bad luck. After Stockport had been in control for almost an hour, Liverpool took the lead when a cross struck a County defender before falling into the path of Joe Fagan who scored with ease from six yards. This had come moments after loud appeals for a County penalty for a foul by Taylor on Alex Herd, with the *Liverpool Echo* admitting that 'Herd was definitely brought down from behind but the referee would not listen to the appeals.' After 70 minutes, Liverpool centre-forward Albert Stubbins ran from the half-way line before shooting. Although Jack Bowles made a magnificent save, the ball fell back to Stubbins and, incredibly, Liverpool were two up. The best goal of the game came in the dying minutes when Herd headed in from Frank Reid's corner. Bert Stewart of the *Stockport Express* summed up the game: 'when officials of a First Division club, which has just beaten a Third Division side, feel it incumbent on themselves to be apologetic about their success, it is a good indication that the success was not merited.'

Merited or not, Liverpool were through and County were out, and perhaps the team found it hard to lift themselves after the cruel way in which they had lost the match. Prior to that game, County were in fifth place, only four points behind leaders Doncaster Rovers. They then managed only four wins in the last 14 games, slipping down to finish in a disappointing tenth place. The

seemingly ageless Alex Herd had a magnificent season, finishing with 19 League and Cup goals.

In 1950-51, County signed centre-forward Andy Black, who, like Herd, was another experienced Scot from Maine Road, and Alan Oliver from Derby County. Surprisingly, they transferred Jimmy McGuigan to Crewe Alexandra shortly after the start of the season before bringing George Dick from Carlisle United and Milton Dixon from Stalybridge Celtic on a month's trial. All these new signings performed well, none more so than Andy Black who scored 18 League and Cup goals. As in 1935-36, County were exempt from the first two rounds of the FA Cup following their march to the fifth round the previous year. After beating Brentford 2-1 at Edgeley Park, County fell to eventual losing Finalists, Blackpool, at Bloomfield Road but not without giving the Seasiders a scare as they went out 2-1. With depressing predictability, County's season went well until they entered the last third. Although Rotherham United ended as runaway champions with a massive 71 points, County had 36 points from their first 28 games whilst their last 16 yielded only 12 points, leaving them in tenth place. The only truly memorable event of the season came in the last game when Alex Herd formed a right-wing partnership with son David at Edgeley Park against Hartlepools United, 17-year-old Herd Jnr beginning his career with the first goal in a 2-0 win. This was also the last of four League games that the schoolboy prodigy, Bryan Brennan, played. Sadly, the young man, who as a schoolboy could not stop scoring, now could not score and, whilst remaining on County's books, never made another first-team appearance.

The following season, 1951-52, saw some of County's finest signings for many years, outside-left Ray Weigh joining from Bournemouth, skilful but injury-prone inside-forward Eddie Moran from Leicester City and, the best-known of all, Jack Connor from Bradford City. Had the perversity that had afflicted County so often not been present, the Edgeley Park club could well have won promotion. After winning their opening two home games and losing their first two away games, County created an all-time League record of seven successive away wins when a Jack Connor goal beat York City on 10 November. During this time, County contrived to draw six, lose one and win one at home, when a reasonable home run would have seen them in first place. Even after this, they put together a run of six consecutive wins between January and February, before ending the season with only one victory in the last eight games to finish in third place. It could and should have been different but at least County's signing of Connor appeared to have been a wise move, the experienced 31-year-old scoring 15 goals in his 31 League appearances. There was no success in the FA Cup, County falling in a first round second replay to Gateshead.

During the season, Alex Herd was presented with a television set by the club in recognition of his 40th birthday, the presentation taking place following County's home win against Mansfield Town on 15 December 1951, a game in which Herd scored the opening goal. The day before, the *Stockport Advertiser* published an account of an angry County chairman who was sick of the 'don't want promotion rumours'. *Plus ça change, plus c'est la même chose* – the more things change, the more they are the same – an apt quote for so many elements of County's

County, 1951-52. Back row (left to right): McCulloch, Glover, Bowles, Kenny, Black, Paterson. Front row: Finney, Cocker, Staniforth, McCaig, Weigh.

Ray Weigh (third from left) scores the first of his two goals in a 3-1 win against Gateshead on 21 February 1953.

history. Shortly before the end of the season, manager Andy Beattie moved to Huddersfield Town for a salary reputed to be £1,500 per annum and, within a matter of weeks, County's highly-rated Ron Staniforth had followed him as did Tommy Cavanagh.

County began 1952-53 with no manager, Dick Duckworth not being appointed until 23 October. Whilst County could not, on this occasion, be accused of throwing away the chance of promotion, they were unable to put together a consistent run of good results. However, the major bonus from the supporters' point of view was that, for the first time in over 15 years, County had a reliable high-scoring centre-forward, Jack Connor scoring 31 League and Cup goals in his first full season. In addition to two hat-tricks, Connor became the first player to score five goals in a match since Billy McNaughton in 1935. Other significant events included the signing of Frank Clempson from Manchester United, a skilful player who would give excellent service to County for over six years, and Bob Murray who was to break the record number of appearances during his 11-year stay. The end of that season saw Jack Bowles finally retire after spending some 15 years at the club.

Prior to the start of the 1953-54 season, it was announced that the County professional staff was to be reduced from 43 to 29, a clear sign that the falling attendances experienced during the previous season were having an effect on the club's finances. New faces at

Edgeley Park included outside-right Chris Anderson from Blackburn Rovers and half-back George Pilkington from Chester. Les Cocker was transferred to Accrington Stanley and full-back Tommy Bell joined Oldham Athletic. Whilst the goals continued to flow for Connor – five hat-tricks, including a hat-trick of hat-tricks – the season provided yet more disappointment, the team as a whole not showing the form of one which could make a promotion challenge. When Connor went through a lean spell, so did County, too much reliance placed upon the centre-forward. In the second game of Connor's hat-trick of hat-tricks, County were away to Crewe Alexandra on 28 November and were trailing 1-0 with 27 minutes left. A remarkable burst of scoring saw five County goals in a 22-minute spell, Oliver and Clempson being the other scorers.

Two weeks later, Connor had the opportunity of creating a record should he score a fourth consecutive hat-trick against Workington in an FA Cup second round tie at Edgeley Park. An outstanding exhibition of goalkeeping by Workington's Monty Newlands restricted Connor to only one goal with the result that, at the end of the match, it was Newlands who was applauded off the pitch and not Connor. At the same time as County fans were waiting to see if Connor could achieve this record, *The Advertiser* revealed that the 'poorly supported team are losing £150 a week'. County's finances could have been helped by progress in the FA Cup but, following a goalless draw at Edgeley Park in the third round against Headington (now Oxford) United, the non-League team won the replay 1-0. A dismal run in the League between January and March saw County fade badly and, by the time Alex Herd finally retired at the end of the season, County had finished tenth, an improvement of only one place over the previous year.

The major news at the beginning of the 1954-55 season was the departure of the long-serving crowd favourite Billy McCulloch to Rochdale together with the receipt of a record transfer fee of £10,000 for Alex Herd's son, David, who had only played 15 League games, to Arsenal. Arnold Jackson was signed from Shrewsbury Town and, in another good season for goals, in addition to Jack Connor's 30, both his inside-forward colleagues reached double figures, Jackson scoring 11 and Eddie Moran 13. Sadly, County's longest serving chairman, Ernest Barlow, died on 4 September 1954, having held the chair for a little over 31 years. Had County not suffered such a bad spell in September when they played eight League games and won only once, they might have been able to mount a serious challenge for promotion. In the event, County fans had to settle for some remarkable high-scoring games, together with another four Connor hat-tricks. By far the most memorable match that season was played on 27 December in the second 'leg' of the Christmas home and away fixture with Chesterfield. On Christmas Day, County had struggled to a 3-2 win over Chesterfield who had been one point above them in the League. Chesterfield equalised twice before Connor scored the winner, 15 minutes from the end. Thus, when County visited the Spireites on Bank Holiday Monday, few expected even a point from the match. Chesterfield got off to a wonderful start, Keith Marsden scoring after only 20 seconds. After 12 minutes, Alan Keen made it 2-0 and the considerable number of travelling County supporters must have looked back nervously at their record 8-1 defeat at Chesterfield 43

years earlier and feared a repeat. But this was to be no 'normal' match. Had George Smith scored when he hit the County post, the result might have been very different, as it might if the Chesterfield goalkeeper, Ron Powell, had not decided to try to stop Arnold Jackson's indirect free-kick. The ball touched Powell before entering the goal and County found themselves back in the game. A diving header by Eddie Moran brought the scores level and, when Gene Wilson was brought down in the penalty area, Frank Clempson calmly converted the spot-kick to put County 3-2 up at half-time. Shortly after the restart, Marsden equalised for Chesterfield, but from the resultant kick-off, Connor burst through and, as centre-half David Blakey tried to get the ball back to Powell, Connor got to it first and restored County's lead. After 55 minutes, Connor scored his second to put County 5-3 in the lead. A stunning shot from Eddie Moran in the 75th minute gave him his second and County their sixth goal. As if to sum up the fact that, what had appeared to start as Chesterfield's day was a cruel deception, ten minutes from the end of the game, a clearance cannoned off referee Wilkinson and dropped at the feet of Arnold Jackson who made it 7-3. An extraordinary game watched by 9,408 had witnessed County's highest-ever away League score, equalled only in an FA Cup-tie against non-League King's Lynn in 1912. Apart from two other six-goal wins against Bradford (Park Avenue), in which Connor scored four goals, and Crewe Alexandra, towards the end of a somewhat crazy season, County scored four goals in three successive away games, but won only one. A 4-4 draw at Gateshead was followed by a 4-1 win at Wrexham and then another 4-4 draw at Crewe. These results came during a seven match unbeaten run when County scored 22 goals but won only three times. In the FA Cup, County were beaten at home in the first round by Carlisle United who had lost 5-2 at Edgeley Park on the opening day of the season. After losing three of their last four games, County ended the season in ninth place, their unpredictability now almost predictable.

The goals did not dry up in 1955-56 as County scored 91 yet still only finished in seventh place, a higher position than seemed likely at the beginning of April 1956. Unusually for County, who were notorious for their poor end-of-season form, they won their last five games and scored 25 goals in the process. Jack Connor had another memorable season, scoring 30 goals. His first hat-trick of the season was historic, coming in a 5-4 home defeat by Workington on 5 September, this being the only occasion on which a County player has scored a hat-trick and finished on the losing side. The following month, County signed Willie Moir, the former captain of Bolton Wanderers and who, as a player, was a great asset, his 16 goals that season taking some of the pressure off Connor. Three weeks after Moir's debut, Connor scored four goals in a 7-0 victory at home to Tranmere Rovers. Knocked out of the FA Cup in the first round by Mansfield Town, County took their revenge in their first match of 1956, Moir scoring a hat-trick in a 7-2 victory at Edgeley Park. The continuing inconsistency was infuriating and, in a detached way, a little amusing; one never knew quite what to expect when watching County. Their end-of-season run began with an overwhelming victory against Carlisle United, a team which had beaten them 4-1 on Boxing Day. Jack Connor scored twice after 16 and 18 minutes before Eddie Moran added a third in the 30th minute.

Connor completed his hat-trick before a goal by Jimmy Whitehouse made it 4-1 at half-time. Numerous chances were missed in the second half before Connor scored a further two goals in the 70th and 75th minutes to take his tally to five. Frank Clempson scored County's seventh after 78 minutes and, in the last minute, Eddie Moran completed the 8-1 rout. Had Jack Connor not had a goal disallowed for offside, he would have become the only County player to score six goals in a match, but a linesman's flag prevented his attaining this record. County's remaining four games were lower-scoring but hardly low-scoring as they won 4-1 at Chester, 4-1 at home to Southport, 5-1 at Scunthorpe and 4-1 at home to York City. Another somewhat bizarre, but entertaining, season had ended.

In 1956-57, the average Edgeley Park attendance rose by over 2,500 as County mounted their last genuine challenge for promotion for some ten years until, once again, a loss of form (or discipline) left them slipping away from the League leaders. Willie Moir had taken over as player-manager in June and County got off to an encouraging start, winning six of their first seven League games. There was both shock and disappointment when Jack Connor was transferred to Crewe Alexandra after playing in only the first two games. Moir was either fortunate or inspired in that the transfer of County's record goalscorer did not affect early results as, initially, Ken Finney made a successful switch to centre-forward. From mid-September, County had a poor run, winning only two games out of nine and the supporters were becoming less than happy with the team's performances. There were, however, distractions during this spell, in the form of 'floodlit football'. County played their first League match under floodlights at Carlisle on 25 September 1956, two goals from Ken Finney and one from Arnold Jackson helping the Hatters to a 3-3 draw. On Tuesday 16 October, County's new floodlights were officially 'switched on' for a friendly against Fortuna '54 Geleen. As the Dutch club were guaranteed £750, an attendance of 10,000 was needed but 14,511 attended the game which County lost 3-0. The attendance was good for County but, as the match was played (unusually then) on a Tuesday evening, there were complaints from the local Darts and Cribbage League that any future Tuesday games would be affected by the absence of darts players for whom that evening had always been set aside.

After protracted negotiations, on 26 October, County finally managed to sign the talented former England 'B' player, Bill Holden, from Sunderland for £6,000. It was a major coup for County although an injury, shortly after his arrival, led to the debut of County's most prolific reserve team goalscorer, Ray Drake. Drake scored the first goal of the game on his debut against eventual champions Derby County, beginning a marvellous run in which he scored 19 goals in 22 League appearances. In addition to the sheer number of goals scored by Drake, on Christmas Day, in only his fourth game, he scored County's fastest-ever goal, only seven seconds after the kick-off against Accrington Stanley at Edgeley Park. By this time, County had already been knocked out of the FA Cup in the first round by non-League New Brighton. County appeared to have done the hard work by holding the Rakers to a 3-3 draw at Rakes Lane, but then lost 3-2 at Edgeley Park in front of a crowd of 16,964. From the time of Ray Drake's debut, County

won 12 of their next 18 games. In February 1957, a fine 5-2 win against Darlington, in which Alan 'Digger' Daley scored a magnificent solo goal, was followed by a Drake hat-trick in a 5-1 win at Gateshead and, in a 4-0 win at Edgeley Park against Wrexham, County's new centre-forward scored all four goals. As Stockport entered the final month of the season, they were hardly favourites for promotion but, with eight games left, including a visit to leaders Derby County, it remained a realistic possibility. Four successive defeats put County out of contention and, whilst acknowledging that three of these were against fellow-promotion contenders, it still came as a great disappointment. Whether or not it was significant, it is of interest that Frank Clempson's absence coincided with County's disastrous collapse.

The major concern in 1957-58 was not simply whether County could win promotion but whether they could finish in the top 12. The Football League had decided to move away from regionalised Third Divisions and create a Third and Fourth Division; the clubs which would make up these Divisions would be determined by those who came in the top and bottom 12 of the Northern and Southern Sections. If nothing else, this maintained interest for the majority of teams in the final weeks of the season when, normally, they would have had little to play for. County made two new full-back signings, Billy Webb

Despite seven Carlisle United players on view, Bill Holden scores with ease in a 4-1 victory for County on 30 November 1957.

from Leicester City and Barry Betts from Barnsley, the latter not being registered to play until November. Betts's appearance was delayed as a result of his retirement through injury during the previous season. Although the former Barnsley player had left football, he continued to train and eventually believed he was fit enough to return to professional football. Signing for County in July 1957, he paid back the £500 compensation he had received, but the wheels of Football League decision-making ground exceedingly slow, Betts unable to make his debut before the 18th game of the season. Stockport's very ordinary start meant that, barring miracles, promotion would be out of the question and County were left to concentrate on trying to have a good FA Cup run and ensuring that they became founder members of the Third Division rather than founder members of the Fourth Division. The atmosphere at the club during the autumn period seemed to be less than harmonious. The previous season's leading goalscorer, Ray Drake, was selected only once and he, Arthur Barnard, Trevor Porteous and Gordon Wilmott all asked for transfers at the end of November. Whilst three

The County team which beat Luton Town 3-0 on 4 January 1958, wearing the Wolves strip of old gold and black. Back row (left to right): Betts, Franklin, Grieves, Holden, Finney. Front row: Davock, Moir, Clempson, Murray, Jackson, Webb.

County in 1958-59. Back row (left to right): Webb, Clempson, Murray, Barnard, Wilmott, Betts, Porteous. Front row: Davock, Jackson, Mulvey, W.M.Kelly, Holden, J.B.Smith, Wilson.

of these four players remained at Edgeley Park, County quite ludicrously lost the services of Drake who eventually moved into non-League football, leaving the club to wait another ten years before finding such a prolific goalscorer. In these circumstances, it was more than a little surprising when, having successfully negotiated the first two rounds of the FA Cup, County achieved their best-ever win against First Division opponents, beating fellow 'Hatters', Luton Town, 3-0 in front of over 18,000 spectators at Edgeley Park. As both Luton and County wore similar strips, white shirts and black shorts, they both had to change, Luton playing in red whilst County played in the famous Wolves kit of 'old gold' and black. An Arnold Jackson goal and two from Bill Holden helped County to their first win over First Division opponents since January 1910. A fourth round tie at eventual Second Division champions West Ham United was County's reward and the Stockport team put up a tremendous fight, Holden and Ken Finney scoring, before losing 3-2. County were then left to fight for a place in the new Third Division and a dreadful run in March, when they gained only one point from five games, saw them fall into the bottom six. During this run, centre-forward Walter Kelly was bought from Doncaster Rovers for £5,000 and Ken Finney was sold to Tranmere Rovers for £2,000. County succeeded in winning three of their last four games, which included an admirable 2-1 victory over champions, Scunthorpe United, and ending the season in ninth place, Bill Holden their top goalscorer with 20 League and Cup goals.

Founder members of simply the 'Third Division' in 1958-59, County were to end the season as one of the first four sides to be relegated from it. The fact that the season was to finish disastrously did not prevent it from being an interesting one, as both players and supporters enjoyed seeing the 'new' teams from the former Third Division

Following a battle to get the Edgeley Park pitch fit to stage the already-postponed FA Cup third-round tie against Burnley on 14 January 1959, Bill Holden, scorer of County's goal, climbs from the snow-covered surface in the 3-1 defeat by the First Division club.

South. Attendances were good, County averaging over 9,000 at Edgeley Park, even through supporters were to witness four home defeats in their first six games. During September, County transferred Walter Kelly to Chester and signed Jimmy Fletcher from Doncaster Rovers. In spite of conceding eight goals, for only the second time in their history, in an 8-2 mauling at Colchester United on 4 October, by Christmas, another good FA Cup run gave the impression that County would be able to hold on to a Third Division place. In the first round of the FA Cup, County had an unexpected win at promotion hopefuls, Hull City, before only just winning by the odd goal in seven at non-League Blyth Spartans. This win gave County a home tie against the increasingly strong First Division Burnley side, and there were hopes of a repeat of the previous season's success against Luton Town. Initially postponed because of snow, on 14 January 1959 County managed to get Edgeley Park fit for the third round clash (although by today's standards, it is highly unlikely that the pitch would have been described as playable), but probably regretted doing so as the First Division team demonstrated their vastly superior skills to win 3-1, despite Bill Holden having equalised before half-time to bring false hope to the supporters. From them until the end of the season, County's form became progressively worse culminating, at a vital stage, in a seven match run from the end of March which yielded only two points. A 4-0 win at home to Southampton in their last match was academic as County were already relegated, the lowest attendance of the season seeing their last rites in the Third Division.

If the County management and supporters believed that 1959-60 would bring an immediate return to the Third Division, such a belief was soon proved erroneous. Had they known then that the club would spend all but three of the next 30 years in the Fourth Division, they might well have given up there and then. A run of five successive wins in October provided a brief period of optimism, but even with four promotion places available, hope evaporated as County won only seven games in the second half of the season. It was particularly disappointing that, whilst having a good defence and a pair of fine wingers in Mike Davock and Gene Wilson,

County were never able to find a successful combination of centre-forward and inside-forwards. Eliminated by Crewe Alexandra in the second round of the FA Cup and a final position of tenth in the Fourth Division were not good enough and Willie Moir was sacked following a board meeting in July 1960.

Before the start of 1960-61, County signed two inside-forwards, the former Scottish schoolboy international, Tom Anderson, from Torquay United and Billy Murdoch from Barrow. There was disappointment when Barry Betts, who County had brought back to League football, was transferred to Manchester City for £8,000 but that was nothing compared to the sadness felt when it was learned that, former favourite, Billy McCulloch had multiple sclerosis. Even though McCulloch had left Edgeley Park six years earlier, his popularity was such that an appeal fund was set up immediately with the express purpose of attempting to pay off his mortgage. As part of the Billy McCulloch appeal, a match was organised at Edgeley Park involving an All Stars team. An attendance of 6,563 saw an excellent All Stars team comprising Ray Wood (Huddersfield Town), Ron Staniforth (Barrow), Joe Walton (Preston North End), Jimmy Scoular (Newcastle United), Jimmy Adamson (Burnley), Tom Finney (formerly of Preston North End), Brian Birch (Oldham Athletic), Ray Pointer (Burnley), Dennis Viollet (Manchester United) and Billy Liddell (Liverpool). County won an entertaining friendly 5-4, but this was inconsequential compared to the money it raised for the McCulloch fund which, following this game, exceeded £1,000 before finally closing after raising £1,220 11s 6d (£1,220.58).

From the playing point of view, it was ironic that managerless County enjoyed an excellent start to the season and were top of the Fourth Division after 12 games when Reg Flewin arrived to take over as manager on 30 September. This season saw the launch of the Football League Cup and in the first round, County beat Carlisle United before travelling the short distance to Maine Road to meet Manchester City in the second round. Two goals from Denis Law and one from Joe Hayes ended County's ambitions in the new competition. Three home ties in the FA Cup resulted in County victories against Workington, Bishop Auckland and Southport. The fourth round took them to Newcastle United on 2 February 1961 where, in front of 48,715, County were easily beaten 4-0. Financial problems were becoming more acute at Edgeley Park with the result that by January, County had only 12 full-time professionals. On 31 March, goalkeeper Harold Lea, a Wigan teacher, broke his leg and was replaced by Alan Smith, an amateur. When new manager Flewin arrived at County on 30 September, County had won eight games; only ten more victories were achieved in the subsequent 34 games, leaving them in a depressing 14th place.

County were now on a downward spiral, 1961-62 giving them little from which to take comfort. The average attendance fell by almost 2,000 as, although managing to score a little more freely than in the previous four years, mainly as a result of new signings Charlie McDonnell from Carlisle United and Derek Ward from Nottingham Forest, they simply won too few games. The defensive stalwarts of Hodder, Murray, Porteous and Webb strove manfully but County found it hard to find a winning formula and, had it not been for an excellent spell

County, 1961-62. Back row (left to right): Beighton, Webb, Murray, Hodder, Birch, Porteous. Front row: Bentley, McDonnell, mascot, Ward, Davock, Partridge.

from early March when they won seven games out of eight, they could well have finished in the re-election area. On that basis, 16th place was an achievement, but taken together with first round dismissals at Edgeley Park by both Leyton Orient and Accrington Stanley (four months before they resigned) in the League Cup and FA Cup respectively, it was an eminently forgettable season. Unfortunately, it was not to be the last one.

Season 1962-63 saw Charlie McDonnell repeat his achievement of 16 League goals, and in spite of the £4,000 purchase of Ron Wylie from Preston North End in November 1962, in simple terms, it became painfully obvious that if County were going anywhere, it was certainly not up. However, it could have been worse: County's excellent achievement in winning four points from their last three games, all of which were against promotion contenders, lifted them two points above the re-election area to finish in 19th place. County's interest in the Cup competitions was short-lived, again eliminated in the first round, losing 4-1 at Chesterfield in the FA Cup and 2-0 at Chester in the League Cup.

County's improvement in 1963-64 could generously be described as 'modest', namely gaining one more point than the previous season whilst progressing no further in either the FA Cup or the League Cup. With dwindling attendances, there was little money to buy players and new arrivals were generally free-transfers. In July 1963, Reg Flewin returned South to manage Bournemouth and long-serving Trevor Porteous was asked to take on the role of player-manager. If it was a dismal season from the spectators viewpoint, from a economic point of view it was disastrous. Amidst the financial crisis which surfaced in December 1963, County offered their ground to the local council. When, in January, the matter was debated in the council chamber at Stockport Town Hall, there was chaos, with many unsympathetic to the plight of the local football club. In February 1964, the Minister of Housing and Local Government ordered a public inquiry into 'Stockport Corporation's application to borrow £20,000 to buy Edgeley Park'. Shortly after this unwelcome and unprofitable publicity, County sold inside-right John Evans to Carlisle United for £1,000 after he had been reprimanded for a somewhat uncomplimentary newspaper article about the club. A win on the last day of the season saw Stockport reach the dizzy heights of 17th place and the club's reward was to 'axe the staff by half'.

During the close-season, County brought a number of young players to the club including Derek Hodgkinson (Manchester City), Ian Sandiford (Blackburn Rovers), Peter Phoenix (Southport), John Nibloe (Doncaster Rovers) and Dennis Hoggart (York City), all of whom were forwards. A number of players were holding out for improved wages and, at the end of July, the chairman, Alderman John Holland resigned. Newly appointed director Vic Bernard (who became chairman in January 1965) wanted the club to have a 'new image' but the way County's season started, there seemed to be a realistic possibility that there would be no County to have any image, be it old or new. A clinical look at the League table that year would have dismissed it as a club that was 'rock-bottom', but strange and tragic things can happen in the face of adversity. County had a history-making start to the season: played 12, drawn 2, lost 10, their first win coming in the 13th match. Luck hardly favoured County in those early weeks as, in three days, they lost 5-4 and 4-3. In their 5-4 game against Chester at Edgeley Park on 4 September, County recovered from being 4-1 down to level the scores at 4-4 before Chester scored the winning goal. Three days later at the Victoria Ground, County equalised three times against Hartlepools United before losing 4-3. In late September, County somehow managed to find the money to buy the experienced and competitive Frank Beaumont from Bury for £4,000 but this made no immediate difference to results. On 29 October, the *Stockport Express* commented that the 'hoodoo sequence of injuries, illness and the rest is incredible. One feels inclined to suggest that an exorcist might do the club more good than a player or two!'

In the FA Cup, County stuttered to a 2-1 win at Edgeley Park against (then) non-League Wigan Athletic. The scorer of County's winning goal, John Nibloe, was tragically killed two weeks later when his car ran off the road as he returned to his Sheffield home in the early hours of 29 November. A John Nibloe Appeal was launched and, on 22 December, a crowd of over 6,000 attended a 'benefit' game between a combined Stoke City & Sheffield United XI (which included Stanley Matthews) and a combined Stockport County & Doncaster Rovers XI. There were so many 'star' players involved that special insurance cover of £150,000 was arranged. The Nibloe appeal finally closed having raised over £2,000.

A little more than a week after Nibloe's death, on Monday, 7 December, County faced Third Division promotion challengers Grimsby Town at Edgeley Park. The game had been abandoned on the Saturday due to fog but, to the surprise of most people, County managed a 1-0 victory, a Derek Hodgkinson goal taking them into the third round where they would meet Third Division leaders, Bristol Rovers.

When County travelled to Eastville to play Bristol Rovers on 9 January, they were still rooted at the foot of the Fourth Division, having won only four League games; not surprisingly they were given little hope of further progress. A thoroughly committed display by the whole Stockport team gained a quite outstanding goalless draw, leaving Rovers to travel to Edgeley Park for a replay on Monday, 11 January, by which time it was known that the winners would meet First Division leaders Liverpool at Anfield. A crowd of just under 20,000 witnessed as

Prior to County's magnificent 1-1 draw against Liverpool in the fourth round of the FA Cup at Anfield on 30 January 1965, the teams observe a minute's silence in tribute to Sir Winston Churchill, who had died six days earlier.

exciting a Cup-tie as one could hope to see and, for the County supporters especially, one that would grip them from the first minute to the last. There could be little argument that Bristol were the more skilful side, but they were playing against a County team which was prepared to give everything, never let their heads drop, even when the game appeared to be slipping away, and one which showed an ability far exceeding what would have been expected of a team in their position. Both teams had chances in a frantic opening but, to the delight of the Stockport supporters, after 30 minutes, Derek Hodgkinson held off two challenges before driving the ball past Rovers' goalkeeper, Bernard Hall. Within a minute, an incredulous crowd watched as Frank Beaumont put County 2-0 in front. Stockport pressed hard in the second half but, within a six-minute spell, magnificent long-range shots from Rovers' Roy Mabbutt and Bobby Jones brought Bristol level. The underdogs reeled as Rovers scented victory whilst stunned County supporters and players could see the game slipping away. Then, with only four minutes remaining, an Ean Cuthbert free-kick found County's 18-year-old centre-forward Ian Sandiford who, having timed his run perfectly, headed the ball over Hall and into the goal. The trite cliché, 'the crowd went wild', at that moment, was the only way to describe the crowd's reaction: uncontrolled pandemonium resulting in a pitch invasion which delayed the restart for three minutes. Although Rovers probably realised that this time there was no way back, for County, the remaining four minutes were nerve-wracking. When referee Fussey of Retford at last blew his whistle for full-time, 'the crowd went wild' again in a combination of hysteria, exhaustion, relief and disbelief. Whereas Derek Hodgson, in the *Daily Express,* summed up the opinion of most visiting journalists that Stockport would 'go to Liverpool to take around £3,000 and an almost certain hiding from the champions', Frank Clough in *The Sun* was 'not so sure it will be the dreadful hiding that the experts are predicting.'

Both before and after the dramatic Bristol match, County seemed unable to emulate that passion in League matches, completing the whole of January with four consecutive defeats, scoring only once. The glory and financial benefits of the Cup run appeared to have become a priority, player-manager Trevor Porteous all too aware that Frank Beaumont, Stockport's most experienced

player, would be suspended for the Anfield tie. Somehow, the Huddersfield Town and former Newcastle United player, Len White, was persuaded to leave Leeds Road and joint the Fourth Division strugglers for £2,500. The signing of White, on 15 January 1965, was probably County's finest since they had brought Joe Smith to Edgeley Park nearly 40 years earlier.

White's third game was in the fourth round at Anfield on 30 January, a match in which 51,851 spectators came close to witnessing the 'impossible' being achieved. The new signing astonishingly headed County into the lead in the 18th minute, and it was not until early in the second half that Gordon Milne equalised for Liverpool. Although the First Division club went close on a number of occasions, they were thwarted by a combination of excellent defending and brilliant goalkeeping and, as had happened in their previous FA Cup meeting 15 years earlier, County were denied a seemingly legitimate appeal for a penalty when Ian Sandiford was brought down. The 'biggest no-hopers of all time' earned a draw and substantial respect which would eventually reap a deserved reward. The replay at Edgeley Park on 3 February was something of an anti-climax, 24,080 seeing two goals by England international Roger Hunt end County's hopes. In the *Daily Express* the following morning, Eric Cooper paid a glowing tribute to the entire County club: 'Farewell Stockport. For them the FA Cup 1965 is but a magnificent memory. But it need not be so. The deeds of this tiny club against the might of Merseyside must linger on, indeed live on. The fans must make it so by turning out, as they did last night, in their inspired thousands. Not for this season at least, merely for Cup glory, but to encourage their team in the depths of the Fourth Division.'

Amazingly, Stockport supporters did maintain commitment, no matter that their team was bottom of the Fourth Division. A victory against Halifax Town on 22 March lifted them off the foot of the table for the first time since the beginning of the season. Four days later, they returned to the bottom and remained there until the end of the season. This was followed by a first application for re-election since before World War One, but few worried about the outcome. The FA Cup run had achieved more than a couple of headlines and a welcome injection of money. No matter that County had finished in 24th place in their worst ever season, the club and its supporters were filled with optimism; attendances had increased by 30 per cent and, after re-election on 29 May, there was a 400 per cent increase in the number of season-tickets sold for the following year. New chairman Vic Bernard's 'Go-Go-Go County' slogan had taken off.

Before the beginning of the 1965-66 season, County were signing good players, Johnny Price 'the pint-size winger' from Burnley, Keith Allen and Billy Haydock (Grimsby Town), David Shawcross (Manchester City) and Len Allchurch (Sheffield United). In August, Stockport had a three game tour in Germany, playing against Bochum (1-3), SV Frankfurt (2-2) and Ruesselsheim (0-2). Even when County kicked off the new season with two defeats and suffered an early dismissal from the League Cup at home to Workington, there was a strange (and unrealistic) conviction that they were destined to win promotion. On 18 September, County recorded their highest ever away win (and, at the

County, 1965-66. Back row (left to right): Cuthbert, Shawcross, Beaumont, Mulhearn, Beighton, Allen, Parry, Bunner, Sandiford. Front row: Hodgkinson, Tillotson, Roberts, White, Collins, Price, Young.

same time, inflicted their host's heaviest ever defeat at Valley Parade) against a Bradford City team who had suffered a humiliating 7-1 away defeat at Crewe Alexandra only three days earlier. A superb Len White hat-trick, together with goals from Dick Young, Keith Allen, Johnny Price and an Alex Smith own-goal, gave County a 7-1 victory. An Edgeley Park crowd of over 15,000 saw another Len White goal defeat Barnsley the following week to add to supporters' optimism before inconsistency set in, County conceding far too many goals to maintain a place in the promotion race. After a run of five games without a win, in January 1966, centre-forward Frank Lord was signed from Plymouth Argyle and scored in his first four games, all of which County won, but the season petered out to the disappointment of the over-optimistic supporters. Objectively, a final position of 13th following the previous season's 24th together with a 2,000 increase in Edgeley Park attendances were quite creditable and could, and would, provide the platform for success.

Stockport travelled to Merseyside again in the FA Cup, this season to play Tranmere Rovers where a Johnny Price goal from 20 yards gave them victory. Southport were their second round opponents and, after a stirring 3-3 draw at Haig Avenue, County were beaten 2-0 in a physical game at Edgeley Park in front of 15,416.

A determination to correct the defensive weaknesses of the previous season led to the signing of two tough and experienced central defenders, Eddie Stuart (Tranmere Rovers) and Matt Woods (Luton Town). The two players provided the defensive backbone needed when the 1966-67 season began with one draw and five wins. Early exits from both Cup competitions prevented distractions of any kind and there was an uncompromising resolve in the way County went about seeking promotion. Although Frank Lord was sold to Blackburn Rovers, County bought Keith East from Swindon Town and former England international Derek Kevan from Luton Town in an exchange deal which took Keith Allen to Kenilworth Road. Another exchange deal took County's skilful half-back David Shawcross to Halifax Town in return for the Shaymen's slim forward, Bill Atkins. It may appear dismissive to describe County's last championship success in a few words, but a brief summary of their season was, simply, that they rarely lost. Of 26 victories, 17 were by single goal margins, of which 12 were 1-0

wins. They achieved the desired goal and, after the trauma of previous seasons, deserved full credit for doing so, but their style was similar to that of their promotion team exactly 30 years earlier.

Promotion was achieved by a 35 yard goal from Albert Harley and an 82nd minute equaliser from Bill Atkins in a 2-2 draw at Notts County on 26 April, whilst a Johnny Price penalty and a Bert Lister goal produced the same scoreline at The Racecourse against Wrexham three days later to win the Fourth Division championship. The Fourth Division trophy was presented at Edgeley Park prior to the last match of the season against bottom club Lincoln City, thus providing the final element of the remarkable coincidence of County having the same opponents in the final game of all three championship seasons. Normally, the County manager and coach would have been sorely unimpressed by their defence conceding five goals, either at home or away, but a carnival atmosphere was accompanied by a carnival match, Lincoln thoroughly enjoying the festivities to win 5-4.

County's ambition did not stop after promotion, the club seemingly carried away by euphoria, believing that further success was not simply attainable but almost destined. In July 1967, the Stockport supporters' special train, the 'County Arrow', was unveiled, ensuring that the club remained in the news. At the beginning of 1967-68, when their talented young goalkeeper, Ken Mulhearn, was transferred to Manchester City, Stockport themselves obtained an excellent goalkeeper, Alan Ogley, in a £25,000 exchange deal. A fee of £7,500 to Torquay United brought Jim Fryatt, a bustling 'old-fashioned' centre-forward to Edgeley Park where he quickly formed an excellent partnership with Bill Atkins and, in the process, became the first County played to score 20 League goals in a season since Jack Connor 12 years earlier. Fryatt made his debut in a pulsating 4-3 win at Edgeley Park against rivals Southport, scoring the first goal with Atkins (2) and Kevan getting the other goals. The season saw a number of richly entertaining and exciting games at Edgeley Park, the Southport match, a 4-2 win against Shrewsbury Town and a 5-2 victory over Tranmere Rovers being three of the best. However, whilst their home record was identical to the previous season's, their away form was dismal which, in a very tight Third Division, condemned them to 14th place, despite them being only ten points behind champions, Oxford United. In the FA Cup, County suffered an embarrassing first round 2-1 defeat at Moss Lane, Macclesfield, after being held to a draw by the non-League side at Edgeley Park. The League Cup gave Stockport the opportunity to see how far they had developed when competing against First Division opposition. After beating Crewe Alexandra 3-1 in a replayed tie at Edgeley Park, Bill Atkins scoring County's only hat-trick in this competition, they enjoyed a richly entertaining game against Sheffield Wednesday before eventually losing 5-3.

Even by County's standards over the years, 1968-69 provided a ludicrously unbalanced season. If the first half of the season had been repeated in the second, County would have been promoted; conversely, had the first half been the same as the second half, they would have finished at the foot of the League. County's form until the New Year was excellent, as they played open and

A trickle of fans entering Edgeley Park on 12 December 1970 after County had raised admission prices by nearly 70 per cent from 6s (30p) to 10s (50p). The attendance for the game against Northampton Town was 1,846, less than half the 3,753 who had attended the previous home game against Newport County.

attractive football, initially continuing to score goals regularly in spite of the sale of Jim Fryatt to Blackburn Rovers. Following Fryatt's departure, in his first game as an emergency centre-forward, Fred Goodwin scored four goals in a 5-2 win against Orient. In both the League Cup and the FA Cup, County reached the third round before losing at Derby County and Blackburn Rovers respectively. However, problems were beginning to surface as, with the club becoming increasingly concerned about the disappointing attendances at Edgeley Park, players other than Fryatt were obviously open to offer. Nonetheless, County appeared to have scored a major coup when they signed Alex Young, the former Everton 'Golden Vision', from Glentoran for £15,000. Unfortunately for both the player and County, Young suffered persistent injuries during his stay, forcing him to retire within nine months of his arrival. The cost to the team of the loss of Fryatt now seemed to come to the fore as County's form fell apart, attendances dropping as did County's position. In March, the chairman claimed that 'the public are responsible. They are forcing us to sell players.' By the end of that month, County's top goalscorer, Bill Atkins had been transferred to Portsmouth for £9,000 and manager Jimmy Meadows had been asked to resign; he did so and Walter Galbraith took over as caretaker-manager.

On the surface, an end-of-season ninth position was good, an improvement upon County's first season back in the Third Division. However, for those who witnessed the second half of the season, County's ninth place was a depressingly good example of 'appearances being deceptive'. By the end of May 1969, the exact reverse of events four years previously was occurring. In May 1965, despite the team finishing at the bottom of the Fourth Division, everyone connected with the club was optimistic; conversely, in 1969, when County finished in a 'respectable position' in the Third Division, the majority of supporters, and others at the club, could see that the 'County Arrow' was about to come off the track. Chairman Vic Bernard resigned to be replaced by hotelier, Dragan Lukic whilst, on the playing side, Len Allchurch, amongst others, was freed. In the same month, a Football League decision that there would be a clampdown on Friday night football was one which meant that Stockport's well-known 1960s slogan 'Friday night is County night' was dead. The slogan was associated with County and when it disappeared into oblivion, the club virtually went with it. Whilst this gives all the appearance of 'being wise after the event', an examination of season-ticket sales reveals that this is not the case; in 1964, prior to the season in which County finished bottom of the Fourth Division, 111 season tickets were sold; in 1965,

after they had finished bottom, 681 were sold. By 1968, after some fluctuation, the number had risen to 709, but after finishing ninth in 1969, the number of season-tickets sold fell to 428, a decrease of almost 40 per cent.

If the prophets of doom had wanted evidence to support their predictions, they did not have to wait long. To proclaim that 1969-70 was a disastrous season would be generous. Occasionally, other teams have been able to escape from the position in which County found themselves towards the end of October: played 16, won 1, drawn 4, lost 11. Only eight goals were scored during this run, of which one was an own-goal. It might be argued that County had experienced similarly bad spells, but this one was very different; the team was not only embarrassingly weak, but appeared resigned to failure. In the League Cup, County were beaten in the first round by Blackburn Rovers, whilst in the FA Cup, they managed, with a little good fortune, to reach the second round. They had begun with a 1-1 draw with non-League Mossley at Edgeley Park before winning a dour replay 1-0 at a mist-shrouded Seel Park. Drawn at home in the second round to Scunthorpe United, County escaped with a goalless draw before being beaten 4-0 at the Old Show Ground, where a young Kevin Keegan scored one of the goals. On the only occasion County scored three goals in a match, it both followed and preceded runs of *totalling* three goals in seven games. There was nothing to lift the supporters, nothing to give them any hope. County's only achievement was to enter the record books as the lowest-scoring side over 46 games, with a mere 27 goals. Twenty-five scoreless League games and a convincing bottom place provided unequivocal confirmation of just how pitiful a season it was. Coincidentally, the second and third teams from the bottom that season were the second and third teams to be promoted behind County in 1967; what became increasingly worrying was that both of these clubs, Barrow and Southport, failed to gain re-election in the 1970s. The omens were not good.

The 20 year period between 1969 and 1989 was such a thoroughly depressing one that it would be forgivable to dismiss it in one short sentence. However, to do so would be unjust, both to those players who toiled manfully during this period and to those whose skill brought the occasional glow and brief moment of hope to a diminishing number of spectators, before they were brought back to reality. It would also be unfair to the astounding achievements of the club during the past five

County, 1972-73. Back row (left right): Bingham, Russell, Ingle, Wilson, Davidson, Griffiths. Middle row: S.Fleet (coach), A.Kirk (vice chairman), Spratt, Ormrod, Ryden, Ogley, Clarke, Ashworth, Lawther, Hart, J.Mulvaney (coach). Front row: Ingham, Collier, Fogarty, B.Doyle (manager), Golder, Crowther, Garbett.

years, which to be fully appreciated, must be put in context. But, a description of every one of those 20 seasons would be repetitive beyond belief; there are only so many times that a season can be described as 'disappointing', 'very disappointing', 'dismal' or, very occasionally, 'moderate'. A stark statement of County's League positions from 1969-70 to 1988-89 provides more than ample evidence of this: 24th, 11th, 23rd, 11th, 24th, 20th, 21st, 14th, 18th, 17th, 16th, 20th, 18th, 16th, 12th, 22nd, 11th, 19th, 20th, 20th.

Throughout Stockport's history, in most seasons there

has been at least an infrequent 'highlight' but for almost two decades these can be remembered with remarkable clarity, notable for their rarity value. Those who not only supported County but watched them for any length of time between 1969 and 1989, are unlikely to yearn to return to those days. Fourteen managers, one of whom, Colin Murphy, 'enjoyed' two stays, emphasises the lack of stability at the club and, for much of the period, a loss of League status seemed inevitable, re-election appearing to be merely a stay of execution. Financial crises became almost matter-of-fact as did either re-election or close shaves from a re-election place. A highest position of 11th, achieved on three occasions, was hardly a platform on which to mobilise the Stockport public; an almost unbelievable record of finishing 18th or lower on no less than 12 occasions in 20 years brands supporters of the team as either showing loyalty above and beyond the call of duty or as extreme masochists.

Apart from the infrequent memorable Cup-tie, there were two or three occasions when the club threatened to achieve something, but such false hopes were practically always extinguished well before the end of the season. On County's return to the Fourth Division, three of the first six years ended in applications for re-election. On each occasion, fears of failure to canvas enough votes to remain in the Football League grew larger. In 1974-75, between their second and third application, County only escaped another re-election place on the last day of the season with a priceless goalless draw away at Scunthorpe

County, 1975-76. Back row (left to right): E.Hopkinson (trainer), McNeill, McNab, Lawther, Brown, Hollis, Coleman, Olynick, J.Meadows (manager). Middle row: Cross, Massey, Price, T.McCreery (secretary), F.Pye (joint chairman), A.Kirk (president), P.Lukic (joint chairman), W.Adams (vice chairman), Smith, Fogarty, Buckley. Front row: Jones, Turner, Campbell, Flanagan, Bradley, Vernon.

United. Few people will remember this achievement, but that result represented relative success and summarised perfectly that period of the 1970s.

In the League, six wins in the first eight games of 1976-77 saw what appeared to be a useful County team on top of the League until the middle of October but by the end of the season, they had won no more games than in the previous season when they had finished in the re-election zone. After a poor start the following season, 1977-78, a good run between late September and late February took them from 20th to fourth place but, incredibly, they then dropped 14 places in the last 14 games, of which they lost 11, finishing 18th. County's most promising season was 1985-86, one which immediately followed their last application for re-election. The season began with five away League games, a result of Edgeley Park's failure to be granted the required safety certificate following the Bradford City fire in May. In October 1985, County's experienced full-back, Les Chapman, took over the role of player-manager following Colin Murphy's sudden departure to Saudi Arabia. From 19th position at the end of October, Chapman inspired a tremendous run over the next five months. County climbed to fifth place, a position they retained for the whole of March, winning 14 and losing only four of 25 games. With very limited resources, the achievement of Chapman's team was all the more worthy and, had the club been able to provide him with even a small amount of money to buy one or two players, rather than relying on loan players, Stockport could have attained a promotion place. However, from the last day of March to the end of the season, County took only two points from their last eight games, slipping down to 11th place. To an outsider, Chapman's subsequent dismissal appeared incomprehensible, even more so with the advent of the Melia team which followed.

The four re-election seasons speak for themselves, the nervous wait to see if County had survived verging on the unbearable. But 1986-87 was different. For the first time, there was to be no re-election, simply automatic relegation to the Conference and possible obscurity. The most remarkable element of the last day escape of Rochdale, Tranmere Rovers, Burnley and Torquay United, was that County were actually safe. Similarities between County's early season form of 1986-87 and 1969-70 were depressingly obvious: one win and seven goals in the first 15 games. The only less worrying factor in 1969 was that demotion would be to the Fourth Division, whereas in 1986 it would involve leaving the Football League completely. The positive difference between these two strangely similar seasons was that in 1969, there was a blind resignation to the club's fate, whereas in 1986 there was at least someone on the board prepared to fight. The return of Colin Murphy motivated the team to an unbelievable extent; the players may not have enjoyed Murphy's harsh discipline; the spectators may not have witnessed the most skilful football but what they did see was a spirit and a passion which had not been evident for many years. Forty-five points from the last 31 games was a fantastic achievement, saving the club from automatic relegation and potential oblivion.

The League Cup provided County with probably their best moments during this 20-year period. In 1972-73, County enjoyed their best-ever run when, after three

George Best's second inswinging corner in quick succession causes such panic in the Swansea City defence that goalkeeper Steve Potter can only help the ball into the net for County's first goal in a 3-2 victory at Edgeley Park on 28 November 1975.

games, they succeeded in overcoming Bradford City in the first round. A visit to First Division Crystal Palace awaited them in the second round. After Ian Lawther, County's former Northern Ireland international, had missed a penalty in the 32nd minute following a foul on Hugh Ryden, nine minutes later it was Ryden who rose to head the only goal of the game. Although Palace played very poorly, it was still an excellent win for County, their first ever away victory against a First Division team in either the FA or League Cup. County's reward for the win was a visit by one of the most attractive teams in the country, West Ham United, whose sixth place in the First Division at the end of that season represents the Hammers' second highest position in the last 20 years. County's 2-1 victory, earned as a result of goals from Malcolm Russell and a penalty from Tommy Spratt, was fully merited. 'Stockport's forwards did all that was required of them in the first half,' reported Eric Todd in *The Guardian*. 'In the second, it was the turn of their defenders among whom Hart, Ashworth and Ogley in particular, were nothing short of magnificent.' Into the fourth round for the first and only time, County had another home tie against a First Division club, Norwich City. On 1 November, a crowd of 16,535, County's highest attendance since the Liverpool FA Cup replay in 1965, did not witness a third consecutive victory against a First Division side; a skilful and breathtakingly quick Norwich team overwhelmed County with goals from David Cross (2), Dave Stringer, Trevor Howard and Jimmy Bone. Ian Lawther's consolation goal was a brief gesture of defiance in a game in which there was never any real doubt about the outcome. Although Norwich reached the League Cup Final, County could lament the fact that they played the Canaries then rather than a little later, when the Norfolk club went through a spell of 19 games without a win.

Although County repeated their League Cup victory over Crystal Palace in 1973-74, their 1-0 win was at Edgeley Park and the London team had dropped down to the Second Division. One of Stockport's most accomplished performances in the competition was on 1 September 1976 when, with maximum points from their first three League games, they visited Second Division Blackburn Rovers. The Ewood Park programme referred to 'lady luck being on our side' with regard to the draw, having been given home advantage against a Fourth Division side. That was how it appeared when, after only

County, 1978-79. Back row (left to right): Lee, Thompson, Bradd, Cassidy, Rogan, Smith, Prudham, Loadwick, Thorpe. Front row: Park, Rutter, Fogarty, Summerbee, Halford, Goodfellow.

Derek Loadwick (number ten, in background) cannot bear to watch as Alan Thompson calmly places a penalty past Manchester United's Paddy Roach to put County on level terms in the second round of the League Cup on 30 August 1978.

four minutes, following a cross from Rovers' winger David Wagstaffe, there was a collision between County's goalkeeper Ian Holbrook and captain Alan Thompson, leaving Ken Beamish the simple task of side-footing the ball into an unguarded goal. County fought their way back into the game, hitting the bar once and making other opportunities. In the second half, the Stockport forwards repeatedly looked dangerous, Daniels, Fletcher and Massey breaking through the Blackburn defence with embarrassing ease. Their superiority was eventually rewarded after 62 minutes when Peter Fletcher headed in a John Rutter cross to equalise. Six minutes later, Barney Daniels switched play from the left to the right to find Steve Massey. The 18-year-old cut inside the Blackburn full-back before delicately chipping the ball over goalkeeper Paul Bradshaw, putting County 2-1 up with a goal of supreme style. Rovers made desperate attempts to get back into the game but it was Massey who scored again, heading in Dave Lennard's free-kick, to put the tie beyond Blackburn. County's reward for this 3-1 victory was a home tie against Everton who, whilst somewhat negative, were simply too strong for the Fourth Division side, a first-half goal from Bob Latchford enough to put

the Goodison club through to the fourth round.

With typical contrariness, County's most memorable League Cup match was one which was lost; one which still enrages those who saw it; one whose referee is unlikely to be forgotten by Stockport supporters. In August 1978, after beating eventual Third Division champions Shrewsbury Town over two legs, County were drawn at home to Manchester United. For financial reasons, a decision to switch the tie to Old Trafford was taken which, to say the least, was unpopular with many fans. It was a 'dream draw', but by switching venues, it gave the impression that the club believed they had no chance, whilst supporters of the likes of Stockport have to believe that it will be their club who will provide the 'shock result'. The supporters' views were ignored and, on 30 August, nearly 42,000 spectators saw United take a tenth minute lead when Joe Jordan headed in an Ashley Grimes cross. Although County were to have yet another poor season, they did have a number of skilful players and, before half-time, they created a number of opportunities. The Reds were less than impressive and, with Lou Macari and County's player-manager Mike Summerbee seemingly intent on re-enacting past Manchester 'derby' battles, United's most dangerous forward was playing himself out of the game. With the supporters uplifted by their team's performance, the second half saw County go close on a number of occasions before, in the 59th minute, United goalkeeper, Paddy Roche, felled Stuart Lee and Alan Thompson confidently equalised from the resultant penalty. 20 minutes later, with United still unable to impose their authority on the game, County's Terry Park picked up possession on the left wing, went round Brian Greenoff and curled the ball delightfully round Roche and inside the far post. Unadulterated joy! County did not fall back on defence, but pressed for another goal with the result that, in the 85th minute, United's Scottish international central defender, Gordon McQueen, brought down Derek Loadwick with a scything tackle. Referee Peter Willis of County Durham had little option but to send off McQueen, who departed with considerable petulance. Three minutes later, Mr Willis awarded the Reds a free-kick, seemingly given against County goalkeeper Mike Rogan and, with no United player near, possibly for time-wasting. Sammy McIlroy took the free-kick which after a deflection, rolled agonisingly past Rogan to equalise. In the 90th minute, Peter Willis guaranteed himself a place in the memories of Stockport supporters by awarding United a penalty for a foul by Thompson on Jordan. It would be churlish to dispute the validity of the decision, but it was certainly a rare event to

Tommy Sword scores the winning goal against Sunderland from the penalty spot in a 2-1 win at Roker Park in a second-round second-leg League Cup match on 3 September 1980.

see a penalty awarded in front of the Stretford End with virtually no appeal from the crowd nor from the players. Jimmy Greenoff calmly scored and United had won. United fans graciously applauded as Mike Summerbee led his players on a lap of honour but, whilst County supporters were rightly proud of their team, many were overwhelmed by a feeling of having witnessed a gross injustice. Such games will remain in the memory of supporters of smaller clubs such as County for the simple reason that, unlike the 'big' clubs, they have far fewer opportunities to rectify perceived injustices.

Two years after the Old Trafford game, County had their last League Cup success against a First Division team. By 1980, the Football League had already introduced the two-leg format for the second round, a change which is weighted heavily against the lower division teams. After a 1-0 extra-time victory against Chester, County were drawn to play First Division Sunderland. The first leg at Edgeley Park was not a 'classic', but a hard-fought game ending in a 1-1 draw, Sunderland's Kevin Arnott equalising after David Sunley had put County ahead. The majority of the 17,635 spectators who attended Roker Park on 3 September came to see Sunderland 'finish off the job' but the chances that came were evenly divided. The First Division team had more possession, as expected, but Les Bradd (twice), David Sunley and Oshor Williams all had good chances for County. With the game still goalless after half-time, Sunderland's nerve seemed to have been settled when, after 69 minutes, their smallest player, Stan Cummins, scored with a brave diving header. Whilst County's spirit, admirably, did not flag, Sunderland inexcusably relaxed and, within five minutes, a flowing Stockport move ended with Les Bradd putting David Sunley through to fire a low shot past Chris Turner. In the 78th minute, a careless back-pass from Sunderland's Shaun Elliott gave Sunley possession and, as the Stockport striker moved towards goal, Elliott brought him down. Referee Hutchinson of Harrogate immediately awarded a penalty and, though loudly jeered by the Roker crowd, Tommy Sword kept his nerve to place the ball past Chris Turner and give County a 2-1 lead. Sunderland were unable to fight their way back into the game and, despite the disadvantage of the two-leg tie, County were through to the third round. A home tie against Arsenal guaranteed a good gate but little else, the well-organised Gunners gaining a comfortable 3-1 win

with goals from John Hollins, Alan Sunderland and Frank Stapleton whilst Les Bradd scored County's consolation.

Stockport's only other creditable performance in the competition came during their 1984-85 re-election season in a second round match against European Cup winners, Liverpool. After a goalless draw at Edgeley Park, County batted to hold Liverpool to 0-0 at Anfield before eventually succumbing during extra-time.

The FA Cup provided even less to cheer about than County's League performances in this seemingly endless 20 year struggle. Stockport reached the third round on only three occasions, the last against Leyton Orient in 1987-88 when they were unlucky to lose 2-1 in a thoroughly absorbing full-blooded Cup-tie.

The only shocks that County provided were on those occasions when they did not lose to non-League teams. Of all the embarrassing dismissals, none were quite as appalling as that on 15 November 1985 when they travelled to Caernarfon Town of the Multipart League in Colin Murphy's first match after replacing Jimmy Melia. If Murphy had any doubt about the scale of the task which confronted him, County's shambolic performance in North Wales ended such doubt. Some dreadful misses by the Stockport forwards encouraged Caernarfon who, after 31 minutes, to the jubilation of their fans, took the lead when Austin Salmon drilled a shot beyond County goalkeeper Gary Walker to give the Welsh team a 1-0 lead. Although County created numerous chances, they were denied either by Caernarfon goalkeeper, Ross Hughes, or by their own woeful finishing. A demoralising defeat was compounded by the disgraceful behaviour of a number of Stockport 'fans' who shamefully instigated a number of fights. If County could not wait to get out of Caernarfon, Caernarfon could not wait to be rid of County.

Of the thousand or so games played in this 20 year spell, two other games are worthy of mention, both for their novelty elements. In late 1975, two years after walking out on Manchester United, the incomparable George Best decided to attempt a comeback. Keen to demonstrate that he had retained the skills which had made him the greatest footballer (unarguably in the United Kingdom, probably in Europe and possibly the world) in modern times, he was persuaded to join County on a match-by-match contract, making his debut at Edgeley Park against Swansea City on 28 November 1975. Stockport's previous home game had been against Huddersfield Town, watched by a crowd of 2,789, a reasonable proportion of whom had crossed the Pennines. The 'George Best game' attracted 9,220 and, whilst the spectators were left in little doubt as to Best's skills, albeit less finely honed than a few years earlier, the match had an eerie quality. Probably less than 30 per cent of the spectators were County fans whilst the overwhelming majority of the crowd had no interest in Stockport, simply coming to Edgeley Park to watch one player. Best did not disappoint. Though having a poor away record, Swansea were a useful side, whilst County, with the exception of Ken Fogarty and Steve Massey, had little to offer. Best was the centre of attraction, demonstrating skills, the like of which had never been seen at Edgeley Park. After 20 minutes, the first of Best's three in-swinging corners in succession forced Swansea goalkeeper, Steve Potter, to push round the post. The second brought a saving header

County, 1981-82. Back row (left to right): Thorpe, Uzelac, Lloyd, Stafford, Booth. Middle row: Rutter, Fowler, Sword, Smith, Sherlock.
Front row: Coyle, Park, Williams, Sunley, Wardrobe.

from a now panic-stricken defence whilst the third spun viciously towards the near post and Potter could only help the ball in to put County in front. Best created County's second goal when he set up Lee Bradley to score in the 55th minute and after 72 minutes, the crowd were treated to the goal they had come to see. Ian Seddon knocked the ball down to Best who scored with a powerful left-foot half-volley from the edge of the penalty area. A magnificent goal from a magnificent player and, although Swansea scored twice in the last seven minutes to leave County hanging on, virtually the sole topic of conversation of the departing crowd was the performance of George Best. For Stockport, seemingly safe at the beginning of April 1976, five consecutive defeats resulted in them having to seek re-election on goal-average.

On Saturday 25 April 1981, County were involved in a bizarre, but important, game at Gigg Lane, Bury. Fifth from the bottom with three games left, two of the clubs below had two home games left whilst County had only one. Nigel Smith was selected for his first game of the season as Stockport were deprived of Terry Park, their most skilful player, who was getting married that afternoon having arranged the date in the belief that the Bury game would take place on the Friday night. Although the weather in the Lancashire town was bright and sunny, on the Yorkshire side of the Pennines, it was wintry, causing havoc on the roads. Manager Jimmy McGuigan and centre-forward Les Bradd were held up coming from Chesterfield and Nottingham respectively, whilst County's other forward, David Sunley, and

midfield player, Chris Galvin, rang Gigg Lane minutes before the game to report that they were stuck behind a snow-plough on the M62. Physiotherapist and former player-manager, Trevor Porteous, was left in charge as County came out with only nine players, referee Vic Callow of Solihull having decreed that the match could and would start. Bury, who had crushed Scunthorpe United 6-1 seven days earlier, were in a position to at least repeat a similar kind of scoreline but, strangely, could not find any rhythm. With Tony Coyle as County's lone forward, the Stockport side held out with surprising ease for 43 minutes when Galvin and Sunley arrived. Had Bradd arrived, he would have been unable to appear as Sunley had been named as a substitute and had come on with a number 12 on his shirt. For Bury, the embarrassment of being unable to break down a nine-man team was compounded when, midway through the second half, Coyle crossed for Smith to head the ball down to Martin Fowler, who drove home an unstoppable shot from the edge of the penalty area. County held out for the remainder of the game and, in the strangest of circumstances, ended Bury's 17 match unbeaten home run. The 'Gigg Lane farce wasn't funny for Bury' was the headline in the *Bury Times* but, for County, it was not a matter for amusement, only delight with the precious two points which virtually assured them of escaping the re-election area.

When Danny Bergara took over at County in March 1989, there were no obvious signs of better things to come. For most Stockport fans, he was just another

County, 1984-85. Back row (left to right): Hendrie, Emerson, Thorpe, Evans, Rutter. Middle row: Buxton, Taylor, Sherlock, Bowles, Salmon, Sword, Power, Coyle. Front row: Kerr, G.White (director), E.Webster (manager), A.Kirk (chairman), B.Taylor (director), Williams.

Although out of the League Cup, County players acknowledge the applause of the crowd at Anfield following their extra-time defeat by Liverpool on 9 October 1984. From left to right are Thorpe, Salmon (partly hidden), Taylor, Kerr, Evans, Hendrie, Sword, Buxton and Williams.

manager, the major difference being that it was a Uruguayan who was replacing the Scottish Asa Harford. It was a time when, unusually for County, they had an abundance of strikers, Brett Angell, Tony Caldwell, Bob Colville, Tony Hancock and Rodger Wylde. With Stockport in 15th place and virtually assured of safety, Bergara used the remaining matches to assess the players he had inherited, changing the team continually. Whilst understandable, it hardly endeared him to County fans who, after all, were turning up at Edgeley Park to see their best team perform, rather than their manager experiment. With constant changes, it was not surprising that the team performed, at best, moderately, failing to win any of their last 12 matches and finishing the season, as they had done the previous year, in 20th place. Of the five forwards Bergara had played, Colville and Hancock, seemingly the most talented, were transferred, whilst the unimpressive Brett Angell was retained. Whatever problems had

existed in his two-year reign, Hartford had built the nucleus of a better than average side, and many fans must have shaken their heads when discovering who had been retained and who had been transferred.

For the start of the 1989-90 season, Bergara brought in players whom he knew from his time at Rochdale: Chris Beaumont, Malcolm Brown and, then record-signing, David Frain. In addition, young unknowns were added to the squad: Ian McInerney from Huddersfield Town and Paul R.Williams from Leicester City. Barry Siddall, a vastly experience goalkeeper, was signed from Blackpool, his eighth club, and strikers George Oghani from Burnley

County's Cheadle End Stand in the latter stages of demolition in July 1985. The wooden stand, less than 20 years old, was a victim of the requirements of a safety certificate following the tragic fire at Valley Parade, Bradford, in May that year.

Queen's Park Rangers in the League Cup left County only 2-1 down with the home leg to play. Their unbeaten League record came to an end at Aldershot, a game which Stockport should have won. Before the next home game, against Scarborough, County signed Keith Edwards, one of the League's most consistent goalscorers, for £50,000 from Hull City. Many considered that this signing alone would see County promoted as, in addition to the quality of the player acquired, it demonstrated an ambition which had seemed dormant for over two decades. Within seven minutes of his debut, Edwards had rifled in his first goal for the club as County edged out

and Gary McDonald from Darlington replaced the departed Colville and Hancock. County started the season with an uninspiring three successive draws, made worse by injuries to new signings Beaumont and Frain in the first game. Consecutive away victories at Wrexham and League newcomers, Maidstone United, resulted in the less committed supporters wondering if there was something worth seeing at Edgeley Park. The attendance for the following home game saw an increase of over 1,000 for the visit of point-less Hartlepool United. The Pool were crushed 6-0, with Brett Angell becoming the first player to score four goals in a game for over 20 years. On 20 September, a battling performance at Loftus Road against

Scarborough 3-2. Despite managing only a goalless draw against Queen's Park Rangers in the League Cup, Edwards and Brett Angell develop an excellent understanding as County won four League games in succession, the last an exciting 1-0 win against leaders, Southend United. Two weeks later, County were on top of the Fourth Division, an unique experience for the majority of supporters. Three successive away defeats in December were followed by four wins in five games, keeping County on course for a promotion position. The last of these involved a superb encounter against Burnley at Edgeley Park, where the Clarets had come from behind to win 2-1 two months earlier in an FA Cup first round

County, 1987-88. Back row (left to right): Robinson, Entwistle, Marples, Mossman, McKenzie. Middle row: L.Cantello (assistant manager), Evans, Williams, Bullock, Sword, Pickering, Sertori, Cronin, C.Wych (physiotherapist). Front row: Hodkinson, Hendrie, A.Hartford (player-manager), Edwards, Bailey.

Brett Angell turns away in delight after giving County the lead in their 3-0 win against Hartlepool United on 24 October 1988. Rodger Wylde, kneeling on the left of Angell, scored County's third goal.

replay. On this occasion, it was County who came from behind, trailing to a Winston White goal before the debut introduction of winger Darren Knowles gave County extra width. A frenzied period of attacking produced three County goals in the last 15 minutes, the pick of which was a thunderous volley from full-back David Logan. Four games without a win, including an avenging 5-0 defeat at Hartlepool, took County out of the top four, but they recovered to record an excellent 3-0 win at York City. Shortly after another 5-0 defeat, this time at Scunthorpe, Bergara signed central defender, Jim Gannon, from Sheffield United. Gannon made a less than impressive debut as County fell to a 2-0 defeat at Edgeley Park to bottom club, Wrexham. By March 1990, Frain and Beaumont had both returned from injury and, although neither was showing the promise of the pre-season, Beaumont scored a wonderful individual goal at Hereford United to give County a much needed win.

There was a worryingly inconsistent spell, not helped by changes of goalkeeper and a 'falling out' between Bergara and Keith Edwards which resulted in the latter leaving Edgeley Park on loan. If nothing else, the goalkeeping problem was solved, by the late loan signing of Scott Barrett, but these events came at a critical stage of the season, a run of six games without a win seeing County slide down to ninth. In a matter of five weeks, County had moved from an automatic promotion place to one where hopes of even a Play-off position were receding. Three of their last four games were against fellow Play-off contenders, the first being against fourth placed Carlisle United. Jim Gannon was recalled, surprisingly taking a midfield role, and scored the first of County's goals in a 3-1 win. Three days later, Stockport travelled to the Abbey Stadium to face a Cambridge United side who, with

games in hand after a marvellous run which had seen them reach the sixth round of the FA Cup, had won their previous four games and were making a dramatic late charge up the table. Two goals from leading scorer, Brett Angell, gave County an excellent and priceless win. Fifth placed Chesterfield were County's last opponents at Edgeley Park in the League, the visitors taking the lead through Jamie Hewitt before a Lee Rogers own-goal brought Stockport back into the game before half-time. In the second half, a Chris Beaumont header and a superbly struck free-kick by David Logan gave County a 3-1 win and put them into fourth place.

On the last day of the season, whilst the champions and runners-up positions were settled, the remaining automatic promotion spot was open to any one of five clubs and eight clubs remained in contention for the four Play-off places. If County could win their last game at Halifax, Southend United, who were in third place and away at one of the other Play-off hopefuls, Peterborough United, had to win at London Road to prevent Stockport going up.

On 5 May in glorious hot sunshine, in excess of 3,000 County fans made the short journey across the Pennines, not only swelling The Shay to its highest attendance of the season, but outnumbering Halifax fans by three to one. A nervous looking Stockport were unable to get their game together and, in the 22nd minute, Halifax's Neil Matthews received the ball from a throw-in and sent a magnificent 25 yard shot past the helpless Scott Barrett to put the Shaymen in front. Half-time news from London Road, that Southend were winning 2-0, further depressed the large travelling County support, which seemingly transmitted itself on to the pitch as the second half began with the team playing no better than before the break. However, mid-way through the second half, Stockport

In his first game of the season, Mark Samways, the Doncaster Rovers goalkeeper, caps a wonderful display by saving a well-struck penalty from County's Mark Payne in the near top-of-the-table clash on 21 December 1990. The game ended goalless.

suddenly began to raise their game and create chances, but Brett Angell missed opportunities which, for most of the season, he would normally have taken. Danny Bergara made what had become his standard substitution, replacing Darren Knowles with Ian McInerney. With under 20 minutes left, McInerney released David Frain who broke through the Halifax defence and, as he rounded goalkeeper David Brown, was brought down. The linesman waved his flag to indicate a penalty but, when referee Brian Hill of Kettering did not immediately acknowledge it, inexplicably and, to the County fans, unforgivably, he stopped waving his flag. Although the vocal appeals by the players achieved nothing, the apparent injustice fired them up. With 16 minutes left, Malcolm Brown found Frain who checked before crossing for Chris Beaumont to turn and sweep the ball home for the equaliser. County supporters invaded the pitch, more with relief than joy before, shortly after the restart, Brookman passed to McInerney who cut inside before driving a left-foot shot past David Brown from 16 yards. The celebrations bordered upon the ecstatic as County ended 2-1 winners in a game which had contained little flair but great drama. Rumours that Peterborough had pulled back two goals spread around the ground and,

for a few short minutes, County believed they were promoted. When it was learned that Southend had held on to win 2-1, there was huge disappointment, but at least Stockport were in the Play-offs as they finished in fourth place.

County's first experience of a Play-off semi-final could hardly have been worse. On 13 May 1990, they travelled to Chesterfield without regular full-back Malcolm Brown and central defender Bill Williams. Although Stockport started brightly, when Calvin Plummer opened the scoring for Chesterfield, they simply fell apart. Plummer went on to score a hat-trick and a goal from David Ryan gave the home team a 4-0 victory and, barring miracles, a place in the Final. County were further weakened by an injury to David Logan and when, three days later, the Spireites came to Edgeley Park for the second leg, goals from Plummer and Chiedozie brought the aggregate score to a comprehensive 6-0 win for Chesterfield. Although it was a sobering and painful experience, it was only when the dust had settled that County supporters realised just how quickly the previous 20 years had been forgotten and how much had been achieved: Stockport County – fourth in the League and a place in the Play-offs. This was more than simple rehabilitation: the County bandwagon was on the move.

Prior to the start of season 1990-91, County fans were disappointed to learn that leading scorer, Brett Angell, had been transferred to Southend United, the team that had just pipped County for promotion. There was also extreme dissatisfaction with a tribunal decision to value Angell at only £100,000, although this was the highest fee received for a Stockport player. The major captures were the £70,000 signing of Neil Matthews, who had scored Halifax's goal against County just two months earlier, and that of Paul Cooper, a reliable goalkeeper with a wealth of First Division experience. Less well-known were Alan Finley from Shrewsbury Town, two former Hartlepool trainees, Tony Barras and Lee Todd, and, from the same club, defender Paul A.Williams who, from the outset at Edgeley Park, played as a striker. Two Paul Williams certainly

A magnificent strike by Andy Kilner (second from left) gives County their sixth consecutive victory, a 2-1 win against fellow promotion challengers Torquay United on 23 April 1991.

provided the opportunity for confusion, further complicated by the continued presence of cultured defender Bill Williams. There was, in fact, only one League game in which all three Williams's played: against Gillingham at Edgeley Park on New Year's Day 1991, Paul A.Williams scoring County's goal in a 1-1 draw.

After long years of suffering, Stockport supporters wondered whether the previous season had been a 'one-off' or the basis on which to mount an even stronger challenge for promotion. Although the season started with a dull 0-0 draw at Halifax, there was soon ample evidence that County would remain among the front-runners of the Fourth Division. One of the most significant improvements in County's game was that they had become very difficult to beat, not in a defensive way but by developing a spirited refusal to accept defeat. In the first two months of the season, County trailed 2-0 at home to Burnley and drew 2-2, 3-0 at Cardiff and drew 3-3, 1-0 at home to Peterborough and won 2-1 and 2-0 at Aldershot and drew 2-2. Defender turned striker, Paul A.Williams, began well, before injury put him out of the side for over two months, a period which coincided with County's leanest scoring spell. Neil Matthews was unable to reproduce the form he had shown when playing against County and the early season signing of Keith Alexander from Grimsby Town was unsuccessful. Nonetheless, with Chris Beaumont in fine form, the end of the year saw them lying in sixth place. If every club needs a little luck to achieve success, County's appeared by way of a Christmas present – Andy Kilner. Returning from Sweden, Kilner was looking for a club in the North-West and, almost accidentally, arrived at Stockport, signing a month's contract on 20 December 1990. He happened to be in the right form at the right time at the right place and, after scoring twice on his full debut, became County's most important player, giving them an extra attacking dimension. With striker Williams back in the side, County became the first team to win at Walsall's new Bescot Stadium, Williams's two goals giving Stockport a 2-0 win in an exceptional performance which took them to the top of the table. A 5-1 demolition of Halifax Town the following Friday confirmed their position, but they then dropped to fourth place after suffering three away defeats in seven days.

The weather interrupted County's programme, during which time Bergara continued his search for another striker. The 6ft 3ins Jason Lee arrived on loan from Charlton Athletic whilst the 6ft 7ins Kevin Francis was bought from Derby County for £60,000. As County suffered a number of postponements, they arranged a friendly at Runcorn in which both Lee and Francis played. Whilst Lee looked skilful and deadly in the penalty area, Francis looked awkward and anything but lethal. Lee played when County returned to League football at Sincil Bank, Francis coming on as substitute in the second half. Two magnificent second half goals from Chris Beaumont, one as a direct result of a Francis run and cross, helped County to a 3-0 win. Jason Lee played one more game before rejecting County's terms, electing instead to join Lincoln City.

In spite of dropping points, County kept in touch with the leading group, Neil Matthews earning an extended run in the side whilst Williams continued to score impressive goals. It still came as a considerable surprise when, on

transfer-deadline day, a desperate West Brom, struggling near the bottom of the Second Division, signed Paul A.Williams for a record £250,000. Although this was extremely good business, bearing in mind that Williams had arrived on a free transfer, it was too late for County to sign another replacement which meant that Kevin Francis took Williams's place. The day after Williams left, County played Hartlepool United on Good Friday. Stockport's football that night was quite outstanding, the Hartlepool defence frequently ripped apart in a devastating attacking display. Unfortunately for County, Kevin Poole, the Hartlepool goalkeeper, was in superb form and their defenders seemed to be on the goal-line whenever Poole was beaten. Unbelievably, the visitors escaped the siege three times and scored three goals. Another wonderful goal from Chris Beaumont was not enough. Somehow, County had lost 3-1. Although their display at Doncaster on Easter Monday was dismal, it was equalled by that of the home team but a freak wind-assisted goal from the side-line left Stockport without a point.

The County records show how often they finish a season poorly but, if they were to have a chance of promotion, they needed a good run. Six successive victories, which took them up to second place, included a 2-1 win against promotion-chasing Northampton Town in which Francis scored his first goal, 3-1 away victories at Gillingham and Wrexham and a thrilling 2-1 win against another promotion rival, Torquay United, Andy Kilner scoring a quite stunning winner. Neil Matthews scored in all six games, invariably at hand to finish off chances created by others. Their winning run ended at another form team, Blackpool, losing an open and exciting game 3-2. Two goals from Andy Kilner gave County a 2-0 win at York City and put them in a position where they knew that they would be promoted if they won the last game against Scunthorpe United at Edgeley Park.

A Play-off place was guaranteed, but so close were the top teams that at 4.40pm on 11 May 1991, County could have finished anywhere in the top five. With Scunthorpe already in the Play-offs, they brought few supporters to Edgeley Park which meant that, whilst many County supporters could not get into the ground, it was nowhere near full. Stockport began with the determination of a team that had narrowly failed the year before. Within a minute, Neil Matthews had headed against the bar, and in the sixth minute, the same player followed up to score when Chris Beaumont's shot was parried into his path by Scunthorpe goalkeeper, Paul Musselwhite. By the tenth minute, persistent pressure ended with Kevin Francis heading in County's second goal. Although the game was thoroughly one-sided and County had a number of chances to increase their lead, when Scunthorpe's Andy Flounders created an isolated opportunity, it was clear that even a 2-0 lead did not guarantee victory. Within two minutes of the re-start, Matthews ran on to a long clearance from goalkeeper, David Redfern, and headed over Musselwhite to score County's third. A fourth goal after 52 minutes dispelled any doubts of a possible Scunthorpe recovery, Alan Finley heading in from Andy Kilner's long throw-in. County completed the scoring when, from an Andy Kilner cross, Kevin Francis scored his second goal with a magnificent far-post header. The remainder of the game was pure carnival, the crowd

Stoke City score their winning goal against County in the 1992 Autoglass Trophy Final.

City the following week, which included wonderful goals from both Andy Kilner and Kevin Francis, put County in third place. However, two dreadful defeats followed: 3-0 to Birmingham City at St Andrews, where Beaumont and Francis were both injured, Andy Kilner missed a penalty and was then sent off for dissent; the second was a far more embarrassing 4-0 defeat at Edgeley Park to lowly Chester, not helped by County fielding a team packed with defenders. In a battling performance at Leeds Road the

singing delightedly whilst the players awaited the final whistle. After 21 years, County were back in the Third Division and the wild celebrations which followed were for the achievement rather than for the one-sided match. As leaders Darlington had beaten Rochdale, County had to settle for the runners-up spot: they were happy to do so.

Bergara's achievement in such a short time was remarkable but, whilst the supporters were overjoyed with promotion, they were wary of what lay ahead of them; there were no illusions of taking the Third Division 'by storm' and even the most optimistic supporter would have been content with a year of consolidation. The major transfer during the close season involved Peter Ward joining County from Rochdale for £35,000 plus Mark Payne. The former Hereford United player, Paul Wheeler, a hardworking forward, also joined County three days before the start of the season.

When the first League match of 1991-92 brought Swansea City to Edgeley Park, after 21 years in the Fourth Division, County did not know what to expect. What it brought was the same scoreline as in their promotion-winning match against Scunthorpe three months previously, the only difference being that Swansea offered even less resistance. Whilst no one believed the Third Division could be that easy, four wins and a draw in County's first five games exceeded their wildest dreams. Shortly after suffering their first League defeat at West Brom, ironically to a Paul A.Williams goal, County bought goalkeeper Neil Edwards from Leeds United. Edwards, though only 5ft 8ins, proved an excellent buy, developing into a first-rate shot-stopping goalkeeper. Mark Lillis also joined County to provide the type of experience necessary at the higher level.

Again, Stockport were proving a very difficult team to 'kill off', coming from behind twice in their first away game at Leyton Orient to draw 3-3. At Springfield Park, after trailing 1-0 at half-time, a dazzling second-half display gave them a 3-1 win against Wigan Athletic. Towards the end of September, Stockport visited the highly fancied Stoke City for the first time since October 1926. In spite of going two goals down inside the first 27 minutes, County fought back in the second half and, after Mark Lillis pulled a goal back on his debut, Kevin Francis equalised in the 87th minute. A 4-1 victory over Bradford

following week, by becoming the first team to score at Huddersfield that season, County atoned for their dismal performance in the Chester game, a Jim Gannon header giving them a 1-0 win. The subsequent five months saw County remain in the top six, enjoying some excellent results, but without being able to string together a run of victories which could take them into an automatic promotion place.

In December, striker Andy Preece, who was languishing in Wrexham's reserve team, was bought for £10,000 and became a regular goalscorer. Unfortunately, the hero of the promotion season, Andy Kilner, had lost his way as had Neil Matthews. Other than at the start of the season, County's only hat-trick of victories came shortly after the turn of the year. On 4 January, a fantastically exciting game against League leaders Brentford was deservedly won in the last minute by a Kevin Francis header. The following week, County visited Hull where second half goals from Andy Preece and the consistently improving Francis gave them a 2-0 win. Their third successive win was against struggling Darlington who battled hard to keep County scoreless until the last 20 minutes, when Peter Ward scored his first goal for the club and Andy Preece added a second. At the end of March, four wins in five games, the last of which was a comprehensive 3-0 victory against pre-season promotion favourites West Brom, took County into third place. Barring complete disaster during the last six games, a Play-off position was almost assured and, with leaders Stoke and second-place Birmingham still to visit Edgeley Park, automatic promotion remained a possibility.

However, whilst County had been knocked out of the major Cup competitions early on, their interest in what was now called the Autoglass Cup was increasing. Although heavily beaten by Carlisle in a preliminary round in front of a meagre attendance of 894, County had progressed to the first round proper as a result of a Jim Gannon hat-trick against York City. The first round took them back to Brunton Park, where a fine Kevin Francis hat-trick gave Stockport a 3-1 win, avenging their earlier 4-0 defeat. County earned a place in the Northern Section semi-final when another Francis hat-trick defeated Hartlepool United 3-0. On 17 March 1992, they visited Gresty Road for what appeared to be a tough game against a skilful Crewe team. Stockport's greater strength shone through and brilliantly taken goals by Peter Ward and Paul Wheeler helped County to a 2-1 win and a place in the two leg Northern Section Final against Fourth Division leaders Burnley.

Thus, by the beginning of April, in their first season in the Third Division, County were making a serious challenge in two competitions. In the League, a dreadful performance at Plainmoor on 4 April saw them lose 2-0 to a Torquay team which seemed condemned to relegation. Three days later, Stockport visited Turf Moor for the first leg of the Autoglass Northern Section Final. As County and Burnley had met frequently in various competitions since the Clarets descent to the Fourth Division, there was no little 'needle' between the clubs. A crowd of over 13,000 witnessed a tremendous performance by County as they won the match through a single Francis header after 33 minutes when their play deserved a more conclusive victory. In between the two legs, an eventful League game against Exeter City at Edgeley Park took place, three goals in the last nine minutes giving County a 4-1 win. On 15 April, Stockport had the opportunity of making history, a visit to Wembley in the Autoglass Final, providing they took advantage of their 1-0 win the previous week. Any tension County felt at the start was quickly dispelled when, after only six minutes, Francis headed in a right-wing corner as he had done in the first leg. There was too much at stake for the game to be a classic and when Burnley's John Pender brought the aggregate score to 2-1 after 22 minutes, Wembley still seemed a long way away. However, Burnley threatened less than expected and, in the 73rd minute, a scrappy goal from Jim Gannon assured County of a visit to Wembley for the first time, where they would meet Stoke City who beat Peterborough United the same evening.

There was, or should have been, little time to relax, as there were still 12 points to play for in the League, points which could promote County into the Second Division for the first time in 54 years. It is impossible to know whether or not the players were distracted by thoughts of Wembley, but the following three games saw a less passionate and less adventurous County fail to score, gaining only two points, one of which was in a well-attended but poor game against Stoke City. The chance of automatic promotion had been lost carelessly and County now found themselves in a position where they had to win their last game just to guarantee a Play-off place. The final League match was at Edgeley Park against Birmingham City who, although already promoted, would be champions if they beat County. Recapturing some of their early season form, Stockport ended Birmingham's hopes within 12 minutes, Gannon and Francis giving County a 2-0 lead which City never threatened. The way the results went that last Saturday of the season meant that County finished fifth, one point behind fourth place fellow-Autoglass Finalists, Stoke City. The two teams would have to play each other three times in six days.

On 10 May, the first leg of the Play-off semi-final against Stoke took place at Edgeley Park. With Stoke no doubt aggrieved at having thrown away automatic promotion with two successive defeats in their final League games, an explosive and unnecessarily unpleasant game saw their captain Carl Beeston sent off for the second game in succession. Further aggravation by the

vocally aggressive petulance of some of his colleagues and a number of theatrical activities by others, hardly helped the atmosphere. A first half swerving free-kick from Peter Ward found the top left hand corner of Ronnie Sinclair's goal, to give County a deserved and precious one goal lead to take to the Victoria Ground. Three days later, over 16,000 spectators attended the second leg, the majority of whom fully expected Stoke to overturn the 1-0 first-leg deficit. The Victoria Ground was stunned when, in the first minute, Kevin Francis robbed Noel Blake of the ball and set up Chris Beaumont to score. County kept their heads, only conceding a late goal to Mark Stein which was both too little and too late for the Potteries team. Unbelievably, County found themselves in two Wembley Finals within a week.

The animosity which had developed in the Play-off matches took much of the gloss from County's first Wembley appearance, an occasion when opposing sets of supporters normally mingle with each other without antagonism. There was no such friendliness on this occasion. Nonetheless, the 16 May was a proud moment for Danny Bergara as he became the first South American to lead out an English team at Wembley. The game as a whole, played in sweltering heat, was disappointing, County having the better of the first half and having an early goal disallowed when Paul Wheeler, replacing the Cup-tied Andy Preece, was alleged to have fouled Stoke goalkeeper Peter Fox before the ball went over the line. Video replays and the commentary on Sky Television seemed to show that Fox had simply been guilty of an error of judgment, dropping the ball before it found the back of the net. The game was littered with fouls, many of which went unpunished, before, in the 68th minute, Mark Stein, Stoke's most dangerous player (and most vocal critic of decisions) found himself in space on the right hand side of the penalty area and sent in an unstoppable shot to put City 1-0 in front. Unfortunately for County, as their defenders ran out of the penalty area prior to the ball being returned for Stein's goal, the linesman failed to notice that Wayne Biggins was running back from an offside position when the ball was played forward into the area. The goal therefore stood and Stoke finished as 1-0 victors.

Disappointing though this was, County knew that it would be only eight days before they returned to Wembley for the bigger prize of promotion. Another hot day saw County and Peterborough United fight out a hard but fair contest, with the Posh having the better of the first half. In the 51st minute, Peterborough's Ken Charley headed a corner against the bar which bounced down before David Frain hooked it clear. To the disbelief of both the players and supporters, the linesman flagged for a goal. 'Was it over the line?' was the simple, but intriguing, reference to this controversial decision in the *Rothman's Football Yearbook*. As the second half wore on, County fought desperately for the equaliser. Francis had a 'goal' disallowed for a highly questionable offside before, finally, County's pressure paid off, Francis scoring in the 87th minute, after Peterborough goalkeeper, Fred Barber, failed to hold an Andy Preece shot. The Stockport fans were ecstatic as, totally in command, they immediately pressed for the winning goal. Then, in the last minute, Preece lost possession on the right wing, a long ball found Ken Charley who evaded Tony Barras's

Ecstatic County fans and players celebrate Kevin Francis's 88th-minute equaliser in the 1992 Play-off Final against Peterborough United.

challenge before brilliantly lobbing the winning goal over Neil Edwards. From ecstasy to abject misery inside two minutes. Players and supporters were stunned, incredulous that the game had been lost after such a passionate fightback. As the County fans returned to their coaches still in a state of shock, the vast majority of Peterborough fans, though predictably delighted with their own success, sportingly applauded their opposite numbers, a far cry from events the previous week.

What the players and supporters found particularly galling was that, during the two Wembley games, there had been four crucial decisions, of which every one had gone against County. But the decisions, for better or for worse (obviously the latter), had been made and County, at the final hurdle, were left with nothing. Once more, the supporters tended to be a little forgetful of the monumental achievements of their team, which had exceeded all pre-season expectations.

As after Bergara's first season, a major concern was whether, after what in fact had been a magnificent season, the team would be able to maintain the fighting qualities it had developed and repeat the challenge for promotion. Season 1992-93 saw the introduction of an elitist FA 'Premier' League (the previous season's First Division), and the remaining Football League Divisions renamed. The result was, that when County kicked off the season, they were, by name at least, a Second Division club. Despite the nonemclature, to the supporters, County were a Third Division club as opposed to a Fourth Division one. Whether or not it was to general approval, Bergara loyally kept faith with the side which had come so close to success on two fronts. Thus, there were no significant

signings in the summer, the previous season's team left to prove whether they could not only repeat, but exceed, their achievements.

Stockport opened the season with an impressive win at Springfield Park, two outstanding individual goals by Chris Beaumont helping County to a 2-1 win against Wigan Athletic. Although County's first defeat came in their third away game at West Brom, as it had the previous season, five wins in the first eight games represented an excellent start. Successive away victories at Bradford City and Chester City, with Beaumont, Kevin Francis and John Muir (who had arrived from Doncaster Rovers in the spring) all scoring for the third game on the run, gave the impression that, in addition to having developed a potent strike force, County could repeat the challenge of 1991-92.

Following a first round League Cup win against Chester in which Stockport became the first team to win at the new Deva Stadium, the draw brought a second round tie against Nottingham Forest. Two richly entertaining games with Brian Clough's attractive Forest team ended with elimination but not before the Premier side were given a fright both at Edgeley Park and at the City Ground where only an unfortunate Jim Gannon own-goal ensured victory for the home team. Overall, these high-profile games seemed to distract County from the more important League fixtures as they failed to win any of the five games subsequent to the first leg against Forest and, worryingly, scored only once. Stockport had dropped to 11th place but two resounding home wins against Huddersfield Town (5-0) and Preston North End (3-0), ended the goal-drought and began a run of 16 games in

The only Stockport player in the photograph, Jim Gannon, turns away in delight after equalising just before half-time against West Brom on 20 February 1993. Gannon scored again in County's 5-1 home win over the eventual Play-off winners.

which only three games were lost. Towards the end of this run, there were important successive home victories against other promotion challengers, Bolton (2-0), Port Vale (2-0) and West Brom (5-1). The last of these three games proved particularly satisfying for Paul A.Williams, who had returned to County from West Brom in early January 1993. Although he had scored against Stockport 15 months earlier, Williams had a miserable spell at The Hawthorns and was delighted to return to Edgeley Park (for one-tenth of the fee West Brom had paid for him) where he had been a very popular figure. Not surprisingly, he was delighted when, after coming on as substitute, his 87th minute goal against Albion completed the 5-1 rout and this after the Baggies had scored first. However, as is often the case, 'going back' does not succeed, and his second spell was unproductive, Williams used only as a substitute or when principal striker, Kevin Francis, was missing.

By transfer-deadline day, Bergara had brought other new faces to Edgeley Park: wingers Michael Wallace (from Manchester City in September), Darren Ryan (from Chester in an exchange deal which took Paul Wheeler to the Deva Stadium in January) and Martin James (from Preston for £50,000); defender Mike Flynn (also from Preston, for a Stockport record fee of £125,000), forward Peter Duffield (on loan from Sheffield United) and midfielder Brian McCord (from Barnsley). Initially, McCord was used as cover for midfield regulars, David Frain and Peter Ward. After playing for the injured Ward, he kept his place, alongside the two regulars, and, in his

first such role, gave a very impressive performance in a fine 2-0 victory at Rotherham. Three days later, on 5 March, his career was ended when he suffered an horrific broken leg in a challenge by Swansea's John Cornforth at Vetch Field.

Having reached the third round of the FA Cup, after away victories at York and Macclesfield, Stockport were drawn against Derby at the Baseball Ground. Although going behind to a Craig Short goal in the first half, McCord came on as a late substitute and headed an equaliser in the 84th minute. Not for the last time, County's luck was out, David Miller (who had been signed from Carlisle the previous March) scoring an own goal in injury time. In the League, following McCord's last match, County's third away game in seven days took them to leaders, Stoke City. Although fortunately lacking some of the previous year's spite, at the end of a disappointing match which Stoke won 2-1, an ugly incident involving Mark Stein and Stockport's Jim Gannon ended with Stein striking Gannon. Although the FA took no action, criminal charges of assault were initiated against Stein, all of which hardly augured well for the return at Edgeley Park three weeks later. In between the Stoke games, after being held to an 0-0 draw by an unambitious Brighton, County registered three successive wins, which took them into the top three for the first time since the opening week of the season. The first two wins were notable for the fact that debutant, Peter Duffield, scored twice both at Preston (3-2) and at Edgeley Park against Hartlepool (4-1). The last of the three victories was at Home Park where, for the only time in their history,

Chris Beaumont helps Kevin Francis celebrate his hat-trick goal at Home Park in County' 4-3 win over Plymouth Argyle on 27 March 1993.

Stockport drew level three times before beating Plymouth Argyle 4-3, which included an incisive hat-trick from Kevin Francis. The game also saw the debut of goalkeeper Phil Kite, on loan from Sheffield United, who surprisingly displaced the popular Neil Edwards, a move that did Kite no favours as many supporters were unhappy with the change and made their feelings obvious.

Once again, County found themselves chasing honours in both the League and the Autoglass Trophy. After beating Chesterfield (twice), Chester, Hartlepool and Bradford City (in a pulsating 4-3 victory at Valley Parade), County found themselves in the competition's Northern Section Final. A miserable performance at Springfield Park was rescued by a late Jim Gannon goal with the result that County were only one goal in arrears for the second leg. Following the Plymouth game, Stoke visited Edgeley Park on 3 April when the fans were 'treated' to a generally squalid game, which whilst unforgivable, was totally predictable in the light of what had occurred in previous games. Leaders Stoke were happy with a point in the 1-1 draw and, in the circumstances, County should not have been too despondent as they were unlikely to catch the leaders. But this match was a turning-point, leading, just three days later, to a strange formation, which included David Frain playing alongside Francis to face a rampant Bolton who sliced through County, almost at will, despite only winning 2-1. From being third in the League, County's form slid away alarmingly as they won only one of their last nine games to finish a disappointing sixth, claiming a Play-off place only on goals scored. At least Stockport had succeeded in overturning their one-goal deficit in their Autoglass tie with Wigan, Peter Ward's beautifully controlled 'chip' over Nigel Atkins bringing the tie level. A 54th minute goal by Francis, his 38th of the season, took County back to Wembley in the Autoglass Final where they would meet Port Vale. Heartbreakingly for the Vale, having been in second place for three months, their four wins and a draw in their last five games could not match Bolton's five successive wins, and they finished in

Kevin Francis in familiar pose, celebrating another goal, this time against Port Vale in the 1993 Autoglass Trophy Final.

third place despite amassing 89 points. Quite extra-ordinarily, County would now have to play Port Vale three times in six days. The chances of this occurring cannot be high, but for Stockport to play the two Potteries teams three times in six days in successive seasons almost defied belief. Thankfully, however, despite the end result being no better, the three games were all played in a good spirit. In the Play-off semi-final, a 1-1 draw at Edgeley Park was followed by an 84th minute Martin Foyle winner at Vale Park giving the Potteries club a place in the Final. County battled particularly hard in the second leg and, despite being hampered by the absence of Kevin Francis, through suspension, did have opportunities to cause an upset. Although disappointing, it was hard to begrudge Vale their place after the way they had just missed out on promotion. The injustice of the Play-off lottery, which could have led to County embarrassingly beating Vale, in spite of finishing 17 points behind them, was left to West Brom to inflict ten days later. The (generally) friendly banter between supporters which should accompany a Wembley Final, unlike the previous year, was present when County and Vale played the last of their three matches on 22 May. With midfield player David Frain still out of favour, County played the ideal system – for Vale. A one-sided first-half saw goals from Paul Kerr and Bernie Slaven put Vale two goals up, but the second half at least found Stockport playing a system which could be more effective. Although Port Vale had appeared in complete control, for no apparent reason, sections of the County followers suddenly began chanting, inspiring almost all their other supporters to join in. As the volume of the vocal support increased, the team responded; it was now County who were looking dangerous and Vale's stroll to victory looked decidedly more shaky. With a little over 20 minutes left, a Peter Duffield cross drew out Paul Musselwhite, and Francis, timing his run to perfection, headed over the stranded Port Vale goalkeeper to put County back into the game. The remainder of the game was played in the Vale half, as Stockport, now roared on by their supporters, strove for the equaliser. A header by substitute, Andy Preece, went agonisingly wide but a now nervous Vale clung on to win 2-1. A third defeat at Wembley within 12 months was hard for everyone, but the team had gone through a stale patch and had looked jaded for the previous six weeks. Ironically, Port Vale would no doubt have happily forsaken their Autoglass Trophy in return for a Play-off Final victory but at least they, unlike County the previous season in their two trips to Wembley, had won something.

Another season empty-handed, yet still one of achievement, as the side to which Bergara had been loyal had almost repaid that loyalty. There were other positive factors. Kevin Francis, so often mocked, was almost a celebrity and, more importantly, had scored 39 goals, a feat previously excelled by only Joe Smith and Alf Lythgoe. County had acquired an excellent centre-half in Mike Flynn, had developed a young defender, Sean Connelly and, in Darren Ryan, they had a wide forward player who was extremely promising. However, well before the start of the 1993-94 season, there was a distinct air of pessimism amongst Stockport supporters. In both local pre-season friendlies and in an Isle of Man competition in July, an unambitious and sterile looking County were thoroughly unimpressive. There had been no influx of new players and, if doubts had existed prior to the previous season about County being able to maintain their momentum, these had multiplied by August 1993.

When County opened their League season at Home Park, it was with some amazement that supporters saw an attacking formation (with Martin James and Darren Ryan, two recognised wingers) play flowing, attractive football. Additionally, former captain David Frain, who had been dropped for all three Port Vale matches and appeared to be out of favour, was back in the team. Two goals from Kevin Francis and an excellent half-volley from Andy Preece gave County a 3-0 lead and, although Plymouth Argyle scored twice in the last minute to give the score an impression of respectability, the home team had been comprehensively outplayed. Although James was unfortunately omitted after the first five games, County's start to the season was more than a little impressive. There was a double disappointment at Hartlepool: the first a freak dismissal in the League Cup following a last-minute goal and 95th minute speculative 40-yard lob by Brian Honour; the second a 1-0 League defeat in an appalling display. However, apart from these two games, by the beginning of November, Stockport not only had a splendid record but were playing exciting and attractive football and looked genuine promotion material, winning 11 of their opening 15 games whilst losing only once. By early November, they seemed quite unstoppable at Edgeley Park, their 4-0 defeats of Exeter and Swansea both flattering the opposition. Not only was Kevin Francis continuing to score regularly, but his striking partner, Andy Preece, had become County's leading scorer. An unfortunate defeat at Cardiff was followed by the first loss of points at Edgeley Park, Bristol Rovers beating County 2-0. Whilst the West Country team were helped by Jim Gannon missing a twice-taken penalty, they were well-worth their win and looked a very good team. One of the most unfortunate consequences of these successive defeats was that not only was the previously impressive Darren Ryan omitted, but County abandoned the use of a genuine wide player. By the time Ryan reappeared 20 games later, the absence of a genuine midfield player resulted in him getting neither the service nor the support he needed.

It was time for County to have their annual stutter and this they duly did, gaining an unambitious point at Cambridge and suffering a second successive home defeat, this time to Plymouth Argyle. Well-beaten at Reading, they only narrowly overcame bottom club, Barnet, through a 78th minute goal by Francis who also earned them a point with an 87th minute equaliser at Brentford. By this time, apart from reaching the Northern quarter-final of the Autoglass Trophy following convincing victories against Wigan, Bury and Rochdale, there was a more novel distraction in the form of an FA Cup third round meeting with Queen's Park Rangers at Edgeley Park. In the earlier two rounds, County had come from behind to beat Rotherham 2-1 at Millmoor with a 90th minute goal from Andy Preece and then overcome Halifax Town at Edgeley Park. Although relegated to The Conference at the end of 1992-93, Halifax had produced the shock result of the first round by comprehensively beating West Brom at The Shay. However, there were no surprises at Edgeley Park where County ran out easy 5-1 winners. As a result of heavy frost, the tie against Queen's

County, 1993-94. Back row (left to right): Flynn, Gannon, P.A.Williams, Finley, Barras, W.R.Williams, Carstairs. Middle row: James, Connelly, Edwards, Ironside, Wilkinson, Miller, Beaumont, Ryan. Front row: Francis, Frain, Wallace, D.Bergara (manager), Ward, Todd, Preece.

Park Rangers was in doubt until the late morning of 8 January 1994. The attractive London side were not impressed by the decision of Sheffield referee John Key to play the match and were not impressive when play began at 3.00pm. Nonetheless, in their first serious attack, the Premier League team took the lead in the 19th minute through a well-struck goal by Simon Barker. Although enjoying most of the possession, County had to wait until the 39th minute for a controversial equaliser, Kevin Francis scoring when defender Tony Barras was lying injured in an offside position. Referee Key rejected Rangers's appeals and the teams went in level at half-time. Although County dominated the second-half, they had to wait until the 74th minute for what turned out to be the winning goal, a spectacular Andy Preece volley from a Peter Ward free-kick. An overjoyed Edgeley Park crowd celebrated County's win, only their fourth FA Cup victory against First (or Premier) Division teams since they first entered the competition in 1892. On the surface, the draw for the fourth round could hardly have been better, a home tie against Liverpool or Bristol City. County's most famous Cup-ties had been against the Anfield team and there was a genuine belief that the Hatters could, at last, gain revenge for 1950 and 1965. The fact that Liverpool had escaped from Ashton Gate with a fortunate draw was ignored on the basis that the Premier club had overcome the possible pitfall of an away defeat. Blind assumptions were made about the forthcoming 'Liverpool game'

which did not materialise, Bristol winning the replay. The fourth round tie was postponed, the Edgeley Park pitch now in an appalling state, but this resulted in County knowing that, if they beat Bristol, they would have another home tie against Charlton Athletic or Blackburn Rovers. Four days before the re-arranged Cup-tie took place, County played Fulham at Edgeley Park and the visitors took full advantage of both the home team's profligacy in front of goal and their own four chances, all of which they converted to win 4-2. On 9 February, Bristol scored an invaluable early goal which put pressure on the home side who both squandered chances and were denied by the magnificent display of Keith Welch, City's goalkeeper. With County pushing forward at the beginning of the second half, Bristol punished the home team with incisive breaks from defence, Wayne Allison scoring an 18-minute hat-trick to complete a 4-0 win for the First Division team.

That distraction over, County gained a valuable away point at Port Vale before returning to Edgeley Park to earn a convincing 3-0 win over Huddersfield Town, the team they would play ten days later in the Northern semi-final of the Autoglass Trophy, Stockport having easily beaten Scunthorpe in the quarter-final. However, Huddersfield were a very different proposition in the Cup-tie and, in spite of the fact that County missed a number of good chances, Huddersfield's total commitment gave them a well-merited victory. Their only other distraction eliminated, County could now 'concentrate on the League'. This seemed to be confirmed by successive victories at home to Hartlepool, when Andy Preece ludicrously got himself sent off with County leading 5-0, and at Wrexham, together with a hard-earned point at Turf Moor against Burnley. There then followed successive home defeats, first to a very confident York City side and then to a considerably less-deserving Bournemouth team who came to Edgeley Park for a point and were astonished to take away three. In the latter game, the only memorable event was the substitute debut of Eric Cantona's brother, Joel. Glimpses of skill were evident but Cantona was not given the opportunity to start a game and show whether he could perform satisfactorily. Three days after the Bournemouth game, a nerve-settling 3-1 victory against Brentford appeared to have eased any anxiety. However, quite inexplicably, an over-cautious team went to relegation-threatened Blackpool and lost not only Peter Ward for the last ten games as a result of injury, but also all three points.

It is a matter of fact that County did not lose any of their last ten games, but six of them were drawn, one incredibly carelessly (and crucially) when they threw away a two-goal lead at home to Cardiff City, and others, when they seemed content with a point, at Barnet, Leyton Orient and Bristol Rovers, none of whom could be described as 'form' teams. There was no recognised midfield player, Ward being injured whilst Frain was left out as was Dean Emerson, who had returned to Edgeley Park before Christmas. Whatever disappointment was to follow, it should be borne in mind that, from the end of August to the end of April, automatic promotion was in County's own hands. In normal circumstances, they could not have expected Port Vale to win eight of their last nine games (their only defeat being at Edgeley Park) to take the second promotion place behind Reading, but after Vale's experience the previous season, it should not have come as a total surprise. Postponements and the consequences, seven games in 16 days, were undoubtedly a factor, but had County been committed to beating inferior teams rather than committed to avoiding defeat, they would probably have gained automatic promotion. The result of an away draw at Bristol Rovers on the last day of April left County, for the first time in eight months, in a position where they had to rely on others dropping points. This did not happen and, whilst Stockport accumulated their highest points total (85), they still finished the League programme in the Play-offs for the third consecutive season.

As a result of a poor goalless draw at home to Hull City on the last day of the season, County finished level on points with Plymouth Argyle but having scored fewer totals and thus ended in fourth place. The two legs of the Play-off semi-final against York City were both tense affairs. Thankfully, after ten games without a 'proper' midfield, Peter Ward was fit and, surprisingly, was supported by the recalled David Frain. In the first match, at Bootham Crescent, York had the better chances but were denied by the excellent goalkeeping of recently acquired John Keeley, once an expensive signing by Oldham, but who had been reduced to unsuccessful loan spells before drifting into non-League football. His consistent performances were one of the few bright spots at Stockport in the end of season run-in. In the second leg at Edgeley Park, County had the better of the game, but following an excellent save by Keeley near the end of the match, Chris Beaumont broke free into the penalty area before clinically curving the ball wide of York's Dean Kiely and into the goal to take Stockport into their second Play-off Final. Their surprise opponents were Burnley who, having finished 12 points behind both Plymouth and County, were held by Argyle to a goalless draw at Turf Moor but had then gone to Home Park and won 3-1.

With no love lost between the two teams, nor between some of the supporters, it was not predicted to be the friendliest of games; on the other hand, it was not predicted to be the shambolic occasion that transpired. Whilst some believed that Stockport were destined to never enjoy victory at Wembley, many believed that justice would be done, even within the absurdities of the Play-off system, as County had ended 12 points above Burnley. The team, whilst not over-confident, were determined not to fail this time and the omens were reasonably good. However, after witnessing the excellent unobtrusive refereeing of Roger Milford of Bristol in the Play-off semi-final, it was less than heartening to learn that the official for Wembley was to be David Elleray of Harrow who, after millions of television viewers had witnessed his officiating in the FA Cup Final, hardly inspired confidence. Within marginally less than two minutes of the kick-off, Chris Beaumont gave County the perfect start, scoring with a diving header from David Frain's free-kick and leaving Burnley goalkeeper, Marlon Beresford, helpless.

Following this goal, the bare facts are: County's Michael Wallace was sent off after 13 minutes; Burnley's David Eyres struck a fine equaliser after 28 minutes; County's Chris Beaumont was sent off after 61 minutes; and, whilst Adrian Heath was in an offside position, Burnley's Gary Parkinson scored their winning goal after 65 minutes, his deflected shot rolling past John Keeley. Thankfully, after 104 minutes of 'play', Mr Elleray blew the final whistle.

It is tempting, in the light of both direct observation and video evidence, to examine the minutiae of this excuse for a football match, but it is a pointless exercise.

Nonetheless, certain comments are necessary, beyond mere references to the Play-off travesty which, in addition to providing the farcical opportunity, for clubs such as Burnley, to gain both undeserved promotion *and* a trophy for finishing in sixth place, is by its very nature potentially explosive. The game itself was a genuine contest for only 13 minutes. Disturbingly, whilst many of the uglier sides of professional football were evident, the punishment for much of the nastiness was neither evenly nor, more importantly, fairly distributed. In factual terms, the 'shame' lay on County's Beaumont and Wallace but this belies the fact that, on the basis of the way Mr Elleray refereed the game, certain Burnley players should have been taking the proverbial 'early bath'. The fact that they did not can be ascribed to good fortune, subtlety of offending, poor officiating or a combination of such factors. It is certainly the case that County players and supporters were left to rue the fact that the excellent Rodger Milford took charge of the First Division Play-off rather than the Second Division one. Had he been in charge of the Burnley contest, the match as a whole would have been very different, although, of course, the result

Chris Beaumont (on ground) gives Stockport County a magnificent start against Burnley in the 1994 Play-off Final. Alas, Beaumont was one of two Stockport players later dismissed by referee David Elleray, and yet again County were destined to leave Wembley in bitter disappointment.

might have been the same. However, for those non-Stockport supporters who believe this summary to be an example of blind prejudice, they should ask how it was that County, the team with the best disciplinary record in the Second Division, could become the first to have two players sent off in a Wembley Final.

There could hardly be a finer understatement than to describe this last game of 1993-94 as 'disappointing'. During Bergara's five and a half year stay at Edgeley Park, whatever criticisms can be levelled at either his tactics or team selection or, indeed, some of his players, there is little doubt that fate has been cruel to both him and his players. To have won nothing in the three years since promotion, has been, quite simply, unjust.

Yet, however angry or disappointed all true supporters of the club might be, they should feel enormous gratitude for the partnership of chairman Brendan Elwood and Danny Bergara, a partnership which has helped to re-write County's history in a way undreamed of five years ago. To say they have won nothing is not merely an over-simplification, but disregards the quite remarkable achievements made on an extremely tight budget. The club has always struggled to survive and it would be tragic if the frustration of near successes, culminating in the 1994 Play-off Final, were to end in the club's disintegration. The nucleus of the team which so nearly succeeded, will probably now be dismantled as changes are inevitably made. Andy Preece's rise to the Premier Division with Crystal Palace is unlikely to be the only departure from Edgeley Park and, for the sake of both the supporters and those who have helped to revitalise the club, it can only be hoped that, in the near future, justice will be done and deserved tangible success achieved.

County Managers

Fred Stewart
(August 1900-May 1911)

BORN in Oldham in 1873, Fred Stewart had been involved in the administrative side of County for seven years before becoming the club's first manager following their successful application to join the Football League in May 1900. In 33 years as a manager, Stewart was in charge of only two clubs, County for the first 11 years and Cardiff City for 22 years, creating record stays at both clubs.

The early years at Stockport were extremely difficult and, despite Stewart's shrewd dealings in the transfer market, limited resources meant that survival was precarious. County applied for re-election in all of their first four seasons in Division Two, ironically their highest position being third from the bottom in 1903-04, the season in which they failed to gain re-election. In 1904-05, in spite of having to sell their two 'stars', Tommy Brittleton and Tommy Green, County won the Lancashire Combination convincingly, so helping them to regain their League status.

On their return to Division Two, Stewart not only guided County to tenth place, their best-ever League position, but also helped the club to make a profit of £500 on the season. Stewart's next five seasons at County continued to be difficult although the club succeeded in avoiding any of the re-election places. He maintained the ability to develop players before, by necessity, having to let them go to wealthier clubs. Besides receiving other 'handsome' fees, Bob Carter and Bob Suart went to Fulham for £550 whilst Bert Elkin moved to Spurs for £500. Nonetheless, Stewart continued to bring in good replacements to ensure County's survival.

In May 1911, it was announced that Stewart had 'declined a Cardiff appointment' but within a week he accepted Cardiff's offer. The *Cheshire Daily Echo* justifiably gave due praise to Stewart's service, stating that his years in charge had 'been full of anxiety and very trying work. Mr Stewart has always taken those hard trials with a good heart and an unflinching spirit and that fact alone must have earned for him in the estimation of his colleagues a very high place'.

Stewart's achievement in keeping County in the Football League was nothing compared to the success he enjoyed at Cardiff. Within two seasons, Cardiff moved from the Second to the First Division of the Southern League but it was on the resumption of professional football after the war that City's golden era began. Following election to the Football League in 1920, they were promoted to Division One in their first season, finishing second on goal-average to champions, Birmingham. In the same season, they reached the FA Cup semi-finals, losing the all-Second Division tie to Wolves 3-1 in a replay at Old Trafford. Cardiff reached the quarter-finals in two of the next three seasons before Stewart at last took the Welsh club to the Cup Final in 1925. Although they lost 1-0 to Sheffield United, they returned to Wembley in 1927 when a Hugh Ferguson goal beat Arsenal to take the FA Cup out of England for the one and only time.

Stewart was cruelly deprived of the League championship on the last day of the 1923-24 season. If Cardiff could win at Birmingham, the title was theirs; if they drew, Huddersfield Town, their closest rivals, had to beat Nottingham Forest 3-0 to take the title. Huddersfield did beat Forest 3-0 whilst Cardiff were held to a goalless draw at St Andrew's. Cardiff even missed a late penalty and were thus denied the championship by 0.02 of a goal.

City could never repeat this form and in 1929, two years after their historic FA Cup win, they were relegated to Division Two before, two years later, being relegated to the Third Division South. When Cardiff finished in a miserable 19th place in 1933, Fred Stewart retired after a long and eventful career. He remained in Cardiff until his death in 1954.

Harry Lewis
(June 1911-April 1914)

ROTHERHAM-born Harry Lewis was in charge of County for only three seasons following Fred Stewart's departure to Cardiff. County finished 16th in Lewis's first season and 12th in his third season but, in between, in 1912-13, they had to apply for re-election for the first time since their return to the Football League in 1905. Although recording their highest-scoring away win in the FA Cup (7-2 against non-League King's Lynn), the re-election season was generally disastrous with players suspended by the club, the termination of a senior player's contract and the suspension of Tommy Charlton 'until further notice' following a sending-off in the 'derby' match with Glossop.

However, Lewis was responsible for introducing three of County's longest serving players, Fred Garrett, Harold Crossthwaite and the rapidly developing talent of Norman Rodgers. In April 1914, Lewis left County for Barnsley where he displayed his managerial qualities in taking the Oakwell club to their highest ever League position, third in Division Two, in his first season. He left Barnsley before the resumption of post-war football, eventually acquiring the manager's job at Hull City in July 1921. His first season at Anlaby Road ended with Hull attaining fifth place, but he was unable to repeat this success in the following two seasons, finally leaving Hull in January 1923. Although this was Lewis's last managerial position, he did advise Rotherham County in their early Football League years.

David Ashworth
(April 1914-December 1919)

DESPITE David Ashworth being in charge at Edgeley Park for over five years, only a season and a half of League football was played either side of World War One. Born in Waterford, Ireland, in 1868, Ashworth was one of the smallest ever managers, standing only five feet tall, earning him the somewhat predictable nickname of 'Little Dave'. After his playing days with Newchurch Rovers, Ashworth joined the Football League list as a referee, before taking up his first managerial post in 1906 with Oldham Athletic, then a Lancashire Combination club. His success at Boundary Park was nothing short of remarkable. In his first season, the Latics won the Lancashire Combination and were elected to the Football League. Their first three seasons saw them finishing third, sixth and second in Division Two, thereby gaining promotion to the First Division. In four seasons in Division One, Ashworth guided the Latics to seventh, eighteenth, ninth and a magnificent fourth along with an FA Cup semi-final appearance in 1913.

Surprisingly, in April 1914 'Little Dave' left Oldham to take charge at Stockport for the last season before the Football League was suspended for the remainder of World War One. During that season, he made few changes to the County team but saw the still improving Norman Rodgers become the first Stockport player to score 20 League goals in a season. Although County could only finish in 14th place, they secured their then highest number of points (37).

He continued in charge throughout the war before returning to Division One as manager of Liverpool whom he led to the League championship in 1921-22. 'Little Dave' continued to surprise as, with Liverpool well on the way to a second successive championship, in January 1923 he returned to Oldham Athletic. Unable to repeat his earlier success at Boundary Park, after 16 months Ashworth left to become Manchester City's first secretary-manager. With restrictions on buying new players, his reign at Maine Road ended in November 1925, a season that saw City both relegated and reach the FA Cup Final.

Walsall became his next and last League club, a 12-month spell leading to the sack in February 1927 after the Midlands club had to seek re-election. Ashworth then moved into non-League management, first with Caernarfon for three years and then Llanelli. In 1938, Ashworth turned his talents to scouting for Blackpool where he remained until his death on 23 March 1947.

Albert Williams
(December 1919-November 1924)

BORN in Stockport in 1883, Albert Williams signed professional forms for County in September 1903. Although not a regular member of the first team, he made six appearances in 1903-04, primarily as a centre-half. Forced to retire from playing as a result of injury, he became first assistant trainer and then trainer in 1914. When Ashworth left County in 1919, Albert Williams was promoted to manager, a position he held for almost five years.

The first 18 months of his managerial career coincided with a disastrous spell for the club. The financial benefits from the sale of Rodgers to Blackburn and Crosshwaite to Stoke for a combined total of £4,500 did not compensate for a depleted forward line, County sliding down the table to finish in 16th place having won only four of their last 20 games. Williams brought in the youthful Harry Hardy and Jimmy Walsh in 1920-21 but, despite the return of the experienced Gault from Cardiff, only three

wins in the first 26 games virtually assured bottom place and automatic relegation. Crowd trouble against Sheffield Wednesday in April 1921 resulted in County's second ground suspension, leaving them to play their last fixture at Old Trafford.

Fortunately, 1921 saw the Third Division North established, of which County were not only founder members, but ultimately the Section's first champions. Williams' introduction of Joe O'Kane, who had been at the club for some 15 months, together with the re-signing of Crossthwaite from Stoke and the late transfer of Wilf Woodcock from Manchester City ensured that County's tight defence was well supported by their attack. In April 1922, County clinched the championship against Darlington in front of nearly 18,500 at Edgeley Park.

County's return to Division Two proved no easier than in earlier years and only a wonderful three wins in the last four games saved Stockport from relegation for the second time in three years. Although Williams had helped to develop the exciting talent of winger Eddie Critchley to supplement a solid defence, County found the standard of Second Division football rising consistently. Following a respectable 13th place in 1923-24, a dreadful string of results in the autumn of 1924 saw Williams enforced resignation.

Before his introduction to management, Albert Williams ran a newsagent's shop in Cheadle to which he returned until his death in Stockport in 1940.

Fred Scotchbrook
(November 1924-February 1926)

BORN in Horwich in 1886, Scotchbrook spent his career as a player in and around his home town. Spells with Gymnasium FC and Horwich FC were followed by a late step up to League football at the age of 28 with Bolton Wanderers just before the outbreak of World War One. After only five games with Bolton, Scotchbrook felt that he was not good enough for this standard of football and retired to concentrate on coaching. He remained at Burnden Park as coach and then assistant secretary before being offered the manager's post at Stockport County in November 1924.

Although County had a number of highly talented players including Eddie Critchley, Billy Bocking, Harry Hardy, Billy Johnston and Ernie Simms, Scotchbrook was unable to find a winning formula. The 1924-25 season was, therefore, a very disappointing one for the club as they finished in 19th place, only three points above the relegation position. Scotchbrook's second season with the club was even worse, beginning with six defeats in the first seven games, and, by the time he was sacked in February, County looked doomed to finish bottom of Division Two. This they duly did, by a margin of seven points, failing to win any of their away games.

However, his record at Edgeley Park did not deter Wolves from appointing him manager in March 1926. In his one full season in charge at Wolves, Scotchbrook took the club from the previous season's fourth place to a disappointing 15th in Division Two. He did have a good FA Cup run during this season, Wolves reaching the sixth round before being beaten 2-1 by eventual Finalists, Arsenal. Scotchbrook laid the blame for Wolves bad season upon the club's directors and left after criticising club policy at their annual meeting in 1927.

Lincoln Hyde
(June 1926-April 1931)

HYDE'S appointment as manager came some 12 years after his debut for County as a centre-forward, a debut that provided the newspapers with the dream headline, 'Lincoln beats Lincoln at Lincoln', Hyde scoring the first goal in a 3-1 win at Sincil Bank in December 1913. Hyde made 13 League appearances for County before the outbreak of war and played in nine wartime fixtures, his only goal being the one scored on his debut.

Although none of Lincoln Hyde's five years at Edgeley resulted in promotion, he succeeded in producing immensely attractive high-scoring County teams. As other managers before (and after) him had found, whenever talented players were developed, they needed to be sold to 'balance the books'. However, unlike some of his predecessors and successors, he continually managed to replace these players. It was Hyde who developed the skilful Billy Johnston before he departed to Old Trafford; it was Hyde who brought Bolton's captain, the famous Joe Smith, to Edgeley; and it was Hyde who introduced the prolific goalscoring talents of Harry Burgess (later to become an England international) and Frank Newton, both of whom continued to score goals in higher grade football.

On the basis of the teams Hyde put together, he was desperately unlucky not to see County promoted as they finished runners-up in successive seasons in 1928-29 and 1929-30 and sixth, third and seventh in his three other full seasons. In April 1931, he accepted the offer of the manager's job at Preston but Hyde did not see out the season as North End failed to challenge for promotion and he believed that he had too little control of the buying and selling of players. After leaving football, Lincoln Hyde ran a successful business in Belfast.

April 1931-July 1932
No manager

Andrew Wilson
(July 1932-May 1933)

BORN in Irvine, Ayrshire on 10 December 1880, Andrew Wilson was a prolific goalscorer during an illustrious playing career. At the age of 17, Wilson was a big powerful forward weighing over 13 stone. After learning his craft with Irvine Meadow, he had one season with Clyde before beginning a long and successful career with Sheffield Wednesday in 1900.

By the time he retired in 1920, Wilson had made 546 appearances, scored 216 goals for the Owls and had been leading scorer in eight of his 16 peacetime seasons. He picked up championship medals in 1902-03 and 1903-04 with Wednesday and played in the club's FA Cup victory over Everton at Crystal Palace in 1907. It was around this time that he won the first of six Scotland caps, making his debut against England in April 1907 at Newcastle.

As a manager it was always a case of what might have been. His first managerial post took him to Bristol Rovers in June 1921 but in his five seasons at Eastville he only once got the club above halfway in the Third Division South. He resigned in May 1926 when Rovers had just avoided re-election. After a year out of the game, in July 1927 he was offered a return to management by Second Division Oldham Athletic, leading them to seventh place in his first season. The nearest he got to promotion was in

1929-30, when Athletic finished third, only two points behind promoted Chelsea, but having squandered their chances by taking only two points in their last five games.

After leaving Oldham, at the age of 52, Wilson took charge of his last club, Stockport County, in time for the 1932-33 season. After finishing a disappointing 12th the previous season, Wilson led the club to within five points of the championship, finishing third behind Hull and Wrexham. Perhaps his greatest legacy in his short spell was the introduction of four of County's best forwards in the 1930s: Jabez Foulkes, Alf Lythgoe, Jimmy Stevenson and Percy Downes. County scored 99 goals that season including eight in Wilson's last match in charge, an 8-5 victory over Chester. He died on 13 March 1945.

May 1933-May 1934
No Manager

Fred Westgarth
(May 1934-September 1936)

BORN in South Shields in 1887, Fred Westgarth never played League football but enjoyed a relatively successful career in management. He first came to County from South Shields as trainer in 1926 but it was eight years before he took over as manager. Although he was not in charge of the club at the time of their historic 13-0 win against Halifax Town, Westgarth inherited most of the players who had gone so close to the championship in 1934. He brought the popular Billy Bocking back from Everton but could not stop the transfer of the record-breaking goalscorer, Alf Lythgoe. It was inevitable that County

would not be able to resist Huddersfield's £3,000+ offer but the fact that Lythgoe finished joint top-scorer with 15 goals having made only ten appearances was a critical factor in their disappointing seventh place in 1934-35.

However, Edgeley Park was not a dull place that season, Westgarth producing the best Cup-fighting team the club had ever produced. It took them seven games to do so, but County at last managed to battle their way through to the fifth round of the FA Cup, only to lose 5-0 to West Brom. As some consolation, Westgarth did see County beat Walsall 2-0 at Maine Road to win the Northern Section Cup.

Whilst the club tried to plan for rebuilding the grandstand destroyed by fire in July 1935, Westgarth tried to build a championship-winning side but a seemingly respectable fifth place at the end of the 1935-36 season was disappointing as was the £3,000 loss during that season. On 10 September 1936, Westgarth resigned and was replaced in November by Bob Kelly of Carlisle United. On 17 December, Carlisle replaced Kelly with Fred Westgarth!

Westgarth spent 15 months at Carlisle, leading them to a marginal improvement on their previous year's position, before moving on to Bradford City in March 1938. Consistently a strong side, Westgarth took City to third place in the Third Division North in the last season before the war.

It was somewhat surprising when, in 1943, Westgarth left Bradford to take on the manager's position at the less well supported Hartlepools United. After a number of seasons in the lower regions of the Third Division North, by 1954-55 Westgarth had assembled an increasingly strong team which finished fifth, followed by fourth place the following season. Sadly, as Hartlepools mounted their most serious title challenge in their history, Fred Westgarth died on 4 February 1957, the season in which the club finished as runners-up.

Bob Kelly
(November 1936-July 1938)

TWO months after Fred Westgarth's resignation, County appointed Bob Kelly as their new manager. Unlike Westgarth, Kelly had enjoyed an illustrious career in professional football. Born in Ashton-in-Makerfield on 16 November 1894, Kelly's teenage career was outside League football whilst working as a miner until his growing reputation resulted in a move to Burnley in 1913. A highly gifted inside-forward with a famous body swerve and the ability to score a high quota of goals in such a position, Kelly made almost 300 League and Cup appearances for the Turf Moor club whilst scoring 97 goals.

Although missing out on Burnley's FA Cup triumph over Liverpool in the 1914 Cup Final, he made 37 appearances and scored 20 goals in Burnley's First Division championship success in 1920-21. Kelly remained with Burnley for another four and a half seasons, years that saw Burnley's fortunes change dramatically for the worse. In December 1925, Kelly was transferred to Sunderland for £6,500, helping the Roker Park club to finish in third place in both his two seasons there. He joined Huddersfield Town for £3,500 in February 1927 and, though making up for his absence in the 1914 FA Cup Final by playing in two Finals within three years, Town were beaten on both occasions. Approaching the age of 38, Kelly moved to Preston in July 1932 where, in his second season, he helped North End to promotion to the First Division.

At the age of 40, Kelly made his final move, joining Carlisle United as player-manager in March 1935. By the time his playing career finally ended, he had chalked up over 600 League appearances and scored over 150 goals, a monumental feat when taking into account the four seasons lost to wartime football.

His move to County in 1936 coincided with the club's

success in at last winning the Third Division North championship on the final day of the season. Although the foundations of the title-winning team had been laid by Westgarth, Bob Kelly deserved considerable credit for finally succeeding in moulding a team which found the consistency previous teams had not enjoyed, albeit without the exciting flair of the earlier free-scoring sides. Unfortunately, County's return to the Second Division was short-lived and whilst the crowds flocked to Edgeley Park to see the big-name teams they had missed for over ten years, they finished in bottom place and were relegated. Kelly resigned on 31 July 1938.

Having won 14 international caps for England in his distinguished career, Kelly became involved in coaching abroad after World War Two before becoming a publican in Blackpool where he died at the age of 74 on 22 September 1969.

August 1938-March 1939
No Manager

Bobby Marshall
(March 1939-February 1949*)

BORN in Hucknall, Nottinghamshire, on 3 April 1903, Robert Samuel Marshall was a skilful ball-playing inside-forward with an excellent goalscoring record for his two League clubs, Sunderland and Manchester City. After

signing for Sunderland from Hucknall Olympic in 1920, Marshall went on to score 71 goals in 205 appearances. The North East club were continually challenging for the First Division championship during his stay, finishing runners-up once in 1922-23 and third on three more occasions.

After his move to Manchester City in March 1928 things got even better. By May, Marshall's signing had helped the Blues to the Second Division championship. Five years later, Marshall was part of the side beaten 3-0 by Everton in the FA Cup Final, but was there again a year later when City beat Portsmouth 2-1. In 1937, having been successfully converted to centre-half, Marshall at last won a League championship medal in City's first-ever League title success. During his stay at Maine Road, he had made 355 appearances and scored 80 goals.

After finishing his playing career, Marshall was immediately appointed Stockport's manager on 22 March 1939, but within six months of arriving at Edgeley Park, war broke out and the Football League was suspended. Less than two weeks after the outbreak of war, he left for Reading to join the army's physical training staff.

He returned to Stockport in 1945 and, on the resumption of League football in 1946-47, guided County to fourth place in the Third Division North, introducing the future England international Ron Staniforth to a generally experienced side. The following season saw the post-war attendance explosion reflected at Edgeley Park but an average home attendance of over 11,000 watched Marshall's County complete their worst season in the Northern Section when finishing in 17th place. This could have been even worse had Marshall not signed Alex Herd with whom he had played in two Cup Finals whilst at Maine Road. Herd's inspiration provided County with seven wins in the final 12 games of the season.

Following improving results in 1948-49, in February 1949, Marshall left to manage Second Division Chesterfield, helping them to finish sixth. Two years later, Chesterfield were relegated and at the end of 1951-52, having finished 13th in the Third Division North, Marshall left Chesterfield and football management for good.

*Note: As Bobby Marshall was absent from Stockport for a considerable part of the war, management responsibilities were very much on an *ad hoc* basis. Although the precise period of his managerial control is unknown, Harry Catterick (senior) was unquestionably in charge at various times between 1941 and 1945. Born in the North-East in 1899, Catterick had played for and trained Chilton Colliery, guiding them to the third round of the FA Cup in 1925-26 for the only time in their history. A number of League clubs had tried to persuade him to turn professional, without success, and he only came to Edgeley Park before the start of the 1926-27 season when lured by County's offer of combining playing with a job as assistant-trainer. He made 14 League and Cup appearances as a centre-half, scoring one goal.

Andy Beattie
(March 1949-April 1952)

BORN in Kintore, Aberdeenshire, on 11 August 1913, Beattie played locally for Inverurie Loco before signing for Preston in March 1935 for a £150 fee. A solid- tackling defender, he appeared in successive FA Cup Finals, gaining a runners-up medal in 1937 when Preston lost 3-1 to Sunderland, and a winners' medal the following year in North End's 1-0 extra-time victory over Huddersfield Town, a club with which he was later to have success as a manager.

In 1937 he gained the first of seven Scotland caps, playing full-back against England. Like many players of this era, Beattie's appearances were affected by the war and, although he spent all his professional playing career at Deepdale, he made only 125 League appearances.

Although a one-club player, Andy Beattie's move into management began a 20-year career that encompassed no fewer than nine clubs. In 1947, his playing days over, Beattie became secretary-manager of Barrow in the Third Division North. A disagreement between the manager and the club's chairman in 1948 led to Beattie resigning. His res-
ignation was not accepted and, although it was Barrow's chairman who departed, before the end of the season Beattie left to manage Stockport County. In his first full season, County finished in tenth place but equalled their best FA Cup run, losing in the fifth round to an embarrassingly fortunate Liverpool team in front of Edgeley Park's highest ever gate.

In 1950-51, County finished in the same position but the following season climbed to third place. Beattie's departure to Huddersfield Town in the middle of April 1952, at a reported salary of £1,500 per annum came during a disastrous end of season run-in, County winning only one of their last eight games.

Beattie could not stop Huddersfield's relegation to Division Two but, in his first full season, he guided them back into Division One. The following season, Town finished third in Division One, only six points behind champions, Wolves. By 1956, however, they were relegated and, in November, Beattie's deferred resignation was accepted.

Before this, Beattie had taken control of the Scottish national side during the 1954 World Cup, but resigned claiming lack of support. Following this, he was surprisingly given a second chance in 1959, but was sacked in 1960 after watching a League match in preference to watching Scotland.

After leaving Huddersfield, Beattie took charge of Carlisle United for 18 months, Nottingham Forest for three years and then held two caretaker manager positions at Plymouth Argyle and Wolves. In December 1965 he joined Notts County as professional advisor and general manager before resigning to become assistant manager at Sheffield United in 1967. He later scouted for Brentford, Wolves, Walsall, Liverpool and Notts County before his death at Rushcliffe on 20 September 1983.

Dick Duckworth
(October 1952-May 1956)

RICHARD Duckworth was born in Bacup, Lancashire, on 6 June 1906 and played most of his professional football in the Third Division North. Although starting his career as a full-back, he developed into a defensive half-back spending periods at Carlisle United, Rochdale and Oldham Athletic before making his League debut in 1929 for Chesterfield where he won a Third Division North championship medal. After spells at Southport, Chester and Rotherham United, Duckworth moved to York City in 1936. This was to be his last club and his best playing days were spent there. As a key defender, he captained York in their superb FA Cup run of 1937-38 which saw City reach the sixth round before being beaten, after a replay, by Huddersfield Town the eventual losing Finalists.

In 1939 he became player-manager of Newark Town before taking up a coaching position at Chesterfield after the war. In March 1950 he returned, now as manager, to York City who were at the foot of the Third Division North. By the time he left York to join County on 23 October 1952, he had successfully transformed City, leaving them in a healthy fourth place.

Dick Duckworth's term as County manager was helped by the presence of centre-forward, Jack Connor, who was at Edgeley Park throughout the Duckworth period. If nothing else, he was able to rely on 30 goals a season from the popular Connor. Frank Clempson was transferred from

Manchester United to provide midfield support to what was a fairly settled side. Duckworth managed to achieve a remarkably consistent marginal improvement in Stockport's League position during his four-year stay, County finishing eleventh, tenth, ninth and then seventh in 1955-56, their highest position since the first post-war season. In this, his final season at Edgeley Park, Duckworth succeeded in persuading the former Bolton Wanderers star, Willie Moir, to join County.

In May 1956, Dick Duckworth left Edgeley Park to become chief scout at Sheffield United before returning to management in October 1957, taking over at Darlington. His three years at Feethams were largely unsuccessful, Darlington finishing in the bottom half of the Third Division North or Fourth Division at the end of each season. However, in his first season, Duckworth inspired the Quakers to their best-ever FA Cup run. Although they were beaten 6-1 by Wolves in the fifth round, they achieved a wonderful result in the previous round, holding First Division Chelsea to a 3-3 draw at Stamford Bridge before winning the replay 4-1.

From Darlington, Duckworth moved to Second Division Scunthorpe United in May 1960. United performed well in his first three seasons, finishing ninth, fourth and ninth again but, in 1963-64, following a tight battle at the foot of the Second Division, Scunthorpe were relegated. In November 1964, with Scunthorpe struggling in the lower regions of the Third Division, Dick Duckworth left the Old Show Ground, finally retiring from the game after 40 years as player and manager. He died in Sheffield on 9 April 1983.

Willie Moir
(June 1956-July 1960;
Player-manager June 1956 to May 1958)

BORN in Bucksburn, Aberdeenshire, on 19 April 1922, Willie Moir was a product of Scottish junior football. He signed amateur forms for Bolton Wanderers in 1943 when he was stationed in Lancashire with the RAF during World War Two. He made his first team debut for Wanderers in attack in 1946, and although small in stature, established himself over the next ten years as an excellent ball player and marksman in the First Division. As an inside-right, he formed a formidable partnership with Nat Lofthouse, scoring 134 goals in 358 games for the Burnden Park club.

He gained his sole Scottish cap against England in 1950

and, as club captain, led the team out at Wembley in the legendary 1953 'Matthews Final'. The fact that Moir scored one of Bolton's goals was of little consolation as his depleted side lost 4-3 to Blackpool.

Two years later, in September 1955, Moir joined Stockport for £2,500, playing alongside the prolific Jack Connor in a County side which scored 90 and 91 goals respectively over the next two seasons. His reputation as a leader saw him elevated to the manager's seat for the start of the 1956-57 season whilst continuing to play until February 1958.

In his first season in charge, County finished in fifth place and then ninth in 1957-58. Although Moir's third season saw County 'qualify' for the newly formed Third Division, this was followed by relegation to Division Four. Moir's failure to gain immediate promotion in 1959-60 led to his being sacked on 20 July 1960 and signalled the end of his managerial career.

Willie Moir died on 9 May 1988 aged 66, but as a player will always be remembered fondly by supporters of both Bolton and Stockport.

Reg Flewin
(1960-1963)

BORN in Portsmouth on 28 November 1920, Reg Flewin spent virtually all of his life on the South Coast, other than the period as manager of Stockport County. Almost 6ft tall and weighing over 13st, Flewin was a solid and dependable centre-half for his one and only club, Portsmouth. After representing Pompey schoolboys as captain at the age of 14, he signed amateur forms for the Fratton Park club at 15, playing for Ryde Sports, a nursery club used by Pompey to blood young players. Having signed as a full-time professional at 17, Flewin made his debut in April 1938 at Grimsby Town, where he had to mark the Mariners' Welsh international, Pat Glover.

At the age of 20 he joined the Marines and, being based in Plymouth and then Portsmouth, was able to turn out for Pompey on and off during the war. Although the war limited him to 167 appearances, he led Portsmouth as captain to two League championships in successive seasons, in 1948-49 and 1949-50. His first team playing career was cut short by a serious injury in 1951 after which he spent some seven years as a coach and then assistant manager to Eddie Lever. Following Lever's departure in 1958, Flewin didn't see eye-to-eye with the new management and applied for the advertised position at Edgeley Park, which he was immediately offered.

He took charge on 30 September 1960 and, although in his first season County reached the FA Cup fourth round before losing to Newcastle United at St James' Park, the club finished a disappointing 13th. He added Graham Beighton, Derek Ward and Charlie McDonnell for the next season, but the club never really recovered from a bad start. Had it not been for an exchange deal that brought George Whitelaw from Carlisle United which helped County to seven wins in eight games late in the season, they would have finished even lower than 16th.

During 1962-63, Flewin bought the experienced Ron Wylie for £4,000 from Preston but County fared even worse than in the previous season, ending in 19th place. Amid disaffection at Edgeley Park, Flewin left County and returned to the South Coast in July 1963 as manager of Bournemouth. Although his tenure at Stockport had been singularly unsuccessful, he describes his time at Edgeley Park as 'thoroughly enjoyable', loving the northern hospitality and the set-up at Stockport. He remained at Bournemouth for three seasons – his first being his most successful when the club came near to promotion to Division Two – before being forced to resign due to severe eye problems. As a result, he was unable to drive long distances to carry out any scouting missions, and so Reg Flewin left football completely, entering into a partnership in a holiday camp venture. After a take-over of the business, he remained as general manager until his retirement in 1990 to the Isle of Wight where he still lives.

Trevor Porteous
(September 1963-October 1965;
Player-manager September 1963 to May 1965†)

DESPITE being sacked by Stockport County three times, leaving of his own accord more than once and having major heart surgery, Trevor Porteous is well on the way to a 40-year association with Edgeley Park. Born in Hull on 9 October 1933, as a schoolboy he was a promising inside-forward. By the time he was 14, he had played for Hull City Boys and, at 15, for Yorkshire Boys, where he played alongside Ron Flowers, later of Wolves, and Graham Shaw, later of Sheffield United, both of whom became full England internationals.

After leaving school, Porteous sought work at Hull docks while signing for Hull City as an amateur. On his 17th birthday, Hull City's manager, Raich Carter, the former Sunderland and England inside-forward, signed him on professional terms, having now successfully turned him into a wing-half. In five and a half years at Hull, he played 61 times, but lost almost two years during 1952-1954 when he was called up for National Service with the Army, serving with the 17/21st Lancers at Catterick. With a playing squad of 40, breaking into the Hull City side restricted his appearances, and in the summer of 1956 he signed for Stockport County for a fee of £1,500.

Over the next nine seasons, Trevor Porteous, a whole-hearted defender, became only the fourth player in County's history to play over 300 League games, ultimately ending his career having made 364 appearances and scoring nine goals. At the end of his seventh season, when Reg Flewin left for Bournemouth, Porteous's holiday in his native Hull was interrupted and he was asked to take over as caretaker-manager before officially becoming player-manager in September 1963.

Amid financial and boardroom crises and with little back-room staff or money, he helped County to improve upon their previous season's League position, albeit marginally. The following season, 1964-65, ended with County finishing at the bottom of Division Four, forced to apply for re-election for the first time in over 50 years. However, the same season saw Porteous leading County

out at Anfield in the fourth round of the FA Cup. Aided by his signing of the inspirational 34-year-old Len White two weeks earlier, County drew 1-1 before 24,000 saw Liverpool win the replay 2-0 at Edgeley Park.

Notwithstanding their disastrous League placing, when Trevor Porteous retired from playing to concentrate on a drive for new players, there was a real mood of optimism at Edgeley Park. In October 1965, having guided County to their highest ever away win at Valley Parade, Porteous became the first County player to secure a testimonial of £1,000 plus when an attendance of over 5,000 saw First Division Stoke City win 6-3 at Edgeley. However, before the end of the month, following a disagreement with the chairman, Vic Bernard, Porteous was sacked. He became assistant manager to Ernie Tagg at Crewe Alexandra but, after only one season at Gresty Road, he was invited back to County to take up a similar position in support of County's new manager, Jimmy Meadows. After two encouraging seasons in Division Three, Porteous was sacked again, this time following a 4-1 home defeat by Fulham. A few months of unemployment followed, until his services were required again when he was asked to run 'The County Club'. This he did successfully for three years before leaving football completely to enter a number of business ventures.

In 1975, he was asked back to Edgeley Park, this time as physiotherapist. Six managers and seven years later, Trevor Porteous took up the post of deputy officer at the Elderly Patients' Home for Stockport Social Services. During this time, he still returned to help manager Eric Webster two days a week, willing to do anything for the benefit of Stockport County. Another five years on, he was asked back yet again to become the club's youth development officer under Asa Hartford. It took major heart by-pass surgery in 1990 to sever finally his official ties with the club that he had served so well in many different positions over 35 years.

Now 60, and still living in Stockport, a remarkably young-looking and cheerful Trevor Porteous remains a regular and popular face at all County games, whether they involve first, reserve or youth teams.

†Note: During the managerial periods of both Trevor Porteous and Eddie Quigley, **Bert Trautmann** had certain management positions at Edgeley Park, variously termed 'administrative' and 'general'. It is difficult to assess the degree of influence which Trautmann exerted in team matters but there is little doubt that he had some authority.

Bert Trautmann remains one of the best known post-war players. Born in Bremen on 22 October 1923, he was a German prisoner-of-war who succeeded in overcoming what was perhaps a natural hostility in post-war England. Tall and athletic, he began his career with St Helens Town in March 1948 before moving to Manchester City in November 1949. He developed into one of the most commanding goalkeepers in the country and enjoyed immense popularity in his 14 years at Maine Road. He made 545 appearances for the Blues and played for the Football League in 1960. He will probably be best remembered for his heroic performance in City's 1956 FA Cup Final win against Birmingham City, when he played with a broken neck for the last 15 minutes of the match.

His period at Edgeley Park coincided with the arrival of the flamboyant Vic Bernard who tried, with some success, to turn 'Friday Night' into 'County Night', but Trautmann left before Stockport won promotion in 1967. Subsequently, he helped coach all over the world and remains a popular figure, still seen at Maine Road.

Eddie Quigley
(October 1965-October 1966 & May 1976-April 1977)
BORN in Bury on 13 July 1921, Eddie Quigley joined his home town club as a full-back in 1941, but through necessity was converted to an attacker. Although on his debut as a centre-forward he scored five goals, his best position turned out to be inside-forward, where he was able to control the attack, lying deep and having the ability to split defences with inch perfect long passes. In October 1947 he joined Sheffield Wednesday for £12,000 and he scored 50 goals in 76 League appearances at Hillsborough. In December 1949, Preston North End paid a British record transfer fee of £26,500 for him. Quigley found goalscoring at North End more difficult, but while at Preston he won a Second Division championship medal and represented England 'B' twice against Holland and Italy.

A two-year spell at Deepdale ended when a struggling Blackburn Rovers paid £20,000 for his services. In his five years at Ewood Park, he netted a remarkable 92 goals in only 159 appearances, but with the club failing repeatedly to win promotion, the presence of ageing players was used as a possible cause. As Quigley was 35, it was a surprise when he was placed on the transfer list at £2,500. After the Football League reduced the fee to £1,000, he re-signed for Bury in August 1956 where he only made ten League appearances before retiring at the end of the 1956-57 season with a Football League career record of 180 goals from 337 appearances.

He moved into non-League football with Mossley, where he spent two seasons as player-manager and four seasons as manager. In 1962, Quigley returned to Bury yet again, as youth team coach, demonstrating his talents by unearthing, amongst others, Colin Bell and Alec Lindsay. Although Bert Trautmann had been appointed Stockport's 'administrative manager' from October 1964 and continued to be 'general manager' until 1966, in October 1965, following the departure of Trevor Porteous, Quigley was offered his chance to manage a League club.

Over a 12-month period at Edgeley Park, Quigley put together a side that would end up Fourth Division champions, success being based upon his signings of the vastly experienced central defenders Matt Woods and Eddie Stuart. In October 1966, he was offered the assistant manager's job at Blackburn, and when Rovers manager, Jack Marshall, left in February 1967 Quigley took over. Other than in that season, Rovers hardly threatened to make a serious promotion challenge and, in October 1970, with the Ewood club heading for relegation to the Third Division for the first time in their illustrious history, Quigley moved sideways to become general/administrative manager, but was sacked a little over six months later.

In May 1976, he returned to Edgeley Park and, for a short time, it looked as if he could repeat his success of ten years earlier. County won five of their first six matches and were in third position at Christmas before an appalling string of results saw them slump to a miserable 14th place and before the season had finished he was sacked. In 1979

he went back to Blackburn Rovers as chief scout but following Bobby Saxton's appointment as manager in May 1981, Eddie Quigley was again dismissed before moving to Blackpool in a similar capacity.

Jimmy Meadows
(October 1966-March 1969 & May 1974-August 1975)
BORN in Bolton on 21 July 1931, Jimmy Meadows began his career with Southport, making 60 appearances and scoring six goals. Although as a player he is best remembered as a full-back, it was for an outside-right that

Manchester City paid Southport £11,000 in March 1951. His signing began an association of almost 15 years with the Maine Road club, the majority of his 141 League and Cup appearances being at outside-right, or occasionally centre-forward. It was only in what turned out to be his last season that he emerged as a full-back, winning an international cap in 1955.

During his one Cup Final appearance for City against Newcastle United in 1955, the infamous Wembley jinx struck again, Meadows rupturing knee ligaments. His career as a player was cruelly ended at the age of 24 and he did not share City's success the following season when his long-time friend and playing colleague, Bert Trautmann, helped the Blues to an FA Cup Final win against Birmingham City. Whilst Trautmann continued to play until 1964, Meadows remained on the training staff at Maine Road for much of this period. After Trautmann became administrative/general manager at Stockport in October 1964, it was not surprising that, when long-serving trainer Billy Newton left Edgeley in December 1965, Trautmann turned to his former Maine Road colleague to replace him.

When Eddie Quigley left for Blackburn Rovers, Jimmy Meadows was promoted to manager and guided County through their best spell for 30 years, his first season seeing County as champions of Division Four. Two seasons in Division Three followed, the second of which saw County for some time looking good promotion prospects. This was achieved by a man known for his shrewd man management skills with a small squad but, whilst having little money to spend in the transfer market, he successfully signed the twin strikers Bill Atkins and Jim Fryatt who were fed by two excellent wingers, Len Allchurch and Johnny Price. However, as County slid away from the promotion positions in 1969, on 30 March Meadows was sacked with the then chairman Victor Bernard stating that 'this club is aiming for the Second Division. It is now certain this will not be achieved and so a new face and approach are required. Jimmy has left Stockport County on good terms.'(!) And the outcome? Within a year, County had finished bottom with a meagre 23 points and were back in Division Four.

After leaving Edgeley Park, Meadows had spells as assistant manager at Bury and Blackpool, and manager's jobs at both Bolton and Southport, before returning to County in May 1974 following a season in which they had finished bottom of Division Four. With a struggling team and few players of any quality, Meadows' return saw County lose more games than the previous season but escaping the re-election zone on the last day of the season. Having been back at Edgeley Park for only 15 months, Meadows was sacked in August 1975.

The misfortune which had dogged Jimmy Meadows' playing and managerial career was summed up by his last post as caretaker-manager of Blackpool between February and May 1978 following the surprising dismissal of Allan Brown. With five games of the season remaining, Blackpool were in ninth place. Four defeats and one draw in a fortnight, together with a combination of freak results involving other clubs, saw the Seasiders crash to 20th and relegation to the Third Division for the first time.

Although he retained football connections in the area, sadly on 1 January 1994 Jimmy Meadows died in Manchester at the age of 62 .

Walter Galbraith
(March 1969-April 1970)

WALTER McMurray Galbraith was born in Glasgow on 26 May 1918 and, although best known as a manager, was a stylish left back in the lower divisions. He made over 200 appearances, all whilst over 30, for three English clubs. In 1939 he joined his first club, Clyde, before moving to New Brighton on 15 September 1948. After two seasons as a player, Galbraith became player-manager of the Rakers but this first venture ended disastrously, the club finishing bottom of Division Three North, failing to gain re-election and being replaced in the Football League by Workington.

He was signed as a player by Grimsby Town and in the first of his two seasons helped the Mariners to run-ners-up in Division Three North. After making 82 League and Cup appear-ances, in June 1953 Accrington Stanley offered him another chance as a player-manager. He retired from playing at the end of his first season at Peel Park but remained as manager for another four seasons and was instrumental in providing Accrington with their best-ever spell in the Football League. In those four seasons, Stanley were twice runners-up and twice in third place. Such was the unexpected nature of this success that in the first of these seasons, 1954-55, Accrington attracted a staggering average home attendance of almost 10,000.

Galbraith's reputation for recruiting players from his native Scotland earned him the totally appropriate nickname of 'Mr McStanley'. Within 12 months of taking over at Peel Park, of the squad he had inherited, only two of the 23 players used remained. Of the 21 new players, an extraordinary 17 were Scottish, 12 of whom were recruited directly from the smaller Scottish clubs.

His success led him to reject the opportunity of becoming manager of Kilmarnock in 1957 but his confidence in Stanley was misplaced. Accrington's runners-up position in 1958 was not enough to dissuade the directors from making economies and led a hugely disappointed Galbraith to resign in August. By November he had become manager of Bradford who had just been 'relegated' to the restructured Fourth Division. He remained at Park Avenue until January 1961 when, with the club set for promotion, he moved to take over at lowly Tranmere but was unable to prevent Rovers' relegation at the end of the 1961-62 season.

In December 1961, for the first and only time, Galbraith moved back to Scotland to take over the manager's job at Hibernian. In his three years at Easter Road, he made the club almost £300,000 from players he had discovered, groomed and then sold on for substantial fees. In 1965, he returned as general manager to Bradford who were now back in Division Four. He remained at Park Avenue until May 1967 before joining Stockport County, his final club, as chief scout in July 1968.

After being coach of the successful side managed by Jimmy Meadows, he eventually replaced Meadows as manager at the end of March 1969. In his one and only season at Edgeley Park, Galbraith was unable to repeat his earlier success at Accrington and the season was an unmitigated disaster. A woeful County team looked like relegation candidates from the start and, predictably, they finished in bottom place, winning only six games. Galbraith was given no opportunity to rebuild the side for their return to Division Four, being sacked in April 1970 whereupon he retired from football after 30 years as a player and manager.

Matt Woods
(April 1970-December 1971)

BORN in Skelmersdale on 1 November 1931, Matt Woods played centre-forward for Skelmersdale Council School until he left at 14 to work in a shoe factory. He continued to play football in the local Sunday School league for Upholland West End and it was whilst there that he received a letter from the Everton manager, Theo Kelly asking him to go to Goodison for a trial. Now a wing-half, Woods signed apprenticeship forms at 15 and professional forms in 1949 at 18. Actually christened Maurice, it was whilst at Everton that he was forced to change his name. Another Maurice, who was also playing wing-half, was causing confusion for the Everton coaching staff, and to resolve the problem a coin was tossed, Matt lost, and subsequently adopted his new name, which remained with him.

Like others of his generation, shortly after signing professional terms, his career was interrupted by National Service. With few first-team opportunities, Woods was signed by Blackburn Rovers for £8,000 after only eight appearances and one goal. Now a centre-half and flanked by Ronnie Clayton and Mick McGrath, there followed the most successful spell of his playing career, Woods making 307 appearances for the Ewood Park club in seven seasons. He helped Rovers to promotion from Division Two and received a runners-up medal in Blackburn's 3-0 defeat by Wolves in the 1960 FA Cup Final. During this time he also represented the Football League against the League of Ireland.

In 1963, after being allowed to leave Blackburn on a

free transfer out of respect for his long service to the club, Matt Woods left for a two-year spell in Australia with Hakoah. Although supposedly returning to England only temporarily in the summer of 1965, he participated in pre-season training with his former club, Blackburn, until George Martin beat a host of interested clubs to sign Woods for Luton Town. In December of that season Luton travelled to play Stockport in a League match. Following the game which County won 4-1, Woods had a drink with Eddie Quigley, whom he had known at Blackburn, and Bert Trautmann – whom he used to watch playing for St Helens Town when at Skelmersdale. The two County men sold the club to Woods, suggesting that he was the player they needed to base an assault on the Fourth Division championship the following season. Woods was convinced and at the end of that season, joined County in July 1966 as captain.

Nine months later, County were champions, Woods having played in every game, forming a formidable partnership with Eddie Stuart. He played 39 games the following season before a serious knee injury finished his playing career at the age of 37. He did sign for Drumcondra in the Irish League, flying over at weekends for the games, but his knee got no better and Woods went into management with Altrincham. Within six months, he was sacked, but returned to Edgeley Park as coach to Walter Galbraith. Another six months later and Woods found himself as manager of Stockport.

By now the club had been relegated back to Division Four and in his first season, County's inability to find a reliable goalscorer, other than midfielder Sammy McMillan, ended with a respectable if disappointing 11th place. By December of his second season, County had won only five League games and having lost to Blyth Spartans in the FA Cup (their second defeat in successive seasons to non-League clubs), he was sacked. His main achievement had been to blood a 17-year-old local player, Paul Hart, Woods helping Hart to become one of the most consistent centre-halves in the First Division with both Leeds United and Nottingham Forest.

Following his departure from Edgeley Park, Matt Woods left football, spending the next 20 years running his own haulage company and remaining behind the wheel into his 60s. He still lives locally in Heald Green.

Brian Doyle
(March 1972-May 1974)

JOHN Brian Doyle was born in Salford on 15 July 1930 and, whilst playing for non-League Lostock Gralam, was spotted by Stoke City for whom he signed in July 1951. In over three years at the Victoria Ground, full-back Doyle made only 17 League appearances before moving to Exeter City in April 1954. Although Exeter had a fairly wretched time during his three-year spell, from a playing point of view, it was undoubtedly Doyle's best period, making 104 appearances for the Grecians.

In August 1957, he moved to Second Division Bristol Rovers and made 43 League appearances in another three-year spell before injury ended his playing career. After spending time coaching for Carlisle United, he was appointed manager of Workington in July 1968. Although Workington improved from 23rd to 12th place during Doyle's tenure, he left at the end of the 1968-69 season. Following another coaching spell at Blackpool in 1971, he

was appointed manager of County in March 1972, three months after the departure of Matt Woods. He could do little to save County from finishing next to bottom and re-election but the next season he led them to a much improved 13th place.

1972-73 saw Doyle's County make their best impression in the Football League Cup, reaching the fourth round after two wonderful wins against First Division teams, away at Crystal Palace and at home to West Ham United. Although finally bowing out to Norwich City, this period was the highlight of Doyle's managerial career, as it was followed by another disastrous season in 1973-74, County finishing bottom whilst winning only seven games. As County applied for re-election for the second time in three years, Doyle was sacked in May 1974.

Brian Doyle then disappeared from the League scene and died at the age of 62 on 22 December 1992.

(May 1974-August 1975
Jimmy Meadows – see above)

Roy Chapman
(September 1975-May 1976)

BORN in Birmingham on 18 March 1934, Roy Clifford Chapman played locally for Kynoch, before signing amateur forms for Aston Villa in November 1951 and becoming a professional in February 1952. With first team opportunities restricted, over the next five seasons he made only 19 appearances and scored seven goals before moving to Lincoln City in November 1957 for the first of two spells with the Imps. Chapman scored 45 goals from 105 games, an excellent strike rate, but one that he would better during the remainder of his playing career. In 1959, during his first spell at Lincoln, his son Lee was born, who in the 1980s and 1990s, was to follow in his father's goalscoring footsteps, albeit at a higher level, with Stoke City, Arsenal, Sheffield Wednesday, Nottingham Forest,

Leeds United, Southampton and West Ham United, although never quite reaching his father's strike rate of a goal every other match.

In August 1961, Mansfield Town's manager Raich Carter paid £7,000 to bring Chapman to Field Mill. There he formed a formidable striking partnership with Ken Wagstaff, the pair scoring 184 League and Cup goals in four seasons. In his second season, Mansfield were promoted to Division Three and in the season he left, Town missed promotion to Division Two on goal-average. During that season, Chapman returned to Lincoln City in January 1965 to take over as player-manager from the long-serving Bill Anderson. His consistent goalscoring continued there – 31 goals from 69 League appearances – and during his stay at Port Vale from 1967 to 1969 where he scored 38 times in 77 appearances. He played briefly for Chester at the beginning of the 1969-70 season before taking over the manager's job at non-League Stafford Rangers in October 1969.

Chapman enjoyed six successful seasons at Stafford, winning the FA Trophy and reaching the fourth round of the FA Cup for the first time, having knocked out County in a replay. These achievements inevitably brought attention to his managerial ability and when Stockport were seeking a replacement for Jimmy Meadows, County director Freddie Pye persuaded Chapman to sign a three-year contract at Edgeley Park on 2 September 1975.

The former goalscoring inside-forward believed, as he had at Stafford, that the game should be played going forward, home or away. In a vain attempt to find some success, Chapman used 32 players, many of them on loan, but he will be remembered for bringing one particular player to the club; George Best, seeking a comeback, turned out for County on three occasions, a major coup by all connected with the club, including Chapman himself. Unfortunately, on the tight budget he had to contend with, he was unable to find anybody with anything like his own ability to score goals and County failed to score in 20 of their 46 League matches. Five successive defeats at the end of the season dropped County to 21st place and the need to apply for re-election for the third time in five years. In the circumstances, it was not surprising that at the season's end, the man who had achieved so much as player and non-League manager was sacked.

Justifiably disillusioned with life at the bottom of the Football League, Roy Chapman returned to non-League management with Stafford before his unfortunate death in March 1983 when he suffered a heart attack whilst playing five-a-side football. He was only 49 years old.

(May 1976-April 1977
Eddie Quigley see above)

Alan Thompson
(Player-manager April 1977-March 1978)
ALAN William Thompson was born in Liverpool on 20 January 1952, becoming an apprentice at Sheffield Wednesday at the age of 15 and turning professional when he was 17. In six seasons, he made almost 170 appearances for the Owls before Eddie Quigley brought him to County in August 1976. A strong and classy central defender, Thompson's move to Edgeley Park started encouragingly with the team playing attractive attacking football but by Christmas, hopes of promotion were fading as County slid down the table.

When Quigley was sacked in April 1977, it came as a

huge surprise to find Thompson appointed player-manager at the age of 25, making him by far County's youngest manager. During the close season, he brought in the widely experienced Mike Summerbee from Blackpool and, supported by the developing talents of Terry Park and Steve Massey, and despite a poor start, County enjoyed their best spell for many years. From mid-September, they lost only five of 25 games, climbing from 20th to fourth place by the end of February 1978. Although three successive defeats brought County down to sixth position, it was a surprise equalling that of his appointment 12 months earlier when Thompson lost his managerial position in March, replaced as player-manager by Mike Summerbee, his own signing. In the event, Thompson's dismissal achieved no benefit, County's last 11 games yielding only five points, leaving them in a frustratingly disappointing 18th place.

Thompson continued at Edgeley Park as a player for another year, scoring 18 goals in his total of 108 appearances before trying his luck in the United States in April 1979. On his return to the England, he joined Bradford City, making over 30 appearances before finally ending his career with 11 appearances for Scunthorpe United in 1982.

After leaving football for good, Alan Thompson moved into insurance in Sheffield.

Mike Summerbee
(Player-manager March 1978-October 1979)
BORN in Cheltenham on 15 December 1942, Michael George Summerbee was a conventional outside-right during his schoolboy days before signing apprentice forms with Swindon Town in August 1959. Before the end of his first season, he had turned professional and went on to make over 200 appearances for Town during his six-year stay, helping them to their first-ever promotion to Division Two in 1963.

In August 1965, Summerbee became Joe Mercer's first signing for Manchester City at a fee of £30,000. He became more than a traditional winger, constantly roving and displaying a (generally) controlled aggression. During the late 1960s, he became an indispensable member of the

City trio of himself, Francis Lee and Colin Bell who could at last rival (and beat) the internationally acclaimed Old Trafford trio of Law, Best and Charlton. In ten successful years at Maine Road, Summerbee won a League championship medal in 1968, an FA Cup winners' medal in 1969 and a Football League Cup winners' medal in 1970. He added a European Cup-winners' Cup medal in 1970, despite not playing in the Final due to injury, and a championship runners-up medal in 1974. Besides representing the Football League, he won eight caps for England.

After scoring 67 goals in 441 appearances for the Blues, Burnley paid £25,000 for Summerbee in June 1975. He made 61 appearances for Burnley but in his only full season, the Clarets were relegated to Division Two. He moved to Blackpool in December 1976 but made only three appearances before joining Stockport County in August 1977. Following the dismissal of Alan Thompson a little over six months later, Mike Summerbee became player-manager in March 1978.

Although in his first full season he brought the talented Les Bradd and Stuart Lee to Edgeley Park – the striking pair netting 38 goals between them – his managerial career was unsuccessful, County finishing disappointingly in 17th place. Probably his greatest moment with County came during a 3-2 League Cup defeat by Manchester United. In front of a crowd of almost 42,000 at Old Trafford, County gave United a monumental scare, leading 2-1 until the dying minutes brought a controversial win for the Reds. Summerbee proudly led his team on a lap of honour around Old Trafford, this being the only high point of the season. After a poor start to the 1979-80 season and following a crushing 6-1 defeat at Bradford City, Mike Summerbee resigned as manager and did not play for County again, having made 99 full appearances and netting seven goals.

He returned briefly as a player in 1980 with Mossley, his final involvement with the game. He is currently running a shirt business and still lives in the Stockport area.

Jimmy McGuigan
(November 1979-April 1982)

GLASWEGIAN-born on 1 March 1924, Jimmy McGuigan began his career with Hamilton Academical before moving to Sunderland in June 1947. After making only three appearances in two seasons at Roker Park, he signed for Stockport in June 1949. A fine outside-right and popular player, McGuigan made 49 League and Cup appearances, scoring four goals as an ever-present in County's record-equalling FA Cup run in 1949-50. It therefore came as something of a surprise when, after only four games of the following season, he moved on to Crewe Alexandra where he was to become a firm favourite. He made over 200 League appearances in his six-year stay at Gresty Road before moving on to his final club, Rochdale, in 1956. After 70 appearances for the Dale, he returned to Crewe, first as trainer and then manager in June 1960.

Jimmy McGuigan became one of the most respected and successful managers in the lower divisions, guiding Crewe to promotion for the first time in their history in 1963 before moving to Grimsby Town in November 1964. Other than at Edgeley Park some 15 years later, his spell at Blundell Park was his least productive. As players were being sold without his being consulted, McGuigan did well to maintain Grimsby as a mid-table Third Division team before, somewhat frustrated, he resigned in July 1967.

Almost immediately, he moved back into management at Chesterfield. Within three years, he had guided the Spireites to the Fourth Division championship and then to fifth in the Third Division the following season. In May 1973, he moved on to Rotherham United and, in 1974-75, steered his third club to promotion from Division Four. Rotherham's second season in the Third Division saw them score 39 goals in 11 wins away from Millmoor only to be deprived of promotion to Division Two on goal-average. However, McGuigan was unable to maintain this momentum and, after six years in charge at Rotherham, moved to Edgeley Park in November 1979.

With his pedigree, the Edgeley Park faithful waited for McGuigan to repeat what he had achieved at his previous clubs but, despite making County's record £25,000 signing, Tony Coyle, success proved as elusive as ever. Soon after his arrival, money ceased to be available to buy new players and this may well have contributed to his losing the enthusiasm he had shown with previous clubs as, in his two seasons at Edgeley Park, County's highest final League position was 16th. With County's seemingly endless struggle continuing, Jimmy McGuigan left his last management post in April 1982. He died in Chesterfield, the town that had been his home for over 20 years, on 30 March 1988.

Eric Webster
(May 1982-May 1985)

NOT many people can have contributed more to the survival of Stockport County in every conceivable way than Eric Webster who, in his 16 years at Edgeley Park, filled almost every non-playing position at the club, some officially, others through necessity. Born in Manchester on 24 June 1931, he played as a winger for Ardwick Lads Club before signing as an amateur with Manchester City. After serving his two years National Service, he signed full-time professional forms at Maine Road in February

1952. While serving his apprenticeship at City, Eric Webster had been switched to wing-half, the position he occupied in his one and only Football League game against Cardiff City at Ninian Park, during the 1951-52 season.

Following his release from Maine Road in June 1953, he spent the rest of his playing career in non-League football with Ashton United, Hyde United, Nantlle Vale, Pwllheli and finally at Stalybridge Celtic. At these last three clubs, Webster's manager was the former Accrington Stanley player, Freddie Pye, and the link between the two continued for over three decades. After Pye was sacked by Stalybridge, Webster was promoted to his first manager's job, but he too was sacked shortly afterwards, returning to Hyde United, the club where he enjoyed his greatest success as a player. Three seasons at Hyde were inevitably followed by the sack, the same fate awaiting him 12 months later at Runcorn before he returned to another former club Ashton United where he resigned after one season.

Meanwhile, Freddie Pye had joined the board of

Stockport County and remembering Webster's commitment and genuine dedication to the game, brought him to Edgeley Park in 1974 to look after the club's youngsters. He moved up to manage the youth team before being appointed as Mike Summerbee's assistant manager in 1978. At this point in Stockport County's history, when managers were rarely lasting more than one season and the club had virtually no money for new players, it was left to the expert eye of Eric Webster to unearth young footballers from local and non-League soccer and free-transfer bargains upon whom the club relied to survive. He supported both Mike Summerbee and Jimmy McGuigan in this capacity before himself becoming manager in May 1982.

It was thanks to Webster's character and vision that he continued to develop and find players for little or no outlay who, because of County's persistent financial problems, could then be sold and bring in much needed money. Along with what was probably his most astute signing, that of Mick Quinn on a free transfer from Wigan Athletic, he brought in money by selling Mike Salmon, Mark Leonard, Dean Emerson and Oshor Williams. The inevitable consequence of having to sell such talented players was that County's struggles went on, their highest position under Webster being 16th in 1983-84. Undoubtedly, the highlight for Webster was the wonderful commitment shown over the two legs of the Milk Cup (League Cup) second round tie against Liverpool in the autumn of 1984. Over 180 minutes, Stockport did not concede a goal to one of the best teams in Europe and it was only during extra-time at Anfield that County's defence was finally breached.

After being replaced by Colin Murphy in August 1985, he continued to support the new manager and his successors, Les Chapman (another player Webster brought to Stockport), Jimmy Melia, Asa Hartford and Danny Bergara. Under Hartford, he recommended Tony Hancock, whom he had seen playing local Sunday football, resulting in a £50,000 profit for a young man who had made only 22 appearances, ten as substitute. After practically living at Edgeley Park for 16 years in his various capacities, which even included groundsman both before and after his spell as manager, he was rewarded with an excellently attended Testimonial match against Manchester City.

Eric Webster, who lives in Warrington, still enjoys watching local football and may yet spot another talented youngster with a future in League football.

Colin Murphy
(August-October 1985 & November 1986-May 1987)
EVEN though his style of management might not have appealed to everyone and his two spells as manager did not even total 12 months, of the 20 or so managers who have experienced tenure at Edgeley Park since the end of the last war, Colin Murphy's name is one that is unlikely to be forgotten.

Born in Croydon on 21 January 1944, Murphy never played in the Football League, his career embracing spells with Cork Hibernian, (then) non-League Wimbledon, Hastings United and Crystal Palace Reserves where injury finished an undistinguished playing career.

At the age of 27, he spent a year coaching at Charlton Athletic before, in November 1972, taking charge of Nottingham Forest's youth team in Dave Mackay's era.

When Mackay moved to Derby County, Colin Murphy followed as coach and, in November 1976, he took over as manager. Although Derby finished 15th in the First Division and reached the sixth round of the FA Cup, this was disappointing for a team who had won the championship only two seasons earlier and, after a dismal start to the following season, he was sacked in September 1977. Within a month he joined Notts County as assistant to Jimmy Sirrel.

When, in November 1978, Murphy took over the manager's job at Lincoln following Willie Bell's departure, the Imps were rooted at the bottom of the Third Division and there they remained until the end of the season. In their first season back in Division Four, Lincoln finished seventh but the following season, 1980-81, saw the club finish as runners-up, City losing only six games. Colin Murphy took Lincoln to fourth place in Division Three, only one point behind a promotion place and in 1982-83 it looked as if he would lead them back into Division Two for the first time in 20 years. By January 1983, they had led the table for some four months but ten defeats in their last 20 matches saw them fall to sixth place. The following two seasons ended with Lincoln finishing 14th and 19th and, in May 1985, Murphy left Sincil Bank.

August 1985 saw him take over at Stockport where, because of problems with Edgeley Park getting a safety certificate following the Bradford City fire, County did not

play until the fifth week of the season. When, in October, Colin Murphy was lured away by a financially attractive offer to coach in Saudi Arabia, Edgeley Park had only seen Murphy's team on four occasions and his famous, almost surrealistic, programme notes twice.

When, in October 1986, Jimmy Melia was sacked, Murphy, after 13 months in the Middle-East, was persuaded to return to Edgeley Park where, even by County's standards, the future looked bleak. 1986-87 saw the introduction of automatic relegation from the Fourth Division and, after 15 games, County had only six points and were not only well adrift at the bottom of the League but did not look as if they had the stomach for a fight. Although Murphy's return was accompanied by a mini-revolt by four County players, subsequent to a private meeting they agreed to pledge themselves to Stockport; three of them, ironically, followed Murphy to Lincoln the next year. Together with the inspired signings of the 19-year-old Les Robinson from Mansfield Town and the 37-year-old Ernie Moss from Chesterfield, Colin Murphy managed to instil a passion and commitment that had been lacking in the first third of the season. A run of only two defeats in 14 games saw County move off the bottom by the turn of the year and although a run of four successive defeats in March took them back to 24th place, six wins in the following nine games climaxed County's greatest escape act ever. Taking into account the demoralised situation that existed at Edgeley Park when he arrived, not helped by County's first round FA Cup defeat at Caernarfon on Murphy's return, his achievement verged on the miraculous.

Shortly after the end of that season, County's 'messiah' resigned in order to return to Lincoln City who had unluckily suffered the first automatic relegation, only occupying 24th place at the end of the last day of that season. Although virtually branded as a traitor by Stockport fans, Murphy's return to Sincil Bank was not so surprising considering his attachment to the Imps and his long successful spell there in the early 1980s. The affection which Edgeley Park had for the deerstalker-hat wearing saviour was short-lived, hardly helped by him taking five County players to Sincil Bank. Once again, Murphy did a tremendous job at Lincoln, bringing them back into the Football League as champions of the Conference, although when he brought his promoted club to Edgeley Park in December 1988, he was not accorded the most pleasant of returns.

In May 1990 he left Lincoln, spending one season as youth-team coach with Leicester City and one as assistant manager at Luton Town. In May 1992 he returned to management with Southend United in the 'new' Division One but, with the club looking firm candidates for relegation, he was sacked as manager in April 1993: although remaining at Roots Hall, it was left to Barry Fry to preserve Southend's First Division status.

It is perhaps the case that, rather than debating his time at Edgeley Park in terms of the extremes of 'hero' or 'villain', an objective conclusion might well be that had Colin Murphy not been persuaded to return in November 1986, there would be no Stockport County in existence today, certainly not as a Football League club.

Les Chapman
(Player-manager October 1985-July 1986)

BORN in Oldham on 27 September 1948, Les Chapman was a trainee accountant when, in September 1966, he signed as an amateur for Oldham Athletic after being on amateur forms at Huddersfield. He turned professional in September 1967 and, although initially starting his career as a winger, developed into a versatile whole-hearted footballer, equally at home playing as a left-sided full-back or in midfield. He was a tenacious tackler, a good passer and striker of the ball and could always be relied upon to give his all.

In between his two spells at Boundary Park where he made over 250 appearances, in September 1969 he moved to Huddersfield Town where he spent six seasons. Playing with the even more durable Frank Worthington, he made sporadic appearances in Town's Second Division championship side but, by the time he had gained a regular place, the club were plunging down from the First to the Third Division in successive seasons. After making 139 appearances for the Leeds Road club, Chapman returned to Boundary Park in December 1974 where he spent a further four and a half seasons.

When, at the end of the 1978-79 season, he was surprisingly given a free-transfer, he moved to Stockport for his first spell at the club. He quickly established himself as a popular player at Edgeley Park and there was general disappointment when, in February 1980, he was sold to Bradford City for £10,000 having made 37 appearances.

After helping Bradford to promotion from Division Four, three years and 158 appearances later, in 1983 Les Chapman left for Rochdale where he made 92 appearances. In July 1985, he returned to Edgeley Park shortly before Colin Murphy took over as manager. Within ten weeks, Murphy had left for Saudi Arabia and Chapman suddenly found himself as player-manager of County. Whether it was his management skills or simply his leadership on the field, his first five months in control saw County's best spell for 20 years. Occupying 19th place when he took over in October, Chapman's team surged up the table to lie in fifth position at the end of March 1986. However, with virtually no resources to enlarge a small permanent squad, County fell away badly, losing six of their last eight games to finish 11th. The fact that County had not finished in a higher position during the previous 17 years did not stop a decision being made to sack Chapman before the start of the following season. The decision seemed a perverse one and, considering what was to follow, was nearly catastrophic for the club.

Apart from anything else, Chapman's loss as a player was crucial, despite him approaching his 38th birthday. He moved to Preston as player/assistant manager, helping North End to promotion from Division Four in his first season and chalking up another 55 League and Cup appearances. In January 1990 he replaced John McGrath as manager at Deepdale but Preston failed to make any impression in the Third Division and, in September 1992, he was sacked. His departure had no positive effect, North End being relegated at the end of the season.

In his long career, Les Chapman played in all four divisions of the Football League, making over 780 League and Cup appearances and, in spite of his limited managerial success (thus far), he will be remembered as a true professional who applied himself to every aspect of the game. He is presently running the Manchester City Reserve team at Maine Road.

Jimmy Melia
(July-November 1986)

SOME successful players are capable of repeating their success on the pitch when taking on the role of manager; more often than not they fail to do so and, unfortunately, Jimmy Melia fell into the latter category.

Liverpool-born on 1 November 1937, at 17 he signed professional forms for the Reds having already represented Liverpool Schools. By 1961-62, Melia was an integral playmaker, renowned for his excellent passing ability in Liverpool's Second Division championship side. By this time, he was on the fringes of the England team but, as he had to compete with the likes of Johnny Haynes and George Eastham, it was not until 1963 that he won the first of his two caps against Scotland at Wembley. With Liverpool heading for the First Division championship, and having scored 78 goals in 287 appearances, Melia left to join Wolves for £55,000 in March 1964. These were bad times for the Molineux club and in November of the same year, Southampton paid a club record £30,000 for him. He won a Second Division runners-up medal with the Saints, playing 139 games in his four-year stay before, in November 1968, he became player-coach at Aldershot, who paid £10,000 for the 31-year-old. By April 1969 he had become player-manager but, after two mediocre seasons, in January 1972, with Aldershot hovering around the re-election zone, Melia was sacked.

Within a month, Jimmy Melia had joined Crewe Alexandra where he ended his playing career, having made nearly 600 League and Cup appearances. He became Alex's manager in May 1972 but the club had to apply for re-election in successive seasons and, in his third season, with Crewe languishing in 21st place, he was sacked in December 1974. Melia took over the manager's job at Southport in July 1975 but lasted only three months and it was more than seven years later, after coaching and scouting jobs in the Middle-East and the United States, that Melia returned to management with Brighton in January 1983.

Under him, Brighton embarked upon a glorious FA Cup run which took them to Wembley for the first time in their history. Had it not been for Gordon Smith's infamous last-minute miss against favourites Manchester United, Melia could well have won the trophy but, in the replayed Final, United's superior talent overwhelmed the Seagulls who were soundly beaten 4-0. In the event, the Cup run had proved a costly distraction, Brighton being relegated from Division One in the same season. In October 1983, within a few months of the Cup Final, Melia resigned, moving abroad to manage Portuguese Beleneses.

Following County's sacking of Les Chapman in July 1986, Melia returned to England to take over at Edgeley Park. Chapman's departure was accompanied by the loss of County stalwarts Tommy Sword and Andy Thorpe and with little money, Melia brought in various players on loan. Not surprisingly, he was unable to produce a team of any quality and, as demoralisation grew, his team looked increasingly incapable of maintaining their Fourth Division status, this being the first year of automatic relegation. At the end of Melia's 14 League games in charge, County's record was W1, D3, L10, F6, A29, and with the writing firmly on the wall and changes in the boardroom, it was no surprise when he was sacked after less than four months in charge.

After a period out of the game, Jimmy Melia returned to the United States in 1992, coaching in Texas.

(November 1986-May 1987
Colin Murphy see above)

Asa Hartford
(Player-manager July 1987-March 1989)
BORN in Clydebank on 24 October 1950 and named after

the American singing star of the first 'talkie', Al (Asa) Jolson, Hartford was one of the best-known, tenacious and creative midfield players of the 1970s. He began his career with West Bromwich Albion, signing professional forms in 1967, making 266 appearances and playing in the first of his three League Cup Finals against Manchester City in 1970 when Albion lost 2-1.

Hartford gained considerable media attention when, in November 1971, a proposed £170,000 move to Don Revie's Leeds United fell through because of a 'hole-in-the-heart' condition. In the event, the medical prognosis that raised question marks about his long-term footballing future proved to be unfounded. Within five months of the cancelled move to Leeds, Asa Hartford won the first of his 50 Scottish caps in a 2-0 win over Peru at Hampden Park.

In August 1974, Hartford joined Manchester City for £225,000 for the first of his two spells at Maine Road which in total accounted for 317 appearances. His City career was a highly successful one. Hartford figured in a 2-1

League Cup Final victory against Newcastle United in 1976 and played in virtually every game the following season when City finished as runners-up to, and only one point behind, First Division champions Liverpool.

In June 1979, Brian Clough paid £500,000 to bring Hartford to Nottingham Forest only to sell him on to Everton within two months for the same fee. Hartford made 98 appearances for an Everton team that was going through a transitional stage before returning to Maine Road in October 1981 for £350,000. City were themselves going through a bleak period and were relegated from the First Division in Hartford's second season. After making few appearances in 1983-84, he had a brief spell in the United States before joining Norwich City in October 1984. He played his third League Cup Final in 1985, his deflected shot giving Norwich a 1-0 win against Sunderland. Both Finalists were relegated and Hartford moved on to Bolton Wanderers as player-coach. The famous old Burnden club were struggling at the wrong end of the Third Division and, despite Hartford's 81 appearances, were relegated at the end of his second season. However, he did make one last Wembley appearance with Bolton in the 1986 Freight Rover Trophy Final although Wanderers lost 3-0 to Bristol City.

Following Colin Murphy's dramatic departure in May 1987, in July Asa Hartford took over as County's player-manager. His period at Edgeley Park was no more successful than those of his predecessors despite him making some good signings, including Brett Angell, Bob Colville, John Cooke, David Logan, Mick Matthews, Mark Payne and Rodger Wylde. In addition, he provided County supporters with the privilege of seeing the evergreen talents of 39-year-old Frank Worthington. At the other extreme, he gave local amateur Tony Hancock the opportunity to demonstrate his exciting potential.

It was perhaps surprising that County fared so badly, finishing 20th in Hartford's only full season in control and promising no real improvement by the time he was dismissed in March 1989. Although still playing at the time of his departure, his influence on the field was not as positive as it had been earlier in his career. County's disciplinary record was poor, Hartford himself not setting a good example. It is, of course, arguable, but taking into account the fact that the players he brought to the club were to form the nucleus of Danny Bergara's play-off team the following season, Hartford may have been better advised to have ceased playing and concentrate on managing.

From Edgeley Park, Asa Hartford moved to Shrewsbury Town as coach before becoming manager at Gay Meadow from January 1990 to January 1991. It was at Shrewsbury that his fine first class playing career finally ended after over 800 League, Cup and international appearances. Following a brief spell playing with non-League Boston United, he joined the coaching staff of Blackburn Rovers under the new regime of Kenny Dalglish.

Danny Bergara
(March 1989-)

DANIEL Alberto Bergara was born in July 1942 in Montevideo, Uruguay. His father, a farmer, had played amateur football but died in 1949, leaving his mother to bring up seven children whose ages ranged from six months to 12 years. However, an inheritance from an uncle eased the pressure on the family and allowed the young Danny Bergara to acquire a private education. He first played competitive football at Colepio private school before, at the age of 14, joining Racing Club and playing for the under-18s.

Bergara was a skilful ball-playing inside-left, capable of scoring more than his fair share of goals. His two elder brothers had, by this time, represented their country; Mario, the eldest, was a full Uruguayan international and played in the 1962 World Cup in Chile whilst Nacho was a youth international. At 15 Danny Bergara signed a professional contract with Racing Club, playing two games in the First Division at that age. He remained at Racing Club until he was 20, playing three times for his country's under-18 side. In 1962, both Danny Bergara and brother Nacho were approached by Real Majorca in Spain. Bergara's £5,000 transfer proved invaluable to the Spanish club, the lively Uruguayan more than repaying the investment over the next five seasons. For three of those seasons he was the club's top scorer, helping them to the Second Division title in 1965. In January 1967, Majorca received a record £25,000 from Seville where Bergara spent another five years. He won another Second Division title and was top scorer during two seasons. At the age of 29, he moved to Tenerife for £8,000 but within 12 months a torn calf muscle brought his playing career to a premature end.

Having an English wife, in 1973 he moved to England with the intention of finding work in the travel business. However, the oil crisis caused severe problems for the travel industry and, unable to get a job, Bergara decided to return to Spain. Before arrangements could be made, his wife's cousin, who was a close friend of the Luton Town manager Harry Haslam, recommended Bergara to chief scout Paddy Sowden, and within a week he was training with the Second Division club. He played for Luton

Reserves in the Football Combination but, when it became clear that his calf injury would not allow him to re-establish a playing career, Haslam offered him the job of youth team coach. Bergara's coaching skills were soon evident, his South American skills and personality resulting in his giving technical demonstrations to both managers and coaches. In 1978, he was promoted to assistant manager, but Haslam was sacked shortly afterwards and, on Ian Porterfield's appointment, Bergara was also sacked.

Although in 1980 he became the first non-Englishman to take charge of the England youth team, the next few years offered little security to Bergara. In 1981 he became involved with working on a coaching video but this venture collapsed when the company funding the project went bankrupt before its completion. By 1984, and with no job, his undoubted coaching talents led to part-time work teaching technique and skills at both Sheffield Wednesday and Manchester United. Bergara then approached Derek Dooley at Sheffield United, but it was through United's chairman, Reg Brealey, that he ended up taking charge of the Brunei national team.

Ten months later, in January 1985, he returned to take up a coaching position with Middlesbrough, then managed by Bruce Rioch. Bergara's bad luck continued as, with the club in crisis, the receivers were brought in and he left after only five months. He returned to Bramall Lane, eventually becoming assistant to manager Billy McEwan. Following McEwan's sacking, in January 1988 Bergara found himself caretaker manager of Sheffield United. After being in charge for two games, both victories, Dave Bassett was appointed as the new manager, much to the disappointment of the ambitious Uruguayan. Bassett inevitably brought in his own back-room staff, and Bergara left Bramall Lane. Shortly after Eddie Gray left Rochdale in June 1988 and, after Brealey had put in his recommendation to the Spotland board of directors, Danny Bergara took over as manager in July 1988. In his ten months at Rochdale, he made the club a £250,000 operating profit with his dealings in the transfer market.

At Edgeley Park, County had a new chairman, Brendan Elwood who had first met Bergara ten years earlier. Following the departure of Asa Hartford, the ambitious Elwood had no doubt about the manager he believed could carry Stockport County away from the lower reaches of the Fourth Division. It would be untrue to say that Bergara was an instant success. Arriving towards the end of 1988-89 and with County safe from the relegation position, he was more concerned with assessing the quality of the players he had inherited from Asa Hartford than the results. The outcome was that, in his first 12 games as manager, County failed to win once, drawing eight times. The cry of 'go back to Rochdale' was not uncommon in Bergara's first two months but, by the early part of the following season, the Edgeley Park faithful realised that the Uruguayan was beginning to mould a potentially successful team. Aided by Elwood's preparedness to make funds available, three former Rochdale players – Chris Beaumont, Malcolm Brown and David Frain – were added to a team which suddenly seemed to develop self-belief.

Bergara's one big-name signing, the highly experienced Keith Edwards, appeared to be a master stroke, but problems developed between the prolific goalscorer and the manager which, unfortunately for County, came at a critical stage of the season. Nonetheless, County reached the Play-offs, and almost promotion, in front of an ecstatic travelling band of supporters at Halifax. Although County were beaten comprehensively by Chesterfield in the semi-final Play-off, Bergara's bandwagon was on the move. 1990-91 saw County promoted from Division Four as runners-up; 1991-92 resulted in a superb fifth place in Division Three, a Play-off Final and Autoglass Final, both at Wembley; 1992-93 ended with County in sixth place, a Play-off semi-final and another Autoglass Final at Wembley; and 1993-94 saw County finish in fourth place, only to lose in the Play-off Final. Even though none of the Wembley visits resulted in victories, Bergara had managed to work miracles getting County to Wembley whilst still on a tight budget and unable to compete with the bigger clubs in the transfer-market.

Bergara has succeeded in mobilising increasingly voc-iferous support, the value of which was seen in the 1993 Autoglass Final when, seemingly on the way to a comprehensive defeat by Port Vale, it was acknowledged, even by the television commentary, that it was the incredible vocal support which dragged County back into the game.

Whilst Bergara's team selection may, on occasion, appear eccentric, it is impossible to deny his prodigious ability to transform unknown or seemingly ordinary players into good players. Those who mocked his signing of the awkward-looking and seemingly unco-ordinated Kevin Francis have been silenced as a result of the work Bergara has done to develop this notoriously tall player into a highly talented attacker who is feared by virtually all opponents.

Bergara's shrewd dealings in the transfer market have seen players such as Beaumont, Edwards, Frain, Gannon, Preece, Todd, Ward, Paul A.Williams, Paul R. Williams, and Kevin Francis all join the club for relatively small fees or on free-transfers. The two Paul Williams, both arriving at Edgeley Park on free transfers, have been sold to West Brom and Coventry for £250,000 and £150,000 respectively, with many of the others likely to command a considerable profit should they leave.

After spending 20 years providing subject-matter for comedians, Bergara has taken County beyond music-hall mockery and, in the process, become the most successful manager ever at Edgeley Park. In April 1994, Bergara became County's second longest-serving manager (excluding wartime periods) and on the basis of resources, in terms of both money and support, his achievements in 1991-92 would have justified him being proclaimed Manager of the Year.

Although Bergara's County have suffered three near-misses in succession, it is to be hoped that this charming but steely Uruguayan, author of programme notes that contain quite unique metaphors, will continue his success at Edgeley Park. It has now become difficult to imagine County without Danny Bergara.

A-Z of County Stars

Note that where the symbol † follows a debut date, this signifies that the player scored on his debut.

Len Allchurch

Born Swansea, 12 September 1933.
County League debut: v Tranmere Rovers (h), 6 September 1965†.
Len Allchurch was not a 'push and run' winger but relied upon guile and close ball control before providing crosses for his forwards. Although making his debut for

Swansea Town at 17, it was not until the end of his National Service at the age of 20 that he established himself in the first team. At 21 he made his international debut for Wales against Northern Ireland in Belfast, forming a left-wing partnership with brother, Ivor, and helping to provide the service for the legendary John Charles to score a hat-trick. He moved to Sheffield United for £18,000 in March 1961 and was immediately involved in helping the Blades to promotion from Division Two. He made 123 League appearances for Sheffield United before, exactly one week short of his 32nd birthday, County paid £10,000 to bring him to Edgeley Park. His four seasons with Stockport were highly successful, County winning the Fourth Division championship in Allchurch's second season and performing creditably in the Third Division. His teasing skills were of particular benefit to the twin-strike force of Bill Atkins and Jim Fryatt but by April 1969, County had lost both of these forwards and, without adequate replacements, Allchurch's talents were some-

what wasted. After making 145 appearances and scoring 16 goals, he returned to Swansea in September 1969, adding 70 appearances to his first spell of 272 before retiring at the age of 37. Len Allchurch opened a hotel before going into the retail business in Swansea where he still lives.

Brett Angell

Born Marlborough, 20 August 1968.
County League debut: v Scarborough (a), 22 October 1988.
Before his transfer to County in October 1988 for the then club record fee of £30,000, Brett Angell had not enjoyed an illustrious career. From being a non-contract player at Portsmouth, he moved to Cheltenham Town before Derby County signed him. He did not make a League appearance for the Rams before

Asa Hartford took what appeared to be a gamble in paying a relatively large sum for the inexperienced 20-year-old forward. Angell was an awkward-looking player who, in his first season at Edgeley Park had to compete for his place with the more experienced Tony Caldwell, Bob Colville, Rodger Wylde, and the precocious talents of Tony Hancock. Five goals in 27 League and Cup appearances, including nine as substitute, did not appear to justify the fee paid for him and initially it was surprising when the newly installed Danny Bergara let Colville and Hancock move on

whilst retaining Angell. However, Bergara's decision was vindicated by Angell's goalscoring exploits the following season, his 23 League goals being a major contribution to County finishing in fourth place, thereby winning a Play-off position.

Although he continued to look somewhat awkward in possession of the ball and rarely scoring 'exciting' goals, Angell had the priceless ability to be in the right place at the right time, most of his goals being scored from within the six-yard box. It was not surprising that County fans were disappointed when, in July 1990, their leading scorer opted to join Southend United, the team that two months earlier had taken an automatic promotion place from County by only one point. Despite lengthy periods of absence through injury, Angell continued to score regularly for Southend, helping them to a second promotion in 1991 and then a healthy position in Division Two (the 'new' First Division). In 1994, Brett Angell was transferred to Everton in a deal worth £500,000 and, as a result of conditions attached to the original tribunal-determined transfer, County will reap further financial benefits from the exploits of their former striker.

Smart Arridge

Born Southwick, near Sunderland 1872. Died Bangor, 20 October 1947.
County League debut: v Middlesbrough (h), 7 September 1901.
Although born in the North-East, Arridge moved to Bangor as a child and started his football career with the North Wales club. Originally a left-winger with Bangor, he was successfully converted to a speedy two-footed left-back, renowned for his shoulder-charges. After four years at Bangor, he was spotted by then Second Division Bootle and transferred to the Merseyside club in 1892. Within 12 months, he had moved on to First Division Everton where he made 56 League and Cup appearances in his four year stay but was bitterly disappointed when, in 1896-97, having played in all the earlier

rounds of the FA Cup, he was omitted from both the semi-final and Final. In 1897 he moved to his third Merseyside club, the ambitious New Brighton Tower, before joining County in the summer of 1901.

Arridge had won eight caps for Wales and County were fortunate to replace their former famous amateur captain, Jack Earp, with another celebrated full-back. Almost 30 when he moved to Stockport, his experience with 'bigger' clubs was a significant bonus for County who were struggling to cope with their newly acquired League status. The unusually named Smart made 67 League and Cup appearances for County at Green Lane and then Edgeley Park where the club moved in 1902. County's struggles continued but Arridge remained a thoroughly reliable full-back, notwithstanding his being one of the four players who missed the train prior to the infamous 8-1 defeat at Chesterfield in April 1902.

Released in 1903, Arridge returned to Bangor where he was engaged in a variety of jobs, the majority having some tie with the sea as he had been a sailor before becoming a professional footballer in 1888, finally working as a stevedore in Port Penrhyn.

Bill Atkins

Born Bingley, 9 May 1939.
County League debut: v Halifax Town (a), 18 March 1967.

Although 6ft tall and good in the air, Bill Atkins was a slim and graceful forward, skilful on the ground and a consistent goal-scorer. He began his playing career at Swindon Town, scoring 28 goals in 75 League appearances before moving on to Halifax Town. His 34 goals in 74 appearances at Halifax persuaded County to sign him on transfer-deadline day in March 1967 in an exchange deal which took the talented David Shawcross to The Shay. Atkins helped County in the

final push for the Fourth Division championship but it was not until the following season that he enjoyed his most productive spell.

With the arrival of Jim Fryatt, a formidable striking partnership emerged, the two forwards consistently well supplied by County's two talented wingers, Len Allchurch and Johnny Price. Their one season together saw the powerful front men share 44 League and Cup goals and although Bill Atkins continued to score when Fryatt moved on to Blackburn Rovers, finishing top-scorer in 1968-69, County failed to provide him with the support he had enjoyed with Fryatt. As County fell away from the promotion places in the second part of that season, Atkins moved to Portsmouth in April 1969. He was unable to repeat his scoring feats at the Fratton Park club, making only 11 appearances before returning to Halifax where he completed 200 appearances. He moved on to Rochdale in December 1972, and then Darlington in September 1973 where he ended his playing career in March 1975.

Chris Beaumont
Born Sheffield, 5 December 1965.
County League debut: v Torquay

United (h), 19 August 1989†.
It was distressing, to say the least, that Chris Beaumont's early goal in the 1993-94 Second Division Play-off Final was later marred by a controversial sending off, for he must rank as one of football's most inoffensive and sporting players. One of Danny Bergara's first signings at both Rochdale and County, Beaumont was an unusually late starter in professional football, playing his first League game three months before his 23rd birthday. On leaving

school, he became an accountant's clerk in Dronfield, playing amateur football for five years. In 1986, he was spotted by Denaby United, the North East Counties League club, for whom he played for two seasons. Whilst at Denaby, he played alongside Simon Bergara, Danny Bergara's son, and when Bergara Senior took over the manager's job at Rochdale, he brought Beaumont to Spotland. Although arriving on a three month trial, within a month he was offered a full-time contract and in August 1988 made his debut as a substitute, scoring in a 3-3 draw with Burnley in the Littlewoods [League] Cup. Before the end of the season, Bergara had moved to Stockport and on 21 July 1989 he brought Beaumont to Edgeley Park for £8,000.

After scoring on his debut against Torquay, Beaumont was badly injured and did not regain a regular place for another six months. Since that time, he has shared in County's upturn in fortunes, invariably playing a significant part in the team's success. His most frequent position has involved supporting the front two players from a wide

position on either side of the pitch but he has also played in a more orthodox midfield role and, on a number of occasions, as a right-back. Chris Beaumont has already passed the 200 appearance-mark in all competitions and is approaching 50 goals for the club. Whilst taking some time to win over supporters, his consistency in his first injury-free season won over any critics and he has always been a tireless worker. He has scored regularly and, whilst never being an out-and-out striker, many of his goals have been spectacular. In addition to playing in all four of County's Wembley appearances, he is the only player to have appeared in all ten Play-off matches for County.

Graham Beighton
Born Sheffield, 1 July 1939.
County League debut: v Hartlepools United (a), 4 September 1961.
Graham Beighton began his career with Sheffield Wednesday but never made a League appearance prior to his transfer to Stockport in June 1961. Although only 5ft 10ins, he was a solid and dependable goalkeeper who, once he had broken into County's team, remained the first choice for over three years. He was unfortunate in that his period with County coincided with their worst spell as they hovered around the re-election zone in each of his three full seasons. When County began the 1964-65 season with their worst-ever run, player-manager Trevor Porteous brought in the 19-year-old Ken Mulhearn and Graham Beighton never regained his position as first-choice goalkeeper. After making 143 League and Cup appearances, he was transferred to Wrexham in January 1966. Although within a week he had returned to Edgeley Park to help his new club to a 4-2 win, it was very much a case of exchanging one re-election club for another, Wrexham finishing bottom of the Fourth Division as County had done the previous year. Having made 23 appearances for Wrexham, Beighton finally dropped out of League football although still only 26 years old.

Barry Betts
Born Barnsley, 18 September 1932.
County League debut: v Tranmere Rovers (a), 9 November 1957.
Barry Betts signed for his home town club in 1950 although he did not get into the Barnsley team until the 1952-53 season. He did not become a regular until 1955-

56, making 38 appearances for the Second Division club. After playing six times at the beginning of the following season, full-back Betts suffered a serious back injury. He was told by doctors that he would have to give up professional football and received £500 compensation from the Football League's insurance scheme. He continued to train whilst working as a clerk and when it became apparent that he could regain his professional career, he agreed to join County on a free transfer in July 1957. However, because of the compensation he had received, there were problems obtaining clearance from the Football League and County were warned that they must not talk to the press about the delay. Although he repaid the £500, it was not until November that he was finally officially registered, Betts only discovering that his registration had been approved by the League when a policeman knocked on his door in Barnsley, this being the only way of contacting the player.

The signing of Betts, an accomplished right back to play alongside County's reliable left back, Billy Webb, allowed Bob Murray to move up to right-half and the former Barnsley player developed into a consistent performer who was highly rated outside the lower divisions. Betts made 122 League and Cup appearances, scoring four goals of which three were penalties. Following an outstanding season, Manchester City paid County £8,000 in June 1960 to take Betts to Maine Road. He captained City in his first season, was their only ever-present and was voted Player of the Year, crowning an outstanding comeback to a career that seemed to have ended some five years earlier. In that same season, the introduction of the Football League Cup brought his old club, County, to Maine Road but he did his former colleagues no favours as City ran out 3-0 winners.

Betts suffered from persistent injuries over his last three years at Maine Road, restricting his appearances to 69 and in August 1964 he was given a free-transfer by City and moved to Scunthorpe United. He made only seven appearances for Scunthorpe before retiring from professional football, this time for good.

Andy Black

Born Stirling, 23 September 1917.
County League debut: v Bradford City (h), 19 August 1950†.
A highly gifted goal-scoring inside-forward, the young Andy Black had already made a name for himself in Scotland before the outbreak of war, having scored 105 goals in only 136 League matches for Heart of Midlothian whom he had joined at the age of 17. At 20, he became the first player to score a hat-trick against Rangers at Ibrox and within a fortnight had won the first of his Scottish international caps against Czechoslovakia. He scored in all his three appearances for Scotland but his professional career, like others of his generation, suffered as a result of the war. He joined Manchester City in June 1946 in

time for the resumption of League football, helping the Sky Blues to win the Second Division championship in his first season with 15 goals in 37 League and Cup appearances. Back in the First Division, Andy Black continued to score freely and he ended the season as top scorer. In his four seasons at Maine Road, he made 146 appearances whilst scoring 52 goals but following City's

relegation in 1949-50, Andy Black made the short move to Edgeley Park teaming up with his fellow Scot and former Maine Road colleague, Alex Herd. Black was a popular player at County, still scoring goals in his three seasons at the club but supported in his last two years by the remarkably prolific Jack Connor. By the time he retired in 1953, Black had scored 39 goals in his 101 League and Cup matches, having enjoyed a notable career in spite of the loss of seven wartime seasons. He became the licensee of a pub in Heald Green which he continued to run until his death.

Ben Boardman

Born Ashton-under-Lyne, 28 April 1899. Died Manchester, 1968.
County League debut: v Oldham Athletic (h), 13 September 1924.
Having moved from Macclesfield and signed professional forms for County in May 1924, Boardman, initially an outside-right, began his career as an understudy to the highly talented Eddie Critchley. Diminutive in height, variously described as being 5ft 4¹/₂ins or 5ft 6ins, Boardman was a staunch servant to County for seven seasons until he was transferred to Manchester City in the summer of 1931. He was regarded as one of the cleverest players of his era, possessing vision, a remarkable turn of speed, and was a brilliant dribbler and passer of the ball. By the time County were relegated to the Northern Section, he had developed into an inside-right, helping to supply free-scoring forwards like Joe Smith, Harry Burgess and Frank Newton. In September 1930, his loyal services were rewarded by a joint-benefit with Bill Bocking - whose career had been contemporaneous with Boardman's - in a match against First Division champions Sheffield Wednesday. The two players had made their County debuts within three weeks of each other and both made their last appearance on 18 April 1931, Boardman having completed 195 League and Cup appearances whilst scoring 33 goals. Whereas Bocking was still only 25, it came as a surprise when, at the age of 31, Boardman was transferred to Manchester City. However, the move helped neither County nor City, Boardman failing to make an appearance in City's first team whilst County experienced their worst season in the Northern Section. It was a sad end to the professional career of one of County's best players.

Bill Bocking

Born Stockport, 11 June 1905.
County League debut: v Crystal Palace (a), 4 October 1925.
After playing junior football in his native Stockport, Bocking played for Hyde United in the Cheshire League before signing amateur forms for County in August 1923. Although he had to wait more than a year for the opportunity to play in the first team, the strong and speedy right-back became a permanent fixture in County's team within three months of his debut. He came to be seen as the most accomplished full-back in the Northern Section and from 1928 to 1931 he captained the County team. After making 276 appearances, his consistency and ability were recognised, Everton

paying a four-figure fee to County to take him to Goodison Park on 30 April 1931. Bocking's first two games for his new club provided a novel statistic. He played his last game for County in the Third Division North and, with Everton already Second Division champions, he made his debut in their final fixture away at Preston together with two other former Stockport players, Charlie Gee and Eddie Critchley. The first game of 1931-32 saw Bocking play in the First Division in a home match against Birmingham with the result that, within three consecutive matches, Bocking had played in all three Divisions of the Football League.

Although he remained at Goodison for three seasons, his League and Cup appearances were limited to only 16 and it came as no surprise when the County

favourite returned to Edgeley Park at the end of August 1934 for a fee of £250. Bocking captained the team in 1934-35 and was a key figure in County's record-breaking FA Cup run which took them to a fifth round home tie against West Brom. With a gale force wind driving down Edgeley Park, Bocking's decision to play against the wind was never forgotten, Albion rushing into an unassailable 5-0 half-time lead. He was not amused by constant reminders of that fateful judgment but, as in his first spell at Edgeley, he continued to display the qualities that made him one of the finest players County had produced. In County's promotion season, he played 32 games before injury forced him out of the club's exciting run-in to the Third Division title and restricted his appearances when Second Division football returned to Edgeley Park. In the summer of 1938, Bill Bocking finally retired from the game having made 396 League and Cup appearances for County, scoring six goals.

Jack Bowles

Born Cheltenham, 4 August 1914.
County League debut: v New Brighton (a), 27 August 1938.
The son of a Worcestershire professional cricketer, Jack Bowles was 17 before he played football. His goalkeeping career began with his home town team, Cheltenham Town, before he was persuaded to sign professional forms with Newport County in May 1936. After making only four League appearances in his one season with

the South Wales club, he was transferred to Accrington Stanley in June 1937. He made only 12 appearances for Stanley, although with thoughts of possibly following in his father's footsteps, he turned out for Accrington Cricket Club as a fast bowler. On 12 July 1938 he was transferred to County in an exchange deal which took goalkeeper John Daniels and centre-forward Sammy Hunt to Peel Park. Bowles' arrival at Edgeley Park began a 15-year association with County where he became one of the club's most popular players, regarded by many as County's finest-ever goal-keeper. Nicknamed 'Tiger' Bowles because he consistently prowled the penalty area, crouching and waving his arms even when County were attacking, he immediately became a permanent fixture in the team in the last pre-war season and for seven post-war seasons. In addition to 306 League and Cup appearances for County, he also made 34 appearances for Stock-port in wartime football. A very agile goalkeeper, his reputation was made by outstanding displays against Barnsley in his first season. His resistance helped County win an FA Cup third round tie at Oakwell and when the two sides met again in a League clash in April 1939, he gave a near miraculous display to ensure Duggie Reid's solitary goal won the match against the Third Division leaders (and subsequent champions). Almost ten years later, Bowles' agility was still evident when he not only saved two penalties from York City's captain and penalty-kick expert Harry Brigham at Bootham Crescent in 1948-49, but repeated the feat in the same fixture the following year. Jack Bowles was 38 when he played his last first-team game in January 1953 before moving to non-League Winsford United. When his football career was over, he initially remained in the Stockport area as a licensee in Romiley before moving on to run an off-licence in Hartley Wintney, Hampshire. He then returned to the Vale of Evesham near to his birthplace.

Les Bradd
Born Buxton, 6 November 1947.
County League debut: v Darlington (h), 19 August 1978†.
When Les Bradd's job as an apprentice mechanic prevented him from playing Saturday football, he became an apprentice welder and joined Hope Valley League team Earl Sterndale for whom the burly 6ft 1in forward scored 75 goals. In March 1966, he was signed by Second Division Rotherham United for whom he only made three appearances before a transfer to Notts County in October 1967 transformed his career. During the following 11 seasons, Bradd made over 400 League and Cup appearances for

Notts County whilst setting a club League scoring record of 125 goals.
In August 1978, County manager Mike Summerbee brought Bradd to Edgeley Park and, in partnership with Stuart Lee, he scored 45 League and Cup goals. In addition to scoring twice on his debut, Bradd's 21 goals included his only hat-trick with County in a remarkable match at Oakwell. After 80 minutes and with Barnsley winning 4-1, Bradd scored his hat-trick in seven minutes to give County a 4-4 draw. Always a committed player, in his three seasons at Stockport, Bradd played a number of games at centre-half as well as in his more orthodox striking position. After scoring 35 goals in 132 League and Cup appearances, Les Bradd moved to Wigan Athletic in July 1981 and, at the age of 34, continued to score freely. He made a brief move to Bristol Rovers for whom he played only once before retiring from the game having made over 600 appearances. He joined the backroom staff at Notts County, holding a number of positions at the club where he enjoyed his greatest success.

Bryan Brennan
Born Halifax, 25 May 1933.
County League debut: v Carlisle United (a), 21 April 1951.
For those who saw him play, Bryan 'Boy' Brennan will be remembered with more than a tinge of sadness and frustration. He was, perhaps, the classic schoolboy prodigy, chosen for England Schoolboys at the age of 13, captain at 14 and a goalscoring phenomenon. At the age of 14 he had the physique of a man and possessed a quite thunderous shot. In 1947-48, he amassed 115 goals for Stockport Boys, 31 of them in the English Schoolboys Trophy, 11

of which came in a first round match against North Staffordshire. The team was good but 'Boy' Brennan was unique, scoring in every round as Stockport reached the two-legged Final against Liverpool. An astonishing 24,000 saw a goalless draw at Edgeley Park and over 40,000 attended the second leg at Anfield where Brennan scored in a 3-3 draw to help Stockport become joint-holders of the trophy. Brennan simply could not stop scoring goals and, with all the big clubs vying for his services, there was considerable amazement when he signed professional forms for County in June 1950. At the age of 17, 'Boy' Brennan played in the last four games of the 1950-51 season but failed to score. Although he remained on County's books for the next three seasons, the schoolboy legend never played another League match. Perhaps, as he grew up, he was unable to cope with the expectations of those around him but, whatever the reasons were for his almost non-existent profes-sional career, it was a momentous loss for himself, the club and the supporters. He was last heard of still living in the Stockport area, driving quarry lorries.

Tommy Brittleton
Born Winsford, 23 April 1882.
Died Winsford, 22 February 1955.
County League debut: v Burslem Port Vale (h), 13 December 1902.
Tommy Brittleton was the first County 'star' to realise a substantial transfer fee. Signed from Winsford United, he began his League career as an outside-right but it was as an inside-right that his reputation grew. Contem-porary sources described him as 'a

class player, noted for his unselfishness, his precision in passing and his shooting powers', and he was doubtlessly one of the most accomplished players ever to play for County. At 5ft 10ins he was a strong player, not easily knocked off the ball, and he quickly established himself as an Edgeley Park favourite. When County failed to gain re-election in May 1904, Brittleton's presence was seen as a critical factor in the club's attempt to regain League status but on 7 January 1905, having scored ten goals in 53 League and Cup appearances, he was transferred to Sheffield Wednesday for £300, the largest amount received for a Stockport player. Having rejected a £200 bid for Brittleton, the financial position of the club was such that the County committee were left with little choice but to let their star attraction depart despite the outraged County fans hastily arranged 'indignation meeting'.
From Brittleton's point of view, the move to Hillsborough gave his career an impetus which could not have been achieved at Edgeley Park. He was successfully transformed into a wing-half, won an FA Cup winners' medal and was made Wednesday's captain before winning the first of five England caps. He spent 12 peacetime seasons at Hills-borough, making 373 League and Cup appearances and scoring 33 goals. On 2 June 1920, Brittleton moved to Second Division Stoke where he played for another five seasons, making 114 League appearances and helping The Potters to win promotion in 1922. The evergreen Tommy Brittleton finally retired from League football in March 1925 to take up the post of player-coach with Winsford United.

Harry Burgess
Born Alderley Edge, 20 August 1904. Died Northwich, 1968.
County League debut: v Hull City (a), 13 March 1926.
Signed as an amateur from Nantwich Ramblers in August 1925, Burgess's career blossomed when he signed professional terms before the start of the 1926-27 season. With high-class inside-forwards Ben Boardman and Billy Johnston alongside him, Burgess scored 28 goals in his first full season and although the arrival of the former Bolton star, Joe Smith, led to his scoring-rate falling in his second season, 1928-29 saw him regain his scoring flair. Seventy-two goals in 121 League and Cup appearances provided sufficient

evidence of his ability to persuade First Division champions Sheffield Wednesday to pay £3,000 for County's goalscoring inside-forward. In his first season at Hillsborough, 19 goals helped Wednesday to another championship and during the following season Burgess won the first of his four England caps. In his six seasons with the Owls, he scored 77 goals in 234 appearances but was surprisingly transferred to Chelsea in March 1935, thus missing out on Wednesday's FA Cup success at Wembley. Penalty specialist Burgess ended his professional career at Chelsea in 1939 after scoring 37 League and Cup goals in his 155 appearances. Although Burgess had left County at a time when they seemed to be able consistently to develop prolific goalscorers, he remained a popular figure at Edgeley Park, and in his late 30s, guested during the war, still good enough to score six times in his seven appearances.

Arthur Burrows (Jnr)

Born Stockport, 4 December 1919.
County League debut: v Wrexham (h), 25 March 1939.

As with many other players of his generation, Arthur Burrows' professional career was affected by the outbreak of war. After signing as an amateur in 1936, he turned professional in 1937 but did not make his first-team debut until March 1939. Following the outbreak of war, he saw service in France before returning to Stockport to work in engineering. He began his career as an inside-left with good ball-control, but played for County in every outfield position other than full-back. Whilst his versatility was such that he was equally at home as an inside-forward or on the

wing, the majority of his appearances were as a wing-half. Although he made only seven League appearances for County, only Ken Shaw and Harry Catterick made more wartime appearances than Burrows who

played in 116 games and scored eight goals. In addition to making guest appearances for Bury and Manchester United, he played right-half in the notorious 'longest match' in March 1946. A serious knee injury restricted his first-team opportunities at Edgeley Park and he was released in 1947, joining Ashton United before moving to Accrington Stanley for whom he made nine appearances between 1948 and 1950. He went on to play for Mossley, Winsford United and Buxton before becoming involved in coaching. When his professional career was over, he returned to his job as an engineering pattern-maker until his retirement. He still lives in Stockport.

His father, also named Arthur, made four appearances for County in 1920 whilst his son, Phil, made over 500 League appearances in his career with York City, Plymouth Argyle, Hereford United and Gillingham.

Joe Butler

Born Horsehay, Shropshire 1879.
Died 30 November 1939.
County League debut: v Burton Swifts (a), 29 September 1900.

After beginning his working life as a miner, Joe Butler joined County in 1898 but did not make a first-team appearance until 1900. However, from the time he secured a regular place as goalkeeper in County's second

season of League football, he became a supporter's player, revered by Stockport fans even when he was playing against County for Clapton Orient and local rivals Glossop. His performances won praise from virtually all footballing journalists of the time, 'Butler's magnificent goalkeeping' being a comment found almost weekly in reports of County matches. His agility and courage frequently gained points for County when their play merited none. Although highly regarded, Butler remained with County following their fall from the Football League, helping them to win the Lancashire Combination and celebrating their success by converting a penalty in their penultimate game in 1904-05. However, following County's successful application to the Second Division, Butler moved to Clapton Orient in June 1905 having made exactly 100 League appearances. When Orient came to Edgeley Park that December, fans were heard to lament 'I wish he

played for County now' as the London club drew 3-3. The lament was answered as Butler returned to Edgeley Park on 1 February 1906 having made only 24 League and Cup appearances for Orient. Joe Butler remained with County for another two years, completing a total of 190 League and Cup appearances before moving to

Glossop on 18 March 1908 for a fee believed to be £150. In his first season, his magnificent goalkeeping ensured Glossop's passage into the FA Cup quarter-finals as he saved two penalties against [Sheffield] Wednesday at Owlerton (now Hillsborough) to assure his team's 1-0 victory. Butler spent four years with the Derbyshire club without missing a game and maintained the same high standards he had set earlier in his career, although following, an incident in a game against Chelsea at the end of the 1911-12 season, he was suspended for the whole of September. After making 152 consecutive League appearances for Glossop, his return from suspension was dramatic, an immediate transfer to Sunderland resulting on 5 October 1912. This became Butler's most successful season as he won a First Division championship medal and an FA Cup runners-up medal as Sunderland narrowly failed to achieve the double, beaten 1-0 by Aston Villa in the Final. Having made 65 League appearances, in 1914 he moved to Lincoln City where he ended his professional career, having missed only one of City's 38 League games. However, Edgeley Park had not seen the last of one of their favourite 'sons' as Butler returned to County in October 1916 in the wartime League. As he had done ten years earlier, he shared goalkeeping responsibilities with Jimmy Molyneux and in three seasons made 37 appearances. It was fitting that, for County's last 'wartime' fixture in April 1919, their custodian should be Joe Butler as, notwithstanding his numerous appearances for other clubs, he was always regarded as a 'County man'.

Harry Catterick (Jnr)

Born Darlington, 26 November 1919. Died Liverpool, 9 March 1985.
County debut (wartime): v Stoke City (a) 28 October 1939†.

Although Harry Catterick was registered with Everton throughout the war and never played League or Cup football for County, his record 'guesting' in wartime football thoroughly justifies his inclusion in this section. His career had only just begun when war broke out and he played for County in every wartime season, demonstrating his considerable talents as a quick and lethal centre-forward by scoring an astonishing 98 goals from only 122 appearances. (Whilst playing for his registered club Everton, he also scored 56 goals in 73 wartime appearances.) His connections with County came through his father who had been both a player and trainer at Edgeley Park and, indeed, managed the club during World War Two.

Whilst Catterick enjoyed some modest success with Everton on

the resumption of League football, he had relatively few first-team opportunites, making only 69 League and Cup appearances and scoring 23 goals in five seasons before ending his playing career with Crewe Alexandra in 1952. However, it was his achievements as a manager for which he will be best remembered. After managing Crewe, Rochdale and then Sheffield Wednesday, he returned to Everton in 1961 and, in addition to guiding his team to an FA Cup win in 1966, built two championship teams during the next ten years, both of which combined flair and a steely desire to win. Following a mild heart attack in 1972, he became general manager until he took over at Preston in 1975. After retiring in 1977, he maintained his lifelong interest in football but in March 1985 he collapsed and died at Goodison Park, the home of his greatest achievements.

Tommy Charlton

Born Middlesbrough.
County League debut: v West Bromwich Albion (h), 1 September 1909.
Signed from Darlington in the summer of 1909, Tommy Charlton rapidly became a popular figure with all Stockport County supporters. In his four seasons at Edgeley Park, he played in every forward position but found his niche as an outside-right and, when at the top of his form, was regarded as the best right-winger in the Second Division. A clever footballer, his artfulness made life

extremely difficult for opposing left backs but he was a somewhat moody player, inclined to be overelaborate and somewhat volatile. However, when in the right frame of mind, he could be a handful and, in addition to being a perfect crosser of the ball, possessed a thunderous shot. He scored 29 goals in his 99 League and Cup appearances before he was sent off following a violent confrontation with Glossop's Stapley at the beginning of February 1913. Three weeks elapsed before he was suspended 'until further notice' but, whilst still serving his suspension, he was transferred to Burnley on 13 March for a fee of £650. He only played seven times for the Turf Moor club, scoring three goals before he was transferred to Blackpool in November. He made 23 appearances for the Seasiders, adding another three goals before suffering a fractured skull in a collision with a Leicester Fosse player on Good Friday 1914. Although his life was in danger, Charlton did in fact recover; however, the injury was sufficient to end his professional career.

Frank Clempson

Born Salford, 27 May 1930. Died Worsley, 1970.
County League debut: v Gateshead (h), 21 February 1953.
The raw potential of Frank Clempson saw him signing professional terms with Manchester United shortly after his 18th birthday, but the abundance of talented youngsters and experienced high-class players at Old Trafford prevented him from gaining a regular place. In his five seasons at Old Trafford, he made only 15 League appearances, scoring twice, his best spell being a run of eight games towards the

end of United's First Division championship success in 1951-52. As the 'Busby Babes' began to be introduced during the following season, Clempson's chances of regular first-team football receded and shrewd County manager, Dick Duckworth, signed the talented inside-forward. Always an

attacking player, Clempson was successfully converted into a lefthalf and became County's regular penalty expert. Whilst not having all the qualities necessary to be a regular player in a top First Division side, Frank Clempson's ability shone through in the Third Division, recognised by his selection for the Third Division North representative side against the Southern section in 1954-55. He gave loyal and consistent service to County for seven seasons, making 261 League and Cup appearances, scoring 37 goals and providing many more for Jack Connor and Bill Holden. In July 1959, he was transferred to Chester where he was immediately made captain but, during his second season, his influence could not prevent the Sealand Road club's slide to the foot of the Fourth Division. After making 69 League appearances with Chester, he retired from professional football in 1961 and ran a grocery business in Salford until his untimely death at the age of 40.

Les Cocker

Born Stockport, 13 March 1924. Died, 4 October 1979.
County League debut: v York City (a), 2 November 1946.
Les Cocker played in every position in the forward line with both County and Accrington Stanley, his only other

professional club. Although he played for Stockport Boys, Cocker had no intentions of making a career in football and had become a painter and decorator before joining the army in 1942. Having seen active service in France in 1944, he returned to Stockport on leave and went to watch County

playing Accrington Stanley in a Western region fixture. When County found themselves one short, Cocker filled the breach as a left-half and, by accident, began an eight year association with the club. He was a versatile and courageous player, always totally committed in every game he played. By the time he left County for Accrington in August 1953, Cocker had made 189 League and Cup appearances and scored 48 goals, three of which helped Stockport to the FA Cup fifth round in 1950. Having begun his County career by accident in a match against Accrington, it was perhaps destiny that his Stanley debut was against Stockport. He was an important player in Accrington's best-ever spell, scoring 49 goals in 132 League and Cup appearances. After he finished playing, Cocker became assistant trainer at Accrington and then at Luton before becoming trainer at Leeds United. At Elland Road, he formed a successful partnership with Don Revie and had spells as coach of the England team, acting as Revie's assistant after the former Leeds boss took over as England manager in 1974. After a short spell abroad, he became assistant manager with Doncaster Rovers and it was whilst with this club that he collapsed and died during a training session, having spent over

30 years in a profession he had entered purely by chance.

Jack Connor

Born Todmorden, 21 December 1919.
County League debut: v Oldham Athletic (h), 20 October 1951.

It is a remarkable coincidence that County's two most famous goalscoring centre-forwards, Jack Connor and Alf Lythgoe, both began their professional career during their mid-20s. A lover of football and particularly the position of centre-forward, Connor would probably have begun his professional career with Rochdale had it not been for the outbreak of war. Whilst stationed in Carlisle, he signed for Ipswich Town in 1944 and on the resumption of League football, he made 12 appearances and scored four goals for the Suffolk club. As he was still travelling back to his home in Carlisle, he needed little persuasion to join United in December 1946. However, appearances with Carlisle were reduced by niggling injuries, restricting him to 39 League appearances and 12 goals in his two year stay at Brunton Park.

Following a loan spell with Ards in Northern Ireland, he was transferred to Rochdale in December 1948 and, at the age of 29, his career suddenly took off. 42 goals in 88 League appearances attracted a host of League clubs and although County were one of those interested, it was Bradford City who succeeded in signing Connor in April 1951.

County's interest in Connor did not wane and the persistence of their officials eventually reaped rewards. On 19 October 1951, Jack Connor and his wife were in a Bradford cinema when a message was flashed on the screen 'would Jack Connor, Bradford City's centre-forward, please go to the foyer'. Initially fearing bad news, Connor was met in the foyer by County manager Andy Beattie and chairman Ernest Barlow, signing there and then for a fee of £2,500 before making his debut at Edgeley Park in front of a crowd of over 24,000. Although he did not score on his debut, Connor, now almost 32, embarked upon his most successful period. Whilst the club never mounted a serious promotion challenge, County could at least provide their supporters with goals, Connor's five seasons seeing him average two goals every three games. Of his 140 League and Cup goals from 217 appearances, Jack Connor scored a record 17 hat-tricks which included four goals in games against Bradford (Park Avenue) and Tranmere Rovers, and five goals in matches against Workington and his former club, Carlisle United. The player, who had a gift for finding space and the ability to shoot with either foot, scored a minimum of 30 goals in all his four full seasons and - in addition to becoming County's leading League goalscorer - in 1953 he shared with Alf Lythgoe the distinction of scoring a hat-trick of hat-tricks. Like his playing colleague, Frank Clempson, Connor was selected for the Third Division North representative team against the Southern section in 1955, scoring in the North's 2-1 victory at Peel Park, Accrington.

In September 1956, Connor had a dispute with player-manager, Willie Moir, and, to the huge disappointment of County supporters, was transferred to Crewe Alexandra. Now 37, he made 27 appearances for the Gresty Road club but was unable to maintain his scoring exploits, finding the net only four times. He had one season at non-League Runcorn before finally retiring from the game in 1958. Connor spent three years as a steward at Reddish Conservative Club before returning to Edgeley Park as pools promoter from 1960 until 1966 when he took on the same role at Rochdale. Another four years and Jack Connor returned to County in 1970 in the same capacity, remaining until 1978. Connor had two very brief experiences of non-League management, the first lasting only four days with Glossop, the second with Droylsden, both in 1969-70. However, whether County supporters saw Jack Connor or just read about him, his goalscoring exploits will never be forgotten.

Tony Coyle

Born Glasgow, 17 January 1960.
County League debut: v Torquay United (h), 21 December 1979.

In many ways a somewhat infuriating player, promising so much but not consistently delivering, Tony Coyle's ability was never in doubt. An almost archetypal Scottish winger, Coyle was at his best taking on defenders with his close control. For a relatively small and slightly-built player, he possessed a tremendous shot, many of his goals being exciting strikes from the angle of the penalty area; however, he was often unable to convert much easier chances. Coyle played football from an early age but ensured that he completed his apprenticeship at Govan shipyards. At 18, he played as a trialist for Aberdeen, Dundee United,

Morton and St Mirren but eventually signed for Albion Rovers on a part-time basis. County manager Jimmy McGuigan had almost signed Coyle whilst managing Rotherham, but he eventually brought the 19-year-old Scot to Edgeley Park for a then record fee of £25,000. Coyle was a regular choice for the next seven seasons, playing either as a traditional outside-left or on the left side of midfield. After making 240 League and Cup appearances and scoring 30 goals, Coyle was given a free transfer in the summer of 1986. He was quickly signed by Chesterfield's John Duncan and made over 80 appearances in the following two seasons. At the end of his first season at Saltergate, he was voted Player of the Year despite the fact he had played in an unaccustomed left-back role. Released by Chesterfield in 1988, a proposed move to Notts County fell through and, with a new season about to start, Coyle asked County manager Asa Hartford if he could train with his old club to keep fit. Hartford agreed and when County suffered with pre-season injuries, Coyle was re-signed on a weekly contract and played at Darlington in the first game of the season, scoring on his second debut. Although injury restricted his appearances, he added another 29 and scored three more goals in his second spell at Edgeley Park before he was again given a free transfer. Coyle spent two seasons with Northwich Victoria, interrupted only by a one month loan to Exeter City where he made one League appearance before leaving football in 1991 to work as a lifeguard at a sports centre. Tony Coyle, who still lives in Stockport, made a brief return to football with Hyde United in 1992 before concentrating on his job as a civil servant in the D.S.S.

Eddie Critchley

Born Stockport, 1903.
County League debut: v Port Vale (h), 9 December 1922.

When the slimly built 18-year-old amateur signed for County in 1921, few would have guessed what the young Eddie Critchley was destined to achieve. He did not make his County debut for over 12 months and only played twice in the 1922-23 season. However, by the time he was 20, he was County's first-choice outside-right, developing an expert control and a quick turn of speed which embarrassed many an experienced full-back in the strong Second Division of that era. In

Critchley's three full seasons at Edgeley Park, County struggled to maintain their status, continuing

the necessary policy of selling their best players, inevitable relegation eventually taking place in 1926. Critchley's stylish play blossomed in front of large crowds and it was not surprising that he was transferred to Everton for £3,000 on 22 December 1926, having scored ten goals in 124 appearances. Within three days of his transfer, he made his debut in front of a Christmas Day crowd of 37,500 at Goodison Park, providing the service for Dixie Dean to score four goals in a 5-4 win against Sunderland. Although Everton narrowly missed relegation, Critchley's first full season saw Everton win the First Division championship and the former County star played a large part in providing the ammunition for the immortal Dixie Dean to score a record-breaking 60 League goals. Eddie Critchley's eight season spell at Goodison was anything but dull; two years after their championship success Everton were relegated in 1930. The following season, the Blues were Second Division champions, scoring 22 goals on their way to an FA Cup semi-final in which Critchley was ruled out because of injury and which Everton lost. The First Division championship was won the following season and, in 1933, Critchley at last played in a semi-final only to lose his place for the Wembley victory against Manchester City. Regarded by many contemporary experts as one of the best wingers never to have been capped and having made 229 League and Cup appearances and scoring 42 goals for Everton, he moved to Preston North End on 9 June 1934. He made 11 appearances in the autumn of 1934 before signing for Port Vale on 13 December. After making 18 appearances at the Vale he ended his distinguished and eventful playing career. For some years he managed a pub in Hazel Grove and now, aged 90, Ted Critchley still lives in Stockport. Fondly remembered, he was a guest of honour when County beat Queen's Park Rangers on 8 January 1994, the sole survivor of the team which had beaten the London club in their only previous FA Cup meeting 69 years earlier.

Harold Crossthwaite

Born Stockport, 9 August 1890.
Died Stockport, 28 November 1939.
County League debut: v Lincoln City (a), 28 December 1912.
Having joined County from Heywood United in the summer of 1912, Crossthwaite was con-

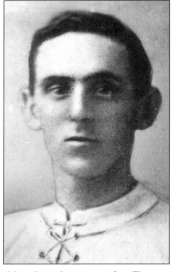

sidered to be cover for Tommy Charlton, but when Charlton was moved to inside-forward, the young Crossthwaite made his debut and retained his place for the rest of the season. Whilst lacking the goalscoring abilities of Charlton, the diminutive Crossthwaite was a clever outside-right and was very quick. Including wartime football, he played for ten seasons at Edgeley Park, becoming a permanent fixture in the team and well-respected by opposing full-backs. He established a remarkable record in wartime football, appearing in 142 of the 144 games County played, missing the other two games only to enable him to play in fund-raising games elsewhere. After playing in the first 29 League fixtures of 1919-20, on 3 March 1920, Stoke paid £1,250 for the now experienced winger. After 30 appearances with the Potters, he rejoined County in September 1921 and helped the club to the first Third Division North championship at the end of that season. Crossthwaite remained for another season, bringing his County appearances up to 131 whilst scoring 11 goals, before retiring from professional football.

Fred Crump

Born Stourbridge.
County League debut: v Chelsea (h), 2 September 1905.
Well-travelled centre-forward Fred Crump was the first County player to reach double-figures in terms of goals in three successive seasons. Before joining County from Stalybridge Rovers on 28 August 1905, Crump had played for Stourbridge, Derby County, Glossop and Northampton Town. With County returning to Second Division football, and having lost Brittleton and Green earlier in the year, they needed a player who

could help them retain their League status. Crump, whilst lacking the class of Tommy Green, was a whole-hearted player who, whilst not a prodigious goalscorer, could be relied upon to score regularly. In each of his three seasons at Edgeley Park, his goals helped County achieve a respectable mid-table position and by the time he was transferred to Brighton in the summer of 1908, he had scored 32 goals in 95 League and Cup appearances. Crump's final move was to Walsall after which he retired from the game.

Mike Davock

Born St Helens, 27 April 1935.
County League debut: v Derby County (a), 13 April 1957.
Michael Davock joined County, his one and only Football League

club, in January 1957 and, whilst not being a first choice in his first three seasons, eventually made the outside-left position his own. A reliable and industrious winger, Davock provided the additional benefit of being able to score, on average, a goal every five games. It was unfortunate that, by the time he had acquired a regular place, the club was going through one of its worst spells, having been relegated from the newly formed Third Division and finding it difficult to come to terms with the Fourth Division. Although County had a regular and competent defence, the goals had dried up and attendances decreased annually. For a winger like Davock, it was difficult to develop a pattern of play when other forwards rarely remained at Edgeley Park for much more than a season. In the circumstances, it was a credit to the player that he retained his commitment to the club for eight seasons, finishing with 46 goals from 252 League and Cup appearances.

Percy Downes

Born Worksop, 19 September 1904.
County League debut: v Darlington (h), 27 August 1932†.
Outside-left Percy Downes was the type of winger fans loved to watch, elusive and skipping over tackles before crossing for his forwards. He began (and ended) his career with Gainsborough Trinity before joining Second Division Blackpool in 1925. He was a key figure in Blackpool's Second Division championship winning team of 1929-30, scoring 13 goals and providing excellent service for the extraordinary goalscoring talents of Jimmy Hampson who finished with 45 goals that season. After making 158 League and Cup appearances and scoring 33 goals, Downes was niggled by injury on Blackpool's return to the First Division and the Seasiders transferred him to Hull City in 1931. After scoring three goals in 11 appearances, Downes was not retained by Hull and he arrived at County on a free transfer in August 1932. Although Downes had only two seasons with County, his influence was substantial as, together with County's other new winger, Jabez Foulkes, constant service was provided for Joe Griffiths and the newly arrived Alf Lythgoe, resulting in County scoring 99 League goals. Downes was made captain in his second season during which County, with the addition of the cultured Joe Hill, scored 115 League goals, 13

of them against Halifax Town. In the Halifax game, Downes became the only genuine outside-left in County's history to score four goals in a match. Having made 90 appearances, scoring 27 goals and playing a major part in one of County's most entertaining eras, Percy Downes left County in May 1934 to join Burnley. He remained at Turf Moor for two seasons, scoring six goals in 69 appearances before joining his last League club, Oldham Athletic on 9 May 1936. Still a very useful player, Downes had made 58 appearances for the Latics and scored four goals when he retired from League football, returning to his first club, Gainsborough Trinity in May 1938.

Ray Drake
Born Stockport, 24 October 1934.
County League debut: v Derby County (h), 1 December 1956.
Shortly after the departure of Jack Connor in September 1956, it appeared that County had found the perfect replacement, one who had averaged more than a goal a game during his three year apprenticeship at Edgeley Park. Through pure determination, Ray Drake, a County supporter from

childhood, had come to terms with the effects of the meningitis he had suffered as a three-year-old which had left him totally deaf in one ear and with only 30 per cent hearing in the other. This disability did not affect his desire to play football and when he took a clerical job at the Stockport Co-op, he played for his works team and then for Bramhall. In 1953 Drake had the confidence to go for a trial at County which resulted in him signing as a semi-professional. He

spent the next three seasons working his way up the reserves, scoring 69 goals in 46 games in 1954-55 and 59 goals in 41 games in the following season which saw him score all eight goals against Cheadle Rovers on Boxing Day 1955. With such a goalscoring record, it was surprising that Drake had to wait until December 1956 to make his first-team debut in which, characteristically, he scored. He was on the scoresheet in all his first four games, the last of these including a goal against Accrington Stanley on Christmas Day, accepted as County's fastest goal ever, referee Arthur Ellis timing it as coming after only seven seconds. In February 1957, a hat-trick in a 5-1 win at Gateshead was followed by Drake scoring all four goals against Wrexham and, by March, strong rumours circulated that he was going to move to Bolton in exchange for Nat Lofthouse. This did not materialise and shortly afterwards, having scored 19 goals in only 23 League appearances, Ray Drake had a disagreement with manager Willie Moir and was transfer-listed. During his five years at Edgeley Park, Drake had achieved the remarkable record of scoring 234 goals in 201 games but his desire to stay in Stockport saw him disappear into non-League football, playing for Altrincham, Hyde United and Cheadle Rovers. On leaving County, Drake took a job at a bookmakers where he remained until his retirement. He still lives near to Edgeley Park where, had he been treated differently, he could well have written himself into County's record books in numerous ways.

Neil Edwards
Born Aberdare, 5 December 1970.
County League debut: v Bury (h), 21 September 1991.
From the time he was a schoolboy, Neil Edwards has always been a goalkeeper, eventually leaving his South Wales home to join a Youth Training Scheme at Leeds United. He was signed as a professional in 1989 and played in the reserves, making only one first-team appearance in a Zenith Data Systems Cup match at Barnsley in November 1989. Although highly regarded at Elland Road, at only 5ft 8ins his height was seen as the one factor which would inhibit his progress and in the summer of 1991 he had the choice of joining County on loan or Blackpool on a contract. After seeking the advice of Elland Road's senior goal-keepers, John Lukic and Mervyn

Day, Edwards opted to join County. After three impressive games, County paid Leeds £10,000 to bring him to Edgeley Park on a permanent basis. Although only in his third season at Stockport, he has developed into an outstanding shot-stopper and his athleticism has helped to make up for his lack of height. Highly popular with the fans, Neil Edwards has already made 139 appearances for County but an injury to his shoulder resulted in him missing the last third of the 1993-94 season.

Dean Emerson
Born Salford, 27 December 1962.
County League debut: v Bournemouth (a), 12 February 1982.
An all-round sportsman in his schooldays, at 16 Dean Emerson had a successful trial for County and, whilst learning his trade as a screen printer, played in the reserve team. His debut was the first of 23 consecutive games as a non-contract player but his displays were so impressive that County signed him as a full-time professional in May 1982. In his four season spell at County, the distinctive red-haired Emerson developed into a fast-raiding midfield player with a tigerish tackle, powerful shot and the ability to make defence-splitting passes. Although mainly noted for his desire to be in the action, he was a very talented midfielder and, given County's never-ending parlous financial position, it became inevitable that he would not remain at Edgeley Park. Following a dismal re-election

season in 1984-85 and with an average attendance falling below 2,000 for the first and only time, County accepted Rotherham United's £30,000 offer for the Player of the Year. Still only 22, Emerson had already made 172 appearances for County and after 15 months at the Millmoor club,

he was transferred to First Division Coventry City in an exchange deal worth £100,000. He held down a regular place at Coventry before a serious knee injury in 1987 led to three operations, resulting in him missing the Sky Blues only FA Cup success at Wembley. Whilst at Coventry, he had a more restrictive role than in his Edgeley days, concentrating on ball-winning rather than furthering the creative side of his game. After five and a half years and well over 100 appearances, Emerson was freed in 1992 and was quickly snapped up by Hartlepool United where, in his one full season, his First Division experience enabled him to dictate the pace of the game. In the autumn of 1993, with Hartlepool suffering from the kind of financial crisis that County had experienced when first letting Emerson move on, the 'County reject' returned to Edgeley Park for a second spell, sharing midfield responsibility with David Frain and Peter Ward.

Clive Evans
Born Birkenhead, 1 May 1957.
County League debut: v York City (h), 27 August 1983.
In a long career in the lower divisions of the Football League, Clive Evans learned that hard work and adaptability were key factors in a player's survival.

When he joined County in 1983, at the age of 26, he had already made over 260 League and Cup

appearances with Tranmere Rovers, Wigan Athletic and Crewe Alexandra, scoring 40 goals as a defensive midfield player. During his five-year spell at Tranmere, he finished top-scorer with 11 goals in their relegation season, 1978-79. In his four full seasons at Edgeley Park, he played on either side of midfield or at full-back, giving him the opportunity to make surging runs and release his extremely strong shot. He remained at County during their relegation-haunted 1986-87 season, helping the Murphy-inspired team to safety. However, in September 1987, having made 181 appearances and scoring 23 goals, Clive Evans followed Colin Murphy to relegated Lincoln City where he played an important role in bringing the Imps back to Division Four. At the end of Lincoln's first season back, Evans finally left League football having given total commitment to every club for whom he played.

Frederick 'Tiny' Fayers
Born King's Lynn, 29 January 1890. Died Huddersfield, 4 February 1954.
County League debut: v Grimsby Town, (a), 30 August 1919.
At only 5ft 5ins, it was remarkable that Frederick 'Tiny' Fayers could have built such a successful career as a centre-half. An England Amateur international, Fayers was at Watford when spotted by Huddersfield Town whom he joined in February 1910. By November, he had signed professional forms and made 164 appearances for Second Division Huddersfield whilst scoring 18

goals before the cessation of professional football in 1915. Although still a Town player, he spent all the war years playing for County, missing only four games and scoring 14 goals in 140 appearances. Both popular and brave, he officially signed for Stockport in August 1919, playing

in all 43 League and Cup games in the first post-war season, scoring once. His consistency in County's Second Division team resulted in the 30-year-old Fayers being transferred to Manchester City in May 1920. He played in virtually all of City's games in 1920-21 as the Maine Road team finished First Division runners-up. Over three years, he made 77 appearances and scored five goals before his final move to Halifax Town in May 1923. Tiny Fayers only appeared for Halifax eight times before retiring in 1924.

Ken Finney
Born St Helens, 10 March 1929.
County League debut:v Lincoln City (a), 3 January 1948.

After impressing as a 17-year-old winger for his home town club St Helens, Ken Finney began his 16 seasons as a professional footballer on 30 December 1947, when he signed for County. Although he made only ten appearances in his first four seasons at Stockport, in the 1950s he became a highly proficient provider for the likes of Bill Holden, Eddie Moran, and Jack Connor. Primarily an outside-right, Finney made a number of appearances as both an inside and centre-forward, scoring 36 goals in 198 games for County. He was twice selected as an outside-right to represent the Northern Section against the Southern Section. During his 11th season at Edgeley Park, Finney and manager Willie Moir agreed that the player needed a fresh challenge with the result that in March 1958, he joined Tranmere Rovers for £2,000. In just over five seasons, Finney gave Rovers, his only other Football League club, the same loyal commitment he had given to County, making almost as many appearances, but in half the time, and scoring 26 League goals.

Ken Fogarty
Born Manchester, 25 January 1955.
County League debut: v Darlington (h), 10 March 1972.
In their long existence, County have produced many defenders of greater ability than the former

Stockport schoolboy, but it is almost impossible to believe that they have produced or could produce one with more passion and commitment to the club. On the basis of his performances on the field, he was a manager's dream: 100 per cent reliable and a spirited competitor who would never admit defeat. From the time

of making his debut shortly after his 17th birthday, he was an automatic choice on the left side of defence, winning honours as an Irish Youth international at 18 and becoming County's youngest Player of the Year at the age of 19. A slightly built player, his guaranteed enthusiasm led to inevitable injuries and when he made the last of his 297 appearances for County, he was still only 24. Although a committed County player during the dismal 1970s, when the club was prepared to accept money for him, Fogarty took the opportunity to move to Fort Lauderdale in March 1979 as the United States tried to develop professional football. Despite his wholehearted approach during his days at Edgeley Park, he had no regrets at his departure, relishing the facilities and way of life that his move had provided.

Jabez Foulkes
Born Fryston, near Castleford, 28 August 1913.
County League debut: v Darlington (h), 27 August 1932.
'Jabber' to the fans, but Jabe to his friends, Foulkes played football for his local Fryston Colliery team where he worked as a miner before signing for Huddersfield Town in 1929. Town were one of the strongest teams in the country at

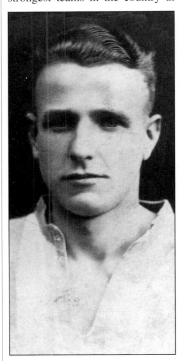

that time and, as an outside-right, the young and light 5ft 6ins Foulkes had to compete with the likes of Alex Jackson, the outstanding Scottish international winger. As a result, he was given a free-transfer and, having attended a practice match at Edgeley Park, signed for County at the age of 18 on 15 August 1932. Foulkes was a hardworking, quick and elusive winger, a brilliant crosser of the ball with the ability to score as well as provide goals. He was very much the right player at the right time for County, an integral part of a formidable attacking team which scored 214 League goals during Foulkes' first two seasons. A key player in the 13-0 defeat of Halifax Town (where, ironically, he finished his professional career), when asked why he hadn't scored more than one goal, the down-to-earth Yorkshireman said: "I just set 'em up for the other buggers." He played in the first Third Division North Challenge Cup Final against Darlington in May 1934, which County lost 4-3, and was adamant that he scored from a shot which went into the goal and came out but which the referee did not see. Foulkes made 162 appearances in his four seasons at Edgeley Park and scored 37 goals before he moved to Bradford (Park Avenue) for £2,000 in the summer of 1936. After two seasons at Park Avenue, he was transferred to Halifax Town where he had only one season as a result of the outbreak of war. He returned to Fryston and spent another 30 years as a miner although he continued to find and encourage young players. Jabez Foulkes retired in 1978 and lives in Airedale, near Castleford.

David Frain

Born Sheffield, 11 October 1962.
County League debut: v Torquay United (h), 19 August 1989.
As a schoolboy, David Frain played for Sheffield Boys as a winger, a position in which he played until beginning his professional career in earnest. Although signing schoolboy forms with Nottingham Forest, Frain was not offered apprenticeship forms, turning instead to gaining plumbing qualifications, football demoted to a weekend activity. At the age of 21, he signed for Dronfield United in the North East Counties League for whom he played until he was offered a trial by Sheffield United. Successfully completing a trial period, Frain signed professional forms in September 1985, eventually making his debut in March 1986. He spent the subsequent two years at Bramall Lane, appearing irregularly, before being released in 1988. Danny Bergara, who had been at Bramall Lane, believed he had successfully transformed Frain into a midfield player and,

when the Uruguayan accepted the manager's job at Rochdale, he immediately brought Frain to Spotland. A very popular player with the Rochdale supporters, in July 1989 Frain followed Bergara to County, signing on the same day as his Sheffield-born Spotland colleague, Chris Beaumont. By now a talented and skilful ball-playing midfielder, Frain's transfer was eventually decided by tribunal, the £50,000 fee almost doubling County's previous record fee. Again, like Beaumont, he was sidelined by injury shortly after his County debut, but his performances over the past five years have more than justified his cost. He has been an integral part of County's midfield, a major influence in County's success and, having taken over the captaincy in 1992, led his team out at Wembley twice in eight days. Seemingly out of favour prior to the beginning of the 1993-94 season, David Frain found himself back in the team and has now made 241 appearances for County. Although he has scored fewer goals than in his brief period at Rochdale, he maintains a high work-rate and is still capable of defence-splitting passes and exciting jinking runs into an opponent's penalty area.

Kevin Francis

Born Moseley, Birmingham, 6 December 1967.
County League debut: (substitute) v Lincoln City (a), 23 February 1991.
Kevin Francis has proved to be the most inspirational of Danny Bergara's signings, providing County supporters with their first-ever 'cult' figure. At 6ft 7ins, references to his height have become both inevitable and

tiresome, but the player who has provided a source of amusement for commentators and been subjected to derision from opposition supporters has responded in the most effective way possible. Excluding wartime football, the predictably nick-named 'Big Kev' has become only the third County player to have scored 100 goals, providing irrefutable evidence of Bergara's ability to transform players. A centre-half in his schooldays, he spent six months on a Youth Training Scheme to learn draughtsmanship before picking up casual work both as a doorman at a nightclub and as a hod-carrier. At 19, Francis's 56 goals for a local pub team led to him joining

Redditch in the Beazer Homes League. Following a move to Mile Oak Rovers, his impressive performances resulted in trials, first with Leicester City and then Derby County for whom he signed in February 1989. In the following two years, he was unable to gain a first-team place, making 13 substitute appearances for the Rams and scoring one goal in an FA Cup defeat by Port Vale, his last of only two full appearances coming in an FA Cup defeat at Newcastle. At the time of his £60,000 transfer to County in February 1991, it did not appear to be the best use of the club's limited resources as they pushed for promotion from the Fourth Division. The most ungainly looking of players, Francis's preparedness to work hard did not look as if it could compensate for a lack of co-ordination, his height proving little benefit to an apparent lack of ability in the air. However, driven on by County's coaching staff and his own ambition, Francis has become one

of the League's most formidable strikers, vastly improved in the air, surprisingly skilful on the ground and possessing remarkable speed. 26 goals in his first full season were followed by a post-war record of 39 goals in 1992-93. He is the only County player to have scored at Wembley (which he has done twice) and, whilst his all-round game has improved immeasurably over three years, his work-rate is quite phenomenal. Kevin Francis is now worth a huge amount of money, and supporters would find it difficult to accept his departure, his physique and style making him an irreplaceable figure.

Jim Fryatt

Born Southampton, 2 September 1940.
County League debut: v Southport (h), 30 October 1967†.
In his own way, Jim Fryatt was as instantly recognisable as Kevin Francis. The burly six-foot striker, with his balding head and huge bushy sideburns, was one of the most powerful headers of the ball of his era. Although he played for eight League clubs, three of them for two spells, he was a dedicated player, immensely strong and seemingly genuinely insulted when left on the ground by an opponent's tackle. Whatever the challenge, he would pick himself up like a boxer afraid of being counted out. Signed by Charlton Athletic at the age of 17, he made only five appearances in three seasons before signing for Southend United. 61 appearances and 24 goals later, he moved to Bradford (Park Avenue) in June 1963 before Southport paid £4,000

in March 1966 to take the now proven goalscorer to Haig Avenue. Twelve months later, £5,000 took Fryatt to Torquay United but County ensured his stay on the Devon Coast was a short one, paying £6,000 to bring him to Edgeley Park in October 1967. His debut came in a thrilling 4-3 encounter with a former club, Southport, Fryatt beginning a productive partnership with striker Bill Atkins. That season, he scored 22 goals in only 32 appearances, obtaining two hat-tricks in the process. With County looking a strong Third Division team, Fryatt's goalscoring brought attention from higher division clubs and, to the fans' disappointment, in October 1968 he was transferred to Blackburn Rovers for £30,000. The period at Ewood Park was Fryatt's least productive and, in February 1970, he moved on to Oldham Athletic, his 24 goals helping the Latics to promotion in his first full season at Boundary Park. His last three moves all involved a return to former clubs: Southport, who he helped to the Fourth Division championship in 1972-73, County, where he scored his last League goal in his one game, and Torquay United, where he finished his League career, only two games short of 500 League appearances. Jim Fryatt had amassed an impressive 189 League goals including one for Bradford which is still credited as being the fastest ever, coming only four seconds after the kick-off.

Jim Gannon

Born Southwark, 7 September 1968.
County League debut: v Wrexham (h), 9 March 1990.
Of Irish parentage, English-born Jim Gannon moved to Dublin with his family at the age of 15. As a centre-half he played in an All Ireland Schools Final and an Irish

FA Youth Cup Final before signing for Dundalk in 1985. In his three year spell with the Irish club, he experienced playing in the European Cup against Red Star Belgrade before buying himself out of the Irish Permanent Defence Force in order to complete a £50,000 move to Sheffield United in April 1989. Unable to break into the first team, Gannon did not make his League debut until a brief loan period with Halifax Town gave him the opportunity in February 1990. Within weeks, County paid £70,000 for the defender but Gannon's first nine months were not particularly happy ones as he failed to impress the supporters. Manager Bergara kept faith with Gannon whose versatility in being able to play in a defensive midfield role or in a position behind the back four resulted in him performing with increased confidence. Having won over the supporters, Gannon became a real favourite, winning awards at the end of every season. Although primarily a defensive player, his ability to get on to the scoresheet has been remarkable with him already 12th in County's list of leading goalscorers. A quiet individual off the field, Jim Gannon has now appeared in 220 games for County and scored 49 goals.

Fred Garrett

Born Stanton Hill, Nottinghamshire, 1889.
County League debut: v Preston North End (a), 2 September 1912.
Signed from Notts County in July 1912, his consistent performances as a centre-half saw him take over the captaincy during his first season at Edgeley Park. He was a keen and intelligent player, popular with the supporters and a loyal servant of the club, enjoying a benefit in 1921 with the wholehearted Albert Waterall and talented Jimmy Mitton. Garrett spent nine consecutive seasons with County, four of them playing in wartime football. By the time League football resumed in 1919, he had been successfully converted into a left-back, partnered by the ever reliable Tommy Robson. Although this position restricted some of the goalscoring opportunities he had enjoyed in his first season, he was a totally dependable full-back, eventually ending his professional career in 1921 when County were relegated from the Second Division, having made 143 League and Cup appearances to which can be added 73 appearances in wartime football.

Ernie Gault

Born Wallsend, 1889.
County League debut: v Birmingham (a), 3 September 1913†.
Although not a regular member of First Division Everton's team, Ernie Gault proved to be an important capture for County in 1913. A small but clever centre-

forward, skilful, fast and with a good shot, he quickly formed a productive partnership with the young Norman Rodgers. He begun his career as a junior with Jarrow Caledonians in the Northern League before being signed by Everton. After scoring 21 goals in 65 appearances for County in peacetime football, his scoring in wartime football was remarkable. Having scored 32 goals in 53 appearances for County, he returned to Goodison for the remainder of the war where he scored an astonishing 86 goals in 68 games. On the resumption of League football, Gault stayed on at Everton until the summer of 1920 before joining County's old manager, Fred Stewart, at Cardiff. With County struggling at the foot of the Second Division, Gault was persuaded to return to Edgeley Park in December 1920 but injury restricted him to only 13 League appearances and County were relegated. At 32, his experience was of critical importance in 1921-22 and, despite a 28 day suspension, he played a major part in County's Third Division (North) championship success. After scoring 33 goals in 107 appearances during his two spells, Ernie Gault finally retired from professional football.

Charlie Gee

Born Reddish, Stockport, 1909. Died 1981.
County League debut: v Halifax

Town (h), 26 October 1929.
Charlie Gee remains a prime example of some of the high-class players from the lower divisions whose skill would remain unrecognised at a national level without a move to a big club. It is inconceivable that he would have played for England two years after his County debut had he remained at Edgeley Park. The Reddish youngster, whom County signed in 1928, waited a year for his debut and played 25 League games in County's Third Division runners-up team of 1929-30. Everton clearly recognised his potential, signing the inexperienced centre-half in July 1930. Gee made his Goodison debut on 1 January 1931 only because of an injury to Everton's regular centre-half, Tommy Griffiths. When he scored in his first game, his meteoric rise was perhaps inevitable. Alongside former County favourite Eddie Critchley, Gee won consecutive Second and First Division championship medals with Everton, and within ten months of his debut won the first of three caps for England against Wales. A totally committed centre-half who concentrated on mastering the elementary, he became a highly popular player at Goodison, although a cartilage operation in 1932 restricted him to seven appearances that season and kept him out of Everton's FA Cup-winning side. Although he remained at Everton until the outbreak of war, he was unable to recapture the form he had shown prior to his operation. Having made 211 League and Cup appearances for the Toffees, he retired from football in 1940, but not before he had returned to County in 1939 'guesting' for three remarkable games in which his old club scored 15 goals and conceded 13.

Fred Goodwin

Born Stockport, 6 January 1944.
County League debut: v Wrexham (h), 14 January 1966.
After playing for Stockport Boys at 13 and representing Cheshire Boys as a winger two years later, Goodwin joined the groundstaff at Wolves before signing professional forms on his 17th birthday. He made his debut in the strong Wolves team of the early 1960s and was selected to play for the England Youth team against West Germany in March 1962. However, Wolves refused to release him as their own youth team were in the semi-final of the Youth Cup. Freddie Goodwin was thus denied the opportunity of

representing his country and although Wolves reached the Youth Cup Final, they were beaten 2-0 by Newcastle United. Developed into a half-back, Goodwin made 44 League appearances for Wolves before, unable to command a first-team place, he asked for a move. County picked him up on a free transfer on 14 January 1966 and over the following four and a half seasons, Goodwin gave wonderful service to the club, literally playing in every position. In February 1968, he replaced the injured Alan Ogley in goal at Orient and, against the same opponents the following season, scored four goals playing as an emergency striker following Jim Fryatt's departure to Blackburn Rovers. In March 1970, with County condemned to relegation, the industrious Goodwin was transferred to Blackburn after making 206 League and Cup appearances. After two seasons at Ewood Park, Goodwin had brief spells with Southport and Port Vale before returning to County at the beginning of the 1974-75 season to complete 200 League appearances for the Hatters before retiring from League football. Goodwin had already acquired his full coaching badge and after moving around non-League circles in various capacities, he emigrated to New Zealand. He spent 13 years coaching club sides and was assistant coach to the national team before returning to Stockport in November 1993.

Ralph Goodwin

Born Hanley, Stoke-on-Trent, 1887.
County League debut: v Leeds City (a), 17 April 1908.
Although not born in Stockport, Ralph Goodwin became an 'honorary Hatter', spending 13 seasons with County, developing into a unflappable right-back, and being sought by a number of other clubs. County had no desire to part with Goodwin and *vice-versa*; indeed by the time he had completed five seasons at County, he was quoted as saying he "would not leave the Edgeley Park Brigade for a pension." A quiet and reliable player, his best seasons were those when he was partnered by Stephen Fagan and then Tommy Robson. He made 188 League and Cup appearances for County and played throughout the war, making a further 136 appearances. On the resumption of League football, he did have a brief spell with Preston North End, making seven appearances before returning to County on 30 September 1920. He made only one further appearance, in December 1920, which, ironically, was in his birthplace against Port Vale. In his long career at Edgeley Park, he was never on the scoresheet, retiring to the athletic outfitter's business he had first acquired in 1912.

Tommy Green

Born Rock Ferry, 25 November 1883.
County debut: (Lancashire Combination) v Southport Central (h), 2 September 1904†; (FA Cup) v Stalybridge Rovers, 29 October 1904; (League) v Blackpool (h), 2 September 1907.
After making Football League appearances for Liverpool and Southern League appearances for Swindon Town, County signed the

20-year-old centre-forward in the summer of 1904 following their failure to gain re-election. The young forward was an instant success, scoring 16 goals in 23 first-team appearances but, as a result of County's financial problems, on 11 February 1905 he was reluctantly sold to First Division Middlesbrough for £300 only five weeks after Tommy Brittleton had moved to Sheffield. Tommy Green remained at Ayresome Park for a little over a year before moving on to Queen's Park Rangers. Unfortunately, unlike Brittleton, he was not able to fulfil the exciting potential he had displayed at County and in July 1907 he returned to Edgeley Park. Although a crowd favourite, sadly he could not recapture his goalscoring touch, moving to outside-right during his second spell. After scoring 16 goals in 70 League and Cup appearances for County, he moved to Exeter City in July 1909 before finishing his career with Preston.

John Griffiths

Born Oldbury, 16 June 1951.
County League debut: v Peterborough United (h), 15 August 1971.
An all-round sportsman, John Griffiths played cricket for Worcestershire boys, was a cross-country runner, won medals at swimming and played football for Worcester Boys. On leaving school, Griffiths began training to be a draughtsman before signing

apprentice forms with Aston Villa in November 1968. In spite of finishing top scorer in Villa's reserve team two years running, the blond centre-forward was restricted to only three first-team appearances, two as substitute. Peter Broadbent, the former Wolves and England international, had joined County in 1969; he had helped Griffiths whilst they were both at Villa Park and recommended the 19-year-old to County who signed him in June 1970. Although he made his debut in August, Griffiths did not open his goalscoring account for 34 matches. He spent much of the following season playing in the unaccustomed role of left winger which did not help him recapture his earlier potential as a goalscorer. Griffiths' third season saw him revert back to a central striking position and he ended the season as top scorer. In his five seasons at the club, John Griffiths made 201 League and Cup appearances, scoring 31 goals before being released in May 1975. Whilst his record shows that he hardly enjoyed a chequered career, it should be viewed in the context of County's fortunes during his stay. These were difficult times for the Edgeley Park club and Griffiths never shirked responsibility, was a constantly committed trier and frequently demonstrated that, had he enjoyed the benefit of playing in a more successful team, he could well have achieved a great deal more than he did.

Tommy Hall

Born Stockport, 1874.
County debut: (Lancashire League) v Rossendale (h), 21 September 1896†; (FA Cup) v Barnton Rovers (h), 31 October 1896; (League) v Chesterfield Town, 18 October 1902.
Tommy 'Bute' Hall was a great servant of County over an 11-year period. Joining County in their pre-League days, he was a dedicated player, guaranteed to give unquestioning commitment in every game in which he participated. Primarily a right-half, he was a permanent fixture in County's attempts to build a side capable of entering League football. From 1896, he played over 100 games in the Lancashire League, inspiring County to the championship in 1900 and seeing them elected to the Football League. 'Bute' Hall took no part in County's first season in League football, having been transferred to Glossop for whom he made 52 appearances. However, on 8 October 1902, he was re-signed and went on to make 97 League and Cup appearances, remaining with County on their return to non-League football in 1904. He amassed a total of 133 appearances in County's non-League days and participated in 21 FA Cup matches, a record bettered by only five other County players. His loyalty to the club, which had surprisingly released him in 1900, was finally rewarded in 1907 by a benefit match, a well-merited

tribute to a thoroughly professional player.

Tony Hancock

Born Manchester, 31 January 1967.
County League debut (substitute) v Torquay United (a), 26 December 1988.

Although his League career lasted no more than 12 months, Tony Hancock appeared to be destined for great things. The speed of his rise to celebrity status was astonishing as he moved from Sunday football to League soccer in a matter of weeks. A regular goalscorer at Stockport Georgians,

his flair and confidence led to regular recommendations to County who finally gave him a trial and had him training with the reserves. After three appearances with County's reserves in December 1988, he spent two days training with the first team who he accompanied to Torquay on Boxing Day. Hancock had five minutes as a substitute in a eminently forgettable match in which County had two players sent off. Another away substitute appearance followed on New Year's Eve before, on 2 January, Edgeley Park rapturously greeted the aptly named 'Hancock's half-hour'. With County leading Exeter City 2-0 and 30 minutes left, Hancock replaced Tony Caldwell. Lack of experience did not affect him as, full of confidence, he demonstrated his precocious talent, thrilling the near 3,000 crowd with a stunning diving header, helping County to a 4-0 win. The HGV driver for his father's haulage business was an instant success, making 22 appearances, ten as substitute, and scoring five goals before the season's end. There was no doubt that Hancock was gifted and that,

with appropriate nurturing, he could have developed into a very special player. Disappointingly, on Danny Bergara's arrival in March 1989, County had an abundance of strikers and in June, the club accepted Burnley's £50,000 offer for him. After 21 appearances for the Clarets (ten as substitute), on 1 January 1991, Lancashire rivals Preston North End paid £50,000 to take Hancock to Deepdale on a two and a half year contract. Before he had played a match for North End, Hancock broke his leg during training which, sadly, effectively put an end to his professional career. In addition to six months spent in Australia with Brisbane United, he has had spells in non-League football with Northwich Victoria, Woodley and Caernarfon. Tony Hancock still lives in Reddish, having now established his own courier company

Harry Hardy

Born Stockport, 14 January 1895.
Died Stockport, 17 February 1969
County League debut: v Cardiff City (a), 4 September 1920.

A product of the well-known local Ward Street Boys, Harry Hardy has remained in the record books throughout County's history as the only player to win an England international cap whilst with Stockport. Whether he was County's best-ever goalkeeper is debatable, but he was undoubtedly one of County's most consistent performers in his five and a half

seasons at Edgeley Park. Having made his debut in September 1920, he made 170 consecutive League appearances, his omission in the 171st game a result of his selection for the Football League against the Irish League on 11

October 1924. A little over eight weeks later he made his one full international appearance against Belgium at The Hawthorns, a match which England won 4-0. In March 1925, he was selected for a Football League representative tour of Australia, thus missing the end of County's League season. Arriving back in London on 31 August, he was expected to return immediately and play against The Wednesday the same day which he duly did but, two months later, his undoubted talents were finally recognised by First Division Everton who signed him for £2,350 on 29 October 1925. He was immediately drafted into Everton's first team but made only six appearances in their 1928 championship team before being transferred to Bury on 3 July. Between 1929 and 1931, Harry Hardy made 27 League appearances for The Shakers before retiring. An accomplished oboist, he spent 13 years as a professional musician.

Paul Hart

Born Golborne, 4 May 1953.
County League debut: v Lincoln City (h), 9 October 1970.

Son of Johnny Hart, the Manchester City inside-forward, Paul Hart was a keen footballer and cricketer, representing Manchester Boys in both sports. At 16, he wrote to a number of

clubs for trials, spending three months at Preston North End before a successful trial period at Edgeley Park resulted in him signing professional forms for County in Spetember 1970. As a 17-year-old, Hart made nine

appearances in his first season and scored his first League goal. The following two seasons saw Hart as a regular in County's first team and, despite being in a poor side, he grew in stature with the inevitable result that he was sold. In June 1973, for the small sum of £25,000, Second Division Blackpool bought the highly promising 20-year-old defender who had already made 100 League and Cup appearances. Although he took time to settle at Bloomfield Road, he established himself in his second season, and his reputation grew. Having made 156 appearances for Blackpool, in March 1978, Leeds United paid £300,000 for Hart to replace Gordon McQueen who had crossed the Pennines to Old Trafford. In his last game for Blackpool at the end of February, the Seasiders were in eighth place; seven weeks later they were relegated. With Leeds United, Hart had another five-year spell and became recognised as one of the country's strongest defenders. After 219 League and Cup appearances with Leeds and 18 goals, two more than he had scored with Blackpool, Hart joined Brian Clough's Nottingham Forest where he stayed for two seasons before moving on to Sheffield Wednesday in June 1985. After 52 appearances with the Owls, Hart was transferred to Birmingham City in December 1986 where a broken leg restricted him to a single appearance. Paul Hart retired in May 1988 after finishing his career with Notts County, having made well over 600 League and Cup appearances, but within six months he had been offered and had accepted the manager's post at Chesterfield. The Spireites had only managed two wins and on Hart's arrival were well adrift at the foot of Division Three. The fighting character Hart had shown as a player was transmitted to the team who almost brought about a miraculous escape, but two defeats in the last two games of the season saw Chesterfield relegated. In the following season, Hart took Chesterfield to the Fourth Division Play-off Final after his club defeated County 6-0 in the two-legged semi-final. After dominating Cambridge United at Wembley, they were beaten by a late goal and this disappointment was followed by a dismal season. With Chesterfield winning only three League games by the end of January, Hart suffered the predictable fate. A brief playing spell at Grantham was succeeded by coaching positions at two of his former clubs, Nottingham Forest and Leeds United.

Billy Haydock

Born Salford, 19 January 1937.
County League debut: v Chester (a), 21 August 1965.

After playing for Eccles Boys as an inside-forward, Haydock was offered terms by Blackpool, but wishing to complete his apprenticeship as a motor engineer, he joined non-League Buxton. He was spotted by Manchester City who, in March 1959, paid Buxton £2,500, a record for the Derbyshire club. After only three

appearances in two and a half years at Maine Road, former County player Jimmy McGuigan paid £7,000 to take Haydock and team-mate Jim Pennington to Crewe Alexandra. Although Haydock's preferred position was half-back, he was classed as a 'utility' player, showing his excellent all-round ability by playing as an inside-forward or full-back, scoring 30 goals in his 142 League appearances. When McGuigan took the manager's job at Grimsby Town, Haydock followed him for a fee of £5,000. After only 21 games and four goals at Grimsby, both County and Oldham Athletic showed interest in signing him but, in August 1965, £4,000 brought him to Edgeley Park where the industrious 28-year-old Haydock spent six seasons. He was successfully switched to right-back and played a key role in County's Fourth Division championship winning team of 1967. Missing only two League matches

in five seasons, Haydock remained loyal to County, seeing the club through its bad times as well as its brief successful period. When he was finally released by County in May 1971, he had amassed 287 League and Cup appearances which, to date, has only been surpassed by 11 Stockport players. After playing and coaching at Port Elizabeth in South Africa, Haydock saw out his English playing career with Southport before retiring at the age of 35. He then opened a guest house in Blackpool, where he still lives, still retaining his links with the game as physiotherapist to the Seasiders. After being promoted to first-team coach, Haydock took the manager's job at ASK Vikinger in Iceland, followed by a move to ASK Tromso in Norway. He then linked up with Eamonn O'Keefe, the former Everton player, for a three-year spell as coach to Cork City in Ireland. In 1988, he returned briefly to Edgeley Park as physiotherapist under Asa Hartford and, when the former County manager moved on to Shrewsbury Town, Haydock followed him as coach. On Hartford's dismissal from Gay Meadow, Haydock left Shrewsbury to coach in Norway and then in Canada. When Hartford joined Kenny Dalglish at Blackburn Rovers, Haydock moved to Ewood Park as second-team physiotherapist whilst also carrying out scouting work.

Alex Herd

Born Bowhill, near Selkirk, 8 November 1911. Died Dumfries, 1982.
County League debut: v Darlington (h), 20 March 1948.

Alex Herd was the younger of two footballing brothers, the older, Andrew, having played for Hearts and Scotland. A highly talented ball-playing inside-forward, Herd joined Hamilton Academical before signing for Manchester City on 1 February 1933. Herd's period at Maine Road was immensely successful as City reached the FA Cup Final in his first season, losing to Everton before returning in 1934 to lift the trophy in a 2-1 win against Portsmouth. As the City team grew stronger, the influential Scot played a major part in their First Division championship win of 1936-37, the season in which their Old Trafford rivals were relegated. However, in true City fashion, the League title was followed the next season by relegation to the Second Division, despite the fact that they were the leading scorers in

Division One. Their fall from grace was compounded by United being promoted in the same season and although in the last peacetime

season City continued their attractive football, finishing as the top-scoring team for the third year running, they failed to gain promotion. Herd's contribution to City's attacking flair was rewarded on the resumption of League football, City being promoted back into Division One. In his 15 years at Maine Road, Alex Herd made 290 League and Cup appearances and scored 124 goals before moving to County on 17 March 1948. He had made one guest appearance for County in March 1946 although nine of his 51 goals in wartime football had been against Stockport. Despite being 36, Herd proved an invaluable acquisition for County, with no less skill or vision than in his younger days. He motivated County in their historic FA Cup run of 1949-50, playing in all six ties, scoring four goals, including one in their unfortunate fifth round defeat against Liverpool. Herd continued playing until shortly after his 40th birthday, his last appearance being on Christmas Day 1951. He had scored a more than respectable 41 goals in 119 League and Cup appearances and thoroughly enjoyed the oft-quoted distinction of having partnered son David on his debut in the last match of 1950-51. After his football career ended, Alex Herd worked as a sales representative for an asphalt company before retiring to his native Scotland.

David Herd

Born Hamilton, 15 April 1934.
County League debut: v

Hartlepools United (h), 5 May 1951†.

Although Alex Herd was living in Manchester, his wife returned to Hamilton for son David's birth so ensuring Herd Junior's eligibility for Scotland. The young David Herd represented Manchester Boys before becoming a member of County's youth team. On leaving school, he worked in a textile company office until he was 17 when he became a professional at County, scoring on his debut two weeks later against Hartlepools United when he formed a right-wing partnership with his father. At the age of 18, National Service with the RAF interrupted his career but, whilst playing at Catterick with Albert Quixall and Dennis Viollet, Herd was already developing his footballing skills, gaining a reputation as a hard-shooting forward. In spite of making only a handful of League appearances, considerable attention was focussed on him. It appeared that Herd would move to Manchester United in a part-exchange deal involving wing-half Bill McGlen but the proposed move fell through when McGlen chose to join Lincoln City. On the day 6ft David Herd was demobbed from the RAF, he was met by Arsenal manager, Tom Whittaker. It was rumoured that when Whittaker asked County how much they were in debt and was told "£10,000", he promptly wrote out a cheque for that amount. Whether or not purely anecdotal, on 24 August 1954, 20-year-old Herd was transferred to Arsenal for precisely that sum, having played only 15 games and scored six goals. Herd was slowly introduced into the Arsenal first team and in his seven seasons at Highbury, he played 180 League and Cup games and scored 107 goals. Whilst not gaining any honours with Arsenal, he did gain the first of five Scottish international caps in 1959. Seven years after his proposed move to Old Trafford had fallen through, Matt Busby finally signed Herd on 26 July 1961 and it was with United that he enjoyed his greatest achievements. He scored twice in United's 3-1 FA Cup Final victory against Leicester City and this was followed by two First Division championship wins in 1965 and 1967. The latter was spoiled by Herd suffering a broken leg in March, an injury from which he never quite recovered. He played irregularly in the following season, missing United's European Cup success against Benfica at Wembley in 1968. Two months later, he signed for Stoke City on a free transfer, having scored 144 goals in 263 appearances for the Reds. Torn ligaments restricted his appearances at Stoke to 44 League games and 11 goals in his two seasons at the Victoria Ground. Following a failed comeback attempt with Waterford, Herd finally gave up playing in 1971 but was offered the manager's job at Lincoln City in March of the same year. His first full season was successful, Lincoln narrowly failing to gain promotion by one point, but in December 1972 he was replaced by Graham Taylor. Following his dismissal, David Herd left football for good, concentrating upon running a garage business he bought in Urmston in 1964 and which he still runs.

Joe Hill

Born Sheffield, 1906.
County League debut: v Carlisle United (a), 26 December 1933†.
Joe Hill began his career at Leeds United but did not make a League appearance until he moved to Barnsley in 1931. He made only eight appearances and scored three goals for the Oakwell club before moving to Queen's Park Rangers in the summer of 1932. Moving between wing-half and inside-right, Hill was not a regular in his one season with Rangers, scoring once in his 16 League and Cup appearances. He joined County in July 1933, but although he waited over four months before making his first appearance, he had the unique experience of making his home debut in the 13-0 match against Halifax Town in which he scored a hat-trick. Even this did not result in a regular place and it was not until Hill's second season that his County career blossomed. Establishing himself as County's regular inside-right, Hill, whilst not a selfish player, was an individualist, a clever dribbler with the ability to find space where he could unleash a splendid shot. His contributions to the team were substantial. In 1935, he scored the winning goal in three of the four FA Cup rounds to take County into the fifth round for the first time. In County's Third Division championship team of 1937, Hill was the only forward who had played in the Halifax match and, in addition to finishing as top scorer in that season, scored the crucial first goal in the memorable last game of the season against Lincoln City. In his five seasons at Edgeley Park, Joe Hill had an excellent return of 71 goals

in 154 League and Cup appearances, a particularly fine achievement for a player who was not regarded primarily as a goalscorer. After failing to secure a regular place in County's Second Division side, on 13 August 1938, Joe Hill was transferred to Walsall where, as with Barnsley, he made only eight appearances, scoring once before retiring from professional football in 1939. He returned to his native Yorkshire where he worked as an assistant to a bookmaker.

Ken Hodder

Born Stockport, 20 August 1930.
County League debut: v Halifax Town (a), 24 March 1952.
A solid and dependable centre-half, Ken Hodder was one of a small number of post-war players to spend his entire career at one club. On leaving school at 14, Hodder began an apprenticeship in decorating and sign-writing until commencing his National Service in 1949, joining the RAF. The previous year, Hodder signed for County as an amateur, captaining

the youth team that year, before becoming a part-time professional on 28 March 1949. He had to wait until 1952 to make his League debut but it was not until 1955-56 that he became a regular choice. Early in 1957-58, Hodder lost his place and it was a credit to his perseverance that he eventually managed to return to the team almost exactly two years later. Ironically, his return was the start of his best spell as he made 101 consecutive League and Cup appearances during which he scored the only goal of his career, a penalty which defeated Don-

caster Rovers on 27 December 1961. In September 1963, Hodder suffered a double fracture of his right leg in a reserve game at Middlesbrough and, on this occasion, there was no way back for the player who had been registered with County for 15 years and who had made 272 League and Cup appearances. By this time a qualified coach, Hodder remained at Edgeley Park helping the apprentices. In 1965, he left to start his own decorating business which he ran until 1974 when he accepted a job as a joiner in Dawlish. Having retired in 1990, Ken Hodder still lives on the Devon coast.

Bill Holden

Born Bolton, 1 April 1928.
County League debut: v Crewe Alexandra (a), 27 October 1956.
After spending his National Service in the Military Police, Bill Holden worked for a Radcliffe company where he was spotted playing for the works team. Although a trial with Everton was unsuccessful, he was recom-

mended to Burnley who signed him in November 1949. From the time he made his debut in September 1950, he was the Clarets' regular centre-forward for five years and scored 79 goals in 199 League and Cup appearances. During his period at Turf Moor, Holden twice played for England 'B'. When, in September 1955, Holden lost his place, he asked for a transfer and in December was signed by Sunderland for £12,000. He made his debut at St James' Park on Boxing Day in front of over 61,000 fans, and although Holden scored after four minutes, Sunderland were beaten 3-1. He did not score in his next nine games and, following a dispute with the management, he was

transfer-listed after making only 19 appearances and scoring five goals. It was a major coup for the Edgeley Park club when Holden agreed to join County for a bargain £6,000, signing on 26 October 1956. During his two and a half year stay at County, the club did not attain the consistency to maintain a serious challenge for promotion, but enjoyed an excellent FA Cup run in Holden's only full season, the forward scoring twice in the 3-0 demolition of First Division Luton Town. In the same season, he was County's top scorer but in March 1959 he joined Bury in a part-exchange deal which brought Jimmy Reid and Bill Ritchie to Edgeley Park. Bill Holden had scored 40 goals in 96 appearances for County and following his departure, a disastrous run saw the club sink into the Fourth Division. Over the next three seasons, Holden made over 100 appearances and scored 33 goals for the Gigg Lane club before moving to his last club, Halifax Town, in the close season of 1962. Having scored 11 goals in 37 appearances, Holden retired from League football in 1963 although he continued to play non-League football with Rugby Town and Hereford United. A variety of jobs followed the end of his football career, Holden running a driving school, becoming a chauffeur, owning a coffee-bar and newsagents, running the recreation centre at Lancaster University, working for the DHSS and buying a guest house. Contrary to published football record-books, 'reports of his death are grossly exaggerated'; Bill Holden is alive and well, living in the Morecambe area.

Arnold Jackson

Born Manchester, 10 November 1925.
County League debut: v Carlisle United (h), 21 August 1954.
In his nine year League career, Arnold Jackson made over 300 appearances with only two clubs, Shrewsbury Town and County. By the time he signed for Shrewsbury, Jackson had spent his footballing days playing non-League football and, at 25, it appeared as though his chance of enjoying a professional career had disappeared. However, the goalscoring inside-forward took his opportunity at Gay Meadow. A regular choice during his four seasons, he scored 40 goals in 144 League appearances. With the inevitable departure of David Herd, County were in need of a goalscoring forward to partner Jack Connor

and, on 19 June 1954, Jackson was signed. As County already had the skilful inside-right, Eddie Moran, Jackson's signing allowed inside-left, Frank Clempson, to drop back to left-half and gave an altogether better balance to the team. Jackson was not always an automatic choice, as he had periods when he had to compete with Willie Moir and Bill Holden, but was to give the club excellent service in his five seasons at Edgeley Park. Although constantly in the shadow of the legendary Jack Connor, Jackson managed virtually a goal every three games, scoring 52 times in his 162 League and Cup appearances, tenth in County's leading scorers until Andy Preece overtook him in 1994.

Fred Jenkinson
Born Chapeltown, Sheffield, 1910.
County League debut v Doncaster Rovers (a), 29 August 1931.
Third in the leading number of appearances for pre-war County, Fred Jenkinson developed into one

of the finest full-backs in their history. Widely regarded as the classiest full-back in the Northern Section, Jenkinson was quick, skilful and a brilliant tackler. After leaving Barnsley Grammar School, he followed his father down the mines whilst playing local football with Intake WMC. He had trials with Sheffield United and Huddersfield Town, where he spent 12 months as an amateur, but it was from Intake that County signed him on 30 December 1930. His debut season was spent covering both full-back positions when established players were injured but, from the beginning of 1932-33, he became an automatic selection until the last season before the war. He played in the free-scoring County team of the early 1930s and missed only one game in their promotion season, although in 1934 he was nearly transferred to Wolves in a deal which would have taken Alf Lythgoe and himself to Molineux. Much to the relief of County fans, Jenkinson preferred to stay at Edgeley Park and the double-transfer fell through. The immaculate defender made 295 League and Cup appearances and scored only once, the first goal in a 3-2 Second Division game against Spurs in front of over 19,000 spectators at Edgeley Park. When his footballing career was over, Fred Jenkinson moved to Bournemouth where he opened a guest house.

Jack Jobson
Born Washington, County Durham, 1903.
County League debut: v Rotherham United (h), 27 August 1927.
An excellent example of the best type of lower division centre-halves, Jack Jobson was a totally committed player who could be relied upon to fight until the final whistle of every game. He began his career with Plymouth Argyle before returning to the North-East to Hartlepools United, where he made 29 League appearances in 1926-27 before joining County on 3 June 1927. County's first choice centre-half for each of his five seasons, his first four years were spent watching his forwards scoring a staggering 399 League goals as the team finished runners-up in consecutive seasons. After making 181 League and Cup appearances and scoring seven goals, Jobson was freed in June 1932 and moved to Queen's Park Rangers. He made only four appearances for Rangers in 1932-33 before a further transfer took him back once more to the North-

East. Jack Jobson spent the last season of his League career at Gateshead with whom he played eight times.

Billy Johnston
Born Edinburgh, 16 January 1901.
Died Salford, November 1964.
County League debut: v Middlesbrough (a), 20 December 1924.
After playing part-time football for Selby, Billy Johnston was signed by First Division Huddersfield Town in November 1920, shortly before Town were to achieve a hat-trick of championships. A wonderfully gifted inside-forward, Johnston had made 50 appearances and scored seven goals for Huddersfield before a fee of £1,500 brought him to County in time to make a joint-debut with

Bob Blood at Ayresome Park. Johnston was handicapped by injuries and inconsistency in his first two seasons, but 1926-27 saw the clever inside-right become an automatic choice, quickly forming an understanding with young centre-forward Harry Burgess in a partnership which, between them, produced 53 League goals. The arrival of the legendary Bolton captain, Joe Smith, late in the season provided County with considerable optimism but the partnership of Johnston, Burgess and Smith was short-lived. On 14 October 1927, Billy Johnston made the short move to Manchester United for £3,000, having scored 27 times in his 74 League and Cup appearances. He went straight into the Old Trafford team, making his debut the day

after he signed, but after two seasons he was transferred to Macclesfield in 1929. Following United's relegation in 1931, Johnston returned to Old Trafford and, by the time he left for good in May 1932, he had an almost identical record to his period at County, having scored 27 goals in 71 appearances. His last League club was Oldham Athletic where he remained for three years, concentrating on being a provider rather than a scorer of goals. When Billy Johnston left Boundary Park in June 1935, he had made 67 appearances for the Latics, scoring seven times. He became player-manager of Frickley Colliery until his retirement from the game in 1936. He became a publican in Manchester before moving to North Wales to run a guest house. Billy Johnston returned to the North-West, running a pub in Salford until his death.

Len Jones
Born Birkenhead, 1910.
County League debut: v Halifax Town (a), 2 September 1933.
Although English by birth, Len Jones was only two weeks old when his family moved back to Holywell in North Wales, which explains why the steady defender twice played in amateur

internationals for Wales. His football career began with his local team, Holywell, before moving to Flint. He then spent eight months, still as an amateur, with Huddersfield Town before joining Rhyl. It was whilst back in North Wales that he won his Welsh caps. After being watched by scouts, Jones signed for County on 10 May 1933. His spent his first season with County playing at left-half before making the centre-half position his own in the autumn of 1934. He was as consistent as his contemporary, Fred Jenkinson, although lacking the style of the right-back. After missing only three games in three years, his last two seasons at County were affected by leg injuries, but he still played in virtually half the League matches. When the war finished his professional career, he had made 226 League and Cup appearances and, like Jenkinson, scored only once, Jones' goal coming in a vital 2-1 win at Gresty Road at the end of County's championship season in 1937. After retiring from football, Len Jones returned to live in Rhyl.

Fred Kenny
Born Manchester, 14 January 1923. Died, 1985.
County League debut: v Gateshead (h), 25 September 1948.
A two-footed player who was equally at home in either full-back position, Fred Kenny had a brief spell with Manchester City but, unable to break into their first team, moved to Edgeley Park in December 1947. When he eventually held a regular place in the latter part of the 1948-49 season, he was seen as having the potential 'to become another Fred Jenkinson'. The following season, Kenny was badly injured and only played in the first round of County's famous FA Cup run. It was a great credit to his fitness and determination that, having played only five games in two years, he succeeded in winning his place back in 1951, a season in which he was an ever-present, forming an excellent partnership with future England full-back Ron Staniforth. His achievements were all the more creditable as he remained a part-time professional whilst first being a labourer and then representing a Manchester wholesale grocery company as a salesman. Although failing to live up to his 'new Fred Jenkinson' tag, he was a thoroughly reliable player, completing 214 appearances by the time he played his final game, an FA Cup tie against New Brighton in November 1956. Kenny had a brief spell as manager of Cheadle Town whilst maintaining a job outside football until he died from a heart-attack in 1985.

Andy Kilner
Born Bolton, 11 October 1966.
County League debut: (substitute) v Gillingham (h), 1 January 1991.
Although an enigmatic player whose last League appearance for County came as substitute a year to the day after making his debut, Kilner's presence during the run-in to the club's promotion from

Division Four was crucial. As a teenager, he was an excellent all-round sportsman, playing football for Salford Boys and the England Youth team, cricket for the English Schools and was a 200 metre record-holder whilst at school. He joined Burnley as an apprentice in 1983, making only five appearances, three as substitute in his two year stay. After he was released at Turf Moor, he went to

Sweden and played for Halmia until 1987, scoring 31 goals in 51 appearances. Recovered from a broken leg suffered in 1988, he joined Vanersborg in 1989 where he scored 18 goals in 21 appearances before moving on to Jonsered, scoring 20 goals in 36 appearances. When the Swedish season finished in the early winter of 1990, he wrote to the *Manchester Evening News* to ask for a piece to appear requesting a club with whom he could train. County coach, John Sainty, contacted Kilner who played in the reserves and, after his first full appearance on 4 January 1991 at Edgeley Park when he scored twice, he was offered an 18 month contract. Quickly establishing himself as a crowd favourite, Kilner added an extra dimension to the County team, almost an old-fashioned left winger with the ability to run at players and turn them, possessing a rasping shot and able to launch long throws in to the danger area. He scored 12 goals, 11 of them in the League during County's dramatic run-in to the season, in only 26 appearances. With County in

Division Three for the first time in 21 years, Kilner started the following season as he had ended his first but then went through a bad run and was unable to maintain his place. Loan spells with Rochdale and Bury did not prove fruitful and after 49 appearances for County, 11 as substitute, Andy Kilner took a job in sales and marketing with the *Bolton Evening News* whilst playing non-League football with Witton Albion, Chorley and Radcliffe Borough.

Ian Lawther
Born Belfast, 20 October 1939.
County League debut: v Crewe Alexandra (a), 14 August 1971.
Although 31 when he joined County, Ian Lawther was still able to give valuable service to the club for five seasons whether playing as a traditional striker or a central defender. Two and a half years into his apprenticeship as a printer, Lawther was playing with Crusaders when he was spotted by

Sunderland for whom he signed in March 1958. The 18-year-old immediately experienced relegation with his new club as Sunderland became the last First Division team to lose their premier status. In a three year stay at Roker Park, Lawther came to prominence when he finished top goalscorer in his last two seasons. Having scored 41 goals in 75 League matches and made two of his four international appearances, in July 1961 he was transferred to Blackburn Rovers where he remained for two years, making 59 League appearances and scoring 21 goals. An almost identical record followed at his third club,

Scunthorpe United, before he joined Brentford in November 1964, reputedly the only player ever to sign for a club in the House of Commons (Brentford's chairman being an MP). Lawther spent almost four seasons at Griffin Park, adding another 43 goals in 139 appearances, before moving to Halifax Town in August 1968. In his first season, he helped The Shay club to their first promotion and in his last season, Halifax came close to Second Division football. After scoring 23 goals in 71 appearances, Lawther joined County, his last club, in July 1971. Lawther did everything that could have been asked of him, finishing joint top-scorer in his first two seasons before being converted to a central defender. Unfortunately for him, his time at Edgeley Park could hardly have been worse, County seeking re-election in three of his five seasons. He was made captain of the side in his last season, retiring in 1976, after making 183 League and Cup appearances for County and scoring 34 goals. Two more games would have given Ian Lawther the distinction of making 600 League appearances which his professionalism surely merited. After leaving football, he concentrated on running a tailor's shop he had bought with Alex Smith, Halifax Town's goalkeeper, whilst at The Shay.

Stuart Lee
Born Manchester, 11 February 1953.
County League debut: v Darlington (h), 19 August 1978.
Stuart Lee was a fine player in the lower divisions of the Football League but, throughout his career, had to contend with the accusation that he could not perform at the higher levels, the majority of his goals being scored in the Third and Fourth Divisions. Quick off the mark, with a good shot, Lee was an enthusiastic player who, whilst having some good seasons, never quite lived up to his promise. He started his career as an apprentice with Bolton Wanderers before turning professional in February 1971. He scored 20 League goals in 85 appearances for Wanderers before Wrexham paid a club record £15,000 for him in November 1975. Although Stuart Lee spent three seasons at The Racecourse, he never really settled in the team, making only 62 appearances and scoring 14 goals which included one against Anderlecht in the European Cup-winners' Cup in 1976. County picked him up on a

free transfer in August 1978 and Lee was an almost instant success, forming a free-scoring partnership with Les Bradd who had arrived at Edgeley Park at the same time. The duo scored 47 League and Cup goals, of which Lee netted 24. After making only 58 League and Cup appearances and adding one more goal, County received a record £80,000 when Malcolm Allison took Lee to Maine Road on 5 September 1979. Again, Lee failed to succeed at the higher level, scoring twice in his seven appearances, City failing to win once. In March 1980, Lee left Maine Road and English football, moving to Portland Timbers in the United States where he saw out the rest of his career.

Andy Lincoln

Born Grangetown, near Middlesbrough, 1905.
County League debut: v Wrexham (a), 31 August 1929.
To describe Andy Lincoln's career as inconsistent would be an understatement. In seven seasons, he played for five League clubs but performed with distinction at only one. The inside-left arrived at County on 3 July 1929 with little pedigree, having played only twice for Northampton Town during the previous season which followed a two-year spell at Millwall where he scored two goals in 12 appearances. The 6ft 1in forward failed to impress in pre-season practice matches yet was surprisingly selected for County's first League game. In the event, Lincoln enjoyed a quite outstanding season, appearing in all 45 League and Cup games and forming a superb striking partnership with Frank Newton, their 66 goals playing a major part in County's second successive challenge for the championship. Scoring a hat-trick on his home

debut, he made full use of his strength and height whilst demonstrating his opportunism and ability to deliver accurate passes to his wingers. Between 25 January and 8 March, Andy Lincoln established a club record of scoring in nine successive League matches, a record which still stands, as he finished the season with 28 goals. In the Northern Section's constantly top-scoring side, it was a considerable disappointment when Lincoln scored only 14 goals in his second season although the team as a whole had an unsatisfactory year. Having made 86 League and Cup appearances and scored 42 goals, Andy Lincoln was freed and moved to the club of his name, Lincoln, in July 1931. Two goals in two appearances with Lincoln City were followed by a transfer, 12 months later, to Gateshead where he made only one League appearance. Sadly, Andy Lincoln returned from whence he came, obscurity.

Brian Lloyd

Born St Asaph, 18 March 1948.
County League debut: v Colchester United (a), 12 April 1968.
Beginning his career at Rhyl, County paid the non-League club £1,000 for the young goalkeeper on 16 March 1967, transfer-deadline day, to provide cover for joint first choices, Ken Mulhearn and Steve Fleet. Brian Lloyd played in the reserves as County won the Fourth Division championship shortly after his arrival,

remaining there for most of the following season when goalkeepers Mulhearn and Alan Ogley swapped clubs. In 1968-69, Lloyd and Ogley shared goalkeeping duties but, at the beginning of County's dreadful 1969-70 season, the club accepted a £10,000 offer from Southend United for the improving and maturing Lloyd.

He was never happy in his two-year spell at Roots Hall and was quick to take the opportunity to return to North Wales when Wrexham offered to buy him. Although sharing duties with David Gaskell, March 1972 saw Lloyd embark upon a quite remarkable run, playing in every game until his last appearance on 20 August 1977. This run consisted of 248 League matches and a record 312 appearances in all competitions. His successful period in the attractive Wrexham team of the 1970s was further boosted by his selection for Wales, Lloyd making three appearances for the national side. Following a change of manager in 1977, Lloyd was dropped and, in September, moved to Chester where he made 94 League appearances and a further 16 whilst on loan to Port Vale. More than 14 years after he arrived at Edgeley Park as a raw 18-year-old, Lloyd returned to County in August 1981 and was to miss only one match in the following two seasons. During this spell, on 10 March 1982, Brian Lloyd became the only County goalkeeper to score a League goal when at Valley Parade, with a gale-force wind behind him, his clearance found the Bradford City net to give County a 1-0 lead at half-time. Unfortunately for County, the gale did not subside in the second-half and City ran out 5-1 winners. At the beginning of 1982-83, Lloyd completed his 500th League appearance but at the end of the season retired, at the age of 35, after completing 133 appearances for County and scoring his unique goal. Following the end of his football career, Brian Lloyd remained in Wrexham working as a design consultant.

Alf Lythgoe

Born Nantwich, 1907. Died, 25 March 1967.
County League debut: v Rotherham United (a), 19 November 1932.
Although it is well over half a century since Alf Lythgoe played his last game for County, his name will be known to almost every County fan, his goalscoring achievements likely to remain forever in the record books. After a brief period as an amateur with Crewe Alexandra, the 5ft 7ins centre-forward was considered 'too small' and, whilst working in the smelting forge at the LMS works, moved into non-League football with Whitchurch, Sandbach and Congleton before returning to Sandbach where he scored a club record 55 goals. In

1931, Lythgoe moved on to Ashton National where his 42 goals aroused the interest of several local League clubs. Signing for County on 3 June 1932, Lythgoe was described as a 'speedy, skilful player who should do the club good service' which must rank as one of the most understated predictions. Lythgoe looked a brilliant player in

County's reserve team but did not make his debut until the younger, but more experienced, Joe R. Griffiths was injured. Initially, he did not remain in the team and failed to score in his first six games. However, once the 26-year-old had scored his first goal, a phenomenal goalscoring career was launched, 19 goals resulting from his last 14 games of the 1932-33 season. After scoring in six consecutive games, Lythgoe came near to a transfer to Wolves but the negotiations for his move broke down. Now established as a tireless worker and a clever and clinical finisher, 1933-34 was Lythgoe's year, a record-breaking 46 League goals in only 39 appearances in his season's total of 52 League and Cup goals in 44 games. The 46 League goals could well have been more as he only scored twice in the 13-0 win over Halifax Town although Lythgoe's performance in that match was featured prominently in reports, praised for his 'unselfishness' and 'generous distribution of the ball'. Lythgoe's five hat-tricks that season included one in a three minute spell against Southport on 4 November 1933 and a 'hat-trick of hat-tricks' in March 1934. When Lythgoe scored five goals on the opening day of the next season, it was obvious that the previous season had been no 'one-off' purple patch and that County would be unable to hold on to him.

In October 1934, with Huddersfield Town winning only two of their first 11 games, Clem Stephenson, their famous manager, went to watch Lythgoe in County's fixture at Barrow. Lythgoe duly delivered with another hat-trick, having reportedly, for one of his goals, dribbled through the Barrow defence, round the goalkeeper, into the net, out again and back to the centre-spot. Stephenson had seen enough and on 23 October 1934, Lythgoe was transferred to Huddersfield for £3,500, scoring on his debut in a 4-0 win over powerful Yorkshire rivals, Sheffield Wednesday. The remarkable Lythgoe ended his first season at Leeds Road with the distinction of being the leading League goalscorer both at Huddersfield with 21 goals and at County with the 15 goals he had scored in his first ten games. In three and a half years at Huddersfield, Lythgoe scored 46 goals in 79 League and Cup games and, in 1935, was selected to play in Belfast for the Football League against the Irish League. On 4 March 1938, with newly-promoted County rooted at the bottom of the Second Division, Alf Lythgoe re-signed for County but this could not prevent the inevitable relegation. Back in the Third Division in 1938-39, Lythgoe added another 20 goals to take his career record with County to a magnificent 110 goals in 129 League and Cup appearances but, although he was now 32, it was a surprise when he was freed at the end of the season. This was academic as the Football League was suspended in September 1939 but could have been proved to be an embarrassing mistake had League football continued. Lythgoe drifted back into non-League football and became involved in coaching and scouting and, as a useful cricketer, played for Stockport and other local clubs. After a lengthy illness, Lythgoe, one of the great late starters in League football, died at the age of 60.

Steve Massey
Born Denton, 28 March 1958.
County League debut: (substitute) v Darlington (h), 28 February 1975†.
In addition to playing schoolboy representative football, Steve Massey was a cross-country runner. Initially coming to County on trial as a midfielder, Massey was persuaded to assume a forward role, due to a shortage of strikers. Whilst still a 16-year-old apprentice, he made his League

debut as a substitute and, in addition to looking an exciting young player, scored County's winning goal. After making eight appearances, he was rewarded with a full-time contract in July 1975 and remained at Edgeley Park for a further three seasons. Massey was a quick and skilful front player, at his best when

attacking defenders from wide positions. Although by no means a prodigious scorer, he did develop the ability to score important goals, half of his 24 goals winning points for County. A player with tremendous skill, many thought him to be one of Edgeley Park's most exciting prospects. He had made 114 League and Cup appearances when a series of moves began with a transfer to Bournemouth in July 1978. By the time Massey ended his League career ten seasons later, he had played for Peterborough United, Northampton Town, Hull City, Cambridge United and, his last club, Wrexham. Whilst he scored four times in his 15 games against County, his most productive spell was with Northampton Town in 1982-83 when he was the Cobblers' top-scorer with 25 goals. Steve Massey scored 101 goals in 405 League and Cup appearances with his seven clubs, constituting a highly respectable career record. However, for those who witnessed the exciting talent he demonstrated as a teenager, it is difficult to feel that he had truly realised his early potential.

Billy McCulloch
Born Edinburgh, 25 June 1922.
Died Manchester, 1961.
County League debut: v Halifax Town (h), 31 August 1946.
Billy McCulloch first appeared for County in wartime football when he was stationed with the RAF, the

tough-tackling Scot impressing from the first of his 47 appearances in December 1943. Although registered with County from 1945, he was not demobbed until 1946 and did not make an appearance in the last season of regionalised football. On the resumption of League football, the influential half-back was made captain and, during the next eight seasons, made 338 League and Cup appearances. The only season in which McCulloch failed to appear in a minimum of 40 games was during 1947-48 when, whilst scoring County's extra-time winner against Shrewsbury Town in an FA Cup second round second replay at Maine Road, he was carried off suffering from severe concussion. A serious operation

was necessary and McCulloch missed the rest of the season. The formidable defender returned and captained County in only their second (and, to date, last) appearance in the fifth round of the FA Cup, in February 1950, when they were beaten by Liverpool in front of Edgeley Park's record attendance. On leaving County in July 1954, the 32-year-old McCulloch spent four seasons with Rochdale where he made 140 League appearances. Such was the popularity he had engendered at Edgeley Park that, when it became known in 1960 that Billy McCulloch had multiple sclerosis, an appeal fund was immediately set up to try to pay off his mortgage. As part of the McCulloch appeal, a crowd of 6,563 saw County win 5-4 against an All Stars XI which attracted many famous players including Ray Wood, Jimmy Scoular, Jimmy Adamson, Tom Finney, Ray Pointer, Dennis Viollet and Billy Liddell. Billy McCulloch's fund was officially closed on 30

November 1960 having raised £1,220, enough for the deeds of his house to be bought and handed over to him. McCulloch died the following year at the age of 39, the financial effects of his death upon his wife and three young children lessened by the supporters of the man they held in such high esteem.

Frank McDonough
Born Easington, County Durham.
County League debut: v Chesterfield (h), 22 December 1934.
Within 24 hours of goalkeeper Frank McDonough joining County from Blackpool on 21 December 1934, he made his debut in a team which had just suffered four consecutive defeats. He arrived in time to participate in County's famous FA Cup run of 1935,

having an outstanding match in the third round, keeping the West Ham forwards at bay at Upton Park. However, along with Bill Bocking, McDonough had special reason to forget the first-half nightmare against West Brom in the fifth round when he conceded five goals. Only 5ft 8½in tall, he was a reliable and experienced goalkeeper, having played in the First Division in over half of his 86 appearances with Blackpool following a move from Third Division Thames. Since the departure of Harry Hardy in 1925, County had not satisfactorily filled the goalkeeping position, none of those who played having stayed for much longer than 18 months. McDonough at last provided the answer to the problem, remaining at County for over three years and, aided by a solid defence, helping them to the Third Division championship in 1937. He had made 149 League and Cup appearances before being released in the summer of 1938 when he joined Macclesfield Town. However, Frank McDonough did re-appear for County in the first season of wartime football when he made 12 consecutive appearances.

Sammy McMillan
Born Belfast, 29 September 1941.
County League debut: v Peterborough United (h), 15 August 1970.
County were the last of five League clubs for whom Sammy McMillan played and, had not a serious back injury forced him to retire prematurely, he would have continued to give excellent service to the club. At the age of 14, he played for Ards reserves before signing amateur forms with Linfield. However, it was whilst with Boyland Boys Club that he was spotted by Manchester United scouts and joined their groundstaff at the age of 16. Signing professional forms at Old Trafford in November 1959, he made his debut two years later in a United side still rebuilding after the Munich air disaster. Playing as an outside-left he scored six goals in 11 appearances in his debut season, but with the arrival of Denis Law to bolster United's attack, McMillan's chances of first-team football receded although he did win two international caps for Northern Ireland. On 24 December 1963, Wrexham paid £8,000 to take him to The Racecourse where he enjoyed his

longest spell, although these were generally dark days for the Welsh club. Converted first to an inside-forward and then a wing-half, McMillan scored 62 goals in 172 League and Cup appearances before Southend United paid £6,000 for him in September 1967. After making 77 League appearances for Southend but scoring only five goals, in December 1969, McMillan moved to Chester. His period at Sealand

Road was hampered by injury, made worse because, with the club short of players, he was forced to play despite a bad muscle injury. In July 1970, County persuaded McMillan to join a club which had just suffered a humiliating relegation. He was made captain and, from his right-sided midfield position, not only helped to create chances but succeeded in becoming County's most reliable goalscorer with a deadly long-range shot, ending both his two seasons as their leading scorer. After only 80 League and Cup appearances and 31 goals from midfield, County's popular Player of the Year in 1971 had to quit the game. Sammy McMillan still lives in the Wrexham area, working as a builder whilst continuing to be involved in coaching.

Billy McNaughton
Born London, 8 December 1905. Died 27 August 1980.
County League debut: v Carlisle United (h), 27 October 1934†.
Three days after Alf Lythgoe's departure to Huddersfield Town, on October 26 1934, centre-forward Billy McNaughton was signed as a direct replacement, on the basis that he was a highly experienced player who had enjoyed considerable goalscoring feats at two of his previous clubs. After playing for Barking Town, Millwall, Peter-

borough United and Northampton Town, McNaughton moved to the North-East where his 22 goals in 24 League games for Gateshead in 1931-32 persuaded Hull City to sign him in the summer of 1932. His first season with Hull saw him score a staggering 39 League goals in only 40 League appearances, which remains a record for the Boothferry Park club, and, although the goals dried up somewhat the following season,

County hoped he would be able to re-discover his goalscoring ability. Injury did not help McNaughton, who made only 20 League and Cup appearances in his first season although he scored 17 goals and was a member of the side which won the Northern Section Challenge Cup in 1935, scoring once in the 2-0 Final win. The following season saw Billy McNaughton play in most of County's matches in which he averaged a goal every other game, his most notable achievement being a five-goal haul against Mansfield Town in December 1935. Whether the County management felt that he was not a sufficiently proficient replacement for Lythgoe, or that they simply needed a younger centre-forward, McNaughton was released in May 1936 after he had made 57 appearances and scored 35 goals. In the event, County were to be Billy McNaughton's last League club, the formerly prolific centre-forward drifting into non-League football following his release.

Tommy Meads
Born Grassmoor, near Chester-field, 1900.
County League debut: v Oldham Athletic (a), 8 December 1923.
Having played for Matlock, Tommy Meads signed for County on 16 November 1923, so beginning a very satisfying career. A powerfully built half-back who County often used as an emergency inside or centre-forward, Meads gave first-rate service to County in his three and a half year stay at Edgeley Park. Most of his career at County involved Second Division football, Stockport consistently struggling to maintain their status before succumbing to the inevitable in 1926, despite Meads' contribution. In March 1927, after making 120 League and Cup appearances for County and having scored 21 valuable goals, Tommy Meads joined First Division Huddersfield Town where he stayed for 18 months before joining Second Division Reading in October 1928. However, within less than a year, he joined Tottenham who had been relegated from Division One the previous season. This was the highpoint in Meads career as, during his six year stay at White Hart Lane, he helped Spurs to eventual promotion and returned to playing First Division football. Finally, after 189 League and Cup appearances, Meads left Spurs in 1935 to join Notts County, his last League club.

Jimmy Mitton
Born Stockport 1890.
County League debut: v Birmingham (h), 13 February 1911.
After beginning his career in the reserves of local rivals Glossop, Jimmy Mitton arrived at County on 25 January 1911 as an inside-forward, but played most of his career as a right-half. Whilst only making five appearances in his first three seasons, his debut provided interest as it took place on a Monday rather than the scheduled Saturday, a result of a two-week ground suspension following 'stone-throwing' by County fans during a match against Blackpool five weeks earlier. When Mitton eventually established himself in the side, he developed into a very skilful half-back, relaxed on the ball and with excellent distribution skills. Jimmy Mitton appeared in three of the four wartime seasons, playing four times alongside his brother Jack, a talented centre-forward, whilst the latter was on leave. Like many others, Mitton was deprived of a successful professional career by the absence of League football, for his potential was such that he could well have played in the First Division. After spending ten years at Edgeley Park, Jimmy Mitton moved to Exeter City in 1921, having played in 44 wartime fixtures in addition to his 90 League and Cup appearances. Following 77 appearances playing at centre-half for the Grecians, he returned to the North, to Nelson, in 1923.

Jimmy Molyneux
Born Port Sunlight, Birkenhead, 1885. Died Stockport, 9 January 1950.
County League debut: v Barnsley (a), 1 April 1906.
Whilst keeping goal for Port Sunlight Works, Jimmy Molyneux was recommended to Stockport by Sammy Dodd, the County centre-half. Following successful trials and having made his debut whilst an amateur, he signed professional terms in September 1906. Initially, he was second-choice to crowd favourite, Joe Butler, but when Butler moved to Glossop in 1908, Molyneux became County's first choice goalkeeper. Molyneux, one of the great characters of that era, became a very popular player at Edgeley Park and, although only 5ft 9ins, was both agile and reliable. After making 94 appearances he was transferred to Chelsea for £550 in the summer of 1910. Whilst with Chelsea,

Molyneux played in three FA Cup semi-finals, only one resulting in a Final appearance in which he had to be satisfied with a runners-up medal following a 3-0 defeat by

Sheffield United at Old Trafford. Molyneux joined up and, whilst stationed in Stockport, made 65 appearances for County in wartime football, sharing goal-keeping responsibilities with his old colleague, Joe Butler. In October 1917, he suffered shrapnel wounds at Ypres and was sent back to England. In December, he was discharged from hospital and, amazingly, within days, turned out for County against Preston North End at Edgeley Park, keeping a clean sheet in a 1-0 victory. When League football resumed in 1919, Molyneux was back at Chelsea, remaining at Stamford Bridge until the summer of 1922 after making 239 League and Cup appearances. On 8 January 1923, he returned to County, helping the younger goalkeepers before, at the age 40, remarkably returning to League football in 1925 when Harry Hardy went to Australia with a Football League repre-sentative side. When Jimmy Molyneux finally retired that summer, he had taken his total appearances for County to 102. He spent the remainder of his working life with for the Stockport Electricity Department.

Eddie Moran
Born Cleland, near Motherwell, 20 July 1930.
County League debut: v Hartle-pools United (a), 27 October 1951.
Whilst playing for Cleland Boys Club, 17-year-old Eddie Moran impressed both Manchester United and Leicester City but it was the latter for whom he signed in

September 1947. Slightly built, Moran was a talented ball-playing inside-forward who Leicester hoped to develop. On his debut as a teenager, he won praise for somehow completing a highly physical game against Grimsby which left Leicester with only three fully fit players, Moran being one. However, opportunities at Filbert Street were few and, after making only eight appearances, the disillusioned 20-year-old returned to Scotland. Having sought a transfer, Moran was staggered to find that Leicester were asking £15,000 for him and made three requests to the Football League for the fee to be reduced. Although a number of clubs showed interest, County's trainer, Jimmy Stevenson, succeeded in persuading Moran to come to Edgeley Park for a club record fee of £5,000. He became a County player on 6 October 1951, shortly before Jack Connor was signed, and he played throughout the Connor era. When manager Andy

Beattie left for Huddersfield Town in April 1952, he wanted to take Moran and Ron Staniforth with him but, although County were persuaded to part with Staniforth, they held on to Moran by requiring £15,000 for the Scotsman. The skilful forward remained with County for six seasons but never enjoyed any long unbroken runs in the team despite the fact that his presence can be shown to have improved Jack Connor's goal-scoring achievements. Moran scored 47 goals in 117 League and Cup appearances, his best run overlapping 1955-56 and 1956-57 when he scored in seven consecutive matches before being transferred to Rochdale on 13 February 1957. Moran played out the remainder of his professional career with Rochdale and Crewe

Alexandra, forced to retire in the summer of 1958 as a result of a knee ligament injury at the relatively young age of 27. With his League career at an end, Eddie Moran returned to Stockport to work for various companies, including British Aerospace, until he was made redundant in 1983. He worked briefly for Shell before moving to a games-machine company in nearby Ashton.

Ken Mulhearn
Born Liverpool, 16 October 1945.
County League debut: v Oxford United (a), 7 October 1964.
Although a wing-half during his early schooldays, Ken Mulhearn's height persuaded him to move to goalkeeper, the position in which he represented both Liverpool and Lancashire Boys. His per-formances brought him into the England Boys squad but he was kept out of the team by Alan Ogley who, coincidentally, was to be part of the exchange deal which took Mulhearn to Manchester City in 1967. He became an apprentice at Everton, but when Gordon West was bought from Blackpool for £27,000, a record fee for a goalkeeper, it was clear that Mulhearn's opportunities would be severely limited and he asked for a transfer. After rejecting an offer from Torquay United, he accepted a move to County and signed in August 1964. Within two months, Mulhearn had taken over from long-serving Graham Beighton and became the first-choice goalkeeper. Athletic and agile, he won a Fourth Division championship medal in 1967, having shared the position with Steve Fleet. As promoted County began the next season in Division Three, Manchester City bought the promising Mulhearn on 21 September for £25,000 plus Alan Ogley who proved to be a wonderfully loyal player for eight seasons. Having made exactly 100 League appearances for County out of a total of 117, Mulhearn made his City debut in a Manchester derby in front of almost 63,000 spectators, 54,000 more than in his last match at Edgeley Park 15 days earlier. Although City lost the derby, their 3-1 win in the return match at Old Trafford in March 1968 set the Blues on their way to the First Division championship, providing Ken Mulhearn with Fourth Division and First Division medals in successive seasons. Major knee surgery in September 1968 kept Mulhearn out of the game for 12 months and, although he played a handful of games in 1969-70, he

never regained his position as first-choice goalkeeper. After 61 League and Cup appearances, he left City on 10 March 1971 to join Shrewsbury Town where he spent ten injury-free seasons and made 370 League appearances. In August 1980 Ken Mulhearn moved to Crewe where, during his two seasons, he chalked up his 600th League appearance before retiring in the summer of 1982. On leaving football, he bought a pub in the Shrewsbury area which he still runs.

Bob Murray
Born Kemnay, near Inverurie, 24 April 1932.
County League debut: v Halifax Town (h), 22 September 1952.
Bob Murray's career began with his local team, Inverurie Locos, where he was learning a trade on the railways. County manager, Andy Beattie, had a brother who lived in Kintore, near Kemnay, and who scouted in and around the Aberdeen area. It was on his

recommendation that Murray was tempted by a two-year contract, the 19-year-old signing for County on 24 November 1951. Bob Murray continued to play football as he completed his National Service, based in Market Drayton. Tall and slim, Murray was an intelligent half-back but, whilst making the majority of appearances in this position, he was more than capable of deputising at full-back and, occasionally, as an inside-forward. He quickly built up an excellent understanding with Billy McCulloch and Gordon Wilmott and later with Frank Clempson, Ken Hodder and Trevor Porteous in a side which could never attain the consistency to challenge for pro-motion. In addition to possessing a tough character, he was committed to keeping fit, both qualities helping him to achieve the remarkable distinction of appearing in 226 consecutive League and Cup games between 28 August 1954 and 14 February 1959. When his professional career finally ended in May 1963, Bob Murray had not missed an FA Cup tie in 11 seasons and had made 495 League and Cup appearances whilst scoring 32 goals. His record number of League appearances (465) remained until Andy Thorpe passed it in 1991. Murray moved into non-League football with Bangor City and then Ashton United and worked with an upholstering firm before returning to British Aerospace where he had completed his apprenticeship when first arriving from Scotland in 1951. As at Edgeley Park, Bob Murray provided similar loyalty to British Aerospace, working there for 27 years before he retired in 1993. He lives with his family in Poynton, Cheshire.

Billy Newton

Born Quebec, County Durham, 6 August 1898. Died Stockport, 29 April 1973.
County League debut: v Rotherham United (h), 27 August 1927.
At the age of 16, Billy Newton moved to Blyth to work in the shipyards and began his football career with Blyth Spartans. Described as a 'terrier-like wing half and a fine distributor of the ball', his qualities attracted a number of League clubs and he joined Newcastle United in 1919.

However, as the Magpies had a playing staff of almost 60, Newton's chances of first-team football were small and in 1920 he joined Cardiff City where he remained for two seasons. Similar to the situation in which he found himself at Newcastle, few first-team opportunities arose and, in May 1922, he accepted a move to

Leicester City. During four seasons at Filbert Street, Billy Newton made 95 League and Cup appearances before moving to Grimsby Town in May 1926. Following an undistinguished season, Newton was transferred to County on 4 July 1927, a move which began a 40-year association with the club. Although narrowly failing to win promotion during his four seasons, these were exciting times at County, the team being one of the most attractive in the Northern Section. As a half-back, Billy Newton was very much the provider for the high-scoring Harry Burgess, Frank Newton and Joe Smith, rather than a goalscorer; in his 160 League and Cup appearances, he scored only twice. In 1931, Newton moved to Hull City but, after making 24 League appearances, returned to Edgeley Park in 1932 as player-coach to the third team. Following the departure of Harry Catterick (Snr), he became the reserve-team trainer and then when Fred Westgarth became manager in 1934, Newton became the first-team trainer, a position he held for 30 years. In October 1956, Newton was honoured by being selected as trainer of the Northern Section XI against their Southern counterparts and in 1969 he and Jimmy Stevenson were given a joint testimonial, a just reward for 40 years service. Billy Newton continued to live in Stockport until his death in 1973.

Frank Newton

Born Romiley, 12 November 1902. Died Tameside, 1977.
County League debut: v Ashington (a), 31 March 1928.
No relation to Billy Newton, at almost 13st, Frank 'Bonzo' Newton was a heavyweight centre-forward in every way, big-hearted and a prodigious goal-scorer with a thunderous shot. After running away to sea as a boy, Newton joined the army where he excelled at a number of sports, representing the service at football, rugby, hockey and boxing. When he left the army, he joined non-League Ashton United before the colourful character brought himself to County's attention. Whilst the County players were training, Newton watched them and whenever the ball came towards him, he kicked it back ferociously. Manager Lincoln Hyde was impressed and, within a week, on 13 January 1928, Newton was a County player. In his first 18 months, Frank Newton's opportunities were limited by the presence of

Joe Smith and Harry Burgess but, even so, he scored an impressive 18 goals in his first 22 appearances, scoring twice on six occasions. In 1929-30, the chance for new forwards to shine arose as Joe Smith had ended his League career and Harry Burgess had moved on to Sheffield Wednesday. Frank Newton partnered new signing Andy Lincoln and although the latter's 28 League and Cup goals was a surprising and worthy achievement, it was Newton who grabbed the headlines as he scored 38 goals in as many games. In September 1929, he became only the second County player to score five goals in a match and added another three hat-tricks during the season. Even more remarkable than Newton's goalscoring exploits was the fact that at the beginning of January 1930, after scoring 21 goals in the first 22 matches of the season, he was actually dropped for seven matches! His replacement, Jack Everest, scored six goals in five games (which included four goals against Carlisle United) before he too was left out, Newton being recalled towards the end of February. In the following season, whilst Andy Lincoln lost his goalscoring touch, 'Bonzo' Newton could not stop scoring, collecting another 37 goals in 41 appearances. After scoring 93 goals in only 101 League and Cup games, it was not surprising that Newton moved on, only that he joined another Third Division team, Fulham, in the summer of 1931 for a mere £575. In his first season at Craven Cottage, Fulham won promotion to the Second Division and followed that by nearly gaining promotion to Division 1, finishing in third place. During these two seasons, Newton demonstrated that he could find the net at higher levels, 74 goals coming from only 75 League and Cup appearances. Without any apparent reason, in September 1933 Frank Newton was transferred to Third Division Reading for £650. Still the scoring went on, 29 goals in 32 League matches before he returned to Fulham in October 1934. A direct result of Newton's transfer to Reading was the dismissal of Fulham's manager, James McIntyre, who alone had been responsible for allowing one of the game's most prodigious scorers to move on for £650 whilst replacing him with a player, Jack Lambert of Arsenal, at a cost of £2,500, who was felt to be clearly past his best. Unfortunately, Newton's return to Craven Cottage took a cruel twist,

the player breaking his leg in a friendly only two months after he had re-signed. At the age of 32 and having scored an incredible 192 goals in 209 League appearances for his three clubs, 'Bonzo' Newton's career was over and he returned to the Stockport area. Burgess, Connor, Lythgoe and Smith were undoubtedly players of greater ability than Newton but, as a goalscoring phenomenon, Frank Newton was unique.

Alan Ogley

Born Barnsley, 4 February 1946.
County League debut: v Tranmere Rovers (a), 22 September 1967.
It is impossible to make an accurate comparison of the strengths of players who have appeared in different eras but, of the numerous goalkeepers who have appeared for County, Alan Ogley will be remembered by those who saw him as ranking as one of the bravest and most agile. As a schoolboy in a strong mining community, Ogley assumed that he would go down the pits, but his sporting talent ensured that he

would follow a different path. He was a more than useful all-round sportsman, playing for Barnsley and England Schoolboys at football and England Schoolboys at cricket, so becoming the first double international at that level. Although a promising fast bowler, at the age of 15 he joined the groundstaff at Barnsley. After nine League games, Ogley signed for Manchester City on 27 July 1963. During his four seasons at Maine Road, he made 57 League and Cup appearances before being involved in an exchange deal which, on 21 September 1967, took County goalkeeper Ken Mulhearn to City and Ogley to Edgeley Park. He suffered a bad injury during the first of his eight seasons, resulting in him missing over 30 games but, when he finally left Edgeley Park in 1975, he had made 269 League and Cup appearances, only 'Tiger' Bowles having made more appearances as a County goalkeeper. At 5ft 10ins, he was not the tallest of goalkeepers but his reflexes were superb and, throughout the relatively dismal seasons in which he played, he was treated with adulation by the fans. County supporters may not have chanted the most original songs heard on football grounds around the country but when they sung 'Here's to you Alan Ogley' to the tune of Simon and Garfunkle's 'Mrs. Robinson', this became the signal for Ogley to face the crowd and go down on his knees as if in prayer, as he soaked up the fans acclaim. After he moved to Darlington in August 1975, his popularity was such that, even when he returned to Edgeley Park with his new club, the same ceremony was carried out, causing considerable confusion to the Darlington fans. Whilst not relating to his performance as a County player, Alan Ogley's ability can be summed up by the response to his performance for Manchester City at The Dell in October 1964. Although City lost 1-0, Ogley received approximately 300 letters from Southampton fans praising his performance in what was described as 'the finest display of goalkeeping ever seen on an English soccer pitch'. When Ogley retired from League football in 1976, he returned to Barnsley to work with a haulage contractor, but visits Stockport annually for the County Present v County Past charity cricket match.

Alan Oliver

Born Blyth, 8 September 1924.
County League debut: v Bradford City (h), 19 August 1950.
Alan Oliver was one of a breed of professional players who quietly did his job to the best of his ability, rarely gaining plaudits for his performances, but who could be relied upon for his consistency. Whilst those around him would receive publicity for their displays, outside-left Oliver was very much an 'unsung hero' in a team in which he was frequently the provider of the goals scored by the likes of Andy Black and Jack Connor. Signed by Derby County on the resumption of League football, Blyth-born Oliver made only 16 League appearances in his four seasons at the Baseball Ground as the Rams were one of the country's leading sides at the time. Transferred to Stockport on 2 August 1950, Oliver's four seasons at Edgeley Park were spent as a regular member of the League side and he made 151 League and Cup appearances whilst, as a winger, scoring a highly acceptable 32 goals. He had a similar record at his last League club, Gateshead, where he moved in July 1954, scoring 36 goals in

146 League appearances. In 1958, he was released by Gateshead and retired from professional football having given excellent service to the two Third Division sides for whom he had played.

Terry Park

Born Liverpool, 7 February 1957.
County League debut: (substitute) v Brentford (h), 23 August 1976.
From the point of view of innate skill, Terry Park was arguably the most gifted midfield player to have appeared for County during the past 30 years. Although almost 6ft tall, Park was very slightly built, a graceful player on the ball, skilful in his distribution and possessing the ability to strike

volleys and half-volleys with both power and accuracy. Joining Wolves as a junior in 1974, Park played in the reserves and 'A' team without ever making a League appearance before moving to Blackpool on a non-contract basis. He had a number of games for the reserve team who were managed by former County manager, Eddie Quigley. When Quigley returned to Edgeley Park for a second spell as manager, he contacted the somewhat disillusioned Park who, in July 1976, signed for County. After finally making a League appearance, within two months Park was forced to have a cartilage operation which ruled him out of first-team football for the rest of that season. Returning to Fourth Division football in August 1977, Park became a regular player in midfield until March 1979 when he, and another County favourite, Ken Fogarty, joined Fort Lauderdale in the United States for a combined fee of £100,000. Both

came back to County to play for two months in the autumn of 1979 before returning to the States. In March 1981, Park returned to Edgeley Park on a permanent basis and appeared in all 50 League and Cup games the following season, still able to lift the crowd, albeit briefly, by demonstrating his wonderful skills. He remained at Edgeley Park until December 1982 when, following a highly unpleasant disagreement with members of the club, he left County for good having scored 24 goals in 181 League and Cup appearances. With County retaining his registration, he had a brief loan spell with Manchester City, making two appearances as a substitute, before joining Bury in the close season. Injuries dogged his stay at Gigg Lane, restricting Park to 21 League appearances and in 1984, the accomplished 27-year-old gave up professional football. Some of those who saw him play felt he was a luxury in the old Fourth Division where toughness was an essential pre-requisite of success; others would simply warm to the way dour encounters could be lifted by his inspired moments of class. An abiding memory for those who witnessed it was the magnificent solo goal he scored at Old Trafford in a 1978 League Cup tie to give County a 2-1 lead. A great loss to football, Terry Park ran a post-office with his wife for seven years before joining a haulage firm in his native Liverpool in 1993.

Colin Parry

Born Stockport, 16 February 1941.
County League debut: v Hartlepools United (a), 17 November 1962.
After leaving school, Colin Parry became an apprentice engineer with an oil company in Stockport, football a weekend activity with Vernon Park in the Manchester Amateur League. Spotted whilst playing for Vernon Park, centre-half Parry signed for County on 27 July 1962, making his debut in November, but was restricted to only one further appearance during the season. With both Ken Hodder and Bob Murray retiring, Parry took his chance and, during the next two seasons, missed only six games. Colin Parry was an uncomplicated and uncompromising centre-half during this period but, unfortunately, was part of a very weak team irrespective of the club's Cup run of 1964-65. However, following their bottom place position in 1965, County were generating considerable

ambition and, with new players arriving, Parry's automatic selection came to an end. After a brief loan spell at struggling Bradford City in September 1965, he returned to Edgeley Park and regained his place. Parry remained as cover for Eddie Stuart and Matt Woods in the championship season of 1966-67 and made 18 League appearances for County on their return to the Third Division. In July 1968, having made 148 League and Cup appearances during his six year stay, Parry moved to Rochdale where he added another 156 League appearances. Colin Parry scored only one goal in his ten years of League football, in a 3-2 victory against Halifax Town in his last season, 1971-1972. Parry spent two seasons with non-League Macclesfield Town before a serious knee injury forced him to quit the game. He still works and lives in Stockport.

Alex Paterson

Born Hardgate, near Clydebank,18 March 1922. Died Stockport, 22 January 1992.
County League debut: v Gateshead (a), 13 March 1948.
After playing wartime football with Alloa Athletic, Alex Paterson joined New Brighton on 15 July 1946 and played for the English club from the time League football resumed in August. Initially a half-back, Paterson was a skilful player, good in the air and was occasionally used as an inside-

forward, the position in which he scored the majority of his ten goals for New Brighton. He had made 70 League and Cup appearances for the Rakers when, immediately before the transfer deadline, he moved to County in March 1948 as part of an exchange deal which took Albert Earl to New Brighton.

Alex Paterson gave consistent performances at left-half in his five years at County, playing in every round of the FA Cup run which took the club to the fifth round in 1950. It was not until 1952 that Paterson lost his place, effectively to Bob Murray, and in July 1953 he was released by County having made 171 League and Cup appearances. He moved to Barrow but did not make a first-team appearance there or at Halifax Town where he spent the last month of his career in September 1954. After leaving professional football, Alex Paterson ran a travel agent's business before becoming a postman and, finally, a porter at Stepping Hill Hospital.

Chris Porter

Born Stockport, 25 October 1885. Died Dardanelles, 1915. County League debut: v Barnsley (h), 14 April 1906.

As has always been the case with amateurs playing in professional football, such players were officially given the respect of having their initials preceding their names. In their early League days, Old Mancunian, T.C. Porter was probably County's most successful and talented amateur, equally adept at any of the inside or centre-forward positions. Chris Porter made his debut within days of joining County on 10 April 1906 and made an immediate impact, scoring three goals in his first four appearances. As an amateur, he played for the love of the game and this was evident in his style of play. Although hardworking, he enjoyed displaying his skills, whether they took the form of scoring goals or the demonstration of clever ball-control. Porter's amateur status also had the unfortunate consequence that he was not always available for games, his business interests preventing him from playing in a number of games. A very popular player with the fans, he scored what was only the second League hat-trick by a County player in April 1908 in a match against Clapton Orient which saw County score six goals for the first time. Whilst not a prolific goalscorer, he did average a goal every three games in his stay of just over three years. In July 1909, having scored 23 goals in 66 League and Cup appearances, Porter moved to local rivals Glossop and scored the only goal of the game for the Derbyshire team when the clubs met in December. Playing with former County favourite, Joe

Butler, Porter spent one season with Second Division Glossop, scoring eight goals in 24 League appearances, before leaving professional football to concentrate on his business. In 1914, Chris Porter joined the army and was tragically killed during the disastrous Gallipoli campaign of 1915.

Andy Preece

Born Evesham, 27 March 1967. County League debut: (substitute) v Preston North End (a), 26 December 1991

An excellent all-rounder as a schoolboy, Andy Preece represented Hereford and Worcester Boys at football and, from the age of 16, Worcestershire Under-19s at cricket. His footballing career began with Worcester City in the Alliance Premier League (the forerunner of the Conference) but after suffering particularly badly from glandular fever, Preece joined Evesham United in the

Midland Football Combination. After two seasons with Evesham and in the close season playing cricket for Worcestershire Second XI, he was paid to go to Australia to play cricket, spending six months near Perth. On his return to England, he rejoined Evesham but, following a trial with Northampton Town in 1988, signed as a non-contract player, making two substitute appearances. After various loan spells with non-League clubs, he returned to Worcester City before Wrexham signed him for £4,000 in March 1990. After scoring ten goals in 53 League and Cup games and languishing in the reserve team, neither Preece nor Wrexham were dismayed when County's Danny Bergara offered £15,000 to bring him to Edgeley Park. Although Preece was cup-tied for County's first Wembley appearance in the 1992 Autoglass Trophy Final, he

returned with County in the Play-off Final eight days later, supplying the cross from which Kevin Francis scored a late equaliser. Thirteen goals in each of his first two seasons suggested that Bergara had made another good signing and this was confirmed in 1993-94 when Andy Preece became only the 11th County player to score 50 goals for the club. Whilst appearing somewhat lethargic at times, Andy Preece springs to life once in the penalty area as his County record demonstrates, scoring his 50th goal in only his 98th appearance (nine of which were as a substitute). Although his partnership with Kevin Francis proved to be a formidable one, following his record £350,000 transfer to Crystal Palace in June 1994, only time will tell whether Andy Preece can maintain such goalscoring feats in the Premier League.

Johnny Price

Born Easington, 25 October 1943. County League debut: v Chester (a), 21 August 1965.

Whilst the current County team have the tallest player in the League, for ten seasons they had the smallest player. At only 5ft 3ins, Johnny Price was a flying outside-left from the North-East who, as a schoolboy, had played as an inside-forward for Durham County Boys. He joined Horden Colliery Welfare Juniors, where he received highly complimentary reviews. In November 1960, he joined the exodus of players to Burnley who were not only one of the best sides in the country, but were also famed for developing players from the North-East. After serving his apprenticeship in the

reserves, he made his League debut in October 1963, but was restricted to 22 League and Cup

games during his four and a half years at Turf Moor. Renewed ambition at County led to them moving quickly for the small winger, Price signing on 13 May 1965. In his first season, he missed only one game in all competitions and was voted County's Player of the Year. With the wily Len Allchurch on the right and Price on the left, chances were constantly created, but the team as a whole were unable to find consistency until Price's second season when County won the Fourth Division championship. The signing of established strikers Bill Atkins and Jim Fryatt gave Price the targets he needed and County enjoyed a brief flirtation with success. However, when the team fell apart in 1969, Johnny Price remained, still darting down the left or right wing but by then more in hope than expectation. Eventually, after making 274 League and Cup appearances, Price moved to Blackburn Rovers in September 1971. He remained at Ewood Park for two and a half years before rejoining County in March 1974. At 31, Price remained a very useful player, particularly in that depressing era. In June 1976, Johnny Price finally hung up his small boots, having made 345 League and Cup appearances and scored 27 goals which actually included the odd headed goal. A regular at Edgeley Park after his retirement, he has remained in the area as a licensee in Stockport.

Richard Prout

Born London, 1888. Died, December 1949. County League debut: v Bolton Wanderers (a), 1 September 1910†.

When Richard Prout ended his first season at Edgeley Park, it appeared that not only had County obtained the services of their best centre-forward to date, but also that Prout would be destined for greater things. One of the relatively few Londoners to join County in their early years, Prout had played amateur football before signing for Fulham in 1908 as an inside-forward. He made only eight appearances, including one against Stockport, before moving north on 12 May 1910. County played him at centre-forward and, after scoring twice on his debut, Prout continued to score regularly, finishing the season with a record 17 goals in 35 League appearances. (He is one of only two County players to have scored the first and last goal of the season.) He was a tireless worker with a deadly shot, but the following season his goalscoring form fell away dramatically, resulting in his being withdrawn to right-half where, in fact, he gave some excellent performances. However, at the beginning of his third season, Prout was one of five players suspended by the club on

27 September 1912 for 'insubordination and breach of training rules', but worse was to follow. On 17 October, Prout was given '14 days notice to terminate his engagement with the club' as a result of 'palpable inefficiency and gross misconduct'. Although Prout's form was undoubtedly poor, what the alleged misconduct consisted of was never publicised. Prout was believed to be considering an appeal but decided against it, instead accepting terms with Plymouth Argyle in the Southern League. He had made only 62 League and Cup appearances and scored 19 goals for County when he left in disgrace, but what was not commonly known was that Prout had been seriously disturbed by the death of his brother whilst playing in a park football match. After leaving Stockport, he made only four appearances for Plymouth before fading into obscurity. At the age of 61, severely depressed by his wife's death, Richard Prout committed suicide during the Christmas period of 1949.

Mick Quinn

Born Liverpool, 2 May 1962.
County League debut: v Peterborough United (h), 28 August 1982.
When he arrived at Edgeley Park on a free transfer in July 1982 as a raw 20-year-old, Mick Quinn had not enjoyed the most auspicious start to a career. He has certainly

made up for this during the past 12 years. After joining Derby County as an apprentice, he began his League career with Wigan Athletic, scoring 19 goals in 69 League appearances during three seasons. Although this was a reasonable strike-rate for a young player, he was freed in 1982 and County manager, Eric Webster, brought him to County. With a similar build to the celebrated centre-forward Frank Newton 50 years earlier, the stocky striker's career took off at Edgeley Park. Quinn was a throwback to centre-forwards of old: aggressive, powerful, good in the air and possessing a powerful shot. He

was a clinical finisher with the priceless ability to turn sharply in the opponents' penalty area and create chances out of nothing. It was a joy for County supporters to at last have a player who was always likely to score for, whenever Quinn had possession of the ball in the opponents' half of the pitch, he had a single-minded desire to get himself on the scoresheet. For a heavily-built player, he was also deceptively quick and few defenders enjoyed playing against such a fast and combative striker. 41 goals in 70 appearances made him a favourite at Edgeley Park and, whilst his aggressive play sometimes went too far, it was part and parcel of the player's hunger for success. Quinn's inevitable move came in January 1984 when he joined Oldham Athletic for £52,000. 37 goals and 86 League and Cup appearances later, he was transferred to Portsmouth for £150,000. In Quinn's first full season at Fratton Park, his 22 goals helped Pompey to promotion from Division Two and, during his

stay, he was rarely out of the news, good and bad, scoring regularly and spending a short period in prison. In June 1989, Mick Quinn moved to Newcastle United for £680,000 but any reservations the Tynesiders had about the 27-year-old striker were quickly dispelled when he scored four goals on his debut against eventual champions, Leeds United. He could not maintain the 34 League and Cup goals in his first season, but had scored 59 League goals for Newcastle in 115 appearances when he was transferred to Coventry City in November 1992. Having already reached the target of 200 League goals, Quinn scored twice on his Coventry debut and finished top-scorer with 17 League goals. The speed he had shown at County may have gone but his desire for goals remains, amply proved by a hat-trick on the opening day of the 1993-94 season at Highbury. A cheerful and colourful character, Mick Quinn plays on, still held in high regard at Edgeley Park where his rise to fame began.

Joe Reid

Born Hebburn, Newcastle-on-Tyne.
County League debut: v Barnsley (h), 23 October 1920.
Beginning his career at South Shields, Joe Reid arrived at Edgeley Park on 19 October 1920 after spending almost 12 months at nearby Manchester City. He went to Maine Road as a half-back but the three appearances he made there were at inside or centre-forward. Reid's first season at County was an unhappy one for both player and club: Reid's appearances restricted to five because of the presence of experienced half-backs Bert Walmsley and Albert Waterall, whilst the club suffered relegation from the Second Division. The following season was successful for Reid, who enjoyed a good run in the half-back line, and for County who won the Third Division North championship. County's return to the Second Division saw a full-back pairing of fellow Geordies, Joe Reid and Billy Richardson, which resulted in a successful partnership, highly regarded throughout the Division. The movement of Reid to left-back proved to be inspired, his obvious footballing skill and vision combining well with the defensive qualities needed. Reid remained at County until they experienced another relegation in 1926, having made 148 League and Cup appearances and scoring

just one goal when playing at inside-right. Afflicted by injuries in his last season, Joe Reid left professional football on his departure from County.

Duggie Reid

Born West Kilbride, 3 October 1917.
County League debut: v Oldham Athletic (h), 3 October 1936.
One of the finest players to be developed by County, Duggie Reid was fanatical about football from being a young boy, playing winter and summer in his home town of Mauchline, where he had moved shortly after his birth. At 15, his sister helped him to get a job as an apprentice plumber in Manchester whilst his brother-in-law introduced him to Heaton Chapel FC. The 6ft 'gentle giant' began as a half-back, but was playing at centre-forward when he was brought to the notice of County. On 9 February 1934, the 16-year-old Reid signed as an amateur and, over the following two years, worked his way up through the 'A' team and then the

reserve team. With the rare combination of power and skill, it was tempting to play the young Reid but County held back until his 19th birthday. Although he did not score on his debut, as a centre-forward, he won two penalties, only one of which was converted in County's 4-1 victory. However promising he was, County only played him when their regular centre-forward was absent with the result that Reid did not play in the championship decider against Lincoln City. On their return to Second Division football, Reid became an integral part of County's team as they struggled to retain their recently won status. Reverting to right-half, Reid lived up to his potential, attracting scouts from numerous First Division clubs. Even when Stockport were relegated in 1938, Reid remained at County, thrilling supporters with his surging runs and his famous free-kicks which, it was accepted, were the hardest hit seen at Edgeley Park. Almost 22 when war broke out, it appeared that the seven years lost would rob Duggie Reid of the opportunity to play higher level football. Whilst on leave, he made 38 appearances in wartime football but remained a much sought after player. In March 1946, County received a record £7,000 from Portsmouth for Reid who had scored 26 goals in 91 League and Cup appearances. As Reid was 28, some thought Portsmouth were taking a risk but he proved to be an inspirational signing. He played for Portsmouth for ten seasons, ending his first as Pompey's highest League scorer with 29 goals, and helping them to consecutive First Division championships in 1948-49 and 1949-50. One of Fratton Park's most popular players, Reid made 309 League appearances and scored 129 goals as an inside-forward. Retiring from playing at the age of 38, although Reid remained at Fratton Park as groundsman, he retained fond memories of his days at Stockport.

Billy Richardson

Born Newcastle-on-Tyne.
County League debut: v Barrow (h), 19 September 1921.
Joining County from Wallsend on 26 August 1921, right-back Billy Richardson enjoyed a successful five years at Edgeley Park. Long-serving full-back Tommy Robson was coming to the end of his career and Richardson slipped naturally into his place, helping County's frugal defence in their Third Division championship

success. On County's return to Second Division football, he formed a solid and reliable partnership with fellow Geordie, Joe Reid. Richardson was an intelligent player who read the game well, was quick to cover and cool when under pressure. He played in the same role throughout his period at County, never being pulled out of position and, therefore, not having scoring opportunities. He remained at County throughout their struggle to stay in the Second Division, finally leaving when County were relegated in 1926 after making 165 League and Cup appearances. Just as he and Joe Reid had been partners at full-back, so too were they on their departure, both transfer-listed on 6 June 1924, both for a fee of £500.

Tommy Robson

Born Scotswood, Newcastle-on-Tyne, 1892.
County League debut: v Preston North End (a), 20 March 1915.
Signed by County in August 1914 as full-back cover for the

consistently reliable duo of Stephen Fagan and Ralph Goodwin, Tommy Robson made only one League appearance in this capacity, waiting five years before he became a regular member of the team. Robson made 69 appearances during wartime football, all but seven of them during the first two years of non-League competition, before he joined the services. On the resumption of professional football in 1919, Robson was widely regarded as one of the finest full-backs in the Second Division, a tough but fair tackler with the ability to make good use of the ball. As with other full-backs of his era, Robson rarely ventured into the opposition's half, concentrating upon his defensive duties. He missed only six games in the first two post-war seasons but, soon after County's demotion to the new Third Division North, an injury gave Billy Richardson the opportunity to play in Robson's place. Richardson immediately grasped his chance and Robson made only one more appearance in the next 20 months before being freed after making 94 League and Cup appearances.

Norman Rodgers

Born Stockport, 1891. Died Stockport, 10 June 1947.
County League debut: v Bradford (Park Avenue) (h), 4 November 1911†.
A local amateur, Norman Rodgers developed into one of County's best-ever goalscoring inside-forwards, all his goals being scored in the top two divisions. At the age of 17, he joined Park Albion in Heaton Norris before moving into the Manchester League with Hooley Hill. As a free-scoring forward, he was persuaded to have a trial with County and, on 21 October 1911, signed as an amateur. Within a fortnight, he had made his debut, scored in his first two games and was an instant success. A versatile player with good control, he was unselfish but never afraid to shoot at any opportunity, capable of scoring with either foot and preferring to hit the ball low into the corners of the goal. Although he could not fail to be aware of the acclaim he was receiving, he remained unaffected, quietly concentrating on maintaining his fitness and improving his game. At the end of his first season, Rodgers finished as County's top scorer with 11 goals in 23 appearances and, on 26 April, he signed professional forms. In the last three seasons prior to the

abandonment of professional football in 1915, Rodgers was a remarkably consistent goalscorer and became the first County player to score 50 League goals. He remained in Stockport through the war years and, in three successive seasons, scored 20 goals, completing wartime football with a record of 70 goals in 115 appearances. On the resumption of

League football, Rodgers continued to score regularly but, only nine days after his benefit game against Leicester City, County found themselves unable to reject an offer of £2,500 for the most gifted inside-forward to have played for them. Having scored 76 goals in 164 League and Cup appearances, on 23 February 1920, Blackburn Rovers signed Rodgers in a desperate attempt to preserve their First Division status. Without a win for ten weeks and looking doomed, Rovers signed three players in the space of nine days. All made a contribution to the fight for survival, but none more than Norman Rodgers who scored a superb 13 goals in 11 games. This, together with a victory by Manchester United at Notts County on the final day of the season, ensured both Rovers' survival and Rodgers' place in the hearts of Blackburn supporters. Rodgers spent another three years at Ewood Park but suffered from a series of bad injuries which restricted him to only 32 League games in which he scored eight goals. In the summer of 1923, Rodgers accepted that his football career was at an end and returned to Stockport where he ran a shop for 12 years before, at the age of 44, going into semi-retirement in Romiley. Norman Rodgers was County's fourth leading League and Cup goalscorer until 1993 when Kevin Francis overtook him, but including his wartime record, Rodgers is County's leading scorer with 146 goals.

John Rutter

Born Warrington, 13 September 1952.
County League debut: v Newport County (a), 21 August 1976.

One of only three players to make over 400 appearances for County, John Rutter was an all-round athlete as a schoolboy. He represented Warrington Boys at football, cross-country and in the 400 metres, in addition to playing Rugby League. When he went on to play football for Cheshire Boys and Warrington Town, it became clear which sport he was going to follow. On leaving school, he accepted an apprenticeship at Wolves but, in his three-year stay, he did not make a first-team appearance. In July 1973, Rutter joined Bournemouth on a free transfer but, after playing in only four League games, he moved to Exeter City 12 months later. In his first season at St. James Park, he established himself as a full-back,

making 31 appearances, but this was followed by a disappointing season with Rutter making only one substitute appearance after having a cartilage operation. Released by Exeter on a free transfer, Rutter remained sufficiently self-confident to communicate with clubs in the North-West, offering himself for a month's trial to prove that he was fully recovered from injury. In August 1976, County took up his offer and, when regular full-back, Ian Buckley, was injured before the start of the season, John Rutter found himself in the first team. As a quick full-back who linked well with the attack, Rutter not only retained his place but became an automatic choice for almost ten

years. He was a player who not only competed in every match, but was enthusiastic, clearly enjoying playing and having an excellent attitude on the pitch. Rutter was never sent off in a League match, the only major blemish on a fine disciplinary record coming when he was dismissed in his 444th game for County in an FA Cup tie against non-League Telford United. During his first five seasons, Rutter only missed seven League games and when he played his last match in April 1986, he had made 451 League and Cup appearances in just ten years, and scored nine goals. With his playing career over, he worked for a property company before returning to Edgeley Park six months later to become involved in a variety of commercial activities. John Rutter still lives in his home town, Warrington, but remains at Edgeley Park in his capacity as commercial manager.

Hugh Ryden

Born Dumbarton, 7 April 1943.
County League debut: v Chesterfield (a), 24 August 1963.

Hugh Ryden began his semi-professional career with Yoker Athletic when, even as a 16-year-old, he was a tremendous striker of the ball. Spotted scoring spectacular goals by a Leeds United scout, he had a successful trial, and joined Leeds in October 1960. His first season was spent in the youth side, but he was in the reserve team when Don Revie became manager in 1961. As Revie built up a strong, large squad in an attempt to lift Leeds out of the Second Division, Ryden had little opportunity to get first-team football. In June 1962, he was transferred to Bristol Rovers for £1,000 but suffered a number of injuries, restricting the centre-forward to eight League games in which he scored four goals. Given a free-transfer, Ryden joined County on 30 July 1963 but, following a good start, which saw him score seven goals in nine games, his form deteriorated and in 1964 he was again given a free transfer. He moved to Chester where he enjoyed his most successful spell, reaching 20 goals in a season for the only time in his career. In November 1967, after scoring 44 goals in 141 League appearances for Chester, Halifax Town paid £5,000 to take Ryden to The Shay. His two year stay at Halifax was not a happy one, Ryden again plagued by injury, and in December 1969, another free transfer brought him back to a demoralised Stockport County.

However, Ryden gave County splendid service in his second spell, consistently dangerous from free-kicks and encouraging the younger players. After 12 years in professional football, Ryden finally made the headlines on the back pages of the national press in September 1972, following a second round League Cup tie against First Division Crystal Palace at Selhurst Park. Shortly after winning a penalty for County and watching the spot-kick missed, Ryden rose to head the only goal of the match, setting up a tie against another First Division team, West Ham United. However, Ryden suffered further injuries and, after making 175 League and Cup appearances and scoring 25 goals in his two spells, he retired from League football in 1973. Still living in Stockport, Hugh Ryden returned to County for 18 months as manager of the youth team.

Ken Shaw

Born Dukinfield, 15 December 1920.
County League debut: v Halifax Town (h) 31 August 1946.

Although making only 51 League and Cup appearances, during World War Two Ken Shaw made more appearances for County than any other player. He began his career in non-League football, playing for Hurst, Stalybridge Celtic, Mossley and Hyde United. Whilst still an amateur, he made

his debut accidentally, having accompanied County's centre-half, his friend Eddie Steele, to watch Stockport play at Everton on Christmas Day 1941. When they arrived at Goodison, County manager Harry Catterick (Snr)

discovered that his team were short of a forward and, following a search to find an amateur form, Ken Shaw signed and played alongside Harry Catterick (jnr), County losing 6-0. Whilst working as a miner in Yorkshire, Shaw signed professional forms on 5 October 1942 and, in the last four seasons of wartime football, made a minimum of 30 appearances each year. Primarily an outside-left, he played in every forward position both during and after the war. A winger who relied mainly on pace, Shaw had a strong left foot and was consistently on the scoresheet in the period before the resumption of League football. Outside-left in the 'longest match' on 30 March 1946, Ken Shaw was a key figure, scoring both County goals in the 2-2 draw at Edgeley Park and, during the lengthening period of extra-time, missing an easy chance to settle the tie when, with the goal at his mercy he shot straight at Doncaster goalkeeper, Hardwick. On the resumption of League football in August 1946, Shaw played regularly, mainly at centre-forward, and was County's top-scorer. He continued playing until December 1947 when, during an FA Cup second replay against Shrewsbury Town at Maine Road, he damaged a cartilage and, only 26, was forced to retire. He assisted County as a scout for some ten years and worked for an engineering company in Denton until his retirement in 1986. Still very fit, Ken Shaw lives in Woodley, Stockport.

Steve Sherlock

Born Birmingham, 10 May 1959.
County League debut: v Walsall (a), 18 August 1979.

After representing Birmingham Boys in a number of age groups, Steve Sherlock signed apprentice forms for Manchester City in May 1977. As a young left-back, Sherlock progressed through to the reserve team and, in 1978, was a member of City's Central League championship team. Unable to displace the highly experienced Willie Donachie, in June 1978 Sherlock joined Luton Town and made his first League appearance on the opening day of the 1978-79 season in a 6-1 win against Oldham Athletic. However, he made only one more appearance for the 'other' Hatters before signing for Stockport, the first Football League Hatters, on a free transfer in August 1979. Sherlock quickly formed an excellent full-back partnership with John Rutter, both of them enjoying attacking down the flanks. Although only

scoring eight goals in his County career, Sherlock had a good shot and was an excellent crosser of the ball. In seven seasons at Edgeley Park, he gave excellent service to the club, making 273 League and Cup appearances before moving to Cardiff City in July 1986. After making only 15 League appearances for Cardiff, he had a brief loan spell with Welsh neighbours, Newport County, joining them permanently in March 1987. His final season in League football, 1987-88, was also Newport's last as they were relegated to the Conference. Steve Sherlock sustained an injury towards the end of Newport's fateful campaign and did not play again.

Ernie Simms

Born South Shields, 1891.
County League debut: v Leicester City (h), 5 January 1924†.
Although joining County towards the end of his career, Ernie Simms was an important signing in County's attempt to remain in the Second Division. Simms was a courageous, exciting and powerful centre-forward who had begun his career with Barnsley. In 1913, he was signed by Luton Town with the express intention of getting them back into the First Division of the Southern League. Simms duly obliged, scoring 37 goals. He remained at Luton until 1922, having scored 109 goals in 160 appearances and, during his last season was rewarded with an England cap against Northern Ireland. On 5 January 1924, Simms joined County from South Shields and was an instant success, scoring six goals in his first three games. Unfortunately, he did not

score again that season but justified his place by helping his other forwards. Although with Stockport he was unable to repeat his earlier goalscoring exploits, in March 1925 he was selected, along with County goalkeeper Harry Hardy, for a Football League tour of Australia where he scored 36 goals in 20 games. His exaggerated celebration on scoring a goal at Blackpool on 21 March was a result of a promise by chairman, Ernest Barlow, to release Simms for the Australian tour if he scored and County won. Ernie Simms remained at County until 1926 when he was released following relegation to the Third Division. The former international had made 66 appearances and scored 21 goals with his last club, retiring on leaving County.

Joe Smith

Born Newcastle-under-Lyme, June 26 1889. Died Blackpool, 11 August 1971.
County League debut v Stoke City (h), 19 March 1927.
A magnificent centre-forward and inspirational captain, Joe Smith was one of a handful of people to enjoy success at the highest level as both a player and a manager. He spent the vast majority of his playing career with Bolton Wanderers whom he joined in 1908 after playing amateur football with Newcastle St. Lukes in the Staffordshire League. Smith spent over 18 years at Burnden Park, winning five international caps and captaining Wanderers in two FA Cup Final wins, the first-ever Wembley Final in 1923 and again in 1926. Whilst at Burnden Park, he scored 38 League goals in a season, a record at Bolton, one which he repeated at County. A very powerful centre-forward, Smith weighed almost 12½st whilst only 5ft 7½in tall and it

was remarkable that he could achieve so much when well into his 30s. When manager, Lincoln Hyde, succeeded in persuading him to join County, his 'signing' on 17 March 1927 was, in every way, sensational. As this famous signing had made 492 appearances for The Trotters and scored 227 goals, it was not surprising that a record crowd of 22,622 packed Edgeley Park to see the former Bolton captain make his debut against League leaders (and eventual champions) Stoke City. The match ended in an exciting 2-2 draw, only chairman Ernest Barlow aware that Smith's registration had not been received by the Football League. County were fined £100 and, for the only time in their history, deducted two points for playing an 'unregistered player'. From then until the end of the season, Smith was only allowed to play in those games which had no bearing on promotion or re-election. When, the following season, Smith was able to play 'unconditionally', his goalscoring achievements were astounding. His 40 goals in 42 League and Cup appearances included a run of 16 goals in six games, which contained four hat-tricks. He was the first County player to score five goals in a match, a feat he repeated at the beginning of the following season, when he was partnered by the young Harry Burgess, before Smith lost his place to the similarly strong Frank Newton. By the time he left County in May 1929, Joe Smith had scored 63 goals in 73 League and Cup appearances and had amassed eight hat-tricks. His superb playing-career over, Joe Smith turned to management, first in 1931 with Third Division Reading, where he was very successful and then, in 1935, with Blackpool. Smith remained as manager at Bloomfield Road for 23 years, building one of the most attractive teams in the country and guiding Blackpool to three FA Cup Finals in six years. Ironically, Blackpool's only victory in the three Finals was in the 'Matthews Final' of 1953 when Smith's old team, Bolton, were defeated. When Joe Smith retired because of ill-health in 1958, the game lost one of its most successful characters, one who had, for two years, graced Edgeley Park with his presence.

Ron Staniforth

Born Newton Heath, Manchester, 13 April 1924.
County League debut: v Tranmere

Rovers (h), 9 November 1946.
Ron Staniforth was probably the finest full-back County produced, deservedly winning international honours which he would certainly not have achieved had he remained at Stockport. After representing Manchester Boys, he played amateur football before joining the navy during World War Two. When he was demobbed, he became a milkman and wrote to County, asking for a trial, which resulted in him signing amateur forms on 21 August 1946. Staniforth's ability was so obvious that within six weeks, on 5 October, he signed professional forms and made his debut five weeks later. A tall and cultured full-back, Staniforth gave some brilliant displays for County and, such was his versatility that he was regularly switched from left-back to right-back, being equally at

home in either position. During his six seasons at Stockport, Staniforth made 245 League and Cup appearances but scored only once, earning a 1-0 win against Accrington Stanley in April 1950. When the County manager, Andy Beattie, left to take charge of Huddersfield Town in April 1952, there was considerable speculation as to whether Staniforth would follow him. The speculation was soon over, Staniforth signing for the Yorkshire club on 20 May 1952 for a reputed £8,000. Within a year of Beattie and Staniforth's arrival at Leeds Road, Huddersfield were promoted to Division One which gave the former Stockport player the stage to display his stylish defensive skills. In 1954, he won eight international caps but lost his

Huddersfield place in 1955 and was transferred to Sheffield Wednesday after making 118 League and Cup appearances. Staniforth remained at Hillsborough for four years, winning Second Division championship medals in his first and last seasons, before leaving to become player-manager of Fourth Division Barrow. He retired from playing in 1960 but remained in management at Barrow until 1964, his new role proving disappointingly unsuccessful. Ron Staniforth had various posts at Sheffield Wednesday until he left the game completely in January 1976.

Jimmy Stevenson

Born New Mains, Lanarkshire, 10 November 1903. Died Stockport, 5 November 1973.
County League debut: v Darlington (h), 27 August 1932†.
Signed from non-League Aldershot on 28 July 1932, Jimmy Stevenson was a vital cog in County's most successful attack. A classic 'schemer', the Scottish inside-forward was the talented link with the half-backs, a wonderful passer of the ball and adept at close control. When Stevenson left school, he began work as an engineer, completing

his apprenticeship after signing for Second Division Third Lanark. By the age of 21, he had moved to the English Second Division with South Shields, where he made 54 League appearances and scored 24 goals. In 1929, Stevenson was transferred to Bradford City who, like South Shields, were a Second Division club, but with much greater potential, averaging gates of 16,000 compared to South Shields 3,500. However, the move

was not a success and Stevenson moved to Southern League Aldershot before arriving at Stockport. He found himself in the company of other new faces, Downes, Foulkes and Lythgoe, and the virtually new forward-line gelled almost immediately, although it was not until the arrival of Joe Hill in December 1933 that the unit was complete. For one who would now be called a 'playmaker', Stevenson had an excellent goalscoring record, scoring 43 times in 110 League and Cup games. Unfortunately for both Stevenson and County, in 1935, serious ligament problems brought his playing career to a sudden end. He had a brief spell managing Macclesfield Town before returning to County as reserve-team trainer and remaining at Edgeley Park in various capacities for another 35 years.

Bob Still

Born Brinscall, near Chorley, 15 December 1912.
County League debut: v Gateshead (h), 29 September 1934.
Beginning his amateur career at Brinscall and then Tocholes, near Darwen, Bob Still played at centre-half for Burnley 'A' before moving to Chorley where he became a part-time professional footballer and, during the summer, played for Chorley Cricket Club. His mature footballing performances attracted a number of scouts, but it was County who persuaded Still to move to Edgeley Park where he signed on 9 May 1934. An unassuming half-back, Still made 38 appearances in his first season, increasing in confidence with each game. He appeared in every game of County's run to the fifth round of the FA Cup, playing an important part in the fourth round replay against Bradford City in front of over 22,000 spectators. Receiving the ball in his own half, he beat player after player before striking the ball so hard that the City goalkeeper could only parry it to Hill who put County 2-1 up. As the ever-improving half-back played in all but two of County's games during their promotion season, a number of First Division clubs pursued him but, with the club now in the Second Division, no inducements could persuade the Edgeley management to part with him. He carried on playing until the war, having made 175 League and Cup appearances and scoring just three goals before being transferred to Crewe Alexandra in August 1939. With

war breaking out less than a month later, Still had to wait seven years for his first appearance for the Gresty Road club, but at the age of 34 was unable to show the form which had won such praise in his County days. That one appearance for Crewe turned out to be Bob Still's last and the reliable and talented half-back finally gave up professional football in that first post-war season.

Bob Suart

Born Stockport, 1885. Died, killed in action 1918.
County League debut: v Gainsborough Trinity (h), 3 October 1903.
Bob Suart signed for his local club, County, on 1 September 1903, the young half-back only making six appearances in his first season, one which saw County fail to gain re-election to the Second Division. With County returning to the Lancashire Combination in

search of an immediate return to League football, Suart took the opportunity of establishing himself as a regular first-team player and was first choice in every match. On County's return to the Second Division, Suart had matured into a more experienced right-half, strong and resolute, but not always reliable in his distribution of the ball. However, his consistent performances in the defensive area of his game persuaded Fulham to negotiate a double transfer, signing both Suart and the exciting Bob Carter (father of Raich Carter) for a fee of £550 on 31 March 1908. Suart had made 119 League and Cup appearances and scored nine goals, excluding the period when County were out of League football. He had a

reputation of being inconsistent with his new club and, four years after his move to London, was signed in 1911 by Burslem Port Vale, at this time a non-League club. Bob Suart remained a Port Vale player although he appeared for County in 22 wartime fixtures before he was killed in the latter stages of World War One.

Tommy Sword

Born Bishop Auckland, 12 November 1957.
County League debut: (substitute) v Walsall (h), 2 November 1979.
At the end of October 1979 and lying in 21st place in Division Four, for County the 1970s were coming to an end as they had begun – dismally. As a result of the failure to replace striker Stuart Lee, the club's leading scorer was central defender, Mike Czuczman. When centre-forward Tommy Sword signed for managerless County at the beginning of

November, he was an unknown non-League player with Bishop Auckland, albeit one who had scored 50 goals for the Northern Football League club. The blond 6ft 2ins striker could not be described as a saviour but his enthusiasm and total commitment were major factors in at least a 'mini-revival'. His full debut saw him return to the North-East to play at Hartlepool in a game which typified the man. With County trailing 1-0, Sword scored twice to give his new team a 2-1 win. Never a player to accept defeat, his passion for the game inspired others around him, bringing him both respect and affection from the supporters and fellow-professionals. Within five months of

Sword's arrival, an injury to centre-half, Les Bradd, himself a converted striker, led to the new centre-forward moving back to central defence. The towering striker enjoyed a successful transition to towering defender, whilst still scoring regularly. After missing only three matches in his first full season, the following season saw him sustain a serious leg fracture in an FA Cup tie against non-League Mossley. Typical of Sword, although his team were winning 3-1, he continued to tackle as if County were losing and was out of the side for 12 months. His character helped him to make a successful comeback, missing only nine games in the three seasons following his return. Seven seasons after he had joined County, he was transferred to Hartlepool United for £5,000 but, a little over six months later, Sword returned, playing his last game in November 1987. He had made 270 League and Cup appearances and of his 55 goals, 25 had been penalties. By far the most successful penalty-taker in County's history, 24 of his conversions had been in League games, the only Cup success being one which gave County a famous 2-1 win at Roker Park against Sunderland. When Tommy Sword retired from football in 1988, moving back to the North-East to run a pub in Newcastle, he was granted a well-deserved testimonial that August against Manchester City. This enabled County fans to show their appreciation for the magnificent service he had given to the club.

Andy Thorpe

Born Stockport, 15 September 1960.
County League debut: v Hartlepool United (a), 8 April 1978.
As a result of his 14 years of service to County, Andy Thorpe broke Bob Murray's record number of appearances, playing in every defensive and midfield position. When released by County in the 1992 close-season, Thorpe had made a magnificent 555 appearances. Signed as an apprentice, he made his way up through the reserve team to make his debut at the age of 17. Following this debut, Thorpe became a regular member of the side for eight seasons, building up an excellent partnership with another County stalwart, Tommy Sword. Whilst his best position was as a central defender, in his younger days he did show considerable potential as a

midfield player. From September 1980 until April 1984, Andy Thorpe made 183 consecutive League and Cup appearances and it was both surprising and disappointing when County let Thorpe move to Tranmere Rovers in August 1986. After making his Tranmere debut against Preston North End, the 'luck of the draw'

saw Andy Thorpe then play against County in his next three games. Within 18 months, manager Asa Hartford brought Thorpe back to Edgeley Park in January 1988 where he remained as reliable and professional as ever for his last four and a half seasons. After spending all his career in the Fourth Division and being a Stockport man through and through, no County player derived more pleasure from, nor was more deserving of, promotion to Division Three in 1991. His last season in League football was spent in the Third Division where he broke Bob Murray's record of League appearances and, despite suffering defeat in both his first and last County games, there was a monumental difference in the setting of these two matches: from the Victoria Ground, Hartlepool, in 1978, to Wembley in the Autoglass Trophy Final in 1992. A prime example of a model professional, Thorpe moved to Australia to play football but, within ten games, suffered an achilles tendon injury, the worst of his career. Returning to England, he made a number of appearances for non-League Witton Albion where he joined former County colleague, Oshor Williams. However, wherever he may be, Andy Thorpe will remain a County man, of whom the club and its supporters can be proud.

Billy Titterington

Born Darwen, 17 December 1911.
County League debut: v Rotherham United (a), 25 April 1935.
After signing professional forms as a centre-half for Blackburn Rovers at 17, Billy Titterington failed to break into the first-team and moved into non-League football with Great Harwood. Following a further move to Fleetwood, Titterington developed into an inside-forward and it was in this role that County signed him on 2 February 1935.

Initially, his appearances were sporadic, covering for the injured Jimmy Stevenson and Bob Green, but Titterington gradually developed into a thoroughly competent and versatile player, equally comfortable as an inside-forward or half-back. In addition to being a clean tackler and good header of the ball, his passing was particularly skilful.

Very much a believer in the philosophy that football should be entertaining, his geniality both on and off the field was well-received by County supporters. Titterington's 117 League and Cup appearances were evenly shared between his position at half-back and inside-forward, and, as only an occasional scorer, he was pleasantly surprised by his 11 goals. Following the suspension of League football in 1939, Billy Titterington continued to play in wartime football, adding a further 57 appearances and scoring five goals, before ending his playing career with his one and only club in November 1943. After working for the Stockport Manufacturing Company, he went into the haulage business, first in Blackburn and then in Liverpool. Retiring in 1974, Billy Titterington moved to Formby where he still lives.

Eddie Vincent

Born Prudhoe, 3 March 1909. Died 1980.
County League debut: v Darlington (a), 30 March 1929.
Signed from Prudhoe Colliery the day before his 19th birthday, Eddie Vincent developed from a 'utility' player into one of the most formidable defenders of his era. His professional career spanned almost 20 years with his two clubs, County and Grimsby Town. Vincent made only four appearances in his first two seasons and only became a first-choice player after three years. At $12\frac{1}{2}$st, he was a very strong defender, a good tackler and reader of the game. Equally at home as a full-back or defensive half-back, Vincent had the additional benefit of being expert at taking free-kicks, possessing a fearsome shot and becoming County's regular penalty-taker in 1931. The only non-forward to score on County's 13-0 win against Halifax Town, Vincent's penalty was one of 23 goals he scored in 143 League and Cup appearances for the Hatters. Three impressive seasons at Edgeley Park resulted in his being transferred to First Division Grimsby Town in June 1934 for a fee of £1,200. He remained at Blundell Park for 13 years, all 144 of his League appearances being in the First Division. Whilst he played for the Mariners in every wartime season, Vincent did make two appearances for County during the Christmas period of 1941. At the age of 38, in March 1947, Eddie Vincent made his last League appearance against Everton, coincidentally the same opponents as in his Grimsby debut over 12 years earlier, before retiring from professional football.

Jimmy Wainwright

Born Stockport 1872.
County debut: (Lancashire League) v Fairfield (h), 7 September 1895; (FA Cup) v Liverpool South End (h), 1 October 1895; (League) v Leicester Fosse (a), 1 September 1900.
After making his debut in County's second season in the Lancashire League, left-back Jimmy Wainwright became the longest-serving player to see Second Division football come to Stockport. A thoroughly consistent and honest player, he was a pivotal figure in County's gradual rise up the Lancashire League. Honoured with the captaincy in August 1896, on the pitch he became the motivating force behind the club's ambitions

which were eventually realised in 1900 when he led County to the championship of the Lancashire League. In his 174 appearances for County, the only occasions on which he did not play at left-back were in November 1897, when on successive Saturdays, County were without their regular goalkeeper, the colourful Joe Lee. The situation was remedied when, with no apparent concern, captain Jimmy Wainwright took over in goal whilst centre-forward, Rimmer Brown replaced him at left-back. County won the first of these two games, an FA Cup fourth qualifying round tie, and drew the second. When County were elected to the Football League in May 1900, Wainwright lost the captaincy to the newly acquired former Wednesday captain, Jack Earp, but played alongside his famous amateur full-back for virtually the whole season. At the end of their first season in the Football League, Jimmy Wainwright was released by County and returned to non-League football.

Jimmy Walsh

Born Stockport, 1901.
County League debut: v Cardiff City (a), 4 September 1920.
Contemporary sports journalists believed that Jimmy Walsh was introduced into League football at too young an age. As a player of undoubted potential, the talented inside-forward signed for County as an amateur at the age of 18, not signing professional forms until 26 September 1920, after he had made his League debut. He appeared in the majority of County's games in his debut season which was clearly hard on the youngster as the club spent the season vainly fighting against relegation. Whilst undeniably possessing the skill to develop into an excellent player, he often appeared lost in the battles which took place that season, by-passed by the frantic urgency of the play. At times, he appeared as an outside-right which was clearly not his best position and, by the end of 1920-21, Walsh looked exhausted. Having apparently made the mistake of overplaying Walsh in the rugged and difficult Second Division, the County management used him only minimally in their Third Division championship season. Although his career this far had seemed to have been misdirected, his ability had not gone unnoticed. On 22 July 1922, Jimmy Walsh was transferred to First Division champions Liverpool for little

more than £100. At Anfield, his inherent ability was nurtured in the reserve team before he appeared in almost every match in 1923-24. As Liverpool's regular inside-left, Walsh scored 19 goals in his first season, including an FA Cup hat-trick against holders Bolton Wanderers in February 1924. He remained at Anfield until 1928, his career dogged by injury which restricted his League and Cup appearances to 77. Walsh moved on to Second Division Hull City where, over the following three seasons, he played out his professional career. County could claim that Jimmy Walsh was 'their' find, but the manner in which he was played ensured that supporters were never given the opportunity to see the player develop in the correct way.

Peter Ward

Born County Durham, 15 October 1964.
County League debut: v Swansea City (h), 17 August 1991.
Following promotion from Division Four in 1991, County manager, Danny Bergara, made one significant signing, that of Peter Ward. Although the midfield player took time to settle into the side, his contribution to the team during the past three seasons has been immense. There is little doubt that Ward is a tenacious battler, and not the kind of

midfield player who has a tendency to drift in and out of a game, but there is much more to his game than this. His ability to direct long accurate passes is often overlooked, as is his close-control when, unfortunately too rarely, he carries the ball into the opposition's penalty area. For a midfield player, it might be argued that Ward does not score as often

as he should, but the goals he has scored can rarely be described as 'ordinary'. Two of his goals have effectively taken County to Wembley: a swerving free-kick in the Play-off semi-final against Stoke City in 1992, and a delicate chip in the second leg of the Autoglass Trophy Northern Final against Wigan Athletic in 1993. He has a wonderful left-foot and, on a number of occasions, has shown that he can make defenders pay dearly for conceding free-kicks near the edge of the penalty area. After beginning his career in his native North-East with Chester-le-Street, Ward signed for Huddersfield Town in January 1987. In two and a half seasons at Leeds Road, he made 37 League appearances, 12 as substitute, before moving to Rochdale in July 1989.

In his first season at Spotland, he was an influential figure in Rochdale's history-making run to the fifth round of the FA Cup where they were beaten, somewhat unfortunately, by eventual Finalists Crystal Palace at Selhurst Park. The resolution he demonstrated in his 99 League and Cup appearances for Rochdale was sufficiently impressive to persuade County to bring him to Edgeley Park in a cash plus player deal which took Mark Payne to Spotland. During his second season at Edgeley Park, Peter Ward was made captain, one who leads by example, and who has now made 150 League and Cup appearances for County.

Albert Waterall

Born Nottingham, 1889.
County League debut: v Fulham (h), 4 October 1913.
In signing Albert Waterall on 23 June 1913, Stockport not only made a coup of the highest order, but also acquired possibly the most loyal player they have ever had. When County signed him, he was the least well-known of three footballing brothers, the others being Isaac and Tommy. He had played alongside Isaac at Notts County and, during wartime football, he frequently formed a left-wing partnership with Tommy, who had played for a number of League clubs, including Bradford, Leicester Fosse and Notts County. Albert Waterall had had considerable First Division experience at Notts County before joining the Hatters following a disagreement with the Nottingham directors. Although he came to County as an inside-forward, he developed into a versatile player who was equally

adept as a half-back. Whilst clearly not lacking in skill, Waterall's greatest asset was his unquenchable drive, a professional who not only loved the game but would have played until he dropped. Whether playing as a half-back or inside-forward, Waterall consistently scored goals and completed one season as County's top-scorer. He played for 13 consecutive seasons which included wartime football when, having entered the mines at the

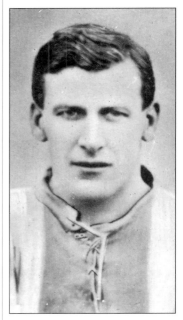

outbreak of war, he could continue to play unpaid football. Both he and brother Tommy, who made 87 wartime appearances for County, were eventually enlisted in February 1918 but, on the resumption of League football, 30-year-old Albert Waterall re-appeared for County to provide the same commitment he had always given. In April 1921, his loyalty was rewarded by a joint-benefit with Fred Garrett and Jimmy Mitton but, as Waterall continued to give sterling service, he was granted another benefit almost exactly four years later in April 1925. Following County's relegation to the Third Division, in the close-season of 1926, Waterall was released by County, having made exactly 300 League and Cup appearances and scored 36 goals, to which can be added another 97 wartime appearances and nine goals. Although 37 years old, Albert Waterall remained in League football, signed by Second Division Leyton Orient for whom he made two appearances and scored one goal. In 1927, this great professional finally retired from League football and returned to Nottingham where he became the landlord of a pub.

Arthur Waters

Born Birmingham, 1879. Died Birmingham, January 1952.
County debut: (Lancashire Combination) v Southport Central, 2 September 1904; (FA Cup) v Staly-bridge Rovers (h), 29 October 1904; (League) v Chelsea (h), 2 September 1905.

After failing to be re-elected to the Football League in May 1904, County attempted to ensure that their team was of sufficient strength to challenge for non-League honours and, whilst forced to introduce a number of young players, persuaded the experienced right-back Arthur Waters to join

them from Swindon Town. Waters had begun his career with Small Heath (Birmingham City) before joining Walsall and had been a member of the Saddlers team which, in 1902, had beaten both Port Vale and Burnley to reach the last 16 of the FA Cup. In order to allow Jimmy Heywood, County's promising young right-back to play in his natural position, Waters took over at left-back and, from his first game, looked as if he had always occupied that position. During his first season, Waters caught pneumonia and, according to a press release on 7 February, 'it was doubtful he would survive until the morning'. The popular Waters not only survived but, within six weeks, was back in County's first team to help them win the Lancashire Combination and regain their League status. A hardworking and inspirational player, Waters was made County's captain in 1906 and remained so for three seasons. During his captaincy, County enjoyed the relative luxury of mid-table respectability, Waters exemplary conduct an important factor in a vastly improved team.

When, after seven seasons at Edgeley Park, Arthur Waters ended his League career in 1911, he had become the first County player to make 150 League appearances, an especially creditable achievement in the light of his near death six years earlier.

Billy Webb

Born Mexborough, 7 March 1932.
County League debut: v Bradford City (a), 24 August 1957.

Although the vast majority of Billy Webb's League career was spent in the Third and Fourth Divisions, it had begun with much greater promise. A quite meteoric rise began when, a month after joining Wath in May 1951, he signed for Rochdale and, before June was out, the left-back was transferred to Second Division Leicester City for £1,250. During a six-year stay at Filbert Street, his place in the first team was interrupted by National Service and, when he returned, he was unable to regain his place other than when covering for injured players. When Leicester won the Second Division championship in 1957, Webb was given a free-transfer and, after making 49 appearances for City, he joined County on 8 June 1957. His signing began an excellent period of loyal and highly consistent service. In his debut season at County he was an ever-present and only missed eight League matches during his first five seasons. The experience of being with a higher level club resulted in Webb being able to shine in the lower divisions of the Football League. He was a model of consistency and, in his earlier seasons, had considerable pace. Webb demonstrated the true art of

the professional, fulfilling his responsibilities quietly, competently and conscientiously. As he had at Leicester, Webb gave six years service, making 262 League and Cup appearances for County without scoring a goal before leaving in July 1963 to join non-League Hyde United.

Len White

Born Skellow, near Adwick-le-Street, 23 March 1930. Died June 1994.
County League debut: v Torquay United (h), 16 January 1965.

At some stage in their history, virtually all lower division League clubs have signed a celebrity from the past, one who is in the twilight of his professional career. County are no exception but, sadly and predictably, most such players have either lost their zest or lost the skills which made them famous. Len White was the most wonderful exception when he joined County, who were in 92nd place in the Football League. Almost 35, White had little to prove, having won an FA Cup winners' medal during a marvellous career with Newcastle United where he proved to be a worthy successor to the idolised Tyneside centre-forward, Jackie Milburn, scoring 153 goals in 269 League and Cup appearances. He was already regarded as a 'veteran' when, in 1961, he joined Huddersfield Town with whom he made 110 appearances and scored 39 goals. In January 1965, despite being in bottom place in the Fourth Division, County had enjoyed a magnificent 3-2 victory against Bristol Rovers in an FA Cup third round replay which set up a fourth round tie at First Division leaders, Liverpool. Frank Beaumont, one of County's most experienced midfield players in a predominantly young and inexperienced team, was suspended for the Anfield tie and, on 15 January, four days after the Bristol game, Stockport splashed out £4,000 to bring Len White to Edgeley Park. Fortunately for County, White had just lost his place at Huddersfield to Tony Leighton and was, therefore, not cup-tied. When the 'no-hopers' visited the First Division leaders at Anfield on 30 January, the *Liverpool Echo* proclaimed that 'victory for Stockport would be day's most impossible result' but, after White headed County in front, they were unlucky only to come away with a 1-1 draw. Despite County losing the replay,

for 58 games White was to show his class in such a way that, whatever County's League position, he warmed the spectators with his innate talent. Age had not dimmed his ability as, still a maestro, White was able to illuminate any game by moments of great craftsmanship. In April 1965, White scored his 200th League goal but he was

unable to save the club from finishing the season in bottom place. His performances inspired those around him and, in 1965-66, a rejuvenated County were a different team. White frequently scored exciting goals, retaining his ability to run gracefully off the ball and to shoot accurately on the turn. He obtained a memorable hat-trick in County's record 7-1 away victory at Bradford City and ended both his seasons as County's top-scorer. After 25 goals in 58 League and Cup appearances, County released White in the summer of 1966, which was particularly disappointing as the Fourth Division championship won the following season, would have been a fitting end to his career. He moved to non-League Altrincham and then to other clubs in his native Yorkshire, playing on into his 50th year. At the end of his professional career, White became an undertaker in the Huddersfield area. For a major part of County's 111-year history, survival has been their major concern and, as a result, they have never had the luxury of being able to insist upon combining victory with flair. Whilst they have had some outstanding players, they have had very few who were simply a joy to watch. Len White was one. A memorable part of County's history went with him when Len White died in the summer of 1994.

Bill Williams

Born Littleborough, 7 October 1960.

County League debut: v Chester City (h), 28 September 1985.

Having completed his ninth season at Edgeley Park, in March 1994 Bill Williams became only the 11th player to have made 300 appearances for County. As his father owned a decorating business, Williams served an apprenticeship which enabled him to join the family firm whilst playing football for local team, Ashe Labs, before signing professional forms forms for Rochdale in August 1981. Initially playing in midfield, Williams was moved into the defence during his second season

at Spotland, and it has been as a central defender that he has blossomed. When Rochdale's Les Chapman was freed in 1985 and moved to Edgeley Park, he recommended Williams to his new club and the slim central defender signed for County on 17 July 1985. The only first-teamer currently at Edgeley Park to have played through some of County's darker days, the cultured defender has been outstanding in his long association with the club, an integral part of the successful team built up during the past five years. The fact that, as a professional player, he has been free to continue in his family business, has not in any way diminished his fitness nor his ability to perform in the Third (now Second) Division. After 120 League and Cup appearances, Bill Williams was transferred to First Division neighbours, Manchester City, for £50,000 in October 1988. Within two months and after making only one substitute appearance in the unfamiliar role of right-back, the defender returned to Edgeley Park for

£30,000. City's loss was County's gain as Williams continued to give wonderful performances in his proper central defensive role. He is, without doubt, the classiest defender to appear for County in the past 30 years, an excellent reader of the game who provides the necessary stability in the heart of the defence. Williams displays the most remarkable coolness on the ball, to the extent that County supporters of a nervous disposition frequently have their hearts in their mouths as he nonchantly plays himself out of trouble in the danger area. The fact that his insistence on taking the stylish way out of hazardous situations leads, on occasion, to the loss of possession, is something the supporters accept as inevitable, but fails to diminish their admiration for the player. In spite of a series of injuries during the last four seasons, Bill Williams has remained a key player, figuring in all four of County's Wembley appearances. At the start of 1993-94, it appeared that Williams might not make another first-team appearance but, to the delight of the fans, on New Year's Day 1994 he returned to the team and, having made 314 appearances for County, it would have been a just reward for his cultured and loyal service if he had entered a tenth season with the club.

Oshor Williams

Born Stockton-on-Tees, 21 April 1958.
County League debut: Tranmere Rovers (a), 31 August 1979.
The first black player to join County, Oshor Williams took little time to become a crowd favourite, the fans approving of his total commitment and powerful running and only disapproving when he was allowed to join Port Vale five years after his arrival. Beginning his career as an apprentice with his local League club Middlesbrough, Williams joined Manchester United in August 1976 where, although elevated to the first-team squad, he failed to make an appearance. Released by United, he returned home to reassess his footballing future, during which time he appeared for Billingham Synthonia. Within a month, Williams was signed by Northern Premier League side, Gateshead, but, as he considered a move to Fort Lauderdale in the United States, a £5,000 move to Southampton materialised in March 1978. He immediately made his League debut in a home

game against Arsenal but in his 17 month stay, only made nine League appearances, three of which were with Exeter City whilst on loan in September 1978. In August 1979, County paid Southampton £10,000 to bring Williams to Edgeley Park, beginning an extremely successful period for the winger/midfielder. County fans took to him quickly and, for the first time in his professional career, Williams was settled and his play improved

immeasurably. Whilst County failed to achieve more than a mid-table place in his five-year spell, Williams enjoyed an excellent understanding with the young Mick Quinn, providing the striker with the ammunition on which he could thrive. He relished the honour of taking over the captaincy when club captain, Tommy Sword, was sidelined by injury and though not overly ambitious, was disappointed in June 1984 when County failed to improve the salary he had received from the time he had first arrived, five years earlier. At the beginning of the 1984-85 season, he played on a month-to-month contract until Port Vale paid £8,000 to take him to the Potteries. Having made 216 appearances and scored 31 goals for County, there was considerable disappointment at Edgeley Park, but Williams' move to Burslem provided him with his first honour, Vale being promoted at the end of his second season. In July 1986, Oshor Williams made his final move, back to the North-West, to Preston North End for a fee of just £2,000. With the Deepdale club, Williams again played in a promotion side which

visited Edgeley Park in October 1986. Stockport fans could only watch in admiration as two magnificent strikes from the former County player helped Preston to a 3-1 victory. Unfortunately, injury ended Williams' playing career at the age of 29, although he remained at Deepdale for three years as Preston's Community Development Officer. After coaching spells at Halifax Town and Winsford United, in July 1993 he moved to Witton Albion. The well-respected and fondly remembered Oshor Williams resides in Cheadle Hulme, as he has done since he first arrived at Edgeley Park 15 years ago.

Gordon Wilmott

Born Brinsley, near Eastwood, Notts., 26 May 1929.
County League debut: v Southport (h), 21 August 1948.
The 19-year-old Nottinghamshire centre-half joined County on 19 June 1948 and, during his 11-season stay, had to consistently fight for his place against more established players. The most resilient of characters, Gordon Wilmott accepted the challenge and, although averaging only 18 games a season during his first five years at Edgeley Park, eventually established himself as County's first choice centre-half in 1953-54. Although a reliable performer, within another two

years Wilmott again found himself second choice to Ken Hodder and then the former England international, Neil Franklin. Another four seasons of irregular selection combined with injury resulted in Wilmott moving to Crewe Alexandra in March 1959, after making 219 League and Cup appearances for County and scoring just one goal in a 3-1 defeat at Tranmere Rovers. Wilmott remained at Gresty Road for a little over two seasons, but after missing County's excellent FA Cup win over First Division Luton Town in 1958, two years later he was in the Crewe side which drew 2-2 with First Division giants, Tottenham Hotspur. Although Crewe were beaten by a massive 13-2 in the replay at White Hart Lane in front of 64,365 spectators, Wilmott was a member of the Fourth Division team which, whilst outclassed, contributed to the entertainment by playing good open football. On retiring in 1961, Gordon Wilmott remained at Crewe as chief scout, before returning to the Stockport area in a similar capacity with amateur team, Cheadle Heath Nomads, whilst working as a foreman in a large local company.

Gene Wilson

Born Sheffield, 11 September 1932.
County League debut: v Grimsby Town (h), 4 September 1954.
Diminutive winger, Gene Wilson, began his footballing career with Worksop Town in the Midland League before serving his National Service in the Far East. On his release from the army, 5ft 4ins Wilson joined Sheffield Wednesday as an amateur before becoming a part-time professional with nearby Rotherham United. It was during his reserve-team experience at Rotherham that he was moved from inside-right to winger, equally comfortable on the

left or right and he was recommended to County manager, Dick Duckworth. On 29 May 1954, Wilson met Duckworth at Chesterfield Station and signed there and then as a part-time professional. After making his debut, Wilson became a firm fixture in County's team, his fast and clever wing-play enabling him to feed prolific goalscorer Jack Connor. When Connor moved on, Wilson kept his place, supplying all the new forwards with excellent service and becoming a regular goalscorer himself. After losing his place to new signing Derek Ward in 1961, he fought his way back in February 1962 only to suffer an ankle injury two games later. Told to get himself fit in the reserves, Gene Wilson set about

this and, in March 1962, played for County's 'A' team against Manchester City 'A'. During the game, a frustrated Wilson lost his composure and was sent off for arguing. Reluctant to leave, he was told by the referee that he had ten seconds to get off the pitch, otherwise the game would be abandoned. Wilson prolonged his walk sufficiently for the referee to carry out his threat, the match being abandoned. After making 239 League and Cup appearances, Gene Wilson was sacked and saw out the remainder of his playing career in non-League football with Stalybridge Celtic, Wigan, Altrincham and Llandudno. He worked as a fork-lift truck driver before being made redundant, suffering a similar fate whilst working with the South Yorkshire Passenger Transport Board. Gene Wilson found new employment with Chesterfield Transport, where he has remained since privatisation, and remains a regular visitor to Edgeley Park.

John Wilson

Born Leadgate, County Durham, 1899.
County League debut: v Leicester City (h), 26 August 1922.
Although beginning his career as a First Division centre-forward, John Wilson's most successful period was spent playing as a half-back with Manchester United. As the Football League prepared to resume in 1919, in May, Wilson was signed by Newcastle United as a centre-forward, appearing in

their first four post-war fixtures. On his third appearance, he scored twice in a 3-0 victory against Arsenal but the young forward lost his place and, during his two-year spell at Newcastle, made only seven League appearances. In 1921, Wilson returned to Leadgate before he was tempted back into League football with Third Division Durham City. On 17 May 1922, County signed the impressive forward who, they believed, would help them to consolidate their status in Division Two following their Third Division championship success weeks earlier. Wilson scored a modest nine goals as an inside-forward in County's first season back in the Second Division but the following year was converted to half-back where he played for the remainder of his County career. A thoughtful and creative player, the strongly-built Wilson attracted the attentions of neighbouring Manchester United and, when County were relegated in 1926, he moved to the First Division club. Wilson had made 134 League and Cup appearances and scored 12 goals in his four seasons with County. He made a similar number of appearances for United, 140 in all, as the Reds struggled in Division One before relegation in 1931. John Wilson left Old Trafford in 1932, moving to Bristol City, for whom he made 21 League and Cup appearances before retiring in the summer of 1933.

Stockport County Season by Season

This section records every competitive league match played by the Stockport County First XI since 1891, the year in which the Club first played league football by being accepted into The Combination. In addition to the period prior to County being elected to the Football League (1891-1900), Lancashire Combination results are included for the single season (1904-05) between failure to gain re-election in May 1904 and subsequent re-election in May 1905. Details of every FA Cup and Football League Cup are also included.

For Football League matches played, the left-hand column indicates a cumulative running number of every game.

One of the consequences of the devestating fire which destroyed the grandstand in July 1935 was that all records were lost. The following information has been gleaned from various sources, in particular contemporary newspapers and Football League records. Dates of matches, opponents, results and goalscorers have been, at the very least, triple-checked but it is acknowledged that goalscorers cited must occasionally be accepted as open to question. The principle followed has been to use the Stockport based *Cheshire Daily Echo* as the primary source for all matches played until the end of 1939, the year in which that newspaper ceased publication, supplemented by the *Stockport Chronicle* published from 1891-1906. Up to ten other newspapers have been consulted in cases where there

appears to be any discrepancy but even this cannot guarantee that every piece of information is 100 per cent accurate. Players' names are taken from official Football League records but, in the case of individuals who played in the early part of this century, the spelling of such names may be inconsistent with newspaper versions.

Official League attendances are given from season 1925-26, this being the first season that the Football League kept such records. All Football League and League Cup attendances given are those recorded by the Football League, even where these conflict with well-publicised published figures, the most notable discrepancy concerning the 'record attendance' at Edgeley Park on May 1st 1937. FA Cup attendances are given for every match since County's first entry in 1892-93 although those given for pre-World War One games are estimated and clearly not official.

Attendances given during the war-years (seasons 1939-40 to 1945-46) are, generally, an exception. Attendances for the two games played in the suspended Division Three North season 1939-40 are official as are those for the first 28 games of season 1945-46 (Division Three Northern Section (Western Region) League and the Western Region Cup Qualifying Competition). All other attendances given during this period are based on published figures but are not official.

Clearly from the state of the pitch and the players' kit, this photograph was taken prior to County's 3-0 victory against Hull City at Boothferry Park on 29 March 1947. Back row (left to right): Brown, Gleave, Morris, Bowles, McCulloch, Redfern. Front row: Staniforth, Earl, Walker, Shaw, Brinton.

1891-92

No	Date	Opponents	Result	Scorers	Bates	Blades Dr	Craig	Eaton	Ferguson	Godwin	Gotheridge	Harrison	Hawes	Heyes	Higson	Hope	Jepson	Jones	Malkin	Merrifield	Muirhead	Perry	Pixton	Ramage	Roberts	Ross	Smith	Talbot	Upton	Urmston	Wallwork	Wright
1	Sep 5	(h) Macclesfield	L 0-3			5	8		2		11						6					7	4	3			9		10	1		
2	12	(h) Stoke Swifts	L 0-3			6	8		2	5	11					10	9					7	4	3						1		
3	19	(a) Wrexham	L 1-3	Upton		5	10		2		11			1			6				3	7	4				8		9			
4	26	(a) Leek	L 2-4	Blades, Smith		5	10		2		11						6				3	7					8	4	9	1		
5	Oct 3	(a) Everton Res	L 0-4			5	10		2		11						6				3	7					8		4	1		9
6	10	(a) Buxton	L 1-2	Wright		5	10		2		11						6				3	7					8		4	1		9
7	17	(h) Chirk	W 2-0	Gotheridge, Blades	9	5	10		2		11						6					7					8		4	1		3
8	Nov 7	(h) Everton Res	L 1-2	Gotheridge		5	10		2		11						6				9						8		4	1	7	3
9	Dec 5	(a) Gorton Villa	L 0-3			5	10		2		11						6				9						8		4	1	7	3
10	25	(a) Macclesfield	L 1-2	Perry			10		2		11						6				3	9					8		4	1	7	5
11	Jan 2	(a) Denton	W 3-1	Muirhead, Smith, Perry		5	10		2								6				9	11					8		4	1	7	3
12	9	(a) Stoke Swifts	W 1-0	Craig		5	9		2		11								4		6	10					8			1	7	3
13	16	(h) Buxton	D 0-0			5	9		2		11						4				6	10					8			1	7	3
14	30	(a) Chirk	L 1-2	Bates	10		9		2								6				5	11					8		4	1	7	3
15	Feb 27	(h) Gorton Villa	D 2-2	Higson, Smith		5	10		2						9		6					11					8		4	1	7	3
16	Mar 5	(h) Chester	W 1-0	Perry		9			2	6							10				5	11			7		8		4	1		3
17	19	(h) Wrexham	L 1-3	Godwin			10		2	5							6				9	11					8		4	1	7	3
18	26	(h) Leek	W 2-0	Perry, Upton		5	10		2								6	9				11					8		4	1	7	3
19	Apr 2	(a) Northwich V	L 1-5	Jones		5	10		2								6	9				11				3	8		4	1	7	
20	15	(h) Northwich V	W 2-0	Perry, Jones			10		2			3	5				6	9				11							4	1	7	8
21	23	(a) Chester	L 0-3					8	2			3					6	9		10		11							4	1	5	7
22	30	(h) Denton	W 7-2	Jones 3, Perry 2, Upton, Eaton		5		8	2			3					6	9		7		11							4	1		10
				Appearances	2	17	19	2	22	3	12	3	1	1	1	1	21	5	1	2	13	20	3	2	1	1	18	1	19	21	13	17
				Goals	1	2	1	1		1	2				1			5			1	7					3		3			1

FINAL LEAGUE POSITION: 11th (out of 12) in The Combination

1892-93

No	Date	Opponents	Result	Scorers	Angus	Barnes	Birchenall	Blades Dr.	Coghlan	Dixon	Entwistle	Ferguson	Gallie	Gaskell	Gittins	Godwin	Grewcock	Heald	Jepson	Perry	Smith	Upton	Urmston	Wilson	Witterance
1	Sep 17	(h) Gorton Villa	W 3-2	Gallie, Entwistle, Grewcock		10		5			8	1	7		3	2	11		6	9		4			
2	24	(h) Everton Res	L 0-4			10		5			8	1	7	3	2		11		6	9		4			
3	Oct 1	(h) Buxton	D 1-1	Entwistle		10	5	9			8	1		3	2		11		6	7		4			
4	8	(a) Leek	L 2-3	Jepson, Grewcock			5			10	8	1		9	2	3	11		6	7		4			
5	Nov 5	(a) Gorton Villa	L 1-3	Coghlan			5		9	10	8	1		3	2		11		6	7		4			
6	Dec 3	(a) Everton Res	L 1-4	Opp own-goal		6	5				8			3	2		11	9		7	10	4	1		
7	10	(h) Chester	D 2-2	Smith 2			5				8			3	2		11	9	6	7	10	4	1		
8	24	(a) Buxton	W 2-1	Smith, Grewcock		6	5				8			3	2		11		9	7	10	4	1		
9	31	(h) Macclesfield	D 1-1	Gaskell			5				8			3	2		11		6	7	10	4	1		9
10	Jan 7	(a) Chester	L 2-4	Birchenall, Entwistle			5				8			3	2		11	9	4	7	10	6	1		
11	14	(h) Dresden U	W 4-0	Smith, Perry, Upton, Grewcock	9		5				8			3	2		11		6	7	10	4	1		
12	21*	(h) Leek	W 3-0	Perry 2, Smith	9	6	5				8			3	2		11			7	10	4	1		
13	28	(h) Stoke Swifts	D 1-1	Entwistle	9	6	5				8			3	2		11			7	10	4	1		
14	Feb 4	(a) Macclesfield	W 3-1	Entwistle, Smith, Grewcock	9	6	5				8			3	2		11		4	7	10		1		
15	11	(a) Nantwich	L 0-1		9	6	5				8			3	2		11			7	10	4	1		
16	18	(h) Chirk	W 2-1	Opp own-goal, Grewcock	9	6	5				8			3	2		11			7	10	4	1		
17	Mar 4	(a) Wrexham	L 0-3		9		5				8			3	2		11	7	6		10	4	1		
18	25	(h) Wrexham	L 0-1		9		5							3	2		11	8	6	7	10	4	1		
19	Apr 1	(a) Dresden U	D 0-0		9		5							3	2		11	8	6	7	10	4	1		
20	8	(h) Nantwich	W 6-0	Perry 4, Grewcock, Angus	9		5				6			3	2		11	7		8	10	4		1	
21	15	(a) Chirk	D 3-3	Grewcock, Heald, Angus	9		5				6			3	2		11	7		8	10	4		1	
22	22	(a) Stoke Swifts	W 1-0	Grewcock		6	5				8			3	2		11		4	7	10	9	1		
				Appearances	11	11	20	3	1	2	20	5	2	21	22	2	22	8	15	21	17	21	15	2	1
				Goals	2		1		1		5		1	1			9	1	1	7	6	1			

FINAL LEAGUE POSITION: 6th (out of 12) in The Combination

Own-goals 2

FA Cup

Round	Date	Opponents	Result	Scorers	Att	Angus	Barnes	Birchenall	Blades Dr.	Coghlan	Dixon	Entwistle	Ferguson	Gallie	Gaskell	Gittins	Godwin	Grewcock	Heald	Jepson	Perry	Smith	Upton	Urmston	Wilson	Witterance
Q1	Oct 25	(h) Halliwell R	W 4-2	Grewcock, Entwistle, Barnes, Upton	500		10	5				8	1		3	2	4	11		6	7		9			
Q2	29	(a) Bury	L 1-8	Grewcock	6,000		10	5		9		8	1		3	2		11		6	7		4			
					Appearances		2	2		1		2	2		2	2	1	2		2	2		2			
					Goals		1					1						2					1			

*Match number 12 was a 'replay' of a match scheduled for November 26. The referee declared the ground unfit but County and Leek played a friendly, drawing 1-1, the team being the same as Match 6.

FA Cup Qualifying round 1 was after extra-time. This was a 'replayed' tie, the clubs having met at Green Lane on 15 October, Stockport winning 4-0 (Upton 2, Grewcock, Entwistle), the team being the same except that Dr Blades had played in place of Godwin. Prior to the kick-off, Halliwell had lodged a protest about the state of the ground and this appeal was upheld by the FA who ordered the tie to be replayed. (According to contemporary newspapers, Halliwell had gained a reputation of lodging protests when they lost a game but, as stated, this particular protest had been lodged *prior* to the tie.) Overall records do *not* therefore include the 'first' tie.

1893-94

#	Date		Opposition	Result	Scorers	Axon	Birchenall	Gaskell	Griffins	Gould	Harvey	Hewitt	Jepson	Leigh	McCombie	Moores	Perry	Smith	Upton	Whitehead
1	Sep 16	(a)	Dresden U	L 0-5			3	2	5	1	7	9		6	11		8	10	4	
2	30	(a)	Stoke Swifts	L 0-3			3	2	5	1	7		9	6	11		8	10	4	
3	Oct 7	(h)	Chester	D 1-1	Leigh		3	2	5	1	7	9		6	11		8	10	4	
4	28	(h)	Leek	W 4-1	Hewitt, Smith 2, Leigh			2	5	1	7	9	3	6	11		8	10	4	
5	Nov 11	(h)	Everton Res	W 4-0	McCombie 3, Perry			2	5	1	7	9	3	6	11		8	10	4	
6	28	(a)	Chester	D 1-1	Hewitt			2	5	1	7	9	3	6	11		8	10	4	
7	Dec 2	(a)	Leek	L 0-1				2	5	1	7	9	3	6	11		8	10	4	
8	9	(a)	Everton Res	L 0-9			3	2		1	7	9		6	11	5	8	10	4	
9	25	(h)	Macclesfield	D 2-2	Smith, Birchenall		3	2	5	1	7	9	8	6	11			10	4	
10	30	(a)	Nantwich	W 4-3	Birchenall, Hewitt, McCombie, Opp own goal		3	2	5	1	7	9		6	11		8	10	4	
11	Jan 13	(h)	Wrexham	W 4-0	Smith, Hewitt 2, McCombie			2	5	1	7	9	3	6	11		8	10	4	
12	20	(h)	Buxton	D 0-0			3	2	5	1		9	7	6	11		8	10	4	
13	Mar 3	(h)	Macclesfield	W 3-0	Birchenall, Whitehead, Opp own goal		3	2	5	1	7	9		6	11			10	4	8
14	23	(h)	Stoke Swifts	D 1-1	Opp own goal		3	2	5	1	7	9		6	11			10	4	8
15	24	(h)	Dresden U	W 2-0	Leigh, Hewitt	5	3	2		1	7	9		6	11			10	4	8
16	26	(a)	Buxton	L 1-4	Whitehead	5	3	2		1	7	9		6	11			10	4	8
17	Apr 7	(a)	Wrexham	D 1-1	Smith	5	3	2		1	7		9	6	11			10	4	8
18	14	(a)	Nantwich	W 5-0	Leigh, Smith, Hewitt, Upton, McCombie	5	3	2		1	7	9		6	11			10	4	8
	FINAL LEAGUE POSITION: 4th (out of 10) in The Combination				**Appearances**	4	13	18	13	18	17	16	9	18	18	1	11	18	18	6
					Goals		3					7		4	6		1	6	1	2

Own-goals 3

FA Cup

#	Date		Opposition	Result	Scorers	Att	Axon	Birchenall	Gaskell	Griffins	Gould	Harvey	Hewitt	Jepson	Leigh	McCombie	Moores	Perry	Smith	Upton	Whitehead
Q1	Oct 14	(h)	Bootle	W w/o																	
Q2	Nov 4	(h)	Tranmere R	W 2-1	McCombie, Hewitt	4,000		3	2	5	1	7	9		6	11		8	10	4	
Q3	Dec 4	(h)	Wrexham	W 7-0	McCombie 2, Smith, Hewitt 3, Perry	'moderate'		3	2	5	1	7	9		6	11		8	10	4	
Q4	16	(h)	Crewe A	D 0-0*		2,000		3	2	5	1	7	9		6	11		8	10	4	
R	23	(a)	Crewe A	W 2-1	McCombie, Smith	2,000		3	2	5	1	7	9		6	11		8	10	4	
1	Jan 27	(h)	Burton W	L 0-1		4,500		3	2	5	1	7	9		6	11		8	10	4	
					Appearances			5	5	5	5	5	5		5	5		5	5	5	
					Goals								4			4		1	2		

Some sources state that Stockport had beaten Rawtenstall 5-0 in the FA Cup Qualifying Round 1. County did beat Rawtenstall 5-0 on 14 October but this was a friendly. In fact, following the draw for the first qualifying round, County's opponents, Bootle, were wound up on 29 August 1893 and County had a walk-over to the second qualifying round.

The Wrexham game in the FA Cup was a 'replayed' tie, the clubs having met at Green Lane on 25 November, Stockport winning 3-2 (Birchenall, McCombie, Hewitt), the team being the same. After the match, Wrexham complained about the state of the pitch and their complaint was, surprisingly, upheld by the FA who ordered the game to be replayed. Again, overall records do not include this original tie.

* After extra-time.

Gorton Villa resigned early in the season before Stockport had played them.

1894-95

#	Date		Opponent	Result	Scorers	Axon	Bailey	Baxter	Chadwick	Coxon	Dunn	Fletcher	Godwin	Gould	Haresnape	Harvey	Henshaw	Heyes	Leigh	Lever	Mann	McCombie	Moss	Smith	Spencer	Upton	Urmston
1	Sep 1	(h)	Chorley	D 2-2	Smith, Coxon	9		2		7		5		1	6			11		3	8			10		4	
2	8	(a)	W Manchester	L 1-4	Coxon		9	2		7		5		1	6			11		3	8			10		4	
3	22	(a)	South Shore	D 1-1	McCombie		9	2				5		1	7			11		3	8	10			6	4	
4	29	(h)	Heywood Cen	W 1-0	Fletcher		9	2	10	7		5		1	6			11		3	8					4	
5	Oct 20	(a)	Accrington	L 0-5		8			2	7		5			9			11		3	10				6	4	1
6	Nov 10	(h)	Accrington	L 2-4	Bailey, Mann	9	10		2			5				4		7	3	11	8				6		1
7	17	(h)	Blackpool	W 1-0	Mann	9	10		2			5			7	4		8		3	11				6		1
8	24	(h)	Clitheroe	W 5-3	Mann, Bailey 3, Haresnape	9	10		2			5			7	4		8		3	11				6		1
9	Dec 1	(h)	South Shore	W 3-2	Baxter, Heyes, Haresnape	9	10	2				5			7	4		8		3	11				6		1
10	15	(a)	Bacup	L 2-6	Heyes 2		9		2			5			7	4		8	11	3	10				6		1
11	22	(h)	Fairfield	D 2-2	Haresnape, Mann		9		2			5			7	4		8	10	3	11				6		1
12	25	(a)	Southport Cen	L 0-3			9		2			5			7	4		8	10	3	11				6		1
13	29	(a)	Heywood Cen	W 9-1	Heyes 2, Haresnape, Fletcher, Leigh 2, Mann 2, Bailey		9		2			5			7	4		8	11	3	10				6		1
14	Jan 5	(a)	Fleetwood R	L 2-7	Fletcher, Mann		9		2			5			7	4		8		3	11				6	10	1
15	12	(h)	Southport Cen	D 3-3	Leigh, Bailey, Opp own-goal*		9					5			7	4		8	11	3	10				6	2	1
16	19	(a)	Rossendale	L 0-4			9					5			7	4		8	11	3	10		2		6		1
17	Feb 2	(a)	Nelson	L 1-5	Bailey		9					5			7	4		8	11	3	10		2		6		1
18	9	(a)	Chorley	L 2-3	Leigh, Haresnape		9					5			7			8	11	3			2		6	4	1
19	16	(h)	Fleetwood R	W 2-0	Heyes, Leigh	9						5			7	4		8	10	3	11		2		6		1
20	23	(h)	Nelson	D 2-2	Haresnape, Opp own-goal*	9						5			7	4	11		10	3	8		2		6		1
21	Mar 2	(a)	Blackpool	L 2-7	Haresnape, Axon	9						5			7	4		8	10	3	11		2		6		1
22	9	(h)	W Manchester	W 2-1	Mann, Axon	9						5			7	4		8	10	2	11				6	3	1
23	23	(a)	Clitheroe	W 2-1	Opp own-goal, Mann	9						5	3		7	4		8	10		11		2		6		1
24	30	(a)	Bacup	W 3-0	Axon, Mann, Haresnape	9						5	2		7	4		8	10	3	11				6		1
25	Apr 6	(h)	Rossendale	W 3-2	Unknown§, Axon 2	9						5	2		7	4		8	10	3	11				6		1
26	20	(a)	Fairfield	L 0-1		9						5	2		7	4		8	10	3	11				6		1
			Appearances			9	17	4	14	4	1	25	4	4	20	25	1	19	22	25	21	6	6	3	24	10	22
			Goals			5	7	1		2		3			8			6	5		10	1		1			

FINAL LEAGUE POSITION: 9th (out of 14) in the Lancashire League

Own-goals 3, Unknown scorer 1

FA Cup

#	Date		Opponent	Result	Scorers	Att.	Axon	Bailey	Baxter	Chadwick	Coxon	Dunn	Fletcher	Godwin	Gould	Haresnape	Harvey	Henshaw	Heyes	Leigh	Lever	Mann	McCombie	Moss	Smith	Spencer	Upton	Urmston
Q2	Oct 13	(h)	Fairfield	L 2-3	Heyes, Fletcher	3,500	9		2				5			7	6		8	11	3	10				4		1
			Appearances				1		1				1			1	1		1	1	1	1				1		1
			Goals										1						1									

These 'own-goals' were not described as such by contemporary newspapers but came about as a result of the goalkeeper being barged over the line.

§ This, and subsequent 'unknown' goalscorers are goals following a 'scrimmage' in front of goal and where the actual scorer has not been identifiable.

1895-96

#	Date		Opponent	Result	Scorers	Axon	Blears	Boulemier	Childs	Ferries	Fletcher	Hareshape	Henshaw	Heyes	Higson	Kirton	Leigh	Lever	Mann	Mycock	Rigby	Robertson	Sawyers	Smith	Spencer	Sutherland	Urmston	Wainwright	Wilson
1	Sep	7 (h)	Fairfield	D 1-1	Smith	9	1			5	7			11			2	10						8	6			3	4
2		21 (h)	Ashton NE	L 2-6	Opp own-goal 2		1			5	7			11	10	2	9							8	6			3	4
3	Oct	19 (h)	Stalybridge R	L 2-3	Fletcher, Sutherland		1			7	5			8		11						10		2	6	9		3	4
4		28 (h)	Chorley	W 2-1	Leigh, Spencer				1	7	5			8			10	2	11						6	9		3	4
5	Nov	9 (a)	Bacup	L 3-4	Ferries 2, Sutherland				1	7	5			8			10	2	11						6	9		3	4
6		16 (a)	Ashton NE	W 6-2	Leigh 2, Sutherland, Ferries 2, Spencer				1	7	5			8			10	2	11						6	9		3	4
7		23 (h)	Bacup	W 4-2	Sutherland 3, Ferries				1	7	5			8			11	2						10	6	9		3	4
8		30 (a)	Stalybridge R	W 2-1	Heyes, Smith				1	7	5			8			11	2						10	6	9		3	4
9	Dec	7 (a)	Clitheroe	W 2-1	Mann, Ferries				1	7	5			8			10	2	11						6	9		3	4
10		14 (h)	W Manchester	L 1-3	Ferries				1	7	5			8			10	2	11					6		9		3	4
11		21 (a)	South Shore	D 1-1	Ferries	6			1	7	5			8			11	2	3					10		9			4
12		25 (a)	Fairfield	L 0-3		6			1	7	5			8			11	2	4					10		9		3	
13		28 (h)	Southport Cen	L 2-4	Sutherland, Leigh	6			1	7	5			10			9	2	11							8		3	4
14	Jan	4 (a)	W Manchester	L 0-2					1	7	5			8			11	2	6					10		9		3	4
15		11 (a)	Chorley	L 1-8	Sutherland				1	7	4			8			10	2	11							9		3	4
16	Feb	1 (a)	Halliwell R	L 1-3	Mann					7	5			9			10		11	2				8	6		1	3	4
17		8 (a)	Southport Cen	L 1-5	Henshaw					7	5	11	9				10		2					8	6		1	3	4
18		15 (h)	Nelson	W 4-0	Smith 3, Heyes					7	5			9			10		11	2				8	6		1	3	4
19		22 (h)	Fleetwood R	W 3-2	Fletcher, Smith, Mann		2		1	7	5			9			10		11					8	6			3	4
20		29 (h)	Rossendale	W 2-0	Smith, Spencer		2		1	7	5			9			10		11					8	6			3	4
21	Mar	7 (h)	Halliwell R	D 2-2	Smith, Fletcher		2		1	7	5			9	4		10		11					8	6			3	
22		14 (a)	Liverpool SE	L 0-2			2		1	7	5			9			10		11					8	6			3	4
23		16 (h)	South Shore	W 1-0	Heyes	4	2		1	7	5			9			10		11					8	6			3	
24		21 (h)	Blackpool	W 2-0	Spencer, Mann	4	2		1	7	5			9			10		11					8	6			3	
25		28 (a)	Nelson	L 0-6		4	2		1	7	5			9			10		11					8	6			3	
26	Apr	3 (h)	Clitheroe	W 8-0	Smith 4, Leigh 2, Heyes 2	10	2		1		5			9			11		7					8	6			3	4
27		4 (a)	Fleetwood R	L 0-3		10	2		1		5			9			11		7					8	6			3	4
28		6 (a)	Blackpool	W 1-0	Leigh	10	2		1		5						11		7		9		8	6			3	4
29		11 (a)	Rossendale	W 2-1	Sawyers, Leigh	10	3		1	8	5			9			11		2				7		6			4	
30		18 (h)	Liverpool SE	L 0-3		10	2		1		5			9			11						7	8	6			3	4

FINAL LEAGUE POSITION: 12th (out of 16) in Lancashire League

Appearances	12	12	3	24	24	30	2	1	27	1	3	28	14	26	1	1	1	3	23	25	13	3	28	25
Goals					8	3		1	5			8		4				1	12	4	8			

Own-goals 2

FA Cup

#	Date		Opponent	Result	Scorers	Axon	Blears	Boulemier	Childs	Ferries	Fletcher	Hareshape	Henshaw	Heyes	Higson	Kirton	Leigh	Lever	Mann	Mycock	Rigby	Robertson	Sawyers	Smith	Spencer	Sutherland	Urmston	Wainwright	Wilson
Q1	Oct	12 (h)	Liverpool SE	W 2-0	Ferries, Sutherland		1			7	5			8					11			10		2	6	9		3	4
Q2	Nov	2 (a)	Fairfield	L 1-5	Heyes				1	7	5			8			10	2	11						6	9		3	4

Appearances	1	1	2	2		2			1	1	2		1		1	2	2		2	2
Goals			1			1											1			

The referee 'adjourned' the match against Rossendale (a) after 70 minutes as a result of a storm of 'cyclonic severity'. When the storm abated, the Stockport players returned but certain Rossendale players had allegedly left the ground and the remainder, although ordered by the referee to return, refused to continue. The referee then abandoned the match. Initially, the Lancashire League agreed to Rossendale's request to replay the match but, having heard the referee's evidence at a subsequent meeting, the League ordered the result to stand.

#	Date		Opponent	Result	Scorers	Axon	Barnes	Blears	Bradbury	Brown	Burgoyne	Carson	Crawford	Evans	Fletcher	Hall	Henshaw	Heyes	Kennedy	Langley	Lee A	Lee J	McDonald	McFetteridge	Smith	Wainwright	Wilson
1	Sep 5	(h)	Stalybridge R	L 0-1		6		2	7	10				11	5							1	9		8	3	4
2	12	(h)	Fairfield	L 1-2	Opp own-goal	9		2	7				6	10	5						11	1			8	3	4
3	21	(h)	Rossendale	W 4-0	Hall, A.Lee, Smith, McDonald	10		2					6		5	7					11	1	8		9	3	4
4	26	(a)	Ashton NE	W 1-0	Henshaw	4		2							5	7	10				11	1			9	3	6
5	Oct 17	(a)	Clitheroe	L 2-3	Hall, A.Lee	10		2					6		5	7					11	1	4	9	8	3	
6	Nov 14	(a)	Fleetwood R	L 0-1		10		2		8					5	7					11	1	6	9		3	4
7	28	(a)	Chorley	L 1-2	Heyes	10		2							5	7		8			11	1	6		9	3	4
8	Dec 5	(a)	Halliwell R	L 0-2		10		2					6		5	7		8			11	1			9	3	4
9	12	(h)	Southport Cen	W 2-1	Brown, Smith	5		2		9						4		8	7		11	1			10	3	6
10	19	(a)	South Shore	W 1-0	Axon	6		2		9						4		8	7		11	1			10	3	5
11	25	(h)	Oldham Co	W 2-1	A.Lee, Brown	6		2		9						4		8	7		11	1			10	3	5
12	26	(a)	Bacup	W 5-4	Heyes 2, Kennedy, Brown, Hall	6		2		9						4		8	7		11	1			10	3	5
13	Jan 1	(h)	Nelson	D 1-1	Brown	6		2		9						4		8	7		11	1			10	3	5
14	2	(a)	W Manchester	W 2-0	Heyes 2	6				9					5	4		8	7		11	1			10	3	2
15	9	(a)	Fairfield	W 4-2	Brown, Smith 2 (1 pen), Heyes	6		2		9						4		8	7		11	1			10	3	5
16	16	(a)	Rossendale	L 1-3	Hall	6		2		9						4		8	7		11	1			10	3	5
17	23	(h)	Fleetwood R	W 7-0	Brown 4, Heyes, Smith 2	6		2		9						4		8	7		11	1			10	3	5
18	30	(a)	Oldham Co	L 1-3	Smith	6		2		9						4		8	7		11	1			10	3	5
19	Feb 6	(a)	South Shore	W 2-0	Brown 2	6		2		9					5	4		8	7		11	1			10	3	
20	13	(h)	Bacup	W 4-1	Smith 2, Wilson, A.Lee	6		2		9					5			8	7		11	1			10	3	4
21	27	(a)	Southport Cen	L 1-6	A.Lee	6		2		9					7	4		8			11	1			10	3	5
22	Mar 6	(h)	Ashton NE	W 3-0	Brown 2, Heyes	6		2		9						4		8	7		11	1			10	3	5
23	13	(h)	Chorley	W 2-0	Fletcher 2	6		2		9					10	4		8	7		11	1				3	5
24	27	(a)	Nelson	W 1-0	Smith	6		2		9					10	4		8	7		11	1				3	5
25	Apr 10	(h)	W Manchester	W 2-0	Fletcher, Smith			2		9					10	4			7	6	11	1			8	3	5
26	16	(h)	Clitheroe	L 0-2		6	3	2		9						4		8	7	10	11	1					5
27	19	(h)	Halliwell R	L 1-2	Heyes	6		2		9						4		8	7	10	11	1				3	5
28	20	(a)	Stalybridge R	L 2-4	Kennedy, A.Lee	6		2		10						4		9	7		11	1			8	3	5
	Appearances					27	1	27	2	20	1	1	4	2	17	26	1	20	18	4	27	28	6	2	23	24	27
	Goals					1				13					3	4	1	9	2		6		1		11		1

FINAL LEAGUE POSITION: 9th (out of 15) in Lancashire League

Own-goal 1

FA Cup

#	Date		Opponent	Result	Scorers	Att	Axon	Barnes	Blears	Bradbury	Brown	Burgoyne	Carson	Crawford	Evans	Fletcher	Hall	Henshaw	Heyes	Kennedy	Langley	Lee A	Lee J	McDonald	McFetteridge	Smith	Wainwright	Wilson
Q1	Oct 31	(h)	Barnton R	W 6-0	Fletcher, Axon 3, McFetteridge, Smith	500	10		2					6		5	7					11	1	4	9	8	3	
Q2	Nov 21	(a)	Welsh Druids	L 2-3	Smith, Unknown	2,000	10		2					6		5	7					11	1		9	8	3	4
	Appearances						2		2					2		2	2					2	2	1	2	2	2	1
	Goals						3									1									1	2		

Unknown Scorer 1

Stockport had decided to 'scratch' the FA Cup Qualifying Round 1 as, due to an error, County had been included in the Cheshire and Wales Section instead of the Lancashire Section and "as the majority of the teams which would have to be opposed are of poor calibre and might necessitate a long railway journey, the County have come to the conclusion that the game is not worth the candle." Additionally, if County succeeded in getting through to the Second Round, they would have had to alter their Lancashire League fixtures which would have entailed a "heavy monetary sacrifice". The committee were of the opinion that the supporters' views would "coincide with the Committee's actions." They did not! The committee gave the matter "further consideration" and decided to play. Had the club not mistakenly failed to post their letter of withdrawal to the FA, County would have failed to participate in the competition for the only time since their first entry.

Qualifying Round 2 was played at Ruabon.

As a result of financial problems, Liverpool South End resigned from the Lancashire League in February 1897 and their records were expunged. Stockport had played the Liverpool club at Green Lane on 4 January and won 8-0 (Heyes 2, Hall, Brown 4, Kennedy), the team being the same as Match 14 except for Smith replacing Wilson at full-back and Henshaw taking Smith's place at inside-left.

1897-98

No.	Date	Opponent	Result	Scorers	Axon	Blears	Bolton	Bridge	Brown	Clibbom	Cooke	Foster	Goddard	Hall	Henshaw	Heyes	Kitchen	Lee A	Lee J	Mann	Massey	Wainwright	Wilks	Wilson	Worrall
1	Sep 4 (h)	Horwich	W 3-0	Brown 2, Worrall	6	2		7	9					4		8		11	1			3		5	10
2	11 (h)	Middleton	W 5-0	Brown 2, Bridge, Worrall, Opp own goal	6	2		7	9					4		8		11	1			3		5	10
3	Oct 2 (a)	Stalybridge R	L 0-1		6	2		7	9					4		8		11	1			3		5	10
4	9 (h)	New Brighton T	W 1-0	Heyes	6	2		7				9		4		8		11	1			3		5	10
5	23 (h)	Ashton NE	W 4-0	Foster 3, Bridge	6		7	2		5		10		4		8		11	1			3			9
6	Nov 6 (a)	New Brighton T	L 0-1		6	2		7	9					4		8		11	1			3		5	10
7	13 (a)	Horwich	W 2-0	Heyes, Bridge	6		7	2				9		4		8		11	1			3		5	10
8	27 (a)	Middleton	D 3-3	Opp own-goal, A.Lee, Heyes	6	2		7	3			10		4		8		11	1					5	9
9	Dec 27 (h)	Chorley	D 2-2	Foster, Worrall	6	2		7				10		5		8		11	1	4		3			9
10	Jan 1 (h)	South Shore	D 0-0			2			6		5	10		4	8			11	1	7		3			9
11	3 (h)	Nelson	W 2-1	A.Lee, Worrall		2		7				10		4		8		11	1	6	5	3			9
12	8 (a)	Rochdale	W 4-0	Heyes, Foster 2, Bridge		2		7				10		4		8		11	1	6	5	3			9
13	15 (h)	Clitheroe	W 7-0	A.Lee, Foster 2, Bridge, Worrall, Hall, Heyes		2	6	7				10		5		8		11	1	4		3			9
14	22 (h)	Southport Cen	W 2-1	Wainwright, Heyes	5	2	10	7				6		4		8		11	1			3			9
15	29 (a)	Ashton NE	W 5-2	Foster 3, Bridge 2		2	4	7		6		10		5		8		11	1			3			9
16	Feb 12 (a)	Clitheroe	W 6-1	Worrall 2, Heyes 2, Bridge, Foster		2	6	7		5		10				8		11	1	4		3			9
17	19 (h)	Rochdale	W 2-1	Heyes, Foster		2	6	7		5		10		4		8		1	11			3			9
18	23 (h)	Wigan Co	L 1-2	Foster		2	6	7		5		10		4		8		11	1			3			9
19	Mar 12 (a)	Southport Cen	W 3-2	Foster, Heyes, Bridge	5	2	6	7				10		4		8	1	11				3			9
20	Apr 2 (h)	Stalybridge R	W 2-0	Foster, Heyes	5	2	6	7				10		4		8	1	11				3			9
21	9 (a)	Chorley	L 0-1			2	6	7				10		4			1	11		5		3	8		9
22	11 (a)	South Shore	L 1-2	Worrall		2	6	7				10		5			1	11		4		3	8		9
23	16 (h)	Halliwell R	W 3-0	Heyes, A.Lee, Foster		2	6	7				10		5		8	1	11		4		3			9
24	20 (a)	Halliwell R	L 0-4			2	6	7				10		5			1	11		4		3	8		9
25	23 (h)	Wigan Co	D 1-1	Goddard		2	6	7				10	8	5			1	11		4		3			9
26	26 (a)	Nelson	L 1-2	Goddard		2	6	7				10	8	5			1	11		4		3			9
		Appearances			12	24	14	25	8	4	2	22	2	25	1	20	8	25	17	13	2	26	3	7	26
		Goals						9	4			17	2	1		12		4				1			8

FINAL LEAGUE POSITION: 3rd (out of 14) in Lancashire League

Own-goals 2

FA Cup

No.	Date	Opponent	Result	Scorers	Att.	Axon	Blears	Bolton	Bridge	Brown	Clibbom	Cooke	Foster	Goddard	Hall	Henshaw	Heyes	Kitchen	Lee A	Lee J	Mann	Massey	Wainwright	Wilks	Wilson	Worrall
Q1	Sep 25 (h)	Chester	W 2-1	Wilson, Worrall		6	2		7	9					4		8		11	1			3		5	10
Q2	Oct 16 (h)	Oswestry	W 2-1	Heyes 2	2,000	6	2		7	9					4		8		11	1			3		5	10
Q3	30 (h)	Rock Ferry	W 2-1	Foster 2	3,000	6	2		7	5			10		4		8		11	1			3			9
Q4	Nov 20 (a)	Aberystwyth	W 5-0	Heyes, Foster 2, A.Lee, Opp own-goal		6	2		7	3			10		4		8		11	1					5	9
Q5	Dec 11 (h)	New Brighton T	L 0-1		7,000	6	2		7	9					4		8		11	1			3		5	10
		Appearances				5	5		5	5			2		5		5		5	4			5		4	5
		Goals											4				3		1						1	1

Own-goal 1

Three clubs withdrew from the Lancashire League this season, Fairfield in October, Oldham County in November and Bacup in February. Stockport had played Oldham County at home on 18 September, winning 2-0 (Brown, Unknown), the team being the same as for Match 2. On 26 December, Stockport beat Bacup 5-0 (Mann 2, Foster, Hall (pen), Worrall) at Green Lane, the team being the same as for Match 10 except Axon played in place of Brown and Heyes played in place of Henshaw.

1898-99

#	Date		Opponent	Result	Scorers	Axon	Betteley	Blears	Bolton	Bridge	Chesworth	Childs	Foster	Goddard	Hall	Harvey	Henshaw	Heyes	Hulme	Johnston	Lee	Lomas	Mann	Moores	Morrow	Pugh	Saer	Smith	Wainwright	Wilks	Worrall
1	Sep 3	(h)	Crewe A	W 3-0	Heyes, Foster, Johnston		2	6	7				10	4				8		5	11								3		9
2	10	(h)	Stalybridge R	L 2-3	Goddard, Foster	5	2	6					10	7	4			8		5	11						1		3		9
3	17	(a)	Chorley	L 1-4	Henshaw		2	6					10	7	4	11		8	1	5									3		
4	24	(a)	South Shore	W 2-1	Foster 2		2	6	7				10		4			8	1	5	11								3		9
5	Oct 1	(a)	Crewe A	L 1-7	Foster		2	6	7				10		4			8	1	5	11								3		9
6	8	(a)	Rochdale	W 3-0	Foster 3	6			7				10	2						5	11	1	4	8					3		9
7	15	(h)	Rochdale	L 1-2	Foster	5		6	7				10							2	11	1	4	8					3		9
8	Nov 12	(a)	Ashton NE	L 0-1		5		6	7				10		4			8		2	11	1							3		
9	Dec 17	(a)	Ashton NE	L 1-2	Goddard	9		6	11				10	7	4			8		2		1	5						3		
10	24	(h)	South Shore	W 5-2	Axon, Betteley 2, Foster 2	9	11	6					8	7	2					5		1	4						3		
11	31	(a)	Stalybridge R	W 6-2	Foster 2, Chesworth 2, Wilks, Goddard	5	11				6		8	7	4					5		1	4						3	9	
12	Jan 2	(h)	Horwich	W 5-0	Betteley 2, Foster 2, Goddard	5	11				6		8	7	4				10	2		1							3	9	
13	7	(h)	Rock Ferry*	W 3-2	Axon, Betteley, Hall (pen)	5	11				6		8	7	4					2		1							3	9	
14	14	(a)	Southport Cen	L 0-2		5					6		8	7	4				9	2	11	1							3		
15	28	(a)	Horwich	W 3-1	Chesworth, Foster 2	5	11				6		8	7	4				9			1						2	3		
16	Feb 4	(a)	Middleton	L 1-2	Foster	5	11		4		6		8	7	2	6			9			1							3		
17	11	(h)	Wigan Co	D 2-2	Foster, Axon	9	11						8	7	4	6			9			1							3		
18	18	(h)	Halliwell R	W 2-1	Chesworth, Axon	9	11				6		8	7	4					5		1						2	3		
19	25	(h)	Southport Cen	W 1-0	Opp own goal	9	11				6		8	7	4	5						1		2					3		
20	Mar 4	(a)	Haydock*	W 3-1	Axon, Chesworth 2	9	11				6		8	7	4	5						1		2					3		
21	18	(a)	Halliwell R	D 1-1	Harvey	9					6		8	7	4	10					5	1						2	3		
22	25	(a)	Wigan Co	L 1-3	Chesworth	9	11				6		8	7	4	5						1							3		
23	Apr 1	(h)	Middleton	W 2-0	Betteley, Chesworth	5	11						8	7	4	9					6	1						2	3		
24	3	(h)	Chorley	L 0-2		5	11						8	7	4	9					6	1						2	3		
			Appearances			20	13	5	20	7	14		24	18	23	8	1	9	3	22	8	13	4	7	1	3	2	5	24	3	7
			Goals			5	6				8		19	4	1	1	1	1		1										1	

FINAL LEAGUE POSTION: 6th (out of 13) in Lancashire League

Own-goal 1

FA Cup

#	Date		Opponent	Result	Scorers	Gate	Axon	Betteley	Blears	Bolton	Bridge	Chesworth	Childs	Foster	Goddard	Hall	Harvey	Henshaw	Heyes	Hulme	Johnston	Lee	Lomas	Mann	Moores	Morrow	Pugh	Saer	Smith	Wainwright	Wilks	Worrall
Q3	Oct 29	(a)	Ashton NE	D 2-2	Worrall, Axon	4,000	5		6		1			10	7	4			8		2	11								3		9
R	Nov 3	(h)	Ashton NE	W 1-0	Foster	600	5		6		1			10	7	4			8		2	11								3		9
Q4	19	(h)	Middleton	W 3-0	Hall (pen), Goddard, Foster	2,000	5		6					10	7	4			8		2	11	1							3		9
Q5	Dec 10	(h)	Glossop NE	L 0-2		5,000	5		6	7				10	8	4			9		2	11	1							3		
			Appearances				4		4	1	2			4	4	4			4		4	4	2							4		3
			Goals				1							2	1	1																1

* On 9 February, Rock Ferry resigned from the Lancashire League and Haydock took over their record and remaining fixtures.

In January, Nelson resigned and their records were expunged. Stockport were due to play away at Nelson on 21 January but received a telegram at 9pm on 20 January which stated "Nelson disbanded. Match cancelled."

1899-1900

No	Date		Opponent	Res	Scorers	Axon	Betteley	Bridge	Chesworth	Davies	Foster	Goddard	Hall	Harding	Harvey	Howcroft	Johnston	Limond	Moores	Parker	Patterson	Pickford	Seale	Singleton	Trotter	Wainwright	Woodhouse	Yates
1	Sep	2 (h)	Liverpool WS	W 6-1	Goddard 2, Hall (pen), Opp own-goal, Foster, Patterson	6	11		10		8	7	4		5		2		1		9					3		
2		9 (h)	Crewe A	W 4-1	Goddard 2, Harvey, Foster	6	11		10		8	7	4		5		2		1		9					3		
3		16 (h)	Horwich	W 3-0	Chesworth, Betteley, Hall (pen)	6	11		10		8	7	4		5		2		1							3	9	
4		30 (a)	Horwich	W 2-0	Patterson, Betteley		11		10		8	7	4	6	5		2		1		9					3		
5	Oct	14 (a)	Chorley	L 0-3			11		10		8	7		6	5		2		1		9		4			3		
6		21 (h)	S Liverpool	W 2-1	Betteley, Patterson		11		10	6	8	7	4		5		2		1		9					3		
7	Nov	4 (h)	Chorley	W 3-0	Betteley, Foster, Goddard		11		10		8	7	4		5		2		1		9			5		3		
8		11 (a)	Crewe A	W 2-1	Betteley, Patterson		11		10		8	7	4		6		2		1		9			5		3		
9		25 (a)	Stalybridge R	L 0-2			11		10		7		4		6		2		1	8	9	5				3		
10	Dec	16 (h)	Southport Cen	W 3-0	Patterson, Betteley 2		11		10		7		4		6		2		1	8	9					3		5
11		23 (a)	Earlestown	W 3-0	Patterson, Foster, Chesworth		11		10		7		4		6		2		1	8	9					3		5
12		25 (h)	Wigan Co	W 5-0	Chesworth 2, Parker 2, Betteley		11		10		7		4		6		2		1	8	9					3		5
13	Jan	1 (a)	Rochdale	D 0-0			11		10		7		4		6		2		1	8	9					3		5
14		6 (h)	Haydock*	W 9-1	Foster, Parker, Betteley, Patterson, Chesworth, Unknown 4		11		10		7		4				2		1	8	9	5	6			3		
15		20 (h)	Darwen	W 3-0	Parker, Patterson, Foster		11		10		7		4		6		2		1	8	9	5				3		
16		27 (h)	Middleton	W 8-0	Patterson 3, Chesworth 2, Foster, Singleton, Wainwright				10		7		4		6		2		1	8	9	5			11	3		
17	Feb	3 (h)	Rochdale	W 3-2	Chesworth 2, Betteley		11		10				4		7		2	6	1	8	9	5				3		
18		24 (a)	Haydock	W 3-1	Betteley, Parker, Foster		11		10		7		4				2	6	1	8	9	5				3		
19		27 (a)	Darwen	D 1-1	Betteley		11		10		7		4				2	6	1	8	9	5				3		
20	Mar	3 (h)	Stalybridge R	D 0-0			11		10		7		4		6		2		1	8	9	5				3		
21		10 (a)	Blackpool§	L 1-4	Chesworth		11		10		7		4		6		2	5	1	8	9					3		
22		17 (a)	Southport Cen	W 1-0	Parker		11		10		7		4		6		2	5	1	8	9					3		
23		24 (a)	Middleton	W 6-0	Foster 2, Limond, Chesworth 3			7	10		8		4		6		2	5	1		9				11	3		
24		31 (h)	Blackpool	W 4-2	Foster 3, Chesworth		11		10		7		4		6		2	5	1	8	9					3		
25	Apr	7 (a)	S Liverpool	W 2-1	Parker, Foster		11		10		7		4		6		2	5	1	8	9					3		
26		13 (a)	Wigan Co	W 4-0	Chesworth 2, Parker, Betteley		11		10		7				6		2	5	1	8	9	4				3		
27		14 (h)	Earlestown	W 3-0	Chesworth 2, Singleton				10		7		4		6		2	5	1	8	9				11	3		
28		16 (a)	Liverpool WS	L 0-2			11		10		7		4		6		2	5	1	8	9					3		
	FINAL LEAGUE POSITION: Champions of Lancashire League – Elected to Division 2 of the Football League				**Appearances**	3	25	1	28	1	27	8	27	9	26		20	11	28	19	27	8	2	3	3	27	1	4
					Goals		13		18		14	5	2		1			1		8	11			2		1		

Own-goal 1, Unknown scorers 4

FA Cup

No	Date		Opponent	Res	Scorers	Att	Axon	Betteley	Bridge	Chesworth	Davies	Foster	Goddard	Hall	Harding	Harvey	Howcroft	Johnston	Limond	Moores	Parker	Patterson	Pickford	Seale	Singleton	Trotter	Wainwright	Woodhouse	Yates
Q3	Oct	28 (a)	Glossop	D 2-2	Foster, Hall (pen)			11		10	6	8	7	4		5		2		1		9					3		
R	Nov	1 (h)	Glossop	W 3-0	Betteley, Chesworth, Foster			11		10		8	7	4		5		2		1		9	6				3		
Q4		18 (a)	Stalybridge R	L 0-2		4,000		11		10		8	7	4				5	2	1		9	6				3		
					Appearances			3		3	1	3	3	3		2		1	3	3		3	2				3		
					Goals			1		1		2		1															

*This game was played in a torrential downpour and, after approximately 65 minutes, with the score at 5-1, Haydock wanted the referee to abandon the match because of the appalling state of the pitch and weather. When the referee refused to abandon the game, six Haydock players walked off. Play continued for another 15 minutes, Stockport scoring another four goals (the four 'Unknown' goalscorers) against the five remaining Haydock players before the referee finally abandoned the game. The Lancashire FA ordered the game to be replayed, but the Lancashire League ordered that Haydock should return to Green Lane and play out the final ten minutes, otherwise the result would stand. Unsurprisingly, Haydock did not return and the result stood.

§In December, Blackpool merged with South Shore whose records were expunged. Stockport had played South Shore away on 23 September, drawing 1-1 (Chesworth), the team being the same as Match 2.

As champions, Stockport played a Rest of the League XI at Green Lane on 21 April, winning 4-1, the scorers being Chesworth, Opp own-goal, Parker, Hall (pen). County's team was Moores; Johnston, Wainwright, Hall, Limond, Pickford, Foster, Parker, Patterson, Chesworth, Betteley. The League was represented by Joe Lee (Haydock); Bunce (Rochdale), Ostick (Chorley), Brown (Blackpool), Liversey (Darwen), Johnson (Stalybridge Rovers), Johnson (Rochdale), Baxendale (Southport Central), Lawson (Stalybridge Rovers), Hulligan (Liverpool White Star), Tinsley (Horwich).

1900-01

First season in Football League. Figures in left-hand column start cumulative numbering.

#	Date		Opponent		Res	Scorers	A	B	Bk	Br	Bu	Bt	C	D	E	Ev	FJ	FW	Ha	Hv	Hu	J	L	M	Mo	P	Pt	Pk	Sh	Si	Sm	St	W
1	Sep	1	(a) Leicester F		D 2-2	Betteley, Smith		11							2			10	6				5		1	9	4				8	7	3
2		3	(a) Burslem PVale		W 1-0	Smith (pen)									2			10	6				5	11	1	9	4				8	7	3
3		8	(h) New Brighton T		L 0-5										2			10	6				5		1	9	4			11	8	7	3
4		15	(a) Gainsboro' T		L 0-2					4		5			2			10	6				3	11	1	9						8	7	
5		22	(h) Walsall		W 4-1	W.J.Foster 4*									2			10	6				5	11	1	9	4				8	7	3
6		29	(a) Burton Swifts		L 2-3	W.J.Foster 2						4		1	2			10	6				5	11		9						8	7	3
7	Oct	6	(h) Barnsley		W 2-1	W.J.Foster, Hulligan						4		1	2			10					5	11		9						8	7	3
8		13	(a) W Arsenal		L 0-2										2			10	6	9			5	11	1		4				8	7	3
9		20	(h) Blackpool		L 0-1										2			8	4	9			5		1	10	7	6			9	11	3
10		27	(h) Chesterfield T		W 3-1	W.J.Foster 2 (1 pen), Patterson		11					1		2			8	4	9			5			10	7	6			3	11	
11	Nov	10	(a) Grimsby T		L 1-5	Brown				5							3	10	4				5			8	7	6			9		
12		24	(h) Newton Heath		W 1-0	Stansfield			5								3	10	6				2		1	8	11	4			9	7	
13	Dec	1	(a) Glossop		L 0-6			6		4	1				2			10					5	11		8	9					7	3
14		8	(a) Lincoln C		L 0-4			6		4	1				2			10					5	11		8	9					7	3
15		15	(a) Burnley		L 1-3	W.J.Foster	9	4			1				2			10					5	11		9	6				8	7	3
16		22	(h) Burslem PVale		D 1-1	Earp	9	4							2			10					5		1	8	11				6	7	3
17		26	(a) Small Heath		L 0-2		9	4							2			10					5		1	8	11				6	7	3
18		29	(h) Leicester F		W 3-1	Ashworth, J.H.Foster, McLachlan	9	4							2			10					5	11	1		6				8	7	3
19	Jan	1	(a) New Brighton T		L 0-3		9	4							2		8	10					5	11	1		6					7	3
20		12	(h) Gainsboro' T		L 1-2	McLachlan	9	4							2		8	10					5	11	1		6					7	3
21		19	(a) Walsall		W 3-1	J.H.Foster, Betteley, Brown	9	11		4	2			3			8	10					5		1		6					7	
22	Feb	9	(a) Barnsley		L 0-2		9	11		4	2						8	10					5		1		6					7	3
23		16	(h) W Arsenal		W 3-1	J.H.Foster 2, Stansfield	9	11		4	2							10							1	8	6					7	3
24		23	(a) Blackpool		L 0-3		9	11		4	2							10							1	8		5			6	7	3
25	Mar	2	(a) Chesterfield T		L 2-4	Ashworth, J.H.Foster	9	11		4	2							10							1	8		5			6	7	3
26		9	(h) Small Heath		D 0-0		9	11			2							10							1	8		5			6	7	3
27		16	(h) Grimsby T		L 0-1		9	11			2							10		4					1	8		5			6	7	3
28		23	(h) Lincoln C		W 1-0	Betteley		11		4	2				9								5		1	8	10	6				7	3
29		30	(a) Newton Heath		L 1-3	Stansfield		11		4	2				9								5		1	8	9	4				7	3
30	Apr	5	(h) Middlesbrough		L 0-1			11			2							10					5		1	8	9	4				7	3
31		6	(h) Glossop		L 1-3	Parker				6	2					7		10					5	11	1	8	9	4			6	7	3
32		13	(a) Middlesbrough		L 0-2		9	11		6	2							10					5	11	1	8	9	4					3
33		20	(h) Burnley		W 3-2	Ashworth 2, Parker	9	11		6	2							10					5		1	8	7	4					3
34		27	(h) Burton Swifts		W 2-0	Parker, Patterson		11		4	2			7									5		1	8	10				6	9	3
	FINAL LEAGUE POSITION: 17th in Division Two - Re-elected					Appearances	15	15	2	23	13	6	1	7	15	1	12	27	2	12	1	1	30	7	28	23	24	23	1	1	25	30	29
						Goals	4	3		2					1		5	10		1				2		3	2				2	3	

FA Cup

#	Date		Opponent		Res	Scorers	Att	A	B	Bk	Br	Bu	Bt	C	D	E	Ev	FJ	FW	Ha	Hv	Hu	J	L	M	Mo	P	Pt	Pk	Sh	Si	Sm	St	W
Q3	Nov	3	(h) Wrexham		W 6-2	Patterson, Parker 2, Earp, Stansfield 2	2,000									2		3	10	6				5		1	8	11	4			9	7	
Q4		17	(h) Crewe A		L 1-3	Stansfield	'moderate'					1				2		3	10	6				5			7	11	4			9	8	
						Appearances						1				2		2	2	2				2		1	2	2	2			2	2	
						Goals										1											2	1					3	

*At least one other report gives the scorers as Foster 3 and Parker.

1901-02

#	Date	Opponents	Result	Scorers	Arridge	Barker	Bentley	Betteley	Booth	Bunce	Butler	Chesworth	Chorlton	Davies	Eaton	Evenson	Hinks	Jeffreys	Longstaff	Madden	Marshall	McLachlan	Parker	Patterson	Perrins	Pickford	Sharpley	Smith	Swann	Wharton
35	Sep 7 (h)	Middlesbrough	L 1-3	Davies	2	7		11				8		10				5		9				4	6			3		1
36	9 (a)	Burnley	L 0-3		2			11				8		10	7			5		9				4	6			3		1
37	14 (a)	Bristol C	L 0-3		3	7		11		2		8		10				5		9				4	6					1
38	21 (h)	Blackpool	W 3-1	Davies 2, Eaton	3		5	11				9		10	7					8				4	6			2		1
39	28 (a)	Burton U	L 2-3	Davies (pen), Chesworth	3		5	11				9		10	7					8				4	6			2		1
40	Oct 5 (a)	Newton Heath	D 3-3	Opp own-goal, Chesworth, Patterson	3		5	11				9		10	7					8				4	6			2		1
41	12 (h)	Glossop	D 0-0		3		5	11			1	9		10	7					8				4	6			2		
42	19 (a)	Doncaster R	L 0-2		3			11			1	9		10	7			5		8					6	4		2		
43	26 (h)	Lincoln C	W 2-1	Chesworth, Betteley	3			11			1	8		10	7	9		5							6	4		2		
44	Nov 9 (h)	W Arsenal	D 0-0		3			11			1	9		10	7			5		8					6	4		2		
45	23 (a)	Leicester F	D 1-1	Davies	3			11			1	8		10	7			5		9					6	4		2		
46	Dec 7 (h)	Burnley	L 1-2	Chesworth	3						1	8		10	7			5		9	11				6	4		2		
47	14 (h)	Burslem PVale	D 1-1	Swann	3			11			1	7		10				5		8					6	4		2	9	
48	21 (h)	Chesterfield T	W 3-0	Davies, Chesworth, Swann	3			11			1	7		10				5		8					6	4		2	9	
49	26 (a)	West Brom A	L 0-3		3			11			1	7		10				5		8					6	4		2	9	
50	28 (a)	Gainsboro' T	D 1-1	Betteley	3			11			1	7		10						8					6	4	5	2	9	
51	Jan 4 (a)	Middlesbrough	L 0-6		3			11			1	7		10						8					6	4	5	2	9	
52	11 (h)	Bristol C	D 1-1	Swann	3			11			1	9		10				5		8					6	4		2	9	
53	18 (a)	Blackpool	L 0-1		3			11			1	9		10				5		7					6	4		2	8	
54	Feb 1 (h)	Newton Heath	W 1-0	Swann	3			11			1	8						5			7	10			6	4		2	9	
55	8 (a)	Glossop	L 1-2	Marshall	3			11	7		1	8						5				10			6	4		2	9	
56	15 (h)	Doncaster R	L 1-2	Booth	3			11	7		1	8						5				10			6	4		2	9	
57	22 (a)	Lincoln C	L 0-5		3			11			1	7						5		8		10			6	4		2	9	
58	Mar 1 (h)	West Brom A	L 0-2		3		10	11			1	8						5	7			2			6	4			9	
59	8 (a)	W Arsenal	L 0-3		3		10	11			1							5	7	8		2			6	4			9	
60	15 (h)	Barnsley	L 2-3	Longstaff, Evenson	3			11			1					10	6	5	7			2	8			4			9	
61	22 (h)	Leicester F	W 2-0	Marshall, Davies	3						1	8		10		4		5	7	9	11				6			2		
62	29 (a)	Preston NE	L 0-4		3			11			1	8		10		4		5		9	7				6			2		
63	31 (a)	Barnsley	L 1-3	Evenson	3			11			1	8		10		4				9	7				6		5	2		
64	Apr 5 (h)	Preston NE	L 0-2		3			11			1	8		10		4				9	7				6		5	2		
65	12 (h)	Burslem PVale	W 4-2	Madden 2, Chesworth, McLachlan	3			11			1	8		10						9		7			6		5	2		
66	14 (h)	Burton U	W 2-0	Madden 2	3			11			1	7	4	10						9		5			6			2		
67	19 (a)	Chesterfield T	L 1-8*	Pickford				11			1			10						9		5			6	4				
68	26 (a)	Gainsboro' T	W 2-1	Longstaff, Betteley	3			11			1	8				6		5	7	9		10				4		2		
	FINAL LEAGUE POSITION: 17th in Division Two – Re-elected			Appearances	33	2	4	29	6	1	28	28	1	29	10	8	1	26	5	23	11	5	1	7	29	27	6	30	14	6
				Goals				3	1			6		7	1	2				2	4	2	1	1		1			4	

Own-goal 1

FA Cup

Round	Date	Opponents	Result	Scorers	Att	Arridge	Barker	Bentley	Betteley	Booth	Bunce	Butler	Chesworth	Chorlton	Davies	Eaton	Evenson	Hinks	Jeffreys	Longstaff	Madden	Marshall	McLachlan	Parker	Patterson	Perrins	Pickford	Sharpley	Smith	Swann	Wharton
Q3	Nov 2 (a)	Buxton	W 2-0	Davies, Eaton	500	3			11			1	9		10	7			5		8					6	4		2		
Q4	20 (h)	Crewe§	W 3-2	Madden 2, Jeffreys	1,000	3			11			1	8		10	7			5		9					6	4		2		
Q5	30 (a)	Glossop	L 0-1			3			11	2		1	8		10	7			5		9					6	4				
				Appearances		3			3	1		3	3		3	3			3		3					3	3		2		
				Goals											1	1			1		2										

*This still represents Stockport's heaviest defeat in peacetime Football League and Cup games (only equalled in their Combination days by an 8-1 defeat at Bury in the second qualifying round of the FA Cup on 29 October 1892) but there were, to say the least, mitigating factors. Four players missed the train to Chesterfield and Stockport took the field with only seven players, three of whom were forwards. During the game, Frank Chesworth broke his ribs with the result that for the majority of the match, County played with only six players. Joe Butler's heroics helped keep the score to what, in the circumstances, was an almost respectable 8-1 defeat. To add insult to injury, Chesterfield reported Stockport to the Football League for playing only seven men and claimed a sum of £20 for loss in gate receipts. The matter was considered and dismissed but County were fined £5 for "playing but seven players".

§This followed a first game on 16 November which was abandoned due to fog at half-time with the score at 0-0, the team being the same.

Although at this time players' shirts were not numbered, for Match 67 when Stockport had only seven players, the numbers do not represent the particular positions in which the players played but simply indicate their 'normal' position.

1902-03

No	Date	Opponent	Result	Scorers	Arridge	Brittleton	Butler	Chorlton	Dixon	Dowdall	Evenson	Foster	Freeborough	Griffin	Hall	Hosie	Hughes	Hunter	Jeffreys	Malone	McKiernan	McLachlan	Middleton	Moir	Pickford	Preston	Raby	Rathbone	Sharpley	Stansfield	Tomkinson	Wallwork
69	Sep 6	(a) Barnsley	L 1-2	Tomkinson	3		1	11		6	7	2													5		10		4	9	8	
70	13	(h) Gainsboro' T	D 1-1	Raby	3		1	11		6	8	2													5		10		4	7	9	
71	15	(a) Lincoln C	L 1-3	Stansfield	3		1	4		11	8	2													5		10	6		9		7
72	20	(a) Burton U	L 1-5	Dowdall	3		1	4		11	8	2									7				5		10	6		9		
73	27	(h) Bristol C	L 0-1		3		1		5	11	4	2									7						10	6		9	8	
74	Oct 11	(h) Manchester U	W 2-1	Raby, Dowdall	3		1	2		11	6										5	4					10		9	8	7	
75	18	(h) Chesterfield T	D 2-2	Raby, Sharpley	3		1	2		11	9										6	5			4		10		8	7		
76	25	(h) Blackpool	L 0-2		3		1	2		11	6										4	5			8		10		9	7		
77	Nov 8	(a) Doncaster R	L 0-2		2		1	11		6			4	9			3	5	8								10			7		
78	10	(a) Burslem P Vale	L 1-3	Stansfield	2		1	4		11	9		6	10			3	5	8											7		
79	22	(a) Small Heath	L 0-2		3		1	11		6	9		2		10			5	8										4	7		
80	29	(h) Leicester F	D 2-2	Evenson, McKiernan	3		1	11		6	9		2					5	8		4									7		
81	Dec 6	(a) Manchester C	L 0-5		3		1	2		11	9				4	6			5		8						10			7		
82	13	(h) Burslem P Vale	L 0-4		3	7	1	11		6					2	4			5								10		8	9		
83	20	(a) Preston NE	L 1-6	Stansfield	3	7	1	9		6					2	5						11			4		10			8		
84	25	(a) Glossop	L 0-3		3	7	1	9		2					4	5						11					10	6		8		
85	Jan 1	(h) W Arsenal	L 0-1			7	1	3		2					4	5			6			11					10		9	8		
86	3	(h) Barnsley	W 4-1	Evenson, Brittleton 2, McLachlan		7	1	3		2	9				4	5						11					10	6		8		
87	17	(h) Burton U	L 0-2			7	1	3		2					4	5						11	9				10		6	8		
88	24	(a) Bristol C	L 1-7	Hosie	3	7	1	11		2	9					5					4						10		6	8		
89	31	(h) Glossop	L 2-3	Evenson, Brittleton		7	1	3		2	9				4	5						11					10	6		8		
90*	Feb 7	(a) Gainsboro' T	D 0-0		3	8		11		9					2	5			4	1							10		6	7		
91	14	(h) Chesterfield T	L 1-4	Hosie	3	8		11		9			2		4	5								1			10		6	7		
92	21	(h) Blackpool§	W 4-0	Stansfield, Hosie, Preston, McLachlan	2	8	1	3							4	5						11				9	10		6	7		
93	28	(a) W Arsenal	L 1-3	Evenson	2		1	3			10				4	5						8				9	11		6	7		
94	Mar 7	(h) Doncaster R	W 1-0	McLachlan	2		1	3			8				4	5						11				9	10		6	7		
95	14	(a) Lincoln C	W 3-1	Stansfield, Evenson, Sharpley	3		1	2			8				4	5					6					9	10		11	7		
96	21	(h) Small Heath	L 1-2	Sharpley	3		1	2			8				4	5					6					9	10		11	7		
97	23	(a) Manchester U	D 0-0		3	8	1	2				4			5	6										9	10		11	7		
98‡	26	(a) Leicester F	W 2-0	Hall, Middleton	3	8	1	2							4	5							6			9	10		11	7		
99	Apr 4	(a) Manchester C	L 0-2		3	8	1	2							4	5						11				9	10		6	7		
100	11	(a) Burnley	L 2-3	Evenson 2	3		1	2			8				4	5					6					9	10		11	7		
101	13	(h) Burnley	W 3-0	Brittleton, Raby, Hall	3	11	1	2			8				4	5					6					9	10			7		
102	18	(h) Preston NE	D 1-1	Preston	3	11	1	2			8				4	5					6					9	10			7		
		Appearances			30	16	32	25	1	16	25	4	14	2	24	25	2	3	17	1	5	12	2	1	9	11	31	6	22	34	3	1
		Goals				4				2	7				2	3					1	3	1			2	4		3	5	1	

FINAL LEAGUE POSITION: 17th in Division Two - Re-elected

FA Cup

Round	Date	Opponent	Result	Att.	Arridge	Brittleton	Butler	Chorlton	Dixon	Dowdall	Evenson	Foster	Freeborough	Griffin	Hall	Hosie	Hughes	Hunter	Jeffreys	Malone	McKiernan	McLachlan	Middleton	Moir	Pickford	Preston	Raby	Rathbone	Sharpley	Stansfield	Tomkinson	Wallwork
Q2	Oct 4	(h†) Stalybridge R	L 0-1	1,500	3		1	11		6		2									5	7			4		10		9	8		
		Appearances			1		1	1		1		1									1	1			1		1		1	1		
		Goals																													

*This match had been played at Gainsborough on 10 January, the score being 1-1 (Raby) and the team being the same as Match 18 except for Middleton playing instead of Evenson. However, over seven days later, the referee reported that he had stopped the game after 86 minutes "because of darkness". The Football League ordered that the game be replayed.

§The first half was played in a deluge and, with Stockport leading 2-0 at half-time, Blackpool came out for the second half with only eight players although a ninth eventually joined them.

‡This was brought forward from 28 March to enable Stockport to play Manchester City in a Manchester Cup semi-final which it was believed would attract between 15,000 and 18,000 spectators. County paid Leicester £40 for the alteration, lost to City 7-0 and, because of the poor weather, the game only attracted 7,000.

†Played at Green Lane, the Rugby Club having preference at Edgeley Park that weekend.

135

1903-04

No	Date	V	Opponent	Res	Scorers	Allan	Aston	Britteton	Broomfield	Brown	Butler	Codling	Cottrell	Fletcher	Freebrough	Hall	Haughton	Heywood	Kaye	McLachlan	Parker	Pass	Price	Raby	Ray	Reynolds	Rooke	Scotson	Sharpley	Stansfield	Suart	Toman	Wallwork	Williams
103	Sep 5	(h)	Preston NE	L 1-5	Raby	2	5	7	9	11	1												8	10	3	4		6						
104	12	(a)	Grimsby T	L 1-2	Raby	2		7	9	11	1			4									8	10	3			6						5
105	19	(h)	Leicester F	W 2-0	Williams, Broomfield	3			9	11	1			4									8	10	2			6				7		5
106	26	(a)	Blackpool	L 1-4	Raby	3		7	9	11	1			4									8	10	2			6						5
107	Oct 3	(h)	Gainsboro' T	L 1-4	McLachlan	3					1			4						11			9	8	2		10	6				7		5
108	10	(a)	Burton U	L 0-7		5			9		1			3	4								8	10	2		11	6				7		
109	17	(h)	Bristol C	D 1-1	Wallwork	3		10			1	6											9	8	2								7	5
110	24	(a)	Manchester U	L 1-3	Pass	7		3			1			4		5				9		11	8	10	2			6						
111	Nov 21	(a)	Barnsley	D 0-0		3		8			1	6				5				11			9	10	2				4	7				
112	28	(h)	Lincoln C	W 4-0	McLachlan 2, Raby, Kaye			8			1	6				5			3	9		11		10	2				4	7				
113	Dec 5	(a)	Burslem PVale	L 0-2				8			1	6				5			3	9		11		10	2				4	7				
114	12	(a)	Bradford C	D 0-0		3		8			1	6			11	5							9	10	2				4	7				
115	19	(h)	Bolton W	W 3-2	Stansfield, Raby, Brittleton	3		8			1	6				5				9		11		10	2				4	7				
116	23	(a)	Lincoln C	L 1-3	Stansfield	3		8			1	6				5				9		11		10	2				4	7				
117	26	(a)	Burnley	L 0-2		3		8			1	6				5				9		11		10	2				4	7				
118	28	(a)	Chesterfield T	L 1-4	Brittleton	3		8			1	6				5				9				10	2				4	7	11			
119	Jan 1	(h)	W Arsenal	D 0-0		3		8			1	6				5				9		11		10	2				4	7				
120	2	(a)	Preston NE	D 1-1	Stansfield	3		10			1	6				5						11	8	9	2				4	7				
121	9	(h)	Grimsby T	D 1-1	Raby	3		11			1	6				5				9			8	10	2				4	7				
122	16	(a)	Leicester F	L 0-3		3		8			1	6				5				9		11		10	2				4	7				
123	23	(h)	Blackpool	W 2-1	Kaye, Price	3					1	6				5				9		11		10	2				4	7	8			
124	30	(a)	Gainsboro' T	D 2-2	Pass, Raby	3		4			1	6				5				11		9		10	2					7		8		
125	Feb 6	(a)	Burton U	D 1-1	Raby	3		4			1	6				5				11		9	8	10	2					7				
126	13	(a)	Bristol C	L 0-6		3		4			1	6				5				9			8	10	2					7	11			
127	27	(a)	Glossop	L 1-5	Hall (pen)			3			1	6				5				11		8			2		10		4	7			9	
128	Mar 5	(h)	Bradford C	W 2-0	Hall, Brittleton			8			1	6	7	3		5				11	10				2							9		4
129	12	(a)	W Arsenal	L 2-5	Toman, Brittleton			8			1	6	3	4		5				11	10				2					7		9		
130	19	(h)	Barnsley	D 2-2	Brittleton, McLachlan			8			1	6	3			5				11	10				2					7		9		4
131	28	(h)	Manchester U	L 0-3				8			1	6	3	4		5				11	10				2					7		9		
132	Apr 1	(h)	Glossop	W 3-0	Pass 2, Brittleton			8			1	6			3	5				11	10	9			2					7	4			
133	2	(a)	Burslem PVale	D 1-1	Pass			8			1	6			3	5				11	10	9			2					7	4			
134	9	(h)	Chesterfield T	W 2-0	McLachlan, Hall (pen)			8			1	6			3	5				11	10	9			2					7	4			
135	16	(a)	Bolton W	W 1-0	Parker			8			1	6				5		3		11	10	9			2					7	4			
136	23	(h)	Burnley	D 2-2	Pass, Suart			8			1	6				5		3		11	10	9			2					7	4			
			Appearances			22	1	29	5	5	34	28	1	4	12	30		2	16	22	5	14	11	21	34	1	16	6	8	24	6	5	6	6
			Goals				6	1								3			2	5	1	6	1	8						3	1	1	1	1

FINAL LEAGUE POSITIONL: 16th in Division Two - Failed to gain re-election

FA Cup

Round	Date	V	Opponent	Res	Scorers	Att	Allan	Aston	Britteton	Broomfield	Brown	Butler	Codling	Cottrell	Fletcher	Freebrough	Hall	Haughton	Heywood	Kaye	McLachlan	Parker	Pass	Price	Raby	Ray	Reynolds	Rooke	Scotson	Sharpley	Stansfield	Suart	Toman	Wallwork	Williams
Q3	Oct 31	(a*)	Heywood	W 4-0	Price 2, Raby, Scotson	3,000	7		3			1					5				11			9	8	4	2		10	6					
Q4	Nov 14	(h)	Burslem PVale	D 0-0		4,000	8		3			1	6			5	4				11			9		2		10			7				
R	19	(a)	Burslem PVale	L 0-6		2,000	2		3			1	6			5	11				4			9	8	10					7				
			Appearances				3		3			3	2			2	3				3			3	2	2		2	1	1	2				
			Goals																					2	1				1						

*Played at Edgeley Park by mutual agreement.

1904-05

League (Lancashire Combination)

No	Date	Venue	Opponent	Res	Score	Scorers
1	Sep 2	(h)	Southport Cen	W	2-1	Green, Price
2	Sep 3	(h)	Manch'r C Res	W	3-1	Green 2, Pass
3	Sep 10	(a)	Stalybridge R	W	1-0	J.T.Brittleton
4	Sep 17	(h)	Preston NE Res	W	1-0	Pass
5	Sep 24	(a)	Bury Res	L	0-2	
6	Oct 1	(a)	Everton Res	W	1-0	Green
7	Oct 8	(a)	Blackb'n R Res	W	1-0	Bardsley
8	Oct 22	(h)	Everton Res	W	4-2	Hall, Suart, Green 2
9	Oct 29	(a)	Bolton W Res	L	1-3	McLachlan
10	Nov 5	(a)	Manch'r U Res	L	0-4	
11	Nov 19	(h)	Manch'r U Res	W	4-0	J.T.Brittleton, Green 3
12	Dec 3	(a)	Rossendale U	W	5-0	J.T.Brittleton, Green, Pass 2, Suart
13	Dec 17	(a)	Earlestown	D	1-1	Bardsley
14	Dec 24	(a)	Ashton T	L	0-1	
15	Dec 31	(a)	St Helens T	W	1-0	J.T.Brittleton
16	Jan 2	(h)	Bolton W Res	W	4-2	Hodgkinson, Pass, Parker, J.T.Brittleton
17	Jan 14	(a)	Darwen	W	1-0	Waters (pen)
18	Jan 21	(a)	Southport Cen	D	1-1	Green
19	Jan 28	(a)	Preston NE Res	W	3-2	Hodgkinson 2, Green
20	Feb 11	(h)	Ashton T	W	4-1	Hall (pen), Suart, Foster, Opp own-goal
21	Feb 18	(h)	Nelson	D	1-1	Hodgkinson
22	Feb 25	(h)	Darwen	D	0-0	
23	Mar 4	(h)	Liverpool Res	L	1-2	Bardsley
24	Mar 11	(a)	Liverpool Res	D	0-0	
25	Mar 18	(h)	Blackb'n R Res	W	5-0	Pass 2, Hodgkinson, Bardsley, Hancock
26	Mar 25	(h)	Earlestown	W	3-2	Hall, Pass, Suart
27	Apr 1	(a)	Manch'r C Res	L	0-1	
28	Apr 3	(h)	Stalybridge R	W	2-0	Parker, Pass
29	Apr 8	(a)	Accrington S	D	1-1	Pass
30	Apr 15	(h)	Accrington S	W	1-0	Pass
31	Apr 18	(a)	Nelson	D	0-0	
32	Apr 22	(h)	Bury Res	W	2-0	Bardsley, Parker
33	Apr 24	(h)	St Helens T	W	6-0	Hancock 2, Pass, Hodgkinson, Butler (pen), Bardsley
34	Apr 29	(h)	Rossendale U	W	3-0	Hancock, Parker, Pass

FINAL LEAGUE POSITION: 1st in Lancashire Combination -
Elected to Division 2 of Football League

Player line-ups (shirt numbers)

No	Ball	Bardsley	Bostock	Brittleton J.T.	Brittleton S.	Butler	Codling	Dowdall	Fletcher	Foster	Green	Hall	Hancock	Haughton	Heywood	Hill	Hodgkinson	Hollingworth	Hughes	McLachlan	Parker	Pass	Perrins	Price	Smith	Suart	Turner	Waters
1		11				1	6				9	5			2						10	7	8	4				3
2		11	8			1	6				9	5			2						10	7			4			3
3		11	8			1	6				9	5			2						10	7			4			3
4		11	8			1	6				9	5			2						10	7			4			3
5		11	8			1	6				9	5			2						10	7			4			3
6		11	8			1	6				9	5			2						10	7			4			3
7		11	8			1	6				9	5			2						10	7			4			3
8		11	8			1	6				9	5			2						10	7			4			3
9	1			8						11	3		4	2			10	5	7	9	6							
10		11	8			1	6				9	5			2		7				10				4			3
11		11	8			1	6				9	5			2		7				10				4			3
12		11	8			1	6				9	5			2		7				10				4			3
13		11	8			1	6				9	5			2		7				10				4			3
14		11	8			1	6				9	5			2		7				10				4			3
15		11	8			1	6				9	5			2		7				10				4			3
16		11	8			1	6				9	5			2		7				10				4			3
17		11				1	6	5	8	9					2		7				10				4			3
18		11				1	6			8	9	5			2		7				10				4			3
19		11				1	6			8	9	5			2		7				10				4			3
20		11				1	6			8		3			2		7			9	10				4	5		
21		11				1	6			8		3			2		7	5		9	10				4			
22		11				1	6			8		3			2		7	5		9	10				4			
23		11				1	6			8		3	9		2		7				10				4	5		
24		11	3			1	6						5		2		7			9	10	8			4			
25		11	3			1	6						5		2		7			9	10	8			4			
26		11				1	6						5		2		7			9	10	8			4			3
27		11				1	6						5		2		7			9	10	8			4			3
28		11				1	6						5		2		7			9	10	8			4			3
29		11				1	6						5		2		7			9	10	8			4			3
30		11				1	6						5		2		7			9	10	8			4			3
31		11				1	6						5		2		7			9	10	8			4			3
32		11				1	6						5		2		7			9	10	8			4			3
33		11				1	6						5		2		7			9	10	8			4			3
34		11				1	6						5		2		7			9	10	8			4			3
Appearances	1	33	2	14	1	33	33	1	2	7	18	32	12	1	33	1	26	3	1	21	27	1	8	1	33	2	27	
Goals		6		5		1				1	12	3	4				6			1	4	13		1		4		1

Own-goal 1

FA Cup

Rnd	Date	Venue	Opponent	Res	Score	Scorers	Att
Q3	Oct 29	(h)	Stalybridge R	W	2-0	Green 2	3,500
Q4	Nov 12	(a)	Glossop	D	1-1	Green	2,500
R	Nov 23*	(h)	Glossop	W	1-0	Bardsley	'moderate'
Q5	Nov 26	(h)	Wrexham	W	4-0	Hall, Pass, Green, Opp own-goal	2,000
Q6	Dec 10	(a)	Chesterfield	L	0-2		

Rnd	Ball	Bardsley	Bostock	Brittleton J.T.	Brittleton S.	Butler	Codling	Dowdall	Fletcher	Foster	Green	Hall	Hancock	Haughton	Heywood	Hill	Hodgkinson	Hollingworth	Hughes	McLachlan	Parker	Pass	Perrins	Price	Smith	Suart	Turner	Waters
Q3		11	8			1	6				9	5			2		7				10				4			3
Q4		11	7			1	6				9	5			2		8				10				4			3
R		11	7			1	6				9	5			2		8				10				4			3
Q5		11	7			1	6				9	5			2		8				10				4			3
Q6		11	7			1	6				9	5			2		8				10				4			3
Appearances		5	5			5	5				5	5			5		4	1			5				5			5
Goals		1									4	1										1						

Own-goal 1

*This followed two abortive attempts to replay the game. The first, on 16 November, was abandoned due to fog during extra-time with the score at 0-0. Although it was believed initially that this constituted a 'replay' and a third match be played at a neutral ground, the FA ruled that the game be treated as abandoned and replayed at Edgeley Park. On 21 November, with the score at 0-0, the tie was abandoned at half-time as a result of a snow-storm.

1905-06

Cumulative numbering resumes

Player columns (left→right): Bardsley, Bostock, Butler, Butterworth, Cresser, Crump, Dodd G.F., Dodd S, Farrant, Frail, Goodwin, Hall, Hancock, Hegarty R, Hegarty T, Heywood, Hodgkinson, Manson, Nixon, Parker, Pass, Pemble, Porter, Roberts, Robinson, Schofield, Suart, Waters, Worsley

No	Date	V	Opponent	Result	Scorers	Bar	Bos	But	Btw	Cre	Cru	DGF	DdS	Far	Fra	Goo	Hal	Han	HgR	HgT	Hey	Hod	Man	Nix	Par	Pas	Pem	Por	Rob(ts)	Rob(n)	Sch	Sua	Wat	Wor
137	Sep 2	(h)	Chelsea	W 1-0	Manson	11				6	8	10				5					2		9							1	7	4	3	
138	9	(a)	Gainsboro' T	D 0-0		11				6	8	10				5					2		9							1	7	4	3	
139	16	(h)	Bristol C	L 2-3	Manson, Bardsley	11					8	10				5	6				2		9							1	7	4	3	
140	23	(a)	Manchester U	L 1-3	Manson	11					9	10				5	6				2		8							1	7	4	3	
141	30	(h)	Glossop	W 5-0	G.F.Dodd, Crump 2, Schofield 2	11					9	10				5	6				2		8							1	7	4	3	
142	Oct 7	(a)	Grimsby T	L 0-2		11					9	10					6				2		7	5						1	8	4	3	
143	14	(a)	Blackpool	L 0-2		11					9	10	8				6				2			5						1	7	4	3	
144	21	(h)	Bradford C	W 1-0		11					9	10					6				2		8	5						1	7	4	3	
145	28	(a)	West Brom A	L 1-3	Manson	11					9	10					6				2		8	5						1	7	4	3	
146	Nov 4	(h)	Leicester F	D 1-1	Waters (pen)	11					9				1		6				2		8	5			10				7	4	3	
147	11	(a)	Hull C	L 0-3		11					9	10			1		6				2		8	5							7	4	3	
148	18	(h)	Lincoln C	W 3-0	Manson, G.F.Dodd 2	11			6			10			1	5					2		8				9				7	4	3	
149	25	(a)	Chesterfield T	L 1-3	Manson	11			6						1	5					2		8			9	10				7	4	3	
150	Dec 2	(h)	Burslem P Vale	W 3-0	Suart, Waters (pen), Crump	11			6		9	10	5		1						2		8								7	4	3	
151	16	(h)	Clapton O	D 3-3	Pass, T.Hegarty 2 (2 pens)	11			6		9		5		1					3	2		8			10					7	4		
152	23	(h)	Burnley	W 1-0	Crump	11			6		9	10	5								2		8							1	7	4	3	
153	25	(a)	Burton U	L 0-2		11			6		9	10	5								2		8							1	7	4	3	
154	26	(h)	Leeds C	W 2-1	Manson, Bardsley	11			6		9	10	5								2		8							1	7	4	3	
155	30	(a)	Chelsea	L 2-4	Pass, Waters				6		9	10	5				11				2					8				1	7	4	3	
156	Jan 1	(a)	Barnsley	L 0-4					6		9	10	5				11				2	7				8				1		4	3	
157	6	(h)	Gainsboro' T	W 2-0	Crump 2	11			6		9	10	5								2					8				1	7	4	3	
158	20	(a)	Bristol C	L 0-7		7			4		9				1	5	8		3								10				11	6	2	
159	27	(h)	Manchester U	L 0-1		11			6							5					2		8			9				1	10	7	4	3
160	Feb 3	(a)	Glossop	L 0-1		11		1	6		9					5					2		8								10	7	4	3
161	10	(h)	Grimsby T	D 2-2	Waters (pen), Robinson	11		1								5		7			2		9				10			8			4	3
162	17	(h)	Blackpool	W 2-1	Suart 2	11		1	6							5	8			4	2					10	7	9					3	2
163	Mar 3	(h)	West Brom A	D 2-2	Robinson, Goodwin	11		1	6			10	5			7					2						9			8			4	3
164	10	(a)	Leicester F	L 0-2		11		1	6			10	5			7					2						9			8			4	3
165	17	(h)	Hull C	W 2-1	Schofield, G.F.Dodd	11	3	1	6			9				7	5				2						10			8			4	
166	24	(a)	Lincoln C	L 0-2		11		1	6		9					7	5				2						10			8			4	3
167	31	(h)	Chesterfield T	D 0-0		11		1			9					7	5				2						10			8			4	3
168	Apr 7	(a)	Burslem P Vale	D 0-0		11		1	6		9					7	5				2						10			8			4	3
169	13	(h)	Leeds C	D 1-1	Waters (pen)	11		1	6		9					5					2		8				10				7		4	3
170	14	(h)	Barnsley	D 0-0		11		1	6		8	10	5								2		9								7	4	3	
171	16	(h)	Burton U	W 2-0	Robinson, G.F.Dodd	11		1	6		9					7	5				2		8				10			7		4	3	
172	17	(a)	Bradford C	W 1-0	Porter	11		1	6							5					2		8				9	10			7	4	3	
173	21	(a)	Clapton O	L 0-1		11		1								5	6				2		8				9	10			7	4	3	2
174	28	(h)	Burnley	W 3-1	Crump, Porter 2	11					8		5				6				2		1				9	10			7	4	3	

FINAL LEAGUE POSITION: 10th in Division Two

	Bar	Bos	But	Btw	Cre	Cru	DGF	DdS	Far	Fra	Goo	Hal	Han	HgR	HgT	Hey	Hod	Man	Nix	Par	Pas	Pem	Por	Rob(ts)	Rob(n)	Sch	Sua	Wat	Wor
Appearances	36	1	14	22	4	23	27	20	2	7	11	16	9	1	2	34	2	19	4	1	15	17	4	3	15	33	38	36	2
Goals	2					7	5				1				2			8			2		3		3	3	3	5	

FA Cup

Rnd	Date	V	Opponent	Result	Scorers	Att	Bar	Btw	Cru	DGF	DdS	Fra	HgT	Hey	Man	Pas	Pem	Rob(n)	Sch	Sua	Wat
Q4	Dec 9	(a)	Walsall	D 3-3	Manson 2, Crump	3,000	11	6	9		5	1		2	8		10		7	4	3
R	14	(h)	Walsall	W 5-0	Manson, Bardsley, T.Hegarty (pen), Crump 2	1,500	11	6	9		5	1	3	2	8		10		7	4	
1	Jan 13	(a)	Lincoln C	L 2-4	Schofield, Bardsley	4,000	11	6	9	10	5			2	8			1	7	4	3

	Bar	Btw	Cru	DGF	DdS	Fra	HgT	Hey	Man	Pas	Pem	Rob(n)	Sch	Sua	Wat
Appearances	3	3	3	1	3	2	1	3	3	1	2	1	3	3	2
Goals	2		3				1		3				1		

1906-07

No	Date	V	Opponent	Result	Scorers	Ambler	Bardsley	Beswick	Bradley	Butler	Buttenworth	Craig	Cresser	Crump	Dodd	Goodwin	Hall	Heywood	Kennedy	Lees	Mitchell	Molyneux	Pass	Porter	Robinson	Smith F	Smith G.R.	Stokes	Suart	Waters	White	Worsley
175	Sep 1	(a)	Clapton O	D 1-1	Porter		11			1	6			8	5				2	10				9					4	3	7	
176	8	(h)	Gainsboro' T	L 1-2	White		11			1	6			8	5				2	10				9					4	3	7	
177	15	(h)	Chesterfield T	D 1-1	Bardsley		11			1	6			8	5				2	10				9					4	3	7	
178	22	(a)	Hull C	L 0-3			11			1	6			8	5				2	10				9					4	3	7	
179	29	(h)	Glossop	W 5-0	Kennedy, Crump 2, Pass, Hall (pen)		11			1	6			9			5		2	10			8						4	3	7	
180	Oct 6	(a)	Blackpool	W 1-0	Suart		11			1	6			9	5				2	10			8						4	3	7	
181	13	(h)	Bradford C	W 2-1	Suart, Pass		11			1	6			9	5				2	10			8						4	3	7	
182	20	(a)	West Brom A	D 1-1	Pass					1	6			9	5			11	2	10			8						4	3	7	
183	27	(h)	Leicester F	W 1-0	Crump					1	6			9	5			11	2	10			8						4	3	7	
184	Nov 3	(a)	Nottingham F	L 1-2	Pass					1	6			9	5			11	2	10			8						4	3	7	
185	10	(h)	Lincoln C	W 1-0	Crump					1	6			9	5			11		10			8		2				4	3	7	
186	17	(a)	Burton U	W 1-0	Waters (pen)					1	6			9	5			11		10			8		2				4	3	7	
187	24	(h)	Grimsby T	W 3-0	Dodd, Pass, Kennedy					1	6			9	5			11	2	10			8						4	3	7	
188	Dec 1	(a)	Burslem PVale	L 0-5						1	6			9	5			11	2	10			8						4	3	7	
189	8	(h)	Burnley	W 2-1	Lees, Crump					1	6			9	5			11	2	10			8						4	3	7	
190	15	(a)	Leeds C	L 1-6	Porter					1	6				5			11	2				8	9	10				4	3	7	
191	22	(h)	Barnsley	D 0-0						1	6			9	5			11	2	10			8						4	3	7	
192	25	(h)	Leicester F	L 0-1						1	6			9	5			11	2	10			8						4	3	7	
193	26	(a)	Wolves	D 1-1	Crump	10				1	6			9	5			11	2				8						4	3	7	
194	29	(h)	Clapton O	D 1-1	Pass					1	6			9	5			11	2				8	10					4	3	7	
195	Jan 1	(h)	Chelsea	L 1-2	Crump					1	6			9	5			11	2				8	10					4	3	7	
196	5	(a)	Gainsboro' T	L 1-3	Pass			9		1	6		4		5			11	2				8	10						3	7	
197	19	(a)	Chesterfield T	W 2-0	Waters (pen), Crump					1	6			8	5			11	2				9	10					4	3	7	
198	26	(h)	Hull C	D 1-1	Pass					1	6			8	5			11	2				9	10					4	3	7	
199	Feb 2	(a)	Glossop	W 3-2	Porter 2, Pass			8		1	6				5		7	11	2				9	10					4	3		
200	9	(h)	Blackpool	D 0-0				8		1	6				5		7	11	2				9	10					4	3		
201	16	(a)	Bradford C	L 0-1				8		1	6				5		7	11	2				9	10					4	3		
202	Mar 4	(a)	Chelsea	L 0-2						1	6			9	5			11	2				8	10					4	3	7	
203	9	(h)	Nottingham F	D 0-0						1	6				5		7	11	2	10			8	9					4	3		
204	16	(a)	Lincoln C	L 1-3	G.R.Smith					1	6				5			11	2	10			8	9			7		4	3		
205	23	(h)	Burton U	W 2-0	Porter, Crump					1	6			8	5			11	2				9	10					4	3	7	
206	29	(h)	Wolves	D 0-0				10		1	6			8	5			11					9						4	3	7	2
207	30	(a)	Grimsby T	L 1-3	Pass			10		1	6			8	5			11					9						4	3	7	2
208	Apr 1	(a)	Barnsley	L 1-3	Crump	4		7			6			9	5			11			1		8	10						3	7	2
209	6	(h)	Burslem PVale	W 3-0	Mitchell, Porter 2			9		1	6				5			11			8			10					4	3	7	2
210	8	(h)	West Brom A	L 0-1				9	2	1	6			8	5			11			10								4	3	7	
211	13	(a)	Burnley	L 0-3		6		9		1				8	5			11	2		10								4	3	7	
212	20	(h)	Leeds C	D 2-2	Mitchell, Crump	6				1				8	5			11			10		9						4	3	7	2
			Appearances			4	7	10	1	37	27	1	8	31	34	5	6	29	18	13	14	1	30	22	5	2	1	1	36	38	32	5
			Goals			1								11	1		1		2	1	2		10	7			1		2	2	1	

FINAL LEAGUE POSITION: 12th in Division Two

FA Cup

No	Date	V	Opponent	Result	Scorers	Gate	Ambler	Bardsley	Beswick	Bradley	Butler	Buttenworth	Craig	Cresser	Crump	Dodd	Goodwin	Hall	Heywood	Kennedy	Lees	Mitchell	Molyneux	Pass	Porter	Robinson	Smith F	Smith G.R.	Stokes	Suart	Waters	White	Worsley
1	Jan 12	(h*)	Fulham	D 0-0		30,000			10		1	6			9	5			11	2				8						4	3	7	
R	Jan 16	(a)	Fulham	L 1-2	Pass	10,000			10		1	6			9	5			11	2				8						4	3	7	
			Appearances						2		2	2			2	2			2	2				2						2	2	2	
			Goals																					1									

*Played at Craven Cottage by mutual agreement, with Stockport being guaranteed £600 in gate receipts.

1907-08

No	Date	V	Opponents	Result	Scorers / Att.	Aaron	Abrams	Ambler	Buller	Butterworth	Carter	Connell	Cook	Craig	Crump	Dodd	Galloway	Goodwin	Green	Hodgkinson	Mitchell	Molyneux	Owen	Porter	Smith	Suart	Waters	Worth	Yuill
213	Sep 2	(h)	Blackpool	D 1-1	Green			1	6	7				2	8	5	10		9		11					4	3		
214	Sep 7	(h)	Gainsboro' T	D 1-1	Abrams		11	1	6	7				2	8	5	10		9							4	3		
215	Sep 9	(h)	Grimsby T	W 3-0	Carter, Crump, Dodd		11	4	6	7				2	9	5						1	10	8			3		
216	Sep 14	(a)	Grimsby T	L 1-2	Crump		10	4	6	7				2	9	5					11	1		8			3		
217	Sep 21	(a)	Glossop	D 1-1	Carter (pen)		10	1	6	11				2	9				7					8	5	4	3		
218	Sep 28	(h)	Leicester F	W 2-1	Crump, Green		10	1	6	11				2	9	5			7					8		4	3		
219	Oct 5	(a)	Blackpool	W 3-1	Crump, Porter 2		10		6	11				2	9	5			7			1		8		4	3		
220	Oct 12	(h)	Stoke	L 1-2	Opp own-goal		10	1	6	11				2	9				7					8	5	4	3		
221	Oct 19	(a)	West Brom A	L 0-2			6	1		11				2	9		10							8	5	4	3		7
222	Oct 26	(h)	Bradford C	D 1-1	Crump		6	1		11				2	9		10		7					8	5	4	3		
223	Nov 2	(a)	Hull C	D 0-0			10	4	1	6	7			2	9						11			8		5	3		
224	Nov 9	(h)	Derby C	W 2-1	Abrams, Opp own goal		10	4	1	6	7	11		2	9									8		5	3		
225	Nov 16	(a)	Lincoln C	D 1-1	Abrams		10		1	6				2	9				7		11			8	4	5	3		
226	Nov 23	(h)	Fulham	W 2-0	Porter, Carter		10	4	1	6	7			2	9						11			8		5	3		
227	Nov 30	(a)	Barnsley	D 0-0			10	4	1	6	7			2	9						11			8		5	3		
228	Dec 14	(a)	Burnley	L 0-4			10	4	1	6	7			2	9						11			8		5	3		
229	Dec 21	(h)	Oldham A	L 2-3	Carter, Crump		10	4	1	6	7			2	9						11			8		5	3		
230	Dec 25	(h)	Leeds C	W 2-1	Suart, Porter		10	4	1	6				2		5			7		11			8		9	3		
231	Dec 26	(a)	Wolves	W 1-0	Green		10	4	1	6				2		5			7		11			8		9	3		
232	Dec 28	(a)	Clapton O	L 1-4	Green		10	6	1	11	8			2	9				7						4	5	3		
233	Jan 1	(h)	Wolves	L 1-3	Dodd			4	1	6	7			2	9	5			8		11			10			3		
234	Jan 4	(a)	Gainsboro' T	L 2-3	Carter, Crump				1	6	7			2	9	5	10				11			8	4		3		
235	Jan 18	(h)	Glossop	W 3-2	Carter, Porter, Suart		8		1	6	7			2	9	5	10				11					4	3		
236	Jan 25	(a)	Leicester F	L 1-2	Carter		10	4	1	6	8			2	9				7		11					5	3		
237	Feb 8	(a)	Stoke C	L 0-1			10		1	6	7			2	8	5			9		11					4	3		
238	Feb 15	(h)	West Brom A	L 1-2	Suart		9		1	6	8			2		5	10		7							4	3	11	
239	Feb 22	(a)	Bradford C	L 0-5			4			6				2	9	10			7			1			5	8	3	11	
240	Feb 29	(h)	Hull C	L 2-3	Aaron, Crump	8				6				2	9	5	10		7			1				4	3	11	
241	Mar 3	(a)	Chesterfield T	L 1-4	Green (pen)					6	9			2	8	5	10		7			1				4	3	11	
242	Mar 7	(a)	Derby C	L 0-3		8	10		1	6	9				5				7						2	4	3	11	
243	Mar 14	(h)	Lincoln C	D 1-1	Green				1	6	8				9	5			7					10	2	4	3	11	
244	Mar 21	(a)	Fulham	W 1-0	Crump		4			6	8			2	9				7	10		1				5	3	11	
245	Mar 28	(h)	Barnsley	W 2-0	Carter, Hodgkinson		4			6	8			2	9				7	10		1				5	3	11	
246	Apr 4	(h)	Chesterfield T	W 1-0	Green		4			6				2	9	5			7	10		1		8			3	11	
247	Apr 11	(h)	Burnley	L 1-3	Hodgkinson		4			6				2	9	5			7	10		1		8			3	11	
248	Apr 17	(a)	Leeds C	L 0-3						6				2	9		4	3	7	10		1		8		5		11	
249	Apr 18	(a)	Oldham A	L 0-5			10			6				2	9		4		7			1		8	3	5		11	
250	Apr 25	(h)	Clapton O	W 6-1	Porter 3, Worth, Crump 2		5			6				2	9		4		7	10		1		8			3	11	
			Appearances			2	23	20	23	37	27	1	4	35	35	19	11	1	30	7	12	15	1	24	15	29	33	13	1
			Goals			1	3				8				11	2			7	2				8		3		1	

FINAL LEAGUE POSITION: 13th in Division Two

Own-goals 2

FA Cup

Round	Date	V	Opponents	Result	Att.	Aaron	Abrams	Ambler	Buller	Butterworth	Carter	Connell	Cook	Craig	Crump	Dodd	Galloway	Goodwin	Green	Hodgkinson	Mitchell	Molyneux	Owen	Porter	Smith	Suart	Waters	Worth	Yuill
R	Jan 11	(h*)	Aston Villa	L 0-3	16,000			4	1	6	8	11		2	9	5			7					10			3		
			Appearances					1	1	1	1	1		1	1	1			1					1			1		
			Goals																										

*Played at Villa Park on the basis of a guaranteed £450 plus 50% of the gross receipts exceeding £900 and all expenses.

1908-09

<table>
<thead>
<tr><th>No</th><th>Date</th><th>Venue / Opponent</th><th>Result</th><th>Scorers</th><th>Andrews</th><th>Angus</th><th>Berry</th><th>Burden</th><th>Butterworth</th><th>Elkin</th><th>Galloway</th><th>Goodwin</th><th>Green</th><th>Hibbert</th><th>Hodgkinson</th><th>Horrocks</th><th>Jones</th><th>Kenyon</th><th>Lomax</th><th>Martin</th><th>Molyneux</th><th>Porter</th><th>Proudfoot</th><th>Settle</th><th>Smith</th><th>Waters</th><th>Whitehouse</th><th>Wilson</th><th>Worth</th></tr>
</thead>
<tbody>
<tr><td>251</td><td>Sep 1</td><td>(a) Grimsby T</td><td>L 0-3</td><td></td><td></td><td></td><td>5</td><td>6</td><td>2</td><td></td><td></td><td></td><td>7</td><td></td><td></td><td>11</td><td></td><td></td><td></td><td>9</td><td>1</td><td>4</td><td>10</td><td></td><td>3</td><td></td><td>8</td><td></td><td></td></tr>
<tr><td>252</td><td>5</td><td>(a) Fulham</td><td>L 1-5</td><td>Martin</td><td></td><td></td><td>5</td><td></td><td>2</td><td>6</td><td></td><td></td><td>7</td><td>8</td><td></td><td>11</td><td></td><td></td><td></td><td>9</td><td>1</td><td>4</td><td>10</td><td></td><td>3</td><td></td><td></td><td></td><td></td></tr>
<tr><td>253</td><td>12</td><td>(h) Burnley</td><td>W 2-1</td><td>Martin, Green</td><td></td><td></td><td>5</td><td>6</td><td>2</td><td></td><td></td><td></td><td>7</td><td>8</td><td></td><td>11</td><td></td><td></td><td></td><td>9</td><td>1</td><td>4</td><td>10</td><td></td><td>3</td><td></td><td></td><td></td><td></td></tr>
<tr><td>254</td><td>19</td><td>(a) Bradford+</td><td>W 1-0</td><td>Porter</td><td></td><td></td><td>5</td><td>6</td><td>2</td><td></td><td></td><td></td><td>7</td><td></td><td></td><td>11</td><td></td><td></td><td></td><td>9</td><td>1</td><td>4</td><td>10</td><td></td><td>3</td><td></td><td>8</td><td></td><td></td></tr>
<tr><td>255</td><td>26</td><td>(h) Wolves</td><td>W 1-0</td><td>Green</td><td></td><td></td><td>5</td><td>6</td><td>2</td><td></td><td></td><td></td><td>7</td><td></td><td>10</td><td>11</td><td></td><td></td><td></td><td>9</td><td>1</td><td>4</td><td></td><td></td><td>3</td><td></td><td>8</td><td></td><td></td></tr>
<tr><td>256</td><td>Oct 3</td><td>(a) Oldham A</td><td>W 1-0</td><td>Whitehouse</td><td></td><td></td><td>5</td><td>6</td><td>2</td><td></td><td></td><td></td><td>7</td><td></td><td></td><td>11</td><td></td><td></td><td></td><td>9</td><td>1</td><td>4</td><td>10</td><td></td><td>3</td><td></td><td>8</td><td></td><td></td></tr>
<tr><td>257</td><td>10</td><td>(h) Clapton O</td><td>D 1-1</td><td>Whitehouse</td><td></td><td></td><td>5</td><td>6</td><td>2</td><td></td><td></td><td></td><td>7</td><td></td><td></td><td>11</td><td></td><td></td><td></td><td>9</td><td>1</td><td>4</td><td>10</td><td></td><td>3</td><td></td><td>8</td><td></td><td></td></tr>
<tr><td>258</td><td>17</td><td>(a) Leeds C</td><td>L 1-2</td><td>Whitehouse</td><td></td><td></td><td>5</td><td>6</td><td>2</td><td></td><td></td><td></td><td>7</td><td></td><td></td><td>11</td><td></td><td></td><td></td><td>9</td><td>1</td><td>4</td><td>10</td><td></td><td>3</td><td></td><td>8</td><td></td><td></td></tr>
<tr><td>259</td><td>24</td><td>(h) Barnsley</td><td>W 2-1</td><td>Whitehouse, Porter</td><td></td><td></td><td>5</td><td>6</td><td>2</td><td></td><td></td><td></td><td>7</td><td></td><td></td><td>11</td><td></td><td></td><td></td><td>9</td><td>1</td><td>4</td><td>10</td><td></td><td>3</td><td></td><td>8</td><td></td><td></td></tr>
<tr><td>260</td><td>31</td><td>(a) Tottenham H</td><td>D 0-0</td><td></td><td></td><td></td><td>4</td><td>6</td><td>2</td><td></td><td></td><td></td><td>7</td><td></td><td></td><td>11</td><td></td><td></td><td></td><td>9</td><td>1</td><td>10</td><td>5</td><td></td><td>3</td><td></td><td>8</td><td></td><td></td></tr>
<tr><td>261</td><td>Nov 7</td><td>(h) Hull C</td><td>W 3-1</td><td>Horrocks, Porter, Whitehouse (pen)</td><td></td><td></td><td>4</td><td>6</td><td>2</td><td></td><td></td><td></td><td>7</td><td></td><td></td><td>11</td><td></td><td></td><td></td><td></td><td>1</td><td>8</td><td>5</td><td>10</td><td>3</td><td></td><td>9</td><td></td><td></td></tr>
<tr><td>262</td><td>14</td><td>(a) Derby C</td><td>L 0-5</td><td></td><td></td><td></td><td>4</td><td>6</td><td>2</td><td></td><td></td><td></td><td>7</td><td></td><td></td><td>11</td><td></td><td></td><td></td><td></td><td>1</td><td>8</td><td>5</td><td>10</td><td>3</td><td></td><td>9</td><td></td><td></td></tr>
<tr><td>263</td><td>21</td><td>(h) Blackpool</td><td>W 1-0</td><td>Horrocks</td><td></td><td></td><td></td><td>6</td><td>2</td><td></td><td>4</td><td></td><td>7</td><td></td><td></td><td>11</td><td></td><td></td><td></td><td>9</td><td>1</td><td></td><td>5</td><td>10</td><td>3</td><td></td><td>8</td><td></td><td></td></tr>
<tr><td>264</td><td>28</td><td>(a) Chesterfield T</td><td>W 2-1</td><td>Horrocks, Whitehouse</td><td></td><td></td><td></td><td>6</td><td>2</td><td></td><td>4</td><td></td><td>7</td><td></td><td></td><td>11</td><td>9</td><td></td><td></td><td></td><td>1</td><td></td><td>5</td><td>10</td><td>3</td><td></td><td>8</td><td></td><td></td></tr>
<tr><td>265</td><td>Dec 5</td><td>(h) Glossop</td><td>W 4-2</td><td>Settle, Whitehouse 2, Porter</td><td></td><td></td><td></td><td>6</td><td>2</td><td></td><td>4</td><td></td><td>7</td><td></td><td></td><td>11</td><td></td><td></td><td></td><td></td><td>1</td><td>8</td><td>5</td><td>10</td><td>3</td><td></td><td>9</td><td></td><td></td></tr>
<tr><td>266</td><td>12</td><td>(h) Bolton W</td><td>W 1-0</td><td>Porter</td><td></td><td></td><td></td><td>6</td><td>2</td><td></td><td>4</td><td></td><td>7</td><td></td><td></td><td>11</td><td></td><td></td><td></td><td></td><td>1</td><td>8</td><td>5</td><td>10</td><td>3</td><td></td><td>9</td><td></td><td></td></tr>
<tr><td>267</td><td>19</td><td>(a) West Brom A</td><td>L 0-2</td><td></td><td></td><td></td><td>5</td><td>6</td><td></td><td></td><td>4</td><td></td><td>7</td><td></td><td></td><td>11</td><td></td><td></td><td></td><td></td><td>1</td><td>8</td><td></td><td>10</td><td>3</td><td></td><td>9</td><td></td><td></td></tr>
<tr><td>268</td><td>25</td><td>(a) Birmingham</td><td>L 2-4</td><td>Green 2</td><td></td><td></td><td>2</td><td>6</td><td></td><td></td><td>4</td><td></td><td>7</td><td></td><td></td><td>11</td><td></td><td></td><td>8</td><td></td><td>1</td><td>9</td><td>5</td><td>10</td><td>3</td><td></td><td></td><td></td><td></td></tr>
<tr><td>269</td><td>26</td><td>(a) Gainsboro' T</td><td>L 2-3</td><td>Horrocks, Martin</td><td></td><td></td><td></td><td>6</td><td></td><td>4</td><td>2</td><td></td><td>7</td><td></td><td></td><td>11</td><td></td><td></td><td>8</td><td>1</td><td>9</td><td>5</td><td>10</td><td></td><td>3</td><td></td><td></td><td></td><td></td></tr>
<tr><td>270</td><td>Jan 1</td><td>(h) Grimsby T</td><td>L 0-1</td><td></td><td>9</td><td></td><td></td><td>6</td><td></td><td>4</td><td>2</td><td></td><td>7</td><td></td><td></td><td>11</td><td></td><td></td><td></td><td>1</td><td></td><td>5</td><td>10</td><td></td><td>3</td><td></td><td>8</td><td></td><td></td></tr>
<tr><td>271</td><td>2</td><td>(h) Fulham</td><td>L 1-2</td><td>Green</td><td>9</td><td></td><td></td><td>6</td><td></td><td>4</td><td></td><td></td><td>7</td><td></td><td></td><td>11</td><td></td><td></td><td></td><td>1</td><td>8</td><td>5</td><td>10</td><td>2</td><td>3</td><td></td><td></td><td></td><td></td></tr>
<tr><td>272</td><td>9</td><td>(a) Burnley</td><td>L 1-5</td><td>Lomax</td><td>9</td><td></td><td>4</td><td>6</td><td></td><td>8</td><td></td><td></td><td>7</td><td></td><td></td><td>11</td><td></td><td></td><td>10</td><td>1</td><td></td><td>5</td><td></td><td>2</td><td>3</td><td></td><td></td><td></td><td></td></tr>
<tr><td>273</td><td>23</td><td>(h) Bradford</td><td>L 0-1</td><td></td><td></td><td></td><td>4</td><td>6</td><td>2</td><td></td><td></td><td></td><td>7</td><td></td><td></td><td>11</td><td></td><td></td><td>10</td><td>1</td><td>8</td><td>5</td><td></td><td></td><td>3</td><td></td><td>9</td><td></td><td></td></tr>
<tr><td>274</td><td>30</td><td>(a) Wolves</td><td>L 0-2</td><td></td><td></td><td></td><td></td><td></td><td>2</td><td>4</td><td></td><td></td><td>7</td><td></td><td></td><td>11</td><td>9</td><td></td><td></td><td>1</td><td>6</td><td>5</td><td>10</td><td></td><td>3</td><td></td><td>8</td><td></td><td></td></tr>
<tr><td>275</td><td>Feb 13</td><td>(a) Clapton O</td><td>L 0-5</td><td></td><td></td><td></td><td>6</td><td>2</td><td>4</td><td></td><td></td><td></td><td>7</td><td></td><td>10</td><td></td><td></td><td></td><td>8</td><td>1</td><td></td><td>6</td><td>5</td><td></td><td>3</td><td></td><td>9</td><td></td><td>11</td></tr>
<tr><td>276</td><td>20</td><td>(h) Leeds C</td><td>W 1-0</td><td>Waters (pen)</td><td></td><td>7</td><td>5</td><td>6</td><td>2</td><td>4</td><td></td><td></td><td></td><td></td><td></td><td>11</td><td></td><td></td><td></td><td>9</td><td>1</td><td>8</td><td></td><td>10</td><td>3</td><td></td><td></td><td></td><td></td></tr>
<tr><td>277</td><td>27</td><td>(h) Barnsley</td><td>L 0-2</td><td></td><td></td><td>7</td><td></td><td></td><td>2</td><td>4</td><td></td><td></td><td></td><td></td><td></td><td></td><td></td><td>8</td><td></td><td>1</td><td></td><td>5</td><td>10</td><td></td><td>3</td><td>9</td><td>6</td><td></td><td>11</td></tr>
<tr><td>278</td><td>Mar 6</td><td>(h) Tottenham H</td><td>L 1-3</td><td>Horrocks</td><td>9</td><td>8</td><td></td><td>6</td><td>2</td><td>4</td><td></td><td>7</td><td>5</td><td></td><td></td><td>11</td><td></td><td></td><td></td><td>1</td><td></td><td></td><td>10</td><td></td><td>3</td><td></td><td></td><td></td><td></td></tr>
<tr><td>279</td><td>8</td><td>(h) Oldham A</td><td>L 1-3</td><td>Jones</td><td>9</td><td>8</td><td>4</td><td></td><td></td><td></td><td></td><td>7</td><td></td><td></td><td></td><td>11</td><td>10</td><td></td><td></td><td>1</td><td></td><td>5</td><td></td><td>2</td><td>3</td><td>6</td><td></td><td></td><td></td></tr>
<tr><td>280</td><td>13</td><td>(a) Hull C</td><td>L 1-4</td><td>Settle</td><td></td><td>7</td><td>4</td><td></td><td>2</td><td></td><td></td><td></td><td></td><td></td><td></td><td>11</td><td>8</td><td></td><td></td><td>1</td><td></td><td>5</td><td>10</td><td>3</td><td></td><td>6</td><td>9</td><td></td><td></td></tr>
<tr><td>281</td><td>20</td><td>(h) Derby C</td><td>W 1-0</td><td>Proudfoot</td><td></td><td>7</td><td></td><td>6</td><td>2</td><td></td><td></td><td></td><td></td><td></td><td></td><td>11</td><td>8</td><td></td><td></td><td>1</td><td></td><td>5</td><td>10</td><td>3</td><td></td><td>4</td><td>9</td><td></td><td></td></tr>
<tr><td>282</td><td>27</td><td>(a) Blackpool</td><td>L 1-2</td><td>Hodgkinson</td><td></td><td>7</td><td></td><td></td><td>2</td><td>4</td><td></td><td></td><td></td><td></td><td>8</td><td></td><td></td><td></td><td></td><td>1</td><td></td><td>5</td><td>10</td><td>3</td><td></td><td>9</td><td>6</td><td></td><td>11</td></tr>
<tr><td>283</td><td>Apr 3</td><td>(h) Chesterfield T</td><td>W 2-0</td><td>Berry, Whitehouse</td><td>9</td><td></td><td>6</td><td></td><td>2</td><td>4</td><td></td><td>7</td><td>10</td><td></td><td></td><td></td><td></td><td></td><td></td><td>1</td><td></td><td>5</td><td></td><td>3</td><td></td><td>8</td><td></td><td></td><td>11</td></tr>
<tr><td>284</td><td>9</td><td>(h) Birmingham</td><td>W 3-2</td><td>Berry, Whitehouse 2</td><td>9</td><td></td><td>6</td><td></td><td>2</td><td>4</td><td></td><td>7</td><td>10</td><td></td><td></td><td></td><td></td><td></td><td></td><td>1</td><td></td><td>5</td><td></td><td>3</td><td></td><td>8</td><td></td><td></td><td>11</td></tr>
<tr><td>285</td><td>10</td><td>(a) Glossop</td><td>L 0-3</td><td></td><td></td><td></td><td>6</td><td></td><td>2</td><td>4</td><td></td><td>7</td><td>10</td><td>8</td><td></td><td></td><td></td><td></td><td></td><td>1</td><td></td><td>5</td><td></td><td>3</td><td></td><td>9</td><td></td><td></td><td>11</td></tr>
<tr><td>286</td><td>12</td><td>(h) Gainsboro' T</td><td>L 0-1</td><td></td><td>9</td><td></td><td>6</td><td></td><td>2</td><td>4</td><td></td><td>7</td><td></td><td></td><td>11</td><td></td><td></td><td></td><td></td><td>1</td><td></td><td>5</td><td>10</td><td></td><td>3</td><td></td><td>8</td><td></td><td></td></tr>
<tr><td>287</td><td>17</td><td>(a) Bolton W</td><td>L 1-4</td><td>Berry</td><td>8</td><td>9</td><td>5</td><td>6</td><td>2</td><td></td><td></td><td>7</td><td></td><td></td><td></td><td></td><td></td><td>10</td><td></td><td>1</td><td></td><td></td><td></td><td>3</td><td>4</td><td></td><td></td><td></td><td>11</td></tr>
<tr><td>288</td><td>24</td><td>(h) West Brom A</td><td>D 0-0</td><td></td><td>9</td><td></td><td>4</td><td>6</td><td>2</td><td></td><td></td><td>7</td><td>10</td><td></td><td></td><td></td><td></td><td></td><td></td><td>1</td><td></td><td>5</td><td></td><td>3</td><td></td><td>8</td><td></td><td></td></tr>
<tr><td colspan="5">Appearances</td><td>3</td><td>3</td><td>12</td><td>21</td><td>32</td><td>31</td><td>21</td><td>2</td><td>31</td><td>1</td><td>10</td><td>32</td><td>3</td><td>3</td><td>11</td><td>38</td><td>16</td><td>34</td><td>26</td><td>10</td><td>32</td><td>29</td><td></td><td>6</td><td>8</td></tr>
<tr><td colspan="5">Goals</td><td></td><td></td><td>3</td><td></td><td></td><td></td><td></td><td></td><td>5</td><td></td><td>1</td><td>5</td><td>1</td><td></td><td>1</td><td>3</td><td></td><td>5</td><td>1</td><td>2</td><td></td><td>1</td><td>11</td><td></td><td></td></tr>
</tbody>
</table>

FINAL LEAGUE POSITION: 18th in Division Two

FA Cup

<table>
<thead>
<tr><th>Rd</th><th>Date</th><th>Venue / Opponent</th><th>Result</th><th>Scorers</th><th>Att.</th><th>Berry</th><th>Butterworth</th><th>Galloway</th><th>Green</th><th>Horrocks</th><th>Lomax</th><th>Martin</th><th>Molyneux</th><th>Porter</th><th>Proudfoot</th><th>Settle</th><th>Smith</th><th>Whitehouse</th><th>Worth</th></tr>
</thead>
<tbody>
<tr><td>1</td><td>Jan 20*</td><td>(a) Grimsby T</td><td>W 2-0</td><td>Whitehouse, Lomax</td><td>5,000</td><td>6</td><td>2</td><td>4</td><td>7</td><td>11</td><td>10</td><td>1</td><td></td><td>5</td><td>8</td><td></td><td>3</td><td>9</td><td></td></tr>
<tr><td>2</td><td>Feb 6</td><td>(h) Glossop</td><td>D 1-1</td><td>Whitehouse (pen)</td><td>13,000</td><td>6</td><td>2</td><td>4</td><td>7</td><td>11</td><td></td><td>1</td><td>8</td><td>5</td><td>10</td><td></td><td>3</td><td>9</td><td></td></tr>
<tr><td>R</td><td>9</td><td>(a) Glossop</td><td>L 0-1§</td><td></td><td>4,500</td><td>6</td><td>2</td><td>4</td><td>7</td><td></td><td>9</td><td>1</td><td></td><td>5</td><td>10</td><td></td><td>3</td><td>8</td><td>11</td></tr>
<tr><td colspan="6">Appearances</td><td>3</td><td>3</td><td>3</td><td>3</td><td>2</td><td>1</td><td>3</td><td>1</td><td>3</td><td>3</td><td></td><td>3</td><td>3</td><td>1</td></tr>
<tr><td colspan="6">Goals</td><td></td><td></td><td></td><td></td><td></td><td>1</td><td></td><td></td><td></td><td></td><td></td><td></td><td>2</td><td></td></tr>
</tbody>
</table>

*This followed a first attempt on 16 January which was abandoned after 75 minutes due to a blizzard and bad light with Stockport leading 2-0 (Green, Whitehouse), the team being the same as for the game played on the 20th with the exception of Porter replacing Lomax.
§After extra-time.
+This, and further references to simply 'Bradford', relate to the club known as Bradford (Park Avenue).

1909-10

No	Date		Opponent	Result	Scorers	Abrams	Andrews	Angus	Bauchop	Berry	Burden	Charlton	Elkin	Galloway	Gettins	Goodwin	Greechan	Green	Kelly	Kennedy	Kenyon	Lomax	Makin	Melville	Molyneux	Moore	Newman	Nixon	Price	Waters	Weir	Whitehouse
289	Sep	1 (h)	West Brom A	L 0-2					11	9		8	2				10		5			4	1				7		3	6		
290		4 (h)	Fulham	L 0-2		6	8		11	9			2						5			4	1	3	10	7					
291		6 (a)	West Brom A	W 1-0	Nixon			9			5	8	2	4	3		10		11			6	1				7					
292		11 (a)	Burnley	D 2-2	Kelly, Greechan (pen)			9			5	8	3	4	2		10		11			6					7	1				
293		18 (h)	Leeds C	D 0-0				9			5	8	3	4	2		10		11			6					7	1				
294		25 (a)	Wolves	L 1-2	Burden						5	8	3	4	2		10		11			6					7	1				9
295	Oct	2 (h)	Gainsboro' T	W 3-0	Greechan, Nixon, Whitehouse			9			4		3	5	2		10		11			6	1				7					8
296		9 (a)	Grimsby T	W 1-0	Whitehouse			9			4		3	5	2		10		11			6	1				7					8
297		16 (h)	Manchester C	L 1-2	Kelly			9			4		3	5	2		10		11			6	1				7					8
298		23 (a)	Leicester F	L 0-1							4		2	5	3		10	9	11			6	1				7					8
299		30 (h)	Lincoln C	D 1-1	Kelly						4		2	5	3		10	9	11			6	1				7					8
300	Nov	6 (a)	Clapton O	L 0-2		6	4				5	8	2	3		9			11				1				10	7				
301		13 (h)	Blackpool	W 2-0	Bauchop, Kelly	6			11		4		2		3			7	5	9	8		1				10					
302		20 (a)	Hull C	D 1-1	Kenyon	6			11		4		2		3			7	5	9	8		1				10					
303		27 (a)	Derby C	D 1-1	Kelly	6			11		4		2		3			7	5	9	8		1				10					
304	Dec	4 (a)	Bradford	W 4-2	Abrams, Newman, Lomax, Bauchop	6			11		4		2		3			9	5	7	8		1				10					
305		11 (a)	Glossop	L 0-1		6			11		4				3			9	5	7	8	2	1				10					
306		18 (h)	Birmingham	D 1-1	Lomax	6			11		4				2			8	5	7	9		1				10		3			
307		25 (a)	Oldham A	L 0-3		6			11		4				2				5	7	8		3	1				10					9
308		27 (a)	Barnsley	L 0-1		6					4				2				11	5	9		3	1				10	7				8
309	Jan	1 (h)	Barnsley	W 5-0	Newman 2, Abrams, Whitehouse, Kenyon	6			11		4				2					5	9		3	1				10	7				8
310		8 (a)	Fulham	L 0-2		6							4	2					11	5	9		3	1				10	7				8
311		22 (h)	Burnley	D 1-1	Newman	6					4			2		11				5	9		3	1				10	7				8
312	Feb	12 (a)	Gainsboro' T	L 0-1		6							4	3	2		9		5		11			1				10	7				8
313		19 (h)	Grimsby T	W 2-1	Newman, Kenyon	6							4	3	2				11	5	9			1				10	7				8
314		26 (a)	Manchester C	L 1-2	Kennedy	6							4	3	2				11	5	9			1				10	7				8
315	Mar	5 (a)	Leeds C	W 2-0	Whitehouse, Kelly	6							4	3	2				11	5	9			1				10	7				8
316		12 (a)	Lincoln C	L 0-1		6				5			4	3	2				11		8			1				10	7				9
317		19 (h)	Clapton O	W 3-0	Abrams 2 (2 pens), Kelly	6	8			4				3					11	5				1				10	7	2			9
318		25 (h)	Oldham A	W 2-0	Nixon, Whitehouse	6	8		11				4	3	2		10					5	1					7				9
319		26 (a)	Blackpool	L 0-2		6	8		11				4		2		10					5	1	3				7				9
320		28 (a)	Wolves	D 1-1	Greechan	6	4							2	10	9	11			5	1					7		3			8
321	Apr	2 (h)	Hull C	L 1-5	Kelly	6	8						4		2	10			11			5	1					7		3		9
322		6 (h)	Leicester F	W 6-2	Makin, Abrams 2 (1 pen), Greechan, Nixon, Whitehouse	6							4		2	10			11				8	5	1			7		3		9
323		9 (a)	Derby C	L 0-1		6							4		2	10			11				8	5	1			7		3		9
324		16 (h)	Bradford	W 2-1	Whitehouse 2	6	8						4		2		10	11					5	1				7		3		9
325		23 (a)	Glossop	W 5-0	Kelly 2, Nixon, Melville, Green	6	8						4		2		10	11					5	1				7		3		9
326		30 (a)	Birmingham	L 0-3		6	8			4					2		10	11					5	1				7		3		9
			Appearances			28	10	6	12	2	23	6	16	22	28	14	16	7	32	18	15	8	2	26	35	2	19	31	3	10	1	26
			Goals			6			2		1						4	1	10	1	3	2	1	1			5	5				8

FINAL LEAGUE POSITION: 13th in Division Two

FA Cup

No	Date		Opponent	Result	Scorers	Att	Abrams	Elkin	Gettins	Kelly	Kennedy	Kenyon	Melville	Molyneux	Newman	Nixon	Whitehouse
1	Jan	15 (h)	Bolton W	W 4-1	Greechan, Whitehouse 2, Newman	8,000	6	4	2	11	5	9	3	1	10	7	8
2	Feb	5 (h)	Leyton	L 0-2		8,000	6	4	2	11	5	9	3	1	10	7	8
			Appearances				2	2	2	2	2	2	2	2	2	2	2
			Goals							1					1		2

1910-11

No	Date		Opponent	Result	Scorers	Abrams	Baggeley	Bauchop	Bird	Bridge	Brown	Burden	Charlton	Galloway	Gettins	Goodwin	Hardy	Hindmarsh	Kelly	Lomax	Makin	Melville	Mitton	Nixon	Price	Proudfoot	Prout	Waters	Whitehouse
327	Sep 1	(a)	Bolton W	D 2-2	Prout 2	6		11						4	3	2	10	7				5			1		9		8
328	3	(h)	Clapton O	L 0-3		6		11						4	3	2		7		10	8	5			1		9		
329	10	(a)	Blackpool	L 1-2	Lomax	6		11						4	3	2		7		10	8	5			1		9		
330	17	(h)	Glossop	W 2-1	Prout, Lomax			11				6		4	3	2			7	10		5			1		9		
331	24	(a)	Lincoln C	L 0-2		6		11						4	3	2			7	10		5			1		9		8
332	Oct 3	(h)	Huddersfield T	W 1-0	Bauchop	6		11					7	4	3	2				10		5			1		9		8
333	8	(a)	Birmingham	W 3-1	Makin, Lomax, Prout	6		11					7	4	3	2				10	8	5			1		9		
334	15	(h)	West Brom A	L 0-1		6		11				5	7	4	3	2				10	8				1		9		
335	22	(a)	Hull C	L 1-4	Lomax	6		11				5	7	4	3	2				10	8				1		9		
336	29	(h)	Fulham	D 1-1	Prout	6		11				5	7	4		2				10	8				1		9	3	
337	Nov 5	(a)	Bradford	L 2-3	Makin, Prout	6		11				5	7	4		2				10	8				1		9	3	
338	12	(h)	Burnley	W 4-2	Kelly, Makin, Lomax 2	6		11				5	7	4		2				10	8				1		9	3	
339	26	(h)	Leeds C	L 0-4					4			5	6			2		11	7	10	8				1		9	3	
340	Dec 10	(a)	Derby C	L 1-4	Bridge	6			7	5				4	3	2		11		10					1		9		8
341	17	(h)	Barnsley	D 2-2	Prout, Lomax	6			7	5				4	3	2		11		10					1		9		8
342	24	(a)	Leicester F	L 1-5	Prout	6			7	5		11		4	3	2				10					1		9		8
343	26	(a)	Wolves	D 0-0		6			7	5		11		4	3	2				10					1		9		8
344	27	(a)	Chelsea	L 0-2		6		11		5			7	4	3	2				10					1		9		8
345	31	(a)	Clapton O	L 0-1				11					7	4	3	2		6		10		5			1		9		8
346	Jan 2	(h)	Chelsea	D 2-2	Bauchop, Charlton			11					7	4	3	2		6		10		5			1		9		8
347	7	(h)	Blackpool	L 1-3	Prout			11					7	4	3	2		6		10		5			1		9		8
348	14	(a)	Huddersfield T	L 1-4	Charlton		1	11					8	4	3	2		6		10		5		7			9		
349	21	(a)	Glossop	L 0-3				11	1				7	4	3	2		6		10	8	5					9		
350	28	(h)	Lincoln C	W 3-2	Prout, Charlton 2			11	1				7	4	3	2		6		10	8	5					9		
351	Feb 4	(a)	Gainsboro' T	D 0-0				11					7	4		2		6		10	8				1	5	9	3	
352	13	(h)	Birmingham	W 3-1	Prout 2 (1 pen), Bauchop			11	1				7			2		6		10	4	5					9	3	8
353	18	(a)	West Brom A	L 2-4	Whitehouse, Charlton			11	1				7			2		6		10	4	5					9	3	8
354	25	(h)	Bolton W	L 0-1				11	1				7	4	3	2		6		10		5					9		8
355	Mar 4	(a)	Fulham	L 2-6	Prout, Hindmarsh			11	1				7			2		6		10	4	5					9	3	8
356	11	(h)	Bradford	W 1-0	Makin			11					7			2		6		10	8	4			1	5	9	3	
357	18	(a)	Burnley	L 3-5	Prout 2, Lomax			11					7		3	2		6		10	8	4			1	5	9		
358	25	(h)	Gainsboro' T	W 1-0	Melville			11					7		3	2		6		10	8	4			1	5	9		
359	Apr 1	(a)	Leeds C	L 0-4				11					7	4	3	2		6		10	8				1	5	9		
360	14	(h)	Wolves	W 1-0	Prout (pen)			11					7		3	2		6		10	8	4			1	5	9		
361	15	(h)	Derby C	W 3-2	Charlton, Whitehouse, Bauchop			11					9		3	2		6		10		4		7	1	5			8
362	22	(a)	Barnsley	D 1-1	Nixon			11					9		3	2		6		10		4		7	1	5			8
363	24	(h)	Hull C	D 1-1	Charlton			11					9		3	2		6		10		4		7	1	5			8
364	29	(h)	Leicester F	W 1-0	Prout			11					7		3	2		6		10		4			1	5	9		8
			Appearances			16	1	29	7	5	2	14	30	23	34	34	1	25	14	28	14	25	3	8	31	10	35	9	20
			Goals					4		1			7					1	1	8	4	1		1			17		2

FINAL LEAGUE POSITION: 17th in Division Two

FA Cup

No	Date		Opponent	Result	Att	Abrams	Baggeley	Bauchop	Bird	Bridge	Brown	Burden	Charlton	Galloway	Gettins	Goodwin	Hardy	Hindmarsh	Kelly	Lomax	Makin	Melville	Mitton	Nixon	Price	Proudfoot	Prout	Waters	Whitehouse
Q4	Nov 19	(a)	Rochdale	D 0-0	2,000	6						5	7		3	2		11		10	8				1		4		9
R*	21	(h)	Rochdale	D 0-0								5			3	2		6	11	10	8			7	1		4		9
2R	28	(n§)	Rochdale	L 0-1		6						5			3	2		11	10	8				7	1		4		9
			Appearances			2						3	1		3	3		1	3	3	3			2	3		3		3
			Goals																										

*Although the referee and linesmen, in consultation with the two captains, decided not to play extra-time because of the hardness of the pitch and the gloom, the match was treated as a replay and a further replay ordered to be played at a neutral ground.

§Played at Boundary Park, Oldham.

1911-12

League (Division Two)

No	Date		Opponent	Result	Scorers	Beech	Charlton	Devlin	Froehlich	Goodwin	Graham J.G.	Graham J.W.	Hiftle	Hindmarsh	Houghton	Lomax	McIver	Melville	Norton	O'Brien	Prout	Rodgers	Rourke	Russell	Smith	Trotter	Warren
365	Sep 2	(a)	Chelsea	D 0-0			7	8				3		6		10	1	4		11	9			5			
366	9	(h)	Clapton O	D 1-1	Devlin		7	8				3		6		10	1	4		11	9			5			
367	16	(a)	Bristol C	L 1-2	O'Brien		7	8				3		6		10	1	4		11	9			5			
368	23	(h)	Birmingham	W 2-0	Lomax, O'Brien	4	7	8		2		3		6		10	1			11	9			5			
369	30	(a)	Huddersfield T	L 0-2		4	7	8		2		3		6		10	1			11	9			5			
370	Oct 7	(h)	Blackpool	L 1-2	Charlton (pen)		7	8		2		3		5		10	1	4		11	9			6			
371	14	(a)	Glossop	D 1-1	Charlton		7	9		2		3	8	6		10	1	4		11				5			
372	21	(h)	Hull C	D 1-1	Hindmarsh		7	8		2		3		6		10	1	4		11				5			9
373	28	(a)	Barnsley	L 1-2	Charlton (pen)		7	8		2		3		6		10	1	4		11				5			9
374	Nov 4	(h)	Bradford	W 1-0	Rodgers		7	8		2		3		6			1			11		10	5	4			9
375	11	(a)	Fulham	L 1-3	Rodgers		7	8		2		3		6			1			11	9	10	5	4			
376	25	(h)	Burnley	L 0-1			7	8		2		3		6		10	1	5		11	9		4				
377	Dec 9	(h)	Wolves	L 1-2	Hiftle		7			2	8	3	10	6			1	5		11	9		4				
378	16	(a)	Leicester F	D 1-1	Norton		7			2		3	10		6	8	1	4	11					5			9
379	23	(h)	Gainsboro' T	L 0-3						2		3	10		6	7	1	4	11	8				5			9
380	25	(h)	Nottingham F	D 2-2	Smith, Charlton		7	8		2				6	3	10	1	5		11				4	9		
381	26	(a)	Grimsby T	D 2-2	Prout, Devlin	5	7	8		2				6	3		1			11	9	10		4			
382	30	(a)	Chelsea	L 0-1		4	7	8	2					6	3		1			11		10		5	9		
383	Jan 1	(h)	Derby C	W 4-0	O'Brien, Lomax 2, Smith	5	7	8	2					6	3	10	1			11				4	9		
384	6	(a)	Clapton O	L 2-4	Smith 2	5	7	8	2					6	3	10	1			11				4	9		
385	20	(h)	Bristol C	W 1-0	O'Brien		7	8		2				6	3	10	1			11				4	9		
386	27	(a)	Birmingham	L 0-2			7	8		2				6	3	10	1	5		11				4	9		
387	Feb 3	(h)	Huddersfield T	W 3-1	Charlton 3 (1 pen)		7			2		3		6		10	1	4		11			8	5	9		
388	10	(a)	Blackpool	W 1-0	Rodgers		7			2		3		6		10	1	4		11			8	5	9		
389	17	(h)	Glossop	W 3-0	Rodgers 2, Smith		7			2		3		6		10	1	4		11			8	5	9		
390	24	(a)	Hull C	W 2-0	Smith, Lomax					2		3		6		10	1	4		11			8	5	9	7	
391	Mar 2	(h)	Barnsley	D 1-1	Rodgers					2		3		6		10	1	4		11			8	5	9	7	
392	9	(a)	Bradford	L 0-1						2		3		6		10	1	4	7	11			8	5	9		
393	16	(h)	Fulham	W 2-1	Rodgers, O'Brien					2		3		6		10	1	5	7	11		4	8		9		
394	23	(a)	Derby C	L 0-2			7			2		3		6		10	1			11		4	8	5	9		
395	30	(a)	Burnley	L 1-4	Lomax					2		3		6		10	1		7	11		4	8	5	9		
396	Apr 5	(h)	Grimsby T	W 3-0	Charlton (pen), Smith, Prout		7			2		3		6		10	1			11		4	8	5	9		
397	6	(a)	Leeds C	D 1-1	Smith		7			2		3				10	1	6		11		4	8	5	9		
398	8	(a)	Nottingham F	W 2-1	Rodgers, Lomax	11				2		3		6		10	1					4	8	5	9	7	
399	13	(a)	Wolves	L 0-4			7			2		3		6		10	1			11		4	8	5	9		
400	15	(h)	Leeds C	D 3-3	Rodgers, Smith 2		7			2		3		6		10	1			11		4	8	5	9		
401	20	(h)	Leicester F	L 2-3	Charlton (pen), Rodgers		7			2		3		6		10	1			11		4	8	5	9		
402	27	(a)	Gainsboro' T	D 0-0			7			2		3		6		10	1			11		4	8	5	9		
					Appearances	6	31	20	3	35	1	31	4	35	9	33	38	22	8	32	20	21	12	27	24	3	3
					Goals		9	2					1	1		6			1	5	2	10			10		

FINAL LEAGUE POSITION: 16th in Division Two

FA Cup

Rnd	Date		Opponent	Result	Scorers	Att	Beech	Charlton	Devlin	Froehlich	Goodwin	Graham J.G.	Graham J.W.	Hiftle	Hindmarsh	Houghton	Lomax	McIver	Melville	Norton	O'Brien	Prout	Rodgers	Rourke	Russell	Smith	Trotter	Warren
Q4	Nov 18	(a)	Chester	W 4-1	Rodgers, Devlin, O'Brien, Lomax			7	8				3		6		10	1	5		11	9	4		2			
Q5	Dec 2	(h)	Catford	W 4-0	Lomax 3, Norton	2,000			8	2			3		6		10	1	4	7	11	9			5			
1	Jan 13	(a)	Lincoln C	L 0-2		8,200	5	7	8	2			3		6		10	1			11		4			9		
					Appearances		1	2	3	2			3		3		3	3	2	1	3	2	3		1	1		
					Goals				1								4			1	1		1					

144

1912-13

League (Division Two)

No	Date		Venue	Opponent	Result	Scorers	Birds	Blair	Bryden	Charlton	Chivers	Cook	Crossthwaite	Davies	Fagan	Froehlich	Garrett	Goodwin	Graham	Hindmarsh	Houghton	McIver	Middleton	Mitton	O'Brien	Proudfoot	Prout	Rodgers	Smith	Tattersall	Trotter
403	Sep	2	(a)	Preston NE	D 1-1	Charlton		10		7				3	5		2		6		1				11		4	8	9		
404		7	(h)	Lincoln C	L 2-4	Rodgers 2		10		7				3	5		2		6		1				11		4	8	9		
405		14	(a)	Nottingham F	L 1-2	Rodgers		10		7				3	5		2		6		1				11		4	8	9		
406		16	(a)	Clapton O	L 1-4	Rodgers				7				3	5		2		6		1				11		4	8	9		
407		21	(h)	Bristol C	L 0-1			10		7					5		2	3		10	6	1			11		4	8	9		
408		28	(a)	Birmingham	D 1-1	Charlton	1	10	11	9				3	5		2		6									8		4	7
409	Oct	5	(h)	Huddersfield T	W 3-1	Cook 3		10			9			3	5		2		6			1			11			8		4	7
410		12	(a)	Leeds C	L 1-2	Rodgers		10		4	9			3	5		2		6			1			11			8			7
411		19	(h)	Grimsby T	D 1-1	Trotter		10			9			3	5		2		6			1			11			8		4	7
412		26	(a)	Bury	L 0-2			10			9			3	5		2		6			1			11			8		4	7
413	Nov	2	(h)	Fulham	W 1-0	Rodgers		10						3	5		2		6			1			11			8	9	4	7
414		4	(h)	Leicester F	L 1-2	Charlton (pen)		10						3	5		2	6				1	4		11			8	9	4	7
415		9	(a)	Barnsley	D 1-1	Cook		10			9			3	5		2	6				1			11			8		4	7
416		16	(h)	Bradford	W 1-0	Garrett					9			3	5		2	6				1			11			8		4	7
417		23	(a)	Wolves	L 0-1						9			3	5		2	6				1			11			8		4	7
418	Dec	7	(a)	Blackpool	D 1-1	Rodgers					9			3	5		2	6				1			11			8		4	7
419		21	(h)	Burnley	L 0-1			6		10				3	5		2					1			11			8	9	4	7
420		25	(a)	Hull C	L 2-3	Charlton (pen), Smith		6		10	9			3	5		2					1			11			8	9	4	7
421		28	(a)	Lincoln C	L 2-3	Charlton, Rodgers		6		7	9			3	5		2					1			11			8	10	4	
422	Jan	1	(h)	Clapton O	W 2-0	O'Brien 2		6		10	9		7		5		2	3				1			11			8		4	
423		4	(h)	Nottingham F	W 2-1	Charlton 2 (1 pen)		6		10	9		7		5		2	3				1			11			8		4	
424		18	(a)	Bristol C	L 2-7	Smith, Charlton		6		10	4		7		5		2	3				1			11			8	9	4	
425		25	(h)	Birmingham	L 0-1			6		10	9		7		5		2	3				1			11			8		4	
426	Feb	1	(a)	Glossop	D 2-2	Blair, Crossthwaite		6		10			7		5		2	3				1			11			8	9	4	
427		8	(a)	Huddersfield T	D 3-3	Charlton, Smith 2		6		7			2		5			3				1	9		11			8	10	4	
428		15	(h)	Leeds C	W 6-0	Charlton, Smith 4, Crossthwaite		6		7			2		5			3			10	1			11			8	9	4	
429		22	(a)	Grimsby T	L 1-4	Smith (pen)						7	2		5			3	6		10	1			11			8	9	4	
430	Mar	1	(h)	Bury	L 1-2	Rodgers						7	8	2	5			3	6			1			11			10	9	4	
431		8	(a)	Fulham	L 0-7			6				7	8	3	5		2					1			11			10	9	4	
432		15	(h)	Barnsley	L 0-3		1					7	10		6		2	3					11	5				8	9	4	
433		21	(h)	Hull C	D 3-3	Rodgers 2, Chivers				6		7	10	3	5		2					1			11			8	9	4	
434		22	(a)	Bradford	L 2-4	O'Brien, Garrett				6		7	10	2	5			3				1			11			8	9	4	
435		24	(h)	Glossop	D 1-1	Garrett (pen)	1			6		7	9	3	5		2					10			11			8		4	
436		29	(h)	Wolves	W 5-1	Garrett, Davies 2, Rodgers, O'Brien	1			6		7	10	2	5			3							11			8	9	4	
437	Apr	5	(a)	Leicester F	L 1-4	Rodgers	1			6		7	10	2	5			3							11			8	9	4	
438		12	(h)	Blackpool	W 2-0	Rodgers 2	1	11		6		7	10	2	5			3										8	9	4	
439		19	(h)	Preston NE	D 1-1	Rodgers	1			6		7	10	3	2		5								11			8	9	4	
440		26	(a)	Burnley	L 2-3	Rodgers, Garrett	1			6		7	10	3	2		5								11			8	9	4	
				Appearances			8	23	1	26	14	10	20	11	34	3	38	27	11	9	10	30	2	2	30	1	4	38	24	30	12
				Goals				1		10	1	4	2	2			5								4			17	9		1

FINAL LEAGUE POSITION: 19th in Division Two - Re-elected

FA Cup

Round	Date		Venue	Opponent	Result	Scorers	Att.	Birds	Blair	Bryden	Charlton	Chivers	Cook	Crossthwaite	Davies	Fagan	Froehlich	Garrett	Goodwin	Graham	Hindmarsh	Houghton	McIver	Middleton	Mitton	O'Brien	Proudfoot	Prout	Rodgers	Smith	Tattersall	Trotter
Q4	Nov	30	(a)	Willenhall P	W 2-0	Charlton, O'Brien	6,000				10	9			3	5		2		6		1				11			8		4	7
Q5	Dec	14	(a)	King's Lynn	W 7-2	Opp own-goal, Rodgers 2, Garrett, Cook 2, Charlton	3,500	6			10	9			3	5		2				1				11			8		4	7
1	Jan	15*	(a)	Everton	L 1-5	Charlton	10,000	6			10	9		7	3	5		2				1				11			8		4	
				Appearances				2			3	1	2	1	3	3		3		1		3				3			3		3	2
				Goals							3		2					1								1			2			

Own-goal 1

*Following an attempt on 11 January which was abandoned after 48 minutes with the score at 1-1 (Tattersall).

1913-14

No	Date	V	Opponent	Res	Scorers	Ashmole	Bertenshaw	Bluer	Chivers	Crosthwaite	Evans	Fagan	Garrett	Gault	Goodwin	Graham	Houghton	Hyde	Lunn	McBain	Mitton	O'Brien	Proctor	Rodgers	Tattersall	Waterall	Wood
441	Sep 3	(a)	Birmingham	L 2-3	Proctor, Gault			6	4		3	5	9	2					1		11	7	8				10
442	Sep 6	(a)	Bristol C	L 0-5				6			3	5	9	2					1		11	7	8	4			10
443	Sep 13	(h)	Leeds C	W 2-1	O'Brien, Wood			6		1	3	5	9	2							11	7	8	4			10
444	Sep 20	(a)	Clapton O	D 1-1	Gault			6		1	3	5	9	2							11	7	8	4			10
445	Sep 27	(h)	Glossop	D 1-1	Wood			6		1	3	5	9	2							11	7	8	4			10
446	Oct 4	(h)	Fulham	L 1-3	Rodgers			6		1	3	4	8	2			5					7	9			11	10
447	Oct 11	(a)	Bradford	W 2-0	Gault 2			6	4	1	3	5	8	2								7	9			10	11
448	Oct 18	(h)	Notts C	L 1-2	Wood			6	4	1	3	5	9	2								7	8			10	11
449	Oct 25	(a)	Leicester F	W 5-2	Waterall 2 (2 pens), Garrett, Wood, Gault				4	1	3	5	9	2	6							7	8			10	11
450	Nov 1	(h)	Wolves	D 0-0					4	1	3	5	9	2	6							7	8			10	11
451	Nov 8	(a)	Hull C	L 0-3				4	7	1	3	5	9	2	6								8			10	11
452	Nov 15	(h)	Barnsley	D 1-1	Rodgers					1	3	5	10	2	6						4	7	8	9			11
453	Nov 24	(a)	Bury	L 0-1				9		1	3	5		2	6						4	7	8			10	11
454	Dec 1	(h)	Huddersfield T	D 0-0				6	7	1	3	5	9	2							4		8			10	11
455	Dec 6	(a)	Lincoln C	W 3-0	Hyde, Ashmole, Waterall	11		5		1	2			10		3		9			4	7	8			6	
456	Dec 13	(h)	Blackpool	D 0-0				5		1	2			10		3		9			4	7	8			6	11
457	Dec 20	(a)	Nottingham F	D 2-2	Wood, Proctor			5		1	2					3		9			4	11	7			6	10
458	Dec 25	(a)	Grimsby T	L 0-2				5		1	2				6	3		9			4	11	7			8	10
459	Dec 26	(h)	Grimsby T	D 2-2	Ashmole 2	11		5		1	2				6	3		9			4	7	8				10
460	Dec 27	(h)	Bristol C	W 5-1	Rodgers 3, Gault 2	11		5		1	2		8			3					4		7	9		6	10
461	Jan 1	(h)	Birmingham	W 2-0	Wood 2	11		5		1	2		8			3					4		7	9		6	10
462	Jan 3	(a)	Leeds C	L 1-5	Ashmole	11				1	2		8		4	3	5						7	9		6	10
463	Jan 17	(a)	Clapton O	L 0-1		11				1	2		8		4	3	5						7	9		6	10
464	Jan 24	(a)	Glossop	D 1-1	Graham	11				1	3		8	2	4		5						7	9		6	10
465	Feb 7	(h)	Fulham	L 0-2		11				1	3		8	2	4		5						7	9		6	10
466	Feb 14	(h)	Bradford	W 3-1	Rodgers, Proctor 2	11		5		1	3		8	2							4		7	9		6	10
467	Feb 21	(a)	Notts C	L 1-2	Ashmole	11		5		1	3		8	2							4		7	9		6	10
468	Feb 28	(h)	Leicester F	W 3-0	Rodgers, Ashmole, Proctor	11		5		1	3		8	2							4		7	9		6	10
469	Mar 7	(a)	Wolves	L 1-3	Opp own-goal	11		5		1	3		8	2							4		7	9		6	10
470	Mar 14	(h)	Hull C	W 2-1	Mitton, Garrett (pen)	11	9		7	1	3	5	8	2	6						4						10
471	Mar 21	(a)	Barnsley	L 0-1		11			7	1	3	5		2	6						4			9		8	10
472	Mar 28	(h)	Bury	W 3-0	Ashmole 2, Wood	11			7	1	3		8	2	5						4			9		6	10
473	Apr 4	(a)	Huddersfield T	W 2-0	Gault, Rodgers	11			7	1	3	5	8	2							4			9		6	10
474	Apr 10	(h)	W Arsenal	W 2-0	Gault, Rodgers	11			7	1	3	5	8	2							4			9		6	10
475	Apr 11	(h)	Lincoln C	L 2-3	Rodgers, Mitton	11			7	1	3	5	8	2							4			9		6	10
476	Apr 13	(a)	W Arsenal	L 0-4		11			7	1	3	5	8	2							4			9		6	10
477	Apr 18	(h)	Blackpool	D 2-2	Wood, Rodgers	11				1	3	5	8	2							4			9		6	10
478	Apr 25	(h)	Nottingham F	W 2-1	Wood, Rodgers	11				1	3	5	8	2							4	7		9		6	10
	FINAL LEAGUE POSITION: 12th in Division Two				Appearances	21	1	20	7	10	36	38	22	33	29	14	9	5	2	1	27	7	28	36	4	31	37
					Goals	8							2	9		1		1			2	1	5	12		3	10

Own-goal 1

FA Cup

No	Date	V	Opponent	Res	Scorers	Att	Ashmole	Bertenshaw	Bluer	Chivers	Crosthwaite	Evans	Fagan	Garrett	Gault	Goodwin	Graham	Houghton	Hyde	Lunn	McBain	Mitton	O'Brien	Proctor	Rodgers	Tattersall	Waterall	Wood
Q4	Nov 29	(a)	Gainsboro' T	L 2-3	Gault, Garrett	4,000			6	7	1	3	5	9	2							4		8			10	11
					Appearances				1	1	1	1	1	1	1							1		1			1	1
					Goals									1	1													

146

1914-15

No	Date		Venue	Opponent	Result	Scorers	Ashmole	Bluer	Crossthwaite	Curtis	Davies	Evans	Fagan	Garrett	Gault	Goodwin	Graham	Harrison	Houghton	Hullock	Hyde	Johnson	Kenyon	Lloyd	Mitton	Proctor	Robson	Rodgers	Waterall	Wood
479	Sep	3	(a)	Hull C	L 0-1			5	7		1	3			8	2	6			4	11							9		10
480		5	(h)	Leeds C	W 3-1	Gault, Wood, Rodgers	11		7		1	3	5		8	2	6			4								9		10
481		12	(a)	Clapton O	L 0-3		11		7		1	3	5		8	2	6			4								9		10
482		19	(h)	Arsenal	D 1-1	Rodgers	11				1	3	5		8	2	6			4								9		10
483		26	(a)	Derby C	L 0-1		11				1	3	5		8	2	6			4					7			9		10
484	Oct	3	(h)	Lincoln C	W 1-0	Wood	11		7		1	3	5			2	6			4								9	8	10
485		10	(a)	Birmingham	W 1-0	Rodgers	11				1	3	5			2	6			4					7			9	8	10
486		17	(h)	Grimsby T	D 1-1	Rodgers	11				1	3	5			2	6			4					7			9	8	10
487		24	(a)	Huddersfield T	L 1-2	Waterall	11		7		1	3	5		8	2				4								9	6	10
488		31	(h)	Bristol C	D 2-2	Rodgers, Gault	11	5	7		1	3			8	2				4								9	6	10
489	Nov	7	(a)	Bury	L 1-2	Ashmole	11		7		1	3	5		9					4								8	6	10
490		14	(h)	Preston NE	W 2-1	Gault, Crossthwaite	11		7		1	3	5		8	2	6			4								9		10
491		21	(a)	Nottingham F	D 1-1	Gault	11		7		1	3	5		8	2	6			4								9		10
492		28	(h)	Leicester F	W 3-0	Gault 2, Waterall			7		1	3	5		8	2	6			4	10							9		11
493	Dec	5	(a)	Barnsley	L 0-2				7		1	3	5		8	2	6			4								9	10	11
494		12	(h)	Glossop	W 2-1	Rodgers, Waterall	11		7		1	3	5			2	6			4								8	9	10
495		19	(a)	Wolves	L 1-4	Rodgers	11		7		1	3	5		8	2	6			4								9		10
496		25	(h)	Blackpool	L 0-2		11		7		1	3	5		8	2	6			4								9		10
497		26	(a)	Fulham	L 0-1						1	3				2	6			4								9		10
498	Jan	1	(h)	Hull C	W 3-0	Kenyon, Proctor, Rodgers (pen)				4	1	3				2							8	11	5	7		9		10
499		2	(a)	Leeds C	W 3-1	Kenyon, Rodgers, Graham				4	1	3				2	6						8	11	5	7		9	10	6
500		16	(h)	Clapton O	W 2-0	Waterall, Rodgers				4	1	3				2	6						8	11	5	7				10
501		23	(a)	Arsenal	L 1-3	Waterall				4	1	3			10	2	6							11	5	7		8	9	
502		30	(h)	Derby C	W 3-2	Waterall 2, Rodgers				4	1	3			10	2	6							11	5	7		8	9	
503	Feb	6	(a)	Lincoln C	D 2-2	Rodgers 2		7		4	1	3			10	2	6							11	5			8	9	
504		13	(h)	Birmingham	W 3-1	Mitton, Rodgers, Gault		7		4	1	3			10	2								11	5			8	9	
505		20	(a)	Grimsby T	L 1-6	Rodgers		6	7	4	1	3			10	2								11	5			8	9	
506		27	(h)	Huddersfield T	W 2-1	Rodgers 2		6	7	4	1	3			10	2								11	5			8	9	
507	Mar	6	(a)	Bristol C	W 2-0	Rodgers, Crossthwaite		6	7	4	1	3			10	2									5			8	9	
508		13	(h)	Bury	W 1-0	Gault	6	7	11	4	1	3			10	2									5			8	9	
509		20	(a)	Preston NE	L 0-2		6	7	11	4	1	3			10										5		2	8	9	
510		27	(h)	Nottingham F	W 1-0	Waterall		6	7	4	1	3			10	2								11	5			8	9	
511	Apr	2	(h)	Fulham	L 0-2			6	7	4	1	3			10	2								11	5			8	9	
512		3	(a)	Leicester F	L 4-5	Waterall 2, Gault, Rodgers			7	4	1	3			10	2	6							11	5			8	9	
513		5	(a)	Blackpool	L 2-4	Rodgers, Graham			7			3			10	2	6			4	11	1			5			8	9	
514		10	(h)	Barnsley	L 1-2	Curtis			7	4		3			10	2	6				11	1			5			8	9	
515		17	(a)	Glossop	D 1-1	Gault	11	4	7		1	3			10	2	6	8							5			9		
516		24	(h)	Wolves	D 2-2	Gault, Rodgers	6		7		1	3	5		10	2				4	11							8	9	
				Appearances			16	12	16	15	16	36	37	14	31	37	26	1		20	8	2	3	10	22	9	1	35	29	21
				Goals			1		2	1					11		2						2		1	1		21	10	2

FINAL LEAGUE POSITION: 14th in Division Two

FA Cup

No	Date		Venue	Opponent	Result	Att	Ashmole	Bluer	Crossthwaite	Curtis	Davies	Evans	Fagan	Garrett	Gault	Goodwin	Graham	Harrison	Houghton	Hullock	Hyde	Johnson	Kenyon	Lloyd	Mitton	Proctor	Robson	Rodgers	Waterall	Wood
1	Jan	9	(a)	Liverpool	L 0-3	8,000				4	1	3				2	6						8	11	5	7		9		10
				Appearances						1	1	1				1	1						1	1	1	1		1		1
				Goals																										

1915-16

#	Date		Opponent	Result	Scorers	1	2	3	4	5	6	7	8	9	10	11
1	Sep	4 (a)	Manchester C	L 1-3	Rodgers	Molyneux	Goodwin	Robson	J.Mitton	Fayers	Suart	Crossthwaite	Gault	Rodgers	A.Waterall	T.Waterall
2		11 (h)	Stoke	W 3-1	Crossthwaite, T.Waterall, Gault	..	Robson	Goodwin	..	..	Graham	..	..	..	..	..
3		18 (a)	Burnley	D 1-1	Rodgers	..	..	..	..	..	..	..	..	..	..	..
4		25 (h)	Preston NE	W 5-0	Gault,A.Waterall 2,Crossthwaite,Kellock	..	..	..	..	..	..	..	..	Kellock	..	..
5	Oct	2 (h)	Rochdale	W 2-0	Gault, T.Waterall	..	..	..	..	..	..	..	..	Rodgers	..	..
6		9 (a)	Liverpool	D 0-0		..	..	..	..	..	..	..	..	..	..	..
7		16 (h)	Bury	L 0-2		..	..	..	..	..	..	..	..	..	..	..
8		23 (a)	Manchester U	L 0-3		..	..	..	Davies	..	..	..	..	..	..	..
9		30 (h)	Blackpool	W 2-1	Rodgers, Gault	..	..	..	J.Mitton	..	Suart	..	..	..	..	..
10	Nov	6 (a)	Southport Cen	L 2-3	Gault (pen), Kellock	..	..	..	..	..	..	..	..	Kellock	..	..
11		11 (h)	Oldham A	W 2-0	Kellock, Gault	..	..	..	..	..	A.Waterall	..	..	Rodgers	Kellock	..
12		20 (a)	Everton	W 5-2	Gault, Rodgers 2, Kellock, T.Waterall	..	..	..	..	Garrett	..	..	..	..	..	..
13		27 (h)	Bolton W	W 4-2	Garrett 2, Rodgers 2 (1 pen)	..	..	..	Suart	Fayers	..	..	Rodgers	Garrett	..	..
14	Dec	4 (h)	Manchester C	D 1-1	Gault	..	..	..	J.Mitton	..	..	..	Gault	Rodgers	..	..
15		11 (h)	Stoke	W 2-0	Kellock, Gault (pen)	..	..	..	Suart	..	..	..	..	..	..	..
16		18 (h)	Burnley	L 0-2		..	..	..	..	..	Graham	..	..	..	..	..
17		25 (h)	Preston NE	W 1-0	Rodgers	..	..	..	..	..	..	..	..	..	Garrett	Kellock
18	Jan	1 (a)	Rochdale	W 1-0	Gault	..	..	..	..	..	..	..	..	..	Kellock	T.Waterall
19		8 (h)	Liverpool	L 1-3	Suart	..	..	..	J.Mitton	..	Suart	..	..	..	..	..
20		15 (a)	Bury	L 1-4	Barnett	..	..	..	..	..	Graham	..	..	Barnett	A.Waterall	..
21		22 (h)	Manchester U	W 3-1	Garrett, Barnett 2	..	..	..	..	..	A.Waterall	..	..	Garrett	Barnett	Kellock
22		29 (a)	Blackpool	L 1-4		..	..	..	..	..	..	..	..	..	..	..
23	Feb	5 (h)	Southport Cen	W 1-0	Gault	..	..	..	..	..	Suart	..	..	A.Waterall	..	T.Waterall
24		12 (a)	Oldham A	L 3-5	Crossthwaite, Nuttall, Gault	..	..	..	A.Waterall	..	..	..	..	Barnet	Nuttall	Kellock
25		19 (h)	Everton	W 3-1	J.Mitton, Rodgers 2	..	..	..	J.Mitton	..	A.Waterall	..	..	Rodgers	..	T.Waterall
26	Apr	24 (a)	Bolton W	L 2-4	Barnett, Kellock	..	Goodwin	Robson	Graham	J.Mitton	..	..	Kellock	Fayers	Barnett	..

FINAL LEAGUE POSITION: 5th (out of 14) in Lancashire Section Principal Tournament

#	Date		Opponent	Result	Scorers	1	2	3	4	5	6	7	8	9	10	11
27	Mar	4 (h)	Manchester C	W 2-0	Nuttall, Kellock	Molyneux	Goodwin	Robson	J.Mitton	Fayers	A.Waterall	Crossthwaite	Gault	Nuttall	Kellock	T.Waterall
28		11 (a)	Everton	L 0-2		..	..	Graham	..	..	..	..	..	..	..	..
29		18 (a)	Oldham A	W 4-2	Gault 2, Barnett (pen), Nuttall	..	..	Cuffe	..	..	..	..	..	..	Barnett	..
30		25 (a)	Liverpool	L 1-2	Barnett	..	..	Garrett	..	..	..	..	Nuttall	Barnett	Graham	..
31	Apr	1 (h)	Manchester U	W 5-3	F.J.Mitton 2, Barnett (pen), Gault, Fayers	Johnson	..	Robson	..	..	Wilde	..	Gault	F.J.Mitton	Barnett	Kellock
32		8 (a)	Manchester C	L 2-3	F.J.Mitton, T.Waterall	Molyneux	..	..	..	..	A.Waterall	..	T.Waterall	..	..	Evans
33		15 (h)	Everton	L 1-2	Barnett	..	..	..	..	..	..	..	Gault	..	..	..
33		21 (a)	Manchester U	L 2-3	Gault, Nuttall	..	..	..	..	..	Suart	..	..	Nuttall	..	T.Waterall
34		22 (a)	Oldham A	D 0-0		..	..	..	Graham	J.Mitton	A.Waterall	..	Nuttall	Garrett	..	..
36		29 (a)	Liverpool	W 2-1	T.Waterall, Barnett	..	..	..	J.Mitton	Fayers	..	..	..	F.J.Mitton	..	..

FINAL LEAGUE POSITION: 5th (out of 6) in Lancashire Section Subsidiary Tournament (Southern Division)

Appearances: H.Crossthwaite 36, R.Goodwin 36, J.Molyneux 35, F.Fayers 34, T.Robson 33, W.E.Gault 31, T.Waterall 31, A.Waterall 30, J.Mitton 29, N.Rodgers 18, W.Kellock 17, J.G.Graham 15, A.Barnett 14, R.Suart 12, T.Nuttall 9, F.H.Garrett 6, F.J.Mitton 4, J.Evans 2, J.Cuffe 1, S.Davies 1, F.Johnson 1, J.Wilde 1.

Goalscorers: Gault 18, Rodgers 10, Barnett 9, Kellock 7, T.Waterall 5, Nuttall 4, Crossthwaite 3, Garrett 3, F.J.Mitton 3, A.Waterall 2, Fayers 1, Suart 1.

1916-17

#	Date	Venue	Opponent	Result	Scorers	1	2	3	4	5	6	7	8	9	10	11
						Molyneux	Goodwin	Robson	A.Waterall	Fayers	Bluer	Crossthwaite	Gault	Rodgers	Nuttall	T.Waterall
1	Sep 2	(h)	Rochdale	W 3-0	T.Waterall, Gault 2	Molyneux	Goodwin	Robson	A.Waterall	Fayers	Bluer	Crossthwaite	Gault	Rodgers	Nuttall	T.Waterall
2	9	(a)	Bolton W	D 1-1	Gault	..	..	..	..	..	..	..	..	..	..	..
3	16	(h)	Burslem PVale	W5-3	Nuttall 2, T.Waterall, Gault 2	..	..	..	..	..	..	..	..	..	..	..
4	23	(a)	Oldham A	D 1-1	Barnett	..	..	..	..	..	..	..	..	..	Barnett	..
5	30	(h)	Preston NE	D 1-1	Nuttall	..	..	..	..	..	..	..	..	Nuttall	..	..
6	Oct 7	(a)	Burnley	L 3-4	A.Waterall 2, Gault	..	..	..	Suart	..	..	..	..	A.Waterall	..	..
7	14	(h)	Manchester U	W 1-0	Rodgers	..	..	..	A.Waterall	..	..	..	..	Rodgers	Nuttall	Evans
8	21	(a)	Liverpool	L 1-3	Nuttall	..	..	..	..	..	..	..	..	T.Waterall	..	..
9	28	(a)	Blackpool	W 2-0	Barnett 2 (1 pen)	Butler	..	..	Mitton	..	..	..	Nuttall	A.Waterall	Barnett	..
10	Nov 4	(h)	Bury	D 1-1	Gault	..	..	..	A.Waterall	..	..	..	Gault	Nuttall	..	..
11	11	(a)	Stoke	L 0-2		Molyneux	..	..	Suart	..	A.Waterall	..	..	Simms	Nuttall	T.Waterall
12	18	(h)	Southport Cen	W 1-0	A.Waterall	..	..	..	Mitton	..	..	..	..	..	..	..
13	25	(a)	Blackburn R	W 4-2	Gault, Rodgers, Crossthwaite 2	..	..	..	A.Waterall	..	T.Waterall	..	Rodgers	Gault	..	Evans
14	Dec 2	(h)	Manchester C	D 0-0		Butler	..	..	..	..	..	..	..	..	..	..
15	9	(a)	Everton	W 1-0	Gault	Molyneux	..	..	..	..	Graham	..	..	..	..	T.Waterall
16	16	(a)	Rochdale	L 0-4		..	..	..	..	..	..	..	..	..	..	..
17	30	(a)	Burslem PVale	W2-1	Crossthwaite 2	Butler	..	..	..	..	Suart	..	..	..	..	..
18	Jan 6	(h)	Oldham A	W 2-0	Rodgers 2 (1 pen)	..	..	..	Davies	..	A.Waterall	..	..	..	..	..
19	13	(a)	Preston NE	L 0-2		Molyneux	..	..	A.Waterall	..	Suart	..	..	..	..	..
20	20	(h)	Burnley	W 1-0	Gault	..	..	..	..	..	Bradley	..	..	..	..	..
21	27	(a)	Manchester U	W 1-0	Gault	..	..	..	..	..	Suart	..	..	..	..	..
22	Feb 3	(h)	Liverpool	D 0-0		..	..	..	Suart	..	A.Waterall	..	..	..	..	..
23	10	(h)	Blackpool	W 6-0	Gault 3, Rodgers, Crossthwaite,A.Waterall	..	..	..	..	..	..	..	..	..	..	..
24	17	(a)	Bury	W 4-1	Rodgers 2, Crossthwaite, Fayers	Butler	..	..	..	..	..	..	Kenyon	Rodgers	..	..
25	24	(h)	Stoke	W 2-0	Rodgers 2	Molyneux	..	..	..	..	..	..	..	..	..	..
26	Mar 3	(a)	Southport C	D 1-1	Fayers	..	..	..	Garrett	..	..	..	..	..	..	..
27	10	(h)	Blackburn R	W 7-1	Rodgers 3, Nuttall, Fayers 2, Kenyon	Butler	..	Newton	A.Waterall	..	T.Waterall	..	..	..	..	Miller
28	17	(a)	Manchester C	W 3-1	Kenyon 2, Francis (pen)	Molyneux	..	Robson	..	..	Francis	..	..	..	..	T.Waterall
29	24	(h)	Everton	W 5-1	Rodgers 2,Kenyon 2, Francis (pen)	..	..	..	..	..	..	..	..	..	..	..
30	Apr 6	(h)	Bolton W	W 2-0	Rodgers 2	Butler	..	Newton	..	..	..	..	..	..	..	..

FINAL LEAGUE POSITION: 2nd (out of 16) in Lancashire Section
Principal Tournament

#	Date	Venue	Opponent	Result	Scorers	1	2	3	4	5	6	7	8	9	10	11
31	Mar 31	(h)	Liverpool	D 0-0		Molyneux	Goodwin	Newton	A.Waterall	Fayers	Francis	Crossthwaite	Kenyon	Rodgers	Nuttall	T.Waterall
32	Apr 7	(a)	Southport Cen	W 1-0	Rodgers	..	..	Robson	..	..	..	..	..	..	Jones	Godwin
33	9	(a)	Everton	D 1-1	Rodgers	Butler	..	Newton	..	..	..	..	..	..	Nuttall	T.Waterall
34	14	(a)	Liverpool	L 0-6		..	..	..	T.Waterall	..	..	..	..	..	..	Miller
35	21	(h)	Southport Cen	D 2-2	Rodgers 2	..	..	..	A.Waterall	..	..	..	..	..	..	T.Waterall
36	28	(h)	Everton	W 2-1	Opp own-goal, Crossthwaite	..	..	Chorlton	..	..	Wilson	..	..	..	..	..

FINAL LEAGUE POSITION: 5th (out of 16) in Lancashire Section
Subsidiary Tournament

Appearances: H.Crossthwaite 36, F.Fayers 36, R.Goodwin 36, A.Waterall 35, T.Nuttall 33, T.Waterall 32, T.Robson 29 , N.Rodgers 29, J.Molyneux 24, W.E.Gault 22, J.Kenyon 13, J.Butler 12, A.Bluer 10, R.Suart 9, J.Francis 8, J.Evans 6, W.A.Newton 6, A.Barnett 5, J.G.Graham 2, W.Miller 2, J.Mitton 2, S.Simms 2, N.Bradley 1, T.Chorlton 1, S.Davies 1, F.Garrett 1, R.Godwin 1, P.Jones 1, D.Wilson 1.

Goalscorers: Rodgers 20, Gault 14, Crossthwaite 7, Kenyon 5, Nuttall 5, Fayers 4, A.Waterall 4, Barnett 3, Francis 2, T.Waterall 2, own-goal 1.

1917-18

#	Match	1	2	3	4	5	6	7	8	9	10	11
1	Sep 1 (a) Manchester C L 1-2 Kenyon	Butler	Goodwin	Robson	A.Waterall	Fayers	Francis	Crossthwaite	Kenyon	Rodgers	Bertenshaw	T.Waterall
2	8 (h) Manchester C L 0-1	..	..	Garrett	..	..	Duckworth	..	..	..	Doncaster	..
3	15 (a) Blackburn R W 6-1 Rodgers 3, T.Waterall 2, Francis	Causer	..	..	Taylor	Silto	Francis	..	Fayers	..	A.Waterall	..
4	22 (h) Blackburn R W 6-0 Silto, Fayers, Rodgers 2, T.Waterall 2	..	..	..	..	..	A.Waterall	..	..	..	Nuttall	..
5	29 (a) Blackpool L 1-3 A.Waterall	..	..	..	Thompson	Fayers	Francis	..	Kenyon	..	A.Waterall	..
6	Oct 6 (h) Blackpool W 3-1 Rodgers, Kenyon, A.Waterall	..	..	Newton	Garrett	..	..	..	..	..	..	..
7	13 (h) Rochdale W 1-0 Rodgers	Butler	..	Garrett	A.Waterall	..	..	..	..	..	Newton	..
8	20 (h) Rochdale W 2-0 Rodgers, Fayers	Causer	..	..	..	..	Silto	..	..	..	Crawshaw	..
9	27 (h) Everton D 0-0	..	Garrett	Newton	Davies	..	Francis	..	..	..	A.Waterall	..
10	Nov 3 (a) Everton W 3-2 Rodgers, Crawshaw, Lester	..	Goodwin	Garrett	A.Waterall	..	..	..	T.Waterall	..	Crawshaw	Lester
11	10 (a) Burslem PVale D 2-2 Crossthwaite, Francis (pen)	..	..	..	..	..	..	..	..	Kenyon	..	..
12	17 (a) Burslem PVale W 4-0 Kenyon 2, T.Waterall, Crossthwaite	Butler	..	..	..	..	..	..	Kenyon	Rodgers	Hyde	T.Waterall
13	24 (a) Bolton W L 2-3 Crawshaw. Francis (pen)	..	Garrett	Newton	..	..	..	Kenyon	Halligan	..	Crawshaw	..
14	Dec 1 (a) Bolton W W 3-1 Kenyon, Crossthwaite, Rodgers	..	Goodwin	Garrett	..	..	..	Crossthwaite	Kenyon	..	..	..
15	8 (h) Preston NE W 1-0 Fayers	Molyneux	..	..	..	..	..	..	..	..	..	..
16	15 (h) Preston NE W 1-0 Crossthwaite	Butler	..	..	..	..	..	..	..	..	..	..
17	22 (a) Southport Cen L 2-3 Kenyon, Rodgers	..	..	..	..	..	..	..	..	..	..	..
18	29 (h) Southport Cen W 6-0 Crawshaw 2, Rodgers 2, Crosst'aite, Kenyon	..	..	..	..	..	..	..	..	..	..	..
19	Jan 5 (a) Liverpool L 1-2 Rodgers	..	..	Simpson	..	..	..	..	..	..	..	..
20	12 (a) Liverpool W 1-0 Crawshaw	..	..	Garrett	..	..	..	..	..	..	..	..
21	19 (a) Stoke L 1-2 Crawshaw	..	..	..	..	..	..	..	..	..	..	..
22	26 (h) Stoke L 0-3	..	..	..	..	..	..	..	..	..	Newton	..
23	Feb 2 (a) Bury W 3-0 Kenyon 2, Green	..	..	..	..	..	..	..	..	..	Green	O'Brien
24	9 (h) Bury W 3-2 Fayers, Rodgers 2	..	..	..	Graham	..	..	..	..	..	A.Waterall	T.Waterall
25	16 (a) Oldham A W 2-0 Kerr, Kenyon	..	..	..	A.Waterall	..	..	..	..	..	Green	Kerr
26	23 (a) Oldham A L 0-1	..	..	..	Challinor	..	..	..	..	..	Maden	Williams
27	Mar 2 (h) Burnley D 0-0	..	..	Newton	Manley	..	..	..	..	..	Finnegan	T.Waterall
28	9 (a) Burnley W 2-0 Fayers, Rodgers	Molyneux	..	..	Butterworth	..	..	..	Hughes	..	Williams	Lester
29	16 (a) Manchester U L 0-2	Butler	..	Garrett	Dickenson	..	Bluer	..	Kenyon	..	Hughes	Francis
30	23 (h) Manchester U W 2-1 Rodgers, Crossthwaite	..	..	..	Challinor	..	Francis	..	..	..	..	Hyde

FINAL LEAGUE POSITION: 6th (out of 16) in Lancashire Section Principal Competition

#	Match	1	2	3	4	5	6	7	8	9	10	11
31	Jan 1 (a) Southport Cen W 1-0 Francis	Molyneux	Goodwin	Newton	Suart	Fayers	Francis	Crossthwaite	Kenyon	Rodgers	Stringfellow	Hyde
32	Mar 29 (h) Southport Cen W 2-0 Crossthwaite, Rodgers	Butler	..	Garrett	Challinor	..	..	..	..	..	Hughes	..
33	30 (a) Everton L 0-4	..	..	..	..	..	..	..	..	..	..	..
34	Apr 6 (h) Everton L 0-1	..	..	..	Manley	..	..	..	..	..	..	Dooley
35	13 (h) Liverpool L 1-4 Rodgers	..	..	..	Challinor	..	..	..	Smith	..	..	Hyde
36	20 (a) Liverpool L 2-4 Hughes, Metcalf	Johnson	..	Hewitt	Manley	..	..	..	Metcalf	..	..	Williams

FINAL LEAGUE POSITION: 13th (out of 16) in Lancashire Section Subsidiary Tournament

Appearances: F.Fayers 36, H.Crossthwaite 35, N.Rodgers 35, R.Goodwin 34, J.Francis 33, F.H.Garrett 30, J.Kenyon 30, A.Waterall 25, J.Butler 24, T.Waterall 24, A.Crawshaw 12, A.Causer 8, C.Hughes 8, W.A.Newton 8, L.Hyde 6, T.Challinor 5, H.Lester 3, G.Manley 3, J.Molyneux 3, N.Silto 3, J.Williams 3, J.Green 2, S.Taylor 2, J.Bertenshaw 1, A.Bluer 1, J.Butterworth 1, S.Davies 1, H.Dickenson 1, F.Doncaster 1, W.Dooley 1, J.Duckworth 1, J.Finnegan 1, J.G.Graham 1, W.Halligan 1, Hewitt (Liverpool) 1, F.Johnson 1, L.Kerr 1, J.Maden 1, A.Metcalf (Liverpool) 1, T.Nuttall 1, R.O'Brien 1, T.Robson 1, R.Simpson 1, F.Smith 1, A.Stringfellow 1, R.Suart 1, E.Thompson 1.

Goalscorers: Rodgers 20, Kenyon 10, Crossthwaite 7, Crawshaw 6, Fayers 5, T.Waterall 5, Francis 4, A.Waterall 2, Green 1, Hughes 1, Kerr 1, Lester 1, Metcalf 1, Silto 1.

1918-19

#	Date	Venue	Opp	Result	Scorers	1	2	3	4	5	6	7	8	9	10	11
						Berry	Goodwin	Garrett	Melville	Fayers	Francis	Crossthwaite	Bridge	Rodgers	Crawshaw	Hyde
1	Sep 7	(h)	Preston NE	D 0-0												
2	14	(a)	Preston NE	W 3-0	Rodgers, Crawshaw 2	..	..	..	Manley	..	..	..	..	..	..	Hughes
3	21	(h)	Bolton W	D 2-2	Bridge, Hughes	..	..	..	Mitton	..	..	..	..	..	Hughes	Hyde
4	28	(a)	Bolton W	L 1-3	Rodgers	..	..	..	..	..	..	..	..	..	Hughes	Hyde
5	Oct 5	(h)	Rochdale	D 2-2	Rodgers, Fayers (pen)	Ollerenshaw	.	Johnstone	Manley	..	..	..	Rodgers	Garrett	Bridge	Hughes
6	12	(a)	Rochdale	L 1-4	Rodgers	..	..	Garrett	Freeborough	..	..	..	Manley	Flaherty	Rodgers	..
7	19	(h)	Port Vale	W 3-0	Cunningham, Rodgers, Fayers (pen)	..	..	..	Waterall	..	..	..	Stainwright	Rodgers	Cunningham	..
8	26	(a)	Port Vale	D 2-2	Rodgers, Fayers	..	..	..	..	..	..	Davies	..	..	Bowcock	..
9	Nov 2	(a)	Manchester C	L 0-1		..	..	Johnstone	Manley	Garrett	Cunningham	Crossthwaite	Kenyon	..	Stainwright	..
10	9	(h)	Manchester C	D 1-1	Hughes	..	..	..	Waterall	..	Wilson	..	..	..	Cunningham	..
11	16	(a)	Oldham A	W 3-1	Cunningham, Rodgers, Kenyon	..	..	Garrett	..	Fayers	Francis	..	..	..	..	..
12	23	(h)	Oldham A	W 6-2	Rodgers 3, Cunningham 2, Crossthwaite	..	..	..	..	..	..	..	..	..	..	..
13	30	(a)	Blackburn R	W 4-0	Francis, Hughes, Waterall, Crossthwaite	..	..	..	..	..	..	..	..	..	..	..
14	Dec 7	(h)	Blackburn R	W 1-0	Hughes	..	..	..	Manley	..	..	..	..	..	Graham	..
15	14	(a)	Everton	L 1-2	Hughes	..	..	..	Catlow	..	..	..	..	..	Cunningham	..
16	21	(h)	Everton	D 0-0		Molyneux	..	..	Challinor	..	..	..	..	..	..	..
17	28	(h)	Southport V	W 4-1	Rodgers 3, Cunningham	..	..	..	..	..	..	..	..	..	..	..
18	Jan 11	(h)	Manchester U	W 2-1	Rodgers 2	Ollerenshaw	..	..	Manley	..	..	..	..	..	..	..
19	18	(a)	Manchester U	W 2-0	Crawshaw, Hughes	..	..	..	Cunningham	..	..	..	..	..	Crawshaw	..
20	25	(h)	Stoke	L 0-6		Molyneux	..	..	Waterall	..	..	..	..	..	Cunningham	..
21	Feb 1	(a)	Stoke	L 0-1		Ollerenshaw	..	..	Challinor	..	..	..	..	..	..	..
22	8	(h)	Bury	W 2-0	Cunningham, Rodgers	..	..	..	Catlow	..	..	..	Hughes	..	..	Rigby
23	15	(a)	Bury	D 1-1	Crawshaw	..	..	..	Challinor	..	..	..	Kenyon	..	Crawshaw	Cunningham
24	22	(a)	Blackpool	L 0-2		..	..	..	..	..	Cunningham	..	..	..	..	Hughes
25	Mar 1	(h)	Blackpool	L 1-2	Rodgers	..	..	..	..	..	Mitton	..	..	..	Hughes	Rigby
26	8	(a)	Burnley	L 2-4	Crawshaw 2	..	..	..	..	..	Francis	..	Cunningham	..	Crawshaw	..
27	15	(h)	Burnley	L 0-3		Evans	..	Mitton	..	..	..	..	..	..	..	Hughes
28	22	(h)	Liverpool	W 2-1	Cunningham, Crawshaw	Goodchild	..	..	..	..	..	..	..	..	..	Curtis
29	29	(a)	Liverpool	L 0-3		Mercer	..	..	..	..	..	..	..	..	Rainford	..
30	Apr 1	(a)	Southport V	L 2-7	Rodgers 2	Goodchild	..	..	..	..	..	..	..	..	Crawshaw	..

FINAL LEAGUE POSITION: 8th (out of 16) in Lancashire Section

Preliminary Competition

#	Date	Venue	Opp	Result	Scorers	1	2	3	4	5	6	7	8	9	10	11
						Mercer	Robson	Garrett	Mitton	Fayers	Francis	Crossthwaite	Kellock	Rodgers	Crawshaw	Curtis
31	Apr 5	(h)	Everton	L 0-1												
32	12	(a)	Everton	W 1-0	Green	..	..	..	..	..	..	..	Green	Newton	..	..
33	18	(a)	Southport V	W 1-0	Crawshaw	..	..	..	..	..	..	..	Nuttall	..	..	..
34	19	(a)	Liverpool	L 1-3	Jones	..	..	..	..	..	..	..	Jones	..	..	..
35	21	(h)	Southport V	W 3-1	Crawshaw, Rodgers, Jones	..	..	..	..	..	..	..	..	Rodgers	..	..
36	28	(h)	Liverpool	D 1-1	Fayers (pen)	Butler	..	..	..	..	..	..	..	..	..	..

FINAL LEAGUE POSITION: 2nd (out of 4) in Lancashire Subsidiary Tournament*

*The Subsidiary Tournament incorporated the Lancashire Cup, producing winners from each of the four Lancashire sections who played a knock-out competition. Liverpool topped the group finishing ahead of County who did not therefore qualify for the knock-out stage.

Appearances: F.H.Garrett 36, H.Crossthwaite 35, F.Fayers 34, N.Rodgers 33, J.Francis 32, R.Goodwin 30, C.Hughes 24, C.Cunningham 21, F.Ollerenshaw 19, J.Kenyon 16, A.Crawshaw 15, J.Mitton 13, J.Curtis 9, T.Challinor 7, A.Waterall 7, G.Manley 6, H.Mercer 6, T.Robson 6, F.Bridge 5, F.Berry 4, L.Hyde 3, H.Johnstone 3, W.L.Jones (Manchester City) 3, J.Molyneux 3, W.A.Newton 3, E.Rigby 3, H.Stainwright 3, T.Catlow (Manchester City) 2, J.Goodchild 2, D.Bowcock (Port Vale) 1, J.Butler 1, S.Davies 1, T.L.Evans 1, J.Flaherty 1, J.Freeborough 1, J.G.Graham 1, J.Green 1, W.Kellock 1, D.Melville 1, T.Nuttall 1, J.Rainford 1, D.Wilson 1.

Goalscorers: Rodgers 20, Crawshaw 9, Cunningham 7, Hughes 6, Fayers 4, Crossthwaite 2, Jones 2, Bridge 1, Francis 1, Green 1, Kenyon 1, Waterall 1.

1919-20

No	Date		Opponent	Result	Scorers	Birds	Brennan	Briggs	Bullough	Crossthwaite	Danskin	Davies	Dingwall	Fayers	Garrett	Graham	Halsworth	Harrison	Hartley	Heath	Hodgkiss	Hudson	Huyton	Metcalf	Milton	Newman	Robson	Rodgers	Walker	Waterall
517	Aug 30	(a)	Grimsby T	W 3-0	Dingwall, Metcalf, Rodgers					7	11		9	5	3							1		10	4		2	8		6
518	Sep 1	(h)	Rotherham C	W 4-1	Metcalf, Dingwall, Fayers (pen), Rodgers					7	11		9	5	3							1		10	4		2	8		6
519	6	(h)	Grimsby T	L 1-2	Metcalf					7	11		9	5	3				10			1		8	4		2			6
520	8	(a)	Rotherham C	L 0-1						7	11		9	5	3			8				1		10	4		2			6
521	13	(a)	Bury	W 2-0	Rodgers, Dingwall					7	11		10	5	2							1		9	4		3	8		6
522	20	(h)	Bury	D 1-1	Rodgers					7	11		9	5	3							1		10	4		2	8		6
523	27	(a)	Nottingham F	D 1-1	Crossthwaite	1	9			7	11			5	3									10	4		2	8		6
524	Oct 4	(h)	Nottingham F	D 0-0						7	11			5	3	9						1		10	4		2	8		6
525	11	(a)	Stoke	L 1-2	Metcalf					7	11			5	3	9						1		10	4		2	8		6
526	18	(h)	Stoke	W 3-1	Rodgers, Heath, Waterall					7	11			5	3	6				9	1				4		2	8		10
527	25	(a)	Barnsley	D 0-0						7	11			5	3	6				9	1				4		2	8		10
528	Nov 1	(h)	Barnsley	W 1-0	Danskin					7	11			5	3	6				9	1				4		2	8		10
529	8	(a)	Lincoln C	L 0-2						7	11			5	3	6				9	1				4		2	8		10
530	15	(a)	Lincoln C	W 3-1	Rodgers, Huyton, Danskin					7	11			5	3	6					1		9		4		2	8		10
531	22	(a)	Hull C	L 1-4	Metcalf					7	11			5	3	6					1		9	10			2	8		4
532	29	(h)	Hull C	W 3-1	Fayers, Waterall, Rodgers					7	11			5	3	6		4			1			8			2	9		10
533	Dec 6	(a)	Wolves	D 2-2	Metcalf 2					7	11			5	3	6		4			1			8			2	9		10
534	13	(h)	Wolves	W 4-1	Rodgers 2, Metcalf, Waterall					7	11			5	4	6					1	3		8			2	9		10
535	20	(h)	South Shields	W 1-0	Rodgers					7	11			5	4	6					1	3		8			2	9		10
536	25	(a)	Clapton O	L 1-2	Crossthwaite					7	11	4		5		6					1	3		8			2	9	11	10
537	26	(h)	Clapton O	W 3-1	Crossthwaite, Metcalf 2					7				5	4	6					1	3		8			2	9	11	10
538	27	(a)	South Shields	L 2-3	Walker, Waterall					7				5	4	6					1	3		8			2	9	11	10
539	Jan 3	(h)	Tottenham H	L 1-2	Walker					7	11			5	3	6					1			8			2	9	10	4
540	17	(a)	Tottenham H	L 0-2		1				7	11			5	3	6								8			2	9	10	4
541	24	(a)	Birmingham	D 1-1	Rodgers	1				7	11			5	3	6			10					8			2	9		4
542	Feb 7	(a)	Leicester C	W 2-0	Rodgers, Metcalf	1				7	11			5	3	6			10					8			2	9		4
543	14	(a)	Leicester C	L 0-2		1				7	11			5		6			10			3		8			2	9		4
544	21	(a)	Fulham	L 1-4	Walker	1				7	11			5	3	6			10								2	9	8	4
545	28	(h)	Fulham	W 2-1	Bullough, Waterall	1			9	7	11			5	3	6								8	4		2			10
546	Mar 6	(h)	Coventry C	D 1-1	Briggs	1		7	9		11			5		6						3		8	4		2			10
547	13	(a)	Coventry C	D 1-1	Metcalf	1		7	9		11			5		6			10			3		8	4		2			
548	15	(h)	Birmingham	W 2-1	Danskin, Bullough	1		7	9		11			5	3	6			10					8	4		2			
549	20	(h)	Huddersfield T	L 1-2	Garrett (pen)	1			9		11			5	3	6	7		10					8	4		2			
550	Apr 2	(h)	Port Vale	L 0-4		1					11			5	3	6	7							8	4	10	2	9		
551	3	(h)	Blackpool	D 0-0		1		7	9		11			5	3	6								8	4	10	2			
552	8	(a)	Port Vale	L 0-2		1		7			11			5	3	6			10					8	4		2			9
553	10	(a)	Blackpool	L 0-1		1		7			11			5		6			10			3		8	4		2			9
554	12	(a)	Huddersfield T	L 0-5		1		7			11			5		6			10			3		8	4		2			9
555	17	(a)	Bristol C	L 2-3	Metcalf, Danskin	1			9		11			5	3	6				7				8	4		2			10
556	24	(a)	Bristol C	L 0-1		1		7	9		11			5	3	6								8	4		2			10
557	26	(h)	West Ham U	W 1-0	Waterall	1		7			11			5	3	6				9				8	4		2			10
558	May 5	(a)	West Ham U	L 0-3		1		7			11			5	3	6								8	4	10	2	9		
	FINAL LEAGUE POSITION: 16th in Division Two				Appearances	20	1	5	13	29	40	1	6	42	36	36	2	6	7	6	22	11	2	36	28	3	41	26	6	37
					Goals			1	2	13	4		3	2	1					1			1	13				12	3	6

FA Cup

No	Date		Opponent	Result	Scorers	Birds	Brennan	Briggs	Bullough	Crossthwaite	Danskin	Davies	Dingwall	Fayers	Garrett	Graham	Halsworth	Harrison	Hartley	Heath	Hodgkiss	Hudson	Huyton	Metcalf	Milton	Newman	Robson	Rodgers	Walker	Waterall
R1	Jan 10	(a)	Preston NE	L 1-3	Rodgers	16,000 / 1				7	11			5	3	6								8			2	9	10	4
					Appearances	1				1	1			1	1	1								1			1	1	1	1
					Goals																							1		

After eight matches, Leeds City were disbanded by order of the Football Association and Port Vale took over their fixtures. County had not played Leeds before their enforced resignation on 4 October 1919 and completed both fixtures against Port Vale.

1920-21

Player columns (left to right): Anderson, Beattie, Birds, Brooks, Bullough, Burrows, Cragg, Danskin, Dondawand, Donnelly, Forrest, Garrett, Gault, Goodwin, Graham, Griffiths, Hardy, Heath, Knowles, Layton, Mitton, Newbigging, Newman, Norris, Reid, Robson, Rosbotham, Shelton, Thompson, Walmsley, Walsh, Waterall

No	Date		Opponent	Result	Scorers
559	Aug 28	(h)	Cardiff C	L 2-5	Norris, Danskin (pen)
560	30	(a)	Fulham	L 1-3	Thompson
561	Sep 4	(a)	Cardiff C	L 0-3	
562	11	(h)	Clapton O	W 6-0	Waterall 3, Danskin (pen), Beattie, Mitton
563	13	(h)	Fulham	D 1-1	Walsh
564	18	(a)	Clapton O	L 0-5	
565	25	(h)	Bury	L 1-2	Walsh
566	Oct 2	(a)	Bury	D 1-1	Mitton
567	9	(h)	Bristol C	L 0-2	
568	16	(a)	Bristol C	L 1-5	Newbigging
569	23	(h)	Barnsley	W 3-2	Mitton, Walmsley, Shelton
570	30	(a)	Barnsley	L 0-2	
571	Nov 6	(h)	Rotherham C	L 0-1	
572	13	(a)	Rotherham C	L 0-1	
573	20	(h)	West Ham U	W 2-0	Thompson, Cragg
574	27	(a)	West Ham U	L 0-5	
575	Dec 4	(h)	Port Vale	D 0-0	
576	11	(a)	Port Vale	L 1-6	Walsh
577	18	(h)	South Shields	D 0-0	
578	25	(h)	Wolves	L 1-2	Cragg
579	27	(a)	Wolves	L 0-2	
580	Jan 1	(a)	South Shields	L 1-3	Anderson
581	15	(h)	Birmingham	L 0-3	
582	22	(a)	Birmingham	L 0-5	
583	Feb 3	(a)	Hull C	D 1-1	Cragg
584	5	(h)	Hull C	D 2-2	Waterall, Heath (pen)
585	12	(h)	Leeds U	W 3-1	Gault, Heath (pen), Rosbotham
586	19	(a)	Leeds U	W 2-0	Griffiths, Heath
587	26	(h)	Coventry C	W 3-0	Heath (pen), Waterall 2
588	Mar 5	(a)	Coventry C	D 1-1	Waterall
589	12	(h)	Stoke	W 2-0	Walsh, Walmsley
590	19	(a)	Stoke	L 0-1	
591	25	(a)	Nottingham F	D 1-1	Heath (pen)
592	26	(a)	The Wednesday	L 1-2	Anderson
593	28	(h)	Nottingham F	W 1-0	Griffiths
594	Apr 2	(h)	The Wednesday	L 0-1	
595	9	(a)	Notts C	L 0-3	
596	16	(h)	Notts C	W 1-0	Heath
597	23	(a)	Blackpool	D 1-1	Brooks
598	30	(h)	Blackpool	D 2-2	Anderson, Waterall
599	May 2	(a)	Leicester C	D 0-0	
600	7	(h)	Leicester C	D 0-0	

FINAL LEAGUE POSITION: 22nd in Division Two - Relegated to new Division Three North

Appearances and Goals

	Anderson	Beattie	Birds	Brooks	Bullough	Burrows	Cragg	Danskin	Dondawand	Donnelly	Forrest	Garrett	Gault	Goodwin	Graham	Griffiths	Hardy	Heath	Knowles	Layton	Mitton	Newbigging	Newman	Norris	Reid	Robson	Rosbotham	Shelton	Thompson	Walmsley	Walsh	Waterall
Appearances	24	20	2	8	4	4	21	16	1	1	1	27	13	1	9	18	40	25	2	21	6	15	1	5	5	37	16	3	6	39	34	37
Goals	3	1		1			3	2					1			2		6			3	1		1			1	1	2	2	4	8

FA Cup

No	Date		Opponent	Result	Att.
1	Jan 8	(a)	Everton	L 0-1	25,000

	Anderson	Beattie	Brooks	Garrett	Gault	Hardy	Heath	Layton	Walmsley	Walsh	Waterall
(shirt no.)	4	7	10	2	9	1	11	3	5	8	6
Appearances	1	1	1	1	1	1	1	1	1	1	1
Goals											

1921-22

No	Date	Opponent	Res	Scorers	Brooks	Cockburn	Crossthwaite	Gault	Griffiths	Hardy	Heath	Jones	Kearslake	Layton	O'Kane	Reid	Richardson	Robson	Rosbotham	Steele	Tarbuck	Walmsley	Walsh	Waterall	West	Woodcock	Young
601	Aug 27 (a)	Barrow	W 2-0	Gault, Kearslake				9	11	1	5		7	3		6		2	8			4		10			
602	Sep 10 (a)	Wigan Bor	W 1-0	Gault				9	11	1	5		7	3		6		2	8			4		10			
603	17 (h)	Wigan Bor	W 3-0	Gault, Jones 2				9	11	1	5	10	7	3		6		2				4		8			
604	19 (h)	Barrow	W 2-0	Heath 2 (1 pen)				9	11	1	5	10	7	3		6		2				4		8			
605	24 (a)	Hartlepools U	D 0-0		9		7	8	11	1	5	10		3		6		2				4					
606	Oct 1 (h)	Hartlepools U	W 1-0	Gault			7	8	11	1	5	10		3		6		2				4			9		
607	8 (a)	Southport	L 1-2	Gault			7	8	11	1	5	10		3		6		2				4			9		
608	15 (h)	Southport	W 2-1	Heath (pen), Gault			7	9	11	1	5	10		3		8		2				4		6			
609	22 (a)	Rochdale	W 1-0	Reid			7	9	11	1	5	10		3		8		2				4		6			
610	29 (h)	Rochdale	W 3-0	Jones 2, Gault			7	9	11	1	5	10		3		8		2				4		6			
611	Nov 5 (h)	Grimsby T	L 0-1				7	9	11	1	5	10		3				2	8			4		6			
612	12 (a)	Grimsby T	L 1-2	Jones			7	9	11	1	5	10		3		6		2	8			4					
613	26 (h)	Walsall	W 3-1	O'Kane 3			7		11	1	5	10		3	9	8		2				4		6			
614	Dec 17 (a)	Tranmere R	W 2-0	Walsh, Jones			7		11	1	5	10		3	9		2					4	8	6			
615	24 (h)	Tranmere R	D 0-0		10		7		11	1	5			3	9		2					4	8	6			
616	26 (h)	Halifax T	D 0-0		10		7		11	1	5			3	9		2					4	8	6			
617	27 (a)	Halifax T	L 0-1		10	5	7		11	1				3	9		2					4	8	6			
618	31 (a)	Stalybridge C	W 4-0	Steele, Walmsley, O'Kane 2			7		11	1	5	8		3	10		2			9		4		6			
619	Jan 14 (h)	Stalybridge C	W 4-0	Steele, O'Kane 2, Waterall			7		11	1	5	8		3	10		2			9		4		6			
620	16 (a)	Walsall	W 2-0	Crossthwaite 2			7		11	1	5	8		3	10		2			9		4		6			
621	21 (a)	Durham C	W 2-0	Steele, O'Kane			7		11	1	5	8		3	10		2			9		4		6			
622	28 (h)	Durham C	W 4-0	O'Kane 2, Gault, Jones			7	9	11	1	5	8		3	10		2					4		6			
623	Feb 11 (h)	Wrexham	D 0-0				7	9	11	1	5	8		3	10		2					4		6			
624	18 (a)	Nelson	D 2-2	Heath, Gault			7	9	11	1	5	8		3	10		2					4		6			
625	25 (h)	Nelson	W 3-0	Gault, Waterall, Heath (pen)			7	9	11	1	5	8		3	10		2					4		6			
626	Mar 4 (a)	Chesterfield	W 1-0	O'Kane			7	9	11	1	5			3	10	6	2					4		8			
627	8 (a)	Wrexham	D 0-0				7	9	11	1	5			3	10		2					4		6	8		
628	11 (h)	Chesterfield	W 2-1	Heath (pen), Woodcock			7		11	1	5	8		3	10		2					4		6		9	
629	18 (h)	Crewe A	D 1-1	Steele			7		11	1	5	8		3	10	6	2			9		4					
630	25 (h)	Crewe A	W 1-0	Rosbotham			7		11	1	5			3	10		2		8	9		4		6			
631	Apr 1 (h)	Accrington S	W 2-1	Woodcock 2			7		11	1	5	8		3	10		2					4		6		9	
632	8 (a)	Accrington S	W 3-1	Jones, Heath, Gault			7	9	11	1	5	8		3			2				10	4		6			
633	14 (a)	Ashington	L 0-2				7		11	1	5	8		3	10		2					4		6			9
634	15 (a)	Darlington	L 0-1				7		11	1	5	8		3	10	6	2					4					9
635	17 (h)	Ashington	W 3-2	Woodcock 2, O'Kane			7		11	1	5	8		3	10	6	2					4				9	
636	22 (h)	Darlington	W 1-0	Jones			7		11	1	5	8		3	10	6	2					4				9	
637	29 (h)	Lincoln C	D 2-2	Woodcock (pen), Waterall		5	7		11	1		8		3	10		2					4		6		9	
638	May 6 (a)	Lincoln C	W 1-0	Woodcock			7		11	1	5	8		3	10		2					4		6		9	
	FINAL LEAGUE POSITION: Champions of Division Three North			Appearances	4	2	34	28	19	38	34	34	5	35	16	26	25	13	5	15	1	33	4	32	3	10	2
	- Promoted to Division Two			Goals			2	11			7	9	1		12	1			1	4		1	1	3		7	

FA Cup

No	Date	Opponent	Res	Att	Brooks	Cockburn	Crossthwaite	Gault	Griffiths	Hardy	Heath	Jones	Kearslake	Layton	O'Kane	Reid	Richardson	Robson	Rosbotham	Steele	Tarbuck	Walmsley	Walsh	Waterall	West	Woodcock	Young
Q5	Dec 3 (a)	Lancaster	L 0-2	6,500	10		7		11	1	5			3	9		2					4	8	6			
				Appearances	1		1		1	1	1			1	1		1					1	1	1			
				Goals																							

1922-23

No.	Date		Opponent	Res.	Scorers	Cockburn	Cousins	Critchley	Crossthwaite	Dolphin	Green	Griffiths	Hardy	Heath	Humphrey	Jones	Kearslake	Knowles	Layton	McKechnie	Morrison	Purcell	Reid	Richardson	Robson	Wainsley	Waterall	Wilson	Woodcock
639	Aug 26	(h)	Leicester C	L 4-5	Crossthwaite, Green 2, Woodcock				7		9		1	5		11							3	2		4	6	10	8
640	28	(a)	Bradford C	L 0-2					7		9		1	5		11							3	2		4	6	10	8
641	Sep 2	(a)	Leicester C	L 0-2					7		9		1	5		11							3	2		4	6	10	8
642	4	(h)	Bradford C	W 1-0	Green		8		7	10			1	5		11	6						3	2			4	9	
643	9	(a)	Leeds U	L 0-2			8		7	10			1	5		11	6						3	2			4	9	
644	16	(h)	Leeds U	W 2-1	Wilson, Green (pen)				7		9		1	5		11	6						3	2			4	10	8
645	23	(a)	West Ham U	W 1-0	Woodcock	5			7	10			1			11	6		2				3				4	9	8
646	30	(h)	West Ham U	W 2-1	Woodcock, Wilson	5			7	10			1			11	6						3	2			4	9	8
647	Oct 7	(a)	South Shields	L 0-3		5			7	10			1			11	6						3	2			4	9	8
648	14	(h)	South Shields	D 1-1	Green				7	10	11		1	5			6						3	2			4	9	8
649	21	(h)	Barnsley	W 3-1	Wilson, Green 2	5			7		9		1	6		11							3	2			4	10	8
650	28	(a)	Barnsley	D 1-1	Wilson	5			7		9		1	6		11							3	2			4	10	8
651	Nov 4	(h)	Wolves	D 1-1	Woodcock	5			7		9		1	6		11							3	2			4	10	8
652	11	(a)	Wolves	L 1-3	Green	5			7		9		1	6		11							3	2			4	10	8
653	18	(h)	Coventry C	W 5-1	Green 4 (1 pen), Wilson	6			7		9		1			11							3	2	5		4	10	8
654	25	(a)	Coventry C	L 0-1		6			7		9		1	5		11							3	2			4	10	8
655	Dec 9	(h)	Port Vale	L 0-2				7		11			1			6		9	5	2			3				4	10	8
656	16	(a)	Manchester U	L 0-1		5			7		9		1	6		11							3	2			4	10	8
657	23	(h)	Manchester U	W 1-0	Green	5			7		9		1			11					6		3	2			4	10	8
658	25	(h)	Clapton O	L 0-2		5			7		9		1		11						6		3	2			4	10	8
659	26	(a)	Clapton O	W 2-0	Wilson, Green	5			7		9		1		11						6		3	2			4	10	8
660	30	(a)	Bury	L 0-2		5					9		1		11		7				6		3	2			4	10	8
661	Jan 1	(h)	Blackpool	D 2-2	Wilson, Kearslake (pen)	5	8						1		11		7				6		3	2			4	10	9
662	6	(h)	Bury	W 1-0	Cousins	5	8	7			9		1		11						6		3	2			4	10	
663	13	(a)	Port Vale	W 2-0	Cousins 2	5	9	7					1		11						6		3	2			4	10	8
664	20	(h)	Rotherham C	W 1-0	Wilson	5	9		7				1		11						6		3	2			4	10	8
665	27	(a)	Rotherham C	L 1-2	Crossthwaite	5	9		7				1		11						6		3	2			4	10	8
666	Feb 10	(a)	The Wednesday	L 1-4	Woodcock	5	8		7				1		11						6		3	2			4	10	9
667	17	(h)	Hull C	D 1-1	Green				7		9		1	5	11						6		3	2			4	10	8
668	24	(a)	Hull C	L 0-1		5	8		7		9		1		11						6		3	2			4	10	
669	Mar 3	(h)	Crystal P	D 2-2	Waterall, Green	5	8		7		9		1		11						6		3	2			4	10	
670	10	(a)	Crystal P	L 0-3		9							1	5	11			7			6		3	2			4	10	8
671	15	(h)	The Wednesday	L 0-1		5				10	9		1		11			7			6		3	2			4		8
672	17	(a)	Fulham	L 0-3		5			7	10	9		1		11						6		3	2			4		8
673	24	(h)	Fulham	L 0-2		5			7		9		1		11		6		3					2			4	10	8
674	30	(a)	Blackpool	D 0-0		9					11		1	6			5	3	10	4		2					8	7	
675	31	(a)	Notts C	L 0-2		9					11		1	6			5	3	8	4		2					10	7	
676	Apr 7	(h)	Notts C	D 0-0		5			7		9		1		11		6			2			3				4	10	8
677	14	(a)	Derby C	W 2-1	Knowles, Humphrey	5					9		1		11		6	7		2			3				4	10	8
678	21	(h)	Derby C	W 2-1	Wilson, Woodock	5	8						1		11		6	7		2			3				4	10	9
679	28	(a)	Southampton	L 0-1		5	8						1		11		6	7		2			3				4	10	9
680	May 5	(h)	Southampton	W 3-0	Woodcock 2, Humphrey	5	8	7		10			1		11		6			2			3				4		9
			Appearances			31	14	2	18	11	31	6	42	19	24	14	10	14	3	8	16	2	40	34	1	8	40	36	38
			Goals				3		2		16				2		1	1									1	9	8

FINAL LEAGUE POSITION: 20th in Division Two

FA Cup

No.	Date		Opponent	Res.	Scorers	Att.	Cockburn	Cousins	Critchley	Crossthwaite	Dolphin	Green	Griffiths	Hardy	Heath	Humphrey	Jones	Kearslake	Knowles	Layton	McKechnie	Morrison	Purcell	Reid	Richardson	Robson	Wainsley	Waterall	Wilson	Woodcock
Q5	Dec 2	(a)	Barrow	L 2-3	Woodcock 2	5,400	5			7		9		1	6		11							3	2			4	10	8
			Appearances				1			1		1		1	1		1							1	1			1	1	1
			Goals																											2

155

1923-24

No.	Date	V	Opponent	Res	Scorers	Bro	Car	Coc	Cra	Cri	Edg	Grn	Grf	Har	Hen	Hum	Hut	Jon	Mea	Mor	Pur	Rei	Ric	Sam	Sim	Swa	Tom	Wat	Whi	Wil	Woo
681	Aug 25	(a)	Derby C	L 1-4	Woodcock	2		5		7	3			1	11						4						10	6		8	9
682	27	(h)	Nelson	W 1-0	Waterall	2		5		7	3			1	11						6						10	4		8	9
683	Sep 1	(h)	Derby C	D 0-0		2	6	5		7				1	11							3					9	4		10	8
684	3	(a)	Nelson	D 1-1	Toms			5		7	11			1						6		3	2				9	4		10	8
685	8	(h)	Port Vale	D 0-0				5			11			1						6		3	2	9			8	4		10	7
686	15	(a)	Port Vale	W 1-0	Woodcock			5		7	11			1						6	8	3	2					4		10	9
687	22	(h)	Bradford C	L 1-2	Woodcock (pen)			5		7			11	1						6	8	3	2					4		10	9
688	29	(h)	Bradford C	W 1-0	Purcell			5		7			11	1						6	8	3	2					4		10	9
699	Oct 6	(h)	Barnsley	D 1-1	Woodcock	3		5		7			11	1						6	8		2					4		10	9
690	13	(a)	Barnsley	D 0-0				5		7	11			1						6	8	3	2					4		10	9
691	20	(a)	Manchester U	L 0-3				5		7	11			1						6	8	3	2					4		10	9
692	27	(h)	Manchester U	W 3-2	Waterall, Purcell, Woodcock (pen)			5		7	11			1						6	8	3	2					4		10	9
693	Nov 3	(a)	Bury	L 1-2	Critchley			5		7	11			1						6	8	3	2					4		10	9
694	10	(h)	Bury	W 3-2	Sambrook, Woodcock, Critchley			5		7	11			1						6	8	3	2	9				4		10	
695	24	(a)	South Shields	L 1-3	Critchley			5		7	11			1		6					8	3	2	10				4			9
696	Dec 8	(a)	Oldham A	L 1-3	Wilson			5		7	11			1		6			9			3	2					4		10	8
697	10	(h)	South Shields	W 3-2	Swan 2, Purcell (pen)			5		7	11			1							6	3	2	9	10	8		4			
698	22	(a)	Clapton O	D 1-1	Edgley			5		7	11			1								3	2	10		8		4		6	9
699	25	(h)	Blackpool	W 2-1	Sambrook, Swan			5		7	11			1								3	2	10		8		4		6	9
700	26	(a)	Blackpool	D 0-0				5		7	11			1								3	2	10		8		4		6	9
701	29	(a)	Leicester C	D 1-1	Critchley			5		7	11			1								3	2	10		8		4		6	9
702	Jan 1	(a)	Oldham A	L 0-1				5		7	11			1								3	2	10		8		4		6	9
703	5	(h)	Leicester C	W 3-1	Swan, Simms 2			5		7				1							10	3	2	11	9	8		4			
704	19	(a)	Hull C	W 2-1	Simms, Wilson			5		7				1							10	3	2	11	9	8		4		6	
705	26	(h)	Hull C	W 5-1	Simms 3 (1 pen), Edgley 2			5		7	11			1							10	3	2		9	8		4		6	
706	Feb 2	(a)	Stoke	D 0-0					5	7	11			1							10	3	2		9	8		4		6	
707	9	(h)	Stoke	L 0-1					5	7	11			1							10	3	2		9	8		4		6	
708	16	(a)	Crystal P	D 1-1	Sambrook			5		7	11			1								3	2	10	9	8		4			
709	Mar 1	(a)	The Wednesday	L 0-3				5		7	11			1								3	2	10	9			4		6	8
710	8	(h)	The Wednesday	W 1-0	Waterall			5		7	11			1			10					3	2		9			4		6	8
711	10	(h)	Crystal P	D 2-2	Hutchinson, Woodcock			5		7	11			1			10					3	2		9			4		6	8
712	15	(h)	Coventry C	D 0-0				5		7	11			1				4				3	2		9	8				6	10
713	22	(a)	Coventry C	D 0-0				5		7			11	1				4				3	2		9				6	8	10
714	29	(h)	Bristol C	D 0-0				5		7			11	1				4				3	2		9				6	8	10
715	31	(h)	Clapton O	W 2-0	Griffiths, Purcell			5		7			11	1							6	3	2	9	10	8		4			
716	Apr 5	(a)	Bristol C	L 0-3				5		7			11	1								3	2	9	10	8		4			
717	12	(h)	Southampton	L 2-3	Woodcock (pen), Sambrook			5		7				1				4	10			3	2	11		9				6	8
718	18	(h)	Leeds U	D 1-1	Meads			5		7	11			1					4			3	2	9	8				6	10	
719	19	(a)	Southampton	D 0-0				5		7	11			1					4			3	2	9	8				6	10	
720	21	(a)	Leeds U	L 0-4				5		7	11			1					4			3	2	9	8				6	10	
721	26	(h)	Fulham	W 2-1	White, Edgley			5		7	11			1					4			3	2	9	8				6	10	
722	May 3	(a)	Fulham	L 0-1				5		7	11			1					4		10	3	2	9					6		8
	Appearances					4	1	40	2	37	29	2	7	42	3	6	4	6	7	10	18	41	37	17	20	20	5	35	6	36	27
	Goals									4	4		1				1		1		4			4	6	4	1	3	1	2	8

FINAL LEAGUE POSITION: 13th in Division Two

FA Cup

No.	Date	V	Opponent	Res	Scorers	Att	Coc	Cri	Edg	Har	Hum	Hut	Jon	Pur	Rei	Ric	Sam	Sim	Swa	Wat	Woo
Q5	Dec 1	(h)	Crewe A	W 1-0	Sambrook	10,000	5	7	11	1	6			8	3	2	10			4	9
Q6	15	(a)	Norwich C	L 0-2		11,572	5	7	11	1		10	6		3	2		9	8	4	
	Appearances						2	2	2	2	1	2	1	2	1	2	1	2	1	2	1
	Goals																1				

1924-25

No	Date		Venue/Opp	Result	Scorers	Barlow	Blood	Boardman	Bocking	Craven	Critchley	Dennison	Hardy	Harries	Hooker	James	Johnston	McIntosh	Meads	Mitchell	Molyneux	Morrison	Newman	Reid G	Reid J	Richardson	Simms	Stenliford	Swan	Waterall	White	Wilson
723	Aug 30	(h)	Stoke C	W 2-0	G.Reid, Dennison						7	8	1						6	11				10	2	3	9			4		5
724	Sep 1	(h)	Manchester U	W 2-1	Dennison, Simms						7	8	1	5					4	11				10	2	3	9					6
725	6	(a)	Coventry C	L 2-4	G.Reid 2						7		1						6	11				10	2	3	9		8	4		5
726	13	(h)	Oldham A	W 2-0	Simms, Wilson			7					1						6	11				10	2	3	9		8			5
727	15	(h)	Leicester C	L 0-2				7					1						6	11	4			10	2	3	9		8			5
728	20	(a)	The Wednesday	L 0-3							7		1						6	11				10	2	3	9			4		5
729	27	(h)	Clapton O	L 0-1						5	7	9	1						4	11	6			10	2	3			8			
730	Oct 4	(a)	Crystal P	L 0-3					7				1			9			4	11	6			10	2	3			8		5	
731	11	(h)	Southampton	D 1-1	Dennison			4	5		7		1			9			6	11				10	2	3			8			
732	18	(a)	Chelsea	D 1-1	Simms						7	10						4	6	11	1				2	3	9	5	8			
733	25	(a)	Fulham	L 0-2								10	1						6	11			7		2	3	9	5	8	4		
734	Nov 1	(h)	Portsmouth	L 1-2	James							10	1						6	11			7	8	2	3	9	5		4		
735	8	(a)	Hull C	L 0-3						5	7	10	1			9			6	11					2	3			8	4		
736	15	(h)	Blackpool	W 1-0	Simms								1			8			6	9			7	10	2	3		5		4		11
737	22	(a)	Derby C	L 0-2				7				10	1						6	11					2	3	9	5	8	4		
738	29	(h)	South Shields	D 0-0				7				10	1						6	11					2	3	9	5	8	4		
739	Dec 6	(a)	Bradford C	L 0-3							7	10	1		6					11					2	3	9	5	8	4	10	
740	20	(a)	Middlesbrough	D 1-1	Mitchell		9		7				1						6	11					2	3		5	8	4	10	
741	25	(h)	Barnsley	W 1-0	Mitchell (pen)		9		7				1			8	5		10	11		6			2	3				4		
742	26	(a)	Barnsley	W 1-0	Meads		9		7				1			8	5		10	11		6			2	3				4		
743	27	(a)	Stoke C	L 0-3			9		7				1				5		10	11		6			2	3				4	8	
744	Jan 1	(h)	Wolves	D 1-1	Blood		9	2	7				1			8	5		10	11		6				3				4		
745	3	(h)	Coventry C	D 1-1	Waterall		9	2	7				1				5	8		11		6			10	3				4		
746	17	(a)	Oldham A	D 0-0			9	2	7				1			8			6	11						3	10	4	5		
747	24	(h)	The Wednesday	W 1-0	Meads		9	2	7				1						10	11						3	8	4	5		6
748	Feb 7	(h)	Crystal P	W 1-0	Blood		9	2	7				1						10	11						3	8	4	5		6
749	14	(a)	Southampton	L 1-2	Mitchell		9	2	7				1						10	11						3	8	4	5		6
750	16	(a)	Clapton O	D 1-1	Simms		9	2					1						10	11		7				3	8	4	5		6
751	21	(h)	Chelsea	W 4-0	Meads 3, Mitchell		9	7	2				1						10	11						3	8	4	5		6
752	25	(h)	Port Vale	L 0-2			9	7	2				1						10	11						3	8	4	5		6
753	28	(h)	Fulham	W 4-1	Blood 2, Meads 2		9	7	2				1						10	11						3	8	4	5		6
754	Mar 7	(a)	Portsmouth	D 1-1	Meads		9	7	2				1						10	11						3	8	4	5		6
755	14	(h)	Hull C	L 0-2			9	7	2				1						10	11						3	8	4	5		6
756	21	(a)	Blackpool	W 1-0	Simms		9	7	2				1			10			6	11						3	8	4	5		
757	28	(h)	Derby C	D 0-0			9	7	2				1						10	11						3	8	4	5		
758	Apr 4	(a)	South Shields	W 1-0	Meads		9	7	2							8			10	11	1					3		4	5		6
759	10	(a)	Manchester U	L 0-2			9	7	2							8			10	11	1					3		4	5		6
760	11	(h)	Bradford C	W 3-0	Blood 3		9	2	7							8			10	11	1					3		4	5		6
761	13	(a)	Wolves	L 0-3			9	2	7							8			10	11	1					3		4			6
762	18	(a)	Port Vale	L 1-4	Critchley		9	2	7							8		5	10	11	1					3		4			6
763	25	(h)	Middlesbrough	D 1-1	Meads		9	2	7							8			10	11	1					3		4	5		6
764	May 2	(a)	Leicester C	L 0-4		2	9	5	7							8			10	11	1					3		4			6
			Appearances			1	25	13	22	3	25	11	34	1	1	4	13	8	41	42	8	4	4	11	21	42	23	33	12	34	3	23
			Goals				7				1	3				1			10	4				3			6			1		1

FINAL LEAGUE POSITION: 19th in Division Two

FA Cup

No	Date		Venue/Opp	Result	Scorers	Att	Barlow	Blood	Boardman	Bocking	Critchley	Hardy	James	Meads	Mitchell	Richardson	Simms	Stenliford	Swan	Waterall	Wilson
1	Jan 10	(a)	Queen's Park R	W 3-1	Simms, Waterall, Blood	19,640		9	2	7		1		8	6 11	3		10	4	5	
2	31	(a)	Birmingham	L 0-1		36,000		9	2	7		1			10 11	3		8	4	5	6
			Appearances				2	2	2	2		1		2	2 2	2	2	2	2	2	1
			Goals					1									1			1	

1925-26

No		Date		Opponent	Result	Scorers	Att	Blood	Blunt	Boardman	Bocking	Burgess G	Burgess H	Caddick	Critchley	Hardy	Haslam	Hooker	James	Johnson	Johnston	Jones	Marsland	Meads	Mitchell	Morton	Pearson	Pritchard	Reid	Richardson	Scurr	Simms	Steniford	Waterall	Whitcombe	Whitelaw	Wilson J.T.	Wilson T.
765	Aug	29	(a)	Stoke C	L 0-3		17,341			7	2			4		1						8		10	11					3		9	5				6	
766		31	(h)	The Wednesday	L 0-2		10,848			7	2					1		5				10		9	11					3		8	4				6	
767	Sep	5	(h)	Oldham A	W 1-0	Simms	9,943				2				7	1		5						10	11		9			3		8	4				6	
768		12	(a)	Clapton O	L 1-2	Critchley	12,491	9			2				7	1								10	11					3		8	4		5		6	
769		14	(a)	Swansea T	L 0-4		17,123				2				7	1						8		10	11					3		9	4		5		6	
770		19	(a)	Fulham	L 0-1		7,023				2		5		7	1						8		10	11					3		9	4				6	
771		21	(a)	The Wednesday	L 2-6	Meads, Caddick	12,761				2		5		7	1						8		10	11					3		9			4		6	
772		26	(h)	South Shields	W 4-1	Simms 3, Mitchell	5,239				2		4		7	1						8		10	11					3		9			5		6	
773	Oct	3	(a)	Preston NE	L 3-5	Meads 2, Simms	14,925				2		4		7	1		5				8		10	11					3		9					6	
774		10	(h)	Middlesbrough	L 1-2	Meads	11,762				2				7	1						8		10	9	11				3					4	5	6	
775		17	(h)	Barnsley	D 1-1	Simms	5,850				2	3		4	7	1						8		10	11							9			5		6	
776		24	(a)	Port Vale	L 0-2		9,954				2			4	8	1				7				10	11					3	9				6		5		
777		31	(a)	Hull C	L 0-1		7,445				2				7		1					8		10	11					3		9	4		5		6	
778	Nov	7	(a)	Chelsea	L 2-3	Mitchell, Blood	29,139	9	4		2				7		1							10	11					3		8			5		6	
779		14	(h)	Nottingham F	W 3-0	Mitchell 2 (1 pen), Critchley	7,706	9			2				7		1				10		4		11					3		8			5		6	
780		21	(a)	Southampton	L 0-3		11,079	9			2				7		1				10				11					3		8			4	5	6	
781		28	(h)	Blackpool	W 4-3	Pearson 2, Mitchell (pen), Simms	9,841				2				7		1						4		11		10			3						5	6	8
782	Dec	5	(h)	Darlington	D 1-1	Simms	9,974				2				7		1						4		11		10			3		9				5	6	8
783		12	(h)	Bradford C	D 1-1	Mitchell	9,708				2				7		1						4		11		10			3		9				5	6	8
784		19	(a)	Derby C	L 0-4		11,143				2				7		1					8	4		11		10			3						6	9	5
785		25	(h)	Portsmouth	D 3-3	Whitelaw 2, Johnston	10,455				2				7		1				8		6		10		11		3					4		9	5	
786		26	(a)	Portsmouth	L 0-4		24,807				2				7		1				8		4		10		11		3						5	9	6
787	Jan	1	(a)	Swansea T	L 1-3	Boardman	8,651			11	2				7		1	6					4		10					3		8				5	9	
788		2	(h)	Stoke C	W 2-1	Blood, Jones	6,925	10		11	2			6	7		1				9		4							3					5	8		
789		23	(h)	Clapton O	W 3-2	Jones 3	7,907				2				7		1				8	9	10	4	11					3					5		6	
790		30*	(a)	Oldham A	L 0-3		11,590				2				7		1				8	9	10	4	11					3					5		6	
791	Feb	6	(a)	South Shields	L 2-4	Mitchell 2 (1 pen)	6,955		4			2			7		1				8	9	10		11					3					5		6	
792		9	(h)	Fulham	L 1-2	Mitchell	4,242	10			2				7		1				8	9		4	11					3					5		6	
793		13	(h)	Preston NE	D 1-1	Meads	9,556		4	11	2			5	7		1					9	10							3	8						6	
794		20	(a)	Middlesbrough	L 0-4		7,946			11	2				7		1				8	9	4			10				3					5		6	
795		27	(a)	Barnsley	D 1-1	Blood	7,663	10				2			5	7	1	6		8	9									4	11							3
796	Mar	6	(h)	Port Vale	D 2-2	Jones, Blood	7,889	10				2			5	7	1	6			9	8								4	11							3
797		13	(a)	Hull C	L 0-4		6,522	10				2	8		7		1					9	4							6	11					5		3
798		20	(h)	Chelsea	D 0-0		7,828	8	4			2			7		1					9	6			10				3	11					5		
799		27	(a)	Nottingham F	L 0-2		6,913	8	4			2			7		1					9	6			10					11					5		3
800	Apr	2	(h)	Wolves	W 1-0	Blood	6,423	8	4			2	3		7		1						10								11	9				5		
801		3	(h)	Southampton	L 1-2	Meads	7,666	8	4			2	3		7		1						10								11	9				5		
802		5	(a)	Wolves	L 1-5	Critchley	16,759	8	4			2	3		7		1						10								11	9	5					
803		10	(a)	Blackpool	L 1-4	Meads	7,610		4			2	3	8	7		1						10			6					11	9				5		
804		17	(a)	Darlington	L 2-3	Scurr, Jones	5,464		4	7		2	3	8			1		6			9	10								11							5
805		24	(a)	Bradford C	D 2-2	Blood, Meads	8,630	8		7		2	3				1		4			9	10				5				11					6		
806	May	1	(h)	Derby C	W 3-0	Jones, Blood 2	3,953	8		7		2	3			11	1		4			9	10													5		6	
				FINAL LEAGUE POSITION: 22nd in Division Two - Relegated to Division Three North			**Appearances**	16	10	9	37	13	3	11	38	11	31	6	3	7	13	15	5	39	24	3	11	2	12	21	11	23	10	15	15	8	36	4
							Goals	8		1				1	3						1	7		8	9		2				1	8				2		

FA Cup

No		Date		Opponent	Result		Att	Blood	Blunt	Boardman	Bocking	Burgess G	Burgess H	Caddick	Critchley	Hardy	Haslam	Hooker	James	Johnson	Johnston	Jones	Marsland	Meads	Mitchell	Morton	Pearson	Pritchard	Reid	Richardson	Scurr	Simms	Steniford	Waterall	Whitcombe	Whitelaw	Wilson J.T.	Wilson T.
3	Jan	9	(a)	Sheffield U	L 0-2		33,031	10		11	2			6	7		1						4	9						3				5		8			
							Appearances	1		1	1			1	1		1						1	1						1				1		1			
							Goals																																

Average Home League attendance: 8,086
Average Away League attendance: 12,088
* This was the 'replay' of a game played at Boundary Park on 16 January which was abandoned after 80 minutes due to fog with the score at 2-2 (Marsland, Jones), the team being the same as that of Match 789.

1926-27

No		Date	H/A	Opponent	Result	Scorers	Att	Blood	Boardman	Bocking	Broome	Burgess G	Burgess H	Catterick	Critchley	Fielding	Helliwell	Hooker	Hunter	James	Johnston	Jones	Lamb	Levick	Marsland	Martin	Meads	Odenrode	Pearson	Read	Sanderson	Scurr	Smith	Turner	Walker	Williams
807	Aug	28	(a)	Halifax T	L 1-4	Critchley	8,269			2					7					8	9	4	5				10			6		11			1	3
808		30	(h)	Doncaster R	W 1-0	Critchley	7,397	9		2		8			7						10	4	5							6		11			1	3
809	Sep	4	(h)	Lincoln C	D 3-3	Scurr, H.Burgess, Odenrode	7,474			2			9		7						10	4	5					8		6		11			1	3
810		6	(a)	Doncaster R	W 2-1	H.Burgess, Scurr	4,597			2			9		7	5					10	4						8		6		11			1	3
811		11	(a)	Accrington S	W 4-2	H.Burgess, Johnston, Scurr, James	4,574		7	2			9	5						8	10	4								6		11			1	3
812		18	(h)	Durham C	W 4-0	Johnston 2, H.Burgess, Catterick	7,892		7	2			9	5						8	10	4								6		11			1	3
813		25	(h)	Tranmere R	D 0-0		6,310		7	2			9	5						8	10	4								6		11			1	3
814	Oct	2	(h)	Rochdale	W 3-0	Scurr, H.Burgess, Johnston	10,161		7	2			9	5						8	10	4								6		11			1	3
815		9	(a)	Southport	D 2-2	H.Burgess 2	4,051		7	2			9	5						8	10	4								6		11			1	3
816		16	(a)	Wrexham	L 1-2	H.Burgess	5,640		7	2			9			5					10	4			8					6		11			1	3
817		23	(h)	Wigan Bor	W 4-1	H.Burgess 3, Scurr	8,953		8	2			9	5	7						10	4								6		11			1	3
818		30	(h)	Stoke C	W 1-0	Boardman	12,592		8	2			9	5	7						10	4								6		11			1	3
819	Nov	6	(h)	Rotherham U	W 3-1	Scurr, Johnston, Meads	7,998		8	2			9	5	7						10	4								6		11			1	3
820		13	(a)	Bradford	L 1-3	Johnston	9,002		8	2			9	5	7						10	4								6		11			1	3
821		20	(h)	Walsall	L 0-2		8,152			2		8		5	7						10	4					9			6		11			1	3
822	Dec	4	(h)	Chesterfield	W 4-0	H.Burgess, Johnston 3	7,982		8	2			9	5	7						10					4				6		11			1	3
823		18	(h)	New Brighton	W 1-0	Boardman	7,406		8	2			9	5	7						10					4				6		11			1	3
824		25	(a)	Barrow	W 3-1	Boardman, Odenrode, Scurr	4,967		8	2			9					5			10						4	7	6		1	11				3
825		27	(h)	Barrow	W 7-0	H.Burgess 2, Meads, Boardman 2, Pearson, Johnston	12,530		8	2			9					5			10						4	7	6		1	11				3
826	Jan	1	(h)	Crewe A	W 3-1	Pearson, Boardman 2 (1 pen)	12,144		8	2			9					5			10						4	7	6		1	11				3
827		3	(a)	Hartlepools U	W 2-1	James, Boardman	4,244		8	2			9						4	5	10							7	6		1	11				3
828		8	(a)	Nelson	L 1-6	Martin	4,129		8	2								5			10					9	4	7	6		1	11				3
829		15	(h)	Halifax T	L 1-3	Johnston	9,784		8	2			9								10			5			4	7	6			11			1	3
830		22	(a)	Lincoln C	W 3-1	Odenrode, Johnston, Opp own-goal	3,144		8	2			9						5		10						4	7	6		1	11				3
831	Feb	5	(a)	Durham C	W 5-1	H.Burgess 2, Johnston 2, Odenrode	1,769		8	2			9					11	5		10						4	7	6		1					3
832		8	(h)	Accrington S	D 3-3	Odenrode, Johnston 2	3,689		8	2			9					11	5		10						4	7	6		1					3
833		12	(h)	Tranmere R	W 2-1	Johnston 2	8,487		8	2			9			5		11			10						4	7	6		1					3
834		19	(a)	Rochdale	L 0-2		10,239		8	2			9					11	5		10						4	7	6		1					3
835		26	(h)	Southport	L 2-4	Jones 2 (2 pens)	9,835		8	2								11	5		10	9					4	7	6		1					3
836	Mar	5	(h)	Wrexham	W 3-2	H.Burgess 3	4,757		8	2			9					11	5		10						4	7	6					1		3
837		12	(a)	Wigan Bor	L 0-2		8,659		7	2			9			5			4		10			8					6			11			1	3
838		19	(h)	Stoke C	D* 2-2	Pearson, Scurr	22,622		7	2	3		9					5	4		8								6			11	10	1		
839		26	(a)	Rotherham U	W 2-1	Smith 2	4,176		7	2	3		9					5	4		8								6			11	10	1		
840	Apr	2	(h)	Bradford	L 1-2	Johnston	7,883		7	2	3		9					5	4		10								6			11	8	1		
841		9	(a)	Walsall	L 0-1		3,998		7	2	3							5	4		8						9					11	10	1		6
842		11	(a)	Ashington	D 1-1	Martin	1,521		7	2								5	4		8					9			6			11	10	1		3
843		15	(a)	Crewe A	L 2-3	Johnston 2	9,547		7	2								5	4		8					9			6			11	10	1		3
844		16	(h)	Nelson	W 4-1	H.Burgess 4 (1 pen)	10,546			2		8	9				6	5	4		10								11	7				1		3
845		18	(h)	Hartlepools U	D 3-3	Smith, H.Burgess 2	7,503		7	2			9					5	4		8								6			11	10	1		3
846		23	(a)	Chesterfield	L 0-3		5,292			2	8		9					5	4		10							7	6			11		1		3
847		30	(h)	Ashington	W 6-2	Smith, H.Burgess 2, Johnston 3	5,766		7	2			9						4		8			5					6			11	10	1		3
848	May	7	(a)	New Brighton	W 2-1	Johnston, H.Burgess	4,650		7	2			9					11	5		8								6			10		1		3
				Appearances				1	35	42	3	4	35	13	16	7	4	14	7	25	40	4	5	5	1	4	30	16	25	11	2	35	8	12	19	39
				Goals					8				28	1	2					2	25	2				2	2	2	5	3		8	4			

FINAL LEAGUE POSITION: 6th in Division Three North

Own-goal 1

FA Cup

		Date		Opponent	Result	Scorers	Att	Blood	Boardman	Bocking	Broome	Burgess G	Burgess H	Catterick	Critchley	Fielding	Helliwell	Hooker	Hunter	James	Johnston	Jones	Lamb	Levick	Marsland	Martin	Meads	Odenrode	Pearson	Read	Sanderson	Scurr	Smith	Turner	Walker	Williams
1	Nov	27	(a)	Nelson	L 1-4	Scurr	8,500			2			9	5	7							4						8		6		11			1	3
				Appearances						1			1	1	1							1						1		1		1			1	1
				Goals																											1				

Average Home League attendance: 8,998
Average Away League attendance: 5,780

*County were deducted two points for playing an unregistered player (Joe Smith) in this game.

1927-28

No	Date		Venue/Opponent	Res	Score	Scorers	Att	Boardman	Bocking	Bond	Broome	Burgess G	Burgess H	Cawley	Duffus	Fielding	Hayes	Helliwell	Hooker	James	Jobson	Johnston	Kay	Kirby	Molloy	Newton F	Newton W	Odenrode	Pearson	Ramsden	Scullion	Scurr	Smith	Turner	Whitelaw	Wilson
849	Aug	27 (h)	Rotherham U	W	2-0	Johnston, Smith	11,546	7	2			9						1	6	5		8				4						11	10			3
850		30 (a)	Rochdale	L	1-2	H.Burgess	10,253	7	2			8						1	6	5						4					9	11	10			3
851	Sep	3 (a)	Southport	L	0-4		6,845		2	8		9						1	6	5				7		4						11	10			3
852		10 (h)	Durham C	W	2-1	H.Burgess, Fielding	8,690	7	2		3	9			11			1	6			8	5			4							10			
853		17 (a)	Wrexham	L	0-1		7,211		2					7	11			1	6	5		8				4					9		10			3
854		24 (h)	Chesterfield	W	3-0	H.Burgess (pen), Helliwell 2	6,252	8	2			9			11			1	6	5		10		7		4										3
855	Oct	1 (a)	Bradford	L	0-2		9,838	8	2			9						1	6	4	5	10		7						11						3
856		8 (h)	Tranmere R	W	1-0	Jobson	8,283	8	2			9			11			1	6	4	5	10		7												3
857		15 (a)	Lincoln C	L	0-2		7,468	8	2						11	9		1	6	4	5			7									10			3
858		22 (h)	Halifax T	W	3-0	Boardman, Duffus, Smith	9,291	8	2						11	9		1	6	5						4		7					10			3
859		29 (a)	Bradford C	D	2-2	Odenrode, Smith	13,582	8	2						11	9		1	6	5						4		7					10			3
860	Nov	5 (h)	New Brighton	D	0-0		6,382	8	2						11	9		1	6	5						4		7					10			3
861		12 (a)	Crewe A	L	0-3		4,185	8	2						11	9		1	6	5						4		7					10			3
862		19 (h)	Ashington	W	3-0	Smith, Duffus, Jobson	6,590	7	2						9			1		5	8					4	6					11	10			3
863	Dec	3 (h)	Doncaster R	W	2-1	Smith (pen), Duffus	9,760	7	2						9			1	6	5	8					4						11	10			3
864		17 (h)	Accrington S	D	3-3	Smith 3	7,020		2									1	6	5	8					4		7			9	11	10			3
865		24 (a)	Hartlepools U	L	1-2	Smith	2,033	8	2								1		6	5						4	11	7			9		10			3
866		26 (h)	Barrow	W	4-0	Smith 3, H.Burgess	8,697		2			8					1		6	5						4	11	7			9		10			3
867		27 (a)	Barrow	W	3-2	Wilson, Scullion, H.Burgess	6,225		2			8					1		6	5						4	11	7			9		10			3
868		31 (a)	Rotherham U	W	1-0	Smith	3,625	7	2			8					1		6	5						4	11				9		10			3
869	Jan	2 (h)	Rochdale	W	5-1	Smith 3, W.Newton, Scullion	10,571		2			8					1		6	5						4	11	7			9	10				3
870		7 (h)	Southport	W	6-3	Smith 5, Ramsden	10,384		2			8					1		6	5						4	11	7			9		10			3
871		14 (a)	Wigan Bor	W	3-1	Smith, Ramsden, Bocking (pen)	3,843		2			8					1		6	5						4		7	11		9			1	10	3
872		21 (a)	Durham C	W	2-1	Whitelaw, H.Burgess	1,781		2			8					1		6	5						4		7	11		9			1	10	3
873		28 (h)	Lincoln C	W	2-0	Whitelaw, Scullion	7,478		2			8					1		6	5						4		7	11		9			1	10	3
874	Feb	4 (a)	Chesterfield	D	1-1	Opp own-goal	4,768		2			8					1		6	5						4		7	11		9			1	10	3
875		11 (h)	Bradford	D	2-2	Smith 2	15,775		2			8					1		6	5						4		7	11		9			1	10	3
876		18 (a)	Tranmere R	L	2-5	Scullion, Whitelaw	8,943		2			8					1		6						5	4		7	11		9			1	10	3
877		27 (h)	Wrexham	W	5-0	Smith 4, Ramsden	4,120		2			8					1			5						4	6	7	11		9			1	10	3
878	Mar	3 (a)	Halifax T	W	3-1	H.Burgess, Scullion, Smith	4,770		2			8					1			5						4	6	7	11		9			1	10	3
879		10 (h)	Bradford C	W	3-0	Ramsden, Smith, H.Burgess	9,984		2			8					1			5						4	6	7		11	9			1	10	3
880		17 (a)	New Brighton	D	0-0		4,876		2			8					1			5						4	6	7	11		9			1	10	3
881		24 (h)	Crewe A	W	1-0	Smith	9,766		2			8					1			5					11	4	6	7			9			1	10	3
882		31 (a)	Ashington	L	1-4	Ramsden	2,053	11	2			8					1			5						4	6	7	10		9			1		3
883	Apr	6 (h)	Nelson	W	8-0	Scurr, Ramsden 2, Smith 2, H.Burgess, Boardman 2	8,430	10	2			8					1			5						4	6	7	11		9			1		3
884		7 (h)	Wigan Bor	D	1-1	Bocking (pen)	8,840	10	2			8			11		1			5						4	6	7			9			1		3
885		9 (a)	Nelson	W	4-0	H.Burgess, Bocking (pen), Smith 2	5,441	10	2			8	4				1			5							6	7			9			1		3
886		14 (a)	Doncaster R	W	2-0	Ramsden 2	5,872	10	2			8	4				1			5							6	7			9			1		3
887		21 (h)	Darlington	W	4-0	Pearson, Smith 2, H.Burgess	6,921	10	2			8	4				1			5							6	7			9			1		3
888		23 (a)	Darlington	L	1-3	Opp own-goal	1,925	10	2	6		8					1			5						4					9			1		3
889		28 (a)	Accrington S	L	0-1		5,225	10	2			8					1			5						4	6	7			9			1		3
890	May	5 (h)	Hartlepools U	D	2-2	H.Burgess, Smith	4,991	10	2			8					1			5						4	6	7			9			1		3
			Appearances					24	42	1	1	35	3	6	10	16	18	12	1	40	6	2	1	9	1	36	4	20	21	18	15	40	26		12	41
			Goals					3	3			12			3	1		2			2	1					1	1	1	9	5	1	38		3	1

FINAL LEAGUE POSITION: 3rd in Division Three North

Own-goals 2

FA Cup

No	Date		Venue/Opponent	Res	Score	Scorers	Att	Boardman	Bocking	Burgess G	Duffus	Helliwell	James	Newton F	Pearson	Scurr	Smith	Wilson
1	Nov	26 (h)	Oswestry T	W	5-2	Smith 2 (1 pen), Scurr, Pearson, Duffus	9,368	7	2	8	9	1	5	4	6	11	10	3
2	Dec	10 (a)	Crewe A	L	0-2		9,064	7	2	8	9	1	5	4	6	11	10	3
			Appearances					2	2	2	2	2	2	2	2	2	2	2
			Goals								1				1	1	2	

Average Home League attendance: 8,561
Average Away League attendance: 5,751

1928-29

No	Date	Venue	Opponent	Result	Scorers	Att	Alport	Boardman	Bocking	Burgess	Cawley	Cook	Crowther	Curry	Everest	Fielding	Helliwell	Hooker	Hudspeth	Jobson	Morrison	Newton F	Newton W	Pearson	Pennington	Raisbeck	Smith	Tompkinson	Townsend	Turner	Vincent	Waites	Wilson
891	Aug 25	(h)	Tranmere R	W 4-1	Tompkinson 2, Burgess, Boardman	10,283	2	8		10		1								5			4	6			9	7	11				3
892	Sep 1	(a)	Chesterfield	W 2-1	Burgess, Smith	6,410	2	8		10		1								5			4	6			9	7	11				3
893	3	(a)	Crewe A	L 0-2		4,524		8	2	10		1								5			4	6			9	7	11				3
894	8	(a)	Halifax T	D 1-1	Burgess	7,542		8	2	10		1								5			4	6			9	7	11				3
895	10	(a)	Ashington	W 4-0	Burgess 3, Smith	8,908		8	2	10		1								5			4	6			9	7	11				3
896	15	(h)	Lincoln C	W 7-3	Smith 5, Burgess, Boardman	10,924		8	2	10		1								5			4	6			9	7	11				3
897	22	(a)	Bradford C	L 1-2	Boardman	18,896		8	2	10		1								5			4	6			9	7	11				3
898	29	(h)	Accrington S	W 6-1	Smith 3, Burgess, Boardman, Tompkinson	10,250		8	2	10		1								5			4	6			9	7	11				3
899	Oct 6	(a)	Hartlepools U	D 1-1	Smith*	5,305		8	2	10		1				11				5			4	6			9	7					3
900	13	(h)	Carlisle U	D 2-2	Fielding, Boardman	14,563		8	2	10		1				11				5			4	6			9	7					3
901	20	(h)	Wrexham	W 6-2	Fielding, Tompkinson 2, Burgess 2, Smith	17,930		8	2	10		1				11				5			4	6			9	7					3
902	27	(a)	New Brighton	L 1-4	Fielding	6,051		8	2	10		1				11				5			4	6			9	7					3
903	Nov 3	(h)	Rochdale	W 4-0	Everest, Burgess, Tompkinson, Fielding	11,661		8	2	10			1		9	11	6			5			4					7					3
904	10	(a)	Southport	D 1-1	Smith	3,738		8	2	10			1			11	6	3		5			4				9	7					3
905	17	(h)	Darlington	W 7-3	Opp own-goal 2, Smith 3, Tompkinson, Fielding (pen)	9,002	3	8	2	10			1			11	6			5			4				9	7					
906	Dec 1	(h)	South Shields	W 7-1	Burgess 3, Fielding, F.Newton 2, Tompkinson	10,690		8	2	10			1			11	6			5		9	4					7					3
907	15	(h)	Doncaster R	W 4-1	Fielding, F.Newton 2, Tompkinson	8,629		8	2	10			1			11	6			5		9	4					7					3
908	22	(a)	Barrow	W 4-2	Tompkinson, F.Newton 2, Burgess	3,346		8	2	10			1			11	6			5		9	4					7					3
909	25	(h)	Rotherham U	W 1-0	Burgess	14,238		8	2	10			1			11	6			5		9	4					7					3
910	26	(a)	Rotherham U	D 3-3	F.Newton, Boardman, Burgess	8,629		8	2	10			1			11	6			5		9	4					7					3
911	29	(a)	Tranmere R	L 1-2	Opp own-goal	6,088		8	2	10			1			11	6			5		9	4					7					3
912	Jan 1	(h)	Wigan Bor	W 2-1	Raisbeck, Fielding	18,744			2	10			1			11	6			5		9	4			8		7					3
913	5	(a)	Chesterfield	W 3-1	Burgess, Boardman 2	9,402		8	2	10			1			11	6			5		9	4					7					3
914	19	(h)	Halifax T	W 3-0	F.Newton 2, Burgess	11,799		8	2	10			1	6		11				5		9	4					7					3
915	22	(a)	Nelson	L 1-4	Burgess	2,749		8	2	10			1	6		11				5		9	4					7		7			3
916	26	(a)	Lincoln C	W 2-1	Smith 2	6,643		8		10			1	5		11				5			4				9	7		7			3
917	Feb 2	(h)	Bradford C	W 2-1	Burgess, Boardman	24,311		8		10			1	5		11		3	6		2		4		1		9	7					3
918	9	(a)	Accrington S	L 0-2		5,851		8	2	10				5	9	11		3	6				4		1			7					3
919	16	(h)	Hartlepools U	W 3-0	Smith, Boardman, Hudspeth	7,468		8	2	10				5		11		3	6				4		1		9	7					3
920	23	(a)	Carlisle U	W 5-0	Burgess 2, F.Newton 2, Hudspeth (pen)	10,779		8	2	10				6		11		3	5			9	4		1			7					3
921	Mar 2	(a)	Wrexham	L 1-2	Curry	16,715		8	2	10				6		11		3	5			9	4		1			7					3
922	9	(h)	New Brighton	W 2-1	Burgess, Boardman	12,844		8	2	10				6		11		3	5				4		1		9	7					3
923	16	(a)	Rochdale	W 3-1	F.Newton 2, Fielding	11,281		8	2	10				6		11		3	5				4		1			7					3
924	23	(h)	Southport	W 2-1	Burgess, Opp own-goal	10,737		8	2	10			1	6		11		3	5			9	4					7					3
925	29	(a)	Crewe A	D 2-2	Burgess 2	13,401		8	2	10			1	6		11		3	5			9	4					7					3
926	30	(a)	Darlington	W 3-2	Burgess 2, F.Newton	5,340		8		10			1					3	5			9	4		11			7					3
927	Apr 1	(a)	Wigan Bor	L 0-4		15,162	7	2	8				1			11						9	4			10					6	5	3
928	6	(h)	Nelson	W 3-0	Tompkinson, F.Newton, Burgess	7,916		8	2	10			1			11	6					9	4					7			6	5	3
929	13	(a)	South Shields	W 1-0	F.Newton	5,597		8	2	10			1			11	6			5		9	4					7					3
930	20	(a)	Ashington	W 1-0	Burgess	1,399		8	2	10			1			11	6			5		9	4					7					3
931	27	(a)	Doncaster R	W 2-0	Boardman, Fielding	9,453		8	2	10			1			11	6			5		9	4					7					3
932	May 4	(h)	Barrow	W 3-2	Tompkinson 3	7,197		8	2	10			1			11	6			5		9	4					7					3

FINAL LEAGUE POSITION: 2nd in Division Three North

						Appearances	3	41	37	42	0	9	27	12	2	34	15	3	11	39	2	19	42	13	6	1	22	39	7	1	3	2	30
						Goals		12		31				1	1	10			2			16				1	19	14					

Own-goals 4

FA Cup

No	Date	Venue	Opponent	Result	Scorers	Att	Alport	Boardman	Bocking	Burgess	Cawley	Cook	Crowther	Curry	Everest	Fielding	Helliwell	Hooker	Hudspeth	Jobson	Morrison	Newton F	Newton W	Pearson	Pennington	Raisbeck	Smith	Tompkinson	Townsend	Turner	Vincent	Waites	Wilson
1	Nov 24	(h)	Halifax T	W 1-0	Fielding	8,748			2	10			1			11	6			5			4			8	9	7					3
2	Dec 8	(h)	Southport	W 3-0	F.Newton 2, Burgess	11,000		8	2	10			1			11	6			5		9	4					7					3
3	Jan 12	(a)	Bradford C	L 0-2		30,171		8	2	10				6		11				5		9	4					7					3

						Appearances		2	3	3		1	2	1		3	2			3		2	3			1	1	3					3
						Goals				1						1						2											

Average Home League attendance: 11,947
Average Away League attendance: 7,690

*There was some dispute as to whom this goal should be credited. It has often been credited to Fielding but two players (Smith and Fielding) collided prior to the ball crossing the line. Fielding remembered nothing about the goal and although the referee believed it was Fielding's goal, Joe Smith claimed it.

1929-30

No.	Date		Opponent	Res.	Scorers	Att.	Boardman	Bocking	Brown	Butt	Cawley	Cooper	Crowther	Curry	Everest	Fielding	Gee	Helliwell	Hudspeth	Jobson	Lambourne	Lincoln	Marshall	McGann	Newton F	Newton W	Richardson	Seabrook	Tompkinson	Vincent	Wilson
933	Aug 31	(a)	Wrexham	D 1-1	Fielding	10,768	8	2					1			11	6	5				10			9	4			7		3
934	Sep 2	(h)	Barrow	W 5-0	Tompkinson, Lincoln 3, Boardman	8,965	8	2					1			11	6	5				10			9	4			7		3
935	7	(h)	Wigan Bor	D 1-1	Lincoln	10,419	8	2					1	4		11	6	5				10			9				7		3
936	9	(a)	Barrow	W 4-1	Opp own-goal, Boardman, F.Newton 2	6,865	8	2					1	4		11	6	5				10			9				7		3
937	14	(a)	Carlisle U	W 5-1	F.Newton 2, Lincoln 2, Boardman	10,204	8	2			1	6				11		5				10			9	4			7		3
938	21	(h)	Nelson	W 6-1	F.Newton 5 (1 pen), Fielding	7,789	8	2						4		11	6	5				10			9		1		7		3
939	28	(a)	Southport	W 2-1	Tompkinson, F.Newton	5,544	8	2						4		11	6	5				10			9		1		7		3
940	Oct 5	(h)	Crewe A	L 2-3	F.Newton 2	11,416	8	2						5		11	6					10			9	4	1	7			3
941	12	(a)	York C	W 2-1	Tompkinson, F.Newton	6,189	8	2						5		11	6					10			9	4	1		7		3
942	19	(a)	Tranmere R	L 0-2		7,604	8	2								11	6	5				10			9	4	1		7		3
943	26	(a)	Halifax T	W 6-0	Boardman, Seabrook, F.Newton 3, Opp own-goal	7,586	8	2			4		1			11		5		6		10			9			7			3
944	Nov 2	(a)	Rotherham U	D 2-2	Lincoln, Opp own-goal	5,622	8	2			4		1			11		5		6		10			9			7			3
945	9	(h)	Rochdale	W 4-2	Bocking (pen), Fielding, F.Newton, Lincoln	12,903	8	2					1			11		5		6		10			9	4			7		3
946	16	(a)	South Shields	W 3-2	Helliwell, Boardman, Fielding	4,971	8	2					1			11		5		6		10			9	4			7		3
947	23	(h)	Accrington S	W 1-0	Tompkinson	8,750	8	2					1			11		5		6		10			9	4			7		3
948	Dec 21	(h)	Chesterfield	W 1-0	F.Newton	8,295	8	2					1			11		5		6		10			9	4			7		3
949	25	(a)	Port Vale	W 2-1	Tompkinson, F.Newton	14,494	8	2					1			11		5		6		10			9	4			7		3
950	26	(h)	Port Vale	W 4-2	W.Newton, F.Newton, Lincoln 2	22,668	8	2					1			11		5		6		10			9	4			7		3
951	28	(a)	Wrexham	L 0-1		8,026	8	2					1			11		5	3	6		10			9	4			7		
952	Jan 1	(h)	Lincoln C	D 1-1	Lincoln	9,972	8	2					1			11		5		6		10			9	4			7		3
953	4	(h)	Wigan Bor	W 1-0	Everest	6,131	8	2					1		9	11		5		6		10				4			7		3
954	18	(a)	Carlisle U	W 7-1	Everest 4, Tompkinson 3	11,701	8	2					1		9	11		5		6		10				4			7		3
955	25	(a)	Nelson	W 2-1	Everest, Lincoln	5,217	8	2					1		9	11		5		6		10				4			7		3
956	Feb 1	(h)	Southport	D 2-2	Lincoln, Jobson	10,250	8	2					1		9	11		5		6		10				4			7		3
957	8	(a)	Crewe A	D 1-1	Lincoln	8,590	8	2					1		9	11		5		6		10				4			7		3
958	15	(h)	York C	L 2-3	Lincoln, Marshall	9,434	8	2								11		5		6		10	9	1		4			7		3
959	19	(a)	Darlington	W 2-1	Butt, Lincoln	2,899	7	2		8						11	5			6		10			9	4	1				3
960	22	(h)	Tranmere R	W 3-1	Lincoln 2, F.Newton	9,217	7	2		8						11	5			6		10			9	4	1				3
961	Mar 1	(a)	Halifax T	W 3-0	F.Newton 2, Lincoln	4,118	8									11	5		3	6		10			9	4	1		7		2
962	3	(h)	Hartlepools U	W 5-1	Tompkinson, Lincoln 2, F.Newton, Boardman	4,674	8	2								11	5			6		10			9	4	1		7		3
963	8	(a)	Rotherham U	W 6-1	F.Newton 4, Lincoln 2	9,544		2	8							11	5			6		10			9	4	1		7		3
964	15	(a)	Rochdale	L 1-3	Tompkinson	4,516		2	8							11	5			6		10			9	4	1		7		3
965	20	(a)	Doncaster R	D 1-1	F.Newton	2,952		2	8							11	5			6		10			9	4	1		7		3
966	22	(a)	South Shields	W 2-0	F.Newton, Lincoln	6,021		2		8						11	5			6		10			9	4	1		7		3
967	29	(a)	Accrington S	W 1-0	Fielding	4,552		2		8						11	5			6		10			9	4	1		7		3
968	Apr 5	(h)	Darlington	W 4-0	Jobson, Brown, Gee (pen), Tompkinson	10,736		2	8							11	5			6		10			9	4	1		7		3
969	12	(a)	Hartlepools U	W 1-0	Brown	8,239		2	8							11	5			6		10			9	4	1		7		3
970	18	(a)	New Brighton	L 2-3	Brown, F.Newton	11,370		2	8							11	5			6		10			9	4	1		7		3
971	19	(a)	Doncaster R	W 3-0	F.Newton 3	7,877		2	8							11	5			6		10			9	4	1		7		3
972	23*	(a)	Lincoln C	L 0-1		5,385		2	8							11	5			6		10			9	4	1		7		3
973	26	(a)	Chesterfield	W 3-1	F.Newton, Lincoln, Tompkinson	4,519		2	8							11	5		3	6		10			9	4	1		7		
974	May 3	(h)	New Brighton	W 2-0	F.Newton, Lincoln	4,140		2	8							11	5		3	6		10			9	4	1		7		
			Appearances				30	41	9	5	3	1	20	7	5	41	25	24	3	32	1	42	2	1	35	35	21	3	37	1	38
			Goals				6	1	3	1					6	5	1	1		2		26	1		36	1		1	12		

FINAL LEAGUE POSITION: 2nd in Division Three North

Own-goals 3

FA Cup

No.	Date		Opponent	Res.	Scorers	Att.	Boardman	Bocking	Crowther	Fielding	Gee	Helliwell	Jobson	Lincoln	Newton F	Newton W	Tompkinson	Wilson
1	Nov 30	(a)	Wellington	W 4-1	Gee, F.Newton, Fielding, Tompkinson	7,719	8	2	1	11	5		6	10	9	4	7	3
2	Dec 14	(h)	Barrow	W 4-0	Boardman, F.Newton, Lincoln 2	6,350	8	2	1	11	6	5		10	9	4	7	3
3	Jan 11	(a)	Blackpool	L 1-2	Boardman	14,000	8	2	1	11		5	6	10	9	4	7	3
			Appearances				3	3	3	3	2	2	2	3	3	3	3	3
			Goals				2			1	1			2	2		1	

Average Home League attendance: 9,542
Average Away League attendance: 6,702

*Replay of a game abandoned after 80 minutes because of bad light on 30 September 1929 with the score at 1-1 (Fielding). Team same as for Match 939 except W.Newton played for Helliwell.

1930-31

No.	Date		Venue / Opponent	Result	Scorers	Att.	Bee	Boa	Boc	BrN	BrW	But	Caw	Fan	Gar	Gow	Hel	Hor	Job	Joh	Kea	Lam	Lin	Llo	MCH	MRW	NeF	NeW	Rat	Ric	Sim	Tay	Vin	Web
975	Aug	30	(h) Hull C	W 3-2	Jobson, F.Newton, Lincoln	12,091		8	2						3			6		11			10		5		9	4			1	7		
976	Sep	1	(h) New Brighton	W 2-0	Bocking, F.Newton	7,985	3	8	2									6		11			10		5		9	4			1	7		
977		6	(a) Lincoln C	L 1-6	F.Newton	7,418		8	2						3			6		11			10		5		9	4			1			
978		11	(a) Carlisle U	L 1-5	Lincoln	8,597	3		2		8							6		11			10		7	5	9	4			1			
979		13	(h) Hartlepools U	W 3-1	Webster, N.Brown, F.Newton	6,372	3	8	2	10								6		11			10		7	5	9	4			1			
980		15	(h) Carlisle U	W 3-0	C.H.Matthews, F.Newton 2	5,424			2	10	8							6							7		9	4		1			5	11
981		20	(a) Wigan Bor	L 1-2	Webster	12,516			2	10	8							3					6		7		9	4		1			5	11
982		27	(h) Nelson	W 1-0	F.Newton	6,822			2	10	8							3					6		7		9	4		1			5	11
983	Oct	4	(a) Darlington	W 2-1	F.Newton 2	4,765	3	8	2									3					6		9	4	7		1			5	11
984		11	(h) Halifax T	W 3-0	Webster, F.Newton, Lincoln	7,137		8	2							6	5						10		7		9	4		1				11
985		18	(a) York C	W 2-1	F.Newton, Boardman	4,676		8	2							6	5						10		7		9	4		1			3	11
986		25	(h) Tranmere R	D 1-1	F.Newton	8,411		8	2							6	5						10		7		9	4		1			3	11
987	Nov	1	(a) Chesterfield	D 1-1	F.Newton (pen)	7,177		8	2							6	5						10		7		9	4		1			3	11
988		8	(h) Barrow	W 6-0	Lincoln 3, Jobson, Webster, C.H.Matthews	6,622		8	2							1	6	5					10		7		9	4					3	11
989		15	(a) Southport	L 0-2		3,642		8	2							1	6	5					10		7			4					9	3	11
990		22	(h) Accrington S	W 4-1	F.Newton 2 (1 pen), Jobson, Webster	4,691		8	2								6	5					10		7			4					9	3	11
991	Dec	6	(h) Crewe A	W 2-0	Webster, F.Newton	7,281		8	2							1	6	5					10		7		9	4					3	11
992		17	(a) Wrexham	L 2-3	F.Newton, Webster	4,338		8	2								6	5					10		7		9	4					3	11
993		20	(h) Rotherham U	W 5-2	F.Newton 2 (1 pen), C.H.Matthews 2, Lincoln	5,713	3	8	2								5				6	10		7		9	4		1			3	11
994		25	(h) Gateshead	W 3-1	F.Newton 3	10,663	3	8	2								5				6	10		7		9	4		1				11
995		27	(a) Hull C	D 1-1	C.H.Matthews	9,557	3	8	2							1	6	5					10		7		9	4						11
996	Jan	1	(a) New Brighton	W 2-0	C.H.Matthews 2	4,720	3	8	2							1	5				6	10		7		9	4						11
997		3	(h) Lincoln C	W 4-2	F.Newton 3 (1 pen), Webster	14,804	3	8	2							1	5				6	10		7		9	4						11
998		10	(a) Rochdale	L 0-1		2,553	3	8	2				5			1					6	10		7		9	4						11
999		17	(a) Hartlepools U	W 2-1	Webster, Lincoln	4,624	3	8	2							1	5				6	10		7		9	4						11
1000		24	(h) Wigan Bor	W 4-1	Lincoln, F.Newton 2, C.H.Matthews	7,798	3	8	2							1	5				6	10		7		9	4						11
1001		31	(a) Nelson	D 1-1	Webster	1,593	3	8	2							1	5					10		7		9	4						11
1002	Feb	7	(a) Darlington	L 0-1		7,620		8	2	10		4				1	6	5						7		9						3	11	
1003		14	(a) Halifax T	L 0-3		4,580	3		2	10	8					1	6						7		9	4							11
1004		21	(h) York C	D 0-0		4,982			2					8		6	1	5				10	3	7		9						4	11
1005		28	(a) Tranmere R	L 0-3		4,988		8	2							1	5				6	10	3	7		9	4						11
1006	Mar	7	(h) Chesterfield	W 2-1	Bocking, F.Newton	4,337	3		2				8				1	5				6	10		7		9	4						11
1007		14	(a) Barrow	L 0-1		7,814	3	8	2								1	5				6	10		7		9	4						11
1008		21	(h) Southport	W 2-0	C.H.Matthews, F.Newton	5,410	3	8	2							6	1	5					10		7		9	4						11
1009		28	(a) Accrington S	D 2-2	Lambourne, F.Newton	2,555	3	7	2							6	1				5	10	8		9	4							11
1010	Apr	3	(a) Doncaster R	L 0-2		4,306	3	7	2							6	1				5	10	8		9	4							11
1011		4	(h) Rochdale	D 2-2	Lincoln 2	5,046	3		2				8			6					5	10			9	4	7	1					11
1012		6	(h) Doncaster R	D 2-2	F.Newton 2	3,707	3	7	2							6	1				5	10	8		9	4							11
1013		11	(a) Crewe A	L 0-1		3,488	3	7	2					8		6					5	4	10		9								11
1014		15	(h) Gateshead	L 1-2	Lincoln	2,389	3	8	2												6	10		7	9	4			1				11
1015		18	(h) Wrexham	D 2-2	Vincent (pen), F.Newton	2,953	3	8	2							6					4	10		7	9				1			5	11
1016		25	(a) Rotherham U	W 4-3	Lincoln, C.H.Matthews, F.Newton, Webster	2,813	3						8			6					5	4	10	9					1			2	11
			Appearances				25	33	41	6	4	3	2	3	2	14	22	8	33	6	5	18	39	2	34	4	39	37	2	20	2	2	18	38
			Goals					1	2	1									3		1		13		10		34						1	11

FINAL LEAGUE POSITION: 7th in Division Three North

FA Cup

No.	Date		Venue / Opponent	Result	Scorers	Att.	Boa	Boc	Gow	Hel	Job	Kea	Lin	MCH	NeF	NeW	Ric	Vin	Web
1	Nov	29	(a) Hartlepools U	W 3-2	F.Newton, Lincoln, Webster	6,038	8	2	1	6		5	10	7	9	4	3		11
2	Dec	13	(a) Bristol R	L 2-4	F.Newton 2	17,072	8	2	1	6		5	10	7	9	4	3		11
			Appearances				2	2	2	2		2	2	2	2	2	2		2
			Goals										1		3				1

Average Home League attendance: 6,946
Average Away League attendance: 5,196

1931-32

No.	Date		Opponent	Result	Scorers	Att	Barber	Beedles	Brown	Burns	Farrow	Gale	Griffiths	Hooley	Howe	Inglis	Jenkinson	Jennings	Jobson	Johnson	Jones	Lambourne	Lloyd	McGann	Nelson	Raisbeck	Rigby	Scullion	Shanks	Smith F.	Smith J.R.	Swift	Taylor	Vincent	Webster
1017	Aug 29	(a)	Doncaster R	D 1-1	Webster	6,264	6		10			1					4	2							8			9	3	7				5	11
1018	31	(h)	Crewe A	L 1-2	Vincent (pen)	8,320	6		10			1					4	2							8			9	3	7				5	11
1019	Sep 5	(h)	Southport	L 0-1		5,384	6		11	9		1					4			5			3		8			10		7		2			
1020	7	(h)	Rochdale	W 3-1	Scullion 2, Webster	3,941				9		1					4			5		6	3		8			10		7		2			11
1021	12	(a)	York C	L 0-1		4,130				9		1					4	10		5		6	3		8					7				2	11
1022	15	(h)	Rochdale	L 0-1		4,348				9		1					4	10		5		6	3		8			11		7				2	
1023	19	(h)	Tranmere R	L 0-1		4,676				9		1		7			4	10		5		6	3		8									2	11
1024	26	(a)	Rotherham U	D 1-1	Jennings	4,044		8				1		7			4	9		5			3					10					6	2	11
1025	Oct 3	(h)	Hull C	W 2-0	Swift, Jennings	4,815			10			1					4	8	5			6	3					9		7		2			11
1026	10	(a)	Accrington S	W 3-0	Webster, Brown, Vincent (pen)	5,254			10			1					4	8	5			6	3					9		7				2	11
1027	17	(a)	Lincoln C	W 2-1	Webster, Taylor	7,747			10			1					4	8	5			6	3							7			9	2	11
1028	24	(h)	Chester	D 0-0		8,811			10			1					4	8	5			6	3							7			9	2	11
1029	31	(a)	Hartlepools U	D 2-2	F.Smith, Taylor	3,502			10			1					4	8	5			6	3							7			9	2	11
1030	Nov 14	(a)	Darlington	L 0-2		3,672			10								4	8	5			6	3	1						7			9	2	11
1031	21	(h)	Halifax T	W 2-1	Lambourne 2	4,416			10			1					4		5	6		9	3		8					7				2	11
1032	Dec 5	(h)	Gateshead	D 1-1	Webster	4,081			10	9		1					4	8	5				3							7			6	2	11
1033	12	(a)	Crewe A	D 2-2	Shanks, Scullion	5,272		7				1						8	5				3					9	11	4			6	2	10
1034	19	(h)	Barrow	W 2-0	Opp own-goal, Vincent (pen)	3,267	5					1		7		4						8	3					9	10				6	2	11
1035	25	(h)	Carlisle U	D 0-0		7,142	5		10		8	1				4						6	3					9		7				2	11
1036	26	(a)	Carlisle U	D 1-1	Scullion	8,106	5				8	1				11	4					6	3				7	9						2	10
1037	30	(a)	New Brighton	L 1-2	Brown	1,741	9	3	7		8	1				2			5			6						10	11	4					
1038	Jan 2	(h)	Doncaster R	W 1-0	Lambourne	1,997			10		8	1		7		4			5			6	3					9	11					2	
1039	9	(a)	Walsall	L 1-3	Scullion	2,436	5		10		8	1		7		4						6	3					9	11					2	
1040	16	(a)	Southport	L 0-1		4,344	5		10		8	1		7		4					9	6	3											2	11
1041	23	(h)	York C	W 3-2	Griffiths 3	5,499	5		10			1	9	7		4						6	3		8									2	11
1042	30	(a)	Tranmere R	D 2-2	Griffiths 2	5,163	5		10			1	9			4						6	3		8				7					2	11
1043	Feb 6	(h)	Rotherham U	W 1-0	Brown	6,042	5		10			1	9	7		4						6	3		8									2	11
1044	13	(a)	Hull C	D 4-4	Nelson 2, Brown, Griffiths	6,149	5		10			1	9	7		4						6	3		8									2	11
1045	20	(a)	Accrington S	L 0-2		3,159	5		10			1	9	7		4						6	3		8									2	11
1046	27	(h)	Lincoln C	L 0-1		9,753	5		10			1	9	7		4		2				6	3		8										11
1047	Mar 5	(a)	Chester	L 1-2	Griffiths	6,759			10			1	9	7		4		2	5			6	3		8										11
1048	12	(a)	Hartlepools U	W 3-2	Nelson 3	4,400			10			1	9	7		4		2	5			6	3		8										11
1049	25	(h)	Wrexham	W 5-1	Nelson, Griffiths 2, Hooley, Vincent	5,114		3	10			1	9	7		4			5			6			8									2	11
1050	26	(a)	Darlington	W 1-0	Brown	4,651		3	10			1	9	7		4			5						8								6	2	11
1051	28	(a)	Wrexham	L 1-2	J.R.Smith	6,716						1		7		4			5		10	6	3		8						9			2	11
1052	Apr 2	(h)	Halifax T	D 2-2	Inglis, Griffiths	4,117			10			1	9	7		4			5		6	8	3											2	11
1053	9	(h)	Walsall	L 0-1		3,112			10			1	9	7		4			5		6	8	3											2	11
1054	16	(a)	Gateshead	L 1-2	Griffiths	8,655			10			1	9			4			5			6	3		8		7							2	11
1055	23	(h)	New Brighton	W 3-1	Jones 2, Webster	2,270						1	9			4			5		10	6	3		8				7					2	11
1056	30	(a)	Barrow	L 2-4	Lambourne, Vincent (pen)	3,861		8				1	9			4					10	6	3		7								5	2	11
			FINAL LEAGUE POSITION: 12th in Division Three North		Appearances		16	3	32	6	6	39	15	18	1	35	6	14	27	5	4	29	33	1	19	1	3	15	13	16	1	3	11	33	35
					Goals				5				11	1		1		2			2	4			6			5	1	1	1	1	2	5	6

Own-goal 1

FA Cup

No.	Date		Opponent	Result	Scorers	Att	Barber	Beedles	Brown	Burns	Farrow	Gale	Griffiths	Hooley	Howe	Inglis	Jenkinson	Jennings	Jobson	Johnson	Jones	Lambourne	Lloyd	McGann	Nelson	Raisbeck	Rigby	Scullion	Shanks	Smith F.	Smith J.R.	Swift	Taylor	Vincent	Webster
1	Nov 28	(a)	Crook T	L 1-3	F.Smith	4,990			10			1					4	8	5			9	3							7			6	2	11
					Appearances				1			1					1	1	1			1	1							1			1	1	1
					Goals																									1					

Average Home League attendance: 5,147
Average Away League attendance: 5,009

Wigan Borough resigned from the League on 26 October 1931 which was before County had played them.

1932-33

No	Date	Venue / Opponent	Result	Scorers	Att	Beedles	Carr	Downes	Foulkes	Gale	Griffiths	Howe	Humpish	Jenkinson	Johnman	Johnson	Lambourne	Lloyd	Lythgoe	McCann	Robinson	Stevers	Stevenson	Taylor	Vincent	Watson
1057	Aug 27	(h) Darlington	W 5-1	Griffiths 3, Stevenson, Downes	8,438		5	11	7	1	9		4	2			10	3					8	6		
1058	31	(a) York C	D 2-2	Downes, Lambourne	7,629		5	11	7	1	9		8	2			10	3						6	4	
1059	Sep 3	(a) Doncaster R	D 1-1	Griffiths	4,530		5	11	7	1	9		4	2			10	3					8	6		
1060	5	(h) York C	W 2-0	Stevenson, Downes	6,157		5	11	7	1	9		4	2			10	3					8	6		
1061	10	(h) Hull C	L 3-5	Lambourne, Griffiths 2	7,009		5	11	7	1	9		4	2			10	3					8	6		
1062	14	(a) Chester	D 2-2	Taylor, Griffiths	8,031		5	11	7	1	9		4	2			10	3					8	6		
1063	17	(a) Barnsley	D 2-2	Stevenson, Downes	6,662		5	11	7	1	9		4	2				3					8	10	6	
1064	24	(h) Hartlepools U	W 6-2	Griffiths 4, Downes, Taylor	6,725		5	11	7	1	9		4	2				3					8	10	6	
1065	29	(a) Carlisle U	L 1-2	Foulkes	5,169	3	5	11	7	1	9		4	2									8	10	6	
1066	Oct 1	(a) Halifax T	W 3-1	Stevenson, Griffiths, Foulkes	6,754		5	11	7	1	9		4	2				3					8	10	6	
1067	8	(h) Tranmere R	W 3-0	Humpish, Stevenson, Taylor	3,656		5	11	7	1	9		4	2				3					8	10	6	
1068	15	(a) Wrexham	L 0-2		6,921		5	11	7	1	9		4	2				3					8	10	6	
1069	22	(a) Crewe A	L 1-2	Vincent (pen)	6,610		5	11	7	1	9		4	2				3					8	10	6	
1070	29	(h) Rochdale	L 2-3	Humpish, Taylor	4,292		5	11	7	1	9		4	2				3					8	10	6	
1071	Nov 5	(a) Southport	L 1-2	Griffiths	5,255		10	11	7	1	9		4	2			6	3					8	5		
1072	12	(h) Mansfield T	D 2-2	Griffiths, Downes	5,498		10	11	7	1	9		4	2			6	3					8	5		
1073	19	(a) Rotherham U	L 1-2	Taylor	3,618	3	5	11	7	1			4				6		9				8	10	2	
1074	Dec 3	(a) New Brighton	D 1-1	Stevenson	2,261	3	5	11	7	1			4				6		9				8	10	2	
1075	17	(a) Barrow	W 3-0	Griffiths, Opp own-goal, Foulkes	3,620	3		11	7		9			2			10			1	4	5	8	6		
1076	24	(h) Carlisle U	L 0-1		4,068	3		11	7		9			2			10			1	4	5	8	6		
1077	26	(h) Walsall	W 5-0	Lythgoe 2, Lambourne 3	5,796		2	11									10	3	9	1	4	5	8	7	6	
1078	27	(h) Walsall	D 0-0		8,518	3		11	7		10			2						1	4	5	8	9	6	
1079	31	(a) Darlington	D 1-1	Taylor	3,202	3		11	7		10			2						1	4	5	8	9	6	
1080	Jan 7	(h) Doncaster R	W 5-1	Vincent (pen), Downes, Taylor, Robinson, Stevenson	4,770	3		11	7		10			2						1	4	5	8	9	6	
1081	14	(h) Accrington S	W 2-0	Griffiths, Stevenson	4,488	3		11	7		10			2						1	4	5	8	9	6	
1082	21	(a) Hull C	L 0-3		8,883	3		11			10			2					7	1	4	5	8	9	6	
1083	28	(h) Barnsley	W 5-4	Downes 2, Lythgoe 2, Taylor	3,414			11			10			2					7	1	4	5	8	9	6	
1084	Feb 4	(a) Hartlepool U	D 1-1	Lythgoe	4,027			11			10			2	6			3	9	1	4	5		7		8
1085	11	(h) Halifax T	W 6-0	Lythgoe, Vincent (pen), Griffiths 2, Stevenson, Foulkes	4,198			11	7		10			2				3	9	1		5	8	6	4	
1086	18	(a) Tranmere R	D 2-2	Lythgoe, Griffiths	2,410			11	7		10			2				3	9	1		5	8	6	4	
1087	Mar 3	(h) Crewe A	W 1-0	Lythgoe	5,934			11	7		9			2				3	10	1		5	8	6	4	
1088	11	(a) Rochdale	W 2-0	Lythgoe*, Foulkes	4,151			11	7		9			2				3	10	1		5	8	6		
1089	18	(h) Southport	W 3-1	Stevenson, Lythgoe, Griffiths	6,095			11	7		9		4	2				3	10	1		5	8	6		
1090	25	(a) Mansfield T	W 2-1	Vincent (pen), Stevenson	5,070			11	7		9		4	2				3	10	1		5	8	6		
1091	Apr 1	(h) Rotherham U	W 1-0	Humpish	5,087			11	7		9		8	2				3		1		5	10	6	4	
1092	8	(a) Accrington S	D 1-1	Lythgoe	2,404			11	7				8	2				3	9	1		5	10	6	4	
1093	14	(a) Gateshead	W 3-0	Lythgoe 3	7,041			11	7				8	2				3	9	1		5	10	6	4	
1094	15	(h) New Brighton	D 1-1	Vincent	6,041			11	7				8	2				3	9	1		5	10	6	4	
1095	17	(h) Gateshead	W 4-3	Stevenson, Griffiths, Humpish, Lythgoe	4,959						9	11	7	2				3	8	1		5	10	6	4	
1096	29	(h) Barrow	W 4-1	Vincent 2 (1 pen), Lythgoe, Stevenson	2,501			11	7				8	2				3	9	1		5	10	6	4	
1097	May 1	(a) Wrexham	W 1-0	Lythgoe	6,035			11	7				8	2				3	9	1		5	10	6	4	
1098	6	(h) Chester	W 8-5	Downes 2, Foulkes 2, Lythgoe 2, Humpish 2	4,255			11	7				8	2				3	9	1		5	10	6	4	
		Appearances				11	18	41	36	18	33	1	29	38	1	1	13	32	20	24	9	24	35	42	35	1
		Goals						11	7		21		6				5		19		1		13	8	7	

FINAL LEAGUE POSITION: 3rd in Division Three North

Own-goal 1

FA Cup

No	Date	Venue / Opponent	Result	Scorers	Att	Beedles	Carr	Downes	Foulkes	Gale	Griffiths	Howe	Humpish	Jenkinson	Johnman	Johnson	Lambourne	Lloyd	Lythgoe	McCann	Robinson	Stevers	Stevenson	Taylor	Vincent	Watson
1	Nov 26	(a) Rochdale	W 2-0	Taylor, Vincent (pen)	9,562	3	5	11	7	1			4				6		9				8	10	2	
2	Dec 10	(h) Luton T	L 2-3	Taylor, Foulkes	9,892	3	5	11	7	1	9		4				6						8	10	2	
		Appearances				2	2	2	2	2	1		2				2		1				2	2	2	
		Goals							1															2	1	

Average Home League attendance: 5,210
Average Away League attendance: 5,370

*Some sources give the scorer of this goal as 'Opp own-goal', but it appears that Lythgoe's header was over the line before Rochdale's full-back 'finished it off'.

1933-34

No	Date	V	Opponents	Res	Scorers	Att	Beedles	Downes	Feeney	Finnegan	Foulkes	Hill	Humpish	Jenkinson	Jones F	Jones L	Leckie	Lythgoe	McGann	Pick	Robinson	Stevens	Stevenson	Taylor HW	Taylor J	Vincent	Wilkins
1099	Aug 26	(h)	Accrington S	W 3-0	Vincent, Lythgoe 2	7,301	3	11			7		2	8				9	1			5	10		6	4	
1100	28	(h)	Doncaster R	W 4-3	Lythgoe 2, Humpish, Foulkes	6,428	3	11			7		2	8				9	1			5	10		6	4	
1101	Sep 2	(a)	Halifax T	L 2-4	Downes, Humpish	9,517	3	11			7		2	8		6		9	1			5	10			4	
1102	4	(a)	Doncaster R	W 2-0	Lythgoe, Stevenson	4,933		11			7		3	8		6		9	1		4	5	10			2	
1103	9	(h)	Crewe A	D 1-1	Lythgoe	9,631		11			7		3	8		6		9	1		4	5	10			2	
1104	16	(a)	New Brighton	L 1-2	Downes	5,265		11			7		3	8				9	1		4	5	10		6	2	
1105	23	(h)	Rotherham U	W 3-1	Lythgoe, Stevenson 2	4,763					7		3	8		6	11	9	1		4	5	10			2	
1106	30	(a)	Walsall	L 0-2		5,849		11			7		3	8		6			1		4	5	9			2	10
1107	Oct 7	(h)	York C	W 2-1	Foulkes, Wilkins	5,137		11			7		3	8		6			1		4	5	9			2	10
1108	14	(a)	Chester	D 1-1	Stevenson	6,153		11			7		3	8	9	6			1		4	5	10			2	
1109	21	(h)	Gateshead	W 1-0	Lythgoe	5,378		11			7		3	8		6		9	1		4	5	10			2	
1110	28	(a)	Darlington	W 2-1	Lythgoe 2	3,684		11			7		3	8		6		9	1		4	5	10			2	
1111	Nov 4	(a)	Southport	W 9-2	Stevenson 2, Downes 2, Lythgoe 4, Foulkes	5,242		11			7		3	8		6		9	1		4	5	10			2	
1112	11	(a)	Wrexham	W 1-0	Lythgoe	7,723		11			7		3	8		6		9	1		4	5	10			2	
1113	18	(h)	Hartlepools U	W 5-2	Lythgoe 2, Downes, Stevenson, Foulkes	7,437		11			7		3	8		6		9	1		4	5	10			2	
1114	Dec 2	(h)	Barnsley	D 1-1	Lythgoe	8,359		11			7		3	8		6		9	1		4	5	10			2	
1115	16	(h)	Rochdale	W 4-1	Foulkes, Stevenson, Lythgoe 2	3,790		11			7		3	8		6		9	1		4	5	10			2	
1116	23	(a)	Chesterfield	L 0-1		12,544		11			7		3	8		6		9	1		4	5	10			2	
1117	25	(h)	Carlisle U	W 4-0	Stevenson, Foulkes 2, Lythgoe	9,781		11			7		3	8		6		9	1		4	5	10			2	
1118	26	(a)	Carlisle U	D 2-2	Hill, Lythgoe	7,364		11			7	8		3		6		9	1		4	5	10			2	
1119	30	(a)	Accrington S	W 3-0	Foulkes, Downes, Lythgoe	2,665		11			7	8		3		6		9	1		4	5	10			2	
1120	Jan 6	(h)	Halifax T	W 13-0	Hill 3, Lythgoe 2, Vincent (pen), Foulkes, Downes 4, Stevenson 2	7,807		11			7	8		3		6		9	1		4	5	10			2	
1121	13	(a)	Mansfield T	D 1-1	Lythgoe	5,191		11			7	8		3		6		9	1		4	5	10			2	
1122	20	(a)	Crewe A	D 2-2	Lythgoe 2	7,394		11			7	8		3		6		9	1		4	5	10			2	
1123	27	(h)	New Brighton	W 5-1	Foulkes, Vincent, Stevenson, Lythgoe 2	9,448		11			7	8		3		6		9	1		4	5	10			2	
1124	Feb 3	(a)	Rotherham U	D 1-1	Foulkes	5,284		11			7	8		3		6		9	1		4	5	10			2	
1125	10	(h)	Walsall	W 3-2	Stevenson 2, Vincent (pen)	11,214		11			7	8		3		6		9	1		4	5	10			2	
1126	17	(a)	York C	D 2-2	Hill 2	5,030		11			7	8		3		6		9	1		4	5	10			2	
1127	24	(h)	Chester	W 4-2	Robinson, Vincent 2 (1 pen), Hill	10,973		11			7	8		3		6		9	1		4	5	10			2	
1128	Mar 3	(a)	Gateshead	W 4-0	Humpish, Downes, Foulkes, Lythgoe	2,922		11			7	8	10	3		6		9	1		4	5				2	
1129	10	(h)	Darlington	W 6-0	Lythgoe 3, Downes, Robinson 2	7,394		11			7	8	10	3		6		9	1		4	5				2	
1130	17	(a)	Southport	W 4-1	Lythgoe 3, Hill	3,621		11			7	8	10	3		6		9	1		4	5				2	
1131	24	(h)	Wrexham	W 7-3	Foulkes, Lythgoe 4, Robinson, Vincent	10,911		11			7	8	10	3		6		9	1		4	5				2	
1132	30	(h)	Barrow	W 4-1	Downes, Humpish 2, Lythgoe	17,308		11		1	7		3	8		6		9			4	5	10			2	
1133	31	(a)	Hartlepools U	L 1-3	Downes	4,766		11		1	7		3	8		6		9			4	5	10			2	
1134	Apr 2	(a)	Barrow	L 0-2		8,049		11		1	7		10	3		6		9			4	5			8	2	
1135	7	(h)	Mansfield T	W 3-1	Lythgoe 3	8,789		11		1	7		3	8		6		9			4	5	10			2	
1136	14	(a)	Barnsley	L 0-2		26,366		11		1	7		3	8		6		9			4	5	10			2	
1137	21	(h)	Tranmere R	W 2-1	Downes 2	9,422		11		1	7			3				9			4	5	10	8	6	2	
1138	23	(a)	Tranmere R	D 1-1	Vincent	4,650		11	8	1	7			3		6		9			4	5	10			2	
1139	28	(a)	Rochdale	D 1-1	Stevenson	7,544		11	8	1	7			3		6		9			4	5	10			2	
1140	May 5	(h)	Chesterfield	D 0-0		21,309		11		1	7		3	8		6		9			4	5	10			2	
					Appearances		3	41	2	9	42	14	29	42	1	38	5	39	28	1	39	42	37	1	4	42	3
					Goals			16			13	8	5					46			4		15			7	1

FINAL LEAGUE POSITION: 3rd in Division Three North

FA Cup

No	Date	V	Opponents	Res	Scorers	Att	Downes	Foulkes	Humpish	Jenkinson	Jones L	Lythgoe	McGann	Robinson	Stevens	Stevenson	Vincent
1	Nov 25	(a)	Lancaster	W 1-0	Lythgoe	7,345	11	7	3	8	6	9	1	4	5	10	2
2	Dec 9	(h)	Crystal P	L 1-2	Vincent	17,422	11	7	3	8	6	9	1	4	5	10	2
					Appearances		2	2	2	2	2	2	2	2	2	2	2
					Goals							1					1

Average Home League attendance: 8,944
Average Away League attendance: 6,977

1934-35

Division Three North

No.	Date		Opponent	Res.	Scorers	Att.
1141	Aug 25	(h)	Southport	W 6-1	Lythgoe 5 (1 pen), Foulkes	11,616
1142	29	(a)	York C	L 1-3	Lythgoe (pen)	5,177
1143	Sep 1	(a)	Doncaster R	W 4-3	Caiels, Foulkes 2, Green	10,052
1144	3	(h)	York C	D 0-0		10,519
1145	8	(h)	Hartlepools U	W 3-2	Hill, Lythgoe, Green	9,586
1146	15	(a)	Crewe A	W 3-2	McKenzie 2, Lythgoe	7,104
1147	22	(h)	Mansfield T	L 0-2		5,932
1148	29	(h)	Gateshead	W 5-1	Lythgoe 3, Green, McKenzie	4,548
1149	Oct 6	(a)	Accrington S	L 1-3	Lythgoe	2,792
1150	13	(h)	Darlington	W 3-0	Hill, Stevenson 2	9,165
1151	20	(a)	Barrow	W 4-1	Lythgoe 3, Dunkerley	6,079
1152	27	(a)	Carlisle U	W 2-0	McNaughton, Stevenson	7,578
1153	Nov 3	(a)	Rochdale	W 5-0	McNaughton 2, Dunkerley, Stevenson 2	5,045
1154	10	(a)	Lincoln C	L 1-2	McNaughton	9,950
1155	17	(a)	Tranmere R	L 1-3	Foulkes	9,307
1156	Dec 1	(a)	Halifax T	L 1-2	Welsby	10,024
1157	15	(a)	Walsall	L 1-3	Foulkes	5,973
1158	22	(h)	Chesterfield	W 4-2	Stevenson, Green 2 (1 pen), Foulkes	8,133
1159	25	(a)	Chester	L 1-5	Welsby	7,686
1160	26	(h)	Chester	L 0-1		14,196
1161	29	(a)	Southport	W 2-1	Robinson 2	2,884
1162	Jan 1	(h)	Rotherham U	W 4-0	Urwin, Hill, Stevenson 2	4,661
1163	5	(a)	Doncaster R	W 3-2	Hill 2, Urwin	9,038
1164	19	(a)	Hartlepools U	L 0-4		2,626
1165	Feb 2	(a)	Mansfield T	L 2-3	McNaughton (pen), Stevenson	5,295
1166	6	(h)	Crewe A	W 4-0	McNaughton 2, Stevenson, Opp own-goal	2,739
1167	9	(a)	Gateshead	L 2-3	McNaughton 2	3,924
1168	20	(h)	Accrington S	W 5-1	Hill, McNaughton 2, Green	1,714
1169	23	(a)	Darlington	D 0-0		4,518
1170	Mar 2	(h)	Barrow	W 4-1	Green, Hill, Stanger, McNaughton	7,001
1171	9	(a)	Carlisle U	W 2-1	Collins, Aspinall	5,968
1172	16	(h)	Rochdale	W 3-1	Hill, McNaughton, Stanger	7,735
1173	23	(a)	Lincoln C	L 0-3		3,109
1174	30	(h)	Tranmere R	W 1-0	Dunkerley	9,535
1175	Apr 6	(a)	Wrexham	L 1-2	Green (pen)	3,193
1176	13	(h)	Halifax T	W 2-1	Foulkes, Green	7,257
1177	19	(a)	New Brighton	W 2-1	Robinson, Hill	5,460
1178	22	(h)	New Brighton	D 1-1	Opp own-goal	6,887
1179	25*	(a)	Rotherham U	L 0-2		3,881
1180	27	(h)	Walsall	L 0-3		4,461
1181	29	(h)	Wrexham	W 6-1	Hill 2, Green 2 (1 pen), McNaughton 2	2,147
1182	May 4	(a)	Chesterfield	L 0-5		2,440

FINAL LEAGUE POSITION: 7th in Division Three North

Player columns: Aspinall, Betton, Bocking, Bullock, Caiels, Cant, Collins, Dunkerley, Finnegan, Foulkes, Green, Haigh, Hales, Hill, Jenkinson, Jones, Lumberg, Lythgoe, McDonough, McKenzie Dr, McNaughton, Robinson, Scott, Smith, Stanger, Stevenson, Still, Taylor HW, Taylor J, Titterington, Urwin, Welsby

Appearances: 1, 2, 37, 2, 2, 1, 6, 9, 17, 35, 28, 7, 16, 37, 36, 41, 2, 10, 24, 7, 15, 36, 2, 1, 7, 24, 28, 8, 8, 1, 6, 4

Goals: 1, 1, 1, 3, 7, 11, 12, 15, 3, 15, 3, 2, 10, 2, 2

Wilson played number 3 in match 1179; number 2 in match 1182.

Own-goals 2

FA Cup

No.	Date		Opponent	Res.	Scorers	Att.
1	Nov 24	(a)	Blyth Spartans	D 1-1	Foulkes	7,173
R	28	(h)	Blyth Spartans	W 4-1	Urwin, Stevenson 2, Foulkes	5,905
2	Dec 8	(h)	Darlington	W 3-2	Green 2 (1 pen), Hill	12,113
3	Jan 12	(a)	West Ham U	D 1-1	Foulkes	26,400
R	16	(h)	West Ham U	W 1-0	Hill	17,911
4	26	(a)	Bradford C	D 0-0		30,767
R	31	(h)	Bradford C	W 3-2§	Green, Hill 2	22,096
5	Feb 16	(h)	West Brom A	L 0-5		24,604

Appearances: 8, 3, 7, 6, 5, 8, 8, 8, 5, 2, 8, 3, 8, 5, 4

Goals: 3, 3, 4, 2, 1

Average Home League attendance: 7,352
Average Away League attendance: 5,359

*This was the 'replay' of a game played at Rotherham on 20 April which was abandoned after 77 minutes due to a freak thunderstorm with the score 1-0 to Rotherham. The team was the same as that for Match 1177 with the exception of McNaughton replacing Collins.
§After extra-time.

1935-36

No.	Date		Opponents	Result	Scorers	Att.	Bocking	Brennan	Brown	Daniels	Ferguson	Foulkes	Green	Haigh	Hill	Jenkinson	Jones	Mawson	McDonough	McNaughton	Pollock	Robinson	Scott A	Scott WJ	Smith	Stanger	Stevenson	Still	Sullivan	Taylor	Tidman	Titterington	Torbet
1183	Aug 31	(a)	York C	W 4-0	McNaughton 2, Brennan, Hill	6,605	2	10			7				8	3	5		1	9		4						6		11			
1184	Sep 2	(h)	Rochdale	W 4-0	Tidman 2, Brennan, McNaughton	11,919	2	10			7				8	3	5		1	9		4						6			11		
1185	7	(h)	Barrow	W 2-1	Hill, McNaughton	12,661	2	10			7				8	3	5		1	9		4						6		11			
1186	10	(a)	Rochdale	D 1-1	Robinson	10,238		10			7					3	5		1	9		4	2					6		11	8		
1187	14	(a)	New Brighton	L 0-2		4,969	2	10			7					3	5		1	9		4						6		11	8		
1188	16	(a)	Lincoln C	L 0-3*		7,020	2	10			7					3	5	8	1	9		4						6				11	
1189	21	(h)	Chesterfield	D 2-2	Foulkes, Opp own-goal	9,381	2	10			7					3	5	8	1	9		4						6				11	
1190	23	(h)	Wrexham	W 3-2	McNaughton 2, Hill	6,228		10							8	3	5		1	9		4	2			7		6				11	
1191	28	(a)	Carlisle U	L 1-2	Green (pen)	8,338	2						10		8	3	5		1	9		4				7		6				11	
1192	Oct 5	(a)	Crewe A	W 1-0	McNaughton	6,204	2				7		10		8	3	5		1	9		4						6					11
1193	12	(h)	Accrington S	L 1-2	Torbet	8,066	2				7		10		8	3	5		1	9		4						6					11
1194	19	(h)	Walsall	L 0-1		5,251	2	10		1					8	3	5			9		4						6					11
1195	26	(a)	Tranmere R	L 1-4	Green	8,097	2				7		10		8	3	5		1	9		4						6		11			
1196	Nov 2	(h)	Gateshead	W 3-1	Hill, Green, Tidman	6,028	2						10		8	3	5		1	9		4				7		6			11		
1197	9	(a)	Darlington	L 1-3	Hill	2,990	2						10		8	3	5		1	9		4				7		6			11		
1198	16	(h)	Halifax T	W 1-0	Green (pen)	6,611	2				7	4	10		8	3	5		1	9								6			11		
1199	23	(a)	Oldham A	W 3-1	Foulkes 2, Hill	9,901	2				7	4			8	3	5		1	9								6			11		
1200	Dec 7	(a)	Rotherham U	D 1-1	Green	5,938	2					4	10		8	3	5		1	9	7							6			11		
1201	14	(h)	Mansfield T	W 6-1	McNaughton 5, Robinson	5,268	2					4	10		8	3	5		1	9	7		2					6			11		
1202	21	(a)	Hartlepools U	D 1-1	McNaughton	3,375	2					4	10		8	3	5		1	9	7		2					6			11		
1203	25	(a)	Southport	W 3-2	Green, McNaughton, Hill	3,896	2					4	10		8	3	5		1	9	7		2					6			11		
1204	26	(h)	Southport	W 2-0	Hill 2	8,816	2					4	10		8	3	5		1	9			2			7		6			11		
1205	28	(h)	York C	W 3-2	McNaughton, Hill 2	6,394	2					4	10	6	8	3	5		1	9			2			7					11		
1206	Jan 4	(a)	Barrow	L 0-1		5,784	2					4	10	6	8	3	5		1	9			2			7					11		
1207	18	(h)	New Brighton	D 1-1	Green (pen)	5,226	2						11		8	3	5		1	10	7	9						6	4				
1208	Feb 1	(h)	Carlisle U	W 2-0	A.Scott 2	7,075	2				7	4				3	5		1	9	11		10	8				6					
1209	8	(h)	Crewe A	L 0-1		8,349	2	10			7	4				3	5		1		9							6	11		8		
1210	15	(a)	Accrington S	D 1-1	McNaughton	4,928	2				7		10		8	3	5		1	9								6	4	11			
1211	29	(h)	Darlington§	W 2-0	McNaughton, Hill	3,771	2			1	7				8	3	5			9	11	4						6				10	
1212	Mar 7	(a)	Gateshead	L 0-1		3,639	2			1	7				8	3	5			9	11	4						6				10	
1213	14	(h)	Tranmere R	W 2-1	Hill, Foulkes	11,702	2				7				8	3	5		1	9	11	4						6				10	
1214	21	(a)	Halifax T	D 0-0		5,167			2		7				8	3	5		1	9	11	4						6				10	
1215	28	(h)	Oldham A	W 2-0	Hill, Titterington	8,232	2				7				8	3	5		1	9	11	4	2					6				10	
1216	30	(h)	Chesterfield	D 0-0		8,388					7	4			8	3	5		1	9	11		2					6				10	
1217	Apr 4	(a)	Wrexham	L 0-4		2,208					7	4			8	3	5		1	9	11		2					6				10	
1218	10	(a)	Chester	L 0-2		10,500	2				7				8	3	5		1	9		4						6	11			10	
1219	11	(h)	Rotherham U	L 1-2	Still	5,231	2	10			7	4			8	3	5		1									6	11			9	
1220	13	(h)	Chester	W 2-0	Hill, Tidman	6,750	2				7	9			8	3	5		1			4						6		11	10		
1221	14†	(a)	Walsall	W 1-0	Robinson (pen)	4,298					7	9			8	3			1	9		4	2	5				6		11	10		
1222	18	(a)	Mansfield T	L 1-2	Hill	4,508					7	9	10		8	3			1			4	2	5				6		11			
1223	25	(h)	Hartlepools U	W 2-1	Green, Hill	3,008	2				7		9		8	3	5		1			4						6		11	10		
1224	May 2	(h)	Lincoln C	W 4-0	Hill 2, Sullivan, Titterington	4,509	2				7				8	3	5		1			4						6	9	11		10	
			FINAL LEAGUE POSITION: 5th in Division Three North			**Appearances**	30	10	1	3	15	30	20	3	36	42	40	3	39	35	7	31	3	11	2	7	1	29	4	13	24	17	6
						Goals		2				4	8		19					17		3	2					1	1		4	2	1

Own-goal 1

FA Cup

Rnd	Date		Opponents	Result	Scorers	Att.	Bocking	Brennan	Brown	Daniels	Ferguson	Foulkes	Green	Haigh	Hill	Jenkinson	Jones	Mawson	McDonough	McNaughton	Pollock	Robinson	Scott A	Scott WJ	Smith	Stanger	Stevenson	Still	Sullivan	Taylor	Tidman	Titterington	Torbet
3‡	Jan 11	(h)	Plymouth A	L 2-3	Opp own-goal, McNaughton	16,844						4	10		8	3	5		1	9		11	2			7		6					
						Appearances						1	1		1	1	1		1	1		1	1			1		1					
						Goals														1													

Own-goal 1

Average Home League attendance: 7,166
Average Away League attendance: 6,047

*All three of Lincoln's goals were penalties and this is the only occasion on which County have lost to three penalty goals.

§Fixtures were rearranged on this date as a result of a dispute between the Football League and the Pools' Companies. Stockport were due to play league-leaders Tranmere Rovers.

†This was the 'replay' of a game played at Walsall on 22 February which was abandoned after 34 minutes due to snow and sleet with the score at 0-0, the team being the same as that for Match 1211 with the exception of Stevenson replacing Green.

‡Stockport were exempt from the first two rounds as a result of their Cup feat the previous season in reaching the fifth round.

1936-37

No.	Date	Opponent	Res.	Scorers	Att.	Bocking	Brown	Daniels	Gore	Harker	Hill	Jenkinson	Jones GF	Jones L	Leach	Mantle	McDonough	Molloy	Oxley	Reid	Rice	Scott	Smailes	Stevens	Still	Sullivan	Taylor	Titterington
1225	Aug 29 (h)	Darlington	D 3-3	Smailes, Stevens (pen), Hill	11,039	2					8	3		4	5		1		7				11	9	6			10
1226	Sep 2 (a)	Gateshead	D 0-0		3,978	2					8	3		4	5		1		7				11	9	6			10
1227	5 (a)	Wrexham	D 0-0		8,599	2					8	3		4	5		1		7				11	9	6			10
1228	7 (h)	Gateshead	W 4-2	Hill 2, Stevens, Smails	6,834	2					8	3		4	5		1		7				11	9	6			10
1229	12 (h)	Rochdale	W 3-0	Smailes, Leach 2 (1 pen)	6,722	2					8	3		4	5		1		7				11	9	6			10
1230	14 (a)	Lincoln C	W 2-0	Hill, Stevens	7,011	2					8	3		4	5		1		7				11	9	6			10
1231	19 (h)	Rotherham U	W 4-2	Titterington 2, Hill 2	10,630	2					8	3		4	5		1		7				11	9	6			10
1232	26 (a)	Port Vale	L 0-3		9,407	2					8	3		4	5		1		7				11	9	6			10
1233	Oct 3 (h)	Oldham A	W 4-1	Smailes, Leach (pen), Titterington, Hill	11,958	2			7		8	3		4	5		1						11	9	6			10
1234	10 (a)	Accrington S	L 1-2	Gore	4,066	2			7		8	3		4	5		1			9			11		6			10
1235	17 (a)	Barrow	D 0-0		4,310	2			7		8	3		4	5		1			9			11		6			10
1236	24 (a)	York C	W 6-0	Leach, Hill 3, Oxley, Sullivan	9,835	2		1			8	3		4	5				7	9					6	11		10
1237	31 (a)	Carlisle U	L 0-1		7,946	2					8	3		4	5		1		7					9	6	11		10
1238	Nov 7 (h)	Hartlepools U	D 1-1	Hill	8,092	2					8	3		4	5		1		7				11	9	6			10
1239	14 (a)	Southport	D 1-1	Titterington	6,973	2					8	3		4	5		1		7				11		6	9		10
1240	21 (h)	Tranmere R	W 5-0	Oxley, Opp own-goal 2, Titterington, Sullivan	8,507	2					8	3		5			1	4	7	9					6	11		10
1241	Dec 5 (h)	Mansfield T	W 3-1	Oxley, Scott 2	5,913	2					9	3		5			1		7	4		10			6	11		8
1242	19 (h)	Chester	W 4-0	Scott, Hill 3	13,051	2					8	3		5			1		7			9	10		6	11		4
1243	25 (a)	New Brighton	D 1-1	Sullivan	5,618	2			7		8	3		5			1					9	10		6	11		4
1244	26 (a)	Darlington	D 1-1	Smailes	8,148	2			7		8	3		5			1					9	10		6	11		4
1245	28* (h)	New Brighton	W 3-1	Scott, Sullivan, Hill	5,368	2			7		8	3		5			1					9	10		6	11		4
1246	Jan 2 (h)	Wrexham	W 2-0	Stevens, Smailes	10,164	2					8	3		5			1		7				10	9	6	11		4
1247	9 (a)	Rochdale	D 2-2	Hill, Sullivan	10,034	2					8	3		5			1					9	10	7	6	11		4
1248	16 (a)	Halifax T	D 1-1	Reid	8,918	2					8	3		5			1		7	9			10		6	11		4
1249	23 (a)	Rotherham U	D 1-1	Reid	2,294	2					8	3		5			1			9			10	7	6	11		4
1250	30 (h)	Port Vale	W 1-0	Oxley	10,690	2					8	3		5			1		7	9			10		6	11		4
1251	Feb 6 (a)	Oldham A	W 2-0	Taylor, Mantle	23,142	2						3		5		9	1	4	7						6	11	10	8
1252	13 (h)	Accrington S	W 3-2	Taylor, Titterington, Mantle	13,515	2						3		5		9	1	4	7				11		6		10	8
1253	20 (h)	Barrow	W 4-1	Taylor, Mantle, Smailes 2	10,708		2					3		5		9	1	4	7				11		6		10	8
1254	27 (a)	York C	L 1-2	Mantle	3,993	2						3		5		9	1	4	7				11		6		10	8
1255	Mar 6 (a)	Carlisle U	L 1-2	Hill	12,365	2					8	3		5		9	1		7				11		6		10	4
1256	13 (a)	Hartlepools U	W 4-2	Hill, Mantle, Titterington, Oxley	7,105	2					8	3		5		9	1	4	7				11		6			10
1257	20 (h)	Southport	W 2-1	Mantle, Hill	12,075	2					8	3		5		9	1	4	7				11		6			10
1258	26 (h)	Hull C	W 3-1	Oxley, Mantle, Hill	13,580						8		2	3	5	9	1	4	7						6	11		10
1259	27 (a)	Tranmere R	D 2-2	Sullivan, Oxley	10,008						8		2	3	5	9	1	4	7						6	11		10
1260	29 (h)	Hull C	W 1-0	Sullivan	11,230								2	3	5	9	1	4	7	8					6	11		10
1261	Apr 3 (h)	Halifax T	D 0-0		14,048					4	8		2	3	5		1		7				11	9	6			10
1262	10 (a)	Mansfield T	W 2-0	Stevens, Reid	6,359								2	3	5		1		7	8	11		10	9	6			4
1263	17 (h)	Crewe A	W 1-0	Oxley	10,009								2	3	5		1		7	8	9		10		6	11		4
1264	19 (a)	Crewe A	W 2-1	L.Jones, Smailes	7,503								2	3	5		1		7	8	9		10		6	11		4
1265	24 (a)	Chester	D 1-1	Smailes	15,255								2	3	5		1		7	8	9		10		6	11		4
1266	May 1 (h)	Lincoln C	W 2-0	Hill§, Stevens (pen)	†26,135					4	8		2	3	5		1		7				11	9	6			10
		Appearances				32	1	1	7	2	32	41	9	42	16	10	41	10	32	11	4	6	35	19	40	21	8	42
		Goals							1		21			1	4	7			8	3		4	10	6		7	3	7

FINAL LEAGUE POSITION: Champions of Division Three North - Promoted to Division 2

Own-goals 2

FA Cup

No.	Date	Opponent	Res.	Scorers	Att.	Bocking	Brown	Daniels	Gore	Harker	Hill	Jenkinson	Jones GF	Jones L	Leach	Mantle	McDonough	Molloy	Oxley	Reid	Rice	Scott	Smailes	Stevens	Still	Sullivan	Taylor	Titterington
1	Nov 28 (a)	Carlisle U	L 1-2	Still	12,443	2					9	3		5			1		7	4		10			6	11		8
		Appearances				1					1	1		1			1		1	1		1			1	1		1
		Goals																							1			

Average Home League attendance: 11,011
Average Away League attendance: 8,186

*This was the 'replay' of a game played at Edgeley Park on 12 December which was abandoned after 77 minutes due to fog with the score at 1-1 (Hill), the team being the same as that for Match 1240 with the exception of Leach replacing Reid.

§Stockport's players and manager believed Hill to be the goalscorer although most newspapers reported the scorer to be Smailes.

†The attendance for this game was reported as being either 27,303 or 27,304 but the figure shown is that *officially* recorded by the Football League.

1937-38

No.	Date		Opponent	Result	Scorers	Att.
1267	Aug 28	(h)	Luton T	W 2-1	Smailes, Oxley	19,077
1268	Sep 1	(a)	Nottingham F	W 2-1	Mantle 2	14,087
1269	4	(a)	Barnsley	L 0-2		13,408
1270	6	(h)	Nottingham F	W 1-0	Mantle (pen)	14,124
1271	11	(h)	West Ham U	D 0-0		17,781
1272	13	(a)	Coventry C	L 0-1		18,247
1273	18	(h)	Manchester U	W 1-0	Mantle	24,386
1274	25	(a)	Sheffield U	L 0-2		23,381
1275	Oct 2	(h)	Tottenham H	W 3-2	Jenkinson, Taylor, Titterington	19,069
1276	9	(a)	Burnley	D 0-0		16,423
1277	16	(a)	Southampton	L 1-4	Mantle	20,039
1278	23	(h)	Blackburn R	L 0-1		13,766
1279	30	(a)	Sheffield W	D 3-3	Stevens, Oxley, Hill	14,272
1280	Nov 6	(h)	Fulham	W 2-0	Hill, Reid	15,201
1281	13	(a)	Plymouth A	L 1-2	Kennedy	20,771
1282	20	(h)	Norwich C	D 1-1	Stevens	11,021
1283	27	(a)	Swansea T	W 2-0	Fuller, Stevens	8,993
1284	Dec 4	(h)	Chesterfield	D 1-1	Smailes	10,275
1285	11	(a)	Aston Villa	L 1-7	Reid	27,500
1286	18	(h)	Bradford	L 1-2	Reid	10,375
1287	25	(a)	Newcastle U	D 0-0		29,736
1288	Jan 1	(a)	Luton T	L 4-6	Hunt, Harker 2, Smailes	14,138
1289	15	(h)	Barnsley	L 1-2	Titterington	7,772
1290	22	(a)	West Ham U	L 0-1		19,143
1291	29	(a)	Manchester U	L 1-3	Smailes	31,852
1292	Feb 5	(h)	Sheffield U	D 1-1	Hunt	18,627
1293	19	(h)	Burnley	W 3-1	Opp own-goal, Hill, Smailes	14,097
1294	23	(a)	Tottenham H	L 0-2		11,049
1295	26	(h)	Southampton	D 0-0		13,226
1296	Mar 2*	(h)	Newcastle U	L 1-3	Reid	8,629
1297	5	(a)	Blackburn R	L 0-3		14,980
1298	12	(h)	Sheffield W	W 2-1	Smailes 2	15,282
1299	19	(a)	Fulham	L 0-2		16,426
1300	26	(h)	Plymouth A	L 1-3	Lythgoe	13,794
1301	Apr 2	(a)	Norwich C	L 0-1		10,142
1302	9	(h)	Swansea T	W 1-0	Lythgoe	11,344
1303	15	(a)	Bury	W 3-1	Lythgoe, Reid (pen), Sargeant	12,469
1304	16	(a)	Chesterfield	L 0-1		9,710
1305	18	(h)	Bury	L 0-1		15,064
1306	23	(h)	Aston Villa	L 1-3	Lythgoe	19,987
1307	30§	(a)	Bradford	L 1-4	Reid	6,215
1308	May 7	(h)	Coventry C	D 1-1	Sargeant	9,486

FINAL LEAGUE POSITION: 22nd in Division 2 - Relegated to Division Three North

Player appearances grid

Player columns (left to right): Amey, Beardshaw, Bocking, Brown, Daniels, Fuller, Harker, Hill, Hunt, Jackson, Jenkinson, Jones G.I., Jones L, Kennedy, Lewis, Lumby, Lythgoe, Mantle, McArdle, McDonough, Oxley, Reid, Rice, Rigby, Sargeant, Smailes, Stevens, Still, Sullivan, Taylor, Titterington, West

	Ame	Bea	Boc	Bro	Dan	Ful	Har	Hil	Hun	Jac	Jen	JGI	JoL	Ken	Lew	Lum	Lyt	Man	McA	McD	Oxl	Rei	Ric	Rig	Sar	Sma	Ste	Sti	Sul	Tay	Tit	Wes
Appearances	1	18	5	6	5	3	15	14	11	9	40	21	21	6	1	6	12	12	4	28	36	36	11	9	9	28	9	33	2	11	32	1
Goals						1	2	3	2		1			1			4	5			2	6			2	7	3			1	2	

Woodward played No.10 in matches 1291-1295; No.9 in match 1296; No.10 in match 1300. Own-goal 1

FA Cup

Rd	Date		Opponent	Result	Att.
3	Jan 8	(a)	Middlesbrough	L 0-2	34,757

	Bea	Hil	Jen	JoL	Oxl	Rei	Ric	Sma	Ste	Tit	Wes
Appearances	1	1	1	1	1	1	1	1	1	1	1
Goals											

(FA Cup line values read across grid: Beardshaw 2, Harker 8, Jenkinson 3, Jones L 5, Oxley 1, Reid 7, Rice 4, Smailes 11, Stevens 6, Titterington 9, West 10)

Average Home League attendance: 14,399
Average Away League attendance: 16,809

*This was the 'replay' of a game played at Edgeley Park on 27 December which was abandoned after 75 minutes due to fog with the score at 2-2 (Oxley, Hunt), the team being the same as for Match 1287.

§This match had a kick-off time of 6 pm because of the likely affect of the number of people listening to the 'live' radio transmission of the FA Cup Final between Preston North End and Huddersfield Town.

1938-39

#	Date		Opponent	Res	Scorers	Att	Arthur	Bagley	Bowles	Burrows	Essex	Haigh	Harker	Jackson	Jenkinson	Jones	Law	Lumby	Lythgoe	Owens	Reid	Rigby	Sargeant	Sherwood	Smith	Still	Stock	Titterington	Topping	West
1309	Aug 27	(a)	New Brighton	D 0-0		5,782		7	1		8				2				9		5		11	10	3	6		4		
1310	29	(h)	Accrington S	W 3-0	Bagley, Essex, Sherwood	9,772		7	1		8				2				9		5		11	10	3	6		4		
1311	Sep 3	(h)	Barrow	W 3-1	Lythgoe, Sargeant, Bagley	7,697		7	1		8				2				9		5		11	10	3	6		4		
1312	5	(a)	Halifax T	D 3-3	Lythgoe, Sargeant, Essex	6,822		7	1		8	3			2				9		5		11	10		6		4		
1313	10	(a)	Chester	L 3-4	Reid, Lythgoe, Essex	9,779		7	1		8	3			2				9		5		11	10		6		4		
1314	17	(h)	Bradford C	W 2-0	Bagley, Reid (pen)	10,482		7	1		8				2				9		5		11	10	3	6		4		
1315	24	(a)	Hull C	D 4-4	Essex, Sargeant 2, Sherwood	8,652		7	1		8				2				9		5		11	10	3	6		4		
1316	Oct 1	(h)	Lincoln C	D 3-3	Reid, Lythgoe, Bagley	10,261		7	1		8		5		2				9		4		11	10	3	6				
1317	8	(a)	Southport	L 0-3		6,509		7	1		8				2				9		5		11	10	3	6		4		
1318	15	(h)	Crewe A	W 5-1	Sargeant, Essex, Sherwood, Bagley 2	15,751		7	1		8				2				9		4		11	10	3	6		5		
1319	22	(a)	Carlisle U	L 2-3	Lythgoe, Bagley	5,776		7	1		8		5	6	2				9		4		11	10	3					
1320	29	(h)	Darlington	W 5-2	Lythgoe, Sherwood 2, Sargeant 2	10,182		7			8		6		2	5			9		4	1	11	10	3					
1321	Nov 5	(a)	Hartlepools U	L 2-4	Essex, Lythgoe	6,519		7			8		6		2	5			9		4	1	11	10	3					
1322	12	(h)	Gateshead	W 3-2	Lythgoe 2, Sargeant	9,425		7	1		8		6		2				9		4		11	10	3	5				
1323	19	(a)	Wrexham	L 1-2	Essex	4,923		7	1		8		4		2				9		5		11	10	3	6				
1324	Dec 3	(a)	Rochdale	W 1-0	Sargeant	6,293		7	1		8		5		2				9				11	10	3	6		4		
1325	17	(a)	Doncaster R	L 1-3	West	8,217		7	1		8		5			6				3	4		10	2	11					9
1326	24	(h)	New Brighton	D 1-1	Lythgoe	6,537		7	1		8		5						9	3	4		11	10		6				
1327	27	(h)	Oldham A	W 3-1	Lumby, Reid 2	15,431		7	1		8							4	9	3	2		11	10		6	5			
1328	31	(a)	Barrow	W 2-0	Reid, Lythgoe	7,792		7	1		8				2				9	3	4		11	10		6		5		
1329	Jan 2	(h)	Rotherham U	W 5-0	Bagley, Lythgoe, Essex 2, Reid (pen)	10,044		7	1		8				2				9	3	4		11	10		6		5		
1330	14	(h)	Chester	D 0-0		10,781		7	1		8				2	9				3	4		11	10		6		5		
1331	25	(a)	Bradford C	L 0-4		2,150		7	1		9				2	8				3	4		11	10		6		5		
1332	28	(h)	Hull C	D 2-2	Sargeant, Sherwood	7,638		7	1		8								9	3	4		11	10	2	6		5		
1333	Feb 4	(a)	Lincoln C	L 2-3	Sherwood, Lythgoe	6,202		7	1		8					5			9	3	4		11	10	2			6		
1334	11	(h)	Southport	W 3-1	Sargeant, Reid, Bagley	11,694		7	1		8		3			5			9		4		11	10	2			6		
1335	18	(a)	Crewe A	L 1-2	Lythgoe	7,419		7	1		8		3			5			9		4		11	10	2	6				
1336	25	(h)	Carlisle U	W 3-0	Essex 2, Reid (pen)	6,712		7	1		8					5			9	3	4		11	10	2	6				
1337	Mar 4	(a)	Darlington	L 3-4	Essex, Bagley, Reid (pen)	3,023		7	1		9					5	8			3	4		11	10	2	6				
1338	11	(h)	Hartlepools U	W 5-0	Reid, Bagley, Sargeant, Lythgoe, Still	5,198		7	1		8		6			5			9	3	4		11			2		10		
1339	18	(a)	Gateshead	L 1-4	Lythgoe	3,746		7	1		8		6			5			9	3	4		11			2		10		
1340	25	(h)	Wrexham	W 2-1	Reid (pen), Lythgoe	5,296		7	1	10	8		6			5			9	3	4		11			2				
1341	Apr 1	(a)	York C	W 2-1	Lythgoe, Sargeant	5,262		7	1		8		6			5			9	3	4		11	10		2				
1342	7	(h)	Barnsley	D 1-1	Sargeant	17,860		7	1		8					5			9	3	4		11	10	2	6				
1343	8	(h)	Rochdale	L 1-2	Reid	6,485	7		1		8		6			5			9	3	4		11	10	2					
1344	10	(a)	Barnsley	W 1-0	Reid	19,146	7		1		8		6			5			9	3	4		11	10	2					
1345	15	(a)	Rotherham U	L 2-3	Essex, Harker	4,054		7	1		8		6			5		4	9	3			11	10	2					
1346	17*	(a)	Oldham A	L 1-3	Sherwood	3,195		7	1		8		6			5		4		3			11	10				2	9	
1347	22	(h)	Doncaster R	L 1-2	Sherwood	4,857		7	1		8		6			5		4	9	3			11	10				2		
1348	24	(h)	York C	W 3-1	Lythgoe 2, Sherwood	2,160		7	1							5		4	9				11	10	3	6	8	2		
1349	29	(a)	Accrington S	L 2-3	Sargeant, Bagley	2,338		7	1		8		6			5		4	9	3			11	10						
1350	May 6	(h)	Halifax T	D 3-3	Reid (pen), Bagley, Sargeant	3,351		7	1		8		3			5			9		4		11	10	2	6				
			FINAL LEAGUE POSITION: 9th in Division Three North			Appearances	2	40	40	1	41	2	18	2	24	20	1	9	38	20	37	2	40	39	34	25	1	21	3	2
						Goals		13			13		1					1	20		14		17	10		1				1

FA Cup

#	Date		Opponent	Res	Scorers	Att	Arthur	Bagley	Bowles	Burrows	Essex	Haigh	Harker	Jackson	Jenkinson	Jones	Law	Lumby	Lythgoe	Owens	Reid	Rigby	Sargeant	Sherwood	Smith	Still	Stock	Titterington	Topping	West
1	Nov 26	(a)	North Shields	W 4-1	Bagley, Sargeant 2 (1 pen), Essex	5,715		7	1		8		5		2			4	9				11	10	3	6				
2	Dec 10	(h)	Walthamstow A	D 0-0		11,752		7	1		8		5						9	3	4		11	10	2	6				
R	15	(a)	Walthamstow A	W 3-1	Sargeant 3	12,500		7	1		8		5						9	3	4		11	10	2	6				
3	Jan 7	(a)	Barnsley	W 2-1	Essex, Sargeant	19,281		7	1		8				2				9	3	4		11	10		6		5		
4	21	(a)	Liverpool	L 1-5	Reid (pen)	39,407		7	1		8		10					9		3	4		11		2	6		5		
						Appearances		5	5		5		4		2			1	1	4	4		5	4	4	5		2		
						Goals		1			2										1		6							

Average Home League attendance: 8,934
Average Away League attendance: 6,362

*This was the 'replay' of a game played at Boundary Park on 26 December which was abandoned after 63 minutes due to fog with the score 1-0 to Stockport (Bagley), the team being the same as for Match 1326 with the exception of Titterington replacing Harker.

1939-40

			1	2	3	4	5	6	7	8	9	10	11
1 Aug 26 (h) Halifax T	L 0-3	7,853	Bowles	Smith	Owens	Reid	Seagrave	Jones	Bagley	Groves	Essex	Titterington	Rich
2 Sep 2 (a) Carlisle U	L 0-2	5,072	..	..	..	..	..	Lumby	Morris	Essex	Rich	Groves	L.G.Sullivan

LEAGUE SUSPENDED ON 4 SEPTEMBER FOLLOWING DECLARATION OF WAR

			1	2	3	4	5	6	7	8	9	10	11
3 Oct 21 (h) Liverpool	L 0-3	5,000	Hall	Topping	Winstanley	Reid	Titterington	Lumby	Bagley	Groves	Howe	Crawshaw	Harthill
4 28 (h) Stoke C	L 2-4 Catterick, Howe	2,150	..	..	Owens	..	..	..	..	..	Catterick	Howe	L.G.Sullivan
5 Nov 11 (h) Port Vale	W 2-1 Catterick 2	3,452	..	..	..	..	Neilson	Titterington	..	Lumby	..	Groves	Howe
6 18 (a) New Brighton	L 2-4 Catterick 2	2,170	..	..	..	..	..	..	..	..	..	..	..
7 25 (h) Tranmere R	W 5-0 Reid 4, Neilson	1,700	..	..	Clark	Neilson	Gee	..	..	Reid	..	..	..
8 Dec 2 (a) Manchester C	D 6-6 Catterick 2, Howe 4 (2 pens)	5,774	..	..	..	..	..	..	..	..	..	..	..
9 9 (h) Manchester U	L 4-7 Reid 3 (1 pen), Bagley	3,392	..	..	..	..	..	..	..	..	..	..	L.G.Sullivan
10 23 (a) Chester	L 1-8 Reid	800	..	..	..	..	Gleave	..	..	..	Dean	Woodcock	..
11 Jan 6 (h) Wrexham	L 0-1	3,108	McDonough	..	Owens	..	..	..	..	..	Catterick	Howe	W.Sullivan
12 Feb 24 (h) Stoke C	L 1-5 Bagley	5,507	..	..	..	Reid	Neilson	..	Toseland	Essex	..	Bagley	Howe
13 Mar 2 (h) Crewe A	W 4-1 Howe (pen), Catterick 3	1,946	..	..	Neilson	..	Gleave	..	Bagley	..	..	Howe	L.G.Sullivan
14 9 (a) Port Vale	L 2-6 Woodcock, Howe	1,787	..	..	Owens	Chappell	Neilson	Lumby	Toseland	Bagley	..	Sherwood	Titterington
15 16 (h) New Brighton	W 4-1 Reid 2 (1 pen), Howe, Bagley	2,390	..	..	..	Reid	..	Titterington	..	Essex	..	Bagley	Howe
16 23 (a) Tranmere R	D 2-2 Bagley, Toseland	3,000	..	..	..	Neilson	Gleave	..	..	Reid	Howe	..	Woodcock
17 30 (h) Manchester C	D 1-1 Woodcock	6,481	..	..	..	Chappell	Neilson	..	..	Woodcock	Reid	..	Howe
18 Apr 3 (a) Everton	L 0-7	1,657	..	..	..	..	..	..	..	Reid	Catterick	..	..
19 6 (a) Manchester U	L 1-6 Reid	6,000	..	..	..	..	Titterington	Sherwood	..	..	..	..	..
20 20 (a) Crewe A	L 1-3 W.Sullivan	1,000	..	..	..	Neilson	..	Chappell	..	Woodcock	Reid	..	..
21 May 4 (a) Wrexham	L 2-4 Catterick 2	1,500	..	Owens	Oldham	Topping	Neilson	..	Woodcock	Bagley	Catterick	Sherwood	W.Sullivan
22 11 (a) Liverpool	L 3-4 Titterington, Toseland (pen), Catterick	6,000	..	Topping	Owens	Chappell	..	Lumby	Toseland	..	..	Howe	Pollitt
23 25 (h) Chester	L 1-3 Lumby (pen)	750	Fielding	..	..	..	..	Titterington	..	Woodcock	..	..	Lumby
24 29 (h) Everton	L 1-2 Catterick		..	Sanders	Oldham	..	Ashley	Hollis	Williams	Bagley	..	..	..

FINAL LEAGUE POSITION: 11th (out of 12) in Regional League (Western Section)

Football League War Cup

			1	2	3	4	5	6	7	8	9	10	11
P Apr 13 (a) Wrexham	L 0-3	2,500	Bowles	Topping	Owens	Chappell	Titterington	Lumby	Bagley	Reid	Davies	Sherwood	Woodcock

Football League Appearances: J.C.Bowles 2, J.R.Essex 2, A.Groves 2, P.Owens 2, J.D.Reid 2, L.Rich 2, J.W.Seagrave 2, W.H.Smith 2, T.H.Bagley 1, L.Jones 1, W.C.W.Lumby 1, J.Morris 1, L.G.Sullivan 1, W.Titterington 1.

Regional League and League Cup Appearances: T.H.Bagley 22, H.W.Topping 22, W.Titterington 20, F.Howe (Grimsby Town) 18, R.Neilson (Manchester City) 18, J.D.Reid 18, H.Catterick (Everton) 17, P.Owens 16, F.J.B.McDonough 12, S.Chappell 10, E.Toseland (Sheffield Wednesday) 10, W.C.W.Lumby 9, G.W.Hall (Tottenham Hotspur) 8, A.Groves 7, A.Woodcock 7, G.V.Clark (Manchester City) 4, C.Gleave 4, G.W.Sherwood 4, L.G.Sullivan 4, J.R.Essex 3, C.Gee (Everton) 3, W.Fielding (Cardiff City) 2, G.Oldham 2, W.Sullivan 2, J.Ashley 1, J.C.Bowles 1, C.Crawshaw 1, J.Davies 1, R.Dean 1, C.Harthill 1, H.Hollis (Chester) 1, J.Pollitt 1, R.M.Sanders (Chester) 1, T.R.Williams 1, L.Winstanley 1.

Goalscorers: Catterick 14, Reid 11, Howe 8, Bagley 4, Woodcock 2, W.Sullivan 2, Lumby 1, Neilson 1, Titterington 1, Toseland 1.

1940-41

#	Date / Venue / Opponent	Result & Scorers	Att	1	2	3	4	5	6	7	8	9	10	11
1	Aug 31 (a) Chester	L 3-5 Catterick, Toseland (pen), Howe	1,000	Fielding	Neilson	Topping	Ridgway	Percival	Titterington	Toseland	Lumby	Catterick	Bagley	Howe
2	Sep 7 (a) Oldham A	L 1-4 Toseland	2,500	..	Topping	Butler	Percival	Neilson	..	..	Bagley	..	Burrows	..
3	14 (h) Chester	W 4-0 Catterick 2, Burgess 2	2,000	..	..	..	..	..	Howe	..	Burrows	..	Burgess	Taylor
4	21 (h) Rochdale	W 4-0 Burrows 3, Burgess	3,000	..	..	..	..	..	..	..	..	..	..	..
5	28 (h) Oldham A	L 1-5 Catterick	3,000	..	Haslam	Topping	..	..	..	..	..	..	..	..
6	Oct 5 (a) Burnley	D 2-2 Burgess 2	2,500	..	Stevens	Butler	..	Titterington	Chappell	..	Bagley	Howe	..	..
7	12 (a) Everton	L 2-4 Bagley, Howe (pen)	2,500	..	Topping	..	..	..	Howe	..	..	Burgess	Burrows	Middleton
8	19 (h) Bury	D 1-1 Burgess	2,500	..	..	..	..	..	..	..	..	Reid	Burgess	..
9	26 (h) Liverpool	W 2-0 Middleton 2	2,000	..	..	..	..	..	..	..	..	Catterick	..	..
10	Nov 2 (a) Liverpool	L 0-5	1,000	..	..	Howe	..	..	Burrows	..	..	..	..	..
11	9 (a) Bury	L 2-5 Howe, Self	1,000	..	..	Butler	..	..	Chappell	..	..	..	Self	Noble
12	16 (a) Rochdale	L 3-5 Catterick 3	2,000	..	..	..	..	..	..	..	..	..	Howe	Self
13	23 (h) Wrexham	W 2-1 Howe 2 (2 pens)	1,000	..	Minshull	..	Topping	Howe	..	..	J.Johnson	..	Bagley	Burrows
14	30 (a) Wrexham	D 2-2 Titterington, Taylor	2,000	Bowles	Topping	..	Percival	Neilson	..	..	Burrows	Howe	Titterington	Taylor
15	Dec 7 (h) Burnley	W 1-0 Woodcock	1,500	Fielding	..	Jones	Burrows	Howe	Toseland	Woodcock	Reid	Bagley	..	Taylor
16	14 (h) Manchester C	L 1-9 Titterington	2,000	..	..	..	Percival	..	Butler	Bagley	Reid	Catterick	Titterington	Burrows
17	21 (a) Manchester C	L 2-7 Leighton, Ridgway	3,000	..	Butler	..	..	Gleave	Chappell	Ridgway	Bagley	Williams	Howe	Burrows
18	25 (h) Manchester U	L 1-3 Bagley		Bowles	Topping	..	..	..	..	Bagley	Titterington	Catterick	..	Leighton
19	28 (a) Southport	L 0-8	1,000	..	..	..	..	Kitching	Butler	..	Woodcock	..	..	Taylor
20	Jan 4 (h) Preston NE	D 2-2 Catterick, Bagley	1,000	Fielding	..	Butler	Reid	Howe	Chappell	Toseland	Percival	..	Bagley	Burrows
21	11 (h) Sheffield U	L 1-5 Catterick	1,000	..	..	Lyons	Percival	..	..	J.Johnson	Bagley	..	Maudsley	Burrows
22	18 (a) Crewe A	W 2-1 Reid, Watson	300	..	..	Butler	Reid	..	Moore	..	..	Watson	..	Maudsley
23	25 (h) Southport	W 4-1 Catterick 3, Watson	1,000	..	..	..	Chappell	T.Johnson	..	..	Watson	..	Bagley	Maudsley
24	Mar 8 (h) Chesterfield	W 1-0 Howe	1,500	..	..	..	Percival	Titterington	Chappell	Burrows	J.Johnson	Reid	..	Howe
25	22 (a) Bradford C	L 3-9 Bagley, Watson, Butler (pen)	500	..	..	..	Ridgway	Howe	..	..	Watson	Percival	..	Maudsley
26	Apr 5 (h) Rochdale	D 1-1 Williams	500	..	..	Minshull	..	Green	..	..	Bagley	Williams	Howe	Egerton
27	12 (a) Rochdale	L 1-3 Reid (pen)	1,000	..	..	Lyons	Reid	Titterington	..	..	J.Johnson	Watson	..	Maudsley
28	14 (h) Bradford C	W 5-2 Watson 3, Bagley, Reid		..	Minshull	Topping	Burrows	..	..	Ridgway	..	Reid	Watson	Maudsley
29	26 (a) Wrexham	L 0-3	1,000	..	Topping	Lyons	Newton	..	..	..	Leighton	Williams	Bagley	Park

FINAL LEAGUE POSITION: 35th (out of 36) North Regional League

Football League War Cup

#	Date / Venue / Opponent	Result & Scorers	Att	1	2	3	4	5	6	7	8	9	10	11
P	Feb 1 (h) Blackpool	L 1-3 Watson	2,000	Fielding	Topping	Butler	Reid	Titterington	Chappell	J.Johnson	Watson	Howe	Bagley	Maudsley
P	8 (a) Blackpool	L 2-9 Toseland, Reid	5,000	..	..	..	Chappell	Howe	Maudsley	Toseland	..	Reid	..	J.Johnson

Appearances: H.W.Topping 29, T.H.Bagley 28, W.Fielding (Cardiff City) 28, F.Howe (Grimsby Town) 27, M.P.Butler (Blackpool) 21, J.Percival (Manchester City) 21, S.Chappell 19, A.Burrows 18, H.Catterick (Everton) 17, W.Titterington 17, E.Toseland (Sheffield Wednesday) 16, J.D.Reid 10, J.Johnson 8, R.C.Maudsley 8, T.Taylor 8, H.Burgess (Chelsea) 7, F.Watson 7, R.Neilson (Manchester City) 6, F.Ridgway 6, G.T.Jones (Walsall) 5, J.C.Bowles 3, E.Lyons 3, J.Middleton (Hartlepools United) 3, O.Minshull 3, T.H.Williams 3, C.Gleave 2, L.Leighton 2, Moore (Stoke City) 2, E.R.Self (Hull City) 2, A.Woodcock 2, J.Egerton 1, J.Green 1, H.Haslam (Manchester United) 1, T.Johnson (Sheffield United) 1, N.Kitching (Workington) 1, W.C.W.Lumby 1, W.Newton 1, J.Noble 1, J.B.Park (Wrexham) 1, J.Stevens 1.

Goalscorers: Catterick 12, Watson 7, Howe 6, Burgess 6, Bagley 5, Reid 4, Burrows 3, Toseland 3, Middleton 2, Titterington 2, Butler 1, Leighton 1, Ridgway 1, Self 1, Taylor 1, Williams 1, Woodcock 1.

1941-42

No	Date		Opponent	Result	Scorers	Att	1	2	3	4	5	6	7	8	9	10	11
1	Aug 30	(a)	Chester	L 1-3	Burrows	1,500	Rigby	Lyons	Tagg	Cutting	Titterington	Forrester	Woods	Chappell	Burrows	Watson	Toseland
2	Sep 6	(h)	Chester	L 2-4	Watson 2 (2 pens)	2,500	Fielding	Minshull	H.W.Topping	..	..	Chappell	Williams	Watson	Catterick	Tagg	Howe
3	13	(h)	Manchester U	L 1-5	Catterick	3,000	..	Basford	Howe	..	..	..	Ridgway	..	..	..	Woods
4	20	(a)	Manchester U	L 1-7	Middleton	2,000	..	H.W.Topping	Chappell	..	Howe	Garfoot	Toseland	Leighton	..	Morris	Middleton
5	27	(a)	Tranmere R	L 0-4		3,000	..	Steele	..	..	Lawrence	Titterington	Leighton	Ridgway	..	Howe	Scott
6	Oct 4	(h)	Tranmere R	W 5-2	Watson, Catterick 3, Howe	1,000	..	..	Lyons	..	..	Chappell	Ridgway	Watson	..	..	..
7	11	(h)	Liverpool	L 1-2	Catterick	3,000	..	..	..	..	..	Percival	Bagley	Titterington	..	Burrows	Chappell
8	18	(a)	Liverpool	L 1-6	Catterick	3,000	..	..	H.W.Topping	..	..	Chappell	Shawcross	Watson	..	Percival	Scott
9	25	(a)	Wrexham	L 1-6	Catterick	1,200	..	H.W.Topping	Lyons	Ridgway	..	Percival	..	Titterington	..	Scott	Caldwell
10	Nov 1	(h)	Wrexham	D 3-3	Percival, Howe, Catterick	750	..	Steele	H.W.Topping	Cutting	..	Chappell	Toseland	Percival	..	Howe	Burrows
11	8	(h)	Manchester C	L 4-6	Watson 3, Howe	3,000	..	H.Topping	..	..	..	..	..	..	Watson	..	Scott
12	15	(a)	Manchester C	L 1-2	Ridgway	2,000	..	Steele	..	..	..	..	..	..	Catterick	Scott	Ridgway
13	22	(a)	New Brighton	L 3-6	Percival, Watson, Catterick (pen)	500	Rigby	H.Topping	..	..	..	..	..	..	..	Watson	Woodcock
14	29	(a)	New Brighton	W 7-1	Watson 2, C'rick 2, P'val, Cutting, Reid(pen)	1,000	..	..	..	..	Reid	..	..	Watson	..	Percival	Howe
15	Dec 6	(h)	Stoke C	L 1-6	Catterick	500	Fallows†	..	..	..	Steele	..	..	..	..	Lawrence	Ridgway
16	13	(h)	Stoke C	L 1-3	Howe	2,000	Rigby	..	..	..	..	Titterington	..	..	..	Howe	Noble
17	20	(h)	Everton	D 1-1	Chappell	2,000	..	..	Howe	..	..	Chappell	..	..	..	Percival	Scott
18	25	(a)	Everton	L 0-6			..	..	Howe	Vincent	..	..	Ridgway	Shaw	..	..	..

FINAL LEAGUE POSITION: 38th (out of 38) North Regional League

No	Date		Opponent	Result	Scorers	Att	1	2	3	4	5	6	7	8	9	10	11
19	Dec 27	(a)	Blackpool	L 2-5	Catterick 2	6,000	Rigby	Vincent	H.Topping	Cutting	Steele	Chappell	Toseland	Percival	Catterick	Titterington	Scott
20	Jan 3	(h)	Blackpool	W 2-1	Catterick 2	2,000	..	H.Topping	H.W.Topping	..	..	..	..	Ridgway	..	Percival	..
21	10	(a)	Wrexham	L 1-6	Catterick	2,027	..	Lawrence	H.Topping	..	..	Barber	..	..	..	..	..
22	17	(h)	Wrexham	D 2-2	Catterick (pen), Cutting	2,000	..	H.Topping	Catlin	..	..	Chappell	..	Percival	..	Scott	Maudsley
23	24	(a)	Burnley	L 0-6		2,500	..	..	..	..	..	..	..	Watson	..	Percival	Titterington
24	31	(h)	Burnley	D 0-0		1,200	..	..	..	..	..	..	..	Burrows	..	..	Ridgway
25	Feb 7	(a)	Southport	L 0-5		1,000	..	..	..	..	..	..	..	Titterington	..	..	..
26	14	(h)	Southport	D 1-1	Percival	1,000	..	..	..	Wilson	Cutting	..	..	Reid	..	..	Howe
27	21	(a)	Barnsley	L 1-6	Scott	1,000	..	..	Wilson	Cutting	Steele	..	..	Bagley	..	..	Scott
28	28	(h)	Barnsley	L 3-6	Catterick 3	1,000	..	..	Catlin	..	..	..	Ridgway	Wilson	..	..	Watson

FINAL LEAGUE POSITION: 48th (out of 51) League Cup Qualifying Competition - failed to qualify

Appearances: H.Catterick (Everton) 26, S.W.Cutting (Exeter City) 26, S.Chappell 25, J.Percival (Manchester City) 20, E.C.Steele 19, E.Toseland (Sheffield Wednesday) 19, H.Topping (Bristol Rovers) 17, W.Rigby (Crewe Alexandra) 16, F.Watson 13, F.Howe (Grimsby Town) 12, N.J.Lawrence 12, F.Ridgway 12, A.Scott 12, H.W.Topping 12, W.Fielding (Cardiff City) 11, W.Titterington 10, A.E.Catlin (Sheffield Wednesday) 6, A.Burrows 4, E.Lyons 4, E.Tagg (Bournemouth) 3, C.M.Wilson (Grimsby Town) 3, T.H.Bagley 2, L.Leighton 2, J.D.Reid 2, K.Shawcross 2, N.E.Vincent (Grimsby Town) 2, H.Woods 2, A.Barber 1, S.Basford 1, A.J.Caldwell 1, L.Fallows† 1, O.Forrester 1, C.A.Garfoot 1, R.Maudsley 1, J.Middleton (Hartlepools United) 1, O.Minshull 1, J.Morris 1, J.Noble 1, K.Shaw 1, T.R.Williams 1, A.Woodcock 1.

Goalscorers: Catterick 21, Watson 9, Howe 4, Percival 4, Cutting 2, Burrows 1, Chappell 1, Middleton 1, Reid 1, Ridgway 1, Scott 1.

†Fallows (RAF), joined the side from the spectators when, prior to kick-off against Stoke City (h), it was found that no goalkeeper was available for County. The Potters won the game 6-1.

1942-43

#	Date	V	Opponent	Result	Scorers	Att	1	2	3	4	5	6	7	8	9	10	11
1	Aug 29	(a)	Tranmere R	L 2-4	Swindells 2	1,000	Rigby	O.Lawrence	Birch	Wilson	Vose	Chappell	Worsley	Titterington	Swindells	McKenna	Barrett
2	Sep 5	(h)	Tranmere R	L 2-3	Shaw, Jones	500	..	Topping	..	..	..	Burrows	..	Swindells	Jones	Richardson	Shaw
3	12	(h)	Blackburn R	W 3-2	Shaw 2, Worsley		..	..	..	..	..	Steele	..	Burrows	Swindells	Barrett	..
4	19	(a)	Blackburn R	L 0-4		2,000	..	..	Lyons	..	..	..	..	..	..	Scott	..
5	26	(h)	Blackpool	L 0-6		3,000	..	..	..	Robinson	..	..	..	Wilson	..	Burrows	..
6	Oct 3	(a)	Blackpool	L 2-6	Worsley (pen), Scott	6,000	..	..	..	..	..	..	..	Burrows	..	Scott	..
7	10	(a)	Burnley	D 0-0		2,000	..	..	..	Wilson	..	..	..	Ridgway	Catterick	Swindells	Burrows
8	17	(h)	Burnley	W 4-1	Worsley 3 (2 pens), Scott	1,000	..	..	..	..	Steele	Burrows	..	Hyde	..	Scott	Shaw
9	24	(h)	Manchester U	L 1-4	Hyde	2,000	..	N.J.Lawrence	Birch	..	..	..	..	..	..	..	..
10	31	(a)	Manchester U	L 1-3	Shaw	3,000	Littlemore	Topping	..	..	..	..	..	..	..	..	..
11	Nov 7	(a)	Wrexham	L 1-7	Catterick	3,000	..	..	Lyons	..	..	..	..	..	..	..	..
12	14	(h)	Wrexham	W 5-3	Shaw, Worsley 2, Lancelotte, Swindells	1,000	Rigby	..	..	..	..	..	..	Lancelotte	Swindells	McPhillips	..
13	21	(a)	Rochdale	L 1-3	Reid	1,200	..	..	..	..	..	..	Hyde	..	Reid	Scott	..
14	28	(h)	Rochdale	W 3-2	Swindells 2, Shaw	1,200	..	..	..	..	..	..	Worsley	Hyde	Swindells	Birch	..
15	Dec 5	(a)	Bury	D 3-3	Matthews, Wright, Worsley	1,000	..	..	..	Cutting	..	..	..	..	Wright	Matthews	..
16	12	(h)	Bury	W 4-1	Swindells 3, Wright	1,500	..	Whatley	..	Steele	Moseley	..	..	..	..	Swindells	..
17	19	(a)	Chester	D 1-1	Hyde	500	..	..	..	Cutting	Steele	..	..	..	..	..	..
18	25	(h)	Chester	L 1-2	Worsley (pen)	4,000	..	Redfern	..	..	..	..	..	..	..	Colquhoun	..

FINAL LEAGUE POSITION: 35th (out of 48) North Regional League

#	Date	V	Opponent	Result	Scorers	Att	1	2	3	4	5	6	7	8	9	10	11
19	Dec 26	(a)	Bury	L 0-10		3,489	Rigby	Redfern	N.J.Lawrence	Woodcock	Steele	Burrows	Worsley	Wright	Spencer	Swindells	Shaw
20	Jan 2	(h)	Bury	W 5-3	Shaw 2, Swindells, Worsley 2	1,000	..	Whatley	Redfern	Lievesley	Moseley	..	..	..	Swindells	Lancelotte	..
21	9	(a)	Manchester C	L 1-7	Lancelotte	5,000	Littlemore	Redfern	Lyons	..	Steele	..	..	Hyde	Wright	..	..
22	16	(a)	Manchester C	L 2-5	Opp own-goal, Catterick	2,500	Ashley	Whatley	..	..	Moseley	McKay	..	Catterick	Wright	..	..
23	23	(h)	Rochdale	L 3-4	Catterick, Hyde, Shaw	2,000	..	..	..	Burrows	..	..	..	..	..	Sweeney	..
24	30	(a)	Rochdale	L 0-6		2,601	..	Topping	..	Lievesley	Redfern	..	Burrows	..	..	Swindells	..
25	Feb 6	(a)	Wrexham	L 1-5	Shaw	2,500	..	Whatley	..	Cutting	..	Burrows	Worsley	..	..	Stuart	..
26	13	(h)	Wrexham	W 5-2	Worsley, Shaw, McKay 2, Ridgway	1,600	..	Redfern	..	Lievesley	O.Lawrence	Burrows	Worsley	Ridgway	..	McKay	..
27	20	(h)	Tranmere R	W 4-3	Worsley, Shaw, Catterick 2	1,200	..	..	..	Burrows	..	McKay	..	Hyde	..	Shaw	Harrison
28	27	(a)	Tranmere R	D 1-1	Catterick	1,500	..	..	..	..	..	..	..	..	..	..	..
29	Mar 6	(h)	Crewe A	L 2-3	James, Worsley (pen)	1,500	..	..	..	Cutting	..	..	..	Colquhoun	..	James	Shaw
30	13	(a)	Crewe A	L 3-8	Hyde 3	3,000	Scales	..	N.J.Lawrence	Burrows	..	..	..	Morris	..	Hyde	..
31	20	(a)	Tranmere R	D 1-1	Catterick	2,000	..	Wright	..	Needham	..	Redfern	..	Hyde	..	Shaw	Harrison
32	27	(h)	Tranmere R	W 2-1	Catterick, James	1,500	..	Seddon	Grant	Kirkwood	..	Burrows	..	Shaw	..	James	..
33	Apr 3	(h)	Rotherham U	D 1-1	James	2,000	..	..	N.J.Lawrence	..	Redfern	..	..	Woodcock	..	..	Shaw
34	10	(a)	Rotherham U	L 0-2		600	Redfern	..	..	Burrows	Lievesley	Lyons	..	..	..	..	Shaw
35	17	(a)	Wrexham	L 3-6	Shaw 2, James	1,000	Scales	Lyons	..	Redfern	..	Burrows	..	James	Shaw	Ramscar	Seddon
36	26	(a)	Oldham A	D 1-1	Shaw	1,000	Rigby	..	..	Needham	..	..	..	Gilmour	Shaw	..	James
37	May 1	(a)	Crewe A	L 2-7	Worsley (pen), Shaw	3,200	..	..	..	..	Lievesley	..	..	Seddon	..	James	Brierley

FINAL LEAGUE POSITION: 45th (out of 54) North Regional League - Second Championship*

*Matches 19-28 inclusive constituted the Qualifying Competition of the Football League Cup (North). Stockport County finished 41st (out of 54) and so did not qualify for the first round.

Appearances: K.Shaw 35, H.Worsley 35, A.Burrows 33, E.Lyons 26, W.Rigby (Crewe Alexandra) 20, E.Hyde (Manchester United) 19, H.Catterick (Everton) 18, E.C.Steele 18, F.Redfern 17, H.Swindells 16, L.Lievesley 15, H.W.Topping 14, C.M.Wilson (Millwall) 13, N.J.Lawrence 9, J.Ashley 8, W.McKay (Manchester United) 8, G.C.James (Blackburn Rovers) 7, A.Scott 7, G.Vose (Manchester United) 7, F.Wright (Crystal Palace) 7, N.Birch (Notts County) 6, H.Seddon 6, W.J.Whatley (Tottenham Hotspur) 6, S.W.Cutting (Exeter City) 5, G.Scales (Manchester City) 5, J.Harrison 5, E.Lancelotte (Charlton Athletic) 4, W.A.Moseley (Chelsea) 4, R.Littlemore 3, A.Woodcock (Millwall) 3, L.J.Barrett 2, D.M.Colquhoun (Bradford City) 2, O.Lawrence 2, F.R.Needham 2, F.Ridgway 2, W.Robinson (Manchester City) 2, A.Brierley 1, S.Chappell 1, T.Gilmour 1, J.A.Grant (Everton) 1, B.W.Jones (Manchester United) 1, S.J.Kirkwood (Plymouth Argyle) 1, R.Matthews (Blackpool) 1, J.McKenna 1, L.McPhillips (Cardiff City) 1, J.Morris (Watford) 1, F.Ramscar 1, J.D.Reid 1, R.Richardson 1, F.Spencer 1, A.Stuart (Falkirk) 1, F.Sweeney (Everton) 1, W.Titterington 1.

Goalscorers: Shaw 16, Worsley 15, Swindells 9, Catterick 8, Hyde 6, James 4, McKay 2, Scott 2, Wright 2, Lancelotte 2, Ridgway 1, Jones 1, Matthews 1, Reid 1, Opp own-goal 1.

1943-44

			1	2	3	4	5	6	7	8	9	10	11
1 Aug 28 (a) Manchester U L 0-6		3,200	Liddell	Redfern	Lyons	Lievesley	Needham	Johnstone	Worsley	Burrows	Catterick	Shaw	Harman
2 Sep 4 (h) Manchester U D 3-3	James, Catterick 2	2,000	..	Geddes	..	..	..	Burrows	..	Gallon	..	James	Shaw
3 11 (h) Tranmere R W 5-3	Curran, Titterington, Catterick 2, Shepherd	1,748	..	Redfern	..	..	Charlesworth	Titterington	..	Curran	..	Shepherd	..
4 18 (a) Tranmere R W 3-2	James 2 (1 pen), Catterick	2,000	Martin	..	..	..	..	Needham	..	James	..	Seddon	..
5 25 (a) Blackpool L 2-3	Titterington, Catterick	5,000	..	..	Geddes	..	..	..	..	Titterington	..	James	..
6 Oct 2 (h) Blackpool D 0-0		6,359	..	..	..	..	..	Burrows	James	..	..	A.Stuart	..
7 9 (a) Blackburn R L 1-2	Shaw	5,320	..	..	Lyons	..	..	..	Worsley	..	..	James	..
8 16 (a) Blackburn R L 2-8	Catterick 2	3,000	..	..	Geddes	..	Needham	..	..	..	..	..	..
9 23 (h) Burnley D 1-1	James	3,063	..	..	..	..	Charlesworth	..	Colquhoun	..	..	..	..
10 30 (a) Burnley D 0-0		4,000	..	..	..	..	..	..	Worsley	Shaw	..	Titterington	Colquhoun
11 Nov 6 (h) Wrexham W 1-0	James	2,480	..	..	..	..	..	..	..	Titterington	..	James	Shaw
12 13 (a) Wrexham L 1-4	D.Stuart	1,500	..	..	..	Swindells	..	..	..	Talbot	Shaw	Scholes	D.Stuart
13 20 (h) Rochdale L 1-3	Talbot	1,800	..	..	Lyons	Tabram	..	..	..	Thomson	James	Talbot	Shaw
14 27 (a) Rochdale L 0-2		1,122	..	..	..	Reece	..	Needham	..	Tabram	Woodcock	James	..
15 Dec 4 (h) Bury W 2-1	Shaw, James	2,000	..	..	..	..	..	..	..	Talbot	James	Tabram	..
16 11 (a) Bury L 0-4		2,029	..	..	..	Lievesley	..	Reece	Shepherd	..	..	..	..
17 18 (h) Chester W 1-0	Johnson	1,200	..	..	..	McCulloch	Lievesley	..	Worsley	James	Johnson	Talbot	..
18 25 (a) Chester D 1-1	James	4,000	..	Geddes	..	Burrows	..	..	..	..	..	..	..

FINAL LEAGUE POSITION: 37th (out of 56) North Regional League

			1	2	3	4	5	6	7	8	9	10	11
19 Dec 27 (a) Oldham A W 2-1	Johnson, Shaw	6,776	Martin	Geddes	Lyons	McCulloch	Lievesley	Reece	Worsley	James	Johnson	Talbot	Shaw
20 Jan 1 (a) Oldham A L 1-5	McCulloch	3,521	Liddell	..	..	Lievesley	Charlesworth	..	..	..	McCulloch	..	..
21 8 (h) Manchester U L 2-3	Johnson, Shaw	4,670	..	Redfern	Geddes	..	..	Simpson	..	McCulloch	Johnson	Tabram	..
22 15 (a) Manchester U L 2-4	Johnson, Tabram	4,500	..	..	Lewin	Geddes	Lievesley	Reece	..	Talbot	..	..	Burrows
23 22 (a) Halifax T W 1-0	Catterick	2,000	Martin	..	..	McCulloch	..	..	Johnson	..	Catterick	..	James
23 29 (h) Halifax T W 4-3	Catterick 2 (1 pen), Rawcliffe 2	3,184	..	..	..	..	..	..	..	..	Rawcliffe	..	..
25 Feb 5 (a) Manchester C L 0-4		6,000	..	..	..	..	Charlesworth	..	Shaw	..	..	..	..
26 12 (h) Manchester C W 4-3	Johnson 2, James, Shaw	6,066	..	..	Lyons	..	Lievesley	..	Worsley	..	Johnson	James	Shaw
27 19 (h) Bury W 5-1	Talbot, Worsley, Shaw, Catterick 2	4,632	..	Lewin	..	..	..	..	..	..	Catterick	..	..
28 26 (a) Bury L 2-4	Talbot, Shaw	2,000	..	Redfern	..	..	..	Burrows	Johnson	..	..	..	..
29 Mar 18 (h) Tranmere R W 4-0	Talbot, Shaw, Catterick, Worsley	1,500	..	..	..	Burrows	..	Reece	Worsley	..	..	Seddon	..
30 25 (a) Tranmere R L 1-4	Catterick	1,500	..	..	..	McCulloch	..	Burrows	..	..	..	Lewin	..
31 Apr 1 (h) Crewe A W 3-1	Catterick, Talbot 2	1,768	..	..	Lewin	..	..	Reece	..	..	..	Seddon	..
32 8 (a) Crewe A W 2-1	Butt, Seddon	4,000	..	..	..	..	..	..	Seddon	..	..	Butt	..
33 10 (a) Rochdale W 4-1	Catterick 3, Burrows	5,700	..	..	..	..	..	..	..	Burrows	..	..	..
34 15 (a) Rochdale W 3-2	Reece 2, Shaw	5,000	..	..	..	..	..	..	Thomson	..	..	Paterson	..
35 22 (a) Bolton W L 2-4	Catterick, McCulloch	5,000	..	..	Lyons	..	..	Burrows	Worsley	Gee	..	Talbot	..
36 29 (h) Bolton W L 1-2	Shaw	3,825	..	..	..	..	..	Seddon	Beasley	..	..	Fenner	..
37 May 6 (a) Chester L 1-6	Opp own-goal	800	..	..	..	..	..	Lewin	..	..	..	Shaw	Leigh

FINAL LEAGUE POSITION: 29th (out of 50) North Regional League - Second Championship*

*Matches 19-28 inclusive constituted the Qualifying Competition of the Football League Cup (North). Stockport County were in 33rd position (out of 56) but, as only the top 32 qualified for the first round, County (on goal-average) narrowly failed to qualify.

Appearances: K.Shaw 34, L.Lievesley (Crystal Palace) 32, F.Redfern 32, H.Martin 31, H.Catterick (Everton) 25, H.Worsley 25, G.C.James 22, E.Lyons 21, F.L.Talbot (Walsall) 20, A.Burrows 18, W.D.McCulloch 18, T.J.Reece (Crystal Palace) 18, S.Charlesworth (Grimsby Town) 16, A.Geddes (Burnley) 13, D.R.Lewin (Bradford City) 11, J.Johnson 9, W.Titterington 8, F.B.Needham 7, Tabram 7, J.Liddell (Aldershot) 6, H.Seddon 6, H.Gee (Birmingham City) 3, T.Beasley 2, L.Butt (Blackburn Rovers) 2, D.M.Colquhoun (Bradford City) 2, F.Rawcliffe (Notts County) 2, G.Shepherd 2, A.Thomson (St Mirren) 2, F.Curran (Bristol City) 1, D.W.Fenner (Stenhousemuir) 1, J.W.Gallon (Swansea Town) 1, C.Harman (Brighton & Hove Albion) 1, J.Johnstone (Motherwell) 1, J.J.Leigh (Chester) 1, J.Paterson 1, J.Scholes 1, J.Simpson (Glasgow Rangers) 1, A.Stuart (Falkirk) 1, D.Stuart (Manchester City) 1, H.Swindells 1, A.Woodcock (Charlton Athletic) 1.

Goalscorers: Catterick 20, Shaw 10, James 8, Johnson 6, Talbot 6, McCulloch 2, Rawcliffe 2, Reece 2, Titterington 2, Worsley 2, Burrows 1, Butt 1, Curran 1, Seddon 1, Shepherd 1, D.Stuart 1, Tabram 1, Opp own-goal 1.

1944-45

#	Date	V	Opponent	Res	Scorers	Att	1	2	3	4	5	6	7	8	9	10	11
1	Aug 26	(h)	Liverpool	L 2-3	Catterick, Gee	5,136	Gage	Owens	Lewin	McCulloch	Morris	McKay	Worsley	Gee	Johnson	Catterick	Shaw
2	Sep 2	(a)	Liverpool	L 0-2		12,418	..	..	..	Wilson	Cope	Burrows	..	Bardsley	Catterick	Redfern	..
3	9	(a)	Manchester U	W 4-3	Woodcock 2, Catterick, Shaw	8,000	Ellis	Lewin	Redfern	..	..	..	..	Hill	..	Woodcock	..
4	16	(h)	Manchester U	D 4-4	Barkas 2, Worsley, Catterick	6,247	Gage	Owens	Lewin	..	..	Hill	..	Barkas	..	Woodcock	..
5	23	(h)	Manchester C	L 2-6	Catterick 2	10,005	..	Redfern	..	..	..	McCulloch	..	..	..	Hill	..
6	30	(a)	Manchester C	L 1-5	Hill	12,000	Ellis	..	..	McCulloch	Morris	..	Watters	Hill	..	James	..
7	Oct 7	(a)	Bury	L 1-2	Opp own-goal	3,500	Crompton	Owens	..	Wilson	..	Wilson	..	Gee	Shaw	Hill	Crawford
8	14	(h)	Bury	W 3-2	McCulloch 2, Crawford	2,000	..	Redfern	..	Wilson	..	Burrows	..	James	McCulloch	Gee	..
9	21	(a)	Crewe A	L 2-4	McCulloch (pen), Leicester	5,200	Gage	..	Cope	Burrows	Lievesley	McCulloch	..	..	Leicester	..	..
10	28	(a)	Crewe A	L 1-5	McCulloch	4,060	..	..	Lewin	..	Cope	..	..	..	Watters	..	..
11	Nov 4	(a)	Chester	L 2-5	Gee, McCulloch (pen)	3,000	..	..	..	Lievesley	..	Burrows	Shaw	Wilson	Watters	..	James
12	11	(h)	Chester	W 4-2	Hyde, Gee, Woodcock, McCulloch	3,000	..	..	..	Gleave	Lievesley	..	Watters	James	McCulloch	..	Waring
13	18	(a)	Wrexham	L 0-8		5,200	..	..	..	..	..	Cope	..	Hyde	..	Woodcock	Gee
14	25	(h)	Wrexham	L 0-3		2,000	..	..	..	..	..	..	..	Shaw	..	..	..
15	Dec 2	(a)	Tranmere R	W 4-2	Catterick 3, Watters	2,500	Crompton	..	Cope	..	..	Wheatley	..	Hyde	Catterick	Hill	Shaw
16	9	(h)	Tranmere R	W 2-1	Ireland, Lievesley	2,300	..	..	Lewin	..	..	McCulloch	..	Hill	Ireland	McCulloch	Gee
17	16	(a)	Everton	L 1-6	Catterick	8,690	Gage	..	Bentham	Wilson	Gleave	..	Murphy	..	Catterick	Gee	Park
18	23	(h)	Everton	L 0-7		8,000	..	..	Lewin	Lievesley	Morris	..	Watters	..	..	..	Shaw / Cochrane

FINAL LEAGUE POSITION: 29th (out of 35) North Regional League

#	Date	V	Opponent	Res	Scorers	Att	1	2	3	4	5	6	7	8	9	10	11
19	Dec 26	(a)	Bolton W	L 0-2		3,000	Gage	Redfern	Lewin	Gleave	Morris	McCulloch	Beasley	Hill	Catterick	Gee	Shaw
20	30	(h)	Bolton W	W 2-0	Catterick, Hill	3,750	..	..	..	Lievesley	..	..	Johnson	..	..	Shaw	A.Booth
21	Jan 6	(a)	Liverpool	L 2-3	Catterick, Shaw	3,000	Martin	..	..	Hill	Cope	..	Ridgway	Woodcock	..	Gee	Shaw
22	13	(a)	Liverpool	L 1-4	Shawcross	14,357	Gage	..	..	..	..	..	Shawcross	Hayward	Shaw	Topping	Morrison
23	20	(h)	Everton	L 0-3		1,000	..	..	..	..	..	..	Watters	Wilson	..	Gee	..
24	27	(a)	Everton	L 2-9	Catterick 2	5,000	..	..	..	..	Lievesley	Cope	Shawcross	..	Catterick	Shaw	Makin
25	Feb 3	(a)	Southport	L 1-2	Shaw	2,000	..	..	..	Lievesley	Cope	McCulloch	..	..	Shaw	Hill	Gee
26	10	(h)	Southport	L 2-5	McCulloch, Gee	2,000	..	..	Cope	Hill	Gleave	Lievesley	Shaw	..	McCulloch	Gee	Morrison
27	17	(h)	Tranmere R	W 4-3	Gorrie, Dimond 2, Redfern (pen)	1,500	Blyth	Owens	Lunn	Lievesley	..	McCulloch	Redfern	Shaw	Dimond	..	Gorrie
28	24	(a)	Tranmere R	L 0-4		1,500	..	..	Lewin	Hill	..	..	Shaw	Woodcock	..	Brown	Gorrie
29	Mar 3	(a)	Port Vale	L 0-5		4,000	J.M.Booth	..	Gennoe	Lewin	..	..	Stevenson	Shaw	Johnson	Gee	Mathieson
30	10	(h)	Port Vale	W 3-0	Gee, Shawcross, Johnson	2,000	Rigby	Redfern	Lewin	Burrows	..	..	R.Jones	..	..	..	Shawcross
31	17	(h)	Manchester C	W 4-1	Catterick 4	4,000	..	..	..	..	..	..	..	..	Catterick	..	Gennoe
32	Apr 2	(a)	Manchester C	W 5-1	Catterick 3, Gee, Barkas	18,000	..	Owens	..	..	..	..	Gee	..	..	Barkas	Cochrane
33	7	(a)	Rochdale	W 3-0	Gee, Owens, Catterick	2,000	..	..	Redfern	..	..	Brown	R.Jones	..	..	Gee	Shawcross
34	14	(h)	Rochdale	W 2-0	Barkas 2	1,100	..	..	..	Lievesley	..	..	..	Barkas	..	Gee	Shawcross
35	21	(h)	Crewe A	L 0-1		3,000	..	..	..	..	..	..	..	Quirk	Shaw	Burrows	Shaw
36	28	(a)	Crewe A	L 0-6		3,000	..	Redfern	T.G.Jones	McCulloch	..	Burrows	Gee	Barkas	Morrison	Hill	Shaw
37	May 5	(a)	Tranmere R	L 0-1		3,000	..	..	Burrows	..	..	Brown	Barnes	Woodcock	Leicester	..	Shaw

FINAL LEAGUE POSITION: 50th (out of 60) North Regional League - Second Championship*

*Matches 19-28 inclusive constituted the Qualifying Competition of the Football League Cup (North). Stockport County were in 56th position (out of 60) and, for the fourth year in succession, failed to qualify.

Appearances: F.Redfern 31, K.Shaw 30, W.D.McCulloch 29, D.R.Lewin (Bradford City) 27, H.Gee (Birmingham City) 26, M.Hill (Everton) 21, A.Gage (Fulham) 19, C.Gleave 19, G.Cope (Crewe Alexandra) 18, H.Catterick (Everton) 17, L.Lievesley (Crystal Palace) 16, A.Burrows 14, J.Watters 13, C.M.Wilson 12, E.Owens 11, W.Rigby (Crewe Alexandra) 8, A.Woodcock 7, K.Shawcross 6, T.Barkas (Halifax Town) 5, W.D.Brown 5, G.C.James 5, R.Jones 5, J.Morris 5, H.Worsley (Fulham) 5, J.Crompton (Manchester United) 4, J.Johnson 4, A.C.Morrison (Derby County) 4, J.C.Crawford 3, L.R.Blyth 2, D.Cochrane (Rochdale) 2, S.Dimond (Manchester United) 2, J.Ellis 2, R.A.Gennoe 2, W.Hyde 2, T.G.Jones (Everton) 2, E.Leicester 2, L.Bardsley (Manchester City) 1, J.W.Barnes 1, T.Beasley 1, S.Bentham (Everton) 1, A.Booth 1, J.M.Booth 1, W.Gorrie (Cowdenbeath) 1, D.Hayward (Bury) 1, H.W.Ireland (Reading) 1, G.Lunn (Aston Villa) 1, G.W.Makin (Everton) 1, H.Martin 1, H.Mathieson 1, W.McKay (Manchester United) 1, M.Murphy† 1, T.Park 1, A.C.Quirk 1, F.Ridgway 1, J.Stevenson 1, H.W.Topping 1, J.Waring (Crewe Alexandra) 1, J.Wheatley (Port Vale) 1.

Goalscorers: Catterick 21, Gee 7, McCulloch 7, Barkas 5, Shaw 3, Woodcock 3, Dimond 2, Hill 2, Shawcross 2, Crawford 1, Gorrie 1, Hyde 1, Ireland 1, Johnson 1, Leicester 1, Lievesley 1, Owens 1, Redfern 1, Watters 1, Worsley 1, Opp own-goal 1.

†For the game against Everton (Match 17), Michael Murphy, a soldier on leave who was entering Goodison as a spectator, heard an announcement that County had only nine players and signed amateur forms ten minutes before the game started. A full team was achieved by the addition of Everton's Bentham.

1945-46

#	Match	Att	1	2	3	4	5	6	7	8	9	10	11
1	Aug 25 (h) Barrow L 2-3 Rickards, Gee	3,905	Rigby	Redfern	Trentham	Burrows	Gleave	Brown	Johnson	Coen	Rickards	Shewood	Gee
2	Sep 1 (a) Barrow W 3-2 Rickards, Coen, Shaw	7,295	..	Topping	Redfern	..	..	..	..	Rickards	Shaw	Coen	Trentham
3	8 (a) Crewe A W 2-1 Catterick, Johnson	2,987	Bowles	..	..	..	..	..	..	..	Catterick	..	..
4	15 (a) Crewe A L 4-5 Reid 3 (1 pen), Trentham	4,695	..	Davison	..	Reid	..	Burrows	..	..	Woodcock	Shaw	..
5	22 (h) Rochdale W 7-0 Catterick, Reid 3 (1 pen), Worrall, Rickards, Gee	4,893	..	..	..	..	..	Brown	..	..	Catterick	Gee	Worrall
6	29 (a) Rochdale L 2-4 Woodcock, Brown	3,724	..	..	..	..	..	Burrows	..	..	Woodcock	Brown	Shaw
7	Oct 6 (a) Accrington S L 0-3	4,773	..	..	..	..	..	Cocker	Shaw	..	Oldnall	Clarke	Worrall
8	13 (h) Accrington S D 0-0	4,647	..	..	..	Cocker	..	Brown	Johnson	..	Shaw	..	..
9	20 (h) Wrexham L 1-2 Brown	4,573	..	Topping	..	Burrows	Lawrence	..	..	..	Kinnear	..	..
10	27 (a) Wrexham L 2-3 Bryant, Woodcock	5,715	..	Redfern	Haslam	Gleave	..	..	Bryant	Burrows	Woodcock	..	..
11	Nov 3 (a) Oldham A L 1-4 Worrall	3,222	..	..	..	Davison	..	..	Johnson	Hyde	..	..	..
12	10 (h) Oldham A W 3-1 Johnson 2, Shaw	4,700	..	..	Buckley	Gleave	..	..	Shaw	Rickards	Johnson	..	..
13	Dec 1 (a) Tranmere R L 1-3 Burrows	5,271	..	..	..	..	..	..	..	Burrows	Rickards	..	..
14	15 (h) Southport D 1-1 Burrows	3,317	..	..	..	Burrows	Gleave	..	Rickards	Clarke	Woodcock	Weaver	Hyde
15	22 (a) Southport W 4-0 Rickards 3, Weaver	1,566	..	..	..	..	..	..	Shaw	Stock	Rickards	..	..
16	25 (a) Chester L 2-4 Hyde, Shaw	1,759	..	..	..	..	..	..	..	..	..	..	..
17	26 (h) Chester D 1-1 Woodcock	8,237	Rigby	Williams	Cocker	..	..	..	..	..	Rickards	Woodcock	..
18	29 (a) Tranmere R W 2-1 Hyde, Rickards	4,204	..	..	..	Buckley	..	..	..	..	Stock	Rickards	..

FINAL LEAGUE POSITION: 7th (out of 10) Division 3 Northern Section (Western Region)

#	Match	Att	1	2	3	4	5	6	7	8	9	10	11
1	Dec 8 (a) Chester W 2-0 Woodcock, Hyde	2,566	Bowles	Redfern	Buckley	Brown	Gleave	Burrows	Shaw	Rickards	Woodcock	Weaver	Hyde
2	Jan 12 (a) Chester W 2-1 Woodcock, Rickards	3,538	Rigby	..	..	Gleave	Morris	Weaver	Woodcock	Clarke	Rickards	Brown	Shaw
3	19 (h) Barrow W 5-2 Brown 2, Weaver, Rickards, Clarke	3,072	..	Gleave	..	Burrows	..	..	..	..	..	..	..
4	26 (h) Barrow W 2-1 Brown, Shaw	2,463	..	..	..	..	..	..	..	..	..	..	..
5	Feb 2 (h) Rochdale W 3-2 Rickards, Shaw 2	3,416	..	..	..	..	..	..	..	Stock	..	..	..
6	9 (h) Rochdale D 2-2 Shaw, Stock	6,554	..	..	..	..	..	..	Worrall	..	..	..	..
7	16 (a) Tranmere R L 0-3	5,536	Bowles	..	..	..	..	..	..	..	..	..	..
8	23 (h) Tranmere R W 4-0 Brown, Rickards, Woodcock, Steele	5,364	..	..	..	..	..	..	Woodcock	Rickards	Steele	..	..
9	Mar 2 (a) Crewe A L 2-3 Shaw, Rickards	4,481	Rigby	..	..	Reid	..	Brown	..	..	..	Herd	..
10	9 (h) Crewe A W 4-1 Shaw (pen), Weaver, Brown, Rickards	9,377	Bowles	..	..	Burrows	..	Weaver	..	..	..	Brown	..

FINAL LEAGUE POSITION: 1st (out of 10) Division 3 (Northern Section) - Western Region Cup Qualifying Competition*

#	Match	Att	1	2	3	4	5	6	7	8	9	10	11
1	Mar 23 (a) Doncaster R D 2-2 Shaw, Rickards	12,026	Bowles	Gleave	Buckley	Burrows	Morris	Weaver	Woodcock	Rickards	Steele	Brown	Shaw
2§	30 (h) Doncaster R D 2-2† Shaw 2 (1 pen)	12,730	..	..	..	..	..	..	..	Cocker	Rickards	..	..
R	Apr 4 (a) Doncaster R L 0-4	13,500	..	Williams	..	Gleave	..	Burrows	..	..	..	..	..
3	6 (a) Tranmere R L 0-3	5,000	..	Redfern	..	..	..	Brown	Rickards	Stock	Williams	Weaver	..
4	13 (h) Tranmere R W 6-1 Shaw 3 (1 pen), Weaver 3	4,000	..	Gleave	..	Lumby	..	..	..	..	Shaw	..	Worrall
5	19 (a) Crewe A L 2-4 Shaw 2 (2 pens)	6,000	..	Topping	..	Burrows	Steele	..	..	Cocker	..	..	..
6	20 (h) Halifax T W 1-0 Rickards	3,000	..	Redfern	..	..	Gleave	..	Woodcock	Rickards	..	..	Jones
7	22 (h) Crewe A L 0-1	6,800	..	..	..	..	Morris	..	Cocker	..	..	..	..
8	27 (a) Halifax T W 3-2 Rickards, Shaw 2	3,000	..	..	..	..	..	..	Stock	..	..	..	..
9	May 4 (h) Carlisle U L 1-2 Burrows	3,000	..	..	..	Rickards	..	..	Rawlings	Burrows	..	..	Keenan

FINAL LEAGUE POSITION: 10th (out of 13) Division 3 (Northern Section) Second Championship

FA Cup

#	Match	Att	1	2	3	4	5	6	7	8	9	10	11
1	Nov 17 (h) Rochdale L 1-2 Shaw	5,000	Bowles	Topping	Redfern	Gleave	Lawrence	Burrows	Shaw	Hyde	Johnson	Clarke	Worrall
	24 (a) Rochdale D 1-1 Hyde	6,158	..	Redfern	Rich	..	Morris	..	..	Woodcock	..	Hyde	..

FA Cup played over two legs

*The top eight clubs in both the Western and Eastern regions of the Northern Section Cup qualified for the first round proper. Stockport County and Doncaster Rovers, winners of the Western Region and Eastern Region respectively, were drawn against each other in the first round.

§The two legs against Doncaster Rovers in the Northern Section Cup also constituted the first two games of the Division Three (Northern Section) Second Championship.

†After extra-time. Abandoned because of bad light after 203 minutes with the scores still level. The venue for the replay was decided on the toss of a coin.

Appearances: W.D.Brown 36; C.J.Rickards 36, C.Gleave 31, K.Shaw 31, A.Burrows 29, J.C.Bowles (Mansfield Town) 28, A.Buckley 26, F.Redfern 23, S.Weaver (Chelsea) 23, J.Morris (Aldershot) 18, A.Woodcock 18, J.Worrall 12, W.Clarke 11, J.Johnson 10, W.Rigby 10, H.Stock 9, L.Cocker (Bournemouth) 7, E.W.Hyde 7, A.E.Davison 6, O.Lawrence 6, J.D.Reid 5, E.C.Steele 5, H.W.Topping 4, D.H.Trentham (Everton) 4, F.A.Williams 4, L.Coen (Coventry City) 3, R.Jones 3, H.Catterick (Everton) 2, H.Gee (Birmingham City) 2, C.Haslam 2, W.Bryant (Manchester United) 1, A.Herd (Manchester City) 1, W.G.Keenan (Everton) 1, D.Kinnear (Raith Rovers) 1, W.C.W.Lumby 1, W.J.Oldnall 1, J.S.D.Rawlings (Everton) 1, G.W.Sherwood 1, L.Rich (Exeter City) 1.

Goalscorers: Shaw 19, Rickards 16, Brown 7, Reid 6, Weaver 6, Woodcock 6, Burrows 3, Hyde 3, Johnson 3, Catterick 2, Gee 2, Worrall 2, Bryant 1, Clarke 1, Coen 1, Steele 1, Stock 1, Trentham 1.

FA Cup Appearances: J.C.Bowles 2, A.Burrows 2, C.Gleave 2, E.W.Hyde 2, J.Johnson 2, F.Redfern 2, K.Shaw 2, J.Worrall 2, W.Clarke 1, O.Lawrence 1, J.Morris 1, L.Rich 1, H.W.Topping 1, A.Woodcock 1.

FA Cup Goalscorers: Hyde 1, Shaw 1.

1946-47

No.	Date		Opponent	Result	Scorers	Att.	Bowles	Brinton	Brown	Buckley	Burrows	Chapman	Cocker	Dainty	Earl	Eastham	Glaister	Gleave	Hacking	Jessop	Lodge	McCulloch	Monks	Morris	Noble	Redfern	Shaw	Staniforth	Stock	Walker	Wassall	Weaver
1351	Aug 31	(h)	Halifax T	W 4-1	Chapman, Earl 2, Stock	8,193	1	11	6	3		9			10							4	5			2	7		8			
1352	Sep 7	(a)	Carlisle U	D 1-1	Chapman	12,555	1		6	3		9			10			4				5	7	2	11				8			
1353	9	(h)	Doncaster R	L 1-3	Walker	12,830	1		6	3	11	9				10		5				4				2	7			8		
1354	14	(h)	Accrington S	W 2-0	Walker 2	8,298	1	11	6	3	7	9			10			5				4				2				8		
1355	16	(a)	Doncaster R	W 3-1	Brown 2, Shaw	11,582	1	11	6	3		9						5				4				2	7		8			10
1356	21	(a)	Barrow	L 0-1		9,077	1	11	6	3		9						5				4				2	7		8			10
1357	28	(h)	Bradford C	W 4-0	Earl 2 (1 pen), Brinton, Chapman	10,247	1	11	6	3		9			10			5				4				2	7		8			
1358	Oct 5	(a)	Oldham A	D 0-0		16,607	1	11	6	3		9			10			5				4				2	7		8			
1359	12	(h)	Southport	W 2-0	Shaw, Earl	9,999	1	11	6	3		9			10			5				4				2	7		8			
1360	19	(a)	Rotherham U	L 1-2	Burrows	13,037	1	11	6	3	7							5				4				2	9		8	10		
1361	26	(h)	Chester	L 0-3		11,738	1	11	6	3	7							5				4				2	9		8	10		
1362	Nov 2	(a)	York C	L 2-3	Shaw, McCulloch	6,842	1	11	6				7			4	3	5				8				2	9			10		
1363	9	(h)	Tranmere R	W 4-0	Walker, McCulloch, Shaw, Cocker	6,646	1	11	6				7			4		5				8				2	9	3		10		
1364	16	(a)	Darlington	W 2-1	Walker, Shaw	6,158	1	11	6				7			4		5				8				2	9	3		10		
1365	23	(h)	Hull C	W 2-0	Eastham, Shaw	8,586	1	11	6				7			4		5				8				2	9	3		10		
1366	Dec 7	(h)	Hartlepools U	L 1-2	Cocker	6,928	1	11	6				7			4		5				8				2	9	3		10		
1367	21	(h)	Lincoln C	W 3-2	Cocker 2, Brown	6,824	1	11	8				7		10	4		5				6				2	9	3				
1368	25	(a)	Rochdale	W 4-1	Brown 3, Walker	7,153	1	11	8				7			4		5				6				2	9	3		10		
1369	26	(h)	Rochdale	W 5-2	Walker, Cocker 2, Earl, Brinton	14,408	1	11	3				7		10	4		5				6				2	9			8		
1370	28	(h)	Halifax T	W 2-1	Walker, Cocker	5,820	1	11	3				7		10	4		5				6				2	9			8		
1371	Jan 1	(a)	New Brighton	L 0-1		5,298	1	11	3				7		10	4		5				6				2	9			8		
1372	4	(h)	Carlisle U	W 2-0	Brinton, Earl	10,006	1	11					7		8	4		5				6				2	9	3		10		
1373	15	(a)	Gateshead	W 2-1	Stock, Shaw	2,271	1	11	3						10	4		5				6		7		2	9		8			
1374	18	(a)	Accrington S	L 1-2	Wassall	5,330	1	11					7		10	4		5				6				2	9	3			8	
1375	25	(h)	Barrow	W 2-0	Earl, Brown	8,060	1	11	3	4			7		10			5				6				2	9				8	
1376	Feb 1	(a)	Bradford C	W 2-0	Walker, Brinton	8,258	1	11		4					10			5				6		7		2	9	3		8		
1377	8	(h)	Oldham A	W 4-0	Stock, Earl, Shaw, Wassall	8,105	1	11		4					10			5				6				2	9	3	8		7	
1378	15	(a)	Southport	L 1-4	Morris	3,465	1	11		4					10			5				6		7		2	9	3		8		
1379	22	(h)	Rotherham U	L 1-2	Shaw	7,894	1	11					7		10			5				6		4		2	9	3		8		
1380	Mar 15	(a)	Tranmere R	L 1-2	Shaw	7,019	1	11					7		10			5				6		4		2	9	3		8		
1381	22	(h)	Darlington	W 1-0	Cocker	8,098		11					7		10			5	1		6	4				2	9	3		8		
1382	29	(a)	Hull C	W 3-0	Shaw 2, Walker	17,209	1	11		4					10			5				6		7		2	9	3		8		
1383	Apr 4	(h)	Wrexham	W 1-0	Gleave	12,050	1	11		4					10			5				6		7		2	9	3		8		
1384	5	(a)	Gateshead	W 2-0	Brinton 2	7,693	1	11		4								5				6		7		2	9	3		10	8	
1385	7	(a)	Wrexham	L 1-2	Shaw	10,029	1	11		4								5				6		7		2	9	3		10	8	
1386	12	(h)	Hartlepools U	L 0-1		8,002	1	11		4			7		10			5				6				2	9	3		8		
1387	19	(h)	Crewe A	W 3-2	Shaw 2, Cocker	8,673	1	11		4			7		10			5				6				2	9	3		8		
1388	26	(a)	Lincoln C	L 0-4		5,550	1	11		4			7		10			2				6		5			9	3		8		
1389	May 3	(h)	New Brighton	W 2-0	Earl (pen), McCulloch	5,610	1	11		4			7		10			2				6		5			9	3		8		
1390	10	(a)	Crewe A	L 2-3	Shaw, Brown	3,411	1	11	3	4					10			2				6		5			9			8	7	
1391	24	(a)	Chester	L 0-3		4,563	1	11		4			7		10			5				6				2	9	3		8		
1392	31	(h)	York C	W 4-2	Earl, Dainty 2, Jessop	5,615	1		4					11	10			5		9		6				2	7	3		8		
					Appearances		41	39	35	11	4	9	21	1	30	14	1	33	1	1	1	42	2	25	1	35	30	26	5	35	17	2
					Goals			6	8		1	3	9	2	11	1		1		1		3		1			16		3	10	2	

FINAL LEAGUE POSITION: 4th in Division Three North

FA Cup

No.	Date		Opponent	Result	Scorers	Att.	Bowles	Brinton	Brown	Cocker	Earl	Eastham	Gleave	McCulloch	Redfern	Shaw	Staniforth	Walker
1	Nov 30	(h)	Southport	W 2-0	Brinton, Cocker	10,000	1	11	6	7		4	5	8	2	9	3	10
2	Dec 14	(a)	Halifax T	D 1-1	Shaw	6,000	1	11		7	10	4	5	6	2	9	3	8
R	18	(a)	Halifax T	W 2-1	Earl (pen), Brinton	7,500	1	11		7	10	4	5	6	2	9	3	8
3	Jan 11	(a)	Bolton W	L 1-5	Walker	30,240	1	11		7	10	4	5	6	2	8	3	9
					Appearances		4	4	1	4	3	4	4	4	4	4	4	4
					Goals			2		1	1					1		1

Average Home League attendance: 8,881
Average Away League attendance: 8,059

1947-48

No	Date	Opponent	Result	Scorers	Att	Barkas	Bowles	Brinton	Brown	Cocker	Dainty	Earl	Finney	Glaister	Gleave	Glover	Hacking	Herd	Jackson	Jessop	McCulloch	Monks	Morris	Paterson	Redfern	Shaw	Stanforth	Stock	Swinscoe	Vennard	Walker	Wassall	Waters
1393	Aug 23 (a)	Southport	W 4-0	Jessop, Brinton, Dainty, Brown	9,148	1	11	4			7	8		10	5					9	6	3					2						
1394	25 (h)	Halifax T	W 2-1	Brown (pen), Earl	15,087	1	11	4			7	8		10	5					9	6	3					2						
1395	30 (h)	Lincoln C	D 1-1	Glaister	13,199	1	11	4			7	8		10	5					9	6	3					2						
1396	Sep 1 (a)	Halifax T	L 0-4		8,664	1	11	6			7	8		10	5					9		3					2				4		
1397	6 (a)	Accrington S	L 2-5	Watters, Glaister	7,055	1		6	11					10	2					9	5	3			8						4		7
1398	8 (h)	Wrexham	L 0-1		10,178	1		6	11					10	2					9	4	3		5	8								7
1399	13 (h)	Hull C	D 0-0		9,712	1	11	6				8		10						9	4	3		5			2						7
1400	17 (a)	Wrexham	L 0-2		11,737	1	11	6	7					10						9	4	3		5			2	8					
1401	20 (a)	Carlisle U	L 0-4		13,327	1	11	6						10						8	4	3		5			2		9				7
1402	27 (a)	Bradford C	L 0-1		10,771	1		6						10				2	11	8		3	9	5							4		7
1403	Oct 4 (h)	Barrow	L 2-3	Brinton, Shaw	9,652	1	11	9			6			10	5					8		3				7	2				4		
1404	11 (h)	Rotherham U	D 2-2	Jessop, Brinton	11,576	1	11	8			7			10	5					9	6	3					2				4		
1405	18 (a)	Hartlepools U	D 0-0		6,903	1	11	8			7	10			5					9	6	3					2				4		
1406	25 (h)	Gateshead	D 1-1	Opp own-goal	10,237	1	11				7			10	5					9	6	3					2	8			4		
1407	Nov 1 (a)	Darlington	D 0-0		8,013	1					10			11	5						6	3	9				2	8			4		7
1408	8 (h)	Tranmere R	W 2-0	Shaw, Barkas	10,872	10	1							11	5						6	3	9				2	8			4		7
1409	15 (a)	Oldham A	D 0-0		15,494	10	1							11	5						6	3	9	7			2	8			4		
1410	22 (h)	York C	W 4-2	Barkas 3, Stock	9,282	10	1							11	5						6	3	9	7			2	8			4		
1411	Dec 6 (h)	Chester	W 4-1	Barkas 2, Glaister 2	9,630	10	1							11	5						6	3	9	7			2	8			4		
1412	25 (h)	New Brighton	L 1-2	Jessop (pen)	11,816	1	11		6	8				10	5					9		3		7			2				4		
1413	27 (a)	New Brighton	L 0-1		5,884	1	11				7		9	8	5			3	10								2				6	4	
1414	Jan 3 (a)	Lincoln C	L 0-3		12,777	10	1			9	7	8		11								3		5			2				6	4	
1415	17 (h)	Accrington S	D 1-1	Cocker	8,932	10	1			9				11	5							3		7			2	8			6	4	
1416	31 (a)	Hull C	L 0-1		27,410	10	1							11	5	6				9		3		7			2	8			4		
1417	Feb 7 (a)	Carlisle U	L 2-3	Swinscoe, Barkas	11,135	8	1				10			11	5						4	3					2		9		6		7
1418	14 (h)	Bradford C	D 3-3	Barkas, Glaister, Swinscoe	13,391	10		11			7			9	5		1				4	3					2		9		6		
1419	21 (h)	Barrow	D 0-0		7,169	10	1	11		4				8	5							3		7			2		9		6		
1420	28 (a)	Rotherham U	L 1-4	Dainty	13,339	10	1	11	6	9				8	5							3		7			2				4		
1421	Mar 6 (h)	Hartlepools U	W 2-0	Dainty, Barkas	9,991	10	1			9				11	5	6						3		7			2	8			4		
1422	13 (a)	Gateshead	D 1-1	Glaister	6,967	10	1			9	7			11	5							3					2	8			6		
1423	20 (h)	Darlington	L 1-3	Dainty	12,247	10	1			9				11	5			8			6	3		7			2						
1424	26 (a)	Rochdale	W 2-1	Glaister, Swinscoe	7,183	10	1				7			11				8			6	3		5			2		9		4		
1425	27 (a)	Tranmere R	W 3-2	Swinscoe, Herd, Barkas	8,525	10	1				7			11				8			6	3		5			2		9		4		
1426	29 (h)	Rochdale	W 4-0	Barkas 2, Glaister, Swinscoe	11,002	10	1				7			11				8			6	3		5			2		9		4		
1427	Apr 3 (a)	Oldham A	W 3-0	Herd, Swinscoe, Opp own goal	13,895	10	1				7			11				8			6	3		5			2		9		4		
1428	5 (a)	Mansfield T	W 2-1	Swinscoe, Dainty	12,760	10	1				7			11							6	3		5			2	8	9		4		
1429	10 (a)	York C	L 2-3	Stock, Dainty	7,511	10	1				7			11							6	3		5			2	8	9		4		
1430	14 (a)	Crewe A	L 2-4	Herd (pen), Dainty	6,613	10	1				7			11		4		8			6	3		5			2		9				
1431	17 (h)	Mansfield T	W 5-0	Dainty 2, Swinscoe 2, Glaister	11,039	10	1				7			11				8			6	3		5			2		9		4		
1432	24 (a)	Chester	D 2-2	Dainty 2	3,881	10	1	11			7							8			6	3		5			2		9		4		
1433	26 (h)	Southport	L 0-3		10,339	10	1	11			7					4		8			6	3		5			2		9				
1434	May 1 (h)	Crewe A	W 2-1	Dainty, Herd	8,198	10	1				7			11				8				3		5		6	2		9		4		
	FINAL LEAGUE POSITION: 17th in Division Three North				**Appearances**	25	41	19	13	11	25	12	1	34	24	8	1	10	2	16	17	39	30	10	1	11	40	13	14	5	33	2	5
					Goals	12		3	2	1	12	1		9				4		3						2		2	9				

Own-goals 2

FA Cup

No	Date	Opponent	Result	Scorers	Att	Barkas	Bowles	Brinton	Brown	Cocker	Dainty	Earl	Finney	Glaister	Gleave	Glover	Hacking	Herd	Jackson	Jessop	McCulloch	Monks	Morris	Paterson	Redfern	Shaw	Stanforth	Stock	Swinscoe	Vennard	Walker	Wassall	Waters
1	Nov 29 (h)	Accrington S	W 3-1	Stock 2, Morris	15,016	10	1							11	5						6	3	9	7			2	8			4		
2	Dec 13 (h)	Shrewsbury T	D 1-1*	Barkas	18,000	10	1							11	5						6	3	9	7			2	8			4		
R	20 (a)	Shrewsbury T	D 2-2§	Shaw, Glaister	13,489	10	1							11	5						6	3	9	7			2	8			4		
2R	22(nt)	Shrewsbury T	W 3-2§	Glaister 2, McCulloch	12,812		1				7			11							6	3	5				9	2	8		4	10	
3	Jan 10 (h)	Torquay U	W 3-0	Morris, Barkas 2	17,938	10	1		6	9				11	5							3		7			2	8			4		
4	24 (a)	Charlton A	L 0-3		39,972	10	1		6					11	5							3	9	7			2	8			4		
				Appearances		5	6		2	1	1			6	5				1		4	6	6				4	6	6		6	1	
				Goals		3								3							1		2			1		2					

Average Home League attendance: 11,020
Average Away League attendance: 10,054

*This was the first time the FA had ruled that extra-time be played at the end of the *first* tie. The game at Edgeley Park was abandoned after 112 minutes due to bad light, but the FA ruled that the 'replay' should be at Shrewsbury.

§After extra-time.

†Played at Maine Road, Manchester. Prior to the replay at Shrewsbury, the clubs could not agree where, if a third game was necessary, the 'neutral' ground should be; Shrewsbury favoured St Andrew's, Birmingham whilst Stockport preferred Maine Road, Manchester. The venue was determined by the toss of a coin.

1948-49

No	Date	Opponent	Result	Scorers	Att	Barclay	Barkas	Barker	Bowles	Brown	Cocker	Dainty	Easdale	Finney	Glaister	Glover	Hacking	Herd	Kenny	Maddison	McCulloch	Monks	Morris	Paterson	Ratcliffe	Stanforth	Swinscoe	Walker	Ward	Wilmott
1435	Aug 21 (h)	Southport	D 0-0		11,877		10		1		7				11			8				3		6		2	9	4		5
1436	25 (a)	Chester	L 0-2		7,644		10		1		7				11			8				3		6		2	9	4		5
1437	28 (a)	Crewe A	D 3-3	Barker 3	9,472	9		7	1						10			8	11		4	3		6		2				5
1438	Sep 1 (h)	Chester	D 1-1	Glaister	11,707			7	1						10			8	11	9		3		6		2		4		5
1439	4 (h)	York C	D 1-1	Glaister	12,157			7	1						10			8	11	5		3		6		2	9	4		
1440	8 (a)	New Brighton	W 2-0	Herd, Glaister	9,238		10	7	1						11	4		8			5	3		6		2	9			
1441	11 (a)	Bradford C	D 1-1	Glaister	9,585		10	7	1						11	4		8			5	3		6		2	9			
1442	15 (h)	New Brighton	W 1-0	Glaister	9,525		10	7	1						11	4		8			5	3		6		2	9			
1443	18 (a)	Carlisle U	L 1-2	Swinscoe	12,701		10	7	1				8		11						5	3		6		2	9	4		
1444	25 (h)	Gateshead	W 3-1	Glover, Barkas, Glaister	12,235		10	7	1						11	6		8			5	3				2	9	4		
1445	30 (a)	Doncaster R	L 1-3	Herd (pen)	10,460		10	7	1						11	6		8			5	3				2	9	4		
1446	Oct 2 (a)	Hartlepools U	D 0-0		9,298		10	9	1		7				11	4		8			5	3		6		2				
1447	9 (h)	Halifax T	W 3-1	Barkas 2, Morris	12,904		10	7	1						11	4		8			5	3	9	6		2				
1448	16 (a)	Wrexham	D 0-0		9,129		10	7	1						11	4		8			5	3	9	6		2				
1449	23 (h)	Barrow	L 1-2	Morris	12,221		10	7	1			6			11	4		8			5	3	9			2				
1450	30 (a)	Mansfield T	L 0-4		11,807		10	7	1			6			11	4		8			5	3	9			2				
1451	Nov 6 (h)	Tranmere R	W 4-1	Swinscoe 3, Barkas	9,720		10		1		7				11			8			5	3		6		2	9	4		
1452	13 (a)	Oldham A	L 2-5	Swinscoe, Barkas	11,964		10	7	1						11			8			5	3		6		2	9	4		
1453	20 (a)	Accrington S	W 2-1	Glaister, McCulloch	9,836				1		7	5			11			10			4	3		6		2	9	8		
1454	Dec 4 (h)	Hull C	D 0-0		15,049				1						11			10			4	3	7	6		2	9	8		5
1455	25 (h)	Rochdale	D 2-2	Herd, Barkas	10,641		10		1		7							8	11		4	3		6		2	9			5
1456	27 (a)	Rochdale	L 0-2		10,510		10		1		7							8	11		4	3		6		2	9			5
1457	Jan 1 (h)	Crewe A	W 4-0	Swinscoe 2, Dainty 2	9,779				1		7	5			11			10			4	3		6		2	9	8		
1458	15 (a)	York C	L 0-4		5,487				1		7	5			11			10			4	3		6		2	9	8		
1459	22 (h)	Bradford C	W 5-2	Paterson 2, Swinscoe 3	8,446			7	1		5				11			8	3		4		10	6		2	9			
1460	Feb 5 (h)	Carlisle U	W 2-0	Swinscoe, Barker	9,384		10	7	1						11			8	3		4			6		2	9			5
1461	12 (a)	Rotherham U	L 1-2	Glaister	12,495		10	7	1						11			8	3		4			6		2	9			5
1462	19 (a)	Gateshead	W 1-0	Barker	8,619			7	1						11	10		8	3		4			6		2	9			5
1463	26 (h)	Hartlepools U	W 4-0	Barker 2, Herd (pen), Paterson	6,954			7	1						11	10		8	3		4			6		2	9			5
1464	Mar 5 (a)	Halifax T	W 1-0	Herd	2,944			7	1						11	10		8	3		4			6		2	9			5
1465	12 (h)	Wrexham	W 1-0	Swinscoe	9,173			7							11	10	1		3		4			6		2	9	8		5
1466	19 (a)	Barrow	L 1-2	Barker	3,859			7	1						11	10		8	3		4			6		2	9			5
1467	26 (h)	Mansfield T	W 2-0	Swinscoe, Glaister	8,183			7	1						11	10		8	3		4			6		2	9			5
1468	Apr 2 (a)	Tranmere R	D 0-0		6,020			7	1	10					11			8	3		4			6		2	9			5
1469	9 (h)	Oldham A	L 1-2	Swinscoe	16,898				1	10	7				11			8	3		4			6		2	9			5
1470	15 (a)	Darlington	D 1-1	Opp own-goal	10,037				1	10	7				11			8	3		4			6		2	9			5
1471	16 (a)	Accrington S	L 1-2	Swinscoe (pen)	6,094			7	1	10					11			8	3		5			6		2	9	4		
1472	18 (h)	Darlington	W 2-0	Brown 2	11,010				1	10	7				11			8	3		5			6	4	2	9			
1473	23 (h)	Rotherham U	L 0-1		14,278				1	10	7				11			8	3		5			6		2	9	4		
1474	30 (a)	Hull C	L 1-6	Herd (pen)	38,192			7	1	10	9				11			8	2		5	3		6				4		
1475	May 2 (a)	Southport	L 0-1		6,400			7	1	9					11	6					5	3				2	10	4	8	
1476	7 (h)	Doncaster R	W 5-1	Cocker, Herd, Barker 2, Swinscoe (pen)	7,166			7	1		9				11			8	3		5			6		2	10	4		
		Appearances				1	19	29	41	9	7	10	6	1	40	15	1	39	19	5	40	25	6	37	1	40	30	22	1	18
		Goals					6	10	2	1	2				9	1		7			1			2		3	16			

FINAL LEAGUE POSITION: 8th in Division Three North

Own-goal 1

FA Cup

No	Date	Opponent	Result	Scorers	Att	Barclay	Barkas	Barker	Bowles	Brown	Cocker	Dainty	Easdale	Finney	Glaister	Glover	Hacking	Herd	Kenny	Maddison	McCulloch	Monks	Morris	Paterson	Ratcliffe	Stanforth	Swinscoe	Walker	Ward	Wilmott
1	Nov 27 (a)	Workington	W 3-0	Herd 2, Glaister	10,669				1			5			11			10			4	3	7	6		2	9	8		
2	Dec 11 (a)	Scunthorpe U	W 1-0	Glaister	13,775		10		1						11				7		4	3		6		2	9	8		5
3	Jan 8 (a)	Portsmouth	L 0-7		33,590				1		7	5			11			10			4	3		6		2	9	8		
		Appearances					1		3		1	2			3			2	1		3	3	1	3		3	3	3		1
		Goals													2			2												

Average Home League attendance: 10,912
Average Away League attendance: 10,093

181

1949-50

League matches — player shirt numbers are shown under each player column.

No.	Date	V	Opponent	Result	Scorers	Att.	Barker	Bowles	Brown	Cavanagh	Cocker	Finney	Glaister	Glover	Hacking	Herd	Kenny	Lester	McCulloch	McGann	McGuigan	Monks	Paterson	Reid	Robinson	Sanaghan	Staniforth	Swinscoe	Walker	Ward	Wilmott
1477	Aug 20	(a)	Chester	W 4-0	Brown, McGuigan, Cocker, Glaister	10,026		1	10	9	11								4		7		6	8		2	3				5
1478	24	(h)	Bradford C	W 1-0	Brown	13,657		1	10	9	11								4		7		6	8		2	3				5
1479	27	(h)	Southport	W 3-2	Brown, Herd, Cocker	13,483		1	10	9	11					8			4		7		6			2	3				5
1480	31	(a)	Bradford C	W 1-0	Cocker	10,116		1	10	9	11								4		7		6			2	3				5
1481	Sep 3	(a)	Carlisle U	L 0-2		14,670		1	10	9	11								4		7		6	8		2	3				5
1482	7	(a)	New Brighton	W 3-1	Robinson, Herd, Cocker	6,305		1			9		11			8	3		4		7		6		10	2					5
1483	10	(h)	Doncaster R	L 0-1		15,350		1	10		9			5		8			4		7		6		11	2	3				
1484	14	(h)	New Brighton	L 0-2		10,108		1	10		9					8			4		7	3	6		11	2					5
1485	17	(h)	Gateshead	W 2-1	Lester, Swinscoe	11,948		1			7			5		8	2	9	4		11		6				3	10			
1486	24	(a)	Hartlepools U	L 0-1		10,036		1			7			5			2	9	4		11		6	8			3	10			
1487	26	(a)	Rotherham U	L 1-2	Swinscoe	8,768		1			7			5				9	4		11		6		10	2	3	8			
1488	Oct 1	(h)	Darlington	W 2-1	McGuigan (pen), Lester	11,153		1						5		8		9	4		7		6		11	3	2	10			
1489	8	(h)	Mansfield T	W 1-0	Herd	15,885		1						5		8		9	4		7		6		11	3	2	10			
1490	15	(a)	Accrington S	L 2-4	Opp own-goal, Cocker	7,395		1			7			5		8		9	4		11		6			3	2	10			
1491	22	(h)	Wrexham	W 2-1	Glaister, Herd	11,175		1					11	5		8		9	4	2	7		6				3	10			
1492	29	(a)	Oldham A	D 3-3	McGuigan, Cocker, Herd	16,151		1			9		11	5		8			4	2	7		6				3	10			
1493	Nov 5	(a)	York C	W 3-1	Herd 2, Swinscoe	10,626		1			9		11	5		8			4	2	7		6				3	10			
1494	12	(a)	Tranmere R	L 0-2		7,205		1			9		11	5		8			4	2	7		6				3	10			
1495	19	(h)	Crewe A	W 4-1	Herd, Glaister, Swinscoe, Cocker	15,124					9		11	5	1	8	3		4	2	7		6					10			
1496	Dec 3	(a)	Lincoln C	D 1-1	McGuigan (pen)	7,939		1			9		11	5		8			4	2	7		6				3	10			
1497	17	(h)	Chester	W 3-0	Cocker, Herd 2	8,413		1			9		11	5		8			4	2	7		6				3	10			
1498	24	(a)	Southport			9,100		1			9			5					4	2	7		6		11		3	10			
1499	26	(h)	Halifax T	W 2-0	Cocker, Herd	15,223		1			9			5		8			4		7		6	10		3	2	11			
1500	27	(a)	Halifax T	L 1-3	Cocker	8,851		1			9			5		8			4		7		6	10		3	2	11			
1501	31	(h)	Carlisle U	W 2-0	Cocker, McGuigan	13,026	7	1			9			5		8			4		11		6			3	2	10			
1502	Jan 14	(a)	Doncaster R	L 0-3		23,363	7	1			9			5					4		8		6	10		3	2	11			
1503	21	(a)	Gateshead	L 0-1		7,723		1			9			5		8					7		6	10		3	2	11	4		
1504	Feb 4	(h)	Hartlepools U	W 1-0	Cocker	20,873		1	10	8	9			5					4	2	7		6	11		3					
1505	18	(a)	Darlington	D 1-1	McGuigan (pen)	8,334		1			9			5		8			4		7		6	11		3	2	10			
1506	25	(a)	Crewe A	L 0-1		11,139		1	10		9			5		8				2	7		6	11					4		
1507	Mar 4	(a)	Barrow	L 1-3	Swinscoe	10,818		1			9			5		8			4		7		6	11		3	2	10			
1508	11	(a)	Wrexham	W 2-0	Herd, McGuigan (pen)	7,309		1			9			5		8			4		7		6	11		3	2	10			
1509	18	(h)	Oldham A	L 1-3	Herd	13,734		1			9			5		8			4		7		6	11		3	2	10			
1510	25	(a)	York C	D 1-1	Cocker	6,365		1			9		11	5		8			4		7		6			3	2	10			
1511	Apr 1	(h)	Tranmere R	W 2-1	McGuigan (pen), Herd	8,094		1	10				11	5		8			4		7		6			3	2	9			
1512	7	(h)	Rochdale	D 1-1	Herd	14,751		1	10				11	5		8			4		7		6			3	2	9			
1513	8	(a)	Mansfield T	L 0-3		9,153		1	8		7			5				9	4		11		6			3	2	10			
1514	10	(a)	Rochdale	D 1-1	Robinson	6,711		1			9	10		5		8			4				6		11	3	2	7			
1515	15	(h)	Accrington S	W 1-0	Staniforth	7,304		1			9	10				8			4				6		11	3	2	7	5		
1516	22	(a)	Lincoln C	D 1-1	Finney	10,087		1			7	10	11	5					4	2						3		9			
1517	27	(a)	Barrow	W 1-0	Swinscoe	5,132					8			5					4	2	7		6	11		3		9	10		1
1518	29	(h)	Rotherham U	L 0-2		3,385					8	10							4	2	7	3	6	11		9				1	5
	Appearances						2	39	8	5	37	4	17	33	1	32	4	8	40	13	39	2	42	16	9	39	29	28	4	2	9
	Goals								3		13	1	3			15		2			8				2		1	6			

FINAL LEAGUE POSITION: 10th in Division Three North

Own-goal 1

FA Cup

No.	Date	V	Opponent	Result	Scorers	Att.	Barker	Bowles	Brown	Cavanagh	Cocker	Finney	Glaister	Glover	Hacking	Herd	Kenny	Lester	McCulloch	McGann	McGuigan	Monks	Paterson	Reid	Robinson	Sanaghan	Staniforth	Swinscoe	Walker	Ward	Wilmott
1	Nov 26	(h)	Billingham S	W 3-0	McGuigan 2 (1 pen), Herd	13,075					9		11	5	1	8	3		4	2	7		6					10			
2	Dec 10	(a)	Nottingham F	W 2-0	McGuigan, Herd	18,253		1			9		11	5		8			4	2	7		6				3	10			
3	Jan 7	(h)	Barnsley	W 4-2	Cocker 2, Swinscoe, McGuigan (pen)	23,847		1			9		11	5		8			4		7		6			3	2	10			
4	28	(h)	Hull C	D 0-0		26,600	7	1			9			5		8			4		11		6			3	2	10			
R	Feb 2	(a)	Hull C	W 2-0	Herd, Cocker	24,556		1			9			5		8			4		7		6	11		3	2	10			
5	11	(h)	Liverpool	L 1-2	Herd	*27,833		1			9			5		8			4		7		6	11		3	2	10			
	Appearances						1	5			6		3	6	1	6	1		6	2	6		6	2		4	5	6			
	Goals										3					4					4							1			

Average Home League attendance: 12,003
Average Away League attendance: 9,711

*This is Stockport's highest recorded attendance although it is registered by the Football League as being 28,000 as all tickets were sold.

1950-51

No.	Date		Opponent	Result	Scorers	Att.	Allman	Barker	Black	Bowles	Brennan	Brooke	Cavanagh	Cocker	Dick	Dixon	Emptage	Evans	Finney	Glover	Gualan	Herd A	Herd D	McCulloch	McGann	McGuigan	Monks	Oliver	Paterson	Reid	Sanaghan	Stanforth	Ward	Wilmott
1519	Aug 19	(h)	Bradford C	W 3-1	Black, A.Herd, McGuigan (pen)	14,875		10	9											5		8		4		7	11	6		3	2	1		
1520	21	(a)	Rotherham U	D 0-0		12,235		10	9											5	8			4		7	11	6		3	2	1		
1521	26	(a)	Rochdale	D 1-1	Black	13,075		10	9											5	8			4		7	11	6		3	2	1		
1522	28	(h)	Rotherham U	L 1-3	Cocker	14,937		10	9					8						5				4		7	11	6		3	2	1		
1523	Sep 2	(h)	Chester	L 0-3		10,834		10	9				7	8						5				4			11	6		3	2	1		
1524	4	(a)	Crewe A	W 2-0	Cocker, Oliver	9,469		10	9				7	8						5				4			11	6		3	2	1		
1525	9	(a)	Shrewsbury T	W 3-0	A.Herd 2 (1 pen), Black	9,632		10	9				7	8						5				4	2		11	6		3		1		
1526	11	(h)	Crewe A	W 3-0	Black, Cocker, Barker	8,112		10	9				7	8						5				4			11	6		3	2	1		
1527	16	(h)	Lincoln C	W 2-0	Oliver, Cocker	11,582		10	9				7	8						5				4			11	6		3	2	1		
1528	18	(a)	Gateshead	L 0-2		11,196		10	9				7	8						5				4			11	6		3	2	1		
1529	23	(a)	Darlington	L 1-2	Black	7,146		10	9				7	8						5				4			11	6		3	2	1		
1530	30	(a)	Barrow	L 0-1		4,512		10	9				7	8						5				4			11	6		3	2	1		
1531	Oct 7	(h)	Bradford	W 2-1	Barker, A.Herd	10,640		10	9				7	8						5				4			11	6	3		2	1		
1532	14	(a)	Tranmere R	D 1-1	Paterson	13,584		9					7	10						5		8		4			11	6	3		2	1		
1533	21	(h)	Wrexham	W 2-1	Oliver, Dick	11,719			9					8	10	7				5				4			11	6	3		2	1		
1534	28	(a)	Oldham A	W 3-1	Dick 2, Dixon	18,646		8	9						10	7				5				4			11	6	3		2	1		
1535	Nov 4	(h)	Mansfield T	W 3-1	Dixon, Black, Paterson	12,297		8	9						10	7				5				4			11	6	3		2	1		
1536	18	(h)	Southport	W 3-2	Cocker, Dick, Black	10,744		8	9						10	7				5				4			11	6	3		2	1		
1537	Dec 2	(a)	Carlisle U	L 1-2	Oliver	10,624		8	9						10	7				5				4			11	6	3		2	1		
1538	9	(a)	Accrington S	W 3-2	Black, Dick 2	3,415		8	9						10	7				5				4			11	6	2			1	3	
1539	16	(a)	Bradford C	W 1-0	Black	9,314		8	9						10	7				5				4			11	6	2			1	3	
1540	23	(a)	Rochdale	D 2-2	Dick, Black	10,152		8	9						10	7				5				4			11	6	2			1	3	
1541	25	(a)	New Brighton	L 0-1		2,124			9						10	7				5				4			11	6	2			1	3	
1542	26	(h)	New Brighton	W 4-0	Black 3, Cocker	12,588		8	9						10	7				5	8			4			11	6	2			1	3	
1543	Jan 13	(a)	Shrewsbury T	W 2-0	Dick 2 (2 pens)	10,788		8	9						10	7	6			5				4			3	11			2	1		
1544	20	(a)	Lincoln C	L 0-6		10,521		8	9						10	7	6			5				4			3	11			2	1		
1545	31	(h)	Gateshead	W 5-2	Emptage, Black, Cocker, Oliver, Dick	6,045		8	9						10	7	6			5				4			3	11			2	1		
1546	Feb 3	(h)	Darlington	W 1-0	Black	11,814		8	9						10	7	4			5				3			6	11			2	1		
1547	10	(a)	Hartlepools U	L 0-2		7,162		8				7		9	10		4			5				3			6	11			2	1		
1548	17	(h)	Barrow	W 4-1	Dick 2, Cocker, Oliver	8,202		8	9						10	7	4			5				3			6	11			2	1		
1549	24	(a)	Bradford	L 0-3		10,477		8	9						10	7	4			5				3			6	11			2	1		
1550	Mar 3	(h)	Tranmere R	D 0-0		10,786		8	9						10	7	4	2		5				3			6	11				1		
1551	10	(a)	Wrexham	L 0-2		7,547		8	9						10	7	4			5				3			6	11				1		
1552	17	(h)	Oldham A	L 1-4	Cocker	13,769		8	9						10	7	4			5				3			6			11	2	1		
1553	24	(a)	Mansfield T	L 1-2	Black	10,219		10	9		4	9	7				6			5	8			3				11			2	1		
1554	Mar 26	(h)	Halifax T	W 2-1	A.Herd, Black	6,308	9	10			4		7				6			5	8			3							2	1		
1555	27	(a)	Halifax T	L 0-1		8,272	9	10			4		8		7		6			5				3				11			2	1		
1556	31	(h)	Scunthorpe U	L 1-2	Cocker	6,401	9	10			4		7				6			5	8			3				11			2	1		
1557	Apr 4	(a)	Chester	L 0-3		2,896	9	10	1		4	7	11		8					3					5						2			6
1558	7	(a)	Southport	L 0-2		4,316	9		1		4	7	10				6			5	8			3				11			2			
1559	11	(h)	York C	D 0-0		5,520		10	1		4	7	9				6			5	8			3				11			2			
1560	14	(h)	Accrington S	D 0-0		5,264		10	1		4	7	9				6			5	8			3				11			2			
1561	21	(a)	Carlisle U	D 2-2	Finney, Cocker	10,154		10	1	9	4	7					6	8	5	11				3							2			
1562	28	(h)	York C	W 1-0	Finney	5,658		10	1	9	4	7					6	8	5					3				11			2			
1563	30	(a)	Scunthorpe U	L 0-3		9,175		10	1	9	4					7	6		5	8				3				11			2			
1564	May 5	(h)	Hartlepools U	W 2-0	D.Herd, Finney	6,005						4					10		5	11	8	7	3					6			2			
			Appearances				5	9	42	8	4	1	13	44	25	21	21	1	4	45	2	23	1	46	1	4	17	36	25	7	13	44	38	6
			Goals					2	17					11	12	2	1		3			5	1			1		6	2					

FINAL LEAGUE POSITION: 10th in Division Three North

FA Cup

Rd	Date		Opponent	Result	Scorers	Att.	Barker	Black	Cocker	Dick	Dixon	Glover	Herd A	McCulloch	Monks	Oliver	Paterson	Stanforth	Ward
3*	Jan 6	(h)	Brentford	W 2-1	Cocker, Dixon	16,341	8	9	10	7		5		4	3	11	6	2	1
4	27	(a)	Blackpool	L 1-2	Black	31,190	8	9	10	7	4	5		3		6	11	2	1
			Appearances				2	2	2	2	1	2		2	2	2	2	2	2
			Goals					1	1		1								

Average Home League attendance: 10,006
Average Away League attendance: 8,722

*As in season 1935-36, Stockport were exempt from the first two rounds as a result of their FA Cup feat the previous season in reaching the fifth round.

1951-52

The following table records league fixtures (match number, date, venue, opponent, result, scorers, attendance) followed by the player appearance grid (shirt numbers worn). Player columns, left to right: Allman, Black, Bowles, Cavanagh, Cocker, Connor, Emptage, Finney, Glover, Haddington, Herd A, Herd D, Hodder, Kenny, McCaig, McCulloch, Moran, Oliver, Paterson, Staniforth, Ward, Weigh, Wilmott.

No	Date		Opponent	Result	Scorers	Att	Alm	Blk	Bow	Cav	Coc	Con	Emp	Fin	Glo	Had	HeA	HeD	Hod	Ken	McC	Mcu	Mor	Oli	Pat	Sta	War	Wei	Wil
1565	Aug 18	(a)	Mansfield T	L 0-1		10,753		10	1		9			8	5					3	7	4		11	6	2			
1566	20	(h)	Bradford	W 1-0	Weigh	11,277		10	1		9			8	5					3	7	4			6	2		11	
1567	25	(h)	Rochdale	W 1-0	Weigh	9,544		10	1		9			8	5					3	7	4			6	2		11	
1568	27	(a)	Bradford	L 2-4	Allman, A.Herd (pen)	12,150	7		1		9			8	5		10			3		4			6	2		11	
1569	Sep 1	(a)	Accrington S	W 3-0	Finney 2, McCaig	7,642		10	1		9			8	5					3	7	4			6	2		11	
1570	3	(h)	Chesterfield	W 2-1	A.Herd (pen), Weigh	9,542			1		9			8	5		10			3	7	4			6	2		11	
1571	8	(h)	Carlisle U	D 1-1	Finney	11,914		10	1		9			8	5					3	7	4			6	2		11	
1572	10	(a)	Chesterfield	W 1-0	Cocker	9,893			1		9			8	5		10			3	7	4			6	2		11	
1573	15	(a)	Southport	W 1-0	Black	6,647		10	1		9			8	5					3	7	4			6	2		11	
1574	22	(a)	Workington	W 3-0	Cavanagh, McCaig, A.Herd	8,807			1	8	9				5		10			3	7	4		11	6	2			
1575	29	(h)	Barrow	D 2-2	Paterson, Cocker (pen)	11,000			1	8	9				5			10		3	7	4		11	6	2			
1576	Oct 6	(h)	Gateshead	D 0-0		14,807	9	10	1	8					5					3	7	4		11	6	2			
1577	13	(a)	Darlington	W 2-1	Oliver, Cavanagh	5,845		10	1	8	9				5					3	7	4		11	6	2			
1578	20	(h)	Oldham A	D 0-0		24,473		10	1	8	9	7			5					3		4		11	6	2			
1579	27	(a)	Hartlepools U	W 1-0	Oliver	9,280			1		9	7		8						3		4	10	11	6	2			5
1580	Nov 3	(h)	Bradford C	L 1-2	Connor	10,992		10	1		9	7		8						3		4		11	6	2			5
1581	10	(a)	York C	W 1-0	Connor	10,782		10	1		9	7		8						3		4		11	6	2			5
1582	17	(h)	Chester	D 0-0		11,822		10	1		9	7		8						3		4		11	6	2			5
1583	Dec 1	(h)	Scunthorpe U	D 1-1	Weigh	10,398		10	1			7		8						3		4		11	6	2		9	5
1584	8	(a)	Tranmere R	L 0-2		4,830		10	1			7		8						3		4		11	6	2		9	5
1585	15	(h)	Mansfield T	W 2-1	A.Herd, Haddington (pen)	10,212		10	1		9					8	7			3		4		11	6	2			5
1586	22	(a)	Rochdale	D 0-0		5,857		10	1		9					8	7			3		4		11	6	2			5
1587	25	(h)	Crewe A	W 4-2	Haddington 3 (1 pen), Oliver	11,521		10	1		9					8	7			3		4		11	6	2			5
1588	26	(a)	Crewe A	L 0-1		11,340			1	8	9	7						10		3		4		11	6	2			5
1589	29	(h)	Accrington S	W 6-0	Black 4, Connor 2	11,278		10	1		9	7		8						3		4		11	6	2			5
1590	Jan 5	(a)	Carlisle U	L 1-2	Oliver	10,744					9	7		8					1	3		4	10	11	6	2			5
1591	12	(h)	Halifax T	W 6-2	Finney 4, Oliver 2	10,004			1		9	7		8						3		4	10	11	6	2			5
1592	19	(h)	Southport	W 3-1	Connor 2, Oliver	11,590			1		9	7		8						3		4	10	11	6	2			5
1593	26	(h)	Workington	W 5-0	Oliver 2, Connor 3	9,651			1		9	7		8						3		4	10	11	6	2			5
1594	Feb 9	(a)	Barrow	W 3-1	Connor 3	7,649			1		9	7		8						3		4	10	11	6	2			5
1595	16	(a)	Gateshead	W 2-0	Oliver, Connor	6,591			1		9	7		8						3		4	10	11	6	2			5
1596	23	(h)	Wrexham	D 0-0		15,383			1		9	7		8						3		4	10	11	6	2			5
1597	Mar 1	(h)	Darlington	W 5-0	Moran, Oliver 2, Finney, Connor	12,212			1		9	7		8						3		4	10	11	6	2			5
1598	8	(a)	Oldham A	L 0-1		33,450			1		9	7		8						3		4	10	11	6	2			5
1599	15	(a)	Hartlepools U	L 0-1		11,020			1		9	7		8						3		4	10	11	6	2			5
1600	22	(a)	Bradford C	W 3-2	Black 2, Oliver	11,102		10	1		9	7		8						3		4		11	6	2			5
1601	24	(a)	Halifax T	W 2-1	Cocker, Weigh	5,318		10	1		9	7		8						3		4			6	2		11	5
1602	29	(h)	York C	W 3-1	Black 2, Weigh	6,334		10	1		9	7		8						3		4			6	2		11	5
1603	Apr 5	(a)	Chester	D 0-0		5,606		10	1		9	7		8						3		4			6	2		11	5
1604	11	(a)	Grimsby T	L 0-4		26,605		10	1		9	7		8						3		4			6	2		11	5
1605	12	(h)	Lincoln C	D 1-1	Connor	18,736		8	1		9	7								3		4	10	11	6	2			5
1606	14	(h)	Grimsby T	D 1-1	Weigh	16,300		8	1		9	7								3		4	10		6	2		11	5
1607	19	(a)	Scunthorpe U	D 1-1	Oliver	8,305		8	1		9	7								3		4	10	11	6	2			5
1608	23	(a)	Lincoln C	L 1-2	Weigh	21,501		8	1		9	7								3		4	10		6	2		11	5
1609	26	(h)	Tranmere R	W 2-0	Paterson, Weigh	6,674		8	1		9	7								3		4	10		6	2		11	5
1610	30	(a)	Wrexham	D 0-0		4,716		10	1		9	7		8						3		4			6	2		11	5
			Appearances				2	27	42	14	34	31	10	20	15	11	7	2	1	46	15	41	16	32	40	44	4	21	31
			Goals				1	9		2	3	15		8		4	4				2		1	14	2			9	

FINAL LEAGUE POSITION: 3rd in Division Three North

FA Cup

No	Date		Opponent	Result	Scorers	Att	Alm	Blk	Bow	Cav	Coc	Con	Emp	Fin	Glo	Had	HeA	HeD	Hod	Ken	McC	Mcu	Mor	Oli	Pat	Sta	War	Wei	Wil
1	Nov 24	(h)	Gateshead	D 2-2	Oliver (pen), Weigh	10,798		10	1	8				9						3	7	4		11		2		6	5
R	28	(a)	Gateshead	D 1-1*	Weigh	7,769		10	1	8				6						3	7	4		11		2		9	5
2R	Dec 3(n§)		Gateshead	L 1-2	Glover	6,831		10	1	8				7						3		4		11		2		9	5
			Appearances					3	3	3				2	1					3	2	3		3		3		3	3
			Goals												1									1				2	

Average Home League attendance: 12,030
Average Away League attendance: 10,670

*After extra-time.

§Played at Hillsborough, Sheffield. The two clubs would not agree to toss a coin to decide the preferred venue. Gateshead desiring the replay to be at St James' Park, Newcastle, Stockport wishing the game to take place at Maine Road, Manchester. (Gateshead played in the Newcastle United strip whilst Stockport played in the Manchester City kit.)

1952-53

No	Date	Match	Result	Scorers	Att	Bell	Black	Bodle	Bowles	Clempson	Cocker	Connor	Crosby	Emptage	Evans	Finney	Glover	Goalen	Hodder	Kenny	McCulloch	Monks	Moran	Murray	Oliver	Paterson	Platts	Rowland	Ward	Weigh	Wilmott
1611	Aug 23	(h) Chester	W 4-1	Cocker 2, Moran, Oliver	10,467	2	8		1		7								3	4			10		11	6				9	5
1612	25	(a) Barrow	L 0-1		6,450	2	8		1			7							3	4			10		11	6				9	5
1613	30	(a) Scunthorpe U	D 2-2	Weigh, Connor	8,892	2	8		1		7	9					5		3	4			10			6				11	
1614	Sep 1	(h) Barrow	W 6-1	Connor 2, Weigh 2 (1 pen), Black 2	8,520	2	8		1		7	9					5			4	6		10			3				11	
1615	6	(a) Wrexham	L 2-5	Cocker 2	10,725	2	8		1		7	9					5			4	6		10			3				11	
1616	8	(a) Port Vale	L 0-2		15,188	2	8		1		7	9	6			10	5			4						3				11	
1617	13	(h) Bradford C	W 6-1	Moran 3, Black 2, Connor	8,279	2	8		1		7	9	6				5			4			10			3				11	
1618	15	(a) Port Vale	L 0-2		10,142	2	8		1		7	9	6				5			4			10			3				11	
1619	20	(a) Rochdale	D 2-2	Oliver (pen), Connor	8,623	2	8		1		7	9	6				5			4			10		11	3					
1620	22	(h) Halifax T	D 1-1	Moran	5,914	2	8		1		7	9								4	6		10	3	11						5
1621	27	(a) Darlington	D 2-2	Black, Moran	5,340	2	8		1		7	9								4	6		10	3	11						5
1622	29	(h) Carlisle U	W 3-0	Black, Weigh 2 (1 pen)	3,639	2	8				7	9					5			4	6		10	3	11			1			
1623	Oct 4	(a) Gateshead	L 0-2		7,062	2	8					9				7	5			4	6		10	3	11			1			
1624	11	(h) Grimsby T	D 2-2	Connor, Black	13,260	2	8					9				7	5			4	6		10	3	11			1			
1625	18	(a) York C	L 0-3		9,222	2	8					9				7	5			4	6		10	3	11			1			
1626	25	(h) Tranmere R	W 3-2	Connor, Black, Bodle	8,601	2	8	10	1		7	9					5			4	6			3	11						
1627	Nov 1	(a) Chesterfield	L 1-2	Connor	8,759	2	8	10	1		7	9					5			4	6			3	11						
1628	8	(h) Workington	W 6-0	Connor 5, Black	7,428	2	8	10	1		7	9								4	6			3	11						5
1629	15	(a) Accrington S	W 4-1	Bodle, Connor, Cocker, Oliver	4,974	2	8	10	1		7	9								4	6			3	11						5
1630	29	(a) Mansfield T	D 2-2	Black 2	4,956	2	8	10	1		7	9								4	6			3	11						5
1631	Dec 13	(a) Bradford	D 1-1	Bodle	7,838	2	8	10	1		7	9								4	6			3	11						5
1632	20	(a) Chester	L 0-4		3,144	2	8	10	1		7	9					5			4	6	3			11						
1633	25	(h) Hartlepools U	D 1-1	Connor	8,591	2	8	10	1		7	9					5			4	6	3			11						
1634	27	(a) Hartlepools U	W 2-0	Bodle (pen), Connor	7,387	2	8	10	1			9				7	5			4	6	3			11						
1635	Jan 1	(a) Carlisle U	L 1-2	Bodle	8,919	2	8	10	1			9				7	5			4	6	3			11						
1636	3	(h) Scunthorpe U	D 1-1	Connor	7,999	2	8	10	1			9				7	5			4	6	3			11						
1637	14	(a) Crewe A	L 0-2		2,741	2	8	10	1		7	9								4	6	3			11						5
1638	17	(h) Wrexham	W 3-1	Connor 3	7,227		8				7	9				10				4	6				11		2	1	3		5
1639	24	(a) Bradford C	L 0-3		11,503		8				7	9				10				4	6				11		2	1	3		5
1640	31	(h) Crewe A	L 2-4	Black, Weigh (pen)	4,579		8		1		7	9				10				4	6						2		3	11	5
1641	Feb 7	(h) Rochdale	W 2-0	Connor, Crosby	5,689	2		10			7	9	8							4	6							1	3	11	5
1642	21	(h) Gateshead	W 3-1	Bodle, Weigh 2	9,616	2		10		8	7	9								4	6							1	3	11	5
1643	28	(a) Grimsby T	W 1-0	Weigh	13,148	2		10		8	7	9								4	6							1	3	11	5
1644	Mar 7	(h) York C	D 1-1	Murray	8,811	2		10		8	7	9									6			4				1	3	11	5
1645	14	(a) Tranmere R	L 0-1		6,704			10		8	7	9									6			4			2	1	3	11	5
1646	21	(h) Chesterfield	W 4-1	Oliver 2, Weigh, Connor	8,046			10		8	7	9									6			4	11		2	1	3		5
1647	28	(a) Workington	W 2-0	Connor, Oliver	4,711			10		8	7	9									6			4	11		2	1	3		5
1648	Apr 3	(a) Southport	L 0-3		8,704			10		8	7	9									6			4	11		2	1	3		5
1649	4	(h) Accrington S	W 3-1	Weigh 2, Connor*	7,068			10		8	7	9									6			4			2	1	3	11	5
1650	6	(h) Southport	W 3-0	Connor 2, Opp own-goal	7,940			10		8	7	9									6			4			2	1	3	11	5
1651	11	(a) Halifax T	L 0-3		5,853			10			7	9		6	8									4			2	1	3	11	5
1652	13	(h) Oldham A	D 1-1	Opp own-goal	16,552			10			7	9		6	8									4			2	1	3	11	5
1653	18	(h) Mansfield T	D 2-2	Moran, Clempson	6,503			10		8	7	9					5				6		11	4			2	1	3		
1654	20	(a) Darlington	L 0-1		4,270			10		8	7	9					5				6		11	4			2	1	3		
1655	25	(a) Oldham A	D 1-1	Weigh	27,681					8	7	9									6		10	4			2	1	3	11	5
1656	29	(h) Bradford	W 2-0	Clempson, Connor	3,619			10		8	7	9					5				6			4	11		2	1	3		

FINAL LEAGUE POSITION: 11th in Division Three North

	Bell	Black	Bodle	Bowles	Clempson	Cocker	Connor	Crosby	Emptage	Evans	Finney	Glover	Goalen	Hodder	Kenny	McCulloch	Monks	Moran	Murray	Oliver	Paterson	Platts	Rowland	Ward	Weigh	Wilmott
Appearances	31	25	29	23	13	19	45	4	5	2	9	19	2	3	32	45	6	18	35	39	6	15	18	8	30	25
Goals		12	6		2	5	27	1				9						7	1	6					13	

Own-goals 2

FA Cup

No	Date	Match	Result	Scorers	Att	Bell	Black	Bodle	Bowles	Clempson	Cocker	Connor	Crosby	Emptage	Evans	Finney	Glover	Goalen	Hodder	Kenny	McCulloch	Monks	Moran	Murray	Oliver	Paterson	Platts	Rowland	Ward	Weigh	Wilmott
1	Nov 22	(a) North Shields	W 6-2	Bodle 2, Connor 3, Oliver	7,956	2	8	10	1		7	9								4	6			3	11						5
2	Dec 6	(h) Gillingham	W 3-1	Bodle (pen), Oliver, Connor	12,473	2	8	10	1		7	9								4	6			3	11						5
3	Jan 10	(a) Walthamstow A	L 1-2	Moran	9,541	2		10	1		7	9								4	6	8	11	3							5

	Bell	Black	Bodle	Bowles	Cocker	Connor	Kenny	McCulloch	Monks	Moran	Murray	Oliver	Wilmott
Appearances	3	2	3	3	3	3	2	3	1	3	3	1	3
Goals			3		4					1		2	

Average Home League attendance: 7,993
Average Away League attendance: 8,585

*Some sources refer to this goal as being an own-goal.

1953-54

No.	Date	Opponent	Result	Scorers	Att.	Anderson CS	Anderson PA	Ashe	Clempson	Connor	Corfield	Crosby	Evans	Finney	Glover	Goalen	Herd	Herod	Hodder	Kennedy	Kenny	McCulloch	Moran	Murray	Oliver	Pendlebury	Pilkington	Platts	Rowland	Ward	Weigh	Wilmott	Wright
1657	Aug 19 (h)	Southport	D 1-1	Finney	10,526	7		2	10	8				9				1						4			6		3		11	5	
1658	22 (a)	Accrington S	L 1-2	Clempson	9,133	7		2	10	8				9				1						4			6		3		11	5	
1659	24 (h)	Halifax T	D 1-1	Clempson	8,687	7			8					9				1			2		10	4			6		3		11	5	
1660	29 (h)	Grimsby T	W 3-2	Clempson 2 (1 pen), Oliver	8,698	7			10					9				1			2	6		8	11		4		3			5	
1661	31 (a)	Halifax T	W 1-0	Finney	3,211	7			10					9				1			2	6		8	11		4		3			5	
1662	Sep 5 (a)	York C	D 0-0		8,573	7			10	9								1		2	3	6		8	11		4					5	
1663	7 (h)	Carlisle U	W 3-2	Connor 3	10,157	7			10	9								1		2	3	6		8	11		4					5	
1664	12 (a)	Rochdale	D 0-0		7,634	7			10	9								1		2	3	6		8	11		4					5	
1665	15 (a)	Carlisle U	L 0-2		9,387	7			10	9	8							1	5		2	3		4	11		6						
1666	19 (h)	Wrexham	D 2-2	Clempson, Murray*	10,259	7			10	9								1			2	6		8	11		4		3			5	
1667	21 (h)	Tranmere R	W 6-0	Connor 3, Clempson 2, Weigh	5,041	7			10	9								1			2	6		8			4		3		11	5	
1668	26 (a)	Mansfield T	L 1-3	Connor	8,610	7			10	9								1			2	6		8			4		3		11	5	
1669	29 (a)	Tranmere R	D 2-2	Connor, Murray	4,933	7			10	9								1			2	6		8			4		3		11	5	
1670	Oct 3 (h)	Barrow	W 5-1	Connor, Weigh, Murray 2, Opp own-goal	9,261	7			10	9								1			2	6		8			4		3		11	5	
1671	10 (h)	Workington	W 2-0	Murray, Connor	8,939	7			10	9								1		2		6		8			4		3		11	5	
1672	17 (a)	Gateshead	L 2-4	Clempson, Connor	8,541	7			10	9								1		2		6		8			4		3		11	5	
1673	24 (h)	Hartlepools U	W 1-0	Weigh	8,867	7			8	9		10						1		2		6					4		3		11	5	
1674	31 (a)	Darlington	L 0-1		4,520	7			10	9								1		2		6		8	11		4		3			5	
1675	Nov 7 (h)	Barnsley	W 3-0	Connor 2, Moran	6,530	7			10	9								1				2	8	6	11		4		3			5	
1676	14 (a)	Bradford	L 2-3	Connor 2	12,253	7			10	9								1				2	8	6	11		4		3			5	
1677	28 (a)	Crewe A	W 5-1	Connor 3, Oliver, Clempson	7,983	7			10	9								1				2	8	6	11		4		3			5	
1678	Dec 5 (h)	Chester	W 5-0	Connor 3, Moran, Clempson (pen)	8,252	7			10	9								1				2	8	6	11		4		3			5	
1679	19 (h)	Accrington S	D 1-1	Connor	9,273	7			10	9								1				2	8	6	11		4		3			5	
1680	25 (h)	Chesterfield	W 6-1	Connor 2, Moran, Murray 2, Oliver	8,822	7			10	9								1				2	8	6	11		4		3			5	
1681	26 (a)	Chesterfield	L 0-4		10,668	7			10	9								1			2		8	6	11		4		3			5	
1682	Jan 2 (a)	Grimsby T	L 0-1		8,683				10	9	7							1			3	2	8	6	11		4					5	
1683	16 (h)	York C	L 0-1		5,559	7			8	9								1				2		6	11		4		3			5	10
1684	23 (h)	Rochdale	L 1-2	Murray	6,651	7			10	9												2		8	11	6	4	1	3			5	
1685	Feb 6 (a)	Wrexham	L 0-1		3,895	7			10											3		2		8	11	6	4	1			9	5	
1686	13 (h)	Mansfield T	W 3-2	Clempson, Connor 2	6,371	7			8	9										3		6			10		4	1	2		11	5	
1687	20 (a)	Barrow	L 0-1		6,526				8	9						7					3	2		6	10		4	1			11	5	
1688	27 (a)	Workington	D 0-0		11,176				10	9							8				3	2		6	7		4	1			11	5	
1689	Mar 6 (h)	Gateshead	L 0-1		6,334				10	9							8				3	2		6	7		4	1			11	5	
1690	10 (h)	Scunthorpe U	D 1-1	Weigh	2,939	7			10	9					5						3	2	8	6			4	1			11		
1691	13 (a)	Hartlepools U	L 0-6		5,879				7	9					5		8				3	2	10	6			4	1			11		
1692	20 (h)	Darlington	W 2-0	Opp own-goal, Weigh	5,456					7			6				8		5	2	3			10			4	1		9	11		
1693	27 (a)	Barnsley	L 1-4	Herd	9,367					9			6				8		5	2	3			10	7		4	1			11		
1694	Apr 1 (a)	Scunthorpe U	L 0-2		5,868					9			6				8		5	2	3			10	7		4	1			11		
1695	3 (h)	Bradford	W 4-1	Opp own-goal, Connor 2, Herd	4,676	7				9							10			2	3	6		8	11		4	1				5	
1696	10 (a)	Port Vale	L 0-7		19,513	7				9							10			2	3	6		8	11		4	1				5	
1697	16 (h)	Bradford C	W 5-0	Kennedy (pen), Murray, Opp own-goal, Connor 2	6,691					9							10	1		2		6		8	11		4		3	7		5	
1698	17 (h)	Crewe A	W 1-0	Herd	6,768	7				9							10	1		2		6		8	11		4		3			5	
1699	20 (a)	Bradford C	D 1-1	Weigh	9,522				10	9								1		2		6		8	7		4		3		11	5	
1700	24 (a)	Chester	W 2-1	Herd 2	3,545					9							10	1		2		6		8	7		4		3		11	5	
1701	26 (h)	Port Vale	D 1-1	Weigh	11,840					9							10	1		2		6		8	7		4		3		11	5	
1702	28 (a)	Southport	W 2-1	Moran 2	2,483	7	6		10	9								1		2			8				4		3		11	5	
FINAL LEAGUE POSITION: 10th in Division Three North					Appearances	34	1	2	37	42	2	1	3	5	2	1	12	33	4	20	24	38	12	43	32	2	46	13	30	2	24	40	1
					Goals				11	30				2			5			1			5	9	3						7		

Own-goals 4

FA Cup

Rd	Date	Opponent	Result	Scorers	Att.	Anderson CS	Anderson PA	Ashe	Clempson	Connor	Corfield	Crosby	Evans	Finney	Glover	Goalen	Herd	Herod	Hodder	Kennedy	Kenny	McCulloch	Moran	Murray	Oliver	Pendlebury	Pilkington	Platts	Rowland	Ward	Weigh	Wilmott	Wright
1	Nov 21 (h)	Chester	W 4-2	Clempson, Connor 3	12,363	7			10	9								1				2	8	6	11		4		3			5	
2	Dec 12 (h)	Workington	W 2-1	Opp own-goal, Connor	13,236	7			10	9								1				2	8	6	11		4		3			5	
3	Jan 9 (h)	Headington U+	D 0-0		15,881				10	9	7							1			3	2	8	6	11		4					5	
R	14 (a)	Headington U	L 0-1		9,955	7			10	9								1				2	8	6	11		4		3			5	
					Appearances	3			4	4	1							4			1	4	4	4	4		4		3			4	
					Goals				1	4																							

Own-goal 1

Average Home League attendance: 7,678
Average Away League attendance: 7,909

*Various sources credit Connor with this goal but both Stockport newspapers clearly state that Murray was the goalscorer.

+ Now Oxford United

1954-55

No	Date	Opponents	Result	Scorers	Att	Clempson	Connor	Easthope	Finney	Gilbert	Goalen	Hodder	Jackson	Jarvis	Kay	Kenny	Moran	Murray	Pilkington	Ross	Rowland	Thomas	Turner	Ward	Wilmott	Wilson
1703	Aug 21 (h)	Carlisle U	W 5-2	Opp own-goal, Connor 2, Clempson (pen), Murray	9,817	8	9	11		1			10			3	6	4	2			7			5	
1704	25 (a)	Halifax T	W 2-1	Moran, Connor	8,332	6	9	11		1			10			3	8	4	2			7			5	
1705	28 (a)	Chester	L 0-1		7,431	8	9	11		1			10			3	6	4	2			7			5	
1706	30 (h)	Halifax T	W 2-1	Jackson, Connor	9,865	8	9	11		1			10			3	6	4	2			7			5	
1707	Sep 4 (h)	Grimsby T	D 0-0		10,511	8	9	11		1			10			3	6	4	2						5	7
1708	6 (h)	Darlington	W 3-0	Connor 3	7,741	8	9	11		1			10			3	6	4	2						5	7
1709	11 (a)	Bradford	L 1-2	Jackson	9,275		9	11		1			10		8	3	6	4	2						5	7
1710	15 (a)	Darlington	D 0-0		8,912		9	11		1			10			3	6	4	2						5	7
1711	18 (h)	Rochdale	L 1-4	Ward	9,923		9	11		1			10			3	6	4	2					8	5	7
1712	20 (h)	Hartlepools U	L 0-2		5,152	8	9	11		1			10			3	6	4	2						5	7
1713	25 (a)	Tranmere R	D 1-1	Jackson	5,892	6	9			1	5		10	2		3	8	4	11							7
1714	27 (a)	Hartlepools U	L 1-2	Finney	6,604	6			9	1	5		10	2		3	8	4	11							7
1715	Oct 2 (a)	York C	L 0-4		6,523	6			9	1	5		10	2		3	8	4	11							7
1716	9 (h)	Oldham A	W 3-2	Jackson, Kay, Easthope (pen)	9,994	6		11	9	1			10	2	8	3		4							5	7
1717	16 (a)	Bradford C	W 3-2	Kay 2, Finney	9,855	6		11	9	1			10	2	8	3		4							5	7
1718	23 (h)	Barnsley	W 1-0	Connor	7,325	6	7	11	9	1			10	2	8	3		4							5	
1719	30 (a)	Scunthorpe U	L 0-3		9,956	6	9	11	7	1			10	2	8	3		4							5	
1720	Nov 6 (h)	Wrexham	W 4-0	Jackson, Murray, Easthope, Connor	5,716	6	9	11	7	1			10	2	8	3		4							5	
1721	13 (a)	Accrington S	W 1-0	Jackson	7,023	6	9	11	7	1			10	2	8	3		4							5	
1722	27 (a)	Workington	L 1-4	Jackson	7,138	6	9	11	7	1			10	2	8	3		4							5	
1723	Dec 4 (h)	Barrow	L 1-2	Connor	3,836	6	9		7	1			10	2	8	3		4							5	11
1724	11 (a)	Southport	D 1-1	Wilson	2,972	8	9		7	1			10	2		3	6	4							5	11
1725	18 (a)	Carlisle U	D 3-3	Murray, Wilson, Jackson	3,596	8	9		7	1			10	2		3	6	4							5	11
1726	25 (h)	Chesterfield	W 3-2	Wilson, Moran, Connor	5,557	6	9		7	1			10	2		3	8	4							5	11
1727	27 (a)	Chesterfield	W 7-3	Jackson 2, Moran 2, Clempson (pen), Connor 2	9,408	6	9		7	1			10	2		3	8	4							5	11
1728	Jan 1 (h)	Chester	W 3-0	Connor, Finney, Jackson	8,497	6	9		7	1			10	2		3	8	4							5	11
1729	15 (a)	Grimsby T	L 0-1		5,611	6	9		7	1			10	2		3	8	4							5	11
1730	22 (h)	Bradford	W 6-0	Moran 2, Connor 4	6,370	6	9		7	1			10	2		3	8	4							5	11
1731	29 (h)	Gateshead	W 2-1	Connor 2	8,768	6	9		7	1			10	2		3	8	4							5	11
1732	Feb 5 (a)	Rochdale	L 0-1		9,026	6	9		7				10	2		3	8	4					1		5	11
1733	12 (h)	Tranmere R	W 2-0	Moran, Goalen	5,789	6	9		7		11		10	2		3	8	4					1		5	
1734	21 (h)	York C	L 1-2	Goalen	2,933	6	9		7		11		10	2		3	8	4					1		5	
1735	26 (a)	Oldham A	D 1-1	Connor	9,214	6	9		7		11		10	2		3		4					1	8	5	
1736	Mar 5 (h)	Bradford C	D 1-1	Connor	6,402	6	9		7				10	2		3		4					1	8	5	11
1737	12 (a)	Barnsley	L 0-2		9,485	6	9		7				10	2		3	8	4					1		5	11
1738	19 (h)	Scunthorpe U	W 4-2	Clempson (pen), Connor 3	7,005	6	9		7				10	2		3	8	4					1		5	11
1739	23 (a)	Gateshead	D 4-4	Pilkington, Connor 3	924	6	9		7			2				3	8	4	10				1		5	11
1740	26 (a)	Wrexham	W 4-1	Wilson, Moran 2, Clempson	3,343	6	9		7			2				3	8	4	10				1		5	11
1741	Apr 2 (a)	Accrington S	D 0-0		13,144	6	9		7			2				3	8	4	10				1		5	11
1742	8 (a)	Crewe A	D 4-4	Pilkington, Moran, Murray, Connor	7,254	6	9		7			2				3	8	4	10				1		5	11
1743	9 (a)	Mansfield T	D 0-0		6,387	6	9		7			2				3	8	4	10				1		5	11
1744	11 (h)	Crewe A	W 6-1	Murray, Pilkington, Connor, Moran 2, Wilson	7,713	6	9		7	1		2				3	8	4	10						5	11
1745	16 (h)	Workington	L 0-1		7,452	6	9		7	1		2				3	8	4	10						5	11
1746	23 (a)	Barrow	L 0-2		4,407	6	9		7	1		2				3	8	4	10						5	11
1747	25 (h)	Mansfield T	D 2-2	Moran, Wilson	4,368	6	9		7	1		2	10			3	8	4							5	11
1748	30 (h)	Southport	L 0-2		4,923	6	9		7	1			10	2		3	8	4							5	11
	FINAL LEAGUE POSITION: 9th in Division Three North				Appearances	43	42	9	35	33	12	13	39	25	8	41	26	45	19	9	8	6	13	4	42	34
					Goals	4	30	2	3		2		11		3		13	5	3					1		6

Own-goal 1

FA Cup

No	Date	Opponents	Result	Scorers	Att	Clempson	Connor	Easthope	Finney	Gilbert	Goalen	Hodder	Jackson	Jarvis	Kay	Kenny	Moran	Murray	Pilkington	Ross	Rowland	Thomas	Turner	Ward	Wilmott	Wilson
1	Nov 20 (h)	Carlisle U	L 0-1		10,591	6	9	11	7	1			10	2	8	3		4							5	
					Appearances	1	1	1	1	1			1	1	1	1		1							1	
					Goals																					

Average Home League attendance: 7,339
Average Away League attendance: 6,894

187

1955-56

Player columns (left→right): Beards, Clempson, Connor, Daley, Finney, Goalen, Hamilton, Hodder, Jackson, Jarvis, Kay, Kerry, Littler, Moir, Moran, Murray, Pilkington, Rowland, Seemley, Turner, Ward, Wilmott, Wilson

No.	Date		Opponent	Result	Scorers	Att.	Be	Cl	Co	Da	Fi	Go	Ha	Ho	Ja	Jr	Ka	Ke	Li	Moir	Mn	Mu	Pi	Ro	Se	Tu	Wa	Wm	Ws
1749	Aug 20	(a)	Crewe A	L 1-3	Jackson	5,786	11	6	9		7				8			3		10		4	2			1	5		
1750	22	(h)	Oldham A	D 0-0		9,311		6	9		7				8			3		10		4	2			1	5		11
1751	27	(h)	Hartlepools U	W 4-0	Moran, Jackson, Connor 2	5,942		6	9		7				8			3		10		4	2			1	5		11
1752	30	(a)	Oldham A	L 2-3	Connor, Jackson	6,356		6	9		7				8			3		10		4	2			1	5		11
1753	Sep 3	(a)	Accrington S	L 1-3	Jackson	8,834		6	9		7			2	8			3		10		4				1	5		11
1754	5	(h)	Workington	L 4-5	Connor 3, Jackson	4,951	11	6	9		7			2	8			3		10		4				1	5		
1755	10	(a)	Mansfield T	D 2-2	Murray, Ward	7,104	11	6	9		7			2	8			3		10		4				1	5		
1756	14	(a)	Workington	W 1-0	Finney	5,327	11	6	9		7			2	8			3		10		4				1	5		
1757	17	(h)	Wrexham	W 4-0	Jackson, Connor, Clempson (pen), Ward	6,868		6	9		7			2	8			3		10		4				1	5		11
1758	19	(a)	York C	L 0-1		10,908	11	6	9		7			2	8			3		10		4				1	5		
1759	24	(a)	Halifax T	L 0-1		6,839		6	9		7			2	8		11	3		10		4				1	5		
1760	26	(h)	Scunthorpe U	W 3-2	Murray, Pilkington, Connor	4,146		6	9		7			2	8			3		10		4	5			1			11
1761	Oct 1	(h)	Bradford C	W 1-0	Moir	11,869		6	9		7			2	8			3		10		4	5			1			11
1762	8	(h)	Gateshead	L 1-2	Connor	9,204		6	9		7			2	8			3		10		4	5			1			11
1763	15	(a)	Barrow	L 0-2		5,580		6	9		7			2	8			3		10		4	5			1			11
1764	22	(h)	Tranmere R	W 7-0	Connor 4, Murray, Moir, Moran	7,145		6	9		7			2	8			3		10	11	4	5			1			
1765	29	(a)	Chesterfield	W 3-2	Connor, Clempson, Moir	7,966		6	9		7			2	8			3		10	11	4	5			1			
1766	Nov 5	(h)	Rochdale	D 0-0		9,337		6	9		7			2	8			3		10	11	4	5			1			
1767	12	(a)	Bradford	L 0-2		6,711		6	9		7	11		2	8			3		10		4	5			1			
1768	26	(a)	Carlisle U	L 1-4	Wilson	6,306		6	9					2	8			3	5	10	11	4				1			7
1769	Dec 3	(h)	Chester	W 2-1	Opp own-goal, Connor	5,737		6	8	9				2				3		10	11	4			5	1			7
1770	17	(h)	Crewe A	W 2-1	Murray, Connor	5,196		6	8	9				2				3		10	11	4			5	1			7
1771	24	(a)	Hartlepools U	D 0-0		9,299		6	8	9	7			2				3		10	11	4			5	1			
1772	26	(h)	Derby C	W 2-1	Connor, Moir	11,231		6	8	9	7			2				3		10	11	4			5	1			
1773	27	(a)	Derby C	L 0-2		20,073		6	8	9	7			2				3		10	11	4			5	1			
1774	31	(h)	Accrington S	L 1-2	Connor	12,206		6	8	9	7			2				3		10	11	4			5	1			
1775	Jan 14	(h)	Mansfield T	W 7-2	Moir 3, Finney, Hamilton, Murray, Connor	5,619		6	8	9	7		5	2				3		10	11	4				1			
1776	21	(a)	Wrexham	W 1-0	Moir	5,093		6	10	9	7			2				3		8	11	4			5	1			
1777	28	(a)	Southport	D 1-1	Connor	6,493		6	10	9	7			2				3		8	11	4			5	1			
1778	Feb 4	(h)	Halifax T	W 3-1	Daley 2, Moir	3,552		6	8	9	7			2		11		3		10		4			5	1			
1779	11	(a)	Bradford C	L 1-4	Wilson	6,387		6	8	9	7			2		11		3		10		4			5	1			
1780	15	(h)	Grimsby T	D 0-0		4,000		6	8	9	7			2		11		3		10		4			5	1			
1781	18	(a)	Gateshead	L 1-2	Moir	1,601		6	8		7			2		11		3		10		4			5	1		9	
1782	25	(h)	Barrow	W 4-1	Connor, Clempson 2, (1 pen), Finney	6,437		6	8	9	7			2		11		3		10		4			5	1			
1783	Mar 3	(a)	Tranmere R	L 1-2	Moir	5,981		6	8	9	7			2		11		3		10		4			5	1			
1784	10	(h)	Chesterfield	W 2-1	Connor, Daley	8,171		6	8	9	7			2		11		3		10		4			5	1			
1785	17	(a)	Grimsby T	L 0-3		14,133		6	8	9	7			2		11		3		10		4			5	1			
1786	24	(h)	Bradford	D 0-0		5,381			8	9	7		6	2		11		3		10		4			5	1			
1787	30	(h)	Darlington	W 2-1	Moir, Jackson	7,622		6		9	7			2	8	11		3		10		4			5	1			
1788	31	(a)	Rochdale	D 0-0		4,643		6		9	7			2	8	11		3		10		4			5	1			
1789	Apr 2	(a)	Darlington	D 0-0		5,002		6		9	7			2		11		3		10	8	4			5	1			
1790	7	(h)	Carlisle U	W 8-1	Connor 5, Clempson, Moran 2	4,957		6	9		7			2		11		3		10	8	4			5	1			
1791	14	(a)	Chester	W 4-1	Moir, Wilson, Moran 2	4,425		6	9					2		11		3		10	8	4			5	1			7
1792	21	(h)	Southport	W 4-0	Moran 2, Wilson, Moir	8,364		6	9					2		11		3		10	8	4			5	1			7
1793	26	(a)	Scunthorpe U	W 5-1	Opp own-goal, Moir, Connor, Clempson (pen), Moran	3,780		6	9					2		11		3		10	8	4			5	1			7
1794	28	(h)	York C	W 4-1	Connor 2, Moir, Moran	9,724		6	9					2		11		3		10	8	4			5	1			7
			Appearances				5	45	44	17	41	1	7	27	25	15	1	37	1	33	16	46	12	4	36	46	11	7	29
			Goals					6	30	3	3		1		7					16	10	5	1				2		4

FINAL LEAGUE POSITION: 7th in Division Three North

Own-goals 2

FA Cup

No.	Date		Opponent	Result		Att.	Cl	Co	Fi	Ho	Ja	Ke	Moir	Mn	Mu	Pi	Se	Tu
1	Nov 19	(a)	Mansfield T	L 0-2		8,074	6	9	7	2	8	3	10	11	4	5		1
			Appearances				1	1	1	1	1	1	1	1	1	1	1	1
			Goals															

Average Home League attendance: 7,260
Average Away League attendance: 7,158

1956-57

No	Date		Opponent	Res	Scorers	Att	Barnard	Clempson	Connor	Cox	Daley	Davock	Drake	Dyer	Finney	Hodder	Holden	Jackson	Jarvis	Kenny	McGreevey	Moir	Moran	Murray	Porteous	Rowland	Seemley	Turner	Vairy	Wilmott	Wilson
1795	Aug 18	(h)	Mansfield T	W 2-1	Daley, Moran	6,375		6	9		11					5						10	8	2	4		3	1			7
1796	20	(a)	Bradford	L 2-3	Clempson (pen), Moran	11,152		6	9		11					5						10	8	2	4		3	1			7
1797	25	(a)	Southport	W 1-0	Moir	6,010	1	6			11				9	5						10	8	2	4		3				7
1798	27	(h)	Bradford	W 4-0	Daley, Moran 2, Finney	8,355	1	6			11				9	5						10	8	2	4		3				7
1799	Sep 1	(h)	Chesterfield	W 2-1	Daley, Finney	12,044	1	6			11				9	5						10	8	2	4		3				7
1800	3	(h)	Oldham A	W 2-1	Moran, Finney	12,715	1	6			11				9	5						10	8	2	4		3				7
1801	8	(a)	Chester	W 4-1	Wilson 2, Moran, Finney	9,948	1	6			11				9	5						10	8	2	4		3				7
1802	10	(a)	Oldham A	L 0-2		13,488	1	6			11				9	5						10	8	2	4		3				7
1803	15	(h)	Hartlepools U	L 2-4	Moir, Moran	13,577	1	6			11				9	5						10	8	2	4		3				7
1804	17	(h)	Carlisle U	W 2-0	Jackson, Finney	8,455		6			11				9	5		10				8		2	4		3	1			7
1805	22	(a)	Bradford C	D 1-1	Moir	13,560		6			11				9	5		10				8		2	4		3	1			7
1806	25	(a)	Carlisle U	D 3-3	Finney 2, Jackson	8,072	1	6			11				9	5		10				8		2	4		3				7
1807	29	(a)	Darlington	L 1-3	Opp own-goal	4,680	1	6			11				9	5		10				8		2	4		3				7
1808	Oct 6	(h)	Gateshead	D 1-1	Jackson	9,337	1	6		8	11				9	5		10						2	4		3				7
1809	13	(a)	Wrexham	W 3-2	Daley, Cox 2	13,524		6		8	11				9	5		10						2	4		3	1			7
1810	20	(h)	Hull C	L 1-2	Finney	9,272		6		9	11				10	5						8		2	4		3	1			7
1811	27	(a)	Crewe A	W 1-0	Moir	8,629		6		9	11				10	5						8		2	4		3	1			7
1812	Nov 3	(h)	Scunthorpe U	L 1-3	Clempson (pen)	12,313	1	6			11	9			10	5						8		2	4		3				7
1813	10	(a)	Rochdale	D 2-2	Opp own-goal, Daley	10,394	1	6			11	9			10	5			7			8		2	4		3				
1814	24	(a)	Workington	L 1-4	Moran	6,715	1				11	9							6			10	8	2	4		3			5	7
1815	Dec 1	(h)	Derby C	W 3-2	Drake, Daley, Moir	11,492	1	6			11		9									10	8	2	4		3			5	7
1816	15	(a)	Mansfield T	L 2-4	Drake 2	6,203	1	6			11		9		7	5	10					8		2	4		3				
1817	22	(h)	Southport	W 2-0	Drake, Clempson (pen)	3,698	1	6			11		9		7	5	10					8		2	4		3				
1818	25	(h)	Accrington S	W 2-1	Drake, Wilson	8,902		6			11		9			5	10					8		2	4		3	1			7
1819	29	(a)	Chesterfield	L 0-1		11,543		6			11		9			5	10					8		2	4		3	1			7
1820	Jan 1	(a)	Barrow	W 3-0	Drake 2, Finney	9,022		6			11		9		10	5						8		2	4		3	1			7
1821	5	(h)	Tranmere R	W 3-1	Daley 2, Opp own-goal	9,142		6			11		9			5	10					8		2	4		3	1			7
1822	12	(h)	Chester	W 2-1	Clempson (pen), Drake	8,958		6			11		9			5	10					8		2	4		3	1			7
1823	19	(a)	Hartlepools U	L 1-4	Finney	8,155		6			11		9		10	5						8		2	4		3	1			7
1824	26	(h)	Tranmere R	D 2-2	Holden, Wilson	5,328		6			11		9			5	10					8		2	4		3	1			7
1825	Feb 2	(h)	Bradford C	D 1-1	Jackson	10,925		6			11				7	5	10	9				8		2	4		3	1			
1826	9	(h)	Darlington	W 5-2	Drake, Daley 2, Moir, Holden	10,026		6			11		9		7	5	10					8		2	4		3	1			
1827	16	(a)	Gateshead	W 5-1	Clempson, Moir, Drake 3	3,170		6			11		9		7	5	10					8		2	4		3	1			
1828	23	(h)	Wrexham	W 4-0	Drake 4	8,574		6			11		9		7	5	10					8		2	4		3	1			
1829	Mar 2	(a)	Hull C	L 3-5	Murray, Holden, Daley	12,222		6			11		9			5	10			7		8		2	4		3	1			
1830	9	(h)	Crewe A	W 2-0	Drake, Daley	11,028		6			11		9		7	5	10					8		2	4		3	1			
1831	16	(a)	Scunthorpe U	W 3-2	Jackson, Holden 2	6,829		6			11				7	5	10	9				8		2	4		3		1		
1832	23	(h)	Rochdale	W 3-1	Moir, Holden 2	15,652		6			11		9		7	5	10					8		2	4		3		1		
1833	30	(a)	Halifax T	L 2-3	Holden, Drake (pen)	7,452		6			11		9		7	5	10					8		2	4		3		1		
1834	Apr 6	(h)	Workington	L 0-1		12,162		6			11		9		7	5	10					8		2	4		3		1		
1835	8	(a)	Accrington S	L 0-4		11,266	1	6			11				9		10					8		2	4		3			5	7
1836	13	(a)	Derby C	L 0-2		22,916	1				11	9					10					8		2	4	6	3			5	7
1837	19	(a)	York C	D 0-0		11,681		6			11	9				5	10		7			8		2	4		3	1			
1838	20	(h)	Barrow	W 2-1	Holden, Drake	6,990	1	6			11		9			5	10					8		2	4		3				7
1839	22	(h)	York C	W 3-0	Wilson, Jackson (pen), Moir	7,193	1	6			11						10	9				8		2	4		3			5	7
1840	29	(h)	Halifax T	D 2-2	Finney, Moir	6,049	1				11			6	9	5	10				7	8		2	4		3				
			Appearances				21	37	2	3	40	5	22	1	39	41	22	17	3	1	1	33	22	46	42	1	45	20	5	5	32
			Goals					5		2	12		19		11		9	6				10	8	1							5

FINAL LEAGUE POSITION: 5th in Division Three North

Own-goals 3

FA Cup

No	Date		Opponent	Res	Scorers	Att	Barnard	Clempson	Daley	Finney	Hodder	Jarvis	Moir	Moran	Murray	Porteous	Seemley	Wilson
1	Nov 17	(a)	New Brighton	D 3-3	Finney, Moran 2	10,127	1	6	11	9	5	3	10	8	2	4		7
R	21	(h)	New Brighton	L 2-3	Finney, Daley	16,964	1	6	11	9	5		10	8	2	4	3	7
			Appearances				2	2	2	2	2	1	2	2	2	2	1	2
			Goals						1	2				2				

Average Home League attendance: 9,706
Average Away League attendance: 9,650

1957-58

No.	Date		Venue	Opponent	Result	Scorers	Attendance
1841	Aug	24	(a)	Bradford C	L 1-2	Sowden	14,405
1842		26	(h)	Oldham A	W 3-0	Sowden 2, Holden	15,551
1843		31	(h)	Hull C	W 1-0	Clempson (pen)	13,091
1844	Sep	3	(a)	Oldham A	W 4-2	Wilson, Opp own-goal, Daley, Holden	10,978
1845		7	(h)	Barrow	W 2-0	Clempson (pen), Holden	12,092
1846		9	(a)	Mansfield T	D 2-2	Holden, Wilson	8,549
1847		14	(a)	Halifax T	D 0-0		7,687
1848		16	(h)	Mansfield T	D 3-3	Jackson 3 (1 pen)	8,662
1849		21	(h)	Rochdale	L 0-3		12,480
1850		23	(h)	Gateshead	W 5-1	Sowden 2, Jackson, Holden 2	7,650
1851		28	(a)	Crewe A	W 2-1	Cox 2	7,308
1852	Oct	5	(h)	Wrexham	D 1-1	Jackson	10,066
1853		12	(a)	Southport	L 0-1		5,602
1854		14	(a)	Gateshead	L 0-3		4,024
1855		19	(h)	Accrington S	D 0-0		9,439
1856		26	(a)	Chester	L 0-3		7,518
1857	Nov	2	(h)	Chesterfield	W 4-1	Holden 3, Jackson	9,760
1858		9	(a)	Tranmere R	D 2-2	Finney, Wilson	9,877
1859		23	(a)	Bradford	L 0-1		8,422
1860		30	(h)	Carlisle U	W 4-1	Holden 2, Sowden, Jackson (pen)	9,572
1861	Dec	14	(h)	York C	W 2-1	Holden, Sowden	10,508
1862		21	(h)	Bradford C	L 0-4		11,040
1863		25	(h)	Darlington	W 4-1	Wilson 2, Holden, Opp own-goal	7,326
1864		26	(a)	Darlington	L 0-1		6,660
1865		28	(a)	Hull C	L 0-1		11,719
1866	Jan	11	(a)	Barrow	D 1-1	Jackson	6,050
1867		18	(h)	Halifax T	W 4-2	Jackson, Holden 2, Mulvey	8,108
1868	Feb	1	(a)	Rochdale	L 0-3		7,804
1869		8	(h)	Crewe A	W 5-1	Holden, Finney, Clempson, Murray, Jackson	8,053
1870		12	(a)	Bury	D 1-1	Jackson	15,976
1871		15	(a)	Wrexham	L 0-1		8,790
1872		22	(h)	Bradford	W 3-0	Jackson 2, Wilson	8,035
1873	Mar	1	(a)	Accrington S	L 2-3	Wilson, Jackson	8,185
1874		8	(h)	Chester	D 2-2	Wilson, Daley	7,629
1875		13	(a)	Scunthorpe U	L 0-4		8,446
1876		15	(a)	Chesterfield	L 1-2	Samuels	8,206
1877		22	(h)	Southport	L 1-2	Clempson	7,668
1878		29	(a)	Hartlepools U	W 2-1	Clempson, Kelly	3,070
1879	Apr	4	(h)	Workington	L 0-2		9,757
1880		5	(h)	Bury	W 4-0	Holden, Wilson, Clempson, Kelly	10,518
1881		7	(a)	Workington	D 1-1	Kelly	4,077
1882		12	(a)	Carlisle U	L 1-3	Davock	7,421
1883		14	(h)	Hartlepools U	W 2-1	Wilson, Kelly	8,046
1884		19	(h)	Tranmere R	W 2-1	Wilson, Mulvey	10,849
1885		21	(h)	Scunthorpe U	W 2-1	Jackson, Mulvey	14,005
1886		26	(a)	York C	D 0-0		8,005

FINAL LEAGUE POSITION: 9th in Division Three North

	Ashton	Barnard	Betts	Clempson	Cox	Daley	Davock	Drake	Finney	Franklin	Grieves	Hodder	Holden	Jackson	Kelly	Moir	Mulvey	Murray	Porteous	Samuels	Smith	Sowden	Webb	Wilmott	Wilson
Appearances	13	7	29	40	4	16	25	1	32	20	39	4	40	40	10	4	7	46	21	5	4	15	46	9	29
Goals				6	2	2	1		2				17	15	4		3	1		1		7			11

Own-goals 2

FA Cup

No.	Date		Venue	Opponent	Result	Scorers	Attendance
1	Nov	16	(h)	Barrow	W 2-1	Davock, Wilson	12,625
2	Dec	7	(h)	Hartlepools U	W 2-1	Davock, Sowden	12,500
3	Jan	4	(h)	Luton T	W 3-0	Jackson, Holden 2	18,158
4		25	(a)	West Ham U	L 2-3	Holden, Finney	36,084

	Betts	Clempson	Davock	Finney	Franklin	Grieves	Holden	Jackson	Kelly	Murray	Sowden	Webb	Wilson
1	2	6	11	9	5	1	8	10		4		3	7
2	2	6	11		5	1	10	8		4	9	3	7
3	2	6	11	7	5	1	9	10	8	4		3	
4	2	6	11	7	5	1	9	10	8	4		3	
Appearances	4	4	4	3	4	4	4	4	2	4	1	4	2
Goals			2	1			3	1			1		1

Average Home League attendance: 9,996
Average Away League attendance: 8,208

1958-59

No.	Date	Opponent	Result	Scorers	Att	Acton	Barnard	Betts	Clarke	Clempson	Davock	Guy	Halliday	Heginbotham	Holden	Jackson	Kelly	Lea	Mulvey	Murray	Porteous	Reid	Ritchie	Samuels	Slack	Smith JB	Smith W	Webb	Wilmott	Wilson
1887	Aug 23 (h)	Rochdale	W 1-0	Holden (pen)	12,171	1	2		8	11					10		9			4	6							3	5	7
1888	26 (a)	Bury	D 3-3	Kelly, Holden 2	15,973	1	2		8						10		9			4	6				11			3	5	7
1889	30 (a)	Doncaster R	L 1-4	Murray	10,447	1	2							8			7		10	4	6			9	11			3	5	
1890	Sep 1 (h)	Bury	L 0-1		17,315	1	2			11				8	9				10	4	6							3	5	7
1891	6 (h)	Plymouth A	D 2-2	Holden 2	11,419	1	2		8			9			10		7			4	6				11			3	5	
1892	8 (h)	Norwich C	L 2-3	Kelly, Clempson	9,613	1	2		6						10		7		9	4				8	11			3	5	
1893	13 (a)	Tranmere R	L 1-3	Wilmott	12,607	1	2	11	6						10		7		9	4				8				3	5	
1894	17 (a)	Norwich C	W 3-1	Samuels, Jackson, Holden	22,717	1	2	11	6						10	9	7			4	5			8				3		
1895	20 (a)	Wrexham	L 1-3	Holden	11,472	1	2	11	6						10	9	7			4	5			8				3		
1896	22 (h)	Queen's P'k R	L 2-3	Samuels, Mulvey	12,162	1	2	11	6							9	7		10	4	5			8				3		
1897	27 (h)	Reading	L 0-1		10,432	1	2	11								9	7		10	4	6			8				3	5	
1898	29 (a)	Queen's P'k R	D 0-0		7,458	1	2	11								9	8		10	4	6							3	5	7
1899	Oct 4 (a)	Colchester U	L 2-8	Clarke, Murray	8,298	1	2	11								9	8		10	4	6							3	5	7
1900	6 (h)	Bournemouth	W 3-1	Opp own-goal, J.B.Smith, Wilson	9,640	6	2		11						10	8		1		5	4					9		3		7
1901	11 (h)	Hull C	W 2-1	Clarke, Kelly	9,521	6	2		11						10		8	1		5	4					9		3		7
1902	18 (a)	Brentford	W 4-1	J.B.Smith 2, Holden, Jackson	12,488	6	2		11		3				10	8	7	1		5	4					9				
1903	20 (h)	Southend U	L 0-1		11,950	6	2		11		3				10	8	7	1		5	4					9				
1904	25 (h)	Swindon T	W 2-0	Holden, Jackson	10,544	6	2		11						10	8		1		5	4					9		3		7
1905	Nov 1 (h)	Mansfield T	L 1-2	Clarke	8,275	6	2		11						10	8		1		5	4					9		3		7
1906	8 (h)	Notts C	D 1-1	J.B.Smith	10,181		2	11	6			7			8			1	10	5	4					9		3		
1907	22 (h)	Accrington S	D 0-0		10,219		2	11	6						10	8		1		5	4			7	9			3		
1908	29 (a)	Halifax T	L 3-4	Porteous, Holden, Kelly	4,127	6	2	11							10	8	9	1		5	4							3		7
1909	Dec 13 (a)	Southampton	L 1-2	Holden	14,437		2	11							10	8	9	1		5	4			6				3		7
1910	20 (a)	Rochdale	W 2-0	Jackson, Wilson	4,056		2	11								8	9	1	10	5	4			6				3		7
1911	27 (a)	Southend U	L 1-3	Clarke	15,315		2	11	6						10	8	9	1		5	4							3		7
1912	Jan 3 (h)	Doncaster R	W 2-0	Opp own-goal, Jackson	7,573		2	11	6						10	8		1		5	4					9		3		7
1913	17 (a)	Plymouth A	L 1-2	Clarke	10,099		2	11	6						10	8		1		5	4					9		3		7
1914	31 (h)	Tranmere R	W 1-0	Kelly	7,749		2	11	8								9	1	10	5	4		6	7				3		
1915	Feb 7 (h)	Wrexham	D 2-2	Davock 2	6,453		2		8	11							9	1	10	5	4		6	7				3		
1916	14 (a)	Reading	L 1-2	Opp own-goal	7,180		2		8	11					10		7	1		5	4		6		9			3		
1917	21 (h)	Colchester U	L 0-1		5,811		2		10	11				9	8			1			4		6	7				3	5	
1918	28 (a)	Hull C	L 1-3	Kelly	16,177	1			10	11		2			8					4			9	6	7			3	5	
1919	Mar 2 (h)	Newport C	W 2-1	Davock, Slack	8,079	1			6	11	2				8						10	9	4	7				3		
1920	7 (h)	Brentford	D 1-1	Samuels (pen)	7,973	1			6	11	2				8					5	10	9	4	7				3		
1921	14 (a)	Swindon T	L 0-3		8,458	1	2		6	11					8					5	10	9	4					3		7
1922	21 (h)	Mansfield T	W 4-1	Jackson 2, Ritchie, Samuels (pen)	6,394				6	11	3				10	8		1		5			7	9	4			2		
1923	27 (h)	Bradford C	D 1-1	Ritchie	9,137				6	11	3				10	8		1		5			7	9	4			2		
1924	28 (a)	Notts C	W 2-0	Jackson 2	9,761	1	2	11	6						10	8				5	4		7	9				3		
1925	31 (a)	Bradford C	L 2-4	Ritchie, Reid	12,579	1	2	11	6						10	8				5	4		7	9				3		
1926	Apr 4 (h)	Chesterfield	D 1-1	Reid	7,331	1	2		6	11					10	8				5	4	7	9					3		
1927	11 (a)	Accrington S	D 2-2	Kelly, Opp own-goal	4,538	1	2		6	11					10	8				5	4	7	9					3		
1928	13 (a)	Chesterfield	L 0-1		5,645	1			6	11	2				8					5	4		9	10				3		7
1929	18 (h)	Halifax T	L 0-1		7,134	6	1	4	7	10	11	2		9	8					5								3		
1930	22 (a)	Bournemouth	L 0-2		6,381	1	10		6	11	2				7					5	4	8		9				3		
1931	25 (a)	Newport C	L 0-2		2,447	1	2		6	11					8					5	4	10		7	9			3		
1932	27 (h)	Southampton	W 4-0	Wilson, Ritchie, Mulvey, Davock (pen)	4,060		2		11		8							1	10	5	4		9			6		3		7
				Appearances		8	25	40	25	31	18	2	1	10	25	32	30	21	13	44	37	11	12	20	8	17	1	44	13	18
				Goals					5	1	4				11	9	7		2	2	1		2	4	4	1	4		1	3

FINAL LEAGUE POSITION: 21st in Division Three - Relegated to Division 4

Own-goals 4

FA Cup

No.	Date	Opponent	Result	Scorers	Att	Barnard	Clarke	Clempson	Holden	Jackson	Lea	Murray	Porteous	Ritchie	Smith JB	Webb	Wilson
1	Nov 15 (a)	Hull C	W 1-0	Jackson	17,441	2	11	6	10	8	1	5	4		9	3	7
2	Dec 6 (a)	Blyth Spartans	W 4-3	Wilson, Clarke, Clempson, Jackson	6,724	2	11	6	10	8	1	5	4		9	3	7
3	Jan 14 (h)	Burnley	L 1-3	Jackson	23,147	2	11	6	10	8	1	5	4		9	3	7
				Appearances		3	3	3	3	3	3	3	3		3	3	3
				Goals			1	1		3							1

Average Home League attendance: 9,255
Average Away League attendance: 10,041

1959-60

No	Date	Opponent	Result	Scorers	Att	Acton	Ashton	Betts	Connelly	Davock	Fletcher	Guy	Heginbotham	Hodder	Holland	Kelly GL	Kelly WM	Lea H	Lea W	Lewis	McCusker	Mulvey	Murray	Porteous	Ritchie	Smith	Swannell	Wallace	Webb	Wilson
1933	Aug 22 (a)	Watford	D 0-0		9,849	6		2		11						10	8	1					5	4	9				3	7
1934	24 (h)	Exeter C	W 1-0	Ritchie	9,922			2		11						10	8	1		6			5	4	9				3	7
1935	29 (h)	Oldham A	W 3-1	W.M.Kelly, Ritchie, Davock	11,122			2		11						10	8	1				6	5	4	9				3	7
1936	Sep 2 (a)	Exeter C	L 1-2	Davock	8,729			2		11						10	8	1		6			5	4	9				3	7
1937	5 (a)	Carlisle U	W 4-0	Davock, Wallace, Wilson 2	6,604			2		11							8	1				6	5	4	9			10	3	7
1938	7 (h)	Crystal P	L 0-1		11,882			2		11							8	1				6	5	4	9			10	3	7
1939	12 (h)	Notts C	W 3-1	G.L.Kelly, Davock 2	7,662			2		11						10		1				6	5	4	9			8	3	7
1940	16 (a)	Crystal P	L 1-3	Wallace	18,534			2		11					6	10		1					5	4	9			8	3	7
1941	19 (a)	Walsall	L 1-3	Wallace	11,309			2		11					6	10	7	1					5	4	9			8	3	
1942	21 (h)	Torquay U	L 0-1		8,240			2		11						10		1				6	5	4	9			8	3	7
1943	26 (h)	Hartlepools U	W 2-1	Davock, G.L.Kelly	5,931			2		11		9				8		1				6	5	4	10				3	7
1944	30 (a)	Torquay U	L 0-4		5,571			2		11		9				8				6			5	4	10		1		3	7
1945	Oct 3 (a)	Crewe A	L 2-4	Wilson, Betts (pen)	9,259		10			11		2		5	6			1					8	4	9				3	7
1946	5 (h)	Chester	W 3-0	Davock 2, Ritchie	7,530			2		11				5	8	9		1					4	6	10				3	7
1947	10 (h)	Southport	W 1-0	Ritchie	6,994			2		11				5	8	9		1					4	6	10				3	7
1948	14 (a)	Chester	W 2-1	Holland 2	3,560			2		11				5	8	9		1					4	6	10				3	7
1949	17 (a)	Gillingham	W 2-0	Ritchie, Murray	7,850			2		11				5	8	9		1					4	6	10				3	7
1950	24 (h)	Barrow	W 1-0	Wilson	5,478			2		11				5	8	9		1		10			4	6					3	7
1951	31 (a)	Aldershot	L 0-1		4,798			2		11				5	8	9		1					4	6	10			7	3	
1952	Nov 7 (a)	Darlington	W 1-0	Guy	5,213			2		11		9		5	8			1					4	6	10				3	7
1953	21 (h)	Rochdale	W 2-1	Guy, Wallace	7,629			2		11		9		5	8	10		1					4	6				7	3	
1954	28 (a)	Workington	D 1-1	G.L.Kelly	4,320			2		11		9		5	8	10		1					4	6				7	3	
1955	Dec 12 (a)	Northampton T	D 1-1	Opp own-goal	6,383			2	7	11		9		5	8			1					4	6	10				3	
1956	19 (h)	Watford	W 4-0	Holland 2, Davock, Porteous	4,259			2		11				5	8			1		9			4	6	10				3	7
1957	28 (h)	Millwall	D 2-2	Betts (pen), Wilson	8,867			2		11				5	8			1		9			4	6	10				3	7
1958	Jan 2 (a)	Oldham A	D 0-0		7,447			2		11				5	8			1		9			4	6	10				3	7
1959	9 (a)	Gateshead	L 1-2	Davock	1,868			2		11				5	8			1		9			4	6	10				3	7
1960	16 (a)	Carlisle U	D 0-0		5,203			2		11				5	8			1		9			4	6	10				3	7
1961	23 (a)	Notts C	L 0-3		13,113			2		11	9			5	8			1					4	6	10				3	7
1962	30 (h)	Doncaster R	W 2-0	Murray, Ritchie	4,337			2		11	9			5	8			1					4	6	10				3	7
1963	Feb 6 (h)	Walsall	W 2-0	Betts (pen), Fletcher	8,439			2	7	11	9			5	8			1					4	6	10				3	
1964	13 (a)	Hartlepools U	L 1-2	Ritchie	2,870			2	7	11	9			5	8			1					4	6	10				3	
1965	27 (a)	Southport	L 0-3		3,675			2	7	11	9			5	4	8		1						6				10	3	
1966	29* (h)	Crewe A	W 1-0	G.L.Kelly	5,727			2		11	9			5	4	8		1						6	10				3	7
1967	Mar 5 (h)	Gillingham	D 1-1	Ritchie	6,077			2		11	9			5	8			1					4	6	10				3	7
1968	7§ (a)	Millwall	L 2-3	Fletcher, Wilson	10,317			2		11	9			5	8	10					1		4	6					3	7
1969	12 (a)	Barrow	L 1-5	Murray	4,123		2			11	9			5	8	10					1		4	6					3	7
1970	19 (h)	Aldershot	D 1-1	Fletcher	4,227		2			11	9			5	8			1					4	6	10				3	7
1971	26 (a)	Darlington	W 2-1	Wilson, Fletcher	2,874			2		11	9			5	8			1					4	6	10				3	7
1972	Apr 2 (h)	Gateshead	D 0-0		4,072			2		11	9			5	8			1					4	6	10				3	7
1973	9 (a)	Rochdale	L 0-3		3,917			2		11	9		10	5	8			1					4	6					3	7
1974	15 (h)	Bradford	D 0-0		4,458			2		11	9			5	8			1	10				4	6					3	7
1975	16 (h)	Workington	W 2-0	Fletcher, Smith	3,585						8			5	4			1					2	6	9	10		11	3	7
1976	19 (a)	Bradford	D 1-1	Murray	7,579			2			8			5	10			1					4	6	9			11	3	7
1977	23 (a)	Doncaster R	L 0-1		4,873			2			8			5	10			1					4	6	9			11	3	7
1978	30 (h)	Northampton T	W 3-0	Davock 2, Murray	3,853			2		11	8			5	10			1					4	6	9				3	7
		FINAL LEAGUE POSITION: 10th in Division Four			**Appearances**	1	2	43	4	43	18	7	1	34	24	34	7	43	1	9	2	6	44	46	38	1	1	13	46	38
					Goals			3		12	5	2			4	4	1						5	1	8	1		4		7

Own-goal 1

FA Cup

No	Date	Opponent	Result	Scorers	Att	Acton	Ashton	Betts	Connelly	Davock	Fletcher	Guy	Heginbotham	Hodder	Holland	Kelly GL	Kelly WM	Lea H	Lea W	Lewis	McCusker	Mulvey	Murray	Porteous	Ritchie	Smith	Swannell	Wallace	Webb	Wilson
1	Nov 14 (a)	W Auckland	W 6-2	Guy 2, Betts, Wilson, Ritchie, Davock	1,845			2		11		9		5	8			1					4	6	10				3	7
2	Dec 5 (h)	Crewe A	D 0-0		14,540			2		11		9		5	8			1					4	6				10	3	7
R	9 (a)	Crewe A	L 0-2		12,193			2		11		9		5	8	10		1					4	6					3	7
					Appearances			3		3		3		3	3	1		3					3	3	1			1	3	3
					Goals			1		1		2													1					1

Average Home League attendance: 6,552
Average Away League attendance: 6,931

*This was the 'replay' of a game played at Edgeley Park on 20 February which was abandoned after 57 minutes due to a waterlogged pitch with the score 0-0, the team being the same as that for Match 1965 with the exception of Ritchie replacing Wallace.

§This was the 'replay' of a game played at The Den on 26 December which was abandoned after 65 minutes due to a waterlogged pitch with the score 1-0 to Stockport (Wilson), the team being the same as that for Match 1956.

1960-61

#	Match	Res	Scorers	Att	Anderson	Ashton	Bennion	Birch	Connelly	Cunliffe	Davock	Fletcher	Hodder	Holland	Keelan	Lea	Lovell	Murdoch	Murray	Partridge	Porteous	Ritchie	Smith	Webb	Wilson
1979	Aug 20 (h) Rochdale	W 1-0	Fletcher	6,617	8		4				11	9	5			1		10	2		6			3	7
1980	23 (a) Carlisle U	W 4-1	Davock 2 (1 pen), Anderson, Murdoch	9,261	8		4				11	9	5			1		10	2		6			3	7
1981	27 (a) Mansfield T	D 2-2	Wilson, Anderson	4,072	8		4				11	9	5			1		10	2		6			3	7
1982	29 (a) Carlisle U	W 2-0	Davock, Opp own-goal	9,033	8	2	4				11	9	5			1		10			6			3	7
1983	Sep 3 (a) Northampton T	L 2-4	Murdoch, Fletcher	8,661	8	2	4				11	9	5			1		10			6			3	7
1984	5 (a) Hartlepools U	W 2-0	Davock 2	7,937	8	2	4				11	9	5			1		10			6			3	7
1985	10 (h) Exeter C	D 0-0		8,108	8	2	4				11	9	5	6		1		10						3	7
1986	12 (h) Hartlepools U	D 1-1	Wilson	8,958	8	2	4				11	9	5			1		10			6			3	7
1987	17 (a) Peterboro' U	W 1-0	Anderson	14,614	8	2	4				11	9	5			1		10			6			3	7
1988	21 (a) Wrexham	W 3-1	Murdoch, Anderson, Wilson	8,283	8	2	4				11	9	5			1		10			6			3	7
1989	24 (h) Southport	W 2-0	Anderson, Bennion (pen)	8,746	8		4				11	9	5			1		10	2		6			3	7
1990	26 (h) Wrexham	W 1-0	Porteous	10,582	8		4				11	9	5			1		10	2		6			3	7
1991	Oct 1 (a) Darlington	L 0-2		6,789	8		4				11	9	5			1		10	2		6			3	7
1992	3 (h) Crystal P	W 5-2	Fletcher 2, Murdoch 2, Wilson	10,729	8		4				11	9	5			1		10	2		6			3	7
1993	8 (h) Oldham A	L 0-1		11,374	8		4				11		5			1		10	2		6	9		3	7
1994	15 (a) Workington	L 0-1		3,400	8		4				11		5			1		10	2		6	9		3	7
1995	22 (h) Chester	D 1-1	Fletcher	6,770	8	3	4				11	9	5			1		10	2		6				7
1996	29 (a) Crewe A	L 1-4	Fletcher	8,947	8	3	4					9	5			1	11	10	2		6				7
1997	Nov 12 (a) Accrington S	L 1-4	Fletcher	3,774	8		4		11			9	5			1		10	2		6			3	7
1998	19 (h) Millwall	W 3-1	Anderson 2, Fletcher	4,857	8			4			11	9	5			1		10	2		6			3	7
1999	Dec 10 (a) Bradford	L 2-4	Murdoch, Davock	6,099	8			4			11	9	5			1		10	2		6			3	7
2000	26 (a) Doncaster R	L 1-3	Opp own-goal	7,203	8			4		7	11	9	5			1		10	2		6			3	
2001	27 (a) Doncaster R	W 1-0	Hodder (pen)	7,204	8		4				11	9	5			1		10	2		6			3	7
2002	31 (h) Mansfield T	W 1-0	Anderson	4,723	8		4				11	9	5			1		10	2		6			3	7
2003	Jan 21 (a) Exeter C	L 1-2	Murdoch	4,579	8			4			11	9	5			1		10	2		6			3	7
2004	Feb 2 (h) Peterboro' U	L 0-6		7,068	8			4			11	9	5			1		10	2		6			3	7
2005	11 (a) Southport	L 0-1		3,803			4	8	9		11		5			1		10	2		6			3	7
2006	18 (h) Darlington	W 2-1	Fletcher, Murdoch	4,408	9			4			11	10	5			1		8	2		6			3	7
2007	25 (a) Oldham A	L 0-3		14,962	9		4	8			11	10	5			1			2	7	6			3	
2008	Mar 4 (h) Workington	W 1-0	Fletcher	4,249	9			4			11	10	5			1			2		6			3	7
2009	6 (h) Gillingham	W 2-0	Murdoch, Anderson	4,759	8		4				11	9	5			1		10	2		6			3	7
2010	11 (a) Chester	D 0-0		3,942	8		4				11	9	5			1		10	2		6			3	7
2011	13 (h) York C	W 2-0	Murdoch, Anderson	5,263	8		4				11	9	5			1		10	2		6			3	7
2012	18 (h) Crewe A	L 0-1		5,138	8		4				11	9	5			1		10	2		6			3	7
2013	25 (a) York C	D 0-0		8,221	8		4				11	9	5			1		10	2	7	6			3	
2014	31 (h) Aldershot	W 2-0	Fletcher, Wilson	4,860	8			4			11	9	5			1		10	2		6			3	7
2015	Apr 1 (h) Accrington S	L 0-3		4,190	8			4			10	9	5			1			2	11	6			3	7
2016	3 (a) Aldershot	L 2-3	Partridge, Murdoch	4,523	8			4			11	9	5		1			10	2	7	6			3	
2017	8 (a) Millwall	L 0-3		7,876	8			4			11	9	5					10	2		6		1	3	7
2018	11 (a) Rochdale	D 1-1	Porteous (pen)	3,215	8			4			10	9	5		1				2	11	6			3	7
2019	15 (h) Barrow	W 1-0	Fletcher	3,549	9			4				10	5					8	2	11	6		1	3	7
2020	17 (h) Northampton T	D 1-1	Fletcher	4,307	8			4			11	9	5					10	2		6		1	3	7
2021	23 (a) Gillingham	D 1-1	Davock	4,287	8			4			10	9	5		1				2	11	6			3	7
2022	26 (a) Crystal P	L 1-2	Anderson	15,822	8			4			11	9	5					10	2	7	6		1	3	
2023	29 (h) Bradford	L 2-3	Porteous (pen), Fletcher	4,147	8			4			10	9	5						2	11	6		1	3	7
2024	May 5 (a) Barrow	L 1-3	Murdoch	1,730	8			4			11	9	5					10	2	7	6		1	3	
	Appearances				45	9	26	23	2	1	43	43	46	1	3	37	1	39	39	11	46	2	6	43	40
	Goals				11		1				7	14	1					12		1	3				5

FINAL LEAGUE POSITION: 13th in Division Four

Own-goals 2

FA Cup

#	Match	Res	Scorers	Att	Anderson	Ashton	Bennion	Birch	Connelly	Cunliffe	Davock	Fletcher	Hodder	Holland	Keelan	Lea	Lovell	Murdoch	Murray	Partridge	Porteous	Ritchie	Smith	Webb	Wilson
1	Nov 5 (h) Workington	W 1-0	Anderson	5,548	8		4				11	9	5			1		10	2		6			3	7
2	26 (h) B Auckland	W 2-0	Davock 2	9,668	8	4					11	9	5			1		10	2		6			3	7
3	Jan 7 (h) Southport	W 3-1	Anderson 2, Wilson	9,435	8		4				11	9	5			1		10	2		6			3	7
4	Feb 2 (a) Newcastle U	L 0-4		48,715	8		4				11	9	5			1		10	2		6			3	7
	Appearances				4	1	3				4	4	4			4		4	4		4			4	4
	Goals				3						2														1

League Cup

#	Match	Res	Scorers	Att	Anderson	Ashton	Bennion	Birch	Connelly	Cunliffe	Davock	Fletcher	Hodder	Holland	Keelan	Lea	Lovell	Murdoch	Murray	Partridge	Porteous	Ritchie	Smith	Webb	Wilson
1	Oct 10 (h) Carlisle U	W 2-0	Wilson, Anderson	7,953	8		4				11		5			1		10	2		6	9		3	7
2	18 (a) Manchester C	L 0-3		21,005	8	3	4				11		5	9		1		10	2		6				7
	Appearances				2	1	2				2		2	1		2		2	2		2	1		1	2
	Goals				1																				1

Average Home League attendance: 6,506
Average Away League attendance: 7,043

1961-62

No.	Date	Opponent	Result	Scorers	Att.	Anderson	Ashton	Beighton	Bentley	Birch	Collinson	Davock	Hodder	Lea	McDonnell	Murdoch	Murray	Partridge	Porteous	Ricketts	Ward	Webb	Whitelaw	Wilson
2025	Aug 19	(a) Colchester U	L 0-3		4,318		2		9			10	5	1	8		4		11	6	7	3		
2026	22	(a) Southport	L 1-2	Bentley	4,274	8	2		9			11	5	1	10		4			6	7	3		
2027	26	(h) Carlisle U	L 1-2	Partridge	4,617			9	4				5	1	10	8	2		11	6	7	3		
2028	28	(h) Southport	L 1-4	McDonnell	4,804	9			4				5	1	10	8	2		11	6	7	3		
2029	Sep 2	(a) Bradford C	W 3-1	Anderson, McDonnell, Murdoch	6,872	9			4				5	1	10	8	2		11	6	7	3		
2030	4	(a) Hartlepools U	D 2-2	McDonnell 2	6,313	9		1	4				5		10	8	2		11	6	7	3		
2031	8	(h) Aldershot	W 3-1	Ward, Partridge, McDonnell	5,784	9			4				5	1	10	8	2		11	6	7	3		
2032	16	(h) Gillingham	W 3-1	Partridge, McDonnell, Porteous	4,365	9			4				5	1	10	8	2		11	6	7	3		
2033	18	(a) Millwall	W 3-1	Anderson, Murdoch, Partridge	12,391	9			4				5	1	10	8	2		11	6	7	3		
2034	12	(a) Oldham A	D 0-0		13,624	9			4			10	5	1		8	2		11	6	7	3		
2035	25	(h) Millwall	D 1-1	Porteous	7,505	9			4			10	5	1		8	2		11	6	7	3		
2036	Oct 2	(a) Darlington	L 0-3		6,438	9		1		2		10	5		8		4		11	6	7	3		
2037	7	(a) Mansfield T	L 0-2		10,631	9		1		2		10	5		8		4		11	6	7	3		
2038	9	(h) Darlington	W 3-0	Anderson 2, Davock	4,990	9		1	4			11	5		10	8	2			6	7	3		
2039	14	(h) Barrow	W 3-0	Murdoch, Ward, Anderson	5,205	9		1	4			11	5		10	8	2			6	7	3		
2040	21	(a) Rochdale	D 3-3	Anderson, Ward, Murdoch	4,413	9		1	4			11	5		10	8	2			6	7	3		
2041	28	(h) Crewe A	L 0-1		5,869	9		1	4			11	5		10	8	2			6	7	3		
2042	Nov 11	(h) Wrexham	L 1-2	Murdoch	4,691			1	7	4			5		10	8	2		11	6	9	3		
2043	18	(a) Doncaster R	D 1-1	Partridge	4,056			1	7	4		10	5		8		2	11		6	9	3		
2044	Dec 2	(a) York C	L 0-1		4,697			1	7	4		11	5		8	10	2			6	9	3		
2045	16	(h) Colchester U	L 1-4	Ward	2,825			1	7	4		10	5		8		2	11		6	9	3		
2046	23	(a) Carlisle U	L 0-1		4,658		2	1	9			11	5		10		4	7		6	8	3		
2047	26	(h) Tranmere R	W 3-0	Ward 2, Wilson	2,811		2	1	9				5		10		4		11	6	8	3		7
2048	Jan 6	(a) Exeter C	L 3-4	Davock, Ward, McDonnell	4,135		2	1	9			11	5		10		4			6	8	3		7
2049	13	(h) Bradford C	W 3-1	McDonnell 2, Ward	2,352		3	1	9	4		11	5		10		2	7		6	8			
2050	20	(h) Aldershot	L 1-4	Ward	5,960		2	1	7			11	5		10		4			6	8	3	9	
2051	Feb 3	(a) Gillingham	D 1-1		5,991		2	1				11	5		10		4	7		6	8	3	9	
2052	10	(h) Oldham A	D 1-1	Davock	10,565		2	1				11	5		10		4	7		6	8	3	9	
2053	23	(h) Mansfield T	W 2-1	Ward, Davock	3,005			1				11	5		10		4		2	6	8	3	9	7
2054	Mar 3	(a) Barrow	L 1-3	McDonnell	5,099			1	7			11	5		10		4		2	6	8	3	9	
2055	9	(h) Rochdale	W 5-2	Murray 2, McDonnell, Ward, Whitelaw	4,248			1	7			11	5		10		4		2	6	8	3	9	
2056	12	(h) Chesterfield	W 2-1	Ward, Whitelaw (pen)	4,323			1	7			11	5		10		4		2	6	8	3	9	
2057	17	(a) Crewe A	L 2-3	Whitelaw 2 (1 pen)	5,227			1	7			11	5		10		4		2	6	8	3	9	
2058	19*	(h) Workington	W 3-1	McDonnell 2, Rickets	6,513			1	7			11	5		10		4		2	6	8	3	9	
2059	23	(h) Exeter C	W 1-0	Whitelaw	4,200			1	7			11	5		10		4		2	6	8	3	9	
2060	26	(a) Tranmere R	W 3-1	McDonnell, Ward, Davock	6,875		2	1	9			11	5		10		4			6	8	3	7	
2061	30	(a) Wrexham	W 1-0	Ward	11,261		2	1	9			11	5		10		4			6	8	3	7	
2062	Apr 6	(h) Doncaster R	W 2-1	Bentley, Whitelaw	4,414			1	8			11	5		10		4		2	6	7	3	9	
2063	9	(h) Hartlepools U	D 1-1	Davock	4,024			1	8			11	5		10		4		2	6	7	3	9	
2064	14	(a) Workington	D 1-1	McDonnell	2,940		2	1	9			11	5		10		4			6	8	3	7	
2065	20	(h) Chester	L 0-1		4,388			1	8			11	5		10		4		2	6	7	3	9	
2066	21	(h) York C	W 2-1	Murray, Porteous	2,739		2	1				11	5		10		4		9	6	8	3		7
2067	23	(a) Chester	L 0-2		5,105		2	1	7			11	5		10		4			6	8	3	9	
2068	28	(h) Chesterfield	L 2-3	Whitelaw 2 (2 pens)	3,709		2	1	8		4	11	5		10					6	7	3	9	
		FINAL LEAGUE POSITION: 16th in Division Four		Appearances		15	15	34	27	20	2	34	41	10	38	19	44	20	32	27	44	43	16	3
				Goals		6			2			6			16	5	3	5	3	1	14		8	1

FA Cup

No.	Date	Opponent	Result	Att.	Anderson	Ashton	Beighton	Bentley	Birch	Collinson	Davock	Hodder	Lea	McDonnell	Murdoch	Murray	Partridge	Porteous	Ricketts	Ward	Webb	Whitelaw	Wilson
1	Nov 4	(h) Accrington S	L 0-1	4,797	9		1	4			11	5		8	10	2			6	7	3		
			Appearances		1		1	1			1	1		1	1	1			1	1	1		
			Goals																				

League Cup

No.	Date	Opponent	Result	Att.	Anderson	Ashton	Beighton	Bentley	Birch	Collinson	Davock	Hodder	Lea	McDonnell	Murdoch	Murray	Partridge	Porteous	Ricketts	Ward	Webb	Whitelaw	Wilson
1	Sep 11	(h) Leyton O	L 0-1	7,615	9			4				5	1	8	10	2		11	6	7	3		
			Appearances		1			1				1	1	1	1	1		1	1	1	1		
			Goals																				

Average Home League attendance: 4,738
Average Away League attendance: 6,318

*This was the 'replay' of a game played at Edgeley Park on 27 January which was abandoned after 37 minutes due to fog with the score at 0-0, ther team being the same as that for Match 2051.

Accrington Stanley resigned from the League in March by which time they had played Stockport twice. Although these results were expunged, for completeness the game at Edgeley Park took place on 30 September 1961, Stockport winning 2-0 (McDonnell, Murdoch) before a crowd of 6,630, the team being the same as for Match 2032. On 17 February 1962, at Peel Park, Accrington, Stockport completed the double by winning 2-1 (McDonnell, Whitelaw(pen)) before a crowd of 1,775, the team being the same as for Match 2052 except for Wilson replacing Partridge.

1962-63

No	Date	Venue/Opponent	Result	Scorers	Att	Beighton	Bentley	Buck	Cutler	Davenport	Davock	Evans	Gorrie	Griffiths	Hodder	Lea	McDonnell	Murray	Parry	Porteous	Ricketts	Ward	Webb	Whitelaw	Wylie
2069	Aug 18	(h) York C	D 1-1	Whitelaw	4,461	1	8				11		4		5		10			2	6	7		3	9
2070	25	(a) Chester	W 1-0	Whitelaw	6,718	1	8				11		4		5		10			2	6	7		3	9
2071	27	(a) Rochdale	W 1-0	Whitelaw	6,389	1	8				11		4		5		10			2	6	7		3	9
2072	Sep 1	(h) Crewe A	D 1-1	McDonnell	7,031	1	8		7		11		4		5		10			2	6			3	9
2073	3	(a) Chesterfield	W 2-1	McDonnell 2	7,078	1	8		7		11		4		5		10			2	6			3	9
2074	8	(a) Gillingham	L 0-1		6,605	1	8		7		11		4		5		10			2	6			3	9
2075	10	(h) Chesterfield	L 0-1		6,600	1	8				11		4		5		10			2	6			3	9
2076	15	(h) Newport C	D 1-1	Ward	3,746	1			7		11		4		5		10			2	6		8	3	9
2077	18	(a) Brentford	L 1-2	McDonnell	10,146	1			7		11		4		5		10			2	6		8	3	9
2078	22	(h) Doncaster R	W 2-1	McDonnell, Whitelaw	3,650	1			7		11		4		5		10			2	6		8	3	9
2079	29	(a) Mansfield T	W 1-0	McDonnell	10,082	1			7		11	8	4		5		10			2	6			3	9
2080	Oct 3	(a) Oxford U	D 1-1	Davock	9,019	1			7		11	8	4		5		10			2	6			3	9
2081	6	(a) Bradford C	L 2-3	Ward, McDonnell	5,014	1			7		11		4		5		10			2	6		8	3	9
2082	8	(h) Oxford U	D 1-1	McDonnell	6,364	1			7		11				5		10	4		2	6		8	3	9
2083	13	(h) Tranmere R	D 2-2	Ward 2	4,753	1			7		11				5		10	4		2	6		8	3	9
2084	16	(a) Rochdale	L 0-1		3,797	1			7		11				5		10	4		2	6		8	3	9
2085	20	(a) Torquay U	D 2-2	Bentley, Davock	5,504	1			7		11				5		10	4		2	6		8	3	9
2086	27	(h) Lincoln C	L 1-2	McDonnell	3,228	1			7		11				5		10	4		2	6		8	3	9
2087	Nov 10	(h) Barrow	L 1-3	Davock	2,944	1	9				11	8			5		10			2	6	7		3	4
2088	17	(a) Hartlepools U	L 0-3		3,856	1	9	7			11	8			5		10	2		3	6				4
2089	24	(h) Brentford	W 2-1	Whitelaw, Ward	3,090	1		7			11				5		10	2		3	6		8	9	4
2090	Dec 1	(a) Southport	L 0-2		3,385		9	7			11				5	1	10	2		3	6		8		4
2091	8	(h) Aldershot	W 3-0	Ward, Bentley, McDonnell	1,966	1	9		7		11				5		10	2		3	6		8		4
2092	15	(a) York C	L 1-3	Bentley	2,610	1	9		7		11				5		10	2		3	6		8		4
2093	26	(a) Exeter C	W 1-0	Evans	3,977	1					11	8			5		10	2		3	6	7		9	4
2094	29	(h) Exeter C	W 4-3	Ward, Evans, Whitelaw, Davock	3,324	1					11	8			5		10	2		3	6	7		9	4
2095	Jan 26	(a) Oldham A	L 1-2	Evans	16,472	1					11	8			5		10	2		3	6	7		9	4
2096	Feb 9	(a) Doncaster R	W 2-1	McDonnell, Evans	5,756	1					11	8			5		10	2		3	6	7		9	4
2097	Mar 2	(a) Tranmere R	L 1-3	Davock	7,300	1					11	8			5		10	2		3	6	7		9	4
2098	9	(h) Torquay U	L 1-2	McDonnell	2,687	1			7		11	8			5		10	2		3	6			9	4
2099	16	(a) Lincoln C	D 0-0		3,289	1					11	8		9	5		10	2		3	6	7			4
2100	18	(h) Chester	W 1-0	Evans	3,154	1			7		11	8		9	5		10	2		3	6				4
2101	23	(h) Oldham A	W 2-1	Whitelaw, McDonnell	10,617	1			7		11	8			5		10	2		3	6			9	4
2102	29	(a) Darlington	L 1-5	Opp own-goal	2,152	1				9	11	8			5		10	2		3	6	7			4
2103	Apr 1	(h) Darlington	L 0-1		3,128	1			7		11	8			5		10	2		3	6			9	4
2104	6	(h) Hartlepools U	W 4-1	Evans 2, Whitelaw, McDonnell	2,619	1			7		11	8			5		10	2		3	6			9	4
2105	12	(h) Workington	L 2-3	Evans, Wylie	3,643	1			7		11	8			5		10	2		3	6			9	4
2106	13	(a) Barrow	L 0-1		4,486	1			7	10	11	8	4	9	5			2		3	6				
2107	15	(a) Workington	L 0-4		2,561	1			7	10	11	8	4		5			2		3	6		9		
2108	20	(h) Southport	L 0-2		2,108				7	10	11	8	4		5	1	9	2		3	6				
2109	22	(h) Bradford C	W 3-1	McDonnell, Evans, Whitelaw	2,052				7		11	8			5	1	10	2		3	6			9	4
2110	27	(a) Aldershot	D 2-2	Ricketts, Whitelaw	3,920				7		11	8				1	10	2	5	3	6			9	4
2111	May 4	(a) Newport C	L 1-3	Evans	2,573	1			7		11	8			5		10	2		3	6			9	4
2112	11	(a) Crewe A	W 2-1	Evans, McDonnell	6,878	1			7		11	8			5		10	2		3	6			9	4
2113	18	(h) Gillingham	D 0-0		2,206	1			7		11	8			5		10	2		3	6			9	4
2114	20	(h) Mansfield T	D 1-1	Ricketts	3,637	1			7		11	8			5		10	6		2	8			3 9	4
		FINAL LEAGUE POSITION: 19th in Division Four			**Appearances**	42	22	3	34	4	39	22	18	3	41	4	41	33	2	46	46	24	21	36	25
					Goals		3				5	11					16				2	7		10	1

Own-goal 1

FA Cup

No	Date	Venue/Opponent	Result	Scorers	Att	Beighton	Bentley	Buck	Cutler	Davenport	Davock	Evans	Gorrie	Griffiths	Hodder	Lea	McDonnell	Murray	Parry	Porteous	Ricketts	Ward	Webb	Whitelaw	Wylie
1	Nov 3	(a) Chesterfield	L 1-4	Bentley	9,177	1	7				11				5		10	4		2	6		8	3	9
					Appearances	1	1				1				1		1	1		1	1		1	1	1
					Goals		1																		

League Cup

No	Date	Venue/Opponent	Result	Scorers	Att	Beighton	Bentley	Buck	Cutler	Davenport	Davock	Evans	Gorrie	Griffiths	Hodder	Lea	McDonnell	Murray	Parry	Porteous	Ricketts	Ward	Webb	Whitelaw	Wylie
1	Sep 5	(a) Chester	L 0-2		5,124	1	8		7		11	4			5		10			2	6			3	9
					Appearances	1	1		1		1	1			1		1			1	1			1	1
					Goals																				

Average Home League attendance: 4,061
Average Away League attendance: 5,790

1963-64

No.	Date	Venue / Opponent	Res.	Scorers	Att.	Beighton	Bircumshaw	Collins	Cuthbert	Davenport	Davock	Eckersall	Evans	France	Hodder	Johnston	Lea	McDonnell	Parry	Porteous	Ricketts	Ryden	Stainsby	Ward	Watt	Wylie
2115	Aug 24	(a) Chesterfield	D 1-1	Bircumshaw	7,599	1	11		3				8		5			10		2	6	9			7	4
2116	26	(h) Lincoln C	W 4-0	Evans, Bircumshaw, Ryden 2	7,075	1	11		3				8		5			10		2	6	9			7	4
2117	31	(h) Doncaster R	L 1-3	Ricketts	7,901	1	11		3				8		5			10		2	6	9			7	4
2118	Sep 7	(a) Brighton & HA	W 2-1	Ryden, Evans	6,903	1	11		3				8	10		2			5	3	6	9			7	4
2119	11	(a) Lincoln C	L 0-1		7,822	1	11		3				8	10		2			5	3	6	9			7	4
2120	14	(h) Chester	W 1-0	Ryden	6,134	1	11		3				8	10		2			5	3	6	9			7	4
2121	17	(a) Bradford	D 2-2	Evans, Ryden	6,382	1	11		3				8	10		2			5		6	9			7	4
2122	20	(a) York C	L 0-2		3,956	1	11		3				8			2			5		6	9			7	4
2123	28	(h) Barrow	W 5-0	Ryden 2, Wylie, Evans, Bircumshaw	3,910	1	11		3				8			2			5		6	9	10		7	4
2124	30	(h) Bradford	W 2-1	Bircumshaw, Evans	6,370	1	11		3				8			2			5		6	9	10		7	4
2125	Oct 5	(a) Rochdale	L 0-1		3,995	1	11		3				8			2			5		6	9	10		7	4
2126	8	(a) Workington	D 1-1	Davock	3,771	1	11		3		10		8			2			5		6	9			7	4
2127	12	(h) Aldershot	D 2-2	Evans 2 (1 pen)	5,947	1	11		3		10		8						5	2	6	9			7	4
2128	14	(h) Workington	D 0-0		5,852	1			3	11	10		8						5	2	6	9			7	4
2129	18	(a) Carlisle U	D 0-0		9,507	1			3	11			8					10	5	2	6	9			7	4
2130	21	(h) Oxford U	D 0-0		6,694	1			3	11			8					10	5	2	6	9			7	4
2131	26	(h) Torquay U	D 0-0		5,511	1			3	11			8						5	2	6	9	10		7	4
2132	30	(a) Oxford U	L 0-1		7,137	1			3	11			8						5	2	6	9	10		7	4
2133	Nov 2	(a) Halifax T	L 2-4	Evans, Ryden	3,972	1	11		3				8	10					5	2	6	9			7	4
2134	9	(h) Tranmere R	D 1-1	France	4,178	1	11		3				8	10					5	2	6	9			7	4
2135	23	(h) Hartlepools U	W 1-0	France	3,216	1	11		3				8	10					5	2	6	9			7	4
2136	29	(a) Exeter C	L 0-2		7,058	1	11		3				8	10		2			5	4	6	9			7	
2137	Dec 14	(h) Chesterfield	W 2-1	France, Watt	2,922	1			3				8	10					5	2	6	9		11	7	4
2138	21	(a) Doncaster R	L 1-4	Watt (pen)	4,142	1			3				8	10					5	2	6	9		11	7	4
2139	28	(h) Bradford C	W 2-1	France, Evans (pen)	3,988	1			3		10		8	9					5	2	6			11	7	4
2140	Jan 4	(a) Darlington	W 3-2	Watt, Davock 2	3,416	1			3		10		8	9					5	2	6			11	7	4
2141	11	(h) Brighton & HA	D 1-1	France	3,522	1			3		10		8	9					5	2	6			11	7	4
2142	18	(a) Chester	L 1-2	Porteous	5,403	1			3		10		8	9					5	2	6			11	7	4
2143	25	(h) Southport	L 1-4	France	3,027	1			3		10		8	9					5	2	6			11	7	4
2144	29	(a) Bradford C	L 0-1		3,575	1			4	3	9								5	10	6	8		11	7	2
2145	Feb 1	(h) York C	W 2-0	Davock 2	2,558	1			3	11	4		8	9					5	10	6	7				2
2146	7	(a) Barrow	W 2-1	Ricketts 2	2,383	1			3	11	6			9					5	2	10	8			7	4
2147	15	(h) Rochdale	W 1-0	Davock	3,487	1			3	11	6			9					5	2	10	8			7	4
2148	22	(h) Aldershot	L 0-7		3,872	1			3	11	6			9		2			5	4	10	8			7	
2149	29	(h) Carlisle U	L 1-3		3,645	1			3	11	6		8	9		2			5		10				7	4
2150	Mar 6	(a) Torquay U	L 0-4		4,827			6	3	11	9	8					1		5	10				4	7	2
2151	14	(h) Halifax T	L 1-2	Davenport	1,935				3	11	9			10			1		5	2	6			8	7	4
2152	20	(a) Tranmere R	L 2-4	Opp own-goal, Davenport	5,569	1			3	11	9			10					5	2	6			8	7	4
2153	27	(h) Newport C	W 1-0	Ryden	2,904	1		5	3	11	9	8								2	6	10			7	4
2154	28	(h) Gillingham	W 2-0	Opp own-goal, France	2,649	1		5	3	11	9			10						2	6	8			7	4
2155	30	(a) Newport C	L 1-3	Davenport	2,966	1		5	3	11	9			10		2					6	8			7	4
2156	Apr 4	(a) Hartlepools U	L 0-3		2,641	1		5	3	11	9			10		2					6	8			7	4
2157	11	(h) Exeter C	D 0-0		2,821	1			3	11	10			9		2			5		6	8			7	4
2158	18	(a) Southport	L 0-2		2,308	1			3	11	10			9		2			5		6	8			7	4
2159	22	(a) Gillingham	D 0-0		12,846	1		4	3	11	9	8							5	10	6	7				2
2160	25	(h) Darlington	W 2-0	Opp own-goal, France	2,086	1		4	3	11	9	8							5	10	6	7				2
Appearances						44	17	7	34	12	28	8	30	30	3	26	2	5	40	36	46	38	5	13	38	44
Goals							4			3	6		9	8						1	3	9			3	1

FINAL LEAGUE POSITION: 17th in Division Four

Own-goals 3

FA Cup

No.	Date	Venue / Opponent	Res.	Scorers	Att.	Beighton	Bircumshaw	Collins	Cuthbert	Davenport	Davock	Eckersall	Evans	France	Hodder	Johnston	Lea	McDonnell	Parry	Porteous	Ricketts	Ryden	Stainsby	Ward	Watt	Wylie
1	Nov 16	(a) Barnsley	L 0-1		7,577	1			3				8	10					5	2	6	9			7	4
Appearances						1			1				1	1					1	1	1	1			1	1
Goals																										

League Cup

No.	Date	Venue / Opponent	Res.	Scorers	Att.	Beighton	Bircumshaw	Collins	Cuthbert	Davenport	Davock	Eckersall	Evans	France	Hodder	Johnston	Lea	McDonnell	Parry	Porteous	Ricketts	Ryden	Stainsby	Ward	Watt	Wylie
1	Sep 4	(a) Tranmere R	L 0-2		5,956	1	11						8	10		2			5	3	6	9			7	4
Appearances						1	1						1			1			1	1	1	1			1	1
Goals																										

Average Home League attendance: 4,275
Average Away League attendance: 5,307

1964-65

No	Date	Opponent	Result	Scorers	Att	Beaumont	Beighton	Brooks	Collins	Cuthbert	Eckersall	Harold	Hodgkinson	Hoggart	McGowan	Mulhearn	Nibloe	Parry	Peacock	Phoenix	Porteous	Roberts	Sandiford	Tillotson	Watt	White
2161	Aug 22 (h)	Millwall	L 1-4	Eckersall	5,042	1		2	3	4			8	7			9	5			6		10	11		
2162	26 (a)	Rochdale	L 0-4		4,458	1		2	3	4			8	7			9	5			6		10	11		
2163	29 (a)	Bradford C	D 1-1	Nibloe	4,238	1		2	3	4			8	7			9	5			6		10	11		
2164	Sep 4 (h)	Chester	L 4-5	Eckersall, Hodgkinson, Hoggart 2	4,367	1				4	6	2	8	11			10	5					3		9	7
2165	7 (a)	Hartlepools U	L 3-4	Hodgkinson, Hoggart, Sandiford	6,619	1				4	6	2	8	11			10	5					3		9	7
2166	12 (a)	Torquay U	L 0-1		5,180	1		2		4			8	11	10			5			6		3		9	7
2167	14 (a)	Hartlepools U	L 0-1		5,259	1		2	3	4			8	11	10			5			6				9	7
2168	19 (a)	Chesterfield	L 0-2		6,171	1		2	3				8	11	10			5			6		9			7
2169	25 (h)	York C	L 1-2	Sandiford	4,156	1		2	3				8		10			5		11	6	4	9			7
2170	28 (a)	Oxford U	D 0-0		5,779	4	1	2					8		10			5		11	6	3	9			7
2171	Oct 3 (a)	Lincoln C	L 0-6		5,180	4	1	2					8	10				5		11	6	3	9			7
2172	7 (a)	Oxford U	L 0-2		8,268	8		2	3	4						1	10	5		11	6		9			7
2173	10 (h)	Aldershot	W 2-1	Watt (pen), Hodgkinson	4,040	6			3	4			8			1	10	5		11	2		9		7	
2174	12 (h)	Barrow	W 1-0	Hodgkinson	5,277	6			3	4			8			1	10	5		11	2		9		7	
2175	17 (a)	Bradford	L 0-1		6,542	8			2	3	4		7			1	10	5		11	6		9			
2176	19 (h)	Barrow	W 1-0	Sandiford	2,634	8			2	3	4		7			1	10	5		11	6		9			
2177	23 (h)	Southport	D 2-2	Nibloe, Phoenix	4,825	8	1		2	3	4						10	5		11	6		9			
2178	29 (a)	Notts C	L 0-2		4,312	8	1		6			4	2	7			9	5		11	10	3				
2179	31 (a)	Wrexham	L 1-4	Nibloe	7,783	8	1		6	3	4	2	7				9	5		11	10					
2180	Nov 6 (h)	Tranmere R	L 2-3	Hodgkinson, Nibloe	6,563	8	1		2	3	4		7				9	5		11	6		10			
2181	20 (a)	Crewe A	D 1-1	Hodgkinson	5,387	6	10	2	3	4			7			1	8	5		11			9			
2182	28 (a)	Newport C	L 0-2		3,850	8			2	3	4		7			1	10	5		11	6		9			
2183	Dec 12 (a)	Millwall	L 0-1		6,573	8	7	2	3				10			1		5	6	11	4		9			
2184	26 (a)	Doncaster R	L 0-3		8,497	8			2	3	10		7			1		5	6	11	4		9			
2185	28 (h)	Doncaster R	W 2-0	Beaumont 2	3,083	8			2	3	4		10			1		5	11	7	6		9			
2186	Jan 2 (a)	Chester	L 0-4		7,606	8			2	3	4		10			1		5	6	11			9	7		
2187	16 (h)	Torquay U	L 0-2		7,356	11			2	3	4		10			1		5			6		9		7	8
2188	23 (h)	Chesterfield	L 0-1		5,305				2	3	4		10			1		5	11		6		9	7		8
2189	Feb 6 (a)	York C	L 0-3		5,778	10			4	3	6		7	11		1		5					9	2		8
2190	13 (h)	Lincoln C	W 3-1	White 2, Beaumont	3,400	8			2	3	4		10	11		1		5			6		7			9
2191	15 (h)	Rochdale	L 1-2	Hoggart	8,645	8			2	3	4		10	11		1		5			6		7			9
2192	20 (a)	Aldershot	L 0-2		3,236	8			2	3	4		10	11		1		5			6		7			9
2193	27 (h)	Bradford	L 0-2		5,255	8			2	3	4		10	11		1		5			6				7	9
2194	Mar 6 (a)	Southport	D 1-1	White	2,488	4			5	3			10	7		1		6		11			8	2		9
2195	8 (h)	Bradford C	W 2-0	White, Hoggart	5,949	4			5	3			10	7		1		6		11			8	2		9
2196	12 (h)	Wrexham	W 3-2	White 2, Sandiford	7,747	4			5	3			10	7		1		6		11			8	2		9
2197	15 (a)	Darlington	L 2-3	Hoggart, Sandiford	2,715	4			5	3			10	7		1		6		11			8	2		9
2198	19 (a)	Tranmere R	D 1-1	White	11,210	4			5	3			10	7		1		6		11			8	2		9
2199	22 (h)	Halifax T	W 2-0	Beaumont, Sandiford	6,515	4			5	3			10	7		1		6		11			8	2		9
2200	26 (h)	Darlington	D 0-0		7,330	4			5	3			10	7		1		6		11			8	2		9
2201	Apr 3 (a)	Crewe A	L 2-3	White, Hodgkinson	4,946	4			5	3			10	7		1		6		11			8	2		9
2202	10 (h)	Newport C	W 2-0	Hodgkinson, White	4,497	4			5	3			10	7		1		6		11			8	2		9
2203	16 (h)	Brighton & HA	L 1-4	Hodgkinson	10,334	4			5	3			10	7		1		6		11			8	2		9
2204	17 (a)	Halifax T	W 1-0	Sandiford	2,371	4			2				10	7		1		5		11	6		8	3		9
2205	19 (a)	Brighton & HA	L 1-3	Sandiford	21,442	4			2				10	7		1		5		11	6		8	3		9
2206	23 (h)	Notts C	L 0-1		5,880	4			2				10	7		1		5		11	6		8	3		9
	FINAL LEAGUE POSITION: 24th in Division Four - Re-elected				Appearances	36	15	2	44	37	28	4	45	27	5	31	22	46	5	19	31	13	43	16	17	20
					Goals	4					2		9	6			4			1			8		1	9

FA Cup

No	Date	Opponent	Result	Scorers	Att	Beaumont	Beighton	Brooks	Collins	Cuthbert	Eckersall	Harold	Hodgkinson	Hoggart	McGowan	Mulhearn	Nibloe	Parry	Peacock	Phoenix	Porteous	Roberts	Sandiford	Tillotson	Watt	White
1	Nov 14 (h)	Wigan A	W 2-1	Eckersall (pen), Nibloe	11,570	8			2	3	4		7			1	10	5		11	6		9			
2	Dec 7* (h)	Grimsby T	W 1-0	Hodgkinson	10,163	8	7		2	3	4		10			1		5		11	6		9			
3	Jan 9 (a)	Bristol R	D 0-0		12,156	8			2	3	4		10			1		5		11	6		9	7		
R	11 (h)	Bristol R	W 3-2	Hodgkinson, Beaumont, Sandiford	19,654	8			2	3	4		10			1		5		11	6		9	7		
4	30 (a)	Liverpool	D 1-1	White	51,851				2	3	4		10			1		5		11	6		9		7	8
R	Feb 3 (h)	Liverpool	L 0-2		24,080				2	3	4		10			1		5		11	6		9		7	8
					Appearances	4	1		6	6	6		6			6	1	6		6	6		6	4	2	
					Goals	1					1		2				1						1			1

League Cup

No	Date	Opponent	Result	Scorers	Att	Beaumont	Beighton	Brooks	Collins	Cuthbert	Eckersall	Harold	Hodgkinson	Hoggart	McGowan	Mulhearn	Nibloe	Parry	Peacock	Phoenix	Porteous	Roberts	Sandiford	Tillotson	Watt	White
1	Sep 2 (h)	Rochdale	L 1-3	Hoggart	3,396	1		2	3	4			8	11			10	5			6		9			7
					Appearances	1		1	1	1			1	1			1	1			1		1			1
					Goals									1												

Average Home League attendance: 5,739
Average Away League attendance: 6,178

*This followed a first attempt on 5 December which was abandoned after 50 minutes due to fog with the score at 0-0, the team being the same as on 7 December.

1965-66

FINAL LEAGUE POSITION: 13th in Division Four

No	Date	Opponent	Result / Scorers	Att	Allchurch	Allen	Beaumont	Beighton	Burner	Clarke	Collins	Cuthbert	Eckersall	Fleet	Goodwin	Haydock	Hodgkinson	Hoggart	Lord	Mulhearn	Parry	Price	Roberts	Sandiford	Shawcross	Sykes	Tillotson	White	Young
2207	Aug 21	(a) Chester	L 0-1	9,973		10	12					3			7			**4**		1	5	11			6		2	8	9
2208	23	(h) Notts C	L 1-3 White	11,670		10						3			7			4		1	5	11			6		2	8	9
2209	27	(h) Halifax T	W 3-0 White 2, Price	9,889		10	4				5	3			8					1		11			6		2	9	7
2210	Sep 4	(a) Port Vale	L 0-2	6,780		8	4				5	3			7					1		11	9		6		2	10	
2211	6	(h) Tranmere R	L 1-2 Allchurch	10,107	7	10	12				5	3			8	4				1		11			6		2	9	
2212	10	(h) Crewe A	W 2-0 Young, Haydock	9,263	7		4					3				8				1		11	10		6	5	2		9
2213	16	(a) Notts C	D 1-1 White	6,623	7		4					3			8					1		11			6	5	2	10	9
2214	18	(a) Bradford C	W 7-1 White 3, Young, Opp own-goal, Allen, Price	3,308		8	4					3			7					1		11			6	5	2	10	9
2215	24	(h) Barnsley	W 1-0 White	15,352	7		4					3			8					1		11			6	5	2	9	
2216	Oct 2	(a) Colchester U	L 2-3 White, Haydock	4,968	7	10	4					3				8				1		11			6	5	2		9
2217	4	(a) Darlington	L 0-3	6,436	7	10	4					3			8					1		11			6	5	2		9
2218	9	(h) Doncaster R	L 0-1	8,237	7		4				2	3			8					1		11			6	5		10	9
2219	15	(h) Southport	D 2-2 Opp own-goal, Shawcross (pen)	9,733	7	8	2					3			4					1		11	9		6	5		10	
2220	23	(a) Wrexham	W 4-1 Allen, White, Allchurch, Shawcross	4,266	7	10	2	1				3			4							11			6	5		8	9
2221	29	(h) Bradford	L 2-3 Allchurch, Allen	9,989	7	10	2	1				3			4							11			6	5		8	9
2222	Nov 6	(a) Aldershot	L 0-1	3,761	7	10					2				8					1	4	11			6	5	3		9
2223	20	(a) Torquay U	W 4-1 Allchurch, Allen 2, White	5,040	7	10					2				8					1	4	11			6	5	3		9
2224	22	(h) Darlington	D 1-1 Shawcross (pen)	8,342	7	10	8				2									1	4	11			6	5	3		9
2225	26	(h) Chesterfield	W 2-1 Sykes, Shawcross (pen)	6,654	7	10					2	3			8					1	4	11			6	5		9	
2226	Dec 10	(h) Luton T	W 4-1 Allen 3, Price	7,778	7	10					2	3			8					1	4	11			6	5		9	
2227	17	(a) Southport	L 0-2	2,995	7	10					2	3			8					1	4	11			6	5		9	
2228	Jan 1	(h) Doncaster R	D 1-1 Sandiford	7,120	11	9					2	3			8					1	4			7	6	5		10	
2229	8	(a) Newport C	L 0-1	2,760	7					4	2	3						8		1		11			6	5		10	
2230	14	(a) Wrexham	L 2-4 Young, Allchurch	6,547	7	10					2				8					1	4	11			6	5	3		9
2231	28	(h) Chester	L 0-1	8,138	7	9					2	3			8	10				1	4	11			6	5			
2232	Feb 5	(a) Halifax T	W 1-0 Lord	2,870	7	10				4	2				3				9	1		11			6	5		8	
2233	11	(h) Barrow	W 5-2 Lord 3, Allen, Shawcross (pen)	6,122	7	10				4	2				3				9	1		11			6	5		8	
2234	18	(h) Port Vale	W 3-0 White, Allchurch, Lord	7,400	7	10				4	2				3				9	1		11			6	5		8	
2235	21	(h) Lincoln C	W 2-1 Price, Lord	8,403	7	**10**				4	2				3	12			9	1		11			6	5		8	
2236	Mar 5	(a) Barrow	L 0-1	4,078	**7**					4	2				3	12			9	1		11			6	5		8	10
2237	15	(a) Lincoln C	W 2-1 Shawcross, Lord	2,638						4	2				3				9	1		11	7		6	5		8	10
2238	18	(a) Barnsley	W 2-1 Collins, White	4,944						4	2				3	12			9	1	5	11	7		6			8	
2239	21	(h) Bradford C	D 1-1 Lord	7,627						4	2				3	8			9	1	5	11	7		6				10
2240	25	(a) Colchester U	W 1-0 Clarke	6,430						4	2				3	8			9	1	5	11	7		6				10
2241	Apr 8	(a) Hartlepools U	L 1-2 Clarke	4,393						4	2				3	8				1	6	11	7	10		5			9
2242	9	(a) Rochdale	L 0-4	3,281		10			5	6	8		1	3	9						2	11		12	4				7
2243	11	(h) Hartlepools U	L 1-2 Shawcross	5,453					5	8	2	12			3	9				1	4	11	7		6	10			9
2244	15	(h) Torquay U	W 1-0 Young	4,278			12			5	2				3	8				1	4	11	7		6	9			10
2245	23	(a) Chesterfield	L 1-2 Shawcross (pen)	3,635		8		6		4	2				3					1	5	7			11	9			10
2246	25	(a) Tranmere R	L 2-6 Allchurch, Price	3,348	7	8				5	2				3					1	4	11			6	9			10
2247	29	(h) Rochdale	W 3-1 White, Young, Price	5,503	7					6	2		1								4	11				5	3	9	10
2248	May 4	(a) Crewe A	D 1-1 White	3,380	7					6	2			1	8						4	11				5	3	9	10
2249	7	(a) Luton T	L 0-2	9,524	7					6	2			1	4	8					5	11					3	9	10
2250	16	(h) Aldershot	L 1-2 Sykes	4,058	7						2			1	3	8					4	11			6	5		10	9
2251	20	(h) Newport C	W 2-1 Shawcross (pen), Goodwin	3,586	7					5	2	3		1	8	12					**4**	11			6	9			10
2252	24	(a) Bradford	L 1-3 Sykes	3,563	7					5		3		1	6	4						11			10	9	2	8	
			Appearances		32	26	16	2	3	21	33	22	3	6	23	29	1	3	9	38	25	45	7	4	42	37	19	33	27
			Sub appearances				3							1					4					1					
			Goals		7	9				2	1				1	2			8			6		1	9	3		15	5

Own-goals 2

FA Cup

No	Date	Opponent	Result / Scorers	Att	Allchurch	Allen	Clarke	Collins	Goodwin	Mulhearn	Parry	Price	Shawcross	Sykes	Tillotson	White	Young
1	Nov 13	(a) Tranmere R	W 1-0 Price	10,848	7	9	2		8	1	4	11	6	5	3		10
2	Dec 4	(a) Southport	D 3-3 Allen 2, Shawcross (pen)	7,194	7	9	2	3	8	1	4	11	6	5			10
R	13	(h) Southport	L 0-2	15,416	7	10	2	3	8	1	4	11	6	5		9	
			Appearances		3	3	3	2	3	3	3	3	3	3	1	2	1
			Goals			2						1	1				

League Cup

No	Date	Opponent	Result / Scorers	Att	Allen	Beaumont	Collins	Cuthbert	Goodwin	Mulhearn	Price	Shawcross	Tillotson	White	Young
1	Sep 1	(h) Workington	L 2-3 Price, Opp own-goal	7,474	10	4	5	3	8	1	11	6	2	9	7
			Appearances		1	1	1	1	1	1	1	1	1	1	1
			Goals								1				

Own-goal 1

Average Home League attendance: 7,802
Average Away League attendance: 4,817

1966-67

No	Date	V	Opponent	Result	Scorers	Att	Allchurch	Allen	Atkins	East	Fleet	Goodwin	Harley	Haydock	Henderson	Holden	Jones	Kevan	Lister	Lord	Morrin	Mulhearn	Parry	Prentis	Price	Quixall	Shawcross	Stuart	Sykes	Woods
2253	Aug 20	(a)	Barrow	D 1-1	Opp own-goal	5,020		10				6		2	7		3			9	1				11	8		4		5
2254	26	(h)	York C	W 3-1	Lord, Shawcross 2	7,897	7	10		1				2			3			9					11	8	6	4		5
2255	Sep 2	(a)	Lincoln C	W 1-0	Allen	5,582	7	10		1				2			3			9					11	8	6	4		5
2256	5	(h)	Barnsley	W 2-1	Lord, Shawcross (pen)	9,068	7	10		1				2			3			9					11	8	6	4		5
2257	9	(h)	Chesterfield	W 3-1	Lord, Allchurch, Allen	10,265	7	10		1				2			3			9					11	8	6	4		5
2258	17	(a)	Luton T	W 3-0	Shawcross (pen), Lord 2	5,887	7	10		1	8			2			3			9					11		6	4		5
2259	24	(a)	Rochdale	L 0-1		5,766	7	10		1	8			2			3			9					11		6	4		5
2260	27	(a)	Barnsley	W 2-1	Henderson 2	4,294	7			1				2	8		3			9					11	10	6	4		5
2261	30	(h)	Southport	W 1-0	Lord	13,760		10		1				2	7		3			9					11	8	6	4		5
2262	Oct 7	(h)	Newport C	D 0-0		11,541		10		1				2	7		3			9					11	8	6	4		5
2263	15	(a)	Brentford	L 1-2	Lord	5,714		8		1		3		2	7	4				9					11		10	5		6
2264	18	(a)	Bradford	W 1-0	Sykes	4,878	7	10				3		2	11					9	1					8		4	6	5
2265	21	(h)	Halifax T	W 2-1	Henderson, Allen	11,100	7	10				3		2	11					9	1					8		4	6	5
2266	29	(a)	Hartlepools U	L 0-1		5,976	7	10				3		2	11					9	1					8		4	6	5
2267	Nov 4	(h)	Exeter C	W 1-0	Lord	8,649	7	10				3		2	11					9	1					8	6	4		5
2268	12	(a)	Bradford C	W 1-0	Price	5,808	8	6				3		2	7					9	1				11	10		4		5
2269	14	(h)	Bradford	W 4-0	Price, Lord 2, Sykes	7,526	8					3		2	7			10		9	1			12	11			4	6	5
2270	18	(h)	Tranmere R	W 1-0	Henderson	11,981						3		2	8			10		9	1			7	11			4	6	5
2271	Dec 2	(h)	Wrexham	W 1-0	Allen	9,955	9					3		2	7			10		11	1				8			4	6	5
2272	10	(a)	Aldershot	D 1-1	East	4,893			9			3		2	7			10		11	1				8			4	6	5
2273	16	(h)	Barrow	W 2-1	Opp own-goal, Sykes	9,459	11		9			3		2	7			10			1				8			4	6	5
2274	23	(h)	Chester	D 1-1	Morrin	8,855	7		9			3		2	11			10			1				8			4	6	5
2275	26	(a)	Chester	D 1-1	Allchurch	8,825	7		9			3		2				8				1			11	10		4	6	5
2276	31	(h)	York C	W 2-1	East, Allen	2,446	7	8	9			3		2				10				1				11		4	6	5
2277	Jan 14	(a)	Chesterfield	L 1-2	East	8,354	7	8	9			3		2			10			11		1						4	6	5
2278	20	(h)	Luton T	W 1-0	Sykes	9,555	7	10	9			3		2				8			1				11			4	6	5
2279	Feb 3	(h)	Rochdale	D 2-2	Allen, Morrin	9,908	7	10	9			3		2				11			1							4	8	5
2280	11	(a)	Southport	L 0-4		7,203	7	10	9			3	6	2				11				1	8					4		5
2281	17	(h)	Port Vale	D 1-1	Shawcross	9,756	7		9			3	6	2	8							1			11		10	4		5
2282	25	(a)	Newport C	D 1-1	Price	2,351			9	1	8			2	7		3	10							11		6	4		5
2283	Mar 3	(a)	Brentford	L 1-2	Lister	8,288	7	8		1				2	7		3		9						11		10	4		5
2284	11	(h)	Port Vale	W 2-0	Allchurch, Harley	6,363	7			1	8	3	6	2				9							11		10	4		5
2285	18	(a)	Halifax T	W 1-0	Kevan	6,335	7	10		1	8	3	6	2				9							11			4		5
2286	24	(a)	Crewe A	D 1-1	Atkins	11,280	7	8	9	1	3			2			6	10				12			11			4		5
2287	25	(h)	Southend U	W 4-1	Kevan, Lister 3	9,024		8	9	1	3			2	12		6	10	11						7			4		5
2288	27	(h)	Crewe A	D 1-1	Lister	12,706		8	9	1	3			2	12		6	10	11						7					5
2289	Apr 1	(a)	Exeter C	W 3-0	Price, Lister, Atkins	4,059		8		1	3			2			6	10	11	9		12			7			4		5
2290	7	(h)	Bradford C	W 1-0	Kevan	10,035		8		1	3			2			6	10	11	9					7			4		5
2291	10	(h)	Notts C	W 2-0	Price (pen), Lister	8,856		8		1	3			2			6	10	11	9					7			4		5
2292	11	(a)	Tranmere R	L 0-3		11,244		8	9	1	3			2			6	10	11						7			4		5
2293	21	(h)	Hartlepools U	W 2-0	Goodwin, Price (pen)	8,865		8				3	6	2			9	10	11			1			7			4		5
2294	26	(a)	Notts C	D 2-2	Harley, Atkins	4,536		8				3	6	2			9	10	11			1			7			4		5
2295	29	(a)	Wrexham	D 2-2	Price (pen), Lister	7,485		8				3	6	2			9	10	11			1			7			4		5
2296	May 5	(h)	Aldershot	W 1-0	Lister	9,150		8				3	6	2			9	10	11			1			7			4		5
2297	13	(a)	Southend U	W 1-0	Jones	6,581		8				3		2			6	10	11	9		1			7			4		5
2298	26	(a)	Lincoln C	L 4-5	Harley, Lister 2 (1 pen), Stuart	9,662		8	12			3	9	2			6	10	11			1			7			4		5
			Appearances				25	23	14	11	21	37	16	46	17	1	27	15	16	18	16	25	1	6	36	13	17	44	15	46
			Sub appearances						1									2					1	1	1						
			Goals				3	6	3	3		1	3		4		1	3	11	10	2				7		5	1	4	

FINAL LEAGUE POSITION: Champions of Division Four - Promoted to Division 3

Own-goals 2

FA Cup

No	Date	V	Opponent	Result	Scorers	Att	Allchurch	Allen	Atkins	East	Fleet	Goodwin	Harley	Haydock	Henderson	Holden	Jones	Kevan	Lister	Lord	Morrin	Mulhearn	Parry	Prentis	Price	Quixall	Shawcross	Stuart	Sykes	Woods
1	Nov 26	(a)	Darlington	D 0-0		8,372						3		2	11			10		9	1				8	7		4	6	5
R	29	(h)	Darlington	D 1-1*	Morrin	12,399						3		2	7			10		9	1				8	11		4	6	5
2R	Dec 5 (n§)		Darlington	L 2-4	Opp own-goal, Sykes	5,461	6					3		2	7		4	10			1				8	11			9	5
			Appearances				1					3		3	3		1	2		3	3				3	3		2	3	3
			Sub appearances																											
			Goals																		1								1	

Own-goal 1

League Cup

No	Date	V	Opponent	Result	Att	Allchurch	Allen	Atkins	East	Fleet	Goodwin	Harley	Haydock	Henderson	Holden	Jones	Kevan	Lister	Lord	Morrin	Mulhearn	Parry	Prentis	Price	Quixall	Shawcross	Stuart	Sykes	Woods
1	Aug 24	(a)	Crewe A	L 0-1	3,540		10				6		2	7		3			9	1				11	8		4		5
			Appearances				1				1		1	1		1			1	1				1	1		1		1
			Sub appearances																										
			Goals																										

Average Home League attendance: 9,820
Average Away League attendance: 6,125

*After extra-time.

§Played at Elland Road, Leeds.

1967-68

No.	Date	Venue / Opponent	Res	Score	Scorers	Att	Allchurch	Atkins	East	Fleet	Fryatt	Gallagher	Goodwin	Harley	Hartle	Haydock	Jones	Kevan	Ledgard	Lloyd	Morris	Mulheam	Ogley	Parry	Prentis	Price	Stuart	Thomson	Woods
2299	Aug 19 (a)	Reading	L	0-3		9,819	7	9	11			3	8	12		2	6	10					1				**4**		5
2300	25 (h)	Swindon T	W	2-0	East, Kevan	9,103	7	8	9			3	6			2		10					1	4	11				5
2301	Sep 2 (a)	Shrewsbury T	D	0-0		5,357	7	8	10			3	6			2		9					1	4	11				5
2302	6 (a)	Grimsby T	L	1-3	Kevan	5,711	7	8	10			3	**6**			2		9					1	4	11	12			5
2303	8 (h)	Brighton & HA	W	2-0	East, Goodwin	9,258	7	8	10			3	6		12	2		9					1	4	11				**5**
2304	15 (h)	Bournemouth	W	3-1	Allchurch, East, Kevan	9,153	**7**	8	10			3	6		12	2		9					1	4	11				5
2305	22 (a)	Tranmere R	L	1-2	Atkins	10,195		8	9			3	6		11	2		10					1	4		7			5
2306	25 (h)	Grimsby T	D	1-1	Atkins	8,748		8	9			3	6		11	2		10					1	4		7			5
2307	29 (h)	Orient	W	2-0	Price, Kevan	8,995		8	9			3	6		11	2		10					1	4		7			5
2308	Oct 4 (a)	Gillingham	L	1-3	East	6,292		8	9			3	6		11	2		10					1	4		7			5
2309	7 (a)	Peterboro' U	L	0-2		8,628	7	8	9			3	12		**11**	2	6	10					1	4					5
2310	13 (h)	Mansfield T	W	1-0	Atkins	7,936	7	9	12			3	8		**11**	2	6	10					1	4					5
2311	21 (a)	Watford	L	0-5		8,486	7	9				12	8			2	3	10					1	4	11		6		5
2312	23 (a)	Gillingham	D	1-1	Price (pen)	6,059	7	9	8			12				2		10			6		1	5	3	11	4		
2313	30 (h)	Southport	W	4-3	Fryatt, Atkins 2, Kevan	7,392	7	8			9	3				2		10			6		1		11		4		5
2314	Nov 3 (a)	Scunthorpe U	W	2-0	Atkins, Fryatt	4,338	7	8			9	3				2		10			6		1		11		4		5
2315	10 (h)	Oldham A	L	0-2		14,264	7	8			9	3				2		10			6		1		11		4		5
2316	13 (h)	Shrewsbury T	W	4-2	Kevan 2, Atkins, Fryatt	7,010	7	8			9	3			6			10					1	2	11		4		5
2317	18 (a)	Bristol R	W	2-0	Fryatt, Price	9,551	7	10			9	3				2	6						1	8	11		4		5
2318	24 (h)	Barrow	W	1-0	Price	6,369	7	8			9	3				2	6	10					1	12	11		4		5
2319	Dec 2 (a)	Oxford U	D	2-2	Fryatt, Atkins	7,998	7	8			9	2	3	6		10							1		11		4		5
2320	15 (h)	Reading	W	3-0	Harley, Fryatt 2	5,920		8			9	3	11			2		10					1		7	4	6		5
2321	19 (h)	Swindon T	L	0-2		13,033		8			9	3	11			2	12	10					1		7	4	6		5
2322	26 (a)	Walsall	W	1-0	Fryatt	15,479	7	8			9	3	10			2		5					1		11	4	6		
2323	29 (h)	Walsall	D	0-0		11,415		8			9	3	10			2				7			1	5	11	4	6		
2324	Jan 20 (a)	Bournemouth	L	0-1		5,932	7	8			9	3	10			2							1	5	11	4	6		
2325	26 (h)	Torquay U	D	0-0		8,864	7				9	3	10	11		2		8		12			1	5	11	4	6		
2326	Feb 2 (h)	Tranmere R	W	5-2	Fryatt 3, Atkins, Allchurch	7,215	7	8			9		6			2	3						1	5	11	4	10		
2327	10 (a)	Orient	D	2-2	Fryatt, Allchurch	6,211	7	8			9	12	6			2	3						1	5	11	4	10		
2328	17 (h)	Northampton T	W	4-0	Fryatt 2, Atkins, Harley	7,121	7	8		1	9		6			2	3							4	11		10		5
2329	23 (h)	Peterboro' U	D	2-2	Atkins, Fryatt	8,913	7	8		1	9		10			2	3							4	11		6		5
2330	Mar 2 (h)	Mansfield T	L	0-1		6,459	7	8		1	9	12	6	**11**		2	3	4									10		5
2331	9 (a)	Torquay U	L	0-3		7,783	7	8		1	9		4			2	3			12				6	**11**		10		5
2332	15 (h)	Watford	W	2-0	Fryatt, Woods (pen)	6,687	7	8		1	9	10	6			2	3								11	4			5
2333	19 (a)	Northampton T	L	1-4	Atkins	6,536	7	8		1	9	10	6			2	3								11	4			5
2334	22 (a)	Southport	L	3-4	Woods (pen), Harley, Fryatt	6,148	7	8		1	9			**11**		2	3	10			7				12	4	6		5
2335	29 (h)	Scunthorpe U	W	4-1	Price, Atkins 2, Fryatt	6,779	7	8		1	9					10	3							2	11	4	6		5
2336	Apr 6 (a)	Oldham A	L	1-4	Fryatt	6,666	7	8		1	9	12				3	6							2	11	4	10		5
2337	12 (a)	Colchester U	D	1-1	Atkins	4,059	7	8			9	6				10	3		1					2	11	4			5
2338	13 (h)	Bristol R	W	3-1	Fryatt 3	5,158	7	8			9	6				10	3		1					2	11	4			5
2339	15 (h)	Colchester U	W	1-0	Atkins	7,141	7	8			9	6				10	3		1					2	11	4			5
2340	20 (a)	Barrow	L	0-3		5,593	7	11			9	8				10	3		1					2	12	4	6		5
2341	22 (h)	Bury	W	4-2	Hartle, Haydock, Goodwin 2	12,557	7	8			9	10	6	11	2	3			1							4			5
2342	26 (h)	Oxford U	L	0-4		7,998	7				9	10	6	11	2	3	12	**8**	1							4			5
2343	May 1 (a)	Brighton & HA	L	0-3		6,042	7	8			9	3	10	**11**	2		6		1							4	12		5
2344	4 (a)	Bury	L	3-5	Opp own-goal 2, Harley	11,108	7	10			9		6	11		4			12	3	1	**8**				2			5

FINAL LEAGUE POSITION: 14th in Division Three

							Al	At	Ea	Fl	Fr	Ga	Go	Hy	Ht	Hd	Jo	Ke	Le	Ll	Mo	Mu	Og	Pa	Pr	Pc	St	Th	Wo
					Appearances		38	44	12	9	32	13	32	23	11	46	24	23	3	8	7	1	6	23	18	10	35	33	16	39
					Sub appearances			1				5	2				3	2		1	1			2	2		1			
					Goals		3	16	4		22		3	4	1	1		7							5				2	

Own-goals 2

FA Cup

No.	Date	Venue / Opponent	Res	Score	Scorers	Att	Al	At	Fr	Ga	Go	Hd	Jo	Ke	Og	Pr	Pc	St	Wo
1	Dec 9 (h)	Macclesfield	D	1-1	Atkins	11,120	7	8	9	2	3	10	6		1	11	4		5
R	13 (a)	Macclesfield	L	1-2	Kevan	8,944	**7**	8	9	3	12	2	6	10	1	11	4		5
					Appearances		2	2	2	1	2	2	2	1	2	2	2		2
					Sub appearances						1								
					Goals			1						1					

League Cup

No.	Date	Venue / Opponent	Res	Score	Scorers	Att	Al	At	Ea	Ga	Go	Hd	Ke	Og	Pa	Pr	Wo
1	Aug 23 (a)	Crewe A	D	1-1	Atkins	4,173	7	8	9	3	6	2	10	1	4	11	5
R	28 (h)	Crewe A	W	3-0	Atkins 3	7,160	7	8	9	3	6	2	10	1	4	11	5
2	Sep 13 (h)	Sheffield W	L	3-5	Atkins, Kevan, East	12,203	7	8	9	3	6	2	10	1	4	11	5
					Appearances		3	3	3	3	3	3	3	3	3	3	3
					Sub appearances												
					Goals			5	1				1				

Average Home League attendance: 8,263
Average Away League attendance: 7,714

1968-69

No	Date	Match	Res	Scorers	Att	Allchurch	Atkins	Campbell	Collier	Cooke	Fryatt	Goodwin	Griffiths	Harley	Hartle	Haycock	Kinsella	Ledgard	Lloyd	Low	Milner	Morrin	Mulholland	Ogley	Price	Young
2345	Aug 10 (h)	Reading	D 2-2	Low (pen), Fryatt	6,463	7	8			3	9	10		4		2			1	6	5		12		**11**	
2346	17 (a)	Swindon T	L 0-1		13,547	7	8			3	9	10		4		2			1	6	5				**11**	
2347	23 (h)	Walsall	D 2-2	Atkins 2	7,574	7	8			3	9	4		10		2			1	6	5		12		**11**	
2348	27 (a)	Northampton T	D 1-1	Opp own-goal	9,622	7	8				9	4		10		2			1	6	5				**11**	
2349	31 (a)	Watford	W 1-0	Fryatt	8,517	7	8				9	4		10	3	2			1	6	5				11	
2350	Sep 6 (h)	Crewe A	W 2-1	Goodwin, Fryatt	9,389	7					9	4		10	3	2			1	6	5	8			11	
2351	14 (a)	Bournemouth	L 0-1		8,237	7	8				9	4		10	3	2			1	6	5				11	
2352	16 (h)	Shrewsbury T	W 4-3	Low 2 (1 pen), Fryatt 2	6,871	7	8				9	4		10	3	2			1	6	5				11	
2353	20 (h)	Plymouth A	L 2-3	Goodwin, Low	6,194	7	8				9	4		10	3	2			1	6	5				11	
2354	28 (a)	Hartlepool	D 0-0		5,336	7	8				9	4		10	3	2			1	6	5				11	
2355	Oct 4 (h)	Barrow	W 4-1	Fryatt, Allchurch 2, Atkins	8,243	7	8				9	4		10	3	2			1	6	5				11	
2356	7 (h)	Northampton T	W 1-0	Atkins	7,979	7	8				9	**4**		10	3	2	12		1	6	5				11	
2357	12 (a)	Gillingham	D 0-0		5,314	7	8				9	4		10	3	2			1	6	5		12		**11**	
2358	18 (h)	Orient	W 5-2	Goodwin 4 (1 pen), Atkins	7,329	7	8					4		10	3	2			1	6	5	9			11	
2359	25 (a)	Southport	L 0-5		6,003	7	8					4		10	3	2			1	6	5	9			11	
2360	Nov 1 (h)	Brighton & HA	W 3-1	Allchurch, Atkins, Goodwin	7,774	7	8					4		10	3	2				6	5		9	1	11	
2361	4 (h)	Rotherham U	W 3-1	Atkins 2, Low (pen)	6,645	7	8					4		10	3	2				6	5		9	1	11	
2362	9 (a)	Torquay U	W 1-0	Price	7,852	7						4		10	3	2	8	12		6	5		**9**	1	11	
2363	22 (a)	Tranmere R	D 1-1	Mulholland	8,256	7						4		10	3	2				6	5		9	1	11	
2364	29 (h)	Luton T	W 2-0	Goodwin, Atkins	13,246	7	8					4		10	3	2				6	5		9	1		11
2365	Dec 13 (h)	Gillingham	W 5-0	Atkins 2, Price 2, Harley	7,698	7	8					4		10	3	2				6	5			1	11	9
2366	26 (a)	Barrow	D 3-3	Atkins 2, Lowe (pen)	6,358	7	8					4		10	3	2				6	5			1	11	9
2367	28 (h)	Southport	W 3-0	Low (pen), Atkins, Goodwin	12,454	7	8					4		10	3	2				6	5			1	11	9
2368	Jan 6 (h)	Oldham A	D 0-0		9,818		8					4		10	3	2				6	5		9	1	11	7
2369	11 (a)	Brighton & HA	D 1-1	Young	10,885		8					4		10	3	2				6	5		9	1	11	7
2370	17 (h)	Torquay U	L 1-2	Mulholland	7,847		8					4			3	2				6	5		9	1	11	10
2371	25 (a)	Rotherham U	L 1-4	Goodwin	8,889	7	8					4		10	3	2				6	5		9	1		11
2372	Feb 1 (a)	Mansfield T	D 0-0		13,291	7	8	6				4			3	2	10				5			1	11	9
2373	28 (a)	Reading	L 2-4	Atkins, Young	5,393	7	8	5				4			3	2	10			6				1	11	9
2374	Mar 4 (a)	Oldham A	L 2-5	Mulholland, Atkins	4,437		8	4				7		10	3	2				6	5		11	1		9
2375	8 (h)	Swindon T	W 2-1	Campbell, Price	6,647		8	4				6			3	2	10		1	5					11	9
2376	10 (h)	Mansfield T	D 1-1	Goodwin	5,827	7	8	6				3			4	2	10		1	5					11	9
2377	15 (a)	Walsall	L 0-2		5,803	7		4				9		8	3	2	10		1	6	5				11	
2378	21 (h)	Watford	W 4-2	Young (pen), Campbell, Atkins, Harley	6,866		8	6				4		10	3	2	9		1		5				11	7
2379	26 (a)	Orient	L 0-2		3,303		8	6				4		10	3	2	9		1		5				11	7
2380	29 (a)	Crewe A	D 1-1	Young	5,286		8	6				4		10	3	**9**			1		5		12		11	7
2381	31 (h)	Barnsley	D 1-1	Atkins	4,261	7	8	5				10			3	2			1	4	6				11	9
2382	Apr 5 (h)	Hartlepool	W 1-0	Price	4,375	7						9		8	3	2	4			6	5		10	1	11	
2383	7 (a)	Shrewsbury T	L 1-2	Campbell	5,212	7		5				6	12	10	3	2			1		4		9		11	8
2384	8 (h)	Bristol R	L 0-1		4,486				11			10	4		3	2	12			6	5		9	1	7	8
2385	12 (a)	Plymouth A	D 2-2	Goodwin, Harley	7,266	7						9	4	10	3	2				6	5		8	**1**	7	8
2386	15 (a)	Bristol R	L 0-2		6,053	**7**						8	4	10	3	2		12		6	5		9	1	11	
2387	18 (h)	Bournemouth	L 0-1		4,423		9					8	4	12	3	2				**6**	5		10	1	11	7
2388	21 (h)	Tranmere R	W 1-0	Harley	2,569		5					8	6	10	3	2	4						11	1	7	9
2389	25 (a)	Luton T	L 1-4	Young (pen)	12,055		6					8	2	10	3		4	12			5		11	1	7	9
2390	29 (a)	Barnsley	L 0-2		7,739	7		6				8	4		3	2			10	1	5		11			9

FINAL LEAGUE POSITION: 9th in Division Three

		Allchurch	Atkins	Campbell	Collier	Cooke	Fryatt	Goodwin	Griffiths	Harley	Hartle	Haycock	Kinsella	Ledgard	Lloyd	Low	Milner	Morrin	Mulholland	Ogley	Price	Young
Appearances		36	34	15	1	3	13	46	7	38	42	45	12	1	24	39	41	3	18	22	43	23
Sub appearances										1	1			1	4				3	1		
Goals		3	18	3			6	12		4						7			3		5	5

Own-goal 1

FA Cup

No	Date	Match	Res	Scorers	Att	Allchurch	Atkins	Goodwin	Harley	Hartle	Haycock	Low	Milner	Mulholland	Ogley	Price	Young
1	Nov 16 (h)	Bradford	W 3-0	Atkins, Harley, Low (pen)	8,413	7	8	4	10	3	2	6	5	9	1	11	
2	Dec 7 (h)	Barrow	W 2-0	Young, Atkins	11,645	7	8	4	10	3	2	6	5		1	11	9
3	Jan 4 (a)	Blackburn R	L 0-2		17,604	7	8	4	**10**	3	2	6	5	12	1	11	9
Appearances					3	3	3	3	3	3	3	3	1	3	3	2
Sub appearances													1			
Goals						2		1			1					1

League Cup

No	Date	Match	Res	Scorers	Att	Allchurch	Atkins	Cooke	Fryatt	Goodwin	Harley	Hartle	Haycock	Kinsella	Lloyd	Low	Milner	Mulholland	Price
1	Aug 14 (a)	Bury	D 1-1	Price	6,181	7	8	3	9	10	4		2		1	6	5		11
1R	19 (h)	Bury	W 1-0	Low	6,638	7	8	3	9	10			2		1	6	5	4	11
2	Sep 4 (a)	Derby C	L 1-5	Ledgard	21,549	7			9	4	10	3	2	12	1	6	5	**8**	11
Appearances					3	2	2	2	3		1	3		3	3	3	2	3
Sub appearances													1					
Goals															1	1		1

Average Home League attendance: 7,173
Average Away League attendance: 7,594

1969-70

No	Date	V	Opponent	Result	Scorers	Att	Bebbington	Broadbent	Campbell	Chapman	Coddington	Collier	Elgin	Foley	Goodwin	Griffiths	Hartle	Haydock	Low	Morton	Mulholland	Ogley	Ormrod	Price	Rowlands	Ryden	Smith	Wilson	Young
2391	Aug 9	(a)	Tranmere R	L 0-3		5,381	3		5	10		12			4	8	2	6	9	11		1			7				
2392	15	(h)	Rochdale	L 0-1		5,338	4		5	3		12			9	8	2	6		11	10	1			7				
2393	23	(a)	Barnsley	L 0-1		7,869	3			4		10			6	11	2	5	9			1			7		8		
2394	25	(h)	Gillingham	W 1-0	Morton	3,880	3			4		10			6	11	2	5	9			1			7		8		
2395	30	(h)	Torquay U	L 0-1		3,458	3			4		11		7	6		2	5	9	10		1					8		
2396	Sep 6	(a)	Halifax T	L 0-1		4,927	3			10		11		7	4	6	2	5	9			1					8		
2397	10	(a)	Torquay U	L 0-3		6,819	3			10		11		7	4	6	2	5	9	12		1					8		
2398	13	(h)	Reading	D 2-2	Opp own-goal, Rowlands	2,857				4	3	10	11			8	5	7	2	6		1	12		9				
2399	17	(a)	Plymouth A	L 0-2		9,524	3		5					8	4	7	2	6	11	10		1	12		9				
2400	20	(a)	Southport	D 1-1	Mulholland	2,960			5	3					4	8	2	6	11	12	10	1			7	9			
2401	27	(h)	Fulham	L 1-4	Rowlands	4,274			5	3					4	8	2	6	11	12	10	1			7	9			
2402	Oct 4	(a)	Luton T	L 0-2		15,944	10		5			8			4		3	2	6	11		1			7	9			
2403	6	(a)	Rochdale	L 0-2		7,889			6			8			4		3	2	5	11	10	1			7	9			
2404	11	(h)	Mansfield T	L 1-3	Bebbington	4,039	12	8	5						4		3	2	10	9	11	1			7			6	
2405	13	(h)	Rotherham U	D 1-1	Morton	3,979	10	8	5			11			4		3	2		9		1			7			6	
2406	18	(h)	Shrewsbury T	D 1-1	Collier	3,273	11	8	4			10			6		3	2	12			1			7	9	5		
2407	24	(a)	Doncaster R	W 1-0	Rowlands	12,199		8	5			11	10		4		3	2				1			7	9		6	
2408	Nov 1	(h)	Bury	W 1-0	Rowlands	5,044		8	5			11	10		4		3	2				1			7	9		6	
2409	8	(a)	Bournemouth	L 0-1		4,903		8	5			11	10		4		3	2				1			7	9		6	
2410	22	(h)	Barrow	D 2-2	Goodwin, Collier	3,363		8	4	10		11			6		3	2				1			7	9			5
2411	24	(h)	Bristol R	L 0-1		2,941		8	4	10		11			5		3	2		9		1			7			6	
2412	29	(a)	Bradford C	L 0-1		7,733		8		10		11			4		3	2	5			1			7	9			
2413	Dec 13	(a)	Reading	L 1-3	Elgin	5,029		8				10			4	6	3	2				1			11	9	7		5
2414	26	(h)	Barnsley	W 1-0	Rowlands	4,991		8				11			4		5	3	2			1			7	9	10	6	
2415	Jan 3	(a)	Bury	L 1-4	Rowlands	4,545		8				11			4		5	3	2			1			7	9	10	6	
2416	10	(h)	Southport	D 0-0		3,493	10			5		11			4		3	2				1			7	9	8	6	
2417	13	(a)	Rotherham U	D 0-0		8,398		8				11			4		5	3	2			1			7	9	10	6	
2418	17	(a)	Fulham	D 1-1	Elgin	7,435		8	5			11			4		3	2				1			7	9	10	6	
2419	23	(h)	Brighton & HA	L 0-1		5,109		8	5			11			4		3	2				1			7	9	10	6	
2420	31	(h)	Luton T	D 1-1	Goodwin	3,922		8	5			11	12		4		3	2				1			7	9	10	6	
2421	Feb 2	(h)	Halifax T	L 0-1		3,428	10			4						8	3	2	5			1			11	9	7	6	
2422	21	(h)	Doncaster R	W 3-1	Goodwin, Collier, Opp own-goal	2,662	10					8			4		3	2	5			1			11	9	7	6	
2423	28	(a)	Shrewsbury T	L 1-3	Ryden	3,879		8				10	12		4		3	2	5			1			11	9	7	6	
2424	Mar 2	(h)	Orient	L 0-2		2,850	4	10		3		8						2	5			1			11	9	7	6	
2425	7	(a)	Barrow	L 1-4	Mulholland	3,271	10					5	8		4		3	2			11	1				9	7	6	
2426	14	(h)	Bradford C	L 0-2		3,408		8		10	5	11							2			1		4	7	9		3	6
2427	18	(a)	Brighton & HA	L 0-1		16,668	3	8			5	11			6				2			1		10	7	9		4	
2428	21	(a)	Orient	L 0-3		10,905	3	8			5	11			6				2	12		1		10	7	9		4	
2429	23	(a)	Mansfield T	L 1-4	Broadbent	7,824	4	8			5	10							2	6		1			11	9	7	3	
2430	28	(h)	Walsall	D 2-2	Rowlands, Collier	1,783		10			5	8	7						2			1		4	11	9	12	3	6
2431	30	(h)	Bournemouth	L 0-2		2,143		10				8	7					2	5			1		4	11	9		3	6
2432	Apr 4	(a)	Gillingham	W 2-0	Rowlands, Ryden	5,614		8				10						2	5			1		4	11	9	7	3	6
2433	7	(a)	Bristol R	L 0-1		17,559		10				8						2	5			1		4	11	9	7	3	6
2434	13	(h)	Plymouth A	L 0-2		2,089		8			5	10	7						2	6		1		4	11	9		3	6
2435	22	(a)	Walsall	D 0-0		3,366				10	5	8						11	2			1		2	11	9	7	3	6
2436	24	(h)	Tranmere R	L 0-1		2,282				10	5	8						11	2			1		4	11	9		3	6
	FINAL LEAGUE POSITION: 24th in Division Three - Relegated to Division 4					Appearances	16	31	16	16	13	24	21	3	33	13	35	45	24	12	10	46	10	41	36	21	33	7	
						Sub appearances	1				4									1	2	3		1	1				
						Goals	1	1				4	2		3					2	2				8	2			

Own-goals 2

FA Cup

No	Date	V	Opponent	Result	Scorers	Att	Bebbington	Broadbent	Campbell	Chapman	Coddington	Collier	Elgin	Foley	Goodwin	Griffiths	Hartle	Haydock	Low	Morton	Mulholland	Ogley	Ormrod	Price	Rowlands	Ryden	Smith	Wilson	Young
1	Nov 15	(h)	Mossley	D 1-1	Collier	5,478		8		4		11	10		6		3	2				1			7	9	5		
R	17	(a)	Mossley	W 1-0	Rowlands	4,000		8	5	11		10			4		3	2				1			7	9		6	
2	Dec 6	(h)	Scunthorpe U	D 0-0		4,200		8		12		11	10		4		3	2	5	9		1			7			6	
R	9	(a)	Scunthorpe U	L 0-4		5,646	10	5		12					4	8	11	2	6			1			7	9		3	
						Appearances		4	3	1		2	4		4		4	2				1	4		4	3	4		
						Sub appearances			1	1																			
						Goals						1													1				

League Cup

No	Date	V	Opponent	Result	Scorers	Att	Bebbington	Broadbent	Campbell	Chapman	Coddington	Collier	Elgin	Foley	Goodwin	Griffiths	Hartle	Haydock	Low	Morton	Mulholland	Ogley	Ormrod	Price	Rowlands	Ryden	Smith	Wilson	Young
1	Aug 13	(h)	Blackburn R	L 0-2		5,925			5	3		11			4		10	2	6	9		1			7			8	
						Appearances			1	1		1			1		1	1	1	1		1			1			1	
						Sub appearances																							
						Goals																							

Average Home League attendance: 3,505
Average Away League attendance: 7,854

202

1970-71

No.	Date		Venue	Opponent	Result	Scorers	Att.
2437	Aug	15	(h)	Peterboro' U	D 0-0		4,123
2438		22	(a)	Darlington	L 0-1		2,980
2439		28	(h)	Scunthorpe U	W 2-0	McMillan, Opp own-goal	4,164
2440		31	(h)	Aldershot	W 1-0	Ryden	4,094
2441	Sep	5	(a)	Bournemouth	L 0-2		6,098
2442		11	(h)	Hartlepool U	W 2-1	Rowlands, Brookes	4,146
2443		18	(a)	Southport	L 0-1		4,174
2444		22	(a)	Northampton T	D 1-1	McMillan	7,873
2445		25	(h)	Oldham A	D 1-1	McMillan	9,563
2446		28	(h)	Brentford	W 1-0	Chapman (pen)	4,387
2447	Oct	3	(a)	Crewe A	W 3-2	Collier, Brookes, Elgin	2,804
2448		9	(h)	Lincoln C	W 4-3	Mulvaney 3, McMillan	5,251
2449		17	(a)	Peterboro' U	L 1-5	Ryden	5,504
2450		19	(a)	Cambridge U	D 1-1	Brookes	4,650
2451		23	(h)	Colchester U	D 0-0		5,113
2452		31	(a)	Barrow	D 2-2	Chapman (pen), Ryden	1,812
2453	Nov	6	(h)	York C	W 1-0	Ryden	4,217
2454		9	(a)	Southend U	L 1-2	McMillan	4,836
2455		13	(a)	Workington	W 1-0	Rowlands	2,446
2456		27	(h)	Newport C	W 3-2	McMillan, Mulvaney, Chapman (pen)	3,753
2457	Dec	5	(a)	Grimsby T	W 2-1	McMillan, Rowlands	4,031
2458		12	(h)	Northampton T	D 1-1	McMillan	1,846
2459		18	(h)	Darlington	D 1-1	McMillan	2,432
2460		26	(a)	Chester	L 0-3		5,822
2461	Jan	9	(a)	Brentford	L 0-3		7,340
2462		15	(h)	Cambridge U	L 0-1		2,340
2463		22	(h)	Exeter C	L 0-3		1,992
2464	Feb	5	(h)	Grimsby T	W 1-0	Ryden	1,777
2465		13	(a)	Exeter C	L 1-2	Mulvaney	4,233
2466		19	(h)	Southend U	D 0-0		1,734
2467		22	(h)	Notts C	W 1-0	Smith	2,926
2468		26	(h)	Barrow	W 2-0	Mulvaney, McMillan	2,098
2469	Mar	2	(a)	Newport C	L 1-3	Smith	1,479
2470		12	(h)	Workington	W 1-0	McMillan	1,777
2471		17	(a)	Notts C	L 1-5	McMillan	10,704
2472		19	(a)	York C	L 1-2	McMillan	6,558
2473		26	(h)	Bournemouth	D 1-1	Haydock	1,732
2474	Apr	3	(a)	Scunthorpe U	W 2-1	McMillan, Griffiths	2,881
2475		9	(a)	Hartlepool U	L 0-3		2,702
2476		10	(h)	Chester	L 0-1		2,174
2477		12	(h)	Crewe A	D 2-2	Hart, Ryden	2,075
2478		17	(a)	Lincoln C	D 1-1	McMillan	3,761
2479		23	(h)	Southport	W 3-0	McMillan, Collier, Griffiths	1,508
2480		28	(a)	Aldershot	L 0-5		3,379
2481	May	1	(a)	Oldham A	D 1-1	Mulvaney	11,988
2482		7	(a)	Colchester U	D 1-1	Collier	5,477

FINAL LEAGUE POSITION: 11th in Division Four

Player appearance grid (shirt numbers):

No.	Brookes	Brown	Cartwright	Chapman	Coddington	Collier	Dighton	Elgin	Foley	Griffiths	Hart	Haydock	Lloyd	McMillan	Mulvaney	Ogley	Ormod	Price	Rowlands	Ryden	Smith	Taylor	Tufty	Walker	Wilson
2437			3	11	5				8	10	2		4	9					7	6				1	12
2438			3	11	5				8		2		4	9			10		7	6				1	
2439			3	10	5				8		2		4	9			11		7	6				1	
2440			3	10	5				8		2		4	9					7	6				1	
2441	12		3	8	5					10	2		4	9			11		7	6				1	
2442	11		3		5				8		2		4	10			9	1	7	6					
2443	11		3	12	5				8		2		4	10			9	1	7	6					
2444	11		3	10	5			8			2		4	9				1	7	6					
2445	11		3	10	5			8			2		4	9				1	7	6					
2446	11		3		5	4		8			2			9				1	7	6					
2447	11		3		5	4		8			2			9			10	1	7	6					
2448	10		3		5	6			8		2		4	9			11	1	7						
2449	11		3	12	5				8		2		4	9			10	1	7	6					
2450	11				5	4	3		8		2			9			10	1	7	6					
2451	11	1			5	4	3		8		2			9			10		7	6					
2452	11	1		12	5	4	3		8		2			9			10		7	6					
2453	11	1	3	10	5				8		2		4	9			12		7	6					
2454	11	1	3	10	5				8		2		4	9			12		7	6					
2455		1	3	10	5				8		2		4	9			11		7	6					
2456		1	3	10	5				8		2		4	9			11		7	6					
2457		1	3	10	5				8		2		4	9			11		7	6					12
2458		1	3		5				8	9	2		4	10			11		7	6					
2459		1	3	12	5				8	9	2		4	10			11		7	6					
2460	12	1	3						8	9	2		4	10			11		7	6					
2461	10	1	3		5				8		2		4	9			11		7	5					6
2462	11	1	3	12	5				8		2		4	9			10		7	6					
2463	11	1	3		5				8	9	2		4	10					7	6					
2464		1	3	10	5				8		2		4						7	6					
2465		1	3		5				8		2	9	4	10	11				7	6					
2466		1	3	10	5				8		2	9	4		11				7	6					
2467		1	3		5				8		2	9	4						7	6	11				
2468		1	3		5				8		2	9	4	10					7	6	11				
2469		1	3		5				8		2	9	4	10					7	6	11				12
2470		1	3	12	5				8		2	9	4	10					7	6					
2471	8	1	3		5				12		2	9	4	10					7	6	11				
2472			3		5				8		2	9	4	10			12		7	6					
2473			3		5				8		2	9	4	10			11		7	6				1	
2474			3	10	5				8	9	2		4				11		7	6				1	
2475			3		5				8		2	9	4				11		7	6	10			1	
2476			3		5				8	9	2		4				11		7	6	10				
2477			3		5				8	9	2		4				11		7	6	10				
2478		1	3		5				8		2		4	9			11		7	6	10				
2479		1	3	10	5	6			8	9	2		4				11		7		3				12
2480		1	3		5				8	9	2		4				11		7	6	10				
2481	12	1	3		5				8		2		4		9		11		7	6	10				
2482		1	3		5	4			8	9	2						11		7	6	10				
Appearances	18	26	43	39	28	9	3	1	38	9	46	10	38	33	14	1	34	9	45	45	5	1	1	10	
Sub Appearances	3		1	4	1				2								1	2	1					1	1
Goals	3			3		3		1		2	1	1		16	7				3	6	2				

Own-goal 1

FA Cup

	Date		Venue	Opponent	Result	Scorer	Att.
1	Nov	21	(a)	Grantham	L 1-2	McMillan	3,403

	Brown	Cartwright	Chapman	Coddington	Foley	Hart	Lloyd	McMillan	Ormod	Rowlands	Ryden	
Team	1	3	10	5	8	2	4	9	11/12	7	6	
Appearances	1	1	1	1	1	1	1	1	1	1	1	
Sub appearances									1			
Goals								1				

League Cup

	Date		Venue	Opponent	Result	Att.
1	Aug	19	(h)	Preston NE	L 0-1	4,353

	Cartwright	Chapman	Coddington	Foley	Hart	Lloyd	McMillan	Ormod	Rowlands	Ryden	Walker	Wilson
Team	3	10	5	8	2	4	9	11	7	6	1	12
Appearances	1	1	1	1	1	1	1	1	1	1	1	
Sub appearances												1
Goals							1					

Average Home League attendance: 3,271
Average Away League attendance: 4,936

1971-72

Own-goals 2

#	Date	Opponent	Res	Scorers	Att	Brennan	Chapman	Charter	Chisnall	Clarke	Collier	Fogarty	Gibbons	Golder	Griffiths	Hart	Ingham	Keyes	Lawther	McMillan	Mulvaney	Ogley	Ormod	Price	Renwick	Ryden	Webber	Wilson	Wright
2483	Aug 14 (a)	Crewe A	L 1-3	McMillan	3,710	3	2		1						10	5			9	4				11	7	8	6	12	
2484	20 (h)	Bury	D 2-2	Lawther 2	3,639	3	2		1						11	5			9	4				7	12	10	6	8	
2485	28 (a)	Peterboro' U	L 2-4	Griffiths, Webber	5,934	3	**2**		1						11	4			8	9				6	12	10	5	7	
2486	30 (h)	Reading	L 0-1		2,648	3			1	2					11	5			9	4				7	12	10	6	8	
2487	Sep 3 (h)	Lincoln C	W 4-2	Collier, Chapman (pen), Webber, Griffiths	2,399	3			1	4					11	5							2	7	8	10	6	9	
2488	10 (a)	Northampton T	L 0-2		5,851	3	2		1	4					11				10	6				7	8	9	5	12	
2489	17 (h)	Doncaster R	L 1-2	Ryden	2,894		3		1	2					11				10	4				7	8	9	5	6	
2490	25 (a)	Grimsby T	L 1-4	Collier	9,810	3	2	7	1		11					5			9	4					8	10	6		
2491	27 (a)	Brentford	L 0-2		10,445		3	7	1	2					11	5			10	4					8	9	6		
2492	Oct 1 (h)	Hartlepool	W 2-1	McMillan, Webber	2,573		3	7	1	2					11	5			10	4					8	9	6		
2493	9 (a)	Darlington	W 2-1	McMillan, Webber	2,022		**3**	7	1						11	5			10	4	12		2		8	9	6		
2494	15 (h)	Crewe A	W 3-1	Lawther 3	2,236		2	7	1						11	5			10	4					3	8	9	6	
2495	18 (h)	Barrow	L 1-3	McMillan	2,059		2	7	1						11	5			10	4					3	8	9	6	
2496	23 (a)	Exeter C	L 0-2		3,545		2	7							11	5			9	4	8	1	12		3	10	6		
2497	29 (h)	Workington	D 1-1	Lawther (pen)	2,630		2	7	8						11	5			10	4		1	12		3	9		6	
2498	Nov 6 (a)	Gillingham	L 2-3	McMillan, Chisnall	4,896		2	7							11	5	12		10	4	**9**	1			3	8		6	
2499	12 (h)	Cambridge U	W 3-0	Ryden, Lawther, McMillan	2,389		2		8						11	5	12		10	4		1			3	7	9	6	
2500	26 (a)	Southend U	L 2-4	Lawther, Webber	9,476		2	7								5			10	4		1			3	8	9	11	6
2501	Dec 3 (h)	Colchester U	D 2-2	Lawther (pen), Opp own-goal	2,043		2	7							11	5			10	4		1			3	8	9		6
2502	18 (a)	Lincoln C	L 1-2	McMillan	5,248	4	3		8										9	10		1	2		6	7	11		5
2503	27 (h)	Southport	D 1-1	Opp own-goal	3,421	6	2		8										9	10		1			3	7	11	5	4
2504	Jan 1 (a)	Doncaster R	D 2-2	McMillan 2	3,241	4			8							5			11	10		1			3	7	9	2	6
2505	7 (h)	Peterboro' U	D 0-0		2,218	5	12		8						4				11	10		1			3	7	9	2	6
2506	15 (a)	Chester	D 0-0		2,554	4			8						11	5				10		1			3	7	9	2	6
2507	21 (h)	Brentford	L 0-1		3,247	6	2		8						11	4	12			10		1			3	7	9		5
2508	28 (a)	Barrow	L 2-3	McMillan 2	1,987	6	12		8	2						4	7		10	11		1			3		9		5
2509	Feb 5 (h)	Scunthorpe U	D 0-0		2,452	6	2		8							4	7		10	11		1			3		9		5
2510	12 (h)	Exeter C	L 0-4		2,166	9	7		10			2			4	8			6			1			3	12	11		5
2511	19 (a)	Workington	D 1-1	Wilson	2,491	9	4		8	11							10	5				1	2		3	7		6	
2512	26 (h)	Gillingham	W 2-1	Brennan, Ingham	1,596	10	6		7	11							5		4	9		1	2		3				8
2513	Mar 4 (a)	Cambridge U	L 0-2		3,913	9	11		8	7							5		10	4		1	2		3	12			
2514	10 (h)	Darlington	W 2-1	Renwick, Ryden	1,846	9			8		5				11		10		4			1	2		3	7			6
2515	13 (h)	Chester	D 0-0		2,102	9			8		5				11		10		4			1	2		3	7	12		6
2516	18 (a)	Bury	L 0-4		3,316	9			8		6	12					11		4			1	2		3	7	10		5
2517	24 (h)	Northampton T	W 3-1	Lawther 2, Chisnall	2,262	9			8								10		4	6		1	2		3	7	11		5
2518	31 (a)	Hartlepool	L 0-5		5,537	11			10	12				8					4	6		1	2		3	7	9	**5**	
2519	Apr 1 (a)	Southport	L 0-1		2,582	11	6	3				8			12	5	10		4			1	2			7	9		
2520	3 (h)	Grimsby T	L 0-2		3,926	10	6	3				8			11	5			4		12	1	2			7	9		
2521	8 (a)	Scunthorpe U	W 2-0	McMillan, Mulvaney	7,461	10	6	2				8				5			4	7	11	1			3		9		
2522	11 (h)	Newport C	L 0-1		3,364			8	2	9			1	7		5			4	6	11				3		9		
2523	14 (h)	Southend U	D 2-2	Chapman (pen), Ryden	2,513	9	6	2	1			7				5			4	8	11				3	12	10		
2524	17 (h)	Aldershot	D 0-0		1,882	9	6	3				8			12	5			4	10		1	2			7	11		
2525	21 (a)	Colchester U	L 2-3	Griffiths, McMillan	4,018	9	3	6			11				8	5			4	10		1	2			7	12		
2526	26 (h)	Reading	D 2-2	Griffiths, Webber	3,136	9	6					8			11	5			4	10		1			3	7	12		
2527	28 (h)	Newport C	D 4-4	Webber, Brennan 2, Griffiths	1,824	9	6	**2**	1			8			11	5			4	10					3	7	12		
2528	May 3 (a)	Aldershot	L 0-4		2,179	9	12		1	11	3				8	5	6		4	10			2		7				
	Appearances					18	28	30	30	17	13	13	1		26	36	12	1	43	36	5	29	16	7	30	33	36	27	19
	Sub appearances						1	2			1			1	2	3					2		2			6	4	2	
	Goals					3	2		2		2				5		1		11	13	1				1	4	7	1	

FINAL LEAGUE POSITION: 23rd in Division Four - Re-elected

FA Cup

#	Date	Opponent	Res	Scorers	Att	Chapman	Chisnall	Clarke	Griffiths	Hart	Lawther	McMillan	Ogley	Price	Renwick	Ryden	Webber	Wilson
1	Nov 20 (a)	Doncaster R	W 2-1	McMillan, Lawther	4,590	2	8			5	10	4	1	3	7	9	11	6
2	Dec 11 (a)	Blyth Spartans	L 0-1		5,800		8	2	11	5	10	4	1	3	7	9		6
	Appearances					1	2	1	1	2	2	2	2	2	2	2	1	2
	Sub appearances																	
	Goals										1	1						

League Cup

#	Date	Opponent	Res	Scorers	Att	Brennan	Chapman	Chisnall	Clarke	Griffiths	Hart	Lawther	McMillan	Price	Renwick	Ryden	Webber	Wilson	Wright
1	Aug 18 (h)	Walsall	W 1-0	Lawther	2,652	3	2	1		11	5	10	4	7		9	6	8	
2	Sep 7 (h)	Watford	L 0-1		3,901	3	**2**	1	4	11		10	6	7	8	9	5	12	
	Appearances					2	2	2	1	2	1	2	2	2	1	2	2	1	
	Sub appearances																		1
	Goals											1							

Average Home League attendance: 2,477
Average Away League attendance: 4,640

1972-73

No	Date	Venue/Opponent	Result	Scorers	Att	Ashworth	Bingham	Broomfield	Charter	Collier	Davidson	Fogarty	Garbett	Griffiths	Hart	Ingham	Ingle	Keyes	Lawther	Ogley	Ormrod	Russell	Ryden	Spratt	Wilson
2529	Aug 12 (h)	Peterboro' U	W 3-2	Spratt 2, Ryden	3,382	6			11		7	9	5		2					1	3	4	10	8	
2530	25 (h)	Barnsley	W 2-0	Opp own-goal, Hart	3,923				11		7	9	5		2					1	3	4	10	6	
2531	Sep 1 (a)	Doncaster R	D 2-2	Hart, Garbett	2,222	6		2	11		7		5						8	1	3	10	9	4	
2532	8 (h)	Darlington	W 3-1	Griffiths 2, Lawther	5,905	6		3	8		7	12	5		2				10	1		11	9	4	
2533	11 (h)	Gillingham	L 2-3	Lawther 2	5,074	6		3	11		7	9	5		2				8	1	12	5	10	4	
2534	16 (a)	Exeter C	L 0-3		3,374	6		3	11		7	9	5		2				8	1		10	12	4	
2535	20 (a)	Cambridge U	L 0-1		2,952	6		11			7	9	5		2				10	1	3	8	12	4	
2536	22 (h)	Bury	D 0-0		4,720	6		10	11		7	9	5		2				8	1	3		12	4	
2537	25 (h)	Mansfield T	W 2-1	Griffiths, Ryden	4,543	6		10	11		7	9	5		2					1	3		8	4	
2538	30 (a)	Newport C	L 0-1		3,012	6	12	10	11		7	9	5		2					1	3		8	4	
2539	Oct 7 (a)	Reading	D 0-0		4,909	6		3	11		7	11	9	5	2					1		8	10	4	
2540	9 (h)	Crewe A	D 0-0		5,180	6		3	11		7	9	5		2				12	1		10	8	4	
2541	13 (h)	Torquay U	W 2-0	Garbett, Lawther	5,440	6	11	10			7	9	5		2				8	1	3			4	
2542	21 (a)	Workington	L 0-2		1,444	6	11	10	12		7	9	5		2				8	1	3			4	
2543	25 (a)	Aldershot	L 0-2		4,005	12		10	11	6	7	9	5		2				8	1	3			4	
2544	28 (h)	Lincoln C	W 2-1	Bingham, Ryden	3,623	6	11		10		7		5		2				8	1	3		9	4	
2545	Nov 4 (a)	Mansfield T	L 0-1		5,114		11		10	6	7	9	5		2				8	1	3			4	
2546	10 (h)	Cambridge U	D 2-2	Spratt, Lawther	3,165		11		10	6	7	9	5		2				8	1	3			4	
2547	24 (h)	Southport	W 2-0	Griffiths, Garbett	3,238			8	10	6	7	11	5		2				9	1	3			4	
2548	Dec 1 (a)	Chester	L 0-2		3,419			8	10	6	7	11	5	12	2				9	1	3			4	
2549	16 (a)	Hartlepool	D 0-0		2,448		9	7	10	6		11	5		2				8	1	3			4	
2550	22 (h)	Hereford U	D 1-1	Griffiths	3,033		9	7	8	6	12	11	5		2				10	1	3			4	
2551	26 (a)	Bury	W 2-1	Bingham, Griffiths	4,114	11	8		10	6		9			2				5	1	3		7	4	
2552	29 (h)	Northampton T	D 0-0		3,496	11	8		10	6	12	9			2				5	1	3		7	4	
2553	Jan 6 (a)	Barnsley	W 3-1	Davidson 2, Griffiths	2,864		8	11	10	6	7		5						5	1	3			4	
2554	19 (h)	Doncaster R	W 2-1	Garbett, Spratt	2,586				2	10	6	7	9	5					8	1	3		11	4	
2555	27 (a)	Darlington	L 0-2		1,286		8	11	2	10	6		7	5					9	1	3		12	4	
2556	Feb 3 (a)	Crewe A	W 1-0	Griffiths	2,721		8		2	11	6	7	9	5					10	1	3			4	
2557	9 (h)	Exeter C	W 1-0	Bingham	3,164	11			2	10	6	7	9	5					8	1	3			4	
2558	13 (a)	Northampton T	D 1-1	Garbett	1,180	11			2	10	6	7	9	5					8	1	3			4	
2559	17 (a)	Peterboro' U	W 3-2	Lawther 2, Spratt	5,202	11		12		10	6	7	9	5	2				8	1	3			4	
2560	23 (h)	Hartlepool	L 0-1		3,324	11		12		10	6	7	9	5	2				8	1	3			4	
2561	Mar 2 (h)	Reading	D 2-2	Hart, Griffiths	3,409	11		8		10	6		9	5	2				7	1	3			4	
2462	5 (a)	Bradford C	L 0-1		3,376	11		8	2	10	6		9	5					7	1	3			4	
2563	10 (a)	Torquay U	D 0-0		2,721	11		8	2		6	7	9	5					10	1	3			4	
2564	16 (h)	Workington	W 3-0	Charter, Griffiths, Collier	3,063	11		10	2	12	6		9	5			7		8	1	3			4	
2565	19 (h)	Colchester U	W 2-0	Griffiths, Garbett	3,056			11	2	10	6	7	9	5					8	1	3			4	
2566	24 (a)	Lincoln C	L 3-5	Lawther, Griffiths 2	3,562			10	2	11	6	7	8	5			12		9	1	3			4	
2567	30 (a)	Southport	L 0-1		4,635	12		11	2	10	6	7	9	5					8	1	3			4	
2568	Apr 6 (h)	Chester	W 2-1	Lawther, Spratt (pen)	2,638	12		10	2	11	6	7	9	5					8	1	3			4	
2569	13 (a)	Colchester U	L 0-3		2,772	11			2	9	6	7		5	12				8	1	3	10		4	
2570	18 (a)	Hereford U	L 0-1		10,612			11	2	10		7	9	5	12				6	1	3	8		4	
2571	21 (h)	Bradford C	W 3-1	Lawther 2, Charter	2,204			11	2	10	6	7	9	5					8	1	3			4	
2572	23 (h)	Newport C	W 1-0	Hart	2,785			11	2	10	6	7	9	5					8	1	3			4	
2573	28 (a)	Gillingham	L 0-3		3,130			11	10		3	7	9	5	12				8	1	2			4	6
2574	May 4 (h)	Aldershot	D 1-1	Garbett	4,785		10	11	12		6	7	9	5			2		8	1	3			4	
				Appearances		14	16	8	32	17	39	30	38	42	42		29		41	46	41	11	13	46	1
				Sub appearances		4		2	1	2			2	1			4		1	1		1		4	
				Goals			3		2	1	2		7	13	4				11				3	6	

FINAL LEAGUE POSITION: 11th in Division Four

Own-goal 1

FA Cup

No	Date	Venue/Opponent	Result	Scorers	Att	Ashworth	Bingham	Broomfield	Charter	Collier	Davidson	Fogarty	Garbett	Griffiths	Hart	Ingham	Ingle	Keyes	Lawther	Ogley	Ormrod	Russell	Ryden	Spratt	Wilson
1	Nov 18 (h)	Workington	W 1-0	Spratt (pen)	3,332	11			8		6	7	12	5		2			10	1	3		9	4	
2	Dec 9 (a)	Rotherham U	W 1-0	Davidson	4,539		8		11	6	7	9	5		3				10	1	2			4	
3	Jan 13 (h)	Hull C	D 0-0		8,294	8	10		11	6	7	9	12		2				5	1	3			4	
R	23 (a)	Hull C	L 0-2*		13,593			11	2	10	6	7	9	5					8	1	3		12	4	
				Appearances		1	1	3	1	4	4	4	3	3		3			4	4	4		1	4	
				Sub appearances									1	1									1		
				Goals							1													1	

League Cup

No	Date	Venue/Opponent	Result	Scorers	Att	Ashworth	Bingham	Broomfield	Charter	Collier	Davidson	Fogarty	Garbett	Griffiths	Hart	Ingham	Ingle	Keyes	Lawther	Ogley	Ormrod	Russell	Ryden	Spratt	Wilson
1	Aug 16 (a)	Bradford C	D 1-1	Davidson	3,854	6			11		7	9	5		2				8	1	3	10	12	4	
R	21 (h)	Bradford C	D 1-1*	Lawther (pen)	5,007	6			11		7	9	5		2				8	1	3	10	12	4	
2R	28 (n§)	Bradford C	W 2-0	Russell, Garbett (pen)	2,603	6		2	11		7		5						10	1	3	4	9	8	
2	Sep 6 (a)	Crystal P	W 1-0	Ryden	11,463	6		2	11		7				3				10	1		4	9	8	
3	Oct 4 (h)	West Ham U	W 2-1	Russell, Spratt (pen)	13,410	6		3	11		7	9	5		2					1		10	8	4	
4	Nov 1 (h)	Norwich C	L 1-5	Lawther	16,535	6	11		10		7	9	5		2				8	1	3			4	
				Appearances		6	1	3	6		6	4	6		5				5	6	4	5	3	6	
				Sub appearances																		2			
				Goals					1		1								2			2	1	1	

Average Home League attendance: 3,728
Average Away League attendance: 3,525

*After extra-time.

§Played at Burnden Park, Bolton.

1973-74

Player columns (left→right): Albeson, Broomfield, Charter, Clarke, Collier, Common, Crowther, Davidson, Fogarty, Garbett, Gough, Griffiths, Hollis, Keyes, Kirk, Lawther, Ogley, Ormrod, Price, Shannon, Smith, Spratt, Trevis, Wilson, Young

No	Date	Opponent	Res	Scorers	Att	Alb	Bro	Cha	Cla	Col	Com	Cro	Dav	Fog	Gar	Gou	Gri	Hol	Key	Kir	Law	Ogl	Orm	Pri	Sha	Smi	Spr	Tre	Wil	You
2575	Aug 25 (a)	Doncaster R	D 1-1	Shannon	2,851	8	11		2				10	6	7			9		5		1	3			12		4		
2576	Sep 1 (h)	Peterboro' U	D 1-1	Broomfield	2,836	8	11		2				10	6	7		12	9		5		1	3					4		
2577	8 (a)	Lincoln C	D 1-1	Hollis	4,132	8	11						9	6	7		10	12				1	3			2		4		5
2578	10 (h)	Mansfield T	D 1-1	Hollis	3,665	10	11						8	6	7		12	9				1	3			2		4		5
2579	14 (h)	Northampton T	D 2-2	Hollis 2	3,552		10		12				8	6	7			9		11		1	3			2		4		5
2580	19 (a)	Workington	D 1-1	Davidson	1,341	12	2						4	6	7		8	9		11		1	3						10	5
2581	22 (a)	Barnsley	L 0-4		2,552	10							8	6	7		2	9		11		1	3					4	12	5
2582	28 (h)	Newport C	D 1-1	Davidson	2,780					3			8	6	7		10	9		11		1	2					4		5
2583	Oct 1 (h)	Workington	D 1-1	Griffiths	2,387	12				3			8	6	7		10	9		11		1	2					4		5
2584	6 (a)	Crewe A	W 3-1	Griffiths 2, Hollis	2,979	12	2						7	6			9	8		11		1	3					4	10	5
2585	13 (h)	Swansea C	L 0-1		3,100	12	2						7	6			9	10		11		1	3					4	8	5
2586	20 (h)	Bradford C	L 0-1		2,448	12							7	6			9	10		11		1	3					4	8	5
2587	22 (a)	Mansfield T	L 0-5		3,443	9	2						7	6			8	12		11		1	3					4	10	5
2588	27 (a)	Gillingham	L 1-2	Hollis	5,777	9							7	2	12		8	10		11	5	1	3					4	6	
2589	Nov 2 (h)	Scunthorpe U	W 3-1	Davidson, Hollis 2	2,418		2						8	6	7			9		11	5	1	3					4	10	
2590	10 (a)	Rotherham U	W 2-1	Kirk, Hollis	3,752		2						8	6	12		10	9		11	5	1	3					4		7
2591	12 (h)	Brentford	D 1-1	Trevis	1,948		2						8	6	12		7	9		11		1	3					4	10	5
2592	17 (a)	Colchester U	L 1-3	Kirk	4,966							2	10	6	12		7	9		11		1	3					4	8	5
2593	Dec 1 (a)	Torquay U	D 2-2	Hollis, Trevis	2,336	9	2						10	6	12		11	8	7	5		1	3					4		
2594	8 (h)	Reading	D 0-0		1,618	10	3					2	8	6	12		9		7	11	5	1						4		
2595	15 (h)	Colchester U	L 0-3		1,472	9						2	7	6	8		12			11	5	1	3			10		4		
2596	22 (a)	Newport C	L 1-3	Hollis	2,546	8	3					12		6		11		9			10	1	2				7	4		5
2597	26 (h)	Bury	W 3-2	Lawther, Garbett, Opp own-goal	3,058		3							6	7	8	12	9			11	1	2				10	4		5
2598	29 (h)	Lincoln C	D 2-2	Lawther, Garbett	2,246		3	1						6	7	8		9			12		2				10	4		5
2599	Jan 1 (a)	Peterboro' U	L 2-3	Hollis, Lawther	8,272		3	1					10	7		6		9			12		2				8	4		5
2600	5 (h)	Exeter C	L 0-1		1,803		3	1					4		8	7	12				11	10	2				9		5	6
2601	12 (a)	Northampton T	L 0-2		3,396		3						12	6	7	8	9				11	10	2	1				4		5
2602	20* (h)	Doncaster R	D 0-0		4,050		2						8	6			9		7	10	11	5	3					4		
2603	26 (a)	Darlington	D 1-1	Kirk	1,533	10	2						8	6			4	9		11		5	3				12			7
2604	Feb 3 (a)	Hartlepool	L 0-3		5,747	10	2			4				6			9	8		11		5	3				12			7
2605	10 (h)	Barnsley	D 1-1	Hollis	2,776		2						10	6	12		8	9		11		5	3					4		7
2606	17 (a)	Swansea C	L 0-3		3,414			1	2	3			4	6	7		8				11	9						5	10	
2607	24 (h)	Crewe A	D 0-0		2,208			1	2	3			4	6			8	10			11	9						5		7
2608	Mar 3 (a)	Bury	D 1-1	Garbett	7,214			1	2	3			4	6			8	9			11	10						5		7
2609	10 (h)	Gillingham	W 2-0	Griffiths, Kirk	1,940			1	2	3			4	6			8	9		10	11							5		7
2610	17 (a)	Bradford C	W 1-0	Hollis	4,364			1	2				4	6	7		8	9			11		3	12				5	10	
2611	23 (h)	Rotherham U	L 0-1		1,789			1	2				4	6	11		10	9			12		3	7				5	8	
2612	27 (a)	Exeter C	L 1-2	Hollis	3,337	5	11	1	3	2			10	6	7			9			12							4	8	
2613	30 (a)	Scunthorpe U	L 1-2	Collier	1,900	5		1	3	2			7	6	8			4		9	11			12					10	
2614	Apr 1 (a)	Darlington	L 1-2	Kirk	1,738	5			7	2				6			9			11	8	1	3					4	10	
2615	6 (a)	Brentford	D 0-0		5,625	5	2		7					6			8	9			11	1	3					4	10	
2616	15 (h)	Chester	L 0-1		2,111	5	8		2						7			9			11	10	3	12				4		6
2617	16 (h)	Chester	L 1-2	Garbett	2,590	5	8	1	2	3					7			9			11	10		12				4		6
2618	20 (a)	Reading	D 1-1	Davidson	4,011	5		1	3	2			9	6	8			7				12	10	11				4		
2619	22 (h)	Hartlepool	D 1-1	Griffiths	1,311	5		1	3	2			6	9		11		4		8	10	7								
2620	26 (h)	Torquay U	W 2-1	Lawther, Collier	1,476	5		1	3	12	2		6	7	8		9	4		11	10									
FINAL LEAGUE POSITION: 24th in Division Four - Re-elected					**Appearances**	9	11	25	15	18	2	20	35	42	25	6	30	39	6	34	28	31	35	3	3	7	19	33	14	16
					Sub appearances	5			1	1			2		5		6	2		4	1			1	3	1	1		2	1
					Goals	1				2			4		4		5	15		5	4						1	2		

Own-goal 1

FA Cup

No	Date	Opponent	Res	Scorers	Att	Cro	Dav	Fog	Gar	Gri	Hol	Key	Kir	Ogl	Orm	Tre	You
1	Nov 24 (h)	Port Vale	L 0-1		3,364	2	7	6	8	9	10	12	11	1	3	4	5
				Appearances		1	1	1	1	1	1		1	1	1	1	1
				Sub appearances								1					
				Goals													

League Cup

No	Date	Opponent	Res	Scorers	Att	Alb	Bro	Cha	Cla	Dav	Fog	Gar	Gri	Hol	Kir	Law	Ogl	Orm	Tre	Wil	You
1	Aug 29 (h)	Port Vale	W 2-0	Davidson, Lawther	3,314	8	11		2	10	6	7		9	5		1	3	4		
2	Oct 9 (h)	Crystal P	W 1-0	Charter	8,105	12	2			8	6	7	9		11		1	3	4	10	5
3	31 (a)	Hull C	L 1-4	Trevis	13,753		2			8	6	12	7	9	11	5	1	3	4	10	
				Appearances		1	3		1	3	3	1	2	3	2	2	3	3	3	2	1
				Sub appearances		1							1								
				Goals						1			1			1			1		

Average Home League attendance: 2,380
Average Away League attendance: 3,829

*This was County's first-ever Sunday game, played as a result of the State of Emergency declared in October 1973 in response to strike action by the National Union of Mineworkers. All games had to kick-off at 2.15pm to avoid the use of floodlights and, in December, the Football Association requested special permission from the Home Office to allow matches to be played on Sundays. Notwithstanding strong opposition from some clubs, Sunday Football League matches took place for the first time on 20 January and attracted above average attendances. In County's case, the attendance was their highest of the season, although the match, in keeping with the season, was a dismal 0-0 draw.

1974-75

No	Date	Opponent	Res	Scorers	Att	Albeson	Broomfield	Clarke	Coleman	Crowther	Fogarty	Fryatt	Gilliver	Goodwin	Griffiths	Hollis	Kirk	Lawther	Lee	Lloyd	Massey	McNab	Ogley	Olynik	Price	Smith	Vernon
2621	Aug 17	(a) Doncaster R	L 1-2	Gilliver	2,383	5			10	4			9	11	8		6			7		3	1		12	2	
2622	24	(h) Shrewsbury T	L 0-3		1,903	5			10	4			9	12	8		6			11		3	1		7	2	
2623	31	(a) Darlington	W 2-0	Coleman, Gilliver	2,079	5	7	1	10	4			9	3	8	11	12			6						2	
2624	Sep 6	(h) Workington	L 1-3	Coleman (pen)	2,290	5	9	1	10				8	3	7	11	4			6						2	
2625	13	(a) Barnsley	L 0-2		5,115	5	9	1	10	2			8	3	11		4	7		6							
2626	18	(a) Torquay U	D 2-2	Griffiths, Hollis	2,997	5		1	10	2			9	6	7	12	4	11		8		3					
2627	20	(h) Mansfield T	W 3-2	Gilliver, Griffiths, Crowther (pen)	2,512	5		1	10	2	12		9	6	7	11	4			8		3					
2628	28	(a) Bradford C	L 0-2		3,167	5		1	10	2	12		9	6	7	11	4			8		3					
2629	30	(h) Brentford	D 1-1	Hollis	1,982	5		1	10	2	4			6	7	11	9			8		3					
2630	Oct 4	(h) Rochdale	L 2-3	Lawther, Fryatt	2,354	5			10	2	4	9		6	7	11	12	8				3	1				
2631	11	(a) Northampton T	L 1-4	Hollis	5,846	5			10	2	4			6	7	11	9	8		12		3	1				
2632	19	(h) Scunthorpe U	W 3-2	Gilliver 2, Hollis	1,500	5		1	10				8	6	7	9		11	4			3			12	2	
2633	21	(h) Rotherham U	W 1-0	Griffiths	2,275	5		1	6				9	3	7	10		4	11	8					12	2	
2634	25	(a) Southport	L 1-2	Goodwin	2,136	5		1		12			9	6	7	10		4	11			3			8	2	
2635	28	(h) Hartlepool	D 1-1	Lee	2,047	5		1					9	6	7	10		4	11	8		3			12	2	
2636	Nov 1	(h) Swansea C	W 2-1	Albeson, Hollis	2,086	5		1					9	3	8	10	12	11				6			7	2	
2637	5	(a) Rotherham U	L 0-3		3,797	5		1	6				9	3	8	10	12	11							7	2	
2638	9	(a) Newport C	D 3-3	Coleman (pen), Kirk, Opp own-goal	2,634	5		1	6					3	9	10	11	7		8					12	2	
2639	15	(h) Crewe A	W 1-0	Hollis	2,430	5			6					3	9	10	11	7		8			1		12	2	
2640	30	(a) Chester	L 1-3	Opp own-goal	3,457	2				4		10	5	8	9	11				3			1	6	12	7	
2641	Dec 6	(h) Cambridge U	W 1-0	Hollis	1,843	5			6				12	3	9	10	11	7						1	8	2	
2642	20	(a) Lincoln C	L 0-2		5,636	5			6	4			9	10	7	11	12					3	1		8	2	
2643	26	(h) Barnsley	L 0-3		2,389	5			6	4				10	9	7	11			12		3	1		8	2	
2644	28	(a) Reading	W 3-1	Griffiths 2, Lloyd	3,941	5				4				6	9	10	11			8		3	1		7	2	
2645	Jan 3	(h) Torquay U	D 0-0		2,223	5				4				6	9	10	11	12		8		3	1		7	2	
2646	11	(a) Cambridge U	L 0-1		3,001	5				4				6	9	11	10			8		3	1		7	2	
2647	17	(h) Chester	D 1-1	Hollis	2,721	5				4				6	9	8	11	12		10		3	1		7	2	
2648	20	(h) Lincoln C	D 0-0		2,040	5		12		4				3	9	10	11	6		8			1		7	2	
2649	24	(a) Exeter C	L 1-4	Hollis	4,438	5				3	4				9	10	11	6		8			1		7	2	
2650	31	(h) Newport C	D 1-1	Fogarty	1,926	5				3	4				9	10	11	6		8			1		7	2	
2651	Feb 8	(a) Swansea C	L 0-1		1,673	5		1	8	3					9	10	11	6		4					7	2	
2652	15	(h) Exeter C	W 3-2	Lloyd, Kirk, Hollis	1,551	5		1	4	3	6				12	10	11	9		8					7	2	
2653	22	(a) Crewe A	L 0-2		2,761	5			6	3	4					10	11	9		8			1		7	2	
2654	28	(h) Darlington	W 2-1	Crowther (pen), Massey	1,919	5				3	4				9	10	11	6		8	12		1		7	2	
2655	Mar 8	(a) Hartlepool	D 1-1	Crowther	2,593	5				3	6					10	11	9		4	8		1		7	2	
2656	14	(h) Bradford C	D 1-1	Massey	2,388	5				3	4				12	10	11	6		8	9		1		7	2	
2657	17	(h) Doncaster R	L 0-2		1,995	5				3	4					10	11	6		8	9		1		7	2	
2658	22	(a) Workington	L 0-1		1,409	**5**				3	4		12			10	11	6		8	9		1		7	2	
2659	31	(h) Reading	W 1-0	Crowther (pen)	1,886	5				3	4		12	5		10	11	6		8	9		1		7	2	
2660	Apr 1	(a) Mansfield T	D 1-1	Hollis	10,245	5				3	4		9			10	11	6		8			1		7	2	
2661	4	(h) Southport	D 0-0		2,047	5				3	4		9			10	11	6		8	12		1		7	2	
2662	7	(a) Brentford	L 0-3		4,434	5				3	4		12			10	11	6		8	9		1		7	2	
2663	12	(a) Rochdale	L 0-3		1,880	5		1	12	3	4		8	9		10	11	6							7	2	
2664	18	(h) Northampton T	W 1-0	Griffiths	1,978	5					4		8	3	9	10	12	6					1		7	2	11
2665	22	(a) Shrewsbury T	D 0-0		5,641	5					4		8	3		10		6			9		1		7	2	11
2666	26	(a) Scunthorpe U	D 0-0		1,565	5					4		9	3		10		6		8			1		7	2	11
Appearances						45	3	17	22	22	36	1	22	29	31	45	26	32	13	36	6	18	29	4	27	39	3
Sub appearances								1	2	2			3		4	1	4	4			2	2			7		
Goals						1			3	4	1		1	5	1	6	11	2	1	1	2	2					

FINAL LEAGUE POSITION: 20th in Division Four

Own-goals 2

FA Cup

No	Date	Opponent	Res	Att	Albeson	Broomfield	Clarke	Coleman	Crowther	Fogarty	Fryatt	Gilliver	Goodwin	Griffiths	Hollis	Kirk	Lawther	Lee	Lloyd	Massey	McNab	Ogley	Olynik	Price	Smith	Vernon
1	Nov 23	(h) Stafford R	D 0-0	5,026	5				4			12	3	9	10	11	8	6				1		7	2	
R	26	(a) Stafford R	L 0-1	5,630	5			6	4			9	3	7	10	11			8			1		12	2	
Appearances					2			1	2			1	2	2	2	2	1	2				2		1	2	
Sub appearances												1										1				
Goals																										

League Cup

No	Date	Opponent	Res	Att	Albeson	Broomfield	Clarke	Coleman	Crowther	Fogarty	Fryatt	Gilliver	Goodwin	Griffiths	Hollis	Kirk	Lawther	Lee	Lloyd	Massey	McNab	Ogley	Olynik	Price	Smith	Vernon
1	Aug 21	(h) Blackburn R	L 0-2	4,028	5			10	4			9	12	8		6			7		3	1		11	2	
Appearances					1			1	1			1	1	1		1			1		1	1		1	1	
Sub appearances													1													
Goals																										

Average Home League attendance: 2,099
Average Away League attendance: 3,601

1975-76

No	Date	V	Opponent	Res	Scorers	Att	Best	Blair	Bradley	Brown	Buckley	Coleman	Coyne	Cross	Davids	Davies	Deere	Dixey	Duddy	Fogarty	Hardman	Hollis	Holsgrove	Hopkinson	Hughes	Lawther	Lester	Massey	McCann	McNab	McNeill	Price	Seddon	Smith	Sutcliffe	Taylor	Turner	Vernon
2667	Aug 16	(h)	Crewe A	D 0-0		3,444			1		9	8		3		11				4		10	5				6	12		7				2				
2668	22	(h)	Northampton T	L 1-3	Lawther	2,932			1	10				3		11				4			5			9	6		8	7				2				
2669	30	(h)	Workington	W 4-1	Massey, Davies, Hollis, McNab	1,678			5	1	8					11				7		10				6	4	9		3	12			2				
2670	Sep 6	(a)	Cambridge U	W 1-0	Opp own-goal	2,677			5	1	11					9				7		8				6	4	10		3	12			2				
2671	12	(h)	Bournemouth	D 0-0		3,605			5	1	11					9				7		8				6	4	10		3	12			2				
2672	20	(a)	Brentford	L 1-2	Lester	6,282			5	1	12	11				9				4		8				3	10	6		7				2				
2673	22	(h)	Darlington	D 0-0		3,054			5	1	11	10				6				9						4	8			3	7			2				
2674	26	(h)	Rochdale	L 0-1		3,436			5	1	11					12				6		9				4	10			3	8	7		2				
2675	Oct 4	(a)	Watford	D 1-1	Price	4,143			5	1	11	12				6				10						9	4	8		3		7		2				
2676	11	(h)	Doncaster R	L 1-2	Hollis	3,159			5	1	11					9				6		10				4	8			3	12	7		2				
2677	18	(a)	Bradford C	W 2-1	Bradley, Massey (pen)	2,527			6	1	11					9				4			5				8			3		7		2		10		
2678	22	(a)	Hartlepool	L 0-3		1,683			5	1	11					9				6							8			3		7		2		10	12	
2679	24	(h)	Torquay U	W 1-0	Massey	2,670			5		11									6		7	4	1			10	9	3					2			8	12
2680	31	(a)	Exeter C	L 0-2		2,856			5		3									6		7	4	1			10	9						2			8	11
2681	Nov 3	(h)	Newport C	L 0-1		2,208			5		11					12				6		8	4	1			9			7	10	3		2				
2682	8	(h)	Huddersfield T	L 0-1		2,789			5		11									3	12	4	1				9	8		10	7	6		2				
2683	15	(a)	Barnsley	D 2-2	Hollis 2	2,758			9		3				8					6		11	5				10	12		4		7		1		2		
2684	28	(h)	Swansea C	W 3-2	Opp own-goal, Bradley, Best	9,220	7		5		3	12								6		9		1	4		10			11	8			2				
2685	Dec 6	(a)	Reading	L 0-5		6,899			5		3	9	10							6		8		1	4		12			7	11			2				
2686	12	(h)	Watford	D 2-2	Best, Lawther	4,755	11		5		3	9	10							6		8		1	4		12			7				2				
2687	20	(a)	Scunthorpe U	D 0-0		1,730			4		3	9	10		5					6		12		1	8		11			7				2				
2688	26	(h)	Southport	W 1-0	Hollis	6,321	11		5		3		10		4					6		8		1			9			7				2				
2689	27	(a)	Tranmere R	L 0-5		4,701			5		3		10		4					6		8		1			9			7	11			2				
2690	Jan 1	(h)	Cambridge U	L 0-1		2,789			10		3		11		4					6		8		1	5		9			7				2	12			
2691	9	(a)	Workington	W 2-1	Davies, Cross	1,917			10		3		11	9	5					6		8		1			4							2	7			
2692	16	(h)	Brentford	W 2-0	Hollis, Sutcliffe	2,267			10		3		11	9	5					6		8		1			4	12						2	7			
2693	24	(a)	Bournemouth	L 0-2		3,927			5				10	9						6		8		1					3	4	7			2	11			
2694	30	(h)	Hartlepool	W 2-0	Hughes, Davids	1,565			8		3		10	5	9					6				1	11						4			2	7			
2695	Feb 7	(a)	Newport C	D 2-2	Davies, Hughes	1,652			8		3		10	5	9					6				1	11		12				4			2	7			
2696	14	(a)	Huddersfield T	D 2-2	Davies, Massey	5,307			8		3		10	5	9					6				1	11		12				4			2	7			
2697	20	(h)	Barnsley	D 1-1	Massey (pen)	2,707			8		3		10	5	9					6				1	11		7				4			2				
2698	23	(a)	Darlington	W 1-0	Fogarty (pen)	1,302			8		3		10	5	9					6				1	11						4	7		2				
2699	28	(a)	Torquay U	L 1-4	Bradley	2,217			8		3		10	9	5					6				1	11		12				4	7		2				
2700	Mar 5	(h)	Exeter C	W 2-1	Davies, Hollis	2,440			8		3		10	9	5					6	12			1	11						4	7		2				
2701	13	(a)	Doncaster R	L 1-3	McNeill	4,231			8		3		11	9	5					6				1	12		10				4	7		2				
2702	15	(h)	Bradford C	W 2-1	Cross, Dixey	2,362			12				3	9	5	8		6						1	10		11				4	7		2				
2703	19	(a)	Swansea C	L 0-5		2,692	10						3	9	5	8		6	12					1			11				4	7		2				
2704	26	(h)	Reading	D 1-1	Hughes	2,319	10						3	9	5	8		6						1	11						4	7		2				
2705	29	(h)	Scunthorpe U	D 0-0		2,078	10						3	9	5	8		6	12					1	11						4	7		2				
2706	Apr 3	(a)	Crewe A	L 1-3	Davies (pen)	2,530	4	3	1				9	5	8			7								10	6				12			2			11	
2707	5	(a)	Rochdale	W 3-2	Davies, Bradley, Hardman	1,287	11	8	1	3			9	5				6	7							10				4				2				
2708	12	(h)	Lincoln C	L 0-3		3,703	11	8	1	3			9	5				6	7							10				4				2	12			
2709	16	(a)	Lincoln C	L 0-2		10,906		8		3			9	5				6	11					1			10				4			2	7			
2710	17	(a)	Southport	L 0-2		2,208	8			3			11	9	5			6						1			10				4			2	7			
2711	19	(h)	Tranmere R	L 0-2		2,973		8		3			10		5			6	11					1			9				4			2	7			
2712	23	(a)	Northampton T	L 0-4		7,680		8		3			10		5	7		11						1		6	9				4			2				

FINAL LEAGUE POSITION: 21st in Division Four - Re-elected

							Best	Blair	Bradley	Brown	Buckley	Coleman	Coyne	Cross	Davids	Davies	Deere	Dixey	Duddy	Fogarty	Hardman	Hollis	Holsgrove	Hopkinson	Hughes	Lawther	Lester	Massey	McCann	McNab	McNeill	Price	Seddon	Smith	Sutcliffe	Taylor	Turner	Vernon
Appearances							3	7	39	15	36	6	3	27	5	28	6	14	6	44	6	22	9	30	11	14	8	30	4	12	33	21	4	44	9	1	8	1
Sub appearances									1		1	1	1			2							2	3			1		1	5	1		1	5		2			2
Goals							2		4					2	1	7		1		1	1	7			3	2	1	5		1	1	1				1		

Own-goals 2

FA Cup

No	Date	V	Opponent	Res	Att	Best	Blair	Bradley	Brown	Buckley	Coleman	Coyne	Cross	Davids	Davies	Deere	Dixey	Duddy	Fogarty	Hardman	Hollis	Holsgrove	Hopkinson	Hughes	Lawther	Lester	Massey	McCann	McNab	McNeill	Price	Seddon	Smith	Sutcliffe	Taylor	Turner	Vernon
1	Nov 22	(a)	Hartlepool	L 0-3	3,348			4	3						11				6		8	5	1	10	9				7				2				
Appearances								1	1						1				1		1	1	1	1	1				1				1				
Sub appearances																																				
Goals																																				

League Cup

No	Date	V	Opponent	Res	Scorers	Att	Best	Blair	Bradley	Brown	Buckley	Coleman	Coyne	Cross	Davids	Davies	Deere	Dixey	Duddy	Fogarty	Hardman	Hollis	Holsgrove	Hopkinson	Hughes	Lawther	Lester	Massey	McCann	McNab	McNeill	Price	Seddon	Smith	Sutcliffe	Taylor	Turner	Vernon
1/1	Aug 20	(a)	Southport	L 1-3	Lester	1,501			1		11			3		9				8		10	5				6	4						2		7		
1/2	25	(h)	Southport	L 1-2	Massey (pen)	2,484			1					3		9				10		12	5				6	11	8		4			2		7		
Appearances									2		1			2		2				2		1	2				2	2	1		1			2		2		
Sub appearances																						1																
Goals																											1	1									

Average Home League attendance: 3,238
Average Away League attendance: 3,657

1976-77

No.	Date	Opponent	Result	Scorers	Att.	Baxter	Buckley	Daniels	Darling	Edwards	Feely	Fletcher	Fogarty	Hardman	Holbrook	Hopkinson	Jackson	Johnson	Lennard	Loadwick	Massey	McBeth	McNeill	Morrin	Park	Pimblett	Rutter	Smith	Sutcliffe	Thompson
2713	Aug 21 (a)	Newport C	W 1-0	Thompson	2,757			9				8	6	12	1				4	2	10	7	3				11			5
2714	23 (h)	Brentford	W 2-0	Daniels 2	3,191			9				10	6		1				5	2	11	7	8		12		3			4
2715	27 (h)	Swansea C	W 3-0	Daniels 2, Massey	4,581			9				10	4		1				5	2	11	7	8				3			6
2716	Sep 3 (a)	Darlington	W 2-0	Thompson, Fletcher	2,668			9				10	6		1				5	2	11	7	8				3			4
2717	11 (a)	Bradford C	D 3-3	Daniels 3	4,604			9				10	4		1				5	2	11	7	8		12		3			6
2718	17 (h)	Barnsley	W 2-1	Daniels, Buckley	7,923		8	9					6		1				7	2	11	10	4				3			5
2719	25 (a)	Huddersfield T	L 0-2		5,916	12		9				10	6		1				5	2	11	7	8		4		3			
2720	Oct 1 (h)	Doncaster R	W 2-1	Fogarty 2	7,132			9				10	6		1			12	5	2	11		8		7		3			4
2721	9 (a)	Aldershot	L 0-2		5,543	12		9					6		1			10	5	2	11	7	8				3			4
2722	15 (h)	Southport	D 2-2	Daniels 2	5,391			9					6		1			10	5	2	12	7	8				3		11	4
2723	23 (a)	Torquay U	W 2-1	Daniels, Massey	2,938			9					6		1			10	5	2	11	7	8				3		12	4
2724	25 (h)	Exeter C	D 0-0		5,493			9					6		1			10	5	2	11	7	8				3		12	4
2725	30 (a)	Halifax T	L 1-2	Thompson	2,149			9					6		1			10	5	2	11	7	8				3		12	4
2726	Nov 1 (a)	Hartlepool	D 1-1	Lennard	1,685	5		9					6		1	11		12	10	2							3		7	4
2727	5 (h)	Crewe A	L 1-2	Fogarty (pen)	4,388	5		9					6		1	11			10	2	12		8				3		7	4
2728	12 (a)	Colchester U	L 0-1		3,948			9					6		1	11			5	2		7	8				3	12	10	4
2729	26 (h)	Bournemouth	W 1-0	Thompson	3,221	11		9				10	6		1				5	2		7	8				3			4
2730	Dec 4 (a)	Cambridge U	D 2-2	McBeth, Daniels	3,462	11		9				10	6		1				5	2		7	8				3			4
2731	17 (h)	Scunthorpe U	W 1-0	Lennard	2,827	11		9				10	6		1				5	2		7	8				3			4
2732	27 (a)	Watford	D 1-1	Fletcher	8,299	11		9				10	6		1				5	2			8				3		7	4
2733	29 (h)	Rochdale	L 0-1		3,842	11		9				10	6		1				5	2		7	8				3		12	4
2734	Jan 7 (h)	Workington	W 1-0	Daniels	3,397	11		9				10	6		1				5	2			8				3		7	4
2735	15 (a)	Brentford	L 0-4		3,981	6	12	9			11	10			1				5	2			8				3		7	4
2736	21 (h)	Newport C	W 2-1	Daniels, Fletcher	3,450			9			11	10			1				5	2		7	8				3	6	12	4
2737	28 (a)	Southend U	D 0-0		6,357	12		9		6					1			8	5	2	10	7					3		11	4
2738	31 (h)	Halifax T	D 1-1	Sutcliffe	3,004			9		6					1			8	5	2	10	7					3		11	4
2739	Feb 11 (h)	Darlington	D 2-2	Thompson (pen), Daniels	3,049	12		9				10			1			8	5	2		7					3	6	11	4
2740	26 (a)	Barnsley	L 0-1		5,828	11		9				10			1				5	2	8	7					3	6	12	4
2741	Mar 4 (a)	Huddersfield T	L 2-3	Lennard, Daniels	5,449	3		9	11						1			10	5			7	8				2	6		4
2742	7 (h)	Hartlepool	W 1-0	McBeth	2,649	3		9	11			12			1				5			7	8	10			2	6		4
2743	11 (a)	Doncaster R	L 0-1		6,340	5		9	11			12			1					2		7	8	10			3	6		4
2744	19 (a)	Aldershot	D 0-0		2,382	12		9				10			1	7			11	2			8	4			3	6		5
2745	22 (a)	Swansea C	D 4-4	Buckley, Lennard, Rutter, Opp own-goal	6,383	11		9					6		1				5	2		7	8				3	12		4
2746	26 (a)	Southport	L 0-1		1,770	11		9				12	6		1				5	2		7	8	10			3			4
2747	28+ (h)	Bradford C	D 1-1	Morrin	4,138	11						9	6		1				5		12	7	8	10			3	2		4
2748	Apr 1 (h)	Torquay U	W 2-1	Fletcher 2	2,318	11		9				10			1				5	2	12	7	8				3	6		4
2749	6 (a)	Crewe A	L 1-2	Fletcher	2,870	12	10	11				9			1				5	2		7	8				3	6		4
2750	9 (a)	Rochdale	D 1-1	McBeth	1,489	2	12	11				10			1				4			7	8	9			3	6		5
2751	11 (h)	Watford	D 2-2	Darling, Fletcher	2,536	11	12		8			9			1				5	2		7		10			3	6		4
2752	16 (a)	Exeter C	L 1-2	Darling	4,474			9	11				6		1				5	2	8	7		10			3			4
2753	18 (h)	Southend U	D 0-0		2,391			9	11						1					2	8	7	5	10			3	6		4
2754	22 (h)	Colchester U	D 1-1	Daniels	2,826	11	7	8				9			1			6		2			12	10			3	5		4
2755	30 (a)	Bournemouth	L 0-3		2,573	11	10					9	6		1		12			2	7		5	8			3	4		
2756	May 4 (a)	Workington	D 2-2	Jackson, Fletcher	807	3		9				10	5		1		6		8		11	7					2	4		
2757	6 (h)	Cambridge U	D 0-0		3,004	12	10	11				9	5		1		6		6			7	8		8		3	2		4
2758	14 (a)	Scunthorpe U	D 2-2	Thompson (pen), Fletcher	2,244	12	10	11				9	6		1		8		4			7					3	2		5
Appearances						4	19	43	11	2	2	28	30		37	9	10	6	39	42	19	37	36	13	2		46	18	10	43
Sub appearances						9	2					3		1				1	2		3	1	1		1	1		2	6	
Goals							2	17	2			9	3				1		4		2	3		1			1		1	6

Own-goal 1

FINAL LEAGUE POSITION: 14th in Division Four

FA Cup

No.	Date	Opponent	Result	Att.	Baxter	Daniels	Fogarty	Holbrook	Lennard	Loadwick	Massey	McBeth	McNeill	Rutter	Sutcliffe	Thompson
1	Nov 20 (a) Sheffield W	L 0-2		13,886	10	9	6	1	5	2	11	7	8	3	12	4
Appearances					1	1	1	1	1	1	1	1	1	1		1
Sub appearances															1	
Goals																

League Cup

No.	Date	Opponent	Result	Scorers	Att.	Baxter	Buckley	Daniels	Fletcher	Fogarty	Hardman	Holbrook	Lennard	Loadwick	Massey	McBeth	McNeill	Park	Rutter	Thompson
1/1	Aug 14 (a) Workington	D 0-0		1,996			9	10	4	12	1	6	2	7	5		8	11	3
1/2	18 (h) Workington	D 0-0		3,291			9	10	6		1	3	2	11	7	12	8	4	5
R	30 (n*) Workington	W 2-0	Daniels 2	1,820			9	10	6		1	5	2	11	7	8		3	4
2	Sep 1 (a) Blackburn R	W 3-1	Massey 2, Fletcher	6,264			9	10	4		1	5	2	11	7	8		3	6
3	20 (h) Everton	L 0-1		15,031	12	10		11	6		1	7	2	8	9	5		3	4
Appearances							5	5	5	5		5	5	5	4	4	2		5	5
Sub appearances						1				1							1		
Goals							2	1						2					

Average Home League attendance: 3,851
Average Away League attendance: 3,873

*Played at Deepdale, Preston.

+ This waw the 'replay' of a game played at Edgeley Park on 18 February which was abandoned after 71 minutes, due to a waterlogged pitch with the score Stockport 1 (Opp own-goal) Bradford City 2, the team being the same as for match 2736 except that Hopkinson, Jackson and Buckley played in place of Holbrook, Lennard and Feely.

1977-78

Player columns (left to right): Cassidy, Daniels, Faulkner, Fletcher, Fogarty, Halford, Howard, Jackson, Lawler, Loadwick, Massey, McBeth, Park, Prudham, Rogan, Rutter, Scholfield, Smith, Summerbee, Thompson, Thorpe

No	Date	V	Opponent	Res	Scorers	Att	Cas	Dan	Fau	Fle	Fog	Hal	How	Jac	Law	Loa	Mas	McB	Par	Pru	Rog	Rut	Sch	Smi	Sum	Tho	Thp
2759	Aug 20	h	Watford	L 1-3	Prudham	3,046				10	2			12	4	5	11	**8**		9	1	3			7	6	
2760	24	a	Aldershot	L 1-2	Summerbee	2,190				9	4	8		12	2	5	11			**10**	1	3			7	6	
2761	26	h	Grimsby T	W 2-0	Thompson, Massey	3,054					6	8			2	5	11		9	10	1	3			7	4	
2762	Sep 2	a	York C	L 1-2	Massey	2,244					4	8			2	5	11		9	10	1	3			7	6	
2763	9	h	Doncaster R	D 1-1	Massey	3,614				10	4	8			2	5	11			9	1	3			7	6	
2764	13	a	Northampton T	L 1-2	Rutter	3,880				10	6	8			2	5	11			9	1	3			7	4	
2765	17	a	Huddersfield T	D 0-0		3,740				10	5	8			2	6	11		**9**		1	3	12		7	4	
2766	23	h	Barnsley	W 3-0	Halford, Lawler, Prudham	4,743					6	8			2	5	11		9	10	1	3			7	4	
2767	25	h	Brentford	D 1-1	Prudham	4,121					4	8			2	5	11		9	10	1	3			7	4	
2768	Oct 1	a	Darlington	D 2-2	Prudham, Park	1,776					6	8			**2**	4	11		9	10	1	3	12		7	5	
2769	3	a	Southend U	W 2-0	Massey, Summerbee	6,076					6	8			2	5	11		9	10	1	3			7	4	
2770	7	h	Rochdale	W 2-0	Prudham, Thompson	4,927					6	8			2	5	11		9	10	1	3			7	4	
2771	15	a	Newport C	D 2-2	Summerbee, Massey	4,168					6	8			2	5	11	12	9	10	1	3			7	4	
2772	22	h	Swansea C	W 2-0	Thompson, Lawler	4,028					6	8			2	5	11		9	10	1	3			7	4	
2773	28	h	Southport	W 2-1	Prudham, Lawler	5,122					6	8			2	5	11	12	9	10	1	3			**7**	4	
2774	Nov 5	a	Bournemouth	L 0-1		2,795					6	8			2	5		7	9	10	1	3			11	4	
2775	11	h	Hartlepool U	W 6-0	Halford 2, Prudham 2, Park, Thompson (pen)	4,179					6	8			2	5	11		9	10	1	3			7	4	
2776	19	a	Torquay U	L 0-2		2,383				12	6	8			2	5	11		9	10	1	3	4		7		
2777	Dec 2	h	Wimbledon	D 2-2	Rutter, Prudham	4,958				12	6	8			2	5	11		9	**10**	1	3			7	4	
2778	9	a	Crewe A	D 1-1	Thompson (pen)	3,323			11		**6**	8			2	5		12	9	10	1	3			7	4	
2779	26	h	Reading	W 2-0	Prudham, Rutter	4,777				12		8			2	5	11		9	10	1	3	6		7	4	
2780	27	a	Halifax T	D 1-1	Summerbee	4,087					4	8			2	5	11	12	9	10	1	3	6		7		
2781	30	h	Bournemouth	W 2-1	Prudham, Massey (pen)	5,241						8			2	5	11	4	9	10	1	3	6		7		
2782	Jan 2	a	Scunthorpe U	L 0-3		3,385				12	4	8				5	11	2	**9**	10	1	3	6		7		
2783	6	h	Aldershot	W 2-1	Smith, Park	5,121			**11**		4	8			2	5		12	9	10	1	3	6		7		
2784	13	a	Watford	L 0-1		12,754			**11**		4	8			2	5		12	9	10	1	3	6		7		
2785	21	a	Grimsby T	D 0-0		4,954					5	8			2		11		9	10	1	3	6		7	4	
2786	27	h	York C	W 2-0	Massey, Rutter	4,558				10	6	8				5	11		9		1	3	2		7	4	
2787	Feb 4	a	Doncaster R	L 0-1		2,147					6	8		11		**5**		12	9	10	1	3	2		7	4	
2788	18	a	Barnsley	W 1-0	Smith	6,928					5	8		11				10	6	9	1	3	2		7	4	
2789	24	h	Darlington	W 1-0	Prudham	4,716					6	8		11				5	9	10	1	3	2		7	4	
2790	27	h	Huddersfield T	L 0-1		6,177					6	8		11				5	9	10	1	3	2		7	4	
2791	Mar 4	a	Rochdale	L 1-2	Howard	2,278					6	**8**	11	5				12	9	10	1	3	2				
2792	6	h	Northampton T	L 1-2	Fletcher	3,358				7	6	8	11	5	4				9	10	1	3	2				
2793	10	h	Newport C	W 2-0	Park, Fogarty	3,862		5			6	8	11						9	10	1	3	2		7	4	
2794	17	a	Swansea C	L 1-3	Thompson (pen)	7,400		5		12	6	8	11						**9**	10	1	3	2		7	4	
2795	24	a	Southport	L 0-2		2,673		5		7	6	8	11							**10**	1	3	2			4	
2796	25	h	Halifax T	L 1-3	Fletcher	2,168				9	5	8	11	7	12				6	10	**1**	3	2				
2797	27	a	Reading	L 1-2	Fletcher	3,537	1			12	10	6	**8**	11	5				7	9		3	2				
2798	31	h	Scunthorpe U	D 1-1	Thompson	2,774						8	11		2		7	10	6		1	3	5		9	**4**	
2799	Apr 3	a	Brentford	L 0-4		11,674						8	11	7	2		12	10	6		1	3	5		9	**4**	
2800	8	a	Hartlepool U	L 0-2		2,416						8			10	4	11	7	6		1	3	5		9		2
2801	14	h	Torquay U	W 3-0	Massey 2 (1 pen), Fletcher	2,196				4		8					7	11	6	10	1	3	5		9		2
2802	22	a	Wimbledon	L 0-2		2,763				4		**8**	12		2		9	11	6	10	1	3	5		7		
2803	24	h	Southend U	W 1-0	Massey	2,394				4		8					7	11	6	10	1	3	5		9		2
2804	28	h	Crewe A	L 1-2	Massey (pen)	3,106				**4**		8					7	11	6	10	1	3	12	5	9		2

FINAL LEAGUE POSITION: 18th in Division Four

							Cas	Dan	Fau	Fle	Fog	Hal	How	Jac	Law	Loa	Mas	McB	Par	Pru	Rog	Rut	Sch	Smi	Sum	Tho	Thp
Appearances							1	2	3	15	36	44	12	5	33	31	32	14	43	37	45	46	27		42	34	4
Sub appearances								1		5			1	2	3			4	4					1	2			
Goals										4	1	3	1		3		11		4	12		4		2	4	7	

FA Cup

Rnd	Date	V	Opponent	Res	Scorers	Att	Cas	Dan	Fau	Fle	Fog	Hal	How	Jac	Law	Loa	Mas	McB	Par	Pru	Rog	Rut	Sch	Smi	Sum	Tho	Thp
1	Nov 26	h	Scunthorpe U	W 3-0	Fletcher, Massey, Fogarty	4,512				10	5	8			2	6	11		9		1	3			7	4	
2	Dec 17	a	Shrewsbury T	D 1-1	Summerbee	4,482						8			2	6	10		9	7	1	3	5		11	4	
R	19	h	Shrewsbury T	L 1-2	Prudham	8,370						8			2	5	11		9	10	1	3	6		7	4	
Appearances										1	1	3			3	3	3		3	2	3	3	2		3	3	
Sub appearances																											
Goals										1	1						1			1					1		

League Cup

Rnd	Date	V	Opponent	Res	Scorers	Att	Cas	Dan	Fau	Fle	Fog	Hal	How	Jac	Law	Loa	Mas	McB	Par	Pru	Rog	Rut	Sch	Smi	Sum	Tho	Thp
1/1	Aug 13	a	Wrexham	L 0-1		4,535				8	6	7		**11**	2	3	10	12	**9**		1	5			4		
1/2	17	h	Wrexham	D 1-1	Fogarty	4,926	12		**9**	4	2					5	11	8		10	1	3			7	6	
Appearances									2	2	2			1	1	2	2	1		2	2	2			2	1	
Sub appearances							1											1									
Goals											1																

Average Home League attendance: 4,010
Average Away League attendance: 4,329

1978-79

No	Date	Ven	Opponent	Res	Score	Scorers	Att	Armstrong	Bradd	Cahill	Cassidy	Connor	Edwards	Fogarty	Galvin	Goodfellow	Halford	Henson	Lawson	Lee	Loadwick	Park	Prudham	Rogan	Rutter	Seddon	Smith	Summerbee	Sumner	Thompson	Thorpe
2805	Aug 19	(h)	Darlington	W	3-0	Bradd 2, Opp own-goal	3,626		**9**				6		8	12				11	10	5		1	3			7		4	2
2806	22	(a)	Halifax T	L	1-2	Lee	2,253		9				6		**8**	12				11	10	5		1	3			7		4	2
2807	26	(a)	Newport C	W	2-1	Bradd, Lee	2,659		10			5								11	8	6	9	1	3			7		4	2
2808	Sep 1	(a)	Wimbledon	L	0-1		5,604		9				6		8					11	10	5	12	1	3			**7**		4	2
2809	9	(a)	Bradford C	D	1-1	Thompson	5,001	11	9				6			12				10	8	5		1	3			7		4	2
2810	11	(h)	Hartlepool U	W	4-0	Lee, Edwards, Halford, Thompson	4,259	8	9				6				12			**11**	10	5		1	3			7		4	2
2811	15	(h)	York C	W	2-0	Lee 2	6,103	8	**9**				6							11	10	12	5	1	3			7		4	2
2812	23	(a)	Scunthorpe U	L	0-1		3,084	8	9				5							11	10	12	7	1	3			**4**		6	2
2813	27	(a)	Crewe A	D	2-2	Lee, Prudham	2,777	8					6				7			11	10	5	9	1	3					4	2
2814	29	(h)	Huddersfield T	W	3-1	Bradd 2, Lee	5,554	8	9				6				7			11	10	5		1	3					4	2
2815	Oct 7	(a)	Doncaster R	L	0-2		2,742	8	9				6	12			7			11	**10**	5		1	3					4	2
2816	13	(h)	Barnsley	D	0-0		9,054	8	9				6	4						11		5		1	3			10			2
2817	16	(h)	Bournemouth	W	1-0	Bradd	4,092	8	9				**6**	4			7	12		11		5	10	1	3						2
2818	21	(a)	Northampton T	D	2-2	Lee, Bradd	3,867	8	9				6	4				10		11		5		1	3			7			2
2819	28	(a)	Reading	D	3-3	Lee, Thompson 2	7,289	**8**	10				9	4			7			11		5		1	3		6		12		2
2820	Nov 3	(h)	Wigan A	L	0-1		8,357	**8**	9				6	4			7			11		5		1	3			10			2
2821	11	(a)	Wimbledon	L	0-2		3,177	**8**	9				6	4			7	12		11		5		1	3			10			2
2822	17	(h)	Newport C	D	1-1	Bradd	4,009		9				6	4			7	2		11		5	8	1	3			10			
2823	Dec 4	(h)	Grimsby T	W	2-1	Lee, Edwards	3,300		9				6	4			7	12		11		5	8	1	3			**10**			2
2824	9	(a)	Port Vale	L	1-2	Bradd	3,689		10				6		12	8	7			11		5	9	1	3			4			2
2825	23	(a)	Aldershot	L	2-3	Bradd, Park	3,115						6			12	10			11		5		1	3		2	7	4		
2826	26	(h)	Hereford U	L	0-2		4,630	10	9					4		12	7			11		5		1	3		2	**8**	6		
2827	29	(h)	Portsmouth	W	4-2	Bradd, Lee 2, Summerbee	3,795	8	9					4			7			11		5		1	3		2	10	6		
2828	Jan 12	(h)	Bradford C	W	1-0	Lee	3,573	9	10					4			7			11		5		1	3		2	8	6		
2829	Feb 21	(h)	Doncaster R	L	0-1		2,907	10	9	2	1		6	4			12	7		11		5						**8**			
2830	24	(a)	Barnsley	D	4-4	Bradd 3, Henson	9,153		9	6	1		5	3			8	7		11		10	12		**4**			2			
2831	26	(h)	Scunthorpe U	L	0-2		2,676		9	3	1		4	6			8	7		11		5	10					2			
2832	Mar 2	(h)	Northampton T	W	2-1	Park 2	2,929	10	9		1		5	4						11		6	7		3			8			2
2833	5	(h)	Crewe A	W	4-3	Bradd 2, Lee, Henson	3,102	8	9				6	4				12	1	11		5	7		3			**10**			2
2834	9	(h)	Reading	D	0-0		3,560	10	9				6	4				12	1	11		5	7		3			8			**2**
2835	13	(a)	Hartlepool U	W	3-1	Henson, Halford, Park	2,449		9				6	4			7	11	1			5	10		3			8			2
2836	17	(a)	Wigan A	L	0-2		7,610		9		12		6	4	8				1	11		5			3			7	**10**		2
2837	23	(h)	Halifax T	L	1-2	Bradd	3,033		9		5		4				10	7	1	11					3	12	6	8			2
2838	27	(a)	Darlington	W	1-0	Bradd	1,086	6	9				4				10	7	1	11					3		5	8			2
2839	30	(h)	Torquay U	L	0-1		2,710	6	9				4				10	7	1	11		12			3		5	8			2
2840	Apr 4	(a)	Huddersfield T	D	0-0		2,267	6	9				4				10	7	1	11		5			3			8			2
2841	7	(a)	Grimsby T	L	1-2	Lee	7,745	6	9								5	7	1	11		10			3	4		**8**	12		2
2842	9	(h)	Aldershot	D	2-2	Lee 2 (1 pen)	2,190	6	9								2	7	1	11		10			3			8			5
2843	14	(a)	Hereford U	L	0-1		3,609	6	9				4				2	7	1	11		10			3	12		**8**			5
2844	16	(h)	Rochdale	W	3-0	Henson 2, Lee	2,863	6	9				4				2	7	1	11		10			3			**8**			5
2845	21	(a)	Portsmouth	D	1-1	Lee	8,177	6	9				4				2	7	1	11					3		8	10			5
2846	23	(a)	Bournemouth	L	1-3	Lee	2,285	6	9				4				2	7	1	11					3	12	8	**10**			5
2847	27	(h)	Port Vale	D	0-0		3,345	6	9				4				2	7	1	11					3			10	8		5
2848	May 1	(a)	Rochdale	L	0-2		2,117	6	9				4				2	7	1	11		12			3			10	8		5
2849	5	(a)	Torquay U	L	0-1		2,156	6	9				4				2	7	1	11					3			**10**	8	12	5
2850	14	(a)	York C	L	0-1		2,089	9	10					7			6	2	1	11					3		5	8			4
			Appearances					34	45	3	4	1	40	20	1	2	21	34	18	45	11	29	19	24	45	1	19	33	3	16	38
			Sub appearances							1		1		1	9	2					2	5						3		2	1	
			Goals						18				2				2	5		20		4	1					1		4	

FINAL LEAGUE POSITION: 17th in Division Four

Own-goal 1

FA Cup

No	Date	Ven	Opponent	Res	Score	Scorers	Att	Armstrong	Bradd	Cahill	Cassidy	Connor	Edwards	Fogarty	Galvin	Goodfellow	Halford	Henson	Lawson	Lee	Loadwick	Park	Prudham	Rogan	Rutter	Seddon	Smith	Summerbee	Sumner	Thompson	Thorpe
1	Nov 25	(h)	Morecambe	W	5-1	Prudham, Bradd, Park 3	3,294	11	9				6	4			7					5	8	1	3			10			2
2	Dec 16	(h)	Bradford C	W	4-2	Fogarty, Lee, Bradd, Park	5,739	8	9				6				7			10		5		1	3	2		11	4		
3	Feb 1	(a)	Wrexham	L	2-6	Lee, Park	7,500	10	9				6				7			11		5	12	1	3	2		8	4		
			Appearances					3	3				2	2			3			2		3	1	3	3	2		3	2		1
			Sub appearances																				1								
			Goals						2					1						2		5	1								

League Cup

No	Date	Ven	Opponent	Res	Score	Scorers	Att	Armstrong	Bradd	Cahill	Cassidy	Connor	Edwards	Fogarty	Galvin	Goodfellow	Halford	Henson	Lawson	Lee	Loadwick	Park	Prudham	Rogan	Rutter	Seddon	Smith	Summerbee	Sumner	Thompson	Thorpe
1/1	Aug 14	(a)	Shrewsbury T	L	0-1		2,435		9				6		8					11	10	5		1	3			7		4	2
1/2	16	(h)	Shrewsbury T	W	3-1	Lee 2, Bradd	4,025		9				6		8					11	10	5		1	3			7		4	2
2	30	(h*)	Manchester U	L	2-3	Thompson (pen), Park	41,761		9				6		8					11	10	5		1	3			7		4	2
			Appearances						3				1	2	2	1				3	3	3		3	3			3		3	3
			Sub appearances																												
			Goals						1											2		1								1	

Average Home League attendance: 4,142
Average Away League attendance: 3,390

*Played at Old Trafford, Manchester, by mutual agreement.

1979-80

Player columns (left→right): Booth, Bradd, Chapman, Coyle, Cruczman, Edwards, Fogarty, Galvin, Henson, Lawson, Lee, Lovell, Maloney, Park, Prudham, Rogan, Rutter, Sherlock, Summerbee, Sunley, Sword, Thorpe, Uzelac, Williams

No	Date	V	Opponent	Res	Scorers	Att	Boo	Bra	Cha	Coy	Czu	Edw	Fog	Gal	Hen	Law	Lee	Lov	Mal	Par	Pru	Rog	Rut	She	Sum	Sun	Swo	Tho	Uze	Wil
2851	Aug 18	(a)	Walsall	L 1-2	Henson	3,786		6			5	4			10	9	1	11					3	2	7		8			
2852	20	(h)	Rochdale	D 1-1	Henson	3,554		6			5	**4**			10	9	1	11	12				3	2	7		8			
2853	25	(h)	Wigan A	L 1-2	Lee	3,837		6			5	4	7	10		1	11						3	2	9		8			
2854	31	(a)	Tranmere R	W 1-0	Thorpe	2,771		6			5	4			9	1	11				10		3	2			8	7		
2855	Sep 8	(a)	Portsmouth	L 0-1		14,942	12	6			5	4			10	9						1	3	2	7		8			11
2856	14	(h)	Bournemouth	D 1-1	Henson (pen)	3,146	12	6			5				10	9					8	1	3	2	11			4		7
2857	17	(h)	Darlington	D 1-1	Summerbee	2,579	12	6			5	4			10	9	1				2		3		7		8			11
2858	22	(a)	York C	D 2-2	Henson, Czuczman	2,443	12	6			5	4			10	9	1				11		3		8		2			7
2859	28	(h)	Huddersfield T	L 1-2	Czuczman	5,369		6			5	4	8		10	9	1				11		3	12	7		2			
2860	Oct 2	(a)	Darlington	L 0-3		1,238		6			5	4	8		10	9	1				11	12	3		7		2			
2861	5	(h)	Hereford U	W 2-1	Henson, Czuczman	3,119		6			5	4	8		9	1				7	10		3		12		2			11
2862	9	(a)	Rochdale	W 1-0	Czuczman	2,300		6			5	4	8		9	1				7	10		3		11		2			
2863	13	(a)	Bradford C	L 1-6	Czuczman	5,261		4			5	6	8		9	1				7	10		3	12	11		2			
2864	19	(h)	Doncaster R	L 0-3		3,222	12	6			5		4	11	**9**	1				7	10		3	8			2			
2865	22	(h)	Hartlepool U	D 0-0		1,983	8	6			5			4	9	1				7	10		3	11			2			
2866	27	(a)	Lincoln C	L 0-1		3,786	9	6			5	12	4		10	1				7	8		3	11			**2**			
2867	Nov 2	(h)	Walsall	W 1-0	Bradd	3,323	8	6			5	2	4		9	1				7	10		3	**11**			12			
2868	6	(a)	Hartlepool U	W 2-1	Sword 2	2,639	8	6			5	2	4		9	1				7	10		3		11					
2869	10	(a)	Scunthorpe U	D 1-1	Bradd	1,967	8	6			5	2	4		9	1				7	10		3		11					
2870	16	(h)	Newport C	L 0-5		3,407	8	6			5	**2**	4		9	1				7	10		3	12	11					
2871	30	(h)	Crewe A	W 2-1	Henson (pen), Sword	2,936	9	6			5		4	12	8	1				7	11		2	3			10			
2872	Dec 7	(a)	Port Vale	W 2-1	Sherlock, Sword	2,799	8	10			5		6	11	4	1				7			2	3			9			
2873	21	(h)	Torquay U	W 4-0	Chapman, Opp own-goal, Sword, Henson	2,310	5	10	11	6					4	1					8		2	3			9			7
2874	26	(a)	Northampton T	L 0-2		3,054	5	10	11	6					4	1					8		2	3			9			7
2875	29	(a)	Wigan A	L 1-3	Prudham	6,847	5	10	11	6					4	1					8		2	3			9			7
2876	Jan 11	(a)	Tranmere R	D 2-2	Sherlock, Prudham	2,898		10	11	6	5				4	1					8		2	3			9			7
2877	21	(h)	Peterboro' U	W 1-0	Henson	1,789	5	**10**	11	6					4	1					8		12	3			9	2		7
2878	26	(a)	Aldershot	L 0-2		3,002	4	6	11	5					8	1					10			3			9	2		7
2879	Feb 2	(a)	Bournemouth	L 0-2		3,044	4	8	11	5					6	1					10			3			9	2		7
2880	8	(h)	York C	W 1-0	Prudham	2,533	7	4	10	11	5				6	1					8			3			9	2		
2881	16	(a)	Huddersfield T	L 0-5		7,561	7	4	10	11	5				6	1					10		3				9	2		
2882	22	(h)	Bradford C	D 2-2	Sword (pen), Opp own-goal	3,872		5	10	11		6				1					8		2	3			9	4		7
2883	Mar 1	(a)	Doncaster R	D 1-1	Williams	3,332		5		11	8	6		7		1					9		2	3				4		10
2884	8	(h)	Lincoln C	W 2-1	Prudham, Rutter	2,536		5		11	10	6		8		1					9		2	3				4		7
2885	10	(h)	Portsmouth	D 1-1	Czuczman	2,938		5		11	9	6		10		1							2	3	8			4		7
2886	15	(a)	Hereford U	L 0-2		2,424		5		11	10	6		8		1							2	3	9			4		7
2887	21	(h)	Scunthorpe U	L 1-2	Czuczman	2,215	11	5			9	2		10		1					12			3	8		**4**	6	7	
2888	29	(a)	Newport C	L 1-3	Sunley	4,727	11	**5**				12		10		1							2	3	8	9	4	6	7	
2889	Apr 2	(a)	Torquay U	D 0-0		1,875	11				6			10		1					9		2	3	8	5	4		7	
2890	4	(h)	Northampton T	W 2-0	Prudham, Sword	2,499	11							10		1					9		2	3	8	5	4	6	7	
2891	7	(h)	Peterboro' U	D 1-1	Prudham	4,527	11	8						10		1					9		2	3		5	4	6	7	
2892	11	(h)	Aldershot	L 0-4		2,511	11	9					12	10		1					8		2	3		5	4	**6**	7	
2893	19	(a)	Crewe A	L 0-1		2,789	8							11		1					9		2	3	10	5	4	6	7	
2894	22	(a)	Halifax T	W 3-1	Booth, Sword (pen), Bradd	1,233	11	8						10		1					9		2	3		5	4	6	7	
2895	25	(h)	Port Vale	L 0-1		2,404	11	8						10		1					9		2	3		5	4	6	7	
2896	May 2	(h)	Halifax T	W 4-1	Prudham 3, Booth	1,979	11	8						10		1					9		2	3		5	4	6	7	
	Appearances						12	28	32	14	36	24	14	25	31	44	4	12		13	24	2	40	36	11	7	24	36	9	28
	Sub appearances						4	1		3	1								1	2	2		3	1			1			
	Goals						2	3	1		7				8		1				9		1	2	1	1	8	1		1

FINAL LEAGUE POSITION: 16th in Division Four

Own-goals 2

FA Cup

No	Date	V	Opponent	Res	Att	Boo	Bra	Czu	Edw	Gal	Hen	Law	Par	Pru	Rut	She
1	Nov 24 (a)		Walsall	L 0-2	4,959	8	6	5	4	11	9	1	7	10	2	3
	Appearances					1	1	1	1	1	1	1	1	1	1	1
	Sub appearances															
	Goals															

League Cup

No	Date	V	Opponent	Res	Scorers	Att	Boo	Bra	Coy	Czu	Edw	Fog	Gal	Hen	Law	Lee	Pru	Rut	She	Sum	Swo	Wil
1/1	Aug 11 (h)		Wigan A	W 2-1	Cruczman, Sherlock	5,944	**9**	10	4	5		7	6		1	11		3	12	8	2	
1/2	15 (a)		Wigan A	D 0-0		7,591		10	4	5		7	6		1	11		2	9	8	3	
2/1	29 (h)		Crystal P	D 1-1	Henson	6,293		6		5	4			9	1	11	10	3	2		8	7
2/2	Sep 4 (a)		Crystal P	L 0-7		18,270		6		5	4			9	1	11	10	3	**2**	12	8	7
	Appearances						1	4	4	4	2	4	4	4		2	4	3	2		4	2
	Sub appearances																		1	1		
	Goals									1				1					1			

Average Home League attendance: 2,911
Average Away League attendance: 3,841

1980-81

No	Date	Venue	Opponent	Res	Score	Scorers	Att	Booth	Bradd	Coyle	Fowler	Galvin	Lawson	Leigh	Mountford	Park	Power	Rogan	Rutter	Sherlock	Smith	Sunley	Sword	Thorpe	Uzelac	Williams
2897	Aug 16	(h)	Rochdale	D	2-2	Booth, Sword (pen)	2,739	11	9			10	1						2	3		8	5	4	6	7
2898	20	(a)	Bradford C	D	1-1	Williams	3,660		9	11	4	10	1						2	3		8	5		6	7
2899	23	(a)	Darlington	D	2-2	Sword, Bradd	1,920		9	11	4	10	1						2	3		8	5		6	7
2900	29	(h)	Halifax T	D	1-1	Sword	2,487		9	11	4	10	1						2	3		8	5		6	7
2901	Sep 6	(a)	Wimbledon	W	2-1	Rutter, Bradd	2,018		9	11	4	10	1						2	3		8	5		6	7
2902	3	(h)	Lincoln C	D	0-0		3,289		9	11	4	10	1						2	3		8	5		6	7
2903	15	(h)	Port Vale	W	2-1	Williams, Sword (pen)	3,480	8	9	11	4	10	1						2	3			5		6	7
2904	19	(a)	Scunthorpe U	L	0-2		2,005		9	11	4	10	1						2	3		8	5		6	7
2905	26	(h)	Crewe A	L	1-3	Opp own-goal	3,536	9		11	4	10					1		2	3		8	5		6	7
2906	29	(a)	Port Vale	L	0-2		2,835	9		11	4	10					1		2	3		8	5	12	6	7
2907	Oct 3	(a)	Northampton T	W	1-0	Williams	1,902	12	9		4	11	1						2	3		8	5	10	**6**	7
2908	6	(h)	Peterboro' U	L	3-4	Galvin, Sunley, Williams	1,794		6		4	10	1				9		2	3		8	5	11		7
2909	10	(h)	Hereford U	D	0-0		2,303		6	7	4	11	1				12		2	3		8	5	10		9
2910	18	(a)	York C	L	0-1		2,135		6		4	11	1				9		2	3		8	5	10		7
2911	22	(a)	Torquay U	W	2-1	Williams, Sunley	1,694		6	9	4	11	1						2	3		8	5	10		7
2912	24	(h)	Bournemouth	W	2-1	Sherlock, Williams	2,012		6	9	4	11	1						2	3		8	5	10		7
2913	27	(h)	Hartlepool U	L	0-2		2,066		6	9	4	11	1						2	3		8	5	10		7
2914	31	(a)	Southend U	L	0-2		6,112		6	9	4	11	1						2	3		8	5	10		7
2915	Nov 4	(h)	Peterboro' U	W	2-1	Fowler, Booth	2,776	12	6	9	4	**11**	1						2			8	5	10	3	7
2916	7	(h)	Doncaster R	W	2-1	Mountford 2	2,474		6	11	4		1		9				2			8	5	10	3	7
2917	10	(h)	Bradford C	L	1-2	Galvin	3,248	12	6		4	**11**	1		9				2			8	5	10	3	7
2918	29	(h)	Aldershot	W	1-0	Fowler	1,818		9	11	4	10	1						2			8	5	3	6	7
2919	Dec 6	(a)	Mansfield T	L	0-1		2,808		9	11	4	10	1		12				2			8	5	3	6	**7**
2920	12	(a)	Rochdale	L	1-2	Mountford	1,901	7	6	11	4		1		9				2	3		8	5	10		
2921	19	(h)	Bury	L	1-2	Thorpe	1,941	7	6	11	4		1		9				2	3		8	5	10		
2922	26	(a)	Tranmere R	L	0-1		2,381	7	6	11	4		1		9				2	3		8	5	10		
2923	27	(h)	Wigan A	L	0-1		3,062	**7**	6	11	4		1	12	9				2	3		8	5	10		
2924	Jan 3	(a)	Bournemouth	W	1-0	Leigh	2,822		9	11	4	10	1	7					2	3		8	5		6	
2925	17	(a)	Aldershot	L	0-3		2,020		6	11	4	10	1	7				9	2	3		8	5			
2926	24	(a)	Halifax T	L	0-2		3,286	12	6	11	4	10	1					**9**	2	3		8	5			7
2927	30	(h)	Darlington	L	0-1		1,911		9	11	4	10	1						2	3		8	6	5		7
2928	Feb 7	(a)	Lincoln C	L	0-1		4,434		9	11	**4**	10	1	12					2	3		8	6	5		7
2929	13	(h)	Wimbledon	D	0-0		1,772		9	11	4	10	1						2	3		8	6	5		7
2930	16	(h)	Torquay U	W	4-1	Sword (pen), Coyle, Sherlock, Bradd	1,431		9	11	4	10	1						2	3		8	6	5		7
2931	21	(a)	Crewe A	L	0-2		2,598		9	11	4	10	1						2	3		8	6	5		7
2932	27	(h)	Scunthorpe U	W	2-0	Bradd 2	1,675		9	11	4	10	1	7					2	3		8	6	5		
2933	Mar 6	(a)	Northampton T	L	1-2	Sunley	1,945		9	11	4	10	1	7					2	3		8	6	5		
2934	20	(h)	York C	W	2-0	Bradd 2	1,903		9	11	4	10	1			7			2	3		8	6	5		
2935	28	(a)	Hartlepool U	L	0-1		1,928		9		4	10	1			7			2	3	11	8	6	5		
2936	Apr 3	(h)	Southend U	W	1-0	Bradd	2,278		9		4	10	1			10			2	3		8	6	5		7
2937	10	(a)	Doncaster R	L	1-2	Bradd	6,120		9		4	11	1			10			2	3		8	6	5		7
2938	18	(a)	Wigan A	L	1-2	Bradd	3,980		9		4	11	1			10			2	3		8	6	5		7
2939	20	(h)	Tranmere R	W	1-0	Galvin	2,311		9		4	11	1			10			2	3		8	6	5		7
2940	25	(a)	Bury	W	1-0	Fowler	2,862			11	4	10	1						2	3	9	8†	6	5		7
2941	May 1	(h)	Mansfield T	W	2-1	Rutter, Park	2,236		9		4	11	1			10			2	3		8	6	5		7
2942	6	(a)	Hereford U	L	0-2		1,707		9		4	10	1			11			2	3		8	6	5		7
			Appearances					8	43	34	45	41	44	4	6	8	4	2	46	41	2	45	43	37	17	36
			Sub appearances					4						2	1		1							1		
			Goals					2	10	1	3	3		1	3	1			2	2		3	5	1		6

FINAL LEAGUE POSITION: 20th in Division Four

Own-goal 1

FA Cup

No	Date	Venue	Opponent	Res	Score	Scorers	Att	Booth	Bradd	Coyle	Fowler	Galvin	Lawson	Leigh	Mountford	Park	Power	Rogan	Rutter	Sherlock	Smith	Sunley	Sword	Thorpe	Uzelac	Williams
1	Nov 22	(h)	Sheffield U	D	0-0		7,179		6	11	4		1		9					3		8	5	10	2	7
R	25	(a)	Sheffield U	L	2-3*	Coyle, Sunley	10,428		9	11	4	12	1						2	3		8	5	10	6	7
			Appearances						2	2	2		1		1				1	2		2	2	2	2	2
			Sub appearances									1														
			Goals							1												1				

League Cup

No	Date	Venue	Opponent	Res	Score	Scorers	Att	Booth	Bradd	Coyle	Fowler	Galvin	Lawson	Leigh	Mountford	Park	Power	Rogan	Rutter	Sherlock	Smith	Sunley	Sword	Thorpe	Uzelac	Williams
1/1	Aug 8	(a)	Chester	D	1-1	Sword	2,468		9	11		10	1						2	3		8	5	4	6	7
1/2	11	(h)	Chester	W	1-0*	Sunley	2,720		9	11		10	1						2	3		8	5	4	6	7
2/1	27	(h)	Sunderland	D	1-1	Sunley	6,108		9	11	4	10	1						2	3		8	5		6	7
2/2	Sep 3	(a)	Sunderland	W	2-1	Sunley, Sword (pen)	17,346		9	11	4	10	1						2	3		8	5		6	7
3	22	(h)	Arsenal	L	1-3	Bradd	11,635		9	11	4	10	1						2	3		8	5		6	7
			Appearances						5	5	3	5	5						5	5		5	5	2	5	5
			Sub appearances								1															
			Goals						1													3	2			

Average Home League attendance: 2,335
Average Away League attendance: 2,865

*After extra-time

† As a result of three players being delayed by the weather, County began the game with nine players. Sunley, was down on the team-sheet as the substitute and in fact wore a number '12' shirt.

1981-82

No.	Date	V	Opponents	Res	Scorers	Att	Connor	Coyle	Dwyer	Emerson	Fowler	Lloyd	Park	Phillips	Power	Rutter	Seddon	Sherlock	Smith	Stafford	Sunley	Sword	Thorpe	Uzelac	Vaughan	Wardrobe	Williams
2943	Aug 29	(a)	Blackpool	L 0-2		4,546		9			4	1	10					3		11	12	5	2	6			8	7
2944	Sep 4	(h)	Aldershot	W 4-2	Coyle 2, Uzelac, Williams	2,239		9			4	1	10					3		11		5	2	6			8	7
2945	12	(a)	Bury	L 0-2		3,077		9			4	1	10					3		11		5	2	6			8	7
2946	18	(h)	Peterboro' U	W 3-0	Uzelac, Fowler, Sword	2,382		9			4	1	10			3		11									8	7
2947	21	(h)	Sheffield U	W 1-0	Sword	5,450		9			4	1	10			3		11			12	5	2	6			8	7
2948	26	(a)	Port Vale	L 0-1		2,755		9			4	1	10		2			3		12	11	6	5				8	7
2949	29	(a)	Northampton T	D 0-0		1,865		9			4	1	10		2			3		11	8	6	5					7
2950	Oct 3	(h)	Bournemouth	L 1-2	Power	2,718		9			4	1	10		8	2		3		11	6	5					12	7
2951	10	(a)	Wigan A	L 1-2	Power	4,873					4	1	8	11				3	2	9	10	6	5					7
2952	16	(h)	Crewe A	W 2-0	Williams, Coyle	2,669		9			4	1	10		2			3		11	6	5				8	7
2953	19	(h)	Bradford C	L 2-3	Sword, Williams	3,684		9	3			1	10	8	2				11			4	6	5			7
2954	24	(a)	Rochdale	L 1-4	Fowler	1,778	1	9	3		4		10		2				11			8	6	5			7
2955	30	(h)	Mansfield T	W 3-0	Sunley, Williams, Power	2,081		9			4	1	10	8	2			3		11	6	5			12	7
2956	Nov 4	(a)	Hereford U	D 0-0		2,350		9			4	1	10	8	2			3		11	6	5				7
2957	7	(a)	Darlington	L 0-2		1,556		9			4	1	10	8	2			3		11	6	5				7
2958	13	(h)	Halifax T	W 2-1	Power, Sherlock	2,493		9	3		4	1	10	8	2			11				6	5				7
2959	28	(h)	Torquay U	W 2-1	Fowler, Power	1,821		9	3		4	1	10	8	2			11	6		12					7
2960	Dec 5	(a)	York C	D 2-2	Vaughan, Park	1,754					4	1	10	8	2			3	11		9		5		6		7
2961	Jan 25	(h)	Hartlepool U	L 0-2		1,924		9			4	1	10	8	2			3	11				5		6		7
2962	30	(a)	Peterboro' U	L 0-2		3,525		9			4	1	10	8	2			3	6	11	12		5				7
2963	Feb 1	(h)	Blackpool	L 2-3	Sherlock (pen), Park	2,948		9			4	1	10	8	2			3	6	12	11		5				7
2964	6	(h)	Bury	W 2-1	Park, Power	3,157					4	1	10	8	2			3	6	11	9		5				7
2965	9	(a)	Sheffield U	L 0-4		11,603					4	1	10	8	2			3	6	11	9		5				7
2966	12	(a)	Bournemouth	L 0-1		5,628				4		1	10	8	2			3	6	11	9		5			12	7
2967	15	(h)	Tranmere R	D 1-1	Williams	1,934				4		1	10	8	2			3	6	11	9		5			12	7
2968	19	(h)	Port Vale	L 1-2	Williams	3,001	11			4	9	1	10	8	2			3	6				5				7
2969	26	(h)	Wigan A	L 0-1		5,084	11			4	9	1	10		2			3	6				5				7
2970	Mar 6	(a)	Crewe A	W 2-0	Coyle 2	1,827	11	4			9	1	10		2			3	6	12	8		5				7
2971	10	(a)	Bradford C	L 1-5	Lloyd*	3,941	11	4			9	1	10			2		3	6	12	8		5				7
2972	12	(h)	Rochdale	L 0-4		2,079		4			9	1	10	11		2		3	6		8		5				7
2973	15	(h)	Hereford U	D 1-1	Sunley	1,357		4	2	1	9			9				3	6	11			5				7
2974	20	(a)	Mansfield T	D 2-2	Williams, Emerson	2,161		9				1	10	8	2			3	6	11			5				7
2975	22	(h)	Colchester U	D 0-0		1,740		9				1	10	8	2			3	6	11			5				7
2976	26	(h)	Darlington	W 1-0	Coyle	1,831		9				1	10	8	2			3	6	11			5				7
2977	30	(a)	Scunthorpe U	D 0-0		1,815		9				1	10	8	2			3	6	11			5				7
2978	Apr 2	(a)	Halifax T	L 1-4	Williams	2,135						1	10	8	2			3	6	11	9		5				7
2979	6	(a)	Aldershot	D 1-1	Park	1,304						1	10	8	2			3	6	11	9		5				7
2980	10	(a)	Hartlepool U	D 2-2	Stafford, Coyle	1,506		9				1	10		2			3	6	11	8		5				7
2981	12	(h)	Hull C	L 1-2	Williams	2,450		9			4	12	1	10		2		3	6	11	8		5				7
2982	16	(h)	York C	W 4-1	Phillips 2, Sherlock (pen), Park	1,938		9			4	7	1	10	8	2		3	6	11			5				
2983	20	(a)	Hull C	D 0-0		3,526		9			4		1	10	8	2		3	6	11			5				7
2984	24	(a)	Torquay U	L 0-1		1,486		9			4		1	10	8	2		3	6		11		5				7
2985	30	(h)	Northampton T	D 0-0		1,658		9			4		1	10	8	2		3	6		11		5				7
2986	May 4	(a)	Tranmere R	L 0-2		1,217		9			4		1	10	8	11	2	3	6				5				7
2987	7	(a)	Colchester U	W 1-0	Phillips	2,132		9			4		1	10	8	11	2	3	6				5				7
2988	14	(h)	Scunthorpe U	D 1-1	Phillips	1,945		9			4		1	10	8	11	2	3	6				5				7
	FINAL LEAGUE POSITION: 18th in Division Four				Appearances		1	36	4	23	29	45	46	13	22	39	2	46	31	21	27	16	46	5	2	7	45
					Sub appearances						1									4	4				4		
					Goals			7			1	3	1	5	4	6			3		1	2	3		2	1		9

FA Cup

No.	Date	V	Opponents	Res	Scorers	Att	Connor	Coyle	Dwyer	Emerson	Fowler	Lloyd	Park	Phillips	Power	Rutter	Seddon	Sherlock	Smith	Stafford	Sunley	Sword	Thorpe	Uzelac	Vaughan	Wardrobe	Williams
1	Nov 21	(h)	Mossley	W 3-1	Williams 2, Park	4,216	11	5			6	1	7		10	2		8			12	4	3				9
2	Dec 30	(a)	Port Vale	L 1-4	Smith	4,478	11				4	1	8		9	2		3	10			5			6		7
					Appearances		2	1			2	2	2		2	2		2	1			1	2		1		2
					Sub appearances																1						
					Goals							1							1								2

League Cup

No.	Date	V	Opponents	Res	Scorers	Att	Connor	Coyle	Dwyer	Emerson	Fowler	Lloyd	Park	Phillips	Power	Rutter	Seddon	Sherlock	Smith	Stafford	Sunley	Sword	Thorpe	Uzelac	Vaughan	Wardrobe	Williams
1/1	Aug 31	(a)	Wigan A	L 0-3		5,079		9			4	1	10					3		11		5	2	6		8	7
1/2	Sep 14	(h)	Wigan A	L 1-2	Fowler	2,913		9			4	1	10		2			3		11			5	6		8	7
					Appearances			2			2	2	2		1			2		2		1	2	2		2	2
					Sub appearances																						
					Goals						1																

Average Home League attendance: 2,547
Average Away League attendance: 2,972

*This is the only recorded occasion on which a Stockport County goalkeeper has scored a goal in a Football League or Cup match. Joe Butler, County's popular goalkeeper in their early Football League days, did score a penalty in the penultimate match of 1904-05 in the carnival atmosphere of winning the Lancashire Combination which helped County to be elected to the Football League in May 1905.

1982-83

No.	Date	Opponent	Result	Scorers	Att.	Bowles	Coyle	Emerson	Leigh	Liptrott	Lloyd	Park	Phillips	Power	Quinn	Rutter	Seddon	Sherlock	Smith	Sword	Thorpe	Wardrobe	Williams
2989	Aug 28 (h)	Peterboro' U	D 1-1	Park	2,003	5	11	4			1	10	8		9	12		3	6		2		7
2990	Sep 4 (a)	Torquay U	L 0-3		2,194	5		7			1	8	10		11	2		3	6		2		7
2991	7 (a)	Scunthorpe U	L 0-3		1,335	5	11	4			1	10	8		9	2		3	6		4	12	9
2992	10 (h)	Hull C	D 1-1	Emerson	2,252	5		4			1	10	8		9	3		11	6		2		7
2993	18 (a)	Tranmere R	D 1-1	Quinn	1,449	5		4			1	10	8		9	2		11	6		3		7
2994	24 (h)	Northampton T	L 0-1		1,621	5		4			1	10	8		9	2		11	6		3		7
2995	27 (h)	Rochdale	D 2-2	Williams, Power	1,873		11	4			1	10	8	9		2		3	6		5		7
2996	Oct 2 (a)	Port Vale	W 3-2	Power 2, Phillips	3,474	5		4			1	10	8	9	12	2		3	11		6		7
2997	8 (h)	Hartlepool U	D 1-1	Phillips	1,915	5	11	4			1	10	8	9		3			2		6		7
2998	16 (a)	Aldershot	L 1-2	Coyle	1,417	6	11	5			1			9	10	4		3	2		7		8
2999	19 (a)	Bury	L 2-3	Quinn, Phillips	2,447	4		8			1	7	9	10	11	2		5			3		6
3000	22 (h)	York C	W 2-1	Coyle, Quinn	2,014	5	11	4			1	10	8		9	2		3	6				
3001	30 (a)	Wimbledon	L 1-2	Quinn	2,294	5		4			1	10	8		9	2		3	6				7
3002	Nov 1 (h)	Hereford U	W 2-1	Opp own-goal, Phillips	1,736	5	12	4			1	10	8		9	2		3	12		6	11	7
3003	6 (a)	Bristol C	D 2-2	Quinn, Opp own-goal	4,648	5	11	4			1	10	8		9	2		3	2		6	11	7
3004	12 (h)	Darlington	W 2-1	Quinn 2	1,885	5	11	4			1	10	8		9	2		3			6		7
3005	26 (h)	Swindon T	L 1-2	Phillips	2,197	5	11	4			1	10	8		9	2		3	12		6		7
3006	Dec 4 (a)	Mansfield T	L 0-1		1,662	5	11	4			1	10	8		9	2		3	7		6		
3007	10 (h)	Crewe A	W 3-2	Quinn 3 (1 pen)	1,860	5	11	4			1	10	8		9	2		3	7		6		
3008	17 (a)	Colchester U	L 0-3		1,625	5	11	4	10		1		8		9	2		3	7		6	12	
3009	27 (h)	Blackpool	W 3-0	Phillips 2, Quinn	3,673		11	4			1		8	10	9	2		3	7	5	6	12	
3010	28 (a)	Chester	W 2-0	Power, Quinn (pen)	2,646		11	4			1		8	10	9	2		3	7	5	6		
3011	Jan 1 (h)	Halifax T	W 4-2	Quinn 3, Emerson	2,871		11	4			1		8	10	9	2		3	7	5	6		
3012	3 (a)	Crewe A	L 0-3		2,508	12	11	4			1		8	10	9	2		3	7	5	6		
3013	15 (a)	Peterboro' U	L 0-1		2,911	6	12	4			1		8	10	9	3		7	5	2		11	
3014	21 (h)	Tranmere R	W 3-2	Power, Wardrobe 2	2,198	6		4			1		8	10	9	3		7	5	2		11	
3015	29 (a)	Hull C	L 0-7		5,901	6	11	4			1			10		3		11	5	2	9		7
3016	Feb 5 (a)	Northampton T	W 3-2	Rutter, Power, Phillips	1,982	5	12	6			1		8	9		2		11	4	3	10		7
3017	12 (h)	Scunthorpe U	D 1-1	Coyle	2,232		11	4			1	12		10	9	2		3	8	5	6		
3018	14 (h)	Bury	W 2-1	Williams, Quinn	3,058			4			1		11	10	9	2		3	8	5	6	12	7
3019	19 (a)	Hartlepool U	L 2-3	Quinn 2	1,029		11	4			1			10	9	2		3	8	5	6		7
3020	26 (h)	Aldershot	W 2-1	Quinn 2	1,853		11	4	12		1		8	10	9	2		3		5	6		7
3021	Mar 2 (a)	Hereford U	D 0-0		1,294		11	4			1			10	9	2		3	7	5	6		8
3022	5 (a)	York C	L 1-3	Power	2,883		11	4			1			10	9	2		3	7	5	6		8
3023	11 (h)	Wimbledon	L 1-3	Coyle	2,396		11	4			1	7		10	9	2		3	12	5	6		8
3024	18 (h)	Bristol C	D 2-2	Power, Emerson	2,036		9	4			1		8	10		2		3	11	5	6		7
3025	26 (a)	Darlington	L 1-3	Sword	1,012			4			1		8	10		2		3	11	5	6		7
3026	Apr 1 (a)	Blackpool	D 0-0		3,126		11	4			1			10	9	2		3	8	5	6		7
3027	2 (h)	Chester	D 3-3	Quinn 2, Phillips	2,008			4			1		8	10	9	2		3	11	5	6		7
3028	8 (h)	Mansfield T	D 1-1	Power	2,202		11	4			1			10	9	2		3	8	5	6		7
3029	16 (a)	Rochdale	L 0-1		1,829	6	11				1	4		10	9	2			8	5	3		7
3030	17 (h)	Torquay U	W 1-0	Quinn	1,986	6	11	4			1			10	9	2			8	5	3		7
3031	22 (h)	Colchester U	W 3-0	Smith, Coyle, Quinn	1,733	6	11	4			1			10	9	2			8	5	3		7
3032	30 (a)	Swindon T	L 0-2		2,838	6	11	4			1	12		10	9	2			8	5	3		7
3033	May 6 (h)	Port Vale	L 0-2		5,516			4	2	12	1		8	10	9		3		6		5	11	7
3034	13 (a)	Halifax T	L 0-1		1,522	6	11	4	12		1			10	9	2			7	5	3		8
				Appearances		28	31	45	2		46	18	36	30	38	43	1	35	37	25	45	12	34
				Sub appearances		1	3		2	1		2			1	1		3		1		1	4
				Goals			5	3				1	9	9	24	1			1	1		2	2

FINAL LEAGUE POSITION: 16th in Division Four

Own-goals 2

FA Cup

No.	Date	Opponent	Result	Scorers	Att.	Bowles	Coyle	Emerson	Leigh	Liptrott	Lloyd	Park	Phillips	Power	Quinn	Rutter	Seddon	Sherlock	Smith	Sword	Thorpe	Wardrobe	Williams
1	Nov 20 (a)	Mansfield T	L 2-3	Williams, Park	2,215	5	11	4			1	10	8		9	3		2			6		7
				Appearances		1	1	1			1	1	1		1	1		1			1		1
				Sub appearances																			
				Goals								1											1

League Cup

No.	Date	Opponent	Result	Scorers	Att.	Bowles	Coyle	Emerson	Leigh	Liptrott	Lloyd	Park	Phillips	Power	Quinn	Rutter	Seddon	Sherlock	Smith	Sword	Thorpe	Wardrobe	Williams
1/1	Aug 30 (h)	Wigan A	D 1-1	Emerson	3,418	5		4			1	10	8		9	3		11	6		2		7
1/2	Sep 4 (a)	Wigan A	D 1-1*	Park	4,008	5		4			1	10	8		9	3		11	6		2		7
				Appearances		2		2			2	2	2		2	2		2	2		2		2
				Sub appearances																			
				Goals				1				1											

Average Home League attendance: 2,309
Average Away League attendance: 2,349

*After extra-time. Wigan Athletic won 5-4 on penalties.

1983-84

No	Date	V	Opponent	Res	Scorers	Att	Bowles	Coyle	Emerson	Evans	Jones	Kerr	Leigh	Parker	Power	Quinn	Rutter	Ryan	Salmon	Sherlock	Smith	Sutcliffe	Sword	Taylor	Thorpe	White	Williams
3035	Aug 27	(h)	York C	L 0-2		2,185	11	4	6	8					10	9	2		1	3			5		7		
3036	Sep 3	(a)	Reading	L 2-6	Williams, Rutter	2,689		4		6					10	9	3	**7**	1	11	12		5				8
3037	6	(a)	Mansfield T	W 2-1	Quinn, Sword	2,167		4		2					10	9	3		1	11	8		5		6		7
3038	9	(h)	Colchester U	D 0-0		2,077	11	4		2					**10**	9	3	12	1		8		5		6		7
3039	18	(a)	Northampton T	D 0-0		3,189	11	4		8					10		2		1	3	7		5		6		9
3040	23	(h)	Swindon T	L 1-3	Williams	2,244	11	4		10						9	2		1	3	8		5		6		7
3041	26	(h)	Wrexham	D 1-1	Williams	2,031	6	11	4	10						9	3		1		8		5		2		7
3042	30	(a)	Crewe A	W 3-0	Quinn 3	2,965	5	11	4	2						9	3		1		8		10		6		7
3043	Oct 8	(a)	Chesterfield	L 0-2		3,846	5	11	4	2						9	3		1		8		10		6		7
3044	15	(h)	Darlington	W 2-0	Quinn, Williams	1,360	5	11	4	8						9	2		1	3			10		6		7
3045	17	(h)	Aldershot	D 2-2	Williams, Emerson	1,895	5	11	4							9	3		1	10	8		6		2		7
3046	22	(a)	Chester C	W 4-2	Quinn 2, Jones, Coyle	1,612	5	11	4	10						9	3		1		8		6		2		**7**
3047	29	(h)	Blackpool	L 1-2	Thorpe	2,602	5	11	4	10						9	3		1	12	8		6		2		7
3048	Nov 1	(a)	Bury	L 1-2	Quinn	2,547	5	11	4	10						9	3		1		8	7	6		2		
3049	5	(a)	Rochdale	D 2-2	Sword, Quinn	1,682	5	8	4	10						9	3		1	11			6		2		7
3050	11	(h)	Halifax T	W 4-0	Sword 2, Quinn 2	2,140	5	11								9	2		1	3	4		10		6		7
3051	26	(a)	Peterboro' U	L 0-2		3,240	5		4	8	10					9	3		1	12			6		2	11	7
3052	Dec 2	(h)	Torquay U	W 2-1	Sword, Evans	1,874	5		4	8	10					9	2		1				6	3		11	7
3053	10	(a)	Aldershot	D 1-1	Quinn	1,349	5		4	11	8					9	2		1	3			10				7
3054	16	(h)	Tranmere R	W 2-1	Quinn, Williams	1,644	5		4	11	8					9	2		1	3			10		6		7
3055	26	(a)	Bristol C	L 1-3	Sword	9,246	5		4	11	8					9	2		1	3			10		6		7
3056	27	(h)	Hereford U	W 1-0	Evans	2,287	5	11	4	8						9	2		1	3			10		6		7
3057	31	(a)	Doncaster R	L 1-2	Quinn	3,736	5	11		8	10					9	2		1	3			4		6		7
3058	Jan 2	(h)	Hartlepool U	W 1-0	Jones	1,799	**5**	11	4	8	12					9	2		1	3			10		6		7
3059	6	(h)	Reading	W 3-0	Kerr 2, Quinn (pen)	1,751		11	4	8		10				9	2		1	3			5		6		7
3060	14	(a)	York C	L 1-3	Sword (pen)	3,570	5	**11**	4	8	12	9					2		1	3			10		6		7
3061	20	(h)	Northampton T	W 1-0	Kerr	1,846	5	11	4	8	2	9							3		1		10		6		7
3062	28	(a)	Colchester U	D 1-1	Sword	2,213	5	11	4	8	2	9							3		1		10		6		7
3063	Feb 3	(h)	Crewe A	L 2-3	Coyle, Sword	2,775	5	11	4	8	2	9							3		1		10		6		7
3064	11	(a)	Swindon T	L 1-2	Evans	3,219	5	**11**	4	8	2	9		12					3		1	7	10		6		
3065	13	(h)	Bury	D 1-1	Kerr	2,281	5		4	8	2	9							3		1	11	10		6		7
3066	24	(h)	Chester C	W 2-1	Evans 2	2,006	5	11	4	8	2	9		12					3		1	7	**10**		6		
3067	Mar 5	(a)	Rochdale	W 2-1	Kerr, Evans (pen)	2,115	5	11	4	8	2	9							3		1	10			6		7
3068	9	(a)	Halifax T	L 0-2		1,261	5	11	4	8	2	9							3		1		7	12	10		
3069	16	(h)	Chesterfield	W 2-0	Sword (pen), Taylor	2,010	5	11	4	8	12	9							3		1		6	10	**2**		
3070	30	(a)	Wrexham	W 2-1	Taylor, Evans	1,252	5	11	4	9	8								3		1		6	10	2		
3071	Apr 6	(h)	Mansfield T	L 0-4		1,933	6	11	4	8		9							3		1		5	10	2		7
3072	10	(a)	Blackpool	D 1-1	Taylor	3,971	5	11	4	8		9							3		1		6	10	2		7
3073	14	(a)	Torquay U	D 1-1	Kerr	1,503	5	11	4	8		9							3		1		5	10	2		7
3074	21	(h)	Bristol C	D 0-0		2,645	6	11	4	8		9							3		1		5	10	2		7
3075	23	(a)	Hereford U	L 0-2		3,728	6	11	4	8		9					2		1	3			5	10			7
3076	27	(h)	Peterboro' U	W 4-1	Coyle 2, Taylor 2	1,753	6	11	4	8		9							1	3			5	10	2		7
3077	May 2	(a)	Darlington	L 0-1		1,102		11	4	8	2	9							1	3			5	10	6		7
3078	5	(a)	Hartlepool U	W 2-1	Taylor, Coyle	790	6	11	4	8		9							1	3			5	10	2		7
3079	7	(h)	Doncaster R	L 0-2		2,993	6	11	4	8		9							1	3			5	10	2		7
3080	12	(a)	Tranmere R	L 0-1		1,467	6	**11**	4	8	7	9							1	3			5	10	2		12
	FINAL LEAGUE POSITION: 12th in Division Four				Appearances		38	38	44	31	32	21			5	24	41	1	46	24	19		45	12	45	4	36
					Sub appearances						3		1	1				1		2	1	1					1
					Goals			5	1	7	2	6				15	1						10	6	1		6

FA Cup

No	Date	V	Opponent	Res	Scorers	Att	Bowles	Coyle	Emerson	Evans	Jones	Kerr	Leigh	Parker	Power	Quinn	Rutter	Ryan	Salmon	Sherlock	Smith	Sutcliffe	Sword	Taylor	Thorpe	White	Williams
1	Nov 19	(a)	Telford U	L 0-3		2,470	5		4	8						9	2		1	3			10		6	11	7
					Appearances		1		1	1						1	1		1	1			1		1	1	1
					Sub appearances																						
					Goals																						

League Cup

No	Date	V	Opponent	Res	Scorers	Att	Bowles	Coyle	Emerson	Evans	Jones	Kerr	Leigh	Parker	Power	Quinn	Rutter	Ryan	Salmon	Sherlock	Smith	Sutcliffe	Sword	Taylor	Thorpe	White	Williams
1/1	Aug 30	(a)	Rochdale	W 3-0	Quinn 2 (1 pen), Sword	1,839		4	**10**	6					12	9	2	7	1	11			5		3		8
1/2	Sep 12	(h)	Rochdale	D 2-2	Williams 2	2,160	12	10	4	2							3	7	1	11	8		**5**		6		9
2/1	Oct 3	(h)	Oldham A	L 0-2		4,640	5	11	4	2						9	3		1		8		10		6		7
2/2	25	(a)	Oldham A	D 2-2	Emerson 2	3,328	5	11	4	10						9	3		1		8		6		2		7
					Appearances		2	3	4	4						3	4	2	4	2	3		4		4		4
					Sub appearances		1								1												
					Goals				2							2							1				2

Average Home League attendance: 2,098
Average Away League attendance: 2,711

1984-85

No	Date	V	Opponent	Result	Scorers	Att	Bowles	Buxton	Byrom	Coyle	Crawford	Emerson	Evans	Hendrie	Jones	Kerr	Leonard	Lodge	Malley	O'Berg	Power	Raynes	Rutter	Salmon	Sherlock	Smith	Sword	Taylor	Thorpe	Williams	Wroe
3081	Aug 25	(h)	Hartlepool U	W 4-1	Williams, Buxton, Taylor, Sword (pen)	1,619	12	8		11			4	10									2	1	3		5	9	6	7	
3082	Sep 1	(a)	Torquay U	D 0-0		1,484		7		11			4	8	12	9							2	1	3		5	10	6		
3083	7	(h)	Tranmere R	L 0-2		2,825				11		4	10	8									2	1	3		5	9	6	7	
3084	15	(a)	Hereford U	L 0-2		3,395		10		11		4	9	8									2	1	3		5		6	7	
3085	17	(a)	Southend U	D 1-1	Emerson	2,004		12		11		4	10	8									2	1	3		5	9	6	7	
3086	22	(h)	Mansfield T	D 1-1	Sword (pen)	1,635		10		11		4		8	12	9							2	1	3		5	9	6	7	
3087	29	(a)	Wrexham	W 4-3	Coyle 2, Kerr 2	1,516	6			11		4		8		9								1	3		5	10	2	7	12
3088	Oct 1	(h)	Bury	W 2-0	Williams, Kerr	3,546				11		4	2	8		9								1	3		5	10	6	7	
3089	5	(h)	Rochdale	D 1-1	Evans	2,681	12			11		4	2	8		9							3	1			5	10	6	7	
3090	13	(a)	Peterboro' U	L 1-3	Sword	3,739		12		11		4	2	8		9								1	3		5	10	6	7	
3091	19	(h)	Crewe A	L 0-1		2,455			3	11		4	2	8		9		6						1			5	10	7		
3092	23	(a)	Colchester U	L 0-3		2,153			3	11		4	2	8		9		6						1			5	10	7		
3093	27	(a)	Swindon T	L 0-4		2,657			3	11		4	2	8		9		6						1			5	10	7		12
3094	Nov 3	(h)	Port Vale	W 3-1	Hendrie, Coyle, Taylor	2,698				11		4	2	8		9							3	1			5	10	6	7	
3095	10	(a)	Blackpool	L 1-4	Hendrie	3,428				11		4	2	8		9							3	1	12		5	10	6	7	
3096	24	(h)	Exeter C	W 1-0	Kerr	1,335						4	7	8		9				2	10		3	1	11		5		6	12	
3097	Dec 1	(a)	Chesterfield	L 0-3		3,943				11		4	7	8		9					2		3	1			5	10	6		
3098	7	(h)	Blackpool	L 1-3	Opp own-goal	2,428				11		4		8		9					2	7	3	1			5	10	6		
3099	4	(h)	Chester C	W 5-1	Kerr 3, Evans, Hendrie	1,463				11	10	4	2	8		9						7	3	1			5		6		
3100	21	(h)	Darlington	D 0-0		1,861				11	10	4	2	8		9						7	3	1			5		6		
3101	26	(a)	Scunthorpe U	L 0-1		2,881				11	10	4	2	8		9						7	3	1	12		5		6		
3102	Jan 1	(h)	Northampton T	W 4-2	Sword 2 (1 pen), Coyle, Crawford	1,726				11	10	4	2	8		9						7	3	1	12		5		6		
3103	Feb 1	(h)	Wrexham	D 2-2	Sword 2 (1 pen)	1,714					10	4	7	8		9						11	2	1	3		5		6		
3104	15	(h)	Southend U	L 1-2	Sword (pen)	1,039				11			4	8		9	10	12			7		2	1	3		5		6		
3105	22	(a)	Port Vale	L 2-3	Crawford, Power	3,154				11	10			6		9	8				7		2	1	3		4		5		
3106	25	(a)	Aldershot	W 6-0	Coyle 2, Kerr, Evans, Emerson, Opp own-goal	1,220				11		4	7	8		9	10						2	1	3		5		6		
3107	Mar 1	(h)	Swindon T	W 2-1	Kerr, Evans	1,680				11		4	7	8		9	10						2	1	3		5		6		
3108	4	(h)	Colchester U	W 1-0	Evans	1,561				11		4	7	8		9	10						2	1	3		5		6		
3109	9	(a)	Crewe A	L 1-2	Leonard	2,313				11		4	7	8		9	10	12					2	1	3		5		6		
3110	11	(a)	Hereford U	W 2-1	Kerr, Leonard	1,750				11		4	2	7		9	10	8					3	1			5		6		
3111	16	(h)	Peterboro' U	D 1-1	Lodge	1,340				11		4	7			9	10	8	12				2	1	3		5		6		
3112	26	(a)	Bury	L 1-2	Hendrie	3,740				11		4	10	8		9		7					2	1	3		5		6		
3113	30	(a)	Aldershot	L 1-2	Leonard	1,380		7		11		4	2	8		9	12				10			1	3		5		6		
3114	Apr 1	(h)	Torquay U	L 1-2	Sword (pen)	1,365		7		11		4	2	8		10		7						1	3		5		6		
3115	3	(a)	Hartlepool U	L 1-5	Lodge	1,148				11		4		8			10	7					2	1	3	6	5	9			
3116	6	(h)	Scunthorpe U	W 2-0	Sword 2 (1 pen)	1,285				11		4	7	8			10	12					2	1	3	6	9	5			
3117	9	(a)	Northampton T	L 0-4		1,426		7		11		4	2				10	8					3	1		6	9	5			
3118	17	(a)	Mansfield T	L 0-1		1,903		7		11		4	2	8			10						3	1		6	9	5			
3119	20	(a)	Exeter C	W 2-0	Leonard, Evans	1,836				11		4	7	8		9							2	1	3	6	10	5			
3120	23	(a)	Halifax T	L 1-2	Sword (pen)	1,291		12		11		4	7	8		9							2	1	3	5	10		6		
3121	27	(h)	Chesterfield	L 0-1		2,887		10		11		4	7	8		9							2	1	3	6	5				
3122	29	(a)	Tranmere R	L 0-3		1,006		10		11		4	7	8		9							2	1	3	6	5				
3123	May 4	(a)	Chester C	L 1-2	Evans	1,592		12		11		4	7	8		9							2	1	3	6	10	5			
3124	6	(h)	Halifax T	L 0-3		1,480		12				4	7	8		9		11					2	1	3	6	10	5			
3125	8	(a)	Rochdale	D 0-0		1,399		12				4	10	7		9		8					3	1	11	6	5		2		
3126	11	(a)	Darlington	L 1-3	Evans	3,686		7				4	10			9		8					3	1	11	6	5		2		
			FINAL LEAGUE POSITION: 22nd in Division Four - Re-elected		Appearances		1	12	3	38	6	44	44	40	3	26	23	9	3	2	6	2	38	46	31	26	44	14	31	13	1
					Sub appearances		2	6				2						3			2				2	1				3	
					Goals			1		6	2	2	8	4		10	4	2			1						12	2		2	

Own-goals 2

FA Cup

No	Date	V	Opponent	Result	Scorers	Att	Bowles	Buxton	Byrom	Coyle	Crawford	Emerson	Evans	Hendrie	Jones	Kerr	Leonard	Lodge	Malley	O'Berg	Power	Raynes	Rutter	Salmon	Sherlock	Smith	Sword	Taylor	Thorpe	Williams	Wroe
1	Nov 17	(h)	Walsall	L 1-2	Taylor	2,781		12		11		4	2	8		9						7	3	1			5	10	6		
					Appearances					1		1	1	1		1						1	1	1			1	1	1		
					Sub appearances			1																							
					Goals																							1			

League Cup

No	Date	V	Opponent	Result	Scorers	Att	Bowles	Buxton	Byrom	Coyle	Crawford	Emerson	Evans	Hendrie	Jones	Kerr	Leonard	Lodge	Malley	O'Berg	Power	Raynes	Rutter	Salmon	Sherlock	Smith	Sword	Taylor	Thorpe	Williams	Wroe
1/1	Aug 27	(h)	Rochdale	W 3-1	Coyle, Hendrie, Taylor	2,274	5	7		11		4		8	12								2	1	3		9	10	6		
1/2	Sep 4	(a)	Rochdale	W 2-1	Taylor, Buxton	1,497		7		11		4	10	8		9							2	1	3		5	9	6		
2/1	Sep 24	(h)	Liverpool	D 0-0		11,278		7		11		4		8		9							3	1			5	10	2	7	
2/2	Oct 9	(a)	Liverpool	L 0-2*		13,422	6	12		11		4	2	8		9								1			5	10	3	7	
					Appearances		2	3		4		4	2	4		3							3	4	2		4	4	4	2	
					Sub appearances			1							1																
					Goals			1		1				1														2			

Average Home League attendance: 1,895
Average Away League attendance: 2,308

*After extra-time

1985-86

League (Division Four)

No	Date	V	Opponent	Res	Scorers	Att	Cammack	Chapman	Coyle	Devine	Diamond	Evans	Hendrie	Hodkinson	Leonard	Lodge	Matthewson	Mossman	Newton	Poskett	Power	Rutter	Salmon	Sherlock	Smith NG	Smith PM	Sword	Thorpe	Walker	Williams	Wroe	Yates
3127	Aug 17	(a)	Colchester U	L 1-3	P.M.Smith	1,719	3	12						7	9	4					2	1	11	6	10	**5**	8					
3128	23	(a)	Burnley	W 1-0	P.M.Smith	3,909	4	11	8						9							1	3	6	10		2				7	5
3129	26	(a)	Rochdale	L 1-4	Leonard	2,053	4	11	8						9							1	3	6	10	12	2				7	5
3130	Sep 6	(a)	Crewe A	W 1-0	P.M.Smith	2,148		4					8	11	9						2	1	3		10	5	6				7	
3131	13	(a)	Preston NE	W 2-1	P.M.Smith, Hodkinson	3,439		4					8	11	9						2	1	3		10	5	6				7	
3132	16	(h)	Hereford U	D 1-1	Sword (pen)	2,255		4	10				8	11	9						2	1	3			5	6				7	
3133	22	(a)	Northampton T	L 1-3	Sword	1,954		4					8	11	9						2	1	3		10	5	6				7	
3134	28	(h)	Chester C	D 2-2	Leonard, P.M.Smith	1,801		4					8	11	9							1	3		10	5	2				6	7
3135	Oct 1	(a)	Southend U	D 0-0		3,854		4	10				8	7	9		11					1	3			5	2				6	
3136	5	(a)	Torquay U	L 3-4	Sword, Leonard 2	1,178		4	10				8	7	9		11	10				1	3			5	2				6	
3137	11	(h)	Hartlepool U	L 1-3	Hodkinson	1,827		4	10				**8**	7	9		12	11				1	3			5	2				6	
3138	18	(h)	Peterboro' U	D 2-2	Hodkinson, Mossman	1,634		4	10	2			8				6	11				1	3		9			5			7	
3139	22	(a)	Swindon T	L 0-1		7,411		4	10			12	8				6	11				1	3		9		2	5			7	
3140	26	(a)	Orient	W 1-0	Leonard	2,721		4	10				8		9		6				2	1	3		11			5			7	
3141	Nov 1	(h)	Cambridge U	W 3-1	Mossman, Sword, Leonard	1,734		4					8	7	9		6	11	10		2	1	3					5				
3142	4	(h)	Halifax T	W 2-1	Chapman, Mossman	1,673		4				12	8	7	9		6	**11**	10		2	1	3					5				
3143	9	(a)	Port Vale	D 1-1	Leonard	5,248		4					8	7	9		6	11	10		2	1	3					5				
3144	23	(h)	Aldershot	W 3-2	Chapman, Sword (pen), Hendrie	1,354		4	10				8	7	9		6	11				1	3				2	5				
3145	29	(a)	Tranmere R	W 3-2	Leonard 2, Mossman	1,605		4	10			2	8	7	9		3	11				1						5			6	
3146	Dec 6	(a)	Cambridge U	W 2-1	Coyle, Wroe	1,235		4	10			2	8	7	9		3					1						5	6		11	
3147	13	(h)	Wrexham	W 2-0	Coyle, Leonard	2,405		4	10			2	8	7	9		3					1						5	6		11	
3148	20	(h)	Burnley	D 1-1	Leonard	3,472		4	11			2	8	7	9		3					1						5	6			
3149	26	(a)	Mansfield T	L 2-4	Leonard 2	4,206		4	11		10	2	8	7	9		3					1						5	6			
3150	28	(h)	Rochdale	W 3-0	Coyle, Sword 2 (2 pens)	4,005		4	11		10	2	8	7	9		3					1						5	6			
3151	Jan 1	(h)	Scunthorpe U	D 0-0		3,505		**4**	11		10	2	8	7	9		3					1						5	6			12
3152	11	(a)	Exeter C	L 0-1		2,161		11			10	2	8	7	9		3					1						5	6			4
3153	17	(h)	Colchester U	D 1-1	Hodkinson	2,336					10	2	8	7	9		3											5		1	6	
3154	24	(h)	Preston NE	W 2-1	Coyle, Leonard	3,035	10	4	11			2	8	7	9		3						12					**5**		1	6	
3155	31	(h)	Crewe A	W 3-0	Hodkinson, Leonard 2	2,564	11	4				2	8	7	9				10				3					5		1	6	
3156	Feb 3	(h)	Swindon T	L 0-2		3,899	11	4				2	8	7	9				10				3					5		1	6	
3157	21	(h)	Northampton T	W 1-0	Cammack	2,011	12	4	11			2	8	7	9		3		10									5	6	1		
3158	24	(h)	Exeter C	D 1-1	Wroe	2048		4				2	8	7	9		3		10									5	6	1	11	
3159	Mar 1	(a)	Chester C	W 2-1	Wroe 2	2,948		4					8	7	9		3		10	2								5	6	1	11	
3160	3	(h)	Southend U	W 2-1	Sword (pen), Poskett	2,425		4					8	7	9		3		10	2								5	6	1	11	
3161	7	(h)	Torquay U	D 1-1	Sword (pen)	3,014		4					8	7	9		3		10	2								5	6	1	11	
3162	14	(h)	Hartlepool U	D 1-1	Leonard	2,675		4				2	8	7	9		3		10									5	6	1	11	
3163	21	(h)	Orient	L 2-3	Chapman, Sword (pen)	3,119		4	10			2	8	7	9		3		12									5	6	1	**11**	
3164	28	(a)	Scunthorpe U	W 3-2	Leonard 2, Sword (pen)	2,025		10					8	7	9		6						3				2	5		1	11	
3165	31	(h)	Mansfield T	L 0-2		4,635		4				2	8	7	9		11	10					3					5	6	1		
3166	Apr 4	(a)	Halifax T	D 0-0		1,836		4				2	8		9		11	10					3					5	6	1		7
3167	8	(a)	Peterboro' U	L 0-2		1,610		4				2	8	7	9		11	10					3					5	6	1		
3168	11	(h)	Port Vale	L 1-2	Newton	4,691		4				2	8	7	9		3	11	10									5	6	1		
3169	16	(a)	Hereford U	L 2-3	Sword, Hodkinson	1,978		4				2	8	7	9		3	10										5	6	1	11	
3170	19	(a)	Aldershot	L 1-6	Mossman	1,319	8	4				2			9		3	11	10				12					5	6	1	7	
3171	25	(h)	Tranmere R	D 1-1	Evans	1,896	10	4				2	8		9		6	11	12				3					5		1	7	
3172	May 3	(a)	Wrexham	L 0-3		1,355	10	4				2	8		9		6	11					3					5		1	7	
				Appearances			3	38	24	2	6	33	36	41	44	1	34	17	6	8		16	26	23	3	7	39	30	20	22	25	2
				Sub appearances			1		1		2							1			1			1			2		1			1	
				Goals			1	3	4			1		6	19			6	1	1						5	12				4	

FINAL LEAGUE POSITION: 11th in Division Four

FA Cup

No	Date	V	Opponent	Res	Scorers	Att	Cammack	Chapman	Coyle	Devine	Diamond	Evans	Hendrie	Hodkinson	Leonard	Lodge	Matthewson	Mossman	Newton	Poskett	Power	Rutter	Salmon	Sherlock	Smith NG	Smith PM	Sword	Thorpe	Walker	Williams	Wroe	Yates
1	Nov 16	(h)	Telford U	L 0-1		2,994		4				12	8	**7**	9		6	11			2	1	3		10			5				
				Appearances			1						1	1	1		1	1			1	1	1		1			1				
				Sub appearances								1																				
				Goals																												

League Cup

No	Date	V	Opponent	Res	Scorers	Att	Cammack	Chapman	Coyle	Devine	Diamond	Evans	Hendrie	Hodkinson	Leonard	Lodge	Matthewson	Mossman	Newton	Poskett	Power	Rutter	Salmon	Sherlock	Smith NG	Smith PM	Sword	Thorpe	Walker	Williams	Wroe	Yates
1/1	Aug 20	(a)	Bolton W	L 1-4	P.M.Smith	3,311	3						8		9	4					2	1	11	6	10	5					7	
1/2	Sep 2	(h*)	Bolton W	D 1-1	Leonard	2,573	4	11					8	7	9							1	3	6	10	5	2					
				Appearances			2	1					2	1	2	1					1	2	2	2	2	1	2				1	
				Sub appearances																												
				Goals											1											1						

Average Home League attendance: 2,667
Average Away League attendance: 2,634

*Played at Burnden Park, Bolton.

1986-87

No	Date		Opponent	Result	Scorers	Att	Allatt	Bailey	Brannigan	Brown	Cockhill	Edwards	Entwistle	Evans	Farnworth	Glavin	Gorton	Grant	Hendrie	Hodkinson	Leonard	Lester	Marples	Matthewson	McAdam	McKenzie	Melvin	Mitchell	Moss	Mossman	Robinson	Serfori	Stevens	Stokes	Sword	Walker	Wilkes	Williams WR
3173	Aug 23	(a)	Swansea C	L 0-3		4,774		3	2					10		12			8	4	9			5						11							1	7	6
3174	29	(h)	Tranmere R	L 0-2		2,145			2					10		12			8	4	9			5						11							1	7	6
3175	Sep 6	(a)	Exeter C	L 0-4		1,820		10	6			8				12				4	9			5	3					11							1	7	
3176	12	(h)	Rochdale	D 1-1	McAdam	2,192		10	5			**8**		2	1	4				9	11			3	8					11									
3177	15	(h)	Wolves	L 0-2		2,724		10	5					2	1	12		3	4	9	11			3	8					12								7	6
3178	19	(a)	Halifax T	W 2-0	Hodkinson, Glavin	1,071		10	5		8			2	1	12	3			4	9	11		6	8					7									6
3179	30	(a)	Torquay U	D 0-0		1,473		10	5		8			2	1	4			11	9	7			3															6
3180	Oct 3	(a)	Cambridge U	L 0-5		2,820		10	5	8	9			2	1	4			7		11			3		12				9									6
3181	18	(a)	Burnley	L 0-2		2,410	4	10		9		8	2							11				5	3					12									6
3182	20	(h)	Preston NE	L 1-3	Entwistle	2,888	9	10		9		8	2						11					5	3					12							1	7	6
3183	24	(h)	Colchester U	D 1-1	Entwistle	1,281	9	10				8	2	12						6				4	5					11	3						1	7	6
3184	27	(h)	Northampton T	L 0-3		1,729	9	10				8	2	1						6				4	5					11	3								7
3185	31	(a)	Orient	L 0-1		2,172	**9**	10				8	2	1						6				4	5	12				11	3								7
3186	Nov 3	(h)	Hereford U	L 1-2	Stokes	1,338	9	10				8	2	1						6				4	5	7				11	3			12					
3187	9	(a)	Aldershot	L 1-3	Allatt	2,660	9	6		12			10	1					2		10			5	3										6				
3188	22	(h)	Cardiff C	W 2-0	Allatt, Edwards	1,674	9	10		4		8	2						7					4	3	2				**11**				8	5				
3189	28	(a)	Hartlepool U	L 0-1		1,586	9			4		8	2						7					5	3					11				6	1				
3190	Dec 13	(a)	Southend U	D 0-0		2,621	9			4		8	2			1			7					5	3					11	10			6	1				
3191	19	(h)	Wrexham	W 2-1	Evans, Allatt	1,770	9	11		4		8	2			1			7					5	3					11	10			6					
3192	26	(a)	Lincoln C	D 0-0		2,773	9		4				2			1								5	3					10				6					7
3193	27	(h)	Peterboro' U	W 3-1	Allatt 3 (1 pen)	2,120	9			4			2			1			7					5	3	8			11	10				6					
3194	Jan 1	(h)	Crewe A	W 2-1	Evans, Moss	2,955	9			4			2			1			7					5	3	8			11	10									6
3195	3	(a)	Cardiff C	D 1-1	Allatt	3,038	9			4			2			1			7					5	3	8			11	10									6
3196	23	(a)	Exeter C	D 0-0		1,975	9			4			2			1			7					5	3	8			11	10									6
3197	Feb 7	(a)	Wolves	L 1-3	Moss	3,238	9		11	4			2			1			7					5	3	8			11	10									6
3198	14	(h)	Halifax T	W 2-0	Allatt (pen), Moss	1,835	9		11	4			2			1			7					5	3	8				10									6
3199	21	(a)	Scunthorpe U	W 2-1	Evans, Allatt	1,752	9	8	11	4			2			1			7					5	**3**					10									6
3200	27	(h)	Torquay U	D 0-0		2,437	9		11	4			2			1			7					5		8				10			12						6
3201	Mar 2	(h)	Orient	D 2-2	Robinson, Allatt	1,840	9		11				2			1			7					5		8				10	3								6
3202	6	(a)	Colchester U	L 1-5	Edwards	2,001	9		11	12			2			1	4		7					5		8				10	3								6
3203	13	(h)	Burnley	L 0-1		2,500	9		11	**7**	12		2			1								5		8				10	3								6
3204	17	(a)	Preston NE	L 0-3		7,867	12		11				9	7					4					5		8				10				6					2
3205	21	(a)	Northampton T	L 1-2	Entwistle	5,466	12		**11**				9	2					4					5		8	3	10	7		6		1					
3206	27	(h)	Cambridge U	W 3-2	Sword (pen), Brown, Hodkinson	1,622			11	9	2			4	12									5		8	**3**	10			6	7						1
3207	Apr 3	(h)	Aldershot	D 0-0		1,975			11	7	9	2									1	5				3	8		10			6	7					
3208	7	(a)	Tranmere R	W 3-0	Moss, Hodkinson 2 (1 pen)	1,543			11	4	9	2					7				1	5	3			8		10			6			4					
3209	11	(a)	Hereford U	W 2-1	Entwistle, Moss	2,251			11	4	9	2					7				1	5	3			8		10			6								
3210	13	(h)	Scunthorpe U	W 1-0	Moss	1,773			11	4	9	2					7				1	5	3			8		10			6								
3211	17	(a)	Crewe A	L 0-5		2,413			11	4	9	2					7				1	5	3			8		10						6					
3212	20	(h)	Lincoln C	W 1-0	Hodkinson	2,529			11	4	9	2					7				1	5	3			8		10			6								
3213	25	(a)	Wrexham	D 0-0		1,433			11	4	9	2					7				1	5	3			8		10			6								
3214	27	(h)	Swansea C	W 3-1	Entwistle, Moss, Edwards	2,216			11	4	9	2					7				1	5	3			8		10			6								
3215	May 1	(h)	Hartlepool U	L 0-2		2,228			11	4	9	2					7				1	5				8		10			6								
3216	4	(a)	Peterboro' U	D 0-0		2,968			11	4	9	2					3	7			1	5				8		10			3			6					
3217	6	(a)	Rochdale	L 1-2	Hodkinson	4,840			11	4		2					7				1	5	3			8		10	9		6								
3218	8	(h)	Southend U	L 0-2		2,853			11	4		2					7				1	5	3			8		10	9		6								
			Appearances				23	16	8	23	3	28	23	45	10	5	14	1	10	37	6	11	13	45	5	29		2	26	20	30	3	1	17	3	9	8	30
			Sub appearances				1	1		2	1		5			1					1				1		1		2					1		1	1	
			Goals				10		1			3	5	3		1				6					1				7	1				1	1			

B. Williams played number-three in Matches 3203 and 3204.

FA Cup

No	Date		Opponent	Result	Att	Allatt	Bailey	Brown	Cockhill	Edwards	Hendrie	Matthewson	McAdam	Moss	Robinson	Stokes	Sword	Walker
1	Nov 15	(a)	Caernarfon T	L 0-1	1,748	9	10	4	8	2	7	5	3	11		12	6	1
			Appearances			1	1	1	1	1	1	1	1	1			1	1
			Sub appearances												1			
			Goals															

League Cup

No	Date		Opponent	Result	Scorers	Att	Allatt	Bailey	Brannigan	Brown	Evans	Glavin	Hendrie	Hodkinson	Leonard	Lester	Matthewson	McAdam	McKenzie	Mossman	Serfori	Walker	Wilkes	Williams WR
1/1	Aug 26	(h)	Tranmere R	W 2-1	Wilkes, Mossman	1,543		3	2		10	12	8	4	9		5			11		1	7	6
1/2	Sep 2	(a)	Tranmere R	D 3-3	Wilkes, McAdam, Leonard	1,433		10			8	12	4	2	9		3	5		11		1	7	6
2/1	23	(a)	Sheffield W	L 0-3		10,466	10		8		2	1		11	9	7	5	3		12			4	6
2/2	Oct 6 (h*)		Sheffield W	L 0-7		2,089	10			11	2	1	4	6	7	8	5	3	12				9	
			Appearances				4		2	1	4	2	1	1	2	4	3	2		2		2	4	3
			Sub appearances									2							1	1				
			Goals												1			1		1			2	

Average Home League attendance: 2,113
Average Away League attendance: 2,826

*Played at Maine Road, Manchester.

219

1987-88

Player columns (left to right): Bailey, Birch, Bullock, Burke, Chandler, Colville, Crompton, Cronin, Edwards, Entwistle, Evans, Farnaby, Hartford, Hendrie, Hodkinson, Howard, Marples, McKenzie, Mills, Mossman, Pickering, Robinson, Scott, Sertori, Sword, Thorpe, Williams, Willis, Worthington

No	Date	Venue / Opponent	Result	Scorers	Att	Bai	Bir	Bul	Bur	Cha	Col	Crm	Cro	Edw	Ent	Eva	Far	Har	Hen	Hod	How	Mar	McK	Mil	Mos	Pic	Rob	Sco	Ser	Swo	Tho	Wil	Wls	Wor
3219	Aug 15 (h)	Swansea C	L 0-2		2,482	3		7					8	11	9	2		10				1					4	12		5		6		
3220	22 (a)	Darlington	W 2-1	Evans 2	1,744		10		9				8	11		2			7			1		3			4			5		6		
3221	28 (h)	Tranmere R	L 1-2	Hodkinson	2,229			5	9				8	11		2		10	7			1		3			4					6		
3222	Sep 31 (a)	Newport C	W 2-1	Evans, Hodkinson	1,626			5	9				8	11		2		10	7			1		3			4					6		
3223	4 (h)	Carlisle U	W 3-0	Hodkinson, Evans, Cronin	2,257	3		5					8	11		2		10	7			1	9				4					6		
3224	12 (a)	Rochdale	W 1-0	Edwards	2,124	3		5		12				11	9			10	7			1	8				4	2				6		
3225	15 (h)	Leyton O	L 1-2	Hodkinson	2,560	3		5			9			11				10	7			1	8				4	2				6		
3226	19 (h)	Wolves	L 0-2		2,234	3		5	8	9				11					7	10		1	12				4	2				6		
3227	26 (a)	Wrexham	L 1-2	Colville	1,946	7		5			9			11	12							1	3	10			4	2			8	6		
3228	29 (a)	Scunthorpe U	D 0-0		2,191	3		5	11	9								10				1	8				4	2				6		
3229	Oct 2 (h)	Cardiff C	L 0-1		2,332	3		5		8	9		11					10	7			1					4	2				6		
3230	10 (h)	Peterboro' U	L 0-1		1,594	3	11	5	10	8	9		14			2			7			1	12				4					6		
3231	16 (a)	Halifax T	L 0-2		1,696	3	11	5	10	8	9		14				12		7			1					4	2				6		
3232	20 (a)	Crewe A	L 1-3	Colville	2,251	3	11	5	10	8						2			7			1					4	9				6		
3233	23 (h)	Hereford U	L 0-2		1,566	3	11	2	8	9					14		12	10		7		1				5	4					6		
3234	31 (a)	Burnley	D 1-1	Entwistle	6,642	3	11	2		8				12	9			10				1				5	4					6		
3235	Nov 3 (h)	Hartlepool U	W 1-0	Birch	1,408	3	11	2		8					9					12	10	1				5	4					6		
3236	6 (a)	Torquay U	W 2-1	Entwistle, Robinson	1,697	3	11	2		8					9			10				1				5	4			12		6		
3237	21 (a)	Exeter C	L 1-2	Birch	2,217	3	11	2		8				14	9			10				1				5	4	12				6		
3238	27 (h)	Colchester U	D 1-1	Farnaby	1,703	3	11	2		8							10				1						4	5				6		9
3239	Dec 11 (a)	Cambridge U	L 0-2		1,288	3	11	2		8				14					10	12	7	1					4	5				6		9
3240	19 (h)	Scarborough	D 1-1	Worthington	1,779	3	11	2		8					12				10	14	7	1					4	5				6		9
3241	26 (h)	Wrexham	D 1-1	Colville	2,504	3	11	2		8							12		10	7		1					4	5				6		9
3242	28 (a)	Bolton W	L 1-2	Worthington	6,607	3	11	2		8				12	14			10			7	1					4	5				6		9
3243	Jan 1 (a)	Tranmere R	L 0-4		3,670	3		2		8				12				11	14	10	7	1					4				6	5		9
3244	2 (h)	Rochdale	D 1-1	Worthington	2,441		11	2		8				12			3	10	14	7		1					4				6	5		9
3245	16 (a)	Wolves	D 1-1	Worthington	8,872	3	11	2		8			12						7			1					4				5	6	10	9
3246	23 (a)	Leyton O	D 1-1	Colville	4,205	3	11	2		8				12					7			1					4				5	6	10	9
3247	29 (h)	Newport C	W 5-1	Hendrie, Colville 2, Birch, Robinson	2,509	3	11	2		8				14				10	7	12		1					4				5	6		9
3248	Feb 6 (a)	Carlisle U	L 0-2		1,852	3	11	2		8				12				10	7			1					4				5	6		9
3249	12 (h)	Bolton W	L 1-2	Worthington	4,814			2		8				11				10	7	12		1	3				4				5	6		9
3250	19 (h)	Swansea C	D 1-1	Worthington	4,405			2		8					10				7	12		1					4				5	6	11	9
3251	27 (a)	Cardiff C	D 0-0		3,937			2		8			9					10	12	7		1	3				4				5	6	11	
3252	Mar 1 (h)	Scunthorpe U	D 1-1	Colville	1,834			2		8			9					10	12	7		1	3				4				5	6	11	
3253	4 (h)	Halifax T	W 1-0	Colville	2,171					8			9			2		10		7		1	3				4				5	6	11	
3254	12 (a)	Peterboro' U	D 0-0		2,193					8		12	9			2		10		7		1					4				5	6	11	
3255	18 (h)	Burnley	W 2-0	Colville, Hodkinson (pen)	4,423	3	12			8			9			2		10		7		1					4				5	6	11	14
3256	26 (a)	Hereford U	W 1-0	Entwistle	1,695	3				8			9			2		10	11	7		1			4						5	6		
3257	Apr 2 (a)	Torquay U	L 0-3		2,919	3	12			8						2		10	11	7		1			4						5	6		9
3258	4 (h)	Exeter C	W 2-1	Colville, Hodkinson (pen)	2,161	3		2		8	12							10	11	7		1			4						5	6		9
3259	9 (a)	Hartlepool U	W 3-1	Edwards, Colville 2	1,269	3		5		8				10		2			11	7		1									4	6		9
3260	19 (h)	Darlington	D 1-1	Colville	1,620	3				8	12	10				2			11			1								7	4	6		9
3261	22 (h)	Crewe A	D 1-1	Colville	2,090			5		8	12					2		10	11	7		1		3							4	6		9
3262	29 (a)	Colchester U	L 0-2		1,607			5		8	6		9					10	11	7		1		3				2			4			
3263	May 2 (h)	Cambridge U	L 1-2	Colville	1,842			5		8	9	12		14				10	11	7	2	1									4	6		
3264	7 (a)	Scarborough	D 1-1	Williams (pen)	2,236	3		5		8	1	7	9					10	11		2										4	6		
	FINAL LEAGUE POSITION: 20th in Division Four			**Appearances**		34	18	41	5	4	40	2	11	12	15	5	17	30	17	36	2	44	12	5		8	37	15		3	20	45	10	18
				Sub appearances			2			1			4	7	10		5	1	5	3						2				1	1	1		1
				Goals			3				14		1	2	3	4	1		1	6						2						1		6

FA Cup

No	Date	Venue / Opponent	Result	Scorers	Att	Bai	Bir	Bul	Cha	Ent	Hod	Hen	Mar	Pic	Rob	Sco	Tho	Wil	Wor
1	Nov 14 (a)	Telford U	D 1-1	Entwistle	2,758	3	11	2	8	9	10	7	1	5	4			6	
R	17 (h)	Telford U	W 2-0	Colville, Hodkinson (pen)	3,083	3	11	2	8	9	10	7	1	5	4			6	
2	Dec 5 (a)	Runcorn	W 1-0	Colville	3,102	3	11	2	8		10	7	1		4	5		6	9
3	Jan 9 (h)	Leyton O	L 1-2	Colville	4,243	3	11	2	8	12	10	7	1		4		5	6	9
				Appearances		4	4	4	4	2	4	4	4	2	4	1	1	4	2
				Sub appearances						1									
				Goals					3	1	1								

League Cup

No	Date	Venue / Opponent	Result	Att	Bai	Bir	Bul	Cro	Edw	Eva	Har	Hen	Mar	McK	Mil	Rob	Sco	Ser	Swo	Wil
1/1	Aug 18 (h)	Carlisle U	L 0-1	1,476	3			8	11	2	10	7	1			4		9	5	6
1/2	25 (a)	Carlisle U	L 0-3	2,174	10		5	8	11	2		7	1	9	3	4				6
			Appearances		2	1		2	2	2	1	2	2	1	1	2		1	1	2
			Sub appearances																	
			Goals																	

Average Home League attendance: 2,272
Average Away League attendance: 3,008

1988-89

No.	Date	Venue/Opponent	Result	Scorers	Att.	Angell	Batch	Bullock	Butler	Caldwell	Colville	Cooke	Coyle	Dooner	Gorton	Hancock	Hart	Hartford	Hendrie	Howard	Leonard	Logan	Matthews	McKenzie	Payne	Pickering	Scott	Stapleton	Thorpe	Williams	Wylde
3265	Aug 27	(a) Darlington	W 4-1	Payne, Wylde, Coyle, Howard	1,794			2					4		1		3	10	8	11					9		12		5	6	7
3266	Sep 3	(h) Leyton O	D 0-0		1,947		9	2				8	4		1		3	10		11									5	6	7
3267	10	(a) Cambridge U	L 0-1		1,845		12	2				10			1		3		8	11					9			4	5	6	7
3268	16	(h) Burnley	D 0-0		6,676		12	2		8	10				1		3		4	11					9				5	6	7
3269	19	(h) Halifax T	D 1-1	Wylde	2,206		12	2				10	4		1		3		8	11					9				5	6	7
3270	23	(a) Crewe A	D 1-1	Butler	2,975		12	2	11			10	4		1		3		8						9				5	6	7
3271	Oct 1	(h) Doncaster R	W 2-0	Cooke, Wylde	1,959			2				10	4		1		3	12	8	11					9				5	6	7
3272	5	(a) Peterboro' U	L 0-1		2,572		12	2				10	4		1		3		8	11					9		6		5		7
3273	8	(a) Rochdale	D 1-1	Wylde	3,021		12	2	9			10	4		1		3		8								6		5		7
3274	15	(h) Hereford U	L 1-2	Wylde	2,035			2	9			10	4		1		3		12	11					8		6		5		7
3275	22	(a) Scarborough	D 1-1	Hart	2,449	8		2	9		11				1		3	10	4						12		6		5		7
3276	24	(h) Hartlepool U	W 3-0	Angell, Cooke, Wylde	2,098	8		2	9		11		4		1		3	10	14						12		6		5		7
3277	28	(a) Colchester U	D 1-1	Opp own-goal	1,675	8		2	12		9	4			1		3	10		11					14		6		5		7
3278	Nov 5	(h) Grimsby T	W 3-1	Coyle, Caldwell, Wylde	2,064	8		2		9			4		1		3	10	14			11			12		6		5		7
3279	8	(a) Wrexham	L 0-2		1,865	8		2		9	12		4		1		3	10	14			11					6		5		7
3280	11	(h) York C	W 3-2	Colville, Hart, Angell	2,477	9	12	2			8		4		1		3	10	6	11					14				5		7
3281	25	(h) Tranmere R	D 1-1	Wylde	2,958	9	12	2			8		4		1		3		10	14		11			6				5		7
3282	Dec 3	(a) Rotherham U	L 1-2	Wylde	4,005	9		4	2		8				1		3	10				11			12				5	6	7
3283	17	(h) Lincoln C	W 1-0	Williams (pen)	2,355	9		4	2		8	10			1		3					11			7		5			6	
3284	26	(a) Torquay U	L 1-2	Colville	2,838	9		4	2	12	8	10			1	14	3					11			7		5			6	
3285	31	(a) Carlisle U	D 1-1	Caldwell	3,774			2	9	8	4				1	12	3	10				11			7		5			6	
3286	Jan 2	(h) Exeter C	W 4-0	Caldwell, Colville, Cooke (pen), Hancock	2,936	12		4	2	9	8	10			1	14	3					11					5			7	6
3287	7	(h) Scunthorpe U	L 1-2	Hancock	2,656			4	2	9	8	10			1	14	3					11			12		5			7	6
3288	14	(a) Leyton O	W 2-1	Colville, Howard	3,848			4		9	8	11			1	12				10		2	3		7				5	6	
3289	20	(h) Darlington	D 0-0		2,889	12		4		9	8	11			1	14				10		2	3		7				5	6	
3290	28	(h) Burnley	L 0-1		6,942			4	2	9	8	11			1	14				10			3		7				5	6	
3291	Feb 4	(h) Halifax T	D 2-2	Cooke, Caldwell (pen)	1,958	12		2		9	8	11			1	14				10			3	4	7				5	6	
3292	10	(h) Crewe A	L 0-1		5,005			2		9	10	8			1							11	3	4	7				5	6	
3293	17	(h) Rochdale	W 3-0	Angell 2, Wylde	2,848	9		2			8	10			1							11	3	4	7		5			6	12
3294	25	(a) Hereford U	L 1-2	Butler	2,015	9		2			8	10			1	14						11	3	4	7		5			6	12
3295	28	(a) Hartlepool U	D 2-2	Caldwell, Hancock	1,598			2	7	9	8				1	12				10			3	4					5	6	
3296	Mar 4	(h) Scarborough	D 2-2	Colville, Hancock	2,648			2	7	9	8				1					10			3	4					5	6	
3297	11	(a) Grimsby T	L 0-2		4,685	12			7	9	8				1	5				10			3	4					2	6	
3298	13	(h) Colchester U	W 1-0	Cooke	2,027	12			7	9	8	10			1	5				14			3	4			2			6	
3299	17	(h) Cambridge U	D 0-0		2,566	12			7	9	8	10			1	5				14			3	4			2			6	
3300	25	(a) Exeter C	D 2-2	Coyle, Wylde	3,058	10	1			7		8				5				12		11	3	4			2			6	9
3301	27	(h) Torquay U	D 0-0		2,808		1			7		8	12			5				10		11	3	4			2			6	9
3302	Apr 1	(a) Lincoln C	D 0-0		3,400		1			7		8	10			5						11	3	4			2			6	9
3303	4	(a) Scunthorpe U	D 1-0	Cooke	3,958		1			7		8	10			5						11	3	4			2			6	9
3304	7	(a) Carlisle U	D 1-1	Wylde (pen)	2,543		1		4	7		8	10			5						11	3				2			6	9
3305	15	(a) Doncaster R	D 2-2	Hancock, Caldwell	1,363	12	1		7	9						11				10		8	3	4			2			6	
3306	21	(h) Peterboro' U	L 1-2	Williams	2,091	14	1		7	9		12				11				10		8	3	4			2			6	
3307	28	(a) Tranmere R	L 0-1		6,270	9	1	6				12				11				10		8	3	4			2				7
3308	May 1	(h) Wrexham	D 2-2	Matthews, Angell	2,118	9	1	2			12	10	11			14				5		8	3	4						7	6
3309	6	(h) Rotherham U	L 1-3	Leonard	4,313	9	1	2			12	10				14				5	11	8	3	4						7	6
3310	13	(a) York C	L 0-2		2,327	9	1	12			10				11	14				5		8	3	4			7			2	6
				Appearances		17	12	13	32	23	27	31	23	1	34	12	37	12	11	10	11	35	19	10	20	7	8	1	41	35	24
				Sub appearances		9	9		1	4	3					10	1			6					7	2	1	1			2
				Goals		5		2	6	5	6	3				5	2		2	1		1			1					2	12

Own-goal 1

FA Cup

No.	Date	Venue/Opponent	Result	Scorers	Att.	Angell	Batch	Bullock	Butler	Caldwell	Colville	Cooke	Coyle	Dooner	Gorton	Hancock	Hart	Hartford	Hendrie	Howard	Leonard	Logan	Matthews	McKenzie	Payne	Pickering	Scott	Stapleton	Thorpe	Williams	Wylde
1	Nov 19	(a) Scarborough	L 1-2	Colville	2,939	9		2			8		4		1		3	10	6			11	14	12			5				7
				Appearances		1		1			1		1		1		1	1	1			1					1				1
				Sub appearances																			1	1							
				Goals							1																				

League Cup

No.	Date	Venue/Opponent	Result	Scorers	Att.	Angell	Batch	Bullock	Butler	Caldwell	Colville	Cooke	Coyle	Dooner	Gorton	Hancock	Hart	Hartford	Hendrie	Howard	Leonard	Logan	Matthews	McKenzie	Payne	Pickering	Scott	Stapleton	Thorpe	Williams	Wylde
1/1	Aug 29	(h) Tranmere R	L 0-1		2,602			2				12	4		1		3	10	8	11					9		14		5	6	7
1/2	Sep 5	(a) Tranmere R	D 1-1	Wylde (pen)	3,335		9	2				8	12	4	1		3		10	11									5	6	7
				Appearances			1	2			1		2	2	2		2	1	2	2					1				2	2	2
				Sub appearances								2															1				
				Goals																											1

FINAL LEAGUE POSITION: 20th in Division Four

Average Home League attendance: 2,792
Average Away League attendance: 3,054

1989-90

Player columns (left→right): Angell, Barnett, Beaumont, Brookman, Brown, Bullock, Caldwell, Cecere, Cooke, Downes, Edwards, Frain, Gannon, Hope, Howard, Jones, Knowles, Leonard, Logan, Matthews, McDonald, McInerney, Muggleton, Oghani, Payne, Redfern, Ritchie, Robertson, Siddall, Thorpe, Williams PR, Williams WR

League

No	Date		Opponent	Res	Scorers	Att	Angell	Barnett	Beaumont	Brookman	Brown	Bullock	Caldwell	Cecere	Cooke	Downes	Edwards	Frain	Gannon	Hope	Howard	Jones	Knowles	Leonard	Logan	Matthews	McDonald	McInerney	Muggleton	Oghani	Payne	Redfern	Ritchie	Robertson	Siddall	Thorpe	Williams PR	Williams WR
3311	Aug 19	(h)	Torquay U	D 1-1	Beaumont	2,356	9	7	2						10		8													12	4			14	1	6	11	5
3312	26	(a)	Burnley	D 0-0		6,537			2		7				10					11						4	9			12	8			3	1	6		5
3313	Sep 1	(h)	York C	D 2-2	Oghani, Matthews	2,793	11		2		7				10										3	4			12	9	8				1	6		5
3314	5	(a)	Wrexham	W 1-0	Payne	2,333	11		2			12			10										3	4		7		9	8				1	6		5
3315	9	(a)	Maidstone U	W 1-0	Logan	2,020	11		2			12			10										3	4		7		9	8				1	6		5
3316	15	(h)	Hartlepool U	W 6-0	Angell 4 (1 pen), Cooke, Oghani (pen)	3,884	11		2						10										3	4		7		9	8				1	6	12	5
3317	23	(a)	Aldershot	L 1-2	Angell (pen)	1,879	11		2						10										3	4		7		9	8				1	6	12	5
3318	30	(a)	Scarborough	W 3-2	Edwards, McInerney, Angell	3,086	11		2			14			10		9									4		7	12	8	8			3	1	6		5
3319	Oct 7	(h)	Hereford U	W 2-1	Edwards, Angell	3,428	11		2		3				10		9	12				6				4		7			8				1	8		5
3320	14	(a)	Gillingham	W 3-0	Angell 2, Edwards	3,950	11		2		3				10		9					6				4		7			8				1	6		5
3321	16	(h)	Southend U	W 1-0	Angell	6,593	11		2		3				10		9					6				4		7			8				1	6		5
3322	21	(a)	Peterboro' U	L 0-2		4,804	11				3						9	8				6		10		4		7						12	1	2		5
3323	28	(a)	Exeter C	W 2-1	McInerney, Edwards	3,767	11		2		3				10		9					6				4		7			8				1	8		5
3324	Nov 1	(h)	Lincoln C	D 0-0		5,003	11		2		3				10		9					6				4		7			8				1	6		5
3325	3	(h)	Halifax T	L 0-1		5,490	11		2		3				10		9					6				4		7			8				1	6		5
3326	11	(a)	Chesterfield	D 1-1	McInerney	4,585	11		2		3				10		9					6				4		7			8				1	6		5
3327	25	(h)	Scunthorpe U	W 4-2	Payne, Angell 3 (1 pen)	3,259	11		2						10		9	4				6						7			8			3	1	6		5
3328	Dec 2	(a)	Doncaster R	L 1-2	Matthews	3,023	11	7									9					6				4				10	8			3	1	6	12	5
3329	9	(a)	Scarborough	L 0-2		1,780	11	12	2	3					10	14	9	4				6						7			8				1			5
3330	17	(a)	Carlisle U	L 1-3	McInerney	4,970	11	7	2								9	4							3			10			8				1	6		5
3331	26	(h)	Rochdale	W 2-1	Angell, Brown	4,216	11		2						10	8	9	4				6			3			7					1					5
3332	29	(h)	Cambridge U	W 3-1	Downes, Edwards 2	3,915	11		2						10	8	9	4				6			3			7					1					5
3333	Jan 1	(h)	Grimsby T	L 2-4	Beaumont, Edwards	5,717	11	11	2		14				10	8	9	4				6			3			7					1				12	5
3334	5	(a)	Colchester U	W 1-0	Frain	3,598	11		2						10	8	9	4				6			3			7				1						5
3335	13	(h)	Burnley	W 3-1	Payne 2, Logan	5,210	11	12	2							8	9	4		14		6			3	10		7				1						5
3336	20	(a)	Torquay U	L 0-3		2,228	11		2							8	9	4				6			3	10		7				1						5
3337	27	(a)	Maidstone U	L 1-2	McInerney	4,161	11		2	3							9	4				6				10		7						12	1	8		5
3338	Feb 3	(h)	Aldershot	D 1-1	Payne	2,771	11		2						10	8	9	12					14					7			4	1		3		6		5
3339	10	(a)	Hartlepool U	L 0-5		2,938	11		2	14					10	4	12	9					7								8	1		3		6		5
3340	13	(a)	York C	W 3-0	Angell 2, McInerney	2,256	11	7	2	3							9					6						10			8	1		4				5
3341	16	(h)	Doncaster R	W 3-1	Edwards 2, Angell	3,609	11	7	2	3							9					6						10			8	1		4				5
3342	24	(a)	Scunthorpe U	L 0-5		3,280	11	7	2	3							9					6			3			10			8	1		4				5
3343	Mar 2	(h)	Colchester U	D 1-1	Angell	3,452	11	7	2	3			12	4	9	8						6						10	1					4				5
3344	9	(h)	Wrexham	L 0-2		4,177	11	14	2	3					9	8	5					6						10	1	12				4		7		
3345	17	(a)	Hereford U	W 2-1	Payne, Beaumont	2,458	11	9	2								12	6	7						3			10	1	8		14		4				5
3346	19	(h)	Gillingham	W 1-0	Edwards	3,378	14	9	2								11	12	6	7					3			10	1	8				4				5
3347	23	(a)	Southend U	L 0-2		3,917	11	1	2						9			7				6			3			10		8				4			12	5
3348	30	(h)	Peterboro' U	D 0-0		3,651	11	1	9	12	2						6		7						3			10		8				4				5
3349	Apr 7	(a)	Exeter C	D 1-1	Angell	4,818	11	1	9			2					10					5		6	3					8				4				
3350	9	(h)	Lincoln C	D 0-1	Angell	3,394	11	1	9								4					6	7	3						8				4				5
3351	14	(h)	Grimsby T	L 2-4	Logan, McInerney	4,065	11	1	9					12			4					6	7	14	3			10		8				2				5
3352	16	(a)	Rochdale	D 1-1	Frain	3,194	11	1	9	14	2	12					4					6	7		3			10		8				5				
3353	20	(h)	Carlisle U	W 3-1	Gannon, Brown, Angell	3,819	11	1	9	10	2						4	8				6	7		3			12						5				
3354	23	(a)	Cambridge U	W 2-0	Angell 2	4,850	11	1	9	10	2						4	8				6	7		3			12						5				
3355	28	(h)	Chesterfield	W 3-1	Opp own-goal, Beaumont, Logan	5,203	11	1	9	10		6					4	8					7	2	3			12						5				
3356	May 5	(a)	Halifax T	W 2-1	Beaumont, McInerney	4,744	11	1	9	10	2	6					4	8				7	14	3				12						5				
			Appearances				43	10	19	4	37	23			23	10	26	25	7	4	1	25	7	4	25	16	1	36	4	5	33	11		6	21	39	2	37
			Sub appearances				1		3	2		4	2	1	1	1	1	4						2						4		3	1		1	3		1	5
			Goals				23		5						1	1	10	2	1						4	2												

FINAL LEAGUE POSITION: 4th in Division Four - Lost in Play-off Semi-final

Brabin played number-7 in Match 3349 and Hart played number- 3 in Match 3311.   Own-goal 1

FA Cup

	Date		Opponent	Res	Scorers	Att	Angell	Beaumont	Brown	Cooke	Edwards	Frain	Jones	Matthews	McInerney	Payne	Siddall	Thorpe	Williams PR	Williams WR
1	Nov 18	(a)	Burnley	D 1-1	Angell	8,030	11	2	3	10	9	14	12	4	7	8	1	6		5
R	21	(h)	Burnley	L 1-2	Edwards	6,257	11	2	3	10	9	14	12	4	7	8	1	6		5
			Appearances				2	2	2	2	2			2	2	2	2	2		2
			Sub Appearances									2	2							
			Goals				1				1									

League Cup

	Date		Opponent	Res	Scorers	Att	Angell	Barnett	Beaumont	Brown	Cooke	Hope	Howard	Jones	Leonard	Logan	Matthews	McDonald	McInerney	Oghani	Payne	Robertson	Siddall	Thorpe	Williams PR	Williams WR
1/1	Aug 21	(h)	Bury	W 1-0	McDonald	2,851		7	2		10	11	14				8	9		12	4	3	1	6		5
1/2	29	(a)	Bury	D 1-1	Matthews	2,590			2	8	9	12					4	10	14	7		3	1		5	6
2/1	Sep 20	(a)	Queen's Park R	L 1-2	McInerney	6,745	11		2		10				12	3	4		7	9	8		1	6		5
2/2	Oct 2	(h)	Queen's Park R	D 0-0		5,997	11		2	3	10	12		6			4	9	7		8		1			5
			Appearances				2	1	4	2	4	1		1		1	4	3	2	1	3	2	4	4		4
			Sub Appearances									3	1		1				1	1						
			Goals														1	1	1							

Average Home League attendance: 3,899
Average Away League attendance: 3,691

1990-91

Column key (player appearance grid, left to right): Alexander, Barras, Beaumont, Brabin, Brown, Bullock, Cooper, Finley, Frain, Francis, Gannon, Kilner, Knowles, Lee, Maguire, Matthews, McInerney, Payne, Redfern, Robertson, Thorpe, Todd, Williams PA, Williams PR, Williams WR

No	Date	V	Opponent	Result	Scorers	Att	Alex	Barr	Beau	Brab	Brow	Bull	Coop	Finl	Frai	Fran	Gann	Kiln	Know	Lee	Magu	Matt	McIn	Payn	Redf	Robe	Thor	Todd	WiPA	WiPR	WiWR
3357	Aug 25	(a)	Halifax T	D 0-0		2,362			10		2	4	1	6	11		8							7		3	9			5	
3358	Sep 1	(h)	Walsall	W 3-0	Beaumont, Payne, P.A.Williams	2,668			**10**		2	3	1	6	11		4					12		7			5	8	9		
3359	Sep 8	(a)	Rochdale	L 0-1		2,825		14	10		2	3	1		11		4					12		7			5	8	9	6	
3360	Sep 14	(h)	Burnley	D 2-2	Payne 2 (1 pen)	3,523	14	6	10		2	3	1		11		4					12		7			5	8	9		
3361	Sep 17	(h)	Carlisle U	W 3-1	P.A.Williams 2, Payne	3,118		3	10		2		1	6			4	8						7			5	11	9		
3362	Sep 22	(a)	Cardiff C	D 3-3	Matthews, Beaumont, P.A.Williams	3,374	12	3	10		2		1	6			4					8		7			5	11	9		
3363	Sep 29	(a)	Hereford U	D 0-0		2,619	9	14			2	3	1	6			4	8				12	10	7			5	11			
3364	Oct 1	(h)	Maidstone U	W 1-0	Frain	3,207	9		10		2	3	1		11		4	8						7			5			6	
3365	Oct 6	(h)	Peterboro'	W 2-1	Beaumont, Payne	2,924	9		10		2	3					4	8				12		7	1		5	11		6	
3366	Oct 13	(a)	Northampton T	L 0-1		3,927	9	14	10		2	3	1				4	8				12		7			5	11		6	
3367	Oct 19	(a)	Aldershot	D 2-2	Payne 2	2,413	9	2	10			3	1				4	8						7			5	11		6	
3368	Oct 22	(h)	Blackpool	D 0-0		4,337	9	2	10	12		3	1				4	8						7			5	11		6	
3369	Oct 26	(h)	York C	W 2-0	Beaumont, Frain	3,196	9	2	10			3	1		11		4	8						7			5			6	
3370	Nov 3	(a)	Scunthorpe U	L 0-3		2,826	9	2	10			3	1		11		4	8						7			5			6	
3371	Nov 10	(h)	Lincoln C	W 4-0	Beaumont 2, Payne (pen), Gannon	2,644	9		10		2	3	1				4	8				12		7			5	11		6	
3372	Dec 1	(h)	Darlington	W 3-1	P.A.Williams, Gannon, Payne	2,938		6	10		2	3	1		11		4	8						7			5		9		
3373	Dec 7	(a)	Torquay U	D 1-1	Beaumont	2,370		6	10		2	3	1		11		4	8						7			5		9		
3374	Dec 16	(a)	Scarborough	W 2-0	P.R.Williams 2	1,154		6	10		2	3			11		4	8	12					7	1		5			9	
3375	Dec 21	(h)	Doncaster R	D 0-0		3,347		6	10		2	3			11		4	8	14	12				7	1		5		9		
3376	Dec 29	(a)	Chesterfield	D 1-1	P.A.Williams	4,307		6	10		2	3			11		4	8						7	1		5		9		
3377	Jan 1	(h)	Gillingham	D 1-1	P.A.Williams	2,859			10		2	3	1		11		4	8	12					7			5		9	6	
3378	Jan 4	(h)	Wrexham	W 2-0	Kilner 2	3,264		5	10		2	3	1		11		4	8						7					9	6	
3379	Jan 12	(a)	Walsall	W 2-0	P.A.Williams 2	4,364		5	10		2	3	1		11	7	4	8											9	6	
3380	Jan 18	(h)	Halifax T	W 5-1	Gannon, Kilner, Brown (pen), Beaumont, P.A.Williams	4,030		6	10		2	3			11	7	4	8				12			1		5	14	9		
3381	Jan 26	(a)	Burnley	L 2-3	Finley, W.R.Williams	8,946		6	10			3	1	5	11	7	4	8											9		2
3382	Jan 29	(a)	Hartlepool U	L 1-3	P.A.Williams	2,384		6	10		2	3	1		11	7	4	8											9	5	
3383	Feb 2	(a)	Carlisle U	L 0-1		2,750		6	10		2	3	1		11	7	4	8				12							9	5	
3384	Feb 23	(a)	Lincoln C	W 3-0	Kilner, Beaumont 2	3,257		5	10		2	3		6		12	7	11	9						1		4		8		
3385	Feb 26	(h)	Cardiff C	D 1-1	Gannon	3,376		5	10		2	3		6		8	7	11	12	9					1		4				
3386	Mar 2	(a)	Darlington	L 0-1		4,046		5	10		2	3		6			7	11				12			1		4		9	8	
3387	Mar 8	(h)	Scarborough	D 2-2	Matthews 2	3,172		6	10		2	3			4	7		11				8			1		5		9	12	
3388	Mar 13	(a)	Maidstone U	W 3-2	Beaumont, Matthews, P.A.Williams	1,412		5	10		2			6		11	7					8					4		9		3
3389	Mar 16	(h)	Hereford U	W 4-2	Beaumont, P.A.Williams, Kilner 2	2,569		5	10		2	6				11	7	8				12					4		9		3
3390	Mar 23	(a)	Peterboro'	D 0-0		7,047		6	10		2				11	7	4	12				8			1		5		9		3
3391	Mar 26	(h)	Rochdale	W 3-0	Kilner, Frain, P.A.Williams	3,697		6	10		2				11	7	4	8	14			12			1		5		9		3
3392	Mar 29	(h)	Hartlepool U	L 1-3	Beaumont	5,217		6	10		2				11	7	4	8	9						1		5				3
3393	Apr 1	(a)	Doncaster R	L 0-1		3,372		5	10		2			6		7	4	8	9			12			1		11				3
3394	Apr 6	(h)	Chesterfield	W 3-1	Kilner, Beaumont, Matthews	3,044		6	10		2				11	7	4		9			8			1		5	12			3
3395	Apr 9	(h)	Northampton T	W 2-0	Francis, Matthews	3,707		6	10		2	14			11	7	4	12	9			8			1		5				3
3396	Apr 13	(a)	Gillingham	W 3-1	Matthews 2, Gannon	2,927		6	10		2				11	7	4	14	9			8			1		5	12			3
3397	Apr 16	(a)	Wrexham	W 3-1	Matthews 2, Francis	1,918		6	10		2				11	7	4		9			8			1		5	12			3
3398	Apr 19	(h)	Aldershot	W 3-2	Matthews, Francis, Beaumont	4,422		6	10		2				11	7	4		9			8			1		5				3
3399	Apr 23	(h)	Torquay U	W 2-1	Matthews, Kilner	4,466		6	10		2				11	7	4		9			8			1		5	12			3
3400	Apr 27	(a)	Blackpool	L 2-3	Finley, Gannon	8,590		6	10		2				11	7	4		9			8			1		5				3
3401	May 4	(h)	York C	W 2-0	Kilner 2 (1 pen)	3,532		6	10		2				11	7	4		9			8			1		5	12			3
3402	May 11	(h)	Scunthorpe U	W 5-0	Matthews 2, Francis 2, Finley	6,212		6	10		2			14	11	7	4		9			8			1		5				3
	FINAL LEAGUE POSITION: 2nd in Division Four – Promoted to Division 3				Appearances		9	37	45		34	29	22	19	43	11	41	21	6	2		22	1	24	24	1	39	12	24	23	17
					Sub Appearances		2	3		1	1			2				3	6			2		7	1		7		1	2	1	1
					Goals				15		1			3	3	5	6	11				14		9					14	2	1

FA Cup

No	Date	V	Opponent	Result	Scorers	Att	Alex	Barr	Beau	Brab	Brow	Bull	Coop	Finl	Frai	Fran	Gann	Kiln	Know	Lee	Magu	Matt	McIn	Payn	Redf	Robe	Thor	Todd	WiPA	WiPR	WiWR
1	Nov 17	(a)	Rotherham U	L 0-1		4,501	9		10		2	3	1				4	8				12		7			5	11		6	
					Appearances		1		1		1	1	1				1	1						1			1	1		1	
					Sub Appearances																	1									
					Goals																										

League Cup

No	Date	V	Opponent	Result	Scorers	Att	Alex	Barr	Beau	Brab	Brow	Bull	Coop	Finl	Frai	Fran	Gann	Kiln	Know	Lee	Magu	Matt	McIn	Payn	Redf	Robe	Thor	Todd	WiPA	WiPR	WiWR
1/1	Aug 27	(h)	Burnley	L 0-2		2,786			10		2	4	1	6	11		8							7		3	12	14	9	5	
1/2	Sep 4	(a)	Burnley	W 1-0	P.A.Williams	3,910			10		2	3	1	6	11		4							7			5	8	9		
					Appearances				2		2	2	2	2	2		2							2		1	1	2	2	1	
					Sub Appearances																							1	1		
					Goals																								1		

Average Home League attendance: 3,562
Average Away League attendance: 3,597

1991-92

No.	Date	Venue	Opponent	Result	Scorers	Att.	Barras	Beaumont	Carstairs	Edwards	Finley	Frain	Francis	Gannon	Kilner	Knowles	Lillis	Loram	Matthews	Miller	Moore	Muir	Paskin	Preece	Redfern	Thorpe	Todd	Ward	Wheeler	Williams PR	Williams WR
3403	Aug 17 (h)		Swansea C	W 5-0	Kilner 2 (2 pens), W.R.Williams, Francis, Frain	4,241	5	10			4	9	7	11	2				12				1					8		3	6
3404	24 (a)		Leyton O	D 3-3	W.R.Williams, Beaumont, Barras	3,650	5	10			4	9	7	12	2				11				1					8	14	3	6
3405	30 (h)		Preston NE	W 2-0	Barras, Gannon	5,405	5	10			4	9	7	11	2				12				1					8		3	6
3406	Sep 3 (a)		Wigan A	W 3-1	P.R.Williams, Wheeler, Francis	3,567	5				4	9	7	11	2								1		6			8	10	3	
3407	6 (h)		Torquay U	W 2-1	Wheeler, Gannon	5,138	5				4		7	11	2			9	12				1		6			8	10	3	
3408	14 (a)		West Brom A	L 0-1		11,845	5				4	9	7	11	2				12			14	1		6			8	10	3	
3409	17 (a)		Exeter C	L 1-2	Francis	2,833	5				4	9	7	11	2				12			14	1	8					10	3	6
3410	21 (h)		Bury	W 2-0	Francis, Gannon	5,083	5			1		12	9	7	11									8			2	4	10	3	6
3411	28 (a)		Stoke C	D 2-2	Lillis, Francis	12,956	5			1			9	7	12	2	11							8			4	10		3	6
3412	Oct 5 (h)		Bradford C	W 4-1	Paskin , Francis, Kilner, Opp own-goal	5,825	5			1			9	7	11	2	12							8			4	10		3	6
3413	12 (a)		Birmingham C	L 0-3		12,364	5	8		1	14		9	7	11	2	12										4	10		3	6
3414	18 (h)		Chester C	L 0-4		4,838	5			1	2	14		7	11	8	9										4	10	12	3	6
3415	25 (a)		Huddersfield T	W 1-0	Gannon	9,229	5	8		1	2			7	12	9											4	3	10	11		6
3416	Nov 1 (a)		Bournemouth	L 0-1		4,649	5	8		1	4			9										2	3	10	11	12	6		
3417	5 (h)		Bolton W	D 2-2	Frain (pen), Matthews	5,036	5	8		1	12	4		7	9	11								2	3	10				6	
3418	23 (a)		Fulham	W 2-1	Francis, Beaumont	3,680		8	3	1	5		9	7	4	11								2		10				6	
3419	26 (a)		Shrewsbury T	L 1-4	Lillis	3,650		8	3	1	5		9	7	12	4	11							2		10				6	
3420	30 (a)		Reading	D 1-1	Wheeler	3,511	5	8	3	1	6	4	9	7	12									2		10	11				
3421	Dec 14 (h)		Peterboro' U	W 3-0	Francis, Frain, Gannon (pen)	2,768	5	10	3	1	6	4	9	7	11	2								14			8	12			
3422	20 (a)		Leyton O	W 1-0	Francis	2,745	5	10		1	6	4	9	7	11	2								3	8						
3423	26 (a)		Preston NE	L 2-3	Opp own-goal, Gannon	6,801	5	10		1	6	4	9	7	11	2							12	3	8						
3424	28 (a)		Swansea C	L 1-2	Preece	4,353	5	10	3	1	6	4		7	2								8			11				12	
3425	Jan 1 (h)		Wigan A	D 3-3	Preece, Francis, Gannon (pen)	4,149	5	10	3	1		4	9	7	12	2								11	6		8				
3426	4 (h)		Brentford	W 2-1	Gannon, Francis	4,421	5	10		1		4	9	7	2									11		3	8				6
3427	11 (a)		Hull C	W 2-0	Preece, Francis	3,982	5	10		1		4	9	7	2									11		3	8				6
3428	18 (a)		Darlington	W 2-0	Ward, Preece	4,186	5	10		1		4	9	7	2									11		3	8				6
3429	Feb 7 (h)		Huddersfield T	D 0-0		7,596	5	10		1	12	4	9	7	2									11		3	8				6
3430	11 (h)		Reading	W 1-0	Finley	3,720	5	10		1	7	4	9		2									11		3	8				6
3431	15 (a)		Peterboro' U	L 2-3	Barras (pen), Preece	5,301	5	10		1	7	4	9		2									11		3	8				6
3432	18 (a)		Hartlepool U	W 1-0	Francis	2,473	5	10		1		4	9	7	2									11		3	8				6
3433	22 (h)		Hull C	D 1-1	Wheeler	4,490	5	10		1		4	9	7	2									11		3	8	12			6
3434	29 (a)		Brentford	L 1-2	Preece	7,484	5	10	3	1		4			2							12		11	7		8	9			6
3435	Mar 3 (a)		Darlington	W 3-1	Preece 3	2,384		10	3	1	5		9	7	4									11	2		8	12			6
3436	6 (h)		Hartlepool U	L 0-1		4,473		6	3	1	5		9	7	14	4		10						11	2		8	12			
3437	10 (a)		Bolton W	D 0-0		7,365	5	10	3	1	4	12	7											11	2		8	9			6
3438	13 (h)		Bournemouth	W 5-0	Gannon 2 (1 pen), Francis, Barras, Preece	3,576	5	10	3	1	6	4	9	7										2		14	8	12			
3439	20 (a)		Shrewsbury T	W 1-0	Wheeler	3,186	5		3	1	6	4		7	12			14						11		2	10	8	9		
3440	24 (a)		Chester C	L 2-3	Gannon, Preece	3,747	5	12	3	1	6	4		7										11		2	10	8	9		14
3441	27 (h)		Fulham	W 2-0	Gannon, Opp own-goal	4,654	5		3	1		4		7	10							9		11		2		8	12		6
3442	31 (h)		West Brom A	W 3-0	Barras, Frain, Preece	6,090	5		3	1		4	9	7	10	12								11		2		8	12		6
3443	Apr 4 (a)		Torquay U	L 0-2		2,693	5		3	1		4		7	10	12	14	9						11		2		8			6
3444	10 (h)		Exeter C	W 4-1	Gannon 3 (1 pen), Preece	4,546	5	10	3	1		4	9	7		12								11		2		8			6
3445	18 (a)		Bury	D 0-0		4,726	5	10	3	1		4	9	7										11		2		8			6
3446	20 (h)		Stoke C	D 0-0		8,129	5	10	3	1		4	9	7		11	14						12			2		8			6
3447	25 (a)		Bradford C	L 0-1		7,099	5	10	3	1		4		7				14				9				2	12	8	11		6
3448	May 2 (h)		Birmingham C	W 2-0	Gannon, Francis	7,840	5	10		1		4	9	7		2								11			3	8	12		6
			Appearances				42	33	20	39	15	37	34	43	13	28	9	1	4			3	3	23	7	33	17	44	13	12	33
			Sub Appearances					1		3	2	1			5	3	2	3	5	3	1	1	2	2		1	2		9	1	2
			Goals				5	2		1		4	15	16	3		2		1				1	13			1	5	1	2

FINAL LEAGUE POSITION: 5th in Division Three - Lost in Play-off Final

Own-goals 3

FA Cup

No.	Date	Venue	Opponent	Result	Scorers	Att.	Barras	Beaumont	Carstairs	Edwards	Finley	Frain	Francis	Gannon	Kilner	Knowles	Lillis	Loram	Matthews	Miller	Moore	Muir	Paskin	Preece	Redfern	Thorpe	Todd	Ward	Wheeler	Williams PR	Williams WR
1	Nov 15 (h)		Lincoln C	W 3-1	Gannon, Opp own-goal, Francis	3,864	5	8		1		4	9	7	11									2			10			3	6
2	Dec 7 (a)		Wigan A	L 0-2		4,168	6	8		1	5	4	9	7	12											3	10	11	2		
			Appearances				2	2		2	1	2	2	2	1									1		1	2	1	2	1	
			Sub Appearances													1													2		
			Goals										1	1																	

Own-goal 1

League Cup

No.	Date	Venue	Opponent	Result	Scorers	Att.	Barras	Beaumont	Carstairs	Edwards	Finley	Frain	Francis	Gannon	Kilner	Knowles	Lillis	Loram	Matthews	Miller	Moore	Muir	Paskin	Preece	Redfern	Thorpe	Todd	Ward	Wheeler	Williams PR	Williams WR
1/1	Aug 20 (h)		Bradford C	D 1-1	Wheeler	3,834	5	10			4	9	7	11	12								1	2			8	14	3	6	
1/2	28 (a)		Bradford C	L 1-3*	Francis	3,806	5	10			4	9	7					11					1	2			8	12	3	6	
			Appearances				2	2			2	2	2	1				1					2	2			2		2	2	
			Sub Appearances													1												2			
			Goals										1																1		

Average Home League attendance: 4,896
Average Away League attendance: 5,647

*After extra-time

1992-93

No.	Date		Venue/Opponent	Result	Scorers	Att.	Barras	Beaumont	Carstairs	Connelly	Duffield	Edwards	Finley	Flynn	Frain	Francis	Gannon	James	Kite	Knowles	Massfield	Matthews	McCord	Miller	Muir	Preece	Redfern	Ryan	Todd	Wallace	Ward	Wheeler	Williams PA	Williams PR	Williams WR
3449	Aug 15	(a)	Wigan A	W 2-1	Beaumont 2	3,536		10				1	6		4	9	7		2					14	11				3		8				5
3450	22	(h)	Burnley	W 2-1	Gannon (pen), Francis	4,953		10				1	6		4	9	7		2						11				3		8				5
3451	29	(a)	Port Vale	D 0-0		6,340		10	8			1	6		4	9	7		2						11				3						5
3452	Sep 2	(a)	West Brom A	L 0-3		12,305		10	8			1	**6**		4	9	7		**2**			11	14	12					3						5
3453	5	(h)	Exeter C	D 2-2	Finley, Gannon	3,759		10	8			1	6		4	9	7		**2**					5	11				3						
3454	12	(h)	Hull C	W 5-3	Muir, Beaumont 2, Francis 2	4,216		**10**	8			1	6		4	9	7			2				5	11	14			12					3	
3455	15	(a)	Bradford C	W 3-2	Muir, Francis, Beaumont	5,070		10	8			1	6		4	9	7			2					11				3						5
3456	19	(a)	Chester C	W 3-0	Francis, Muir, Beaumont	3,627		10	8			1	6		4	**9**	7			2	12			5	11	14			**3**						
3457	25	(h)	Fulham	D 0-0		4,755		10	8			1	**6**		4	9	7	12		**2**	14			5	11				3						
3458	Oct 3	(h)	Swansea C	D 1-1	Ward	4,943		10				1			4	9	7			2				5	11						8			3	6
3459	10	(a)	Mansfield T	L 0-2		3,840		10				1	6		4	9	7			**2**				5	11				3	14	8				
3460	16	(h)	Blackpool	D 0-0		5,682		10				1			4	9	7		2					5					3	11	8				6
3461	24	(a)	Bournemouth	L 0-1		4,058		10	12						4	14	7			**2**				5		9	1		3	11	8				6
3462	30	(h)	Huddersfield T	W 5-0	Preece 2, Francis 2, Ward	5,405		10				5			4	**9**	7		2					14	11	1			3		8				6
3463	Nov 3	(h)	Preston NE	W 3-0	Francis, Preece, Beaumont	4,860		10				5			4	9	7		2						11	1			3		8				6
3464	7	(a)	Brighton & HA	L 4-2		5,742	12	10				5			4	9	7		**2**						11				3	14	8				6
3465	20	(a)	Plymouth A	W 3-0	Francis 2, Preece	5,377	5	10							4	9	7				14				11	1			2		8			3	6
3466	28	(a)	Hartlepool U	L 2-3	Preece, Francis	2,949	5	10							4	9	7		2		14		8		11	1			3						6
3467	Dec 19	(a)	Reading	W 4-2	Gannon 2, Preece, Francis	3,832	5	10	3		1					9	7						4		11				2		8				6
3468	28	(h)	Leyton O	D 1-1	Beaumont	6,368	5	10	3		1				4	9	7				14				11				2		8				6
3469	Jan 9	(h)	Bradford C	D 2-2	Francis, Opp own-goal	4,999	5	10			1					9	7		12		4				11				2	8	14			3	6
3470	16	(h)	Fulham	L 1-2	Gannon (pen)	3,516	5	10			1			12			7		14		4				11				2	8	9		3	6
3471	22	(h)	Chester C	W 2-0	Francis, W.R.Williams	4,427		10			1				4	9	7				5				11				2	8	14		3	6
3472	30	(a)	Burnley	D 1-1	Beaumont	11,228		10			1				4	9	7				5				11				2	8			3	6
3473	Feb 5	(h)	Wigan A	W 3-0	Francis 2, Beaumont	4,800		10			1				4	9	7				5				11				2	8			3	6
3474	9	(h)	Bolton W	W 2-0	Preece, Francis	7,363		10			1				4	9	7				5				11				2	8	14	3	6	
3475	13	(a)	Exeter C	D 2-2	P.A.Williams, Beaumont	2,795		10			1				4		7				5				11				2	8	9	3	6	
3476	16	(h)	Port Vale	W 2-0	Preece, Beaumont	7,449		10			1	6			4		7				14	5			11				2	8	9	3		
3477	20	(h)	West Brom A	W 5-1	Gannon 2, Francis, Carstairs, P.A.Williams	7,181		10	8		1	6				9	7				4	5			11				2	14	3			
3478	28	(h)	Mansfield T	L 0-1		5,307		10	**8**		1	6		12	9	7				4	5			14				2	11	3			
3479	Mar 2	(a)	Rotherham U	W 2-0	Beaumont, Francis	4,275	6	10			1				4	9	7			11	5							2	8	14	3		
3480	5	(a)	Swansea C	D 2-2	Gannon (pen), Francis	4,755	6	10			1				4	9	7			11	5							2	8	14	3		
3481	9	(a)	Stoke C	L 1-2	Francis	17,479	6	10			1				4	9	7				5	11						2	8	14	3		
3482	13	(h)	Brighton & HA	D 0-0		5,298	6				1				4	9	7				5	11	10	2	12	8	14	3				
3483	20	(a)	Preston NE	W 3-2	Duffield 2, Gannon (pen)	5,255		10	2	11	1	6			4	9	7				5							8	3				
3484	23	(h)	Hartlepool U	W 4-1	Francis, Beaumont, Duffield 2	4,154		10	2	11	1	6			4	**9**	7	14			5							8	3				
3485	27	(a)	Plymouth A	W 4-3	P.R.Williams, Francis 3	6,132		10	2	**11**	6	12		4	9	7	14	1			5							8	3				
3486	Apr 3	(h)	Stoke C	D 1-1	Ward	9,402		10	2	**11**		6		4	9	7	12	1			5							8	14	3		
3487	6	(a)	Bolton W	L 1-2	Francis	13,773	6	10				2	4	9	7	11	1				5					12		8	14	3		
3488	9	(h)	Rotherham U	D 2-2	Francis 2	5,440		10	2			6	4	9	7	11	1				5							8	14	3		
3489	12	(a)	Leyton O	L 0-3		4,641		10	**2**	7		6		9	4	11	1				5					12		8		3		
3490	16	(h)	Reading	D 2-2	Gannon 2	5,001			3		1	6	4	9	7						5			11	2			8	10			
3491	24	(a)	Blackpool	L 0-2		7,205	6	10	3	2	11	1	8	4	9	7					5			14					12			
3492	27	(a)	Hull C	W 2-0	Miller, Gannon	4,079		10		14	1	6	4		9	7					5			11	2	3	8				
3493	May 1	(h)	Bournemouth	D 0-0		5,446		**10**			1	6	5	12	9	7	11				4	14			2	3	8				
3494	8	(a)	Huddersfield T	L 1-2	P.A.Williams	7,673		10			1	6	4			7					5	11			2	3	8		9		

FINAL LEAGUE POSITION: 6th in (New) Division Two - Lost in Play-off Semi-final

						Appearances	12	44	13	7	6	35	22	9	37	41	46	4	5	10	7	1	4	36	7	23	6	3	36	5	35		6	24	22
						Sub Appearances	1		1		1			1	3	1			3		3		1	4	4	1	2	5		1	3	3	1	10	1	1
						Goals		14	1		4		1			28	12							1	3	8					3		3		

Own-goal 1

FA Cup

No.	Date		Venue/Opponent	Result	Scorers	Att.	Barras	Beaumont	Carstairs	Connelly	Duffield	Edwards	Finley	Flynn	Frain	Francis	Gannon	James	Kite	Knowles	Massfield	Matthews	McCord	Miller	Muir	Preece	Redfern	Ryan	Todd	Wallace	Ward	Wheeler	Williams PA	Williams PR	Williams WR
1	Nov 14	(a)	York C	W 3-1	Todd, Francis 2	5,640	5	10							4	9	**7**							12		11	1		2		8			3	6
2	Dec 5	(a)	Macclesfield T	W 2-0	Preece, W.R.Williams	5,700	5	10	8			1			4	9	7							12		11			2				3	6	
3	Jan 2	(a)	Derby C	L 1-2	McCord	17,960	5	10				1			12	9	**7**						14	4		11			2		8		3	6	

						Appearances	3	3	1			2			2	3	3						1			3	1		3		2			3	3	
						Sub Appearances									1								1	2							1				
						Goals										2							1			1			1						1

League Cup

No.	Date		Venue/Opponent	Result	Scorers	Att.	Barras	Beaumont	Carstairs	Connelly	Duffield	Edwards	Finley	Flynn	Frain	Francis	Gannon	James	Kite	Knowles	Massfield	Matthews	McCord	Miller	Muir	Preece	Redfern	Ryan	Todd	Wallace	Ward	Wheeler	Williams PA	Williams PR	Williams WR
1/1	Aug 18	(h)	Chester C	D 1-1	Gannon	2,785		10	**8**			1	6		4	9	7		2					5	14	11			3						
1/2	25	(a)	Chester C	W 2-1	Beaumont, Carstairs	4,505		**10**	8			1	6		4	9	7		2	14				5		11			3						
2/1	Sep 23	(h)	Nottingham F	L 2-3	Francis 2	7,968		10	8			1	6		4	9	7	12	2					5	11				3						
2/2	Oct 7	(a)	Nottingham F	L 1-2	Beaumont	15,573		10				1			4	9	7	12	2					5	11	14			3		8				6

						Appearances		4	3			4	3		4	4	4		2	2				4	2	2			4		1				1
						Sub Appearances												2		1					1	1									
						Goals		2	1							2	1																		

Average Home League attendance: 5,504
Average Away League attendance: 6,265

1993-94

No	Date	Opponent	Result	Scorers	Att	Barras	Beaumont	Cantona	Connelly	Edwards	Emerson	Finley	Flynn	Frain	Francis	Gannon	Ironside	James	Kelley	Miller	Murray	Preece	Quinn	Ryan	Todd	Wallace	Ward	Williams P.A.	Williams W.R.
3495	Aug 14 (a)	Plymouth A	W 3-2	Francis 2, Preece	6,863		14	2	1			6	5	4	9					7		11		10		3	8		
3496	21 (h)	Cambridge U	W 3-1	Preece 2, Francis	3,782			1				6	5	4	9	14				7	2	11		10		3	8		
3497	28 (a)	Huddersfield T	D 1-1	Preece	7,053			1				6	5	4	9	2				7		11		10		3	8		
3498	31 (h)	Bradford C	W 4-1	Opp own-goal, Francis, Ryan, Preece	4,236			1				6	5	4	9	2				7		11		10		3	8		
3499	Sep 4 (h)	Wrexham	W 1-0	Ryan	4,886			1				6	5	4	9	2				7		11		10		3	8		
3500	11 (a)	Hartlepool U	L 0-1		2,473		14	12	1			6	5	4	9	2				7		11		10		3	8		
3501	14 (a)	York C	W 2-1	Ryan, Preece	3,606			12	1			6	5	4	9	2			14	7		11		10		3	8		
3502	18 (h)	Burnley	W 2-1	Preece, Ryan	5,122			6	1				5	4	9	2			14	7		11		10		3	8		
3503	25 (h)	Rotherham U	W 2-0	Preece, Ward	4,903			6	1				5	4	9	2				7		11		10		3	8		
3504	Oct 2 (a)	Bournemouth	D 1-1	Francis	4,294			6	1				5	4	9	2	15			7		11		10		3	8		
3505	9 (a)	Brighton & HA	D 1-1	Preece	5,330			6	1				5	4	9	2			14	7		11		10		3	8		
3506	16 (h)	Exeter C	W 4-0	Ryan, Francis, Frain, Ward	4,349		2	6	1				5	4	9				14	7		11		10	3		8		
3507	23 (h)	Fulham	W 1-0	Preece	3,615		2	6	1				5	4	9					7		11		10	3		8		
3508	30 (h)	Swansea C	W 4-0	Francis (pen), Preece 3	4,641		2	6	1				5	4	9	12				7		11		10	3		8		
3509	Nov 2 (h)	Leyton O	W 3-0	Beaumont, Francis, Ryan	4,323		2	6	1				5	4	9	12			14	7		11		10	3		8		
3510	6 (a)	Cardiff C	L 1-3	Frain	4,738		2	6	1				5	4	9	12			14	7		11		10	3		8		
3511	20 (h)	Bristol R	L 0-2		5,250		2	6	1				5	4	9	7					12	11		10	3		8	14	
3512	27 (a)	Hull C	W 1-0	Francis	7,119		2	6	1				5	4	9				10	7		11				3	8		
3513	Dec 11 (a)	Cambridge U	D 0-0		3,239		10		1	8			5	4	9	6				7		11		12	2	3			
3514	17 (h)	Plymouth A	L 2-3	Preece, Frain	4,174		10		1	8			5	4	9	6				7		11		12	2	3	14		
3515	28 (a)	Reading	L 0-2		11,240		10		1	6			5	4	9				12	7		11			2	3	8		
3516	Jan 1 (h)	Barnet	W 2-1	Francis 2	5,121		10			1			5	4	9				14	7		11		6		3	8	2	
3517	3 (a)	Brentford	D 1-1	Francis	6,410		10			1			5	4	9					7		11		14	2	3	8	6	
3518	22 (h)	Brighton & HA	W 3-0	Preece 3	6,657	6	10			1			5	4	9				12	7		11			2	3	8		
3519	Feb 1 (h)	Blackpool	W 1-0	Francis (pen)	5,288	6	10			1			5	4	9					7		11			2	3	8		
3520	5 (h)	Fulham	L 2-4	Francis, Preece	5,488	6	10			1			5	4	9				14	7		11			2	3	8		
3521	12 (a)	Port Vale	D 1-1	Francis	10,628		10	7					5	4	9		1					11		14	2	3	8	6	
3522	19 (h)	Huddersfield T	W 3-0	Opp own-goal, Francis 2	5,071		10	2					5	4	9	7	1					11		14	3		8	6	
3523	Mar 5 (h)	Hartlepool U	W 5-0	Francis 3, Gannon, Flynn	4,076		12	2		4			5		9	7	1			6		11	14	10		3	8		
3524	8 (a)	Wrexham	W 1-0	Wallace	4,756		10	2		4			5		9	7	1			6		11				3	8		
3525	12 (a)	Burnley	D 1-1	Preece	13,130		10	2		4			5		9	7	1			6		11		12		3	8		
3526	15 (h)	York C	L 1-2	Gannon	3,899		10			4			5		9	7	1			6	14	11		12		3	8	2	
3527	19 (a)	Rotherham U	W 2-1	Gannon, Francis	3,755		10						5	4	9	7	1		14	6		11			2	3	8		
3528	26 (h)	Bournemouth	L 0-2		5,277		10	14	3				5	4	9	7	1		12	6		11			2		8		
3529	29 (h)	Brentford	W 3-1	Ward, Francis 2 (1 pen)	4,361		10	6					5	4	9	7	1		11		12				2	3	8		
3530	Apr 2 (a)	Blackpool	L 0-2		5,235		10	14	6					12	9	7	1		9			11			2	3	8	4	
3531	9 (a)	Barnet	D 0-0		1,798		10	2					5	4	9	7		14	1	6		11				3			8
3532	12 (a)	Swansea C	W 2-1	Wallace, Preece	2,483			2					5		9	7			1	4		11		10	3		8	6	
3533	16 (a)	Leyton O	D 0-0		3,984		10	2					5		9	7			1	4		11		14	3		8	6	
3534	19 (h)	Port Vale	W 2-1	Francis 2	5,910			2					5		9	7		14	1	4		11		10	3		8	6	
3535	23 (h)	Cardiff C	D 2-2	Gannon, W.R.Williams	5,455			2					5	12	9	7		14	1	4		11		10	3		8	6	
3536	26 (a)	Bradford C	W 2-1	Wallace, Preece	5,720			2					5		9	7			1	4		11		10	3		8	6	
3537	28 (h)	Reading	D 1-1	Francis	7,221			2					5		9	7			1	4		11		10	3		8	6	
3538	30 (a)	Bristol R	D 1-1	Opp own-goal	4,189		14	2					5		9	7			1	4		11		10	3		8	6	
3539	May 2 (a)	Exeter C	W 2-1	Francis 2	1,992		12	14	2				5		9	7			1	4		11		10	3		8	6	
3540	7 (h)	Hull C	D 0-0		7,666		14		2				5		9	7			1	4		11		10	3		8	6	

FINAL LEAGUE POSITION: 4th in (New) Division Two - Lost in Play-off Final

					Apps	3	26		30	26	7	7	46	32	45	31	10	9	10	36	2	43		26	31	36	34	16	
					Sub appearances	6	3	2		1		1				4	1	15	2	1		1		6	2	1	1		
					Goals		1						1	3	28	4						21		6		3	3		1

Own-goals 3

FA Cup

No	Date	Opponent	Result	Scorers	Att	Barras	Beaumont	Cantona	Connelly	Edwards	Emerson	Finley	Flynn	Frain	Francis	Gannon	Ironside	James	Kelley	Miller	Murray	Preece	Quinn	Ryan	Todd	Wallace	Ward	Williams P.A.	Williams W.R.
1	Nov 13 (a)	Rotherham U	W 2-1	Todd, Preece	4,836		2	6	1				5	4	9	8				7		11		10	12	3			
2	Dec 4 (h)	Halifax T	W 5-1	Frain, Francis 2, Beaumont, Wallace	5,496		10		1	8			5	4	9	6				7		11		14	2	3			
3	Jan 8 (a)	Queen's P'k R	W 2-1	Francis, Preece	7,569	6	10		1				5	4	9					7		11			2	3	8		
4	Feb 9 (h)	Bristol C	L 0-4		7,691	6	10	12	1				5	4	9				14	7		11			2	3	8		

					Apps	2	4		1	4	1		4	4	4	2				4		4		1	4	3	2		
					Sub appearances			1											1					1	1				
					Goals		1							1	3							2			1	1			

League Cup

No	Date	Opponent	Result	Scorers	Att	Barras	Beaumont	Cantona	Connelly	Edwards	Emerson	Finley	Flynn	Frain	Francis	Gannon	Ironside	James	Kelley	Miller	Murray	Preece	Quinn	Ryan	Todd	Wallace	Ward	Williams P.A.	Williams W.R.
1.1	Aug 17 (h)	Hartlepool U	D 1-1	Ryan	2,915		14		1			6	5	4	9					7	2			10		3	8		11
1.2	24 (a)	Hartlepool U	L 1-2	Francis	2,273		14		1			6	5	4	9	10				7		11			2	3	8		

					Apps		2		2			2	2	2	2	1				2	1			2	1	2	2		1
					Sub appearances		2																						
					Goals										1									1					

Average Home League Attendance: 5,094
Average Away League Attendance: 5,376

Season by Season League Record (excluding wartime football) 1891-1994

Season	P	HOME					AWAY					ALL					Pts	Position
		W	D	L	F	A	W	D	L	F	A	W	D	L	F	A		
1891-92	22	5	2	4	18	15	2	0	9	11	29	7	2	13	29	44	16	11/12 in The Combination
1892-93	22	5	4	2	23	13	3	2	6	15	23	8	6	8	38	36	22	6/12 in The Combination
1893-94	18	6	3	0	24	3	1	3	5	9	29	7	6	5	33	32	20	4/10 in The Combination
1894-95	26	8	4	1	31	21	2	1	10	22	48	10	5	11	53	69	25	9/14 in Lancashire League
1895-96	30	8	2	5	36	27	5	1	9	20	42	13	3	14	56	69	29	12/16 in Lancashire League
1896-97	28	9	1	4	31	11	6	0	8	22	30	15	1	12	53	41	31	9/15 in Lancashire League
1897-98	26	10	3	0	34	6	5	1	7	26	21	15	4	7	60	27	34	3/14 in Lancashire League
1898-99	24	7	1	4	27	16	5	1	6	22	25	12	2	10	49	41	26	6/13 in Lancashire League
1899-00	28	13	1	0	56	8	8	2	4	25	15	21	3	4	81	23	45	1/15 in Lancashire League†
1900-01	34	9	2	6	25	21	2	1	14	13	47	11	3	20	38	68	25	17/18 in Div 2 - Re-elected
1901-02	34	8	3	6	25	20	0	4	13	11	52	8	7	19	36	72	23	17/18 in Div 2 - Re-elected
1902-03	34	6	4	7	26	24	1	2	14	12	50	7	6	21	38	74	20	17/18 in Div 2 - Re-elected
1903-04	34	7	7	3	28	23	1	4	12	12	49	8	11	15	40	72	27	16/18 in Div 2 - not re-elected
1904-05	34	14	2	1	46	12	7	5	5	17	16	21	7	6	63	28	49	1/18 in Lancashire Combination‡
1905-06	38	11	6	2	36	16	2	3	14	8	40	13	9	16	44	56	35	10/20 in Div 2
1906-07	38	8	8	3	26	12	4	3	12	16	40	12	11	15	42	52	35	12/20 in Div 2
1907-08	38	9	4	6	35	26	3	4	12	13	41	12	8	18	48	67	32	13/20 in Div 2
1908-09	38	11	2	6	25	19	3	1	15	14	52	14	3	21	39	71	31	18/20 in Div 2
1909-10	38	9	6	4	37	20	4	2	13	13	27	13	8	17	50	47	34	13/20 in Div 2
1910-11	38	10	4	5	27	26	1	4	14	20	53	11	8	19	47	79	30	17/20 in Div 2
1911-12	38	8	5	6	31	22	3	6	10	16	32	11	11	16	47	54	33	16/20 in Div 2
1912-13	38	8	4	7	32	23	0	6	13	24	55	8	10	20	56	78	26	19/20 in Div 2 - Re-elected
1913-14	38	9	6	4	32	18	4	4	11	23	39	13	10	15	55	57	36	12/20 in Div 2
1914-15	38	12	4	3	33	19	3	3	13	21	41	15	7	16	54	60	37	14/20 in Div 2
1919-20	42	11	4	6	34	25	3	5	13	18	37	14	9	19	52	62	37	16/22 in Div 2
1920-21	42	8	6	7	30	24	1	6	14	12	51	9	12	21	42	75	30	22/22 in Div 2 - Relegated
1921-22	38	13	5	1	36	10	11	3	5	24	11	24	8	6	60	21	56	1/20 in Div 3N - Promoted
1922-23	42	10	6	5	32	24	4	2	15	11	34	14	8	20	43	58	36	20/22 in Div 2
1923-24	42	10	7	4	32	21	3	9	9	12	31	13	16	13	44	52	42	13/22 in Div 2
1924-25	42	10	6	5	26	15	3	5	13	11	42	13	11	18	37	57	37	19/22 in Div 2
1925-26	42	8	7	6	34	28	0	2	19	17	69	8	9	25	51	97	25	22/22 in Div 2 - Relegated
1926-27	42	13	4	4	60	31	9	3	9	33	38	22	7	13	93	69	49*	6/22 in Div 3N
1927-28	42	16	5	0	62	14	7	3	11	27	37	23	8	11	89	51	54	3/22 in Div 3N
1928-29	42	19	2	0	77	23	9	4	8	34	35	28	6	8	111	58	62	2/22 in Div 3N
1929-30	42	15	3	3	67	20	13	4	4	39	24	28	7	7	106	44	63	2/22 in Div 3N
1930-31	42	15	5	1	54	19	5	4	12	23	42	20	9	13	77	61	49	7/22 in Div 3N
1931-32	40	12	3	5	31	15	1	8	11	24	38	13	11	16	55	53	37	12/21 in Div 3N
1932-33	42	16	2	3	69	30	5	10	6	30	28	21	12	9	99	58	54	3/22 in Div 3N
1933-34	42	18	3	0	84	23	6	8	7	31	29	24	11	7	115	52	59	3/22 in Div 3N
1934-35	42	15	2	4	57	22	7	1	13	33	50	22	3	17	90	72	47	7/22 in Div 3N
1935-36	42	15	2	4	45	18	5	6	10	20	31	20	8	14	65	49	48	5/22 in Div 3N
1936-37	42	17	3	1	59	18	6	11	4	25	21	23	14	5	84	39	60	1/22 in Div 3N - Promoted
1937-38	42	8	6	7	24	24	3	3	15	19	46	11	9	22	43	70	31	22/22 in Div 2 - Relegated
1938-39	42	13	6	2	57	24	4	3	14	34	53	17	9	16	91	77	43	9/22 in Div 3N
1946-47	42	17	0	4	50	19	7	2	12	28	34	24	2	16	78	53	50	4/22 in Div 3N
1947-48	42	9	6	6	42	28	4	6	11	21	39	13	12	17	63	67	38	17/22 in Div 3N
1948-49	42	13	5	3	44	16	3	6	12	17	40	16	11	15	61	56	43	8/22 in Div 3N
1949-50	42	14	2	5	33	21	5	5	11	22	31	19	7	16	55	52	45	10/22 in Div 3N
1950-51	46	15	3	5	45	26	5	5	13	18	37	20	8	18	63	63	48	10/24 in Div 3N
1951-52	46	12	9	2	47	17	11	4	8	27	23	23	13	10	74	40	59	3/24 in Div 3N
1952-53	46	13	8	2	61	26	4	5	14	21	43	17	13	16	82	69	47	11/24 in Div 3N
1953-54	46	14	6	3	57	20	4	5	14	20	47	18	11	17	77	67	47	10/24 in Div 3N
1954-55	46	13	4	6	50	27	5	8	10	34	43	18	12	16	84	70	48	9/24 in Div 3N

1955-56	46	16	4	3	65	22	5	5	13	25	39	21	9	16	90	61	51	7/24 in Div 3N
1956-57	46	16	3	4	51	26	7	5	11	40	49	23	8	15	91	75	54	5/24 in Div 3N
1957-58	46	15	4	4	54	28	3	7	13	20	39	18	11	17	74	67	47	9/24 in Div 3N
1958-59	46	9	7	7	33	23	4	3	16	32	55	13	10	23	65	78	36	21/24 in Div 3 - Relegated
1959-60	46	15	6	2	35	10	4	5	14	23	44	19	11	16	58	54	49	10/24 in Div 4
1960-61	46	14	4	5	31	21	4	5	14	26	45	18	9	19	57	66	45	13/24 in Div 4
1961-62	44	13	3	6	42	27	4	6	12	28	42	17	9	18	70	69	43	16/23 in Div 4
1962-63	46	9	7	7	34	29	6	4	13	22	41	15	11	20	56	70	41	19/24 in Div 4
1963-64	46	12	7	4	32	19	3	5	15	18	49	15	12	19	50	68	42	17/24 in Div 4
1964-65	46	8	4	11	30	34	2	3	18	14	53	10	7	29	44	87	27	24/24 in Div 4 - Re-elected
1965-66	46	12	4	7	42	29	6	2	15	29	41	18	6	22	71	70	42	13/24 in Div 4
19666-67	46	16	5	2	41	18	10	7	6	28	24	26	12	8	69	42	64	1/24 in Div 4 - Promoted
1967-68	46	16	5	2	49	22	3	4	16	21	53	19	9	18	70	75	47	14/24 in Div 3
1968-69	46	14	5	4	49	25	2	9	12	18	43	16	14	16	67	68	46	9/24 in Div 3
1969-70	46	4	7	12	17	30	2	4	17	10	41	6	11	29	27	71	23	24/24 in Div 3 - Relegated
1970-71	46	12	8	3	28	17	4	6	13	21	48	16	14	16	49	65	46	11/24 in Div 4
1971-72	46	7	10	6	33	32	2	4	17	22	55	9	14	23	55	87	32	23/24 in Div 4 - Re-elected
1972-73	46	14	7	2	38	18	4	5	14	15	35	18	12	16	53	53	48	11/24 in Div 4
1973-74	46	4	12	7	22	25	3	8	12	22	44	7	20	19	44	69	34	24/24 in Div 4 - Re-elected
1974-75	46	10	8	5	26	27	2	6	15	17	43	12	14	20	43	70	38	20/24 in Div 4
1975-76	46	8	7	8	23	23	5	5	13	20	53	13	12	21	43	76	38	21/24 in Div 4 - Re-elected
1976-77	46	10	10	3	29	19	3	9	11	24	38	13	19	14	53	57	45	14/24 in Div 4
1977-78	46	14	4	5	41	19	2	6	15	15	37	16	10	20	56	56	42	18/24 in Div 4
1978-79	46	11	5	7	33	21	3	7	13	25	39	14	12	20	58	60	40	17/24 in Div 4
1979-80	46	9	7	7	30	31	5	5	13	18	41	14	12	20	48	72	40	16/24 in Div 4
1980-81	46	10	5	8	29	25	6	2	15	15	32	16	7	23	44	57	39	20/24 in Div 4
1981-82	46	10	5	8	34	28	2	8	13	14	39	12	13	21	48	67	49**	18/24 in Div 4
1982-83	46	11	8	4	41	31	3	4	16	19	48	14	12	20	60	79	54	16/24 in Div 4
1983-84	46	12	5	6	34	25	5	6	12	26	39	17	11	18	60	64	62	12/24 in Div 4
1984-85	46	11	5	7	40	26	2	3	18	18	53	13	8	25	58	79	47	22/24 in Div 4 - Re-elected
1985-86	46	9	9	5	35	28	8	4	11	28	43	17	13	16	63	71	64	11/24 in Div 4
1986-87	46	9	6	8	25	27	4	6	13	15	42	13	12	21	40	69	51	19/24 in Div 4
1987-88	46	7	7	9	26	26	5	8	10	18	32	12	15	19	44	58	51	20/24 in Div 4
1988-89	46	8	10	5	31	20	2	11	10	23	32	10	21	15	54	52	51	20/24 in Div 4
1989-90	46	13	6	4	45	27	8	5	10	23	35	21	11	14	68	62	74	4/24 in Div 4 (Play-off Semi-Final)
1990-91	46	16	6	1	54	19	7	7	9	30	28	23	13	10	84	47	82	2/24 in Div 4 - Promoted
1991-92	46	15	5	3	47	19	7	5	11	28	32	22	10	14	75	51	76	5/24 in Div 3 (Play-off Final)
1992-93	46	11	11	1	47	18	8	4	11	34	39	19	15	12	81	57	72	6/24 in Div 2§ (Play-off Semi-Final)
1993-94	46	15	3	5	50	22	9	10	4	24	22	24	13	9	74	44	85	4/24 in Div 2§ (Play-off Final)

† Successfully applied for election to the Football League Division 2.

‡ Successfully applied for election to the expanded Football League Division 2.

* Two points deducted for playing an unregistered player (Joe Smith).

** First season of three points for a win.

§ 'New' Division 2.

Football League Games - Complete Record 1900-1994

	HOME						AWAY					TOTAL				
	P	W	D	L	F	A	W	D	L	F	A	W	D	L	F	A
Accrington Stanley	54	16	8	3	58	24	8	4	15	43	54	24	12	18	101	78
AFC Bournemouth	30	7	4	4	20	13	1	1	13	3	22	8	5	17	23	35
Aldershot	48	13	9	2	43	25	0	5	19	18	63	13	14	21	61	88
Arsenal	12	2	3	1	6	3	0	0	6	4	20	2	3	7	10	23
Ashington	8	4	0	0	16	4	1	1	2	3	7	5	1	2	19	11
Aston Villa	2	0	0	1	1	3	0	0	1	1	7	0	0	2	2	10
Barnet	2	1	0	0	2	1	0	1	0	0	0	1	1	0	2	1
Barnsley	74	18	14	5	60	38	6	11	20	27	59	24	25	25	87	97
Barrow	76	30	2	6	111	37	13	6	19	51	57	43	8	25	162	94
Birmingham City	24	7	2	3	19	12	2	2	8	10	27	9	4	11	29	39
Blackburn Rovers	2	0	0	1	0	1	0	0	1	0	3	0	0	2	0	4
Blackpool	54	12	8	7	38	28	4	7	16	20	46	16	15	23	58	74
Bolton Wanderers	12	3	1	2	9	7	1	2	3	6	10	4	3	5	15	17
Bradford	46	14	3	6	44	20	4	3	16	28	49	18	6	22	72	69
Bradford City	86	25	11	7	86	44	14	10	19	53	74	39	21	26	139	118
Brentford	24	6	4	2	17	10	1	2	9	9	26	7	6	11	24	36
Brighton & HA	14	3	2	2	10	7	1	2	4	5	12	4	4	6	15	19
Bristol City	26	2	6	5	16	17	1	1	11	10	51	3	7	16	26	68
Bristol Rovers	8	1	0	3	3	5	1	1	2	3	4	2	1	5	6	9
Burnley	42	11	5	5	37	25	2	6	13	19	46	13	11	18	56	71
Burton Swifts	12	4	1	1	9	3	1	0	5	6	20	5	1	6	15	23
Bury	42	12	4	5	35	20	4	5	12	24	39	16	9	17	59	59
Cambridge United	24	6	3	3	18	11	3	3	6	8	16	9	6	9	26	27
Cardiff City	10	1	2	2	7	9	0	3	2	5	10	1	5	4	12	19
Carlisle United	60	19	5	6	72	26	5	8	17	44	57	24	13	23	116	83
Chelsea	12	2	2	2	8	5	0	2	4	5	12	2	4	6	13	17
Chester City	76	18	11	9	72	45	10	8	20	46	67	28	19	29	118	112
Chesterfield	72	26	7	3	77	30	9	6	21	41	75	35	13	24	118	105
Colchester United	36	6	9	3	17	15	2	4	12	15	44	8	13	15	32	59
Coventry City	12	2	4	0	11	4	0	3	3	4	8	2	7	3	15	12
Crewe Alexandra	104	29	11	12	98	54	15	11	26	72	95	44	22	38	170	149
Crystal Palace	10	2	2	1	10	7	0	1	4	3	12	2	3	5	13	19
Darlington	102	34	12	5	108	37	16	11	24	58	79	50	23	29	166	116
Derby County	24	9	3	0	24	10	1	0	11	4	31	10	3	11	28	41
Doncaster Rovers	76	22	5	11	64	43	8	9	21	40	65	30	14	32	104	108
Durham City	6	3	0	0	10	1	3	0	0	9	2	6	0	0	19	3
Exeter City	44	13	6	3	33	20	4	3	15	24	42	17	9	18	57	62
Fulham	38	8	3	8	25	27	3	1	15	12	46	11	4	23	37	73
Gainsborough T	22	4	2	5	13	15	0	6	5	8	15	4	8	10	21	30
Gateshead	58	19	8	2	67	28	9	3	17	42	53	28	11	19	109	81
Gillingham	26	8	4	1	23	8	4	4	5	16	15	12	8	6	39	23
Glossop	28	9	3	2	37	14	1	5	8	11	32	10	8	10	48	46
Grimsby Town	50	9	10	6	36	27	4	2	19	21	58	13	12	25	57	85
Halifax Town	92	29	9	8	112	45	14	10	22	53	72	43	19	30	165	117
Hartlepool United	116	35	10	13	121	56	13	16	29	58	105	48	26	42	179	161
Hereford United	28	6	4	4	18	17	3	3	8	8	17	9	7	12	26	34
Huddersfield Town	28	7	2	5	24	13	2	5	7	12	28	9	7	12	36	41
Hull City	64	13	12	7	57	45	7	7	18	34	71	20	19	25	91	116
Leeds City	20	6	3	1	21	13	2	2	6	11	25	8	5	7	32	38
Leeds United	6	2	1	0	6	3	1	0	2	2	6	3	1	2	8	9
Leicester City	36	10	3	5	36	22	3	5	10	21	36	13	8	15	57	58
Leyton Orient	52	12	7	7	50	29	3	8	15	21	53	15	15	22	71	82
Lincoln City	92	26	13	7	99	58	9	9	28	38	91	35	22	35	137	149

Luton Town	10	4	1	0	10	3	1	0	4	8	14	5	1	4	18	17
Maidstone United	4	1	0	1	2	2	2	0	0	4	2	3	0	1	6	4
Manchester City	4	0	0	2	1	4	0	0	2	1	7	0	0	4	2	11
Manchester United	18	7	0	2	11	8	0	2	7	7	21	7	2	9	18	29
Mansfield Town	66	19	9	5	70	42	5	9	19	32	61	24	18	24	102	103
Middlesbrough	8	0	1	3	3	7	0	1	3	1	13	0	2	6	4	20
Millwall	8	1	2	1	7	8	1	0	3	5	8	2	2	4	12	16
Nelson	14	7	0	0	26	2	2	3	2	12	15	9	3	2	38	17
New Brighton	34	10	5	2	30	12	5	4	8	18	21	15	9	10	48	33
New Brighton T	2	0	0	1	0	5	0	0	1	0	3	0	0	2	0	8
Newcastle United	2	0	0	1	1	3	0	1	0	0	0	0	1	1	1	3
Newport County	34	9	6	2	28	20	3	4	10	18	32	12	10	12	46	52
Northampton Town	42	11	5	5	31	19	2	7	12	17	42	13	12	17	48	61
Norwich City	4	0	1	1	3	4	1	0	1	3	2	1	1	2	6	6
Nottingham Forest	18	6	3	0	12	4	2	4	3	11	13	8	7	3	23	17
Notts County	18	4	2	3	10	8	1	2	6	7	20	5	4	9	17	28
Oldham Athletic	54	13	6	8	43	29	5	9	13	29	52	18	15	21	72	81
Oxford United	8	0	3	1	1	5	0	2	2	3	6	0	5	3	4	11
Peterborough Utd	38	7	8	4	30	25	3	4	12	15	34	10	12	16	45	59
Plymouth Argyle	12	1	1	4	10	12	2	1	3	11	13	3	2	7	21	25
Portsmouth	8	1	2	1	9	8	0	2	2	2	7	1	4	3	11	15
Port Vale	54	10	8	9	35	34	7	5	15	22	53	17	13	24	57	86
Preston North End	20	4	3	3	14	15	2	2	6	13	28	6	5	9	27	43
Queen's Park R	2	0	0	1	2	3	0	1	0	0	0	0	1	1	2	3
Reading	30	5	8	2	20	12	2	5	8	21	37	7	13	10	41	49
Rochdale	104	29	12	11	108	58	11	17	24	51	76	40	29	35	159	134
Rotherham United	54	16	3	8	55	29	6	8	13	32	45	22	11	21	87	74
Scarborough	8	1	3	0	8	7	1	2	1	4	4	2	5	1	12	11
Scunthorpe United	56	13	10	5	47	29	7	9	12	27	46	20	19	17	74	75
Sheffield United	4	1	1	0	2	1	0	0	2	0	6	1	1	2	2	7
Sheffield Wed	12	3	0	3	4	5	0	1	5	7	21	3	1	8	11	26
Shrewsbury Town	12	3	1	2	12	13	2	2	2	6	5	5	3	4	18	18
Southampton	12	2	2	2	11	6	0	1	5	3	12	2	3	7	14	18
Southend United	22	5	3	3	12	9	2	4	5	8	14	7	7	8	20	23
Southport	86	26	9	8	91	52	8	7	28	35	75	34	16	36	126	127
Stalybridge Celtic	2	1	0	0	4	0	1	0	0	4	0	2	0	0	8	0
Stoke City	18	4	3	2	13	8	1	2	6	5	14	5	5	8	18	22
Swansea City	24	8	1	3	25	11	2	3	7	13	29	10	4	10	36	40
Swindon Town	14	4	0	3	10	9	0	0	7	1	15	4	0	10	11	24
Torquay United	56	14	7	7	35	21	4	9	15	22	51	18	16	22	57	72
Tottenham Hotspur	6	1	0	2	5	7	0	1	2	0	4	1	1	4	5	11
Tranmere Rovers	90	28	9	8	90	40	6	14	25	47	92	34	23	33	137	132
Walsall	28	7	3	4	25	15	5	2	7	13	17	12	5	11	38	32
Watford	12	3	2	1	15	9	1	3	2	3	8	4	5	3	18	17
West Brom A	18	2	2	5	11	11	1	1	7	5	19	3	3	12	16	30
West Ham United	8	3	1	0	5	1	1	0	3	1	9	4	1	3	6	10
Wigan Athletic	12	1	1	4	7	8	2	0	4	8	11	3	1	8	15	19
Wigan Borough	12	4	2	0	15	5	3	0	3	6	9	7	2	3	21	14
Wimbledon	8	0	2	2	3	6	1	0	3	3	7	1	2	5	6	13
Wolverhampton W	32	5	6	5	20	18	1	4	11	11	36	6	10	16	31	54
Workington	38	10	3	6	37	19	5	8	6	19	25	15	11	12	56	44
Wrexham	80	25	10	5	89	41	13	7	20	46	60	38	17	25	135	101
York City	78	27	6	6	81	37	9	10	20	40	61	36	16	26	121	98
	3540	952	439	379	3263	1853	358	411	1001	1769	3309	1310	850	1380	5028	5161

Stockport's FA Cup Record

	P	W	D	L	F	A
Aberystwyth	1	1	0	0	5	0
Accrington Stanley	2	1	0	1	3	2
Ashton North End	2	1	1	0	3	2
Aston Villa	1	0	0	1	0	3
Barnsley	3	2	0	1	6	4
Barnton Rovers	1	1	0	0	6	0
Barrow	4	3	0	1	10	4
Billingham Synthonia	1	1	0	0	3	0
Birmingham City	1	0	0	1	0	1
Bishop Auckland	1	1	0	0	2	0
Blackburn Rovers	1	0	0	1	0	2
Blackpool	2	0	0	2	2	4
Blyth Spartans	4	2	1	1	9	6
Bolton Wanderers	2	1	0	1	5	6
Bradford	1	1	0	0	3	0
Bradford City	4	2	1	1	7	6
Brentford	1	1	0	0	2	1
Bristol City	1	0	0	1	0	4
Bristol Rovers	3	1	1	1	5	6
Burnley	3	0	1	2	3	6
Burton Wanderers	1	0	0	1	0	1
Bury	1	0	0	1	1	8
Buxton	1	1	0	0	2	0
Caernarfon Town	1	0	0	1	0	1
Carlisle United	2	0	0	2	1	3
Catford	1	1	0	0	4	0
Charlton Athletic	1	0	0	1	0	3
Chester	3	3	0	0	10	4
Chesterfield	2	0	0	2	1	6
Crewe Alexandra	8	3	2	3	7	10
Crook Town	1	0	0	1	1	3
Crystal Palace	1	0	0	1	1	2
Darlington	4	1	2	1	6	7
Derby County	1	0	0	1	1	2
Doncaster Rovers	1	1	0	0	2	1
Everton	2	0	0	2	1	6
Fairfield	2	0	0	2	3	8
Fulham	2	0	1	1	1	2
Gainsborough Trinity	1	0	0	1	2	3
Gateshead	3	0	2	1	4	5
Gillingham	1	1	0	0	3	1
Glossop	8	2	3	3	8	8
Grantham	1	0	0	1	1	2
Grimsby Town	2	2	0	0	3	0
Halifax Town	4	3	1	0	9	3
Halliwell Rovers	1	1	0	0	4	2
Hartlepool United	3	2	0	1	5	6
Headington United*	2	0	1	1	0	1
Heywood	1	1	0	0	4	0
Hull City	5	2	2	1	3	2
King's Lynn	1	1	0	0	7	2
Lancaster	2	1	0	1	1	2
Leyton**	1	0	0	1	0	2
Leyton Orient	1	0	0	1	1	2

	P	W	D	L	F	A
Lincoln City	3	1	0	2	5	7
Liverpool	5	0	1	4	3	13
Liverpool South End	1	1	0	0	2	0
Luton Town	2	1	0	1	5	3
Macclesfield Town	3	1	1	1	4	3
Mansfield Town	2	0	0	2	2	5
Middlesbrough	1	0	0	1	0	2
Middleton	1	1	0	0	3	0
Morecambe	1	1	0	0	5	1
Mossley	3	2	1	0	5	2
Nelson	1	0	0	1	1	4
New Brighton	2	0	1	1	5	6
New Brighton Tower	1	0	0	1	0	1
Newcastle United	1	0	0	1	0	4
North Shields	2	2	0	0	10	3
Norwich City	1	0	0	1	0	2
Nottingham Forest	1	1	0	0	2	0
Oswestry Town	2	2	0	0	7	3
Plymouth Argyle	1	0	0	1	2	3
Port Vale	4	0	1	3	1	11
Portsmouth	1	0	0	1	0	7
Preston North End	1	0	0	1	1	3
Queen's Park R.	2	2	0	0	5	2
Rochdale	6	1	3	2	4	4
Rock Ferry	1	1	0	0	2	1
Rotherham United	3	2	0	1	3	2
Runcorn	1	1	0	0	1	0
Scarborough	1	0	0	1	1	2
Scunthorpe United	4	2	1	1	4	4
Sheffield United	3	0	1	2	2	5
Sheffield Wednesday	1	0	0	1	0	2
Shrewsbury Town	5	1	3	1	8	8
Southport	5	3	1	1	11	6
Stafford Rangers	2	0	1	1	0	1
Stalybridge Rovers	3	1	0	2	2	3
Telford United	4	1	1	2	3	5
Torquay United	1	1	0	0	3	0
Tranmere Rovers	2	2	0	0	3	1
Walsall	4	1	1	2	9	7
Walthamstow Ave	3	1	1	1	4	3
Wellington	1	1	0	0	4	1
Welsh Druids	1	0	0	1	2	3
West Auckland	1	1	0	0	6	2
West Bromwich A.	1	0	0	1	0	5
West Ham United	3	1	1	1	4	4
Wigan Athletic	2	1	0	1	2	3
Willenhall Pickwick	1	1	0	0	2	0
Workington	4	4	0	0	7	1
Wrexham	4	3	0	1	19	8
York City	1	1	0	0	3	1
Home†	104	59	18	27	197	106
Away‡	113	31	20	62	145	217
Neutral	4	1	0	3	6	9
TOTAL	221	91	38	92	348	332

* Now Oxford United.
** The Amateur team and not associated with Leyton Orient.
† Includes two ties where County were drawn at home (v Fulham and Aston Villa) but which, by mutual agreement, were played at the opposition's ground.
‡ Includes one tie where County were drawn away (to Heywood) but which, by mutual agreement, was played at Edgeley Park.

Stockport's League Cup Record

	P	W	D	L	F	A		P	W	D	L	F	A
Arsenal	1	0	0	1	1	3	Oldham Athletic	2	0	1	1	2	4
Blackburn Rovers	3	1	0	2	3	5	Port Vale	1	1	0	0	2	0
Bolton Wanderers	2	0	1	1	2	5	Preston North End	1	0	0	1	0	1
Bradford City	5	1	3	1	6	6	Queen's Park R	2	0	1	1	1	2
Burnley	2	1	0	1	1	2	Rochdale	5	3	1	1	11	7
Bury	4	2	2	0	4	2	Sheffield Wed.	3	0	0	3	3	15
Carlisle United	3	1	0	2	2	4	Shrewsbury Town	2	1	0	1	3	2
Chester City	5	2	2	1	5	5	Southport	2	0	0	2	2	5
Crewe Alexandra	3	1	1	1	4	2	Sunderland	2	1	1	0	3	2
Crystal Palace	4	2	1	1	3	8	Tranmere Rovers	5	1	2	2	6	8
Derby County	1	0	0	1	1	5	Walsall	1	1	0	0	1	0
Everton	1	0	0	1	0	1	Watford	1	0	0	1	0	1
Hartlepool United	2	0	1	1	2	3	West Ham United	1	1	0	0	2	1
Hull City	1	0	0	1	1	4	Wigan Athletic	6	1	2	3	5	8
Leyton Orient	1	0	0	1	0	1	Workington	4	1	2	1	4	3
Liverpool	2	0	1	1	0	2	Wrexham	2	0	1	1	1	2
Manchester City	1	0	0	1	0	3	Home†	46	13	13	20	49	66
Manchester United	1	0	0	1	2	3	Away	37	7	10	20	34	69
Norwich City	1	0	0	1	1	5	Neutral	2	2	0	0	4	0
Nottingham Forest	2	0	0	2	3	5	TOTAL	85	22	23	40	87	135

† This includes three games where County were drawn at home but where the tie was not played at Edgeley Park: v Manchester United, played at Old Trafford by mutual agreement; v Bolton Wanderers, played at Burnden Park as Edgeley Park had not been granted the required safety certificate following the Bradford City fire, and v Sheffield Wednesday, played at Maine Road on the grounds of safety.

Stockport County in 1973-74. Back row (left to right): Lawther, Ogley, Clarke, Russell. Middle row: A.Kirk (president), Shannon, Broomfield, Hollis, Ormrod, Wilson, Collier, Common, J.Mulvaney (trainer), T.McCreery (secretary). Front row: Fogarty, Spratt, Garbett, B.Doyle (manager), Davidson, Charter, Griffiths.

Divisional Competitions

Third Division North Challenge Cup

1933-34
Round 1
23 Jan 1934 v Rochdale (a) 4-2
Lythgoe 2, Stevenson, Foulkes
McGann; Vincent, Jenkinson, Robinson, Stevens, L.Jones, Foulkes, Hill, Lythgoe, Stevenson, Downes.
Att: Unknown
Round 2
19 Feb 1934 v Accrington Stanley (h) 1-0
Hill
McGann; Vincent, Jenkinson, Robinson, Stevens, L.Jones, Foulkes, Hill, Humpish, Stevenson, Downes.
Att: 1,689
Round 3
Bye
Semi-final
16 Apr 1934 v Mansfield Town (h) 4-0
H.W.Taylor 2, Lythgoe 2
Finnegan; Vincent, Jenkinson, Robinson, Stevens, J.Taylor, Foulkes, H.W.Taylor, Lythgoe, Stevenson, Downes.
Att: 3,419
Final
1 May 1934 v Darlington (at Old Trafford) 3-4
Lythgoe, Vincent (pen), Stevenson
Finnegan; Vincent, Jenkinson, Robinson, Stevens, L.Jones, Foulkes, Humpish, Lythgoe, Stevenson, Downes.
Att: 5,000

1934-35
Round 1
27 Feb 1935 v Accrington Stanley (a) 2-1
Collins 2
McDonough; Bocking, Jenkinson, H.W.Taylor, Jones, Still, Stanger, Hill, Collins, Green, Dunkerley.
Att: 500
Round 2
11 Mar 1935 v Halifax Town (a) 0-0
McDonough; Wilson, Jenkinson, Robinson, Jones, J.Taylor, Stanger, Hill, Collins, Green, Dunkerley.
Att: 1,570
Replay
20 Mar 1935 v Halifax Town (h) 3-1
McNaughton, Bullock, Stevenson
McDonough; Bocking, Jenkinson, H.W.Taylor, Jones, J.Taylor, Foulkes, Hill, McNaughton, Stevenson, Bullock.
Att: 2,225
Round 3
25 Mar 1935 v Rochdale (h) 3-0
Dunkerley 2, Hill
McDonough; Bocking, Jenkinson, Robinson, Jones, J.Taylor, Foulkes, Hill, McNaughton, Stevenson, Dunkerley.
Att: 1,400
Semi-final
8 Apr 1935 v Hartlepools United (h) 6-2
Green 2(1 pen), Collins 3, Foulkes
McDonough; Wilson, Jenkinson, Robinson, Jones, J.Taylor, Foulkes, Hill, Collins, Green, Hales.
Att: 1,318
Final
1 May 1935 v Walsall (at Maine Road) 2-0
McNaughton, Opp own-goal
McDonough; Bocking, Jenkinson, Robinson, Jones, Still, Foulkes, Hill, McNaughton, Green, Scott.
Att: 6,000

1935-36
Round 1
26 Sep 1935 v Barrow (a) 0-2
McDonough; Bocking, Jenkinson, Robinson, Jones, Taylor, Pollock, Hill, Mawson, McNaughton, Tidman.
Att: 2,609

1936-37
Round 1
30 Sep 1936 v Crewe Alexandra (a) 3-3
Reid 2, Hill
McDonough; Bocking, Jenkinson, Smith, L.Jones, Still, Gore, Hill, Reid, Harker, Smailes.
Att: 500
Replay
26 Oct 1936 v Crewe Alexandra (h) 4-2
Hill, Stevens, Sullivan 2
Daniels; Bocking, Walton, Molloy, Beardshaw, Still, Gore, Hill, Stevens, Harker, Sullivan.
Att: 700
Round 2
8 Feb 1937 v Port Vale (a) 0-4
McDonough; Beasley, Brown, Molloy, Beardshaw, Still, Gore, Rice, Stevens, Lovery, Sullivan.
Att: 150

1938-39
Did not enter as the competition was restricted to those Division Three North clubs who had not reached the third round of the FA Cup.

Associate Members Cup
(Later the Freight/Rover Trophy (1985-86, 1986-87), the Sherpa Van Trophy (1987-88, 1988-89), the Leyland Daf Cup (1989-90, 1990-91) and the Autoglass Cup (1991-92, Present)

1983-84
Round 1
22 Feb 1984 v Crewe Alexandra (h) 2-2 a.e.t.
Thorpe, Kerr
Salmon; Jones, Rutter, Emerson, Bowles, Thorpe, Smith, Evans, Kerr, Parker(Leigh), Coyle.
Att: 1,692
Stockport lost 3-0 on penalties

1984-85
Round 1 (1st leg)
29 Jan 1985 v Burnley (a) 1-5
Emerson
Salmon; Rutter, Sherlock, Emerson, Sword, Thorpe(Smith), Power(Buxton), Kerr, Hendrie, Crawford, Evans.
Att: 1,432
Round 1 (2nd leg)
4 Feb 1985 v Burnley (h) 0-1
Salmon; Rutter, Sherlock, Emerson, Sword, Smith, Evans, Hendrie, Kerr, Crawford, Raynes.
Att: 1,568

1985-86
Preliminary Round
14 Jan 1986 v Crewe Alexandra (a) 1-4

Leonard (pen)
Walker; Evans, Matthewson, Wroe, Thorpe, Williams, Hodkinson, Hendrie, Leonard, Power, Coyle.
Att: 994

Preliminary Round
20 Jan 1986 v Bolton Wanderers (h) 2-2
Leonard 2
Walker; Evans, Rutter, Chapman, Sword, Thorpe, Hodkinson, Hendrie, Leonard, Power, Coyle.
Att: 1,874

1986-87
Preliminary Round
6 Dec 1986 v Bury (a) 1-3
Entwistle
Walker; Evans, McKenzie, Edwards, Matthewson, Stokes, Hodkinson, Entwistle, Allatt, Robinson, Mossman(Bailey).
Att: 1,261

Preliminary Round
8 Dec 1986 v Carlisle United (h) 0-1
Walker; Evans, McKenzie, Edwards, Matthewson, Stokes, Hodkinson, Entwistle(Bailey), Allatt(Stevens), Robinson, Mossman.
Att: 1,000

1987-88
Preliminary Round
27 Oct 1987 v Preston North End (a) 2-5
Birch, Colville
Marples; Bullock, Bailey, Robinson, Pickering, Williams, Hodkinson, Colville, Entwistle, Hartford, Birch.
Att: 1,968

Preliminary Round
24 Nov 1987 v Bolton Wanderers (h) 1-3
Farnaby
Marples; Bullock, Bailey, Robinson, Scott, Williams, Edwards, Colville, Entwistle(Hodkinson), Farnaby(Hendrie), Birch.
Att: 2,123

1988-89
Preliminary Round
28 Nov 1988 v Crewe Alexandra (h) 1-1
Wylde
Gorton; Butler, Hart, Bullock, Thorpe(Scott), Howard, Wylde, Colville, Angell, Caldwell, Logan(McKenzie).
Att: 1,328

Preliminary Round
5 Dec 1988 v Tranmere Rovers (a) 1-2
Bullock
Crompton; Butler, Hart, Pickering, Thorpe, Williams, Wylde (Howard), Colville, Angell, Bullock, Logan.
Att: 1,494

1989-90
Preliminary Round
28 Nov 1989 v Burnley (a) 2-0
Beaumont, Angell
Siddall; Bullock, Robertson, Frain, Jones, Thorpe, Beaumont, Payne, Edwards(McInerney), Cooke(Downes), Angell.
Att: 3,352

Preliminary Round
13 Dec 1989 v Preston North End (h) 2-4
Angell (pen), Thorpe
Shepherd; Leonard, Logan(Bullock), Frain, W.R.Williams, Thorpe, McInerney, Payne, Edwards(P.R.Williams), Beaumont, Angell.
Att: 1,545

Round 1
9 Jan 1990 v Carlisle United (a) 2-1 a.e.t.
Angell, Edwards
Redfern; Bulock, Logan, Frain, W.R.Williams, Jones, Beaumont (Cooke), Downes, Edwards, McInerney, Angell.
Att: 2,814

Round 2
30 Jan 1990 v Halifax Town (a) 1-3 a.e.t.

Angell
Siddall; Brown, Robertson(P.R.Williams), Downes, W.R.Williams, Thorpe, Payne, Knowles, Beaumont, Frain, Angell.
Att: 1,779

1990-91
Preliminary Round
27 Nov 1990 v Crewe Alexandra (a) 1-1
P.A.Williams
Cooper; Brown, Robertson, Frain, Thorpe, Barras, Payne, Knowles, P.A.Williams, Beaumont, P.R.Williams(Alexander).
Att: 1,927

Preliminary Round
8 Jan 1991 v Burnley (h) 1-1
Gannon
Cooper; Brown, Bullock, Frain, W.R.Williams, Barras, Gannon, Knowles, P.A.Williams, Matthews, Kilner.
Att: 1,707

Round 1
22 Jan 1991 v Burnley (a) 2-3 a.e.t.
Kilner, P.R.Williams
Redfern; Thorpe, Bullock(Beaumont), Frain, Barras, Finley, Gannon, Knowles(P.R.Williams), P.A.Williams, McInerney, Kilner.
Att: 3,578

1991-92
Preliminary Round
19 Nov 1991 v Carlisle United (a) 0-4
Edwards; Thorpe, P.R.Williams(Todd), Frain, Barras, W.R.Williams, Gannon, Beaumont, Francis, Ward, Lillis(Kilner).
Att: 894

Preliminary Round
7 Jan 1992 v York City (h) 3-0
Gannon 3 (1 pen)
Edwards; Thorpe, Knowles, Frain, Barras, Holmes, Gannon, Lillis, Francis, Beaumont(Carstairs), Moore(Kilner).
Att: 1,397

Round 1
14 Jan 1992 v Carlisle United (a) 3-1
Francis 3
Edwards; Knowles, Todd, Frain, Barras, W.R.Williams, Gannon, Ward, Francis, Lillis, Wheeler.
Att: 1,243

Round 2
4 Feb 1992 v Hartlepool United (h) 3-0
Francis 3
Edwards; Knowles, Todd, Frain, Barras, W.R.Williams, Gannon, Ward, Francis, Lillis, Wheeler(Finley).
Att: 2,255

Semi-final
17 Mar 1992 v Crewe Alexandra (a) 2-1
Ward, Wheeler
Edwards; Thorpe, Carstairs, Frain, Barras, Finley, Gannon, Ward, Francis, Todd, Wheeler.
Att: 5,594

Northern Section Final (1st leg)
7 April 1992 v Burnley (a) 1-0
Francis
Edwards; Thorpe, Carstairs, Frain, Barras, W.R.Williams, Gannon, Ward, Francis, Knowles, Wheeler.
Att: 13,259

Northern Section Final (2nd leg)
15 April 1992 v Burnley (h) 2-1
Francis, Gannon
Edwards; Thorpe, Carstairs, Frain, Barras, W.R.Williams, Gannon, Ward, Francis, Beaumont, Wheeler.
Att: 8,260

Final
16 May 1992 v Stoke City (at Wembley) 0-1
Edwards; Knowles, Todd, Frain(Thorpe), Barras, W.R.Williams, Gannon, Ward, Francis, Beaumont, Wheeler(P.R.Williams).
Att: 48,339

1992-93
Preliminary Round
8 Dec 1992 v Chesterfield (a) 3-0
Francis 2, Preece
Edwards; Todd, Carstairs, Frain, Barras, W.R.Williams, Gannon, McCord, Francis, Beaumont(Wallace), Preece.
Att: 1,956
Preliminary Round
15 Dec 1992 v Chester City (h) 2-0
Preece 2
Edwards; Todd, Carstairs, Frain(Wheeler), Barras, Miller (Fitzsimonds), Gannon, Ward, Francis, Beaumont, Preece.
Att: 2,062
Round 1
12 Jan 1993 v Hartlepool United (h) 1-0
Preece
Edwards; Todd, P.R.Williams, Frain, Barras, Gannon, Miller, Ward, P.A.Williams, McCord(Beaumont), Preece.
Att: 2,383
Round 2
2 Feb 1993 v Bradford City (a) 4-3
Ward 2, Francis 2
Edwards; Todd, P.R.Williams, Frain, Miller, W.R.Williams, Gannon, Ward, Francis, Beaumont, Preece.
Att: 2,790
Semi-final
23 Feb 1993 v Chesterfield (h) 2-1
P.A.Williams, Francis
Edwards; W.R.Williams, P.R.Williams, McCord, Miller, Finley, Gannon, Carstairs, Francis, Beaumont, P.A.Williams.
Att: 4,613
Northern Section Final (1st leg)
16 Mar 1993 v Wigan Athletic (a) 1-2
Gannon
Edwards; Knowles(Wallace), P.R.Williams(Carstairs), Frain, Miller, Finley, Gannon, Ward, Francis, Todd, P.A.Williams.
Att: 4,136
Northern Section Final(2nd leg)
20 Apr 1993 v Wigan Athletic (h) 2-0
Ward, Francis
Edwards; Todd, Carstairs, Frain, Miller, Barras, Gannon, Ward (P.R.Williams), Francis, Beaumont, Duffield.
Att: 6,315
Final
22 May 1993 v Port Vale (at Wembley) 1-2
Francis
Edwards; Todd, Wallace, Miller, W.R.Williams, Finley, Gannon, Ward, Francis, Beaumont(Preece), Duffield.
Att: 35,885

1993-94
Preliminary Round
28 Sep 1993 v Wigan Athletic (h) 2-0
Preece, Gannon
Edwards; Gannon, Wallace, Frain, Flynn, Connelly, Miller, Ward, Francis, Ryan, Preece.
Att: 2,393
Preliminary Round
11 Nov 1993 v Bury (a) 3-1
Preece 2, Francis
Edwards; Beaumont, Carstairs, Frain, Flynn, Connelly, Miller, Ward (Gannon), Francis, Ryan(James), Preece.
Att: 1,737
Round 1
30 Nov 1993 v Rochdale (h) 4-0
Beaumont 2, Frain, Preece
Edwards; Beaumont, Todd, Frain, Flynn, Connelly(Barras), Miller, Wallace, Gannon, Ryan(James), Preece.
Att: 2,484
Round 2
11 Jan 1994 v Scunthorpe United (h) 2-0
Preece, Francis
Edwards; Todd, Wallace, Frain, Flynn, Barras, Miller, Ward,

Francis, Beaumont, Preece.
Att: 4,404
Semi-final
1 Mar 1994 v Huddersfield Town (h) 0-1
Ironside; Connelly, Todd, Frain, Flynn, W.R.Williams(Wallace), Gannon, Ward, Francis, Beaumont, Preece(Ryan).
Att: 4,980

Divisional Play-offs
1989-90 - Division 4
Semi-final (1st leg)
13 May 1990 v Chesterfield (a) 0-4
Barrett; Leonard, Logan(Knowles), Frain, Thorpe, Bullock, McInerney, Gannon, Beaumont, Brookman(Brabin), Angell.
Att: 8,277
Semi-final (2nd leg)
16 May 1990 v Chesterfield (h) 0-2
Barrett; Brown(Bullock), P.R.Williams, Frain, Thorpe, Jones, Knowles(Brookman), Beaumont, Brabin, McInerney, Angell.
Att: 7,339

1991-92 - Division 3
Semi-final (1st leg)
10 May 1992 v Stoke City (h) 1-0
Ward
Edwards; Knowles(Wheeler), Todd, Frain, Barras, W.R.Williams, Gannon, Ward, Francis, Beaumont, Preece.
Att: 7,537
Semi-final (2nd leg)
13 May 1992 v Stoke City (a) 1-1
Beaumont
Edwards; Knowles, Todd, Frain, Barras, W.R.Williams, Gannon, Ward, Francis, Beaumont, Preece(Wheeler).
Att: 16,170
Final
24 May 1992 v Peterborough United (at Wembley) 1-2
Francis
Edwards; Knowles, Todd, Frain, Barras, W.R.Williams, Gannon, Ward(Wheeler), Francis, Beaumont, Preece
Att: 35,087

1992-93 (New) Division 2
Semi-final (1st leg)
16 May 1993 v Port Vale (h) 1-1
Gannon (pen)
Edwards; Todd, Wallace, Flynn, W.R.Williams, Finley, Gannon (Miller), Ward, P.A.Williams, Beaumont, Ryan(Duffield).
Att: 7,856
Semi-final (2nd leg)
20 May 1993 v Port Vale (a) 0-1
Edwards; Todd, Wallace, Flynn, Miller, W.R.Williams, Gannon (Miller), Ward, P.A.Williams, Beaumont, Ryan.
Att: 12,689

1993-94 (New) Division 2)
Semi-final (1st leg)
15 May 1994 v York City (a) 0-0
Keeley; Todd, Wallace, Connelly, Flynn, W.R.Williams, Gannon, Ward, Francis, Beaumont, Preece.
Att: 8,744
Semi-final (2nd leg)
18 May 1994 v York City (h) 1-0
Beaumont
Keeley; Todd, Wallace, Connelly, Flynn, W.R.Williams, Gannon, Ward, Francis, Beaumont, Preece.
Att: 6,743
Final
29 May 1994 v Burnley (at Wembley) 1-2
Beaumont
Keeley; Todd, Wallace, Connelly, Flynn, W.R.Williams(Preece), Gannon(Miller), Ward, Francis, Beaumont, Frain.
Att: 44,806

Football League Attendances 1925-1994

Season	Total	Ave	Highest	Lowest	Total	Ave	Highest	Lowest
			HOME				**AWAY**	
				DIVISION TWO				
1925-26	169,811	8,086	11,762 v Middlesbrough	3,953 v Derby County	253,838	12,088	29,139 v Chelsea	5,464 v Darlington
				DIVISION THREE NORTH				
1926-27	188,961	8,998	22,622 v Stoke City	3,689 v Accrington S	121,370	5,780	12,592 v Stoke City	1,521 v Ashington
1927-28	179,711	8,561	15,775 v Bradford	4,120 v Wrexham	120,762	5,751	13,582 v Bradford City	1,781 v Durham City
1928-29	250,897	11,947	24,311 v Bradford City	7,197 v Barrow	161,498	7,690	18,896 v Bradford City	1,399 v Ashington
1929-30	200,383	9,542	22,668 v Port Vale	4,140 v New Brighton	140,749	6,702	14,494 v Port Vale	2,899 v Darlington
1930-31	145,869	6,946	14,804 v Lincoln City	2,953 v Wrexham	109,109	5,196	12,516 v Wigan Boro'	1,593 v Nelson
1931-32	102,945	5,147	9,753 v Lincoln City	1,997 v Doncaster R	100,185	5,009	8,655 v Gateshead	1,741 v New Brighton
1932-33	109,146	5,210	8,438 v Darlington	2,501 v Barrow	112,766	5,370	8,883 v Hull City	2,261 v New Brighton
1933-34	187,822	8,944	21,309 v Chesterfield	3,790 v Rochdale	146,514	6,977	26,366 v Barnsley	2,665 v Accrington S
1934-35	154,398	7,352	14,196 v Chester	1,714 v Accrington S	112,537	5,359	10,052 v Doncaster R	2,440 v Chesterfield
1935-36	150,476	7,166	12,661 v Barrow	3,008 v Hartlepools Utd	126,991	6,047	10,500 v Chester	2,208 v Wrexham
1936-37	231,238	11,011	26,135 v Lincoln City	5,368 v New Brighton	171,897	8,186	23,142 v Oldham Ath	2,294 v Rotherham Utd
				DIVISION TWO				
1937-38	302,383	14,399	24,386 v Manchester Utd	7,772 v Barnsley	352,981	16,809	31,852 v Manchester Utd	6,215 v Bradford
				DIVISION THREE NORTH				
1938-39	187,614	8,934	17,860 v Barnsley	2,160 v York City	133,599	6,362	19,146 v Barnsley	2,150 v BradfordCity
1946-47	186,501	8,881	14,408 v Rochdale	5,610 v New Brighton	169,236	8,059	17,209 v Hull City	2,271 v Gateshead
1947-48	231,410	11,020	15,087 v Halifax Town	8,198 v Crewe Alex	211,131	10,054	27,410 v Hull City	3,881 v Chester
1948-49	229,143	10,912	16,898 v Oldham Ath	6,954 v Hartlepools Utd	211,955	10,093	38,192 v Hull City	2,944 v Halifax Town
1949-50	252,069	12,003	20,873 v Hartlepools U	3,385 v Rotherham Utd	203,939	9,711	23,363 v Doncaster R	5,132 v Barrow
1950-51	230,144	10,006	14,937 v Rotherham Utd	5,264 v Accrington S	200,607	8,722	18,646 v Oldham Ath	2,124 v New Brighton
1951-52	276,684	12,030	24,473 v Oldham Ath	6,334 v York City	245,413	10,670	33,450 v Oldham Ath	4,716 v Wrexham
1952-53	183,830	7,993	16,552 v Oldham Ath	3,619 v Bradford	197,454	8,585	27,681 v Oldham Ath	2,741 v Crewe Alex
1953-54	176,597	7,678	11,840 v Port Vale	2,939 v Scunthorpe Utd	181,903	7,909	19,513 v Port Vale	2,483 v Southport
1954-55	168,801	7,339	13,144 v Accrington S	2,933 v York City	158,568	6,894	9,956 v Scunthorpe Utd	924 v Gateshead
1955-56	166,970	7,260	12,206 v Accrington S	3,552 v Halifax Town	164,267	7,158	20,073 v Derby County	1,601 v Gateshead
1956-57	223,234	9,706	15,652 v Rochdale	3,698 v Southport	221,959	9,650	22,916 v Derby County	3,170 v Gateshead
1957-58	229,905	9,996	15,551 v Oldham Ath	7,326 v Darlington	188,779	8,208	15,976 v Bury	3,070 v Hartlepools Utd
				DIVISION THREE				
1958-59	212,861	9,255	17,315 v Bury	4,060 v Southampton	230,935	10,041	22,717 v Norwich City	2,447 v Newport County
				DIVISION FOUR				
1959-60	150,707	6,552	11,882 v Crystal Palace	3,585 v Workington	159,422	6,931	18,534 v Crystal Palace	1,868 v Gateshead
1960-61	149,639	6,506	11,374 v Oldham Ath	3,549 v Barrow	162,000	7,043	15,822 v Crystal Palace	1,730 v Barrow
1961-62	104,237	4,738	10,565 v Oldham Ath	2,352 v Bradford City	138,987	6,318	13,624 v Oldham Ath	2,940 v Workington
1962-63	93,397	4,061	10,617 v Oldham Ath	1,966 v Aldershot	133,178	5,790	16,472 v Oldham Ath	2,152 v Darlington
1963-64	98,332	4,275	7,901 v Doncaster R	1,935 v Halifax Town	122,050	5,307	12,846 v Gillingham	2,308 v Southport
1964-65	131,991	5,739	10,334 v Brighton & HA	3,083 v Doncaster R	142,097	6,178	21,442 v Brighton & HA	2,371 v Halifax Town
1965-66	179,442	7,802	15,352 v Barnsley	3,586 v Newport County	110,801	4,817	9,973 v Chester	2,638 v Lincoln City
1966-67	225,861	9,820	13,760 v Southport	7,526 v Bradford	140,880	6,125	11,280 v Crewe Alex	2,351 v Newport County
				DIVISION THREE				
1967-68	190,055	8,263	14,264 v Oldham Ath	5,158 v Bristol Rovers	177,424	7,714	15,479 v Walsall	4,059 v Colchester Utd
1968-69	164,978	7,173	13,246 v Luton Town	2,569 v Tranmere R	174,654	7,594	13,547 v Swindon Town	3,303 v Orient
1969-70	80,606	3,505	5,338 v Rochdale	1,783 v Walsall	180,641	7,854	17,559 v Bristol Rovers	2,960 v Southport
				DIVISION FOUR				
1970-71	75,222	3,271	9,563 v Oldham Ath	1,508 v Southport	113,532	4,936	11,988 v Oldham Ath	1,479 v Newport County
1971-72	56,965	2,477	3,926 v Grimsby Town	1,596 v Gillingham	106,716	4,640	10,445 v Brentford	1,987 v Barrow
1972-73	85,736	3,728	5,905 v Darlington	2,204 v Bradford City	81,074	3,525	10,612 v Hereford United	1,180 v Northampton T
1973-74	54,730	2,380	4,050 v Doncaster R	1,311 v Hartlepool	88,078	3,829	8,272 v Peterborough U	1,341 v Workington
1974-75	48,285	2,099	2,721 v Chester	1,500 v Scunthorpe U	82,828	3,601	10,245 v Mansfield T	1,409 v Workington
1975-76	74,474	3,238	9,220 v Swansea City	1,565 v Hartlepool	84,112	3,657	10,906 v Lincoln City	1,287 v Rochdale
1976-77	85,582	3,851	7,923 v Barnsley	2,318 v Torquay United	89,085	3,873	8,299 v Watford	807 v Workington
1977-78	92,240	4,010	6,177 v Huddersfield T	2,168 v Halifax Town	99,571	4,329	12,754 v Watford	1,776 v Darlington
1978-79	95,271	4,142	9,054 v Barnsley	2,190 v Aldershot	90,396	3,930	9,153 v Barnsley	1,086 v Darlington
1979-80	66,959	2,911	5,369 v Huddersfield T	1,789 v Peterborough U	88,347	3,841	14,942 v Portsmouth	1,233 v Halifax Town
1980-81	53,711	2,335	3,536 v Crewe Alex	1,431 v Torquay United	65,904	2,865	6,120 v Doncaster R	1,694 v Torquay United
1981-82	58,583	2,547	5,450 v Sheffield United	1,357 v Hereford United	68,360	2,972	11,603 v Sheffield United	1,217 v Tranmere R
1982-83	53,118	2,309	5,516 v Port Vale	1,621 v Northampton T	54,026	2,349	5,901 v Hull City	1,012 v Darlington
1983-84	48,246	2,098	2,993 v Doncaster R	1,360 v Darlington	62,344	2,711	9,246 v Bristol City	790 v Hartlepool Utd
1984-85	43,593	1,895	3,546 v Bury	1,039 v Southend United	53,074	2,308	3,943 v Chesterfield	1,006 v Tranmere R
1985-86	61,338	2,667	4,691 v Port Vale	1,354 v Aldershot	60,587	2,634	7,411 v Swindon Town	1,178 v Torquay United
1986-87	48,599	2,113	2,955 v Crewe Alex	1,281 v Colchester Utd	64,990	2,826	7,867 v Preston NE	1,071 v Halifax Town
1987-88	52,250	2,272	4,814 v Bolton W	1,408 v Hartlepool U	69,192	3,008	8,872 v Wolves	1,269 v Hartlepools Utd
1988-89	64,223	2,792	6,676 v Burnley	1,947 v Leyton Orient	70,235	3,054	6,942 v Burnley	1,363 v Doncaster R
1989-90	89,677	3,899	6,593 v Southend United	2,356 v Torquay United	84,882	3,691	6,537 v Burnley	1,780 v Scarborough
1990-91	81,937	3,562	6,212 v Scunthorpe Utd	2,569 v Hereford United	82,722	3,597	8,946 v Burnley	1,154 v Scarborough
				DIVISION THREE				
1991-92	112,599	4,896	8,129 v Stoke City	2,745 v Leyton Orient	129,878	5,647	12,956 v Stoke City	2,384 v Darlington
				DIVISION TWO‡				
1992-93	126,585	5,504	9,402 v Stoke City	3,759 v Exeter City	144,105	6,265	17,479 v Stoke City	2,795 v Exeter City
1993-94	117,156	5,094	7,666 v Hull City	3,782 v Cambridge Utd	123,650	5,376	13,130 v Burnley	1,798 v Barnet

‡ 'New' Division Two which, for the general purposes of all records, is incorporated within information on Division Three.

Complete Career Records With Stockport County

The following should be noted when reading players' career details.Under 'Surname', an '*' indicates that the only appearances made were as a guest player during the war years whilst '‡' indicates that, although the player was at some time registered with County, at least one appearance was made as a guest player during the war years. With regard to 'First names', in some cases neither christian names nor initials have been discovered. 'Pos' gives a guide to the position in which individual players normally played. Since the 1966 World Cup, positions have become rather blurred and outfield players have been loosely categorised into 'defenders', 'midfield' and 'forwards'. The abbreviations used are as follows: CF=Centre-forward; CH=Centre-half; D=Defender; F=Forward; F/D=Forward who became a defender; FB=Full-back; GK=Goalkeeper; HB=Half-back; IF=Inside-forward; IL=Inside-left; IR=Inside-right; LB=Left-back; LH=Left-half; M=Midfield; M/D=Midfield player who became a defender; OL=Outside-left; OR=Outside-right; RB=Right-back and RH=Right-half. Within the heading 'Seasons played – No', a number in parenthesis shows the number of 'spells' the player had at the club. The heading 'Divisional' includes the Football League Third Division North Challenge Cup which ran from 1932-33 to 1938-39 (in which County competed every season other than 1937-38, when they were in Division Two, and 1938-39, when the competition was restricted to those clubs who had not reached the third round of the FA Cup) and the Associate Members Cup (variously called the Autoglass Cup, the Leyland Daf Cup, the Sherpa Van Trophy and the Freight/Rover Trophy). It also covers the ten Divisional Play-off matches in which County have been involved between 1989-90 and 1993-94. 'Other' incorporates three groups of matches: (i) all wartime regional league and cup games (1915-19 and 1939-46); (ii) the two Football League games of 1939-40 prior to suspension of the League and (iii) all first team league matches outside the Football League between 1891-1900 and 1904-05. 'Other' does not include Lancashire Cup, Cheshire Senior Cup, Cheshire Bowl and Manchester Senior Cup matches, on the basis that it was not unusual for either club involved to play a 'weak' or reserve team. Neither does it include matches against clubs who withdrew from the league in mid-season and whose records were expunged, nor matches which were abandoned.

Surname	First names	Pos	Seasons played First/Last	No	League App	League Gls	FA Cup App	FA Cup Gls	Lge Cup App	Lge Cup Gls	Divisional App	Divisional Gls	TOTAL App	TOTAL Gls	Other App	Other Gls
Aaron	AF	IR	1907-08	1	2	1	0	0	0	0	0	0	2	1	0	0
Abrams	Lawrence	HB	1907-08/1910-11	3	67	9	4	0	0	0	0	0	71	9	0	0
Acton	Alec E	HB	1958-59/1959-60	2	9	0	0	0	0	0	0	0	9	0	0	0
Albeson	Brian	CH	1973-74/1974-75	2	54	1	2	0	1	0	0	0	57	1	0	0
Alexander	Keith	F	1990-91	1	9/2	0	1	0	0	0	0/1	0	10/3	0	0	0
Allan	Richard	FB	1903-04	1	22	0	3	0	0	0	0	0	25	0	0	0
Allatt	Vernon	F	1986-87	1	23/1	10	1	0	0	0	2	0	26/1	10	0	0
Allchurch	Leonard	OR	1965-66/1968-69	4	131	16	8	0	6	0	0	0	145	16	0	0
Allen	Keith	IF	1965-66/1966-67	2	49	15	4	2	2	0	0	0	55	17	0	0
Allman	George	CF	1950-51/1951-52	2	7	1	0	0	0	0	0	0	7	1	0	0
Allport	Arthur	FB	1928-29	1	3	0	0	0	0	0	0	0	3	0	0	0
Ambler	Alfred	HB	1906-07/1907-08	2	24	0	3	0	0	0	0	0	27	0	0	0
Amery	Charles	LB	1937-38	1	1	0	0	0	0	0	0	0	1	0	0	0
Anderson	Christopher S	OR	1953-54	1	34	0	3	0	0	0	0	0	37	0	0	0
Anderson	Frank	LH	1920-21	1	24	3	1	0	0	0	0	0	25	3	0	0
Anderson	Percy A	LH	1953-54	1	1	0	0	0	0	0	0	0	1	0	0	0
Anderson	Thomas C	IF	1960-61/1961-62	2	60	17	5	3	3	1	0	0	68	21	0	0
Andrews	William	IF	1908-09/1909-10	2	13	0	0	0	0	0	0	0	13	0	0	0
Angell	Brett	F	1988-89/1989-90	2	60/10	28	3	1	2	0	8	4	73/10	33	0	0
Angus	Jack W	CF	1892-93	1	0	0	0	0	0	0	0	0	0	0	11	2
Angus	James	CF	1908-09/1909-10	2	9	0	0	0	0	0	0	0	9	0	0	0
Armstrong	George	M	1978-79	1	34	0	3	0	0	0	0	0	37	0	0	0
Arridge	Stuart	FB	1901-02/1902-03	2	63	0	4	0	0	0	0	0	67	0	0	0
Arthur	John	OR	1938-39	1	2	0	0	0	0	0	0	0	2	0	0	0
Ashe	Armour D	RB	1953-54	1	2	0	0	0	0	0	0	0	2	0	0	0
Ashley	Jack	CH	1939-40	1	0	0	0	0	0	0	0	0	0	0	1	0
Ashley	John	GK	1942-43	1	0	0	0	0	0	0	0	0	0	0	8	0
Ashmole	William G	OL	1913-14/1914-15	2	37	9	0	0	0	0	0	0	37	9	0	0
Ashton	Kenneth J	RB	1957-58/1961-62	4	39	0	0	0	1	0	0	0	40	0	0	0
Ashworth	Joseph	D	1972-73	1	14	0	0	0	6	0	0	0	20	0	0	0
Ashworth	Leonard	CF	1900-01	1	15	4	0	0	0	0	0	0	15	4	0	0
Aspinall	Wilfred	IL	1934-35	1	1	1	0	0	0	0	0	0	1	1	0	0
Aston	James	CH	1903-04	1	1	0	0	0	0	0	0	0	1	0	0	0
Atkins	William M	IF	1966-67/1968-69	3	92	37	5	3	5	5	0	0	102	45	0	0
Axon	Tom	HB	1893-94/1899-00	7	0	0	11	4	0	0	0	0	11	4	87	11
Baggeley	Christopher	RH	1910-11	1	1	0	0	0	0	0	0	0	1	0	0	0
Bagley	Thomas H	OR	1938-39/1941-42	4	40	13	5	1	0	0	0	0	45	14	53	9
Bailey	H	CF	1894-95	1	0	0	1	0	0	0	0	0	1	0	17	7
Bailey	Neil	D	1986-87/1987-88	2	50/1	0	5	0	6	0	2/2	0	63/3	0	0	0
Ball		GK	1904-05	1	0	0	0	0	0	0	0	0	0	0	1	0
Barber	Alan	LH	1941-42	1	0	0	0	0	0	0	0	0	0	0	1	0
Barber	Jack	CH	1931-32	1	16	0	0	0	0	0	0	0	16	0	0	0
Barclay	Robert	CF	1948-49	1	1	0	0	0	0	0	0	0	1	0	0	0
Bardsley	Edwin	OL	1904-05/1906-07	3	43	3	10	2	0	0	0	0	53	5	33	6
Bardsley*	Leslie	IR	1944-45	1	0	0	0	0	0	0	0	0	0	0	1	0
Barkas‡	Thomas	IL	1944-45/1948-49	3	44	18	6	3	0	0	0	0	50	21	5	5

Surname	First names	Pos	Seasons played First/Last	No	League App	League Gls	FA Cup App	FA Cup Gls	Lge Cup App	Lge Cup Gls	Divisional App	Divisional Gls	TOTAL App	TOTAL Gls	Other App	Other Gls
Barker	Leonard	OR	1948-49/1950-51	3	40	12	1	0	0	0	0	0	41	12	0	0
Barker	John	OR	1901-02	1	2	0	0	0	0	0	0	0	2	0	0	0
Barlow	Arthur	RB	1924-25	1	1	0	0	0	0	0	0	0	1	0	0	0
Barnard	Arthur	GK	1956-57/1958-59	3	53	0	2	0	0	0	0	0	55	0	0	0
Barnes	Harry	HB	1892-93/1896-97	2	0	0	2	1	0	0	0	0	2	1	12	0
Barnes	JW	OR	1944-45	1	0	0	0	0	0	0	0	0	0	0	1	0
Barnett	Albert	IF	1915-16/1916-17	2	0	0	0	0	0	0	0	0	0	0	19	12
Barras	Anthony	D	1990-91/*	4	94/4	5	7	0	2	0	19/1	0	122/5	5	0	0
Barrett	Louis J	OL	1942-43	1	0	0	0.	0	0	0	0	0	0	0	2	0
Barrett	Scott	GK	1989-90	1	10	0	0	0	0	0	2	0	12	0	0	0
Basford	Samuel	RB	1941-42	1	0	0	0	0	0	0	0	0	0	0	1	o
Batch	Nigel A	GK	1988-89	1	12	0	0	0	0	0	0	0	12	0	0	0
Bates	James	IF	1891-92	1	0	0	0	0	0	0	0	0	0	0	2	1
Bauchop	William F	OL	1909-10/1910-11	2	41	6	0	0	0	0	0	0	41	6	0	0
Baxter		IF	1894-95	1	0	0	0	0	0	0	0	0	0	0	4	1
Baxter	Stuart W	D	1976-77	1	4	0	0	0	0	0	0	0	4	0	0	0
Beards	Alan	OL	1955-56	1	5	0	0	0	0	0	0	0	5	0	0	0
Beardshaw	Ernest	CH	1936-37/1937-38	2	18	0	0	0	0	0	2	0	20	0	0	0
Beasley	J Edward	RB	1936-37	1	0	0	0	0	0	0	1	0	1	0	0	0
Beasley	T	OR	1943-44/1944-45	2	0	0	0	0	0	0	0	0	0	0	3	0
Beattie	Stephen	OR	1920-21	1	20	1	1	0	0	0	0	0	21	1	0	0
Beaumont	Christopher P	F	1989-90/*	5	167/10	37	10	1	9/2	2	29/2	6	215/14	46	0	0
Beaumont	Frank	HB	1964-65/1965-66	2	52/3	4	4	1	1	0	0	0	57/3	5	0	0
Bebbington	Peter	D	1969-70	1	16/1	1	0	0	0	0	0	0	16/1	0	0	0
Beech	Harry	HB	1911-12	1	6	0	1	0	0	0	0	0	7	0	0	0
Beedles	Norman	LB	1930-31/1933-34	4	42	0	2	0	0	0	0	0	44	0	0	0
Beighton	Graham	GK	1961-62/1965-66	5	137	0	3	0	3	0	0	0	143	0	0	0
Bell	Thomas A	RB	1952-53	1	31	0	3	0	0	0	0	0	34	0	0	0
Bennion	John	RH	1960-61	1	26	1	1	0	2	0	0	0	29	1	0	0
Bentham*	Stanley	LB	1944-45	1	0	0	0	0	0	0	0	0	0	0	1	0
Bentley	E	CH	1901-02	1	4	0	0	0	0	0	0	0	4	0	0	0
Bentley	John	OR	1961-62/1962-63	2	49	5	1	1	1	0	0	0	51	6	0	0
Berry	F	GK	1918-19	1	0	0	0	0	0	0	0	0	0	0	1	0
Berry	William	CF	1908-09/1909-10	2	14	3	0	0	0	0	0	0	14	3	0	0
Bertenshaw	James	CF	1913-14/1917-18	2	1	0	0	0	0	0	0	0	1	0	1	0
Best	George	M	1975-76	1	3	2	0	0	0	0	0	0	3	2	0	0
Beswick	Joseph	IF	1906-07	1	10	0	0	0	0	0	0	0	10	0	0	0
Betteley	William	OL	1898-99/1901-02	4	44	6	6	1	0	0	0	0	50	7	38	19
Betton	Alec	CH	1934-35	1	2	0	0	0	0	0	0	0	2	0	0	0
Betts	James Barry	RB	1957-58/1959-60	3	112	3	10	1	0	0	0	0	122	4	0	0
Bingham	John G	F	1972-73	1	16/4	3	1	0	1	0	0	0	18/4	3	0	0
Birch	Alan	F	1987-88	1	18/2	3	4	0	0	0	2	1	24/2	4	0	0
Birch*	Neville	LB	1942-43	1	0	0	0	0	0	0	0	0	0	0	6	0
Birch	Trevor	RH	1960-61/1961-62	2	43	0	4	0	1	0	0	0	48	0	0	0
Birchenall	Joe	CH	1892-93/1893-94	2	0	0	7	0	0	0	0	0	7	0	33	4
Bircumshaw	Peter B	OL	1963-64	1	17	4	0	0	1	0	0	0	18	4	0	0
Birds	Joseph	GK	1910-11/1920-21	4	37	0	1	0	0	0	0	0	38	0	0	0
Black	Andrew	IF	1950-51/1952-53	3	94	38	7	1	0	0	0	0	101	39	0	0
Blades	Dr	CH	1891-92/1892-93	2	0	0	0	0	0	0	0	0	0	0	20	2
Blair	James	HB	1912-13	1	23	1	2	0	0	0	0	0	25	1	0	0
Blair	Ken	M	1975-76	1	7	0	0	0	0	0	0	0	7	0	0	0
Blears	Harry	FB	1895-96/1898-99	4	0	0	7	0	0	0	0	0	7	0	68	0
Blood	Robert	CF	1924-25/1926-27	3	42	15	3	1	0	0	0	0	45	16	0	0
Bluer	Alfred	HB	1913-14/1917-18	4	32	0	1	0	0	0	0	0	33	0	11	0
Blunt	John	HB	1925-26	1	10	0	0	0	0	0	0	0	10	0	0	0
Blyth	LR	GK	1944-45	1	0	0	0	0	0	0	0	0	0	0	2	0
Boardman	Benjamin	IR	1924-25/1930-31	7	185	31	10	2	0	0	0	0	195	33	0	0
Bocking	William	FB	1924-25/1937-38	11(2)	366	6	24	0	0	0	6	0	396	6	0	0
Bodle	Harold	IF	1952-53	1	29	6	3	3	0	0	0	0	32	9	0	0
Bolton	William Henry	HB	1897-98/1898-99	2	0	0	4	0	0	0	0	0	4	0	34	0
Bond	Sam	LH	1927-28	1	1	0	0	0	0	0	0	0	1	0	0	0
Booth	A	OL	1944-45	1	0	0	0	0	0	0	0	0	0	0	1	0
Booth	David C	F	1979-80/1980-81	2	20/8	4	0	0	0	0	0	0	20/8	4	0	0
Booth	Frank	OL	1901-02	1	6	1	0	0	0	0	0	0	6	1	0	0
Booth	JM	GK	1944-45	1	0	0	0	0	0	0	0	0	0	0	1	0
Bostock	Joseph	FB	1905-06	1	1	0	0	0	0	0	0	0	1	0	2	0
Boullemier		GK	1895-96	1	0	0	1	0	0	0	0	0	1	0	3	0
Bowcock*	D	IL	1918-19	1	0	0	0	0	0	0	0	0	0	0	1	0
Bowles‡	John Charles	GK	1938-39/1952-53	11	275	0	31	0	0	0	0	0	306	0	34	0
Bowles	Paul MA	D	1982-83/1984-85	3	67/3	0	2	0	7/1	0	1	0	77/4	0	0	0
Brabin	Gary	M	1989-90/1990-91	2	1/1	0	0	0	0	0	1/1	0	2/2	0	0	0

Surname	First names	Pos	Seasons played First/Last	No	League		FA Cup		Lge Cup		Divisional		TOTAL		Other	
					App	Gls	App	Gls	App	Gls	App	Gls	App	Gls	App	Gls
Bradbury ·	OR		1896-97	1	0	0	0	0	0	0	0	0	0	0	2	0
Bradd	Les	F/D	1978-79/1980-81	3	116/1	31	6	2	9	2	0	0	131/1	35	0	0
Bradley	Clifford	RB	1906-07	1	1	0	0	0	0	0	0	0	1	0	0	0
Bradley	Lee	M	1975-76	1	39/1	4	1	0	0	0	0	0	40/1	4	0	0
Bradley*	J	LH	1916-17	1	0	0	0	0	0	0	0	0	0	0	1	0
Brannigan	Kenneth	D	1986-87	1	8	0	0	0	0	0	0	0	8	0	0	0
Brennan	Bryan	CF	1950-51	1	4	0	0	0	0	0	0	0	4	0	0	0
Brennan	Michael	F	1971-72	1	18	3	0	0	0	0	0	0	18	3	0	0
Brennan	Thomas	CF	1919-20	1	1	0	0	0	0	0	0	0	1	0	0	0
Brennan	Thomas J	IL	1935-36	1	10	2	0	0	0	0	0	0	10	2	0	0
Bridge	F	OR	1918-19	1	0	0	0	0	0	0	0	0	0	0	5	1
Bridge	Jock	OR	1910-11	1	5	1	0	0	0	0	0	0	5	1	0	0
Bridge	Roger	OR	1897-98/1899-00	3	0	0	6	0	0	0	0	0	6	0	33	9
Brierley	A	OL	1942-43	1	0	0	0	0	0	0	0	0	0	0	1	0
Briggs	John W	OR	1919-20	1	5	1	0	0	0	0	0	0	5	1	0	0
Brinton	John V	OL	1946-47/1947-48	2	58	9	4	2	0	0	0	0	62	11	0	0
Brittleton	J Thomas	IF	1902-03/1904-05	3	45	10	8	0	0	0	0	0	53	10	14	5
Brittleton	Sammy	IR	1904-05	1	0	0	0	0	0	0	0	0	0	0	1	0
Broadbent	Peter A	M	1969-70	1	31	1	4	0	0	0	0	0	35	1	0	0
Broadhurst	Fred	FB	1923-24	1	4	0	0	0	0	0	0	0	4	0	0	0
Brooke	Maurice	CF	1950-51	1	1	0	0	0	0	0	0	0	1	0	0	0
Brookes	John	M	1970-71	1	18/3	3	0	0	0	0	0	0	18/3	3	0	0
Brookes	Thomas	HB	1900-01	1	2	0	0	0	0	0	0	0	2	0	0	0
Brookman	Nicholas A	M	1989-90	1	4/2	0	0	0	0	0	1/1	0	5/3	0	0	0
Brooks	Anthony	IF	1964-65	1	2	0	1	0	0	0	0	0	3	0	0	0
Brooks	Edward A	CF	1920-21/1921-22	2	12	1	1	0	0	0	0	0	13	1	0	0
Broome	Albert H	IF	1926-27/1927-28	2	4	0	0	0	0	0	0	0	4	0	0	0
Broomfield	Ernest	CF	1903-04	1	5	1	0	0	0	0	0	0	5	1	0	0
Broomfield	Ian	F	1972-73/1974-75	3	22/5	1	1	0	1/1	0	0	0	24/6	1	0	0
Brown	Henry	IL	1910-11	1	2	0	0	0	0	0	0	0	2	0	0	0
Brown	J	OL	1903-04	1	5	0	0	0	0	0	0	0	5	0	0	0
Brown	John C	GK	1970-71/1975-76	2(2)	41	0	0	0	2	0	0	0	43	0	0	0
Brown	Malcolm	D	1989-90/1990-91	2	71	3	3	0	6	0	4	0	84	3	0	0
Brown	Norman	IF	1929-30/1931-32	3	47	9	1	0	0	0	0	0	48	9	0	0
Brown	Philip J	M	1986-87	1	23	1	0	0	0	0	0	0	23	1	0	0
Brown	Rimmer	CF	1896-97/1897-98	2	0	0	5	0	0	0	0	0	5	0	28	17
Brown	William	IF	1930-31	1	4	0	0	0	0	0	0	0	4	0	0	0
Brown	William Dewis	HB	1944-45/1949-50	6	65	15	3	0	0	0	0	0	68	15	41	7
Brown	William P	HB	1900-01	1	23	2	0	0	0	0	0	0	23	2	0	0
Brown	William W	FB	1935-36/1937-38	3	8	0	0	0	0	0	2	0	10	0	0	0
Bryant*	William	OR	1945-46	1	0	0	0	0	0	0	0	0	0	0	1	1
Bryden	Thomas	OL	1912-13	1	1	0	0	0	0	0	0	0	1	0	0	0
Buck	George W	OR	1962-63	1	3	0	0	0	0	0	0	0	3	0	0	0
Buckley	Ambrose	LB	1945-46/1946-47	2	11	0	0	0	0	0	0	0	11	0	26	0
Buckley	Ian	M	1975-76/1976-77	2	55/10	2	2	0	1/1	0	0	0	58/11	2	0	0
Bullock	Samuel	OL	1934-35	1	2	0	0	0	0	0	1	1	3	1	0	0
Bullock	Steven	D	1987-88/1990-91	4	106/14	0	7	0	6	0	9/2	1	128/16	1	0	0
Bullough	Dennis R	CF	1919-20/1920-21	2	17	2	0	0	0	0	0	0	17	2	0	0
Bunce	William	FB	1900-01/1901-02	2	14	0	1	0	0	0	0	0	15	0	0	0
Bunner	Henry F	CH	1965-66	1	3	0	0	0	0	0	0	0	3	0	0	0
Burden	Frederick	HB	1908-09/1910-11	3	58	1	5	0	0	0	0	0	63	1	0	0
Burgess	George	FB	1925-26/1927-28	3	18	0	0	0	0	0	0	0	18	0	0	0
Burgess‡	Harry	IF	1925-26/1940-41	5	115	71	6	1	0	0	0	0	121	72	7	6
Burgoyne		IR	1896-97	1	0	0	0	0	0	0	0	0	0	0	1	0
Burke	Steven J	M	1987-88	1	5	0	0	0	0	0	0	0	5	0	0	0
Burns	William	CF	1931-32	1	6	0	0	0	0	0	0	0	6	0	0	0
Burrows (Snr.)	Arthur	RB	1920-21	1	4	0	0	0	0	0	0	0	4	0	0	0
Burrows (Jnr.)	Arthur	HB	1938-39/1946-47	8	5	1	2	0	0	0	0	0	7	1	116	8
Butler	Brian F	D	1988-89	1	32	2	1	0	2	0	2	0	37	2	0	0
Butler	Joseph H	GK	1900-01/1918-19	11(3)	174	0	16	0	0	0	0	0	190	0	70	1
Butler*	Malcolm P	LB	1940-41	1	0	0	0	0	0	0	0	0	0	0	21	1
Butt‡	Leonard H	IR	1929-30/1943-44	3	8	1	0	0	0	0	0	0	8	1	2	1
Butterworth	J	RH	1917-18	1	0	0	0	0	0	0	0	0	0	0	1	0
Butterworth	Thomas	LH	1905-06/1908-09	4	118	0	7	0	0	0	0	0	125	0	0	0
Buxton	Stephen C	M	1984-85	1	12/6	1	0	0	2/1	1	0/1	0	14/8	2	0	0
Byrom	David J	D	1984-85	1	3	0	0/1	0	0	0	0	0	3/1	0	0	0
Caddick	George	HB	1925-26	1	11	1	1	0	0	0	0	0	12	1	0	0
Cahill	Paul G	D	1978-79	1	3	0	0	0	0	0	0	0	3	0	0	0
Caiels	Alfred L	OL	1934-35	1	2	1	0	0	0	0	0	0	2	1	0	0
Caldwell	AJ	OL	1941-42	1	0	0	0	0	0	0	0	0	0	0	1	0
Caldwell	Anthony	F	1988-89/1989-90	2	23/3	6	0	0	0	0	1	0	24/3	6	0	0

Surname	First names	Pos	Seasons played First/Last	No	League App	Gls	FA Cup App	Gls	Lge Cup App	Gls	Divisional App	Gls	TOTAL App	Gls	Other App	Gls
Cammack	Stephen R	F	1985-86	1	3/1	1	0	0	0	0	0	0	3/1	1	0	0
Campbell	Danny	D	1968-69/1969-70	2	31	3	3/1	0	1	0	0	0	35/1	3	0	0
Cant	John L	GK	1934-35	1	1	0	0	0	0	0	0	0	1	0	0	0
Cantona	Joel	M	1993-94	1	0/3	0	0	0	0	0	0	0	0/3	0	0	0
Carr	George	CH	1932-33	1	18	0	2	0	0	0	0	0	20	0	0	0
Carrick	James	LH	1923-24	1	1	0	0	0	0	0	0	0	1	0	0	0
Carson		IL	1896-97	1	0	0	0	0	0	0	0	0	0	0	1	0
Carstairs	James W	D	1991-92/*	3	33/1	1	1	0	3	1	8/2	0	45/3	2	0	0
Carter	Robert	OR	1907-08	1	27	8	1	0	0	0	0	0	28	8	0	0
Cartwright	Ian	GK	1970-71	1	0	0	1	0	0	0	0	0	1	0	0	0
Cassidy	Andrew D	GK	1977-78/1978-79	2	5	0	0	0	0	0	0	0	5	0	0	0
Catlin*	Arthur E	LB	1941-42	1	0	0	0	0	0	0	0	0	0	0	6	0
Catlow*	T	RH	1918-19	1	0	0	0	0	0	0	0	0	0	0	2	0
Catterick (Snr.)	Harry	CH	1926-27	1	13	1	1	0	0	0	0	0	14	1	0	0
Catterick (Jnr.)*	Harry	CF	1939-40/1945-46	7	0	0	0	0	0	0	0	0	0	0	122	98
Causer	A	GK	1917-18	1	0	0	0	0	0	0	0	0	0	0	8	0
Cavanagh	Thomas H	IF	1949-50/1951-52	3	32	2	3	0	0	0	0	0	35	2	0	0
Cawley	Ernest	HB	1927-28/1930-31	4	8	0	1	0	0	0	0	0	9	0	0	0
Cecere	Michael J	F	1989-90	1	0/1	0	0	0	0	0	0	0	0/1	0	0	0
Chadwick	Alfred	FB	1894-95	1	0	0	1	0	0	0	0	0	1	0	14	0
Challinor	Thomas	RH	1917-18/1918-19	2	0	0	0	0	0	0	0	0	0	0	12	0
Chandler	Ian	F	1987-88	1	4/1	0	0	0	0	0	0	0	4/1	0	0	0
Chapman	Edwin	CF	1946-47	1	9	3	0	0	0	0	0	0	9	3	0	0
Chapman	John	D	1969-70/1971-72	3	87/2	5	2/1	0	4	0	0	0	93/3	5	0	0
Chapman	Leslie	M	1979-80/1985-86	2(2)	70	4	2	0	6	0	1	0	79	4	0	0
Chappell	Sidney	HB	1939-40/1942-43	4	0	0	0	0	0	0	0	0	0	0	55	1
Charlesworth*	John Stanley	CH	1943-44	1	0	0	0	0	0	0	0	0	0	0	16	0
Charlton	Thomas	OR	1909-10/1912-13	4	93	26	6	3	0	0	0	0	99	29	0	0
Charter	Raymond	D	1971-72/1973-74	3	87/4	2	4	0	8	1	0	0	99/4	3	0	0
Chesworth	Frank	IF	1898-99/1901-02	3	28	6	6	1	0	0	0	0	34	7	38	26
Childs		GK	1895-96/1898-99	2	0	0	2	0	0	0	0	0	2	0	24	0
Chisnall	Philip	M	1971-72	1	30	2	2	0	0	0	0	0	32	2	0	0
Chivers	William	HB	1912-13/1913-14	2	21	1	1	0	0	0	0	0	22	1	0	0
Chorlton	Thomas	FB	1900-01/1916-17	4	27	0	0	0	0	0	0	0	27	0	1	0
Clark*	Gordon V	FB	1939-40	1	0	0	0	0	0	0	0	0	0	0	4	0
Clarke	Peter A	GK	1971-72/1974-75	3	49	0	0	0	2	0	0	0	51	0	0	0
Clarke	Peter J	HB	1965-66	1	21	2	0	0	0	0	0	0	21	2	0	0
Clarke	Roy J	OL	1958-59	1	25	5	3	1	0	0	0	0	28	6	0	0
Clarke	William	IL	1945-46	1	0	0	1	0	0	0	0	0	1	0	11	1
Clempson	Frank	LH	1952-53/1958-59	7	246	35	15	2	0	0	0	0	261	37	0	0
Clibborn		CH	1897-98	1	0	0	0	0	0	0	0	0	0	0	4	0
Cochrane*	David	OL	1944-45	1	0	0	0	0	0	0	0	0	0	0	2	0
Cockburn	William	CH	1921-22/1923-24	3	73	0	3	0	0	0	0	0	76	0	0	0
Cocker‡	Leslie	CF	1945-46/1952-53	8	173	43	16	5	0	0	0	0	189	48	7	0
Cockhill	Andrew J	M	1986-87	1	3	0	0	0	2	0	0	0	5	0	0	0
Coddington	John W	D	1969-70/1970-71	2	52	0	1	0	1	0	0	0	54	0	0	0
Codling	Roland	LH	1903-04/1904-05	2	28	0	7	0	0	0	0	0	35	0	33	0
Coen*	Lawrence	IR	1945-46	1	0	0	0	0	0	0	0	0	0	0	3	1
Coghlan	HR	CF	1892-93	1	0	0	1	0	0	0	0	0	1	0	1	1
Coleman	Anthony G	M	1974-75/1975-76	2	28/2	3	0	0	1	0	0	0	29/2	3	0	0
Collier	James	M	1968-69/1973-74	6	101/6	12	5	1	3	0	0	0	109/6	13	0	0
Collins	James H	CF	1934-35	1	6	1	0	0	0	0	3	5	9	6	0	0
Collins	John J	FB	1963-64/1965-66	3	84	1	9	0	2	0	0	0	95	1	0	0
Collinson	Roger	RB	1961-62	1	2	0	0	0	0	0	0	0	2	0	0	0
Colquhoun*	Duncan M	IF	1942-43/1943-44	2	0	0	0	0	0	0	0	0	0	0	4	0
Colville	Robert J	F	1987-88/1988-89	2	67/4	19	5	4	1	0	4	1	77/4	24	0	0
Common	Alan R	D	1973-74	1	2/1	0	0	0	0	0	0	0	2/1	0	0	0
Connell	Herbert	CF	1907-08	1	1	0	0	0	0	0	0	0	1	0	0	0
Connelly	Michael	OR	1959-60/1960-61	2	6	0	0	0	0	0	0	0	6	0	0	0
Connelly	Sean	D	1992-93/*	2	37/2	0	1/1	0	0	0	7	0	45/3	0	0	0
Connor	James T	D	1978-79	1	1/1	0	0	0	0	0	0	0	1/1	0	0	0
Connor	John	GK	1981-82	1	1	0	0	0	0	0	0	0	1	0	1	0
Connor	John T (Jack)	CF	1951-52/1956-57	6	206	132	11	8	0	0	0	0	217	140	0	0
Cook	Albert	OL	1907-08	1	4	0	1	0	0	0	0	0	5	0	0	0
Cook	Lawrence	CF	1912-13	1	10	4	2	2	0	0	0	0	12	6	0	0
Cook	Walter	GK	1928-29	1	9	0	2	0	0	0	0	0	11	0	0	0
Cooke		CH	1897-98	1	0	0	0	0	0	0	0	0	0	0	2	0
Cooke	David Frederick	D	1968-69	1	3	0	0	0	2	0	0	0	5	0	0	0
Cooke	John	M	1988-89/1989-90	2	54/4	7	2	0	4/2	0	1/1	0	61/7	7	0	0
Cooper	Harry	OL	1929-30	1	1	0	0	0	0	0	0	0	1	0	0	0
Cooper	Paul D	GK	1990-91	1	22	0	1	0	2	0	2	0	27	0	0	0

Surname	First names	Pos	Seasons played First/Last	No	League App	Gls	FA Cup App	Gls	Lge Cup App	Gls	Divisional App	Gls	TOTAL App	Gls	Other App	Gls
Cope*	George	CH	1944-45	1	0	0	0	0	0	0	0	0	0	0	18	0
Corfield	Ernest	IR	1953-54	1	2	0	1	0	0	0	0	0	3	0	0	0
Cottrell	Ernest P	OR	1903-04	1	1	0	0	0	0	0	0	0	1	0	1	0
Cousins	Harry	IR	1922-23	1	14	3	0	0	0	0	0	0	14	3	0	0
Cox	David	CF	1956-57/1957-58	2	7	4	0	0	0	0	0	0	7	4	0	0
Coxon	E	OR	1894-95	1	0	0	0	0	0	0	0	0	0	0	4	2
Coyle	Anthony	M	1979-80/1988-89	8(2)	238/4	31	7	1	17	1	3	0	265/4	33	0	0
Coyne	John D	F	1975-76	1	3/1	0	0	0	0	0	0	0	3/1	0	0	0
Cragg	Richard	IF	1920-21	1	21	3	1	0	0	0	0	0	22	3	0	0
Craig	Tommy	IF	1891-92	1	0	0	0	0	0	0	0	0	0	0	19	1
Craig	Thomas	RB	1906-07/1907-08	2	36	0	1	0	0	0	0	0	37	0	0	0
Craven	Joseph	CH	1923-24/1924-25	2	5	0	0	0	0	0	0	0	5	0	0	0
Crawford		LH	1896-97	1	0	0	2	0	0	0	0	0	0	0	4	0
Crawford	Andrew	F	1984-85	1	6	2	0	0	0	0	2	0	8	2	0	0
Crawford	James C	OL	1944-45	1	0	0	0	0	0	0	0	0	0	0	3	1
Crawshaw	A	IF	1917-18/1918-19	2	0	0	0	0	0	0	0	0	0	0	27	15
Crawshaw	C	IL	1939-40	1	0	0	0	0	0	0	0	0	0	0	1	0
Cresser	Ernest	LH	1905-06/1906-07	2	12	0	2	0	0	0	0	0	14	0	0	0
Critchley	Edward	OR	1922-23/1926-27	5	118	10	6	0	0	0	0	0	124	10	0	0
Crompton	Jack	GK	1944-45	1	0	0	0	0	0	0	0	0	0	0	4	0
Crompton	Steven G	GK	1987-88	1	2	0	0	0	0	0	1	0	3	0	0	0
Cronin	Denis	F	1987-88	1	11/4	1	0	0	2	0	0	0	13/4	1	0	0
Crosby	Geoffrey J	IF	1952-53/1953-54	2	5	1	0	0	0	0	0	0	5	1	0	0
Cross	Michael J	D	1975-76	1	27	2	1	0	2	0	0	0	30	2	0	0
Crossthwaite	Harold	OR	1912-13/1922-23	10(2)	127	11	4	0	0	0	0	0	131	11	142	19
Crowther	George E	GK	1928-29/1929-30	2	47	0	4	0	0	0	0	0	51	0	0	0
Crowther	Stephen	D	1973-74/1974-75	2	42/2	4	2	0	0	0	0	0	44/2	4	0	0
Crump	Frederick	CF	1905-06/1907-08	3	89	29	6	3	0	0	0	0	95	32	0	0
Cuffe	J	LB	1915-16	1	0	0	0	0	0	0	0	0	0	0	1	0
Cunliffe	James W	CF	1960-61	1	1	0	0	0	0	0	0	1	1	0	0	0
Cunningham	C	IF	1918-19	1	0	0	0	0	0	0	0	0	0	0	21	7
Curran*	Frank	IR	1943-44	1	0	0	0	0	0	0	0	0	0	0	1	1
Curry	Thomas	HB	1928-29/1929-30	2	19	1	0	0	0	0	0	0	19	1	0	0
Curtis	John	OL	1914-15/1918-19	2	15	1	0	0	0	0	0	0	15	1	9	0
Cuthbert	Ean R	LB	1963-64/1965-66	3	93	0	9	0	2	0	0	0	104	0	0	0
Cutler	Reginald V	OR	1962-63	1	34	0	0	0	1	0	0	0	35	0	0	0
Cutting*	Stanley W	RH	1941-42/1942-43	2	0	0	0	0	0	0	0	0	0	0	31	2
Czuczman	Michael	D	1979-80	1	36	7	1	0	4	1	0	0	41	8	0	0
Dainty	Albert	OR	1946-47/1948-49	3	36	16	2	0	0	0	0	0	38	16	0	0
Daley	Alan J	OL	1955-56/1957-58	3	73	17	2	1	0	0	0	0	75	18	0	0
Daniels	Barney	F	1976-77/1977-78	2	45/2	17	1	0	5/1	2	0	0	51/3	19	0	0
Daniels	John Francis	GK	1935-36/1937-38	3	9	0	0	0	0	0	1	0	10	0	0	0
Danskin	Charles	OL	1919-20/1920-21	2	56	6	1	0	0	0	0	0	57	6	0	0
Darling	Malcolm	F	1976-77	1	11	2	0	0	0	0	0	0	11	2	0	0
Davenport	Carl	IF	1962-63/1963-64	2	16	3	0	0	0	0	0	0	16	3	0	0
Davids	Neil G	D	1975-76	1	5	1	0	0	0	0	0	0	5	1	0	0
Davidson	Ian	M	1972-73/1973-74	2	74/4	6	5	1	9	2	0	0	88/4	9	0	0
Davies	G	HB	1899-00	1	0	0	1	0	0	0	0	0	1	0	1	0
Davies	David Walter	IF	1912-13	1	11	2	0	0	0	0	0	0	11	2	0	0
Davies	Jack	CF	1939-40	1	0	0	0	0	0	0	0	0	0	0	1	0
Davies	Joseph	IF	1901-02	1	29	7	3	1	0	0	0	0	32	8	0	0
Davies	Seymour	HB	1914-15/1919-20	6	17	0	1	0	0	0	0	0	18	0	4	0
Davies	Wyn	F	1975-76	1	28/2	7	0	0	2	0	0	0	30/2	7	0	0
Davison	Arthur E	RB	1945-46	1	0	0	0	0	0	0	0	0	0	0	6	0
Davock	Michael	OL	1956-57/1963-64	8	235	41	14	5	3	0	0	0	252	46	0	0
Dean	R	CF	1939-40	1	0	0	0	0	0	0	0	0	0	0	1	0
Deere	Stephen	D	1975-76	1	6	0	0	0	0	0	0	0	6	0	0	0
Dennison	Harry	IF	1924-25	1	11	3	0	0	0	0	0	0	11	3	0	0
Devine	Stephen B	D	1985-86	1	2	0	0	0	0	0	0	0	2	0	0	0
Devlin	William	IR	1911-12	1	20	2	3	1	0	0	0	0	23	3	0	0
Diamond	Barry	F	1985-86	1	6	0	0	0	0	0	0	0	6	0	0	0
Dick	George W	IL	1950-51	1	25	12	2	0	0	0	0	0	27	12	0	0
Dickenson	H	RH	1917-18	1	0	0	0	0	0	0	0	0	0	0	1	0
Dighton	Richard	GK	1970-71	1	1	0	0	0	0	0	0	0	1	0	0	0
Dimond*	Stuart	CF	1944-45	1	0	0	0	0	0	0	0	0	0	0	2	2
Dingwall	George	CF	1919-20	1	6	3	0	0	0	0	0	0	6	3	0	0
Dixey	Richard	D	1975-76	1	14	1	0	0	0	0	0	0	14	1	0	0
Dixon		IL	1892-93	1	0	0	0	0	0	0	0	0	0	0	2	0
Dixon	J	CH	1902-03	1	1	0	0	0	0	0	0	0	1	0	0	0
Dixon	Milton	OR	1950-51	1	21	2	2	1	0	0	0	0	23	3	0	0
Dodd	George F	IF	1905-06	1	27	5	1	0	0	0	0	0	28	5	0	0

Surname	First names	Pos	Seasons played First/Last	No	League App	Gls	FA Cup App	Gls	Lge Cup App	Gls	Divisional App	Gls	TOTAL App	Gls	Other App	Gls
Dodd	Samuel	CH	1905-06/1907-08	3	73	3	6	0	0	0	0	0	79	3	0	0
Dolphin	Alfred	OR	1922-23	1	11	0	1	0	0	0	0	0	12	0	0	0
Donbawand	Albert E	CF	1920-21	1	1	0	0	0	0	0	0	0	1	0	0	0
Doncaster	F	IL	1917-18	1	0	0	0	0	0	0	0	0	0	0	1	0
Donnelly	James	OR	1920-21	1	1	0	0	0	0	0	0	0	1	0	0	0
Dooley	W	OL	1917-18	1	0	0	0	0	0	0	0	0	0	0	1	0
Dooner	Gary J	M	1988-89	1	1	0	0	0	0	0	0	0	1	0	0	0
Dowdall	Walter	OL	1902-03/1904-05	2	16	2	1	0	0	0	0	0	17	2	1	0
Downes	Christopher B	M	1989-90	1	10/1	1	0	0	0	0	2/1	0	12/2	1	0	0
Downes	Percy	OL	1932-33/1933-34	2	82	27	4	0	0	0	4	0	90	27	0	0
Downie	E	FB	1900-01	1	7	0	0	0	0	0	0	0	7	0	0	0
Drake	Raymond B	CF	1956-57/1957-58	2	23	19	0	0	0	0	0	0	23	19	0	0
Duckworth	J	LH	1917-18	1	0	0	0	0	0	0	0	0	0	0	1	0
Duddy	John M	M	1975-76	1	6	0	0	0	0	0	0	0	6	0	0	0
Duffield	Peter	F	1992-93	1	6/1	4	0	0	0	0	2/1	0	8/2	4	0	0
Duffus	John	CF	1927-28	1	6	3	2	1	0	0	0	0	8	4	0	0
Dunkerley	John	OL	1934-35	1	9	3	0	0	0	0	3	2	12	5	0	0
Dunn		OR	1894-95	1	0	0	0	0	0	0	0	0	0	0	1	0
Dwyer	Alan	D	1981-82	1	4	0	1	0	0	0	0	0	5	0	0	0
Dyer	Raymond	OL	1956-57	1	1	0	0	0	0	0	0	0	1	0	0	0
Earl	Albert T	IL	1946-47/1947-48	2	42	12	3	1	0	0	0	0	45	13	0	0
Earp	Martin John	FB	1900-01	1	15	1	2	1	0	0	0	0	17	2	0	0
Easdale	John	HB	1948-49	1	6	0	2	0	0	0	0	0	8	0	0	0
East	Keith MG	F	1966-67/1967-68	2	23/2	7	0	0	3	1	0	0	26/2	8	0	0
Eastham	Stanley	RH	1946-47	1	14	1	4	0	0	0	0	0	18	1	0	0
Easthope	Joseph D	OL	1954-55	1	9	2	1	0	0	0	0	0	10	2	0	0
Eaton		IF	1891-92	1	0	0	0	0	0	0	0	0	0	0	2	1
Eaton	Samuel L	OR	1901-02	1	10	1	3	1	0	0	0	0	13	2	0	0
Eckersall	Michael W	HB	1963-64/1965-66	3	39/1	2	6	1	1	0	0	0	46/1	3	0	0
Edgley	Harold	OL	1923-24	1	29	4	2	0	0	0	0	0	31	4	0	0
Edwards	Keith	F	1989-90	1	26/1	10	2	1	0	0	3	1	31/1	12	0	0
Edwards	Levi	M	1986-87/1987-88	2	40/9	5	1	0	3	0	3	0	47/9	5	0	0
Edwards	Neil R	GK	1991-92/*	3	100	0	8	0	6	0	25	0	139	0	0	0
Edwards	Paul	D	1976-77/1979-80	3	66/3	2	2	0	5	0	0	0	73/3	2	0	0
Egerton	Joseph	OL	1940-41	1	0	0	0	0	0	0	0	0	0	0	1	0
Elgin	Robert	M	1969-70/1970-71	2	30/5	3	4	0	1	0	0	0	35/5	3	0	0
Elkin	Bertram H	FB	1908-09/1909-10	2	47	0	3	0	0	0	0	0	50	0	0	0
Ellis	Jack	GK	1944-45	1	0	0	0	0	0	0	0	0	0	0	2	0
Emerson	Dean	M	1981-82/1993-94	5(2)	163/1	7	4	0	10	3	3	1	180/1	11	0	0
Emptage	Albert T	HB	1950-51/1952-53	3	36	1	2	0	0	0	0	0	38	1	0	0
Entwistle	J	IR	1892-93	1	0	0	2	1	0	0	0	0	2	1	20	5
Entwistle	Wayne P	F	1986-87/1987-88	2	38/11	8	3/1	1	0	0	4	1	45/12	10	0	0
Essex	John R	IR	1938-39/1939-40	2	41	13	5	2	0	0	0	0	46	15	5	0
Evans		OL	1896-97	1	0	0	0	0	0	0	0	0	0	0	2	0
Evans	Andrew Clive	D	1983-84/1987-88	5	158/2	23	2/1	0	11	0	7	0	178/3	23	0	0
Evans	Jack	OL	1915-16/1916-17	2	0	0	0	0	0	0	0	0	0	0	8	0
Evans	John	IR	1962-63/1963-64	2	52	20	1	0	1	0	0	0	54	20	0	0
Evans	Ronald	LH	1950-51/1953-54	2	6	0	0	0	0	0	0	0	6	0	0	0
Evans	Thomas L	GK	1913-14/1918-19	3	72	0	2	0	0	0	0	0	74	0	1	0
Evenson	Isaac	HB	1900-01/1902-03	3	34	9	1	0	0	0	0	0	35	9	0	0
Everest	John	CF	1928-29/1929-30	2	7	7	0	0	0	0	0	0	7	7	0	0
Fagan	Stephen	FB	1912-13/1914-15	3	109	0	5	0	0	0	0	0	114	0	0	0
Fallows	L	GK	1941-42	1	0	0	0	0	0	0	0	0	0	0	1	0
Fantham	John T	IR	1930-31	1	3	0	0	0	0	0	0	0	3	0	0	0
Farnaby	Craig	M	1987-88	1	17/5	1	0	0	0	0	1	1	18/5	2	0	0
Farnworth	Simon	GK	1986-87	1	10	0	0	0	2	0	0	0	12	0	0	0
Farrant	SG	IR	1905-06	1	2	0	0	0	0	0	0	0	2	0	0	0
Farrow	George H	IR	1931-32	1	6	0	0	0	0	0	0	0	6	0	0	0
Faulkner	Stephen A	D	1977-78	1	3/1	0	0	0	0	0	0	0	3/1	0	0	0
Fayers‡	Frederick	CH	1915-16/1919-20	5	42	2	1	0	0	0	0	0	43	2	140	14
Feely	Peter	D	1976-77	1	2	0	0	0	0	0	0	0	2	0	0	0
Feeney	Thomas W	IR	1933-34	1	2	0	0	0	0	0	0	0	2	0	0	0
Fenner*	Donald W	IL	1943-44	1	0	0	0	0	0	0	0	0	0	0	1	0
Ferguson	Daniel	RH	1935-36	1	15	0	1	0	0	0	0	0	16	0	0	0
Ferguson	James H	FB	1891-92/1892-93	2	0	0	2	0	0	0	0	0	2	0	27	0
Ferries		OR	1895-96	1	0	0	2	1	0	0	0	0	2	1	24	8
Fielding	Horace	OL	1926-27/1929-30	4	92	16	6	2	0	0	0	0	98	18	0	0
Fielding*	William	GK	1939-40/1941-42	3	0	0	0	0	0	0	0	0	0	0	41	0
Finley	Alan	D	1990-91/*	4	63/3	5	1	0	5	0	6/1	0	75/4	5	0	0
Finnegan	J	IL	1917-18	1	0	0	0	0	0	0	0	0	0	0	1	0
Finnegan	Richard	GK	1933-34/1934-35	2	26	0	3	0	0	0	2	0	31	0	0	0

Surname	First names	Pos	Seasons played First/Last	No	League		FA Cup		Lge Cup		Divisional		TOTAL		Other	
					App	Gls	App	Gls	App	Gls	App	Gls	App	Gls	App	Gls
Finney	Richard Kenneth	F	1947-48/1957-58	11	191	33	7	3	0	0	0	0	198	36	0	0
Fitzsimonds	Stuart	D	1992-93	1	0	0	0	0	0	0	0/1	0	0/1	0	0	0
Flaherty	J	CF	1918-19	1	0	0	0	0	0	0	0	0	0	0	1	0
Fleet	Stephen	GK	1965-66/1967-68	3	36	0	0	0	0	0	0	0	36	0	0	0
Fletcher	Ernest	LB	1903-04/1904-05	2	4	0	0	0	0	0	0	0	4	0	2	0
Fletcher	Harry	CH	1894-95/1896-97	3	0	0	5	2	0	0	0	0	5	2	72	9
Fletcher	James	CF	1959-60/1960-61	2	61	19	4	0	0	0	0	0	65	19	0	0
Fletcher	Peter	F	1976-77/1977-78	2	43/8	13	1	1	7	1	0	0	51/8	15	0	0
Flynn	Michael A	D	1992-93/*	2	55/1	1	4	0	2	0	10	0	71/1	1	0	0
Fogarty	Kenneth	D	1971-72/1979-80	9	265/4	6	13	2	15	1	0	0	283/4	9	0	0
Foley	Charles	M	1969-70/1970-71	2	6	0	0	0	0	0	0	0	6	0	0	0
Forrest	Albert	OL	1920-21	1	1	0	0	0	0	0	0	0	1	0	0	0
Forrester	O	LH	1941-42	1	0	0	0	0	0	0	0	0	0	0	1	0
Foster	John Henry	IF	1900-01	1	12	5	2	0	0	0	0	0	14	5	0	0
Foster	William Joseph	IF	1897-98/1904-05	6	31	9	9	8	0	0	0	0	40	18	80	51
Foulkes	Jabez	OR	1932-33/1935-36	4	143	31	11	4	0	0	8	2	162	37	0	0
Fowler	Martin	M	1980-81/1981-82	2	74/1	6	4	0	5	1	0	0	83/1	7	0	0
Frail	Joseph	GK	1905-06	1	7	0	2	0	0	0	0	0	9	0	0	0
Frain	David	M	1989-90/*	5	174/10	12	9/3	1	11	0	34	1	228/13	14	0	0
France	Anthony	CF	1963-64	1	30	8	1	0	0	0	0	0	31	8	0	0
Francis	J	LH	1916-17/1918-19	3	0	0	0	0	0	0	0	0	0	0	73	7
Francis	Kevin	F	1990-91/*	4	131/4	76	9	6	8	4	25	18	173/4	104	0	0
Franklin	Neil	CH	1957-58	1	20	0	4	0	0	0	0	0	24	0	0	0
Freeborough	James	FB	1902-03/1918-19	3	26	0	4	0	0	0	0	0	30	0	1	0
Froehlich	William	RB	1911-12/1912-13	2	6	0	2	0	0	0	0	0	8	0	0	0
Fryatt	James E	F	1967-68/1974-75	3(2)	46	29	2	0	2	0	0	0	50	29	0	0
Fuller	Richard J	IF	1937-38	1	3	1	0	0	0	0	0	0	3	1	0	0
Gage*	Albert	GK	1944-45	1	0	0	0	0	0	0	0	0	0	0	19	0
Gale	Thomas	GK	1931-32/1932-33	2	57	0	3	0	0	0	0	0	60	0	0	0
Gallagher	Brian	D	1967-68	1	13	0	1	0	3	0	0	0	17	0	0	0
Gallie		OR	1892-93	1	0	0	0	0	0	0	0	0	0	0	2	1
Gallon*	John W	IR	1943-44	1	0	0	0	0	0	0	0	0	0	0	1	0
Galloway	Thomas	HB	1907-08/1910-11	4	77	0	3	0	0	0	0	0	80	0	0	0
Galvin	Christopher	M	1978-79/1980-81	3	67/1	3	1/1	0	7	0	0	0	75/2	3	0	0
Gannon	James P	D	1989-90/*	5	168/4	39	8	1	9	1	30/1	8	215/5	49	0	0
Garbett	W Edward	M	1972-73/1973-74	2	63/7	11	5	0	7/1	1	0	0	75/8	12	0	0
Garfoot	Claude A	LH	1941-42	1	0	0	0	0	0	0	0	0	0	0	1	0
Garner	Herbert	LB	1930-31	1	2	0	0	0	0	0	0	0	2	0	0	0
Garrett	Frederick H	FB	1912-13/1920-21	9	137	8	6	2	0	0	0	0	143	10	73	3
Gaskell	George	FB	1892-93/1893-94	2	0	0	7	0	0	0	0	0	7	0	39	1
Gault	William Ernest	IF	1913-14/1921-22	6(2)	105	32	2	1	0	0	0	0	107	33	53	32
Geddes*	Alec	LB	1943-44	1	0	0	0	0	0	0	0	0	0	0	13	0
Gee‡	Charles W	CH	1929-30/1939-40	2	25	1	2	1	0	0	0	0	27	2	3	0
Gee*	Harold	IR	1943-44/1945-46	3	0	0	0	0	0	0	0	0	0	0	31	9
Gennoe	RA	LB	1944-45	1	0	0	0	0	0	0	0	0	0	0	2	0
Gettins	Edward	FB	1909-10/1910-11	2	62	0	5	0	0	0	0	0	67	0	0	0
Gibbons	David	D	1971-72	1	1	0	0	0	0	0	0	0	1	0	0	0
Gilbert	William A	GK	1954-55	1	33	0	1	0	0	0	0	0	34	0	0	0
Gilliver	Alan	F	1974-75	1	22/3	5	1/1	0	1	0	0	0	24/4	5	0	0
Gilmour	Tom	IR	1942-43	1	0	0	0	0	0	0	0	0	0	0	1	0
Gittins	W	FB	1892-93/1893-94	2	0	0	7	0	0	0	0	0	7	0	35	0
Glaister	George	OL	1946-47/1949-50	4	92	21	12	5	0	0	0	0	104	26	0	0
Glavin	Ronald M	M	1986-87	1	5/5	1	0	0	1/2	0	0	0	6/7	1	0	0
Gleave	Colin	HB	1939-40/1947-48	6	57	1	11	0	0	0	0	0	68	1	56	0
Glover	Bevil A	CH	1947-48/1953-54	7	137	1	9	1	0	0	0	0	146	2	0	0
Goalen	Harold K	OL	1950-51/1955-56	5	18	2	0	0	0	0	0	0	18	2	0	0
Goddard	Artie	OR	1897-98/1899-00	3	0	0	7	1	0	0	0	0	7	1	28	11
Godwin	Richard	FB	1891-92/1894-95	3	0	0	1	0	0	0	0	0	1	0	9	1
Godwin	R	OL	1916-17	1	0	0	0	0	0	0	0	0	0	0	1	0
Golder	James	M	1971-72	1	0/1	0	0	0	0	0	0	0	0/1	0	0	0
Goodchild	J	GK	1918-19	1	0	0	0	0	0	0	0	0	0	0	2	0
Goodfellow	James	M	1978-79	1	2/1	0	0	0	2	0	0	0	4/1	0	0	0
Goodwin	Frederick J	D	1965-66/1974-75	6(2)	200/5	21	13	0	8	0	0	0	221/5	21	0	0
Goodwin	James W	OR	1905-06/1906-07	2	16	1	0	0	0	0	0	0	16	1	0	0
Goodwin	Ralph	FB	1907-08/1920-21	13(2)	180	0	8	0	0	0	0	0	188	0	136	0
Gore	Leslie	OR	1936-37	1	7	1	0	0	0	0	3	0	10	1	0	0
Gorrie	David A	RH	1962-63	1	18	0	0	0	1	0	0	0	19	0	0	0
Gorrie*	Willie	OL	1944-45	1	0	0	0	0	0	0	0	0	0	0	1	1
Gorton	Andrew W	GK	1986-87/1988-89	2(2)	48	0	1	0	2	0	1	0	52	0	0	0
Gotheridge	J	OL	1891-92	1	0	0	0	0	0	0	0	0	0	0	12	2
Gough	Robert G	M	1973-74	1	6	0	0	0	0	0	0	0	6	0	0	0

Surname	First names	Pos	Seasons played First/Last	No	League App	League Gls	FA Cup App	FA Cup Gls	Lge Cup App	Lge Cup Gls	Divisional App	Divisional Gls	TOTAL App	TOTAL Gls	Other App	Other Gls
Gould	T	GK	1893-94/1894-95	2	0	0	5	0	0	0	0	0	5	0	22	0
Gowland	Norman	GK	1930-31	1	14	0	2	0	0	0	0	0	16	0	0	0
Graham	Joseph G	HB	1911-12/1920-21	9	86	7	2	0	0	0	0	0	88	7	19	0
Graham	JW	FB	1911-12/1912-13	2	42	0	3	0	0	0	0	0	45	0	0	0
Grant*	John A	LB	1942-43	1	0	0	0	0	0	0	0	0	0	0	1	0
Grant	Peter J	D	1986-87	1	1	0	0	0	1	0	0	0	2	0	0	0
Greechan	James	IF	1909-10	1	16	4	2	1	0	0	0	0	18	5	0	0
Green	Arthur William	CF	1909-10	1	7	1	0	0	0	0	0	0	7	1	0	0
Green	Joseph	CH	1940-41	1	0	0	0	0	0	0	0	0	0	0	1	0
Green	Robert E	IL	1934-35/1935-36	2	48	19	7	3	0	0	4	2	59	24	0	0
Green	Thomas	OR	1904-05/1908-09	3(2)	61	12	9	4	0	0	0	0	70	16	18	12
Green	Thomas	CF	1917-18/1922-23	3(2)	31	16	1	0	0	0	0	0	32	16	3	2
Grewcock	E	OL	1892-93	1	0	0	2	2	0	0	0	0	2	2	22	9
Grieves	Kenneth J	GK	1957-58	1	39	0	4	0	0	0	0	0	43	0	0	0
Griffin	Albert	CF	1902-03	1	2	0	0	0	0	0	0	0	2	0	0	0
Griffin	James	RB	1923-24	1	2	0	0	0	0	0	0	0	2	0	0	0
Griffiths	Douglas James	D	1968-69/1969-70	2	20/1	0	0	0	0	0	0	0	20/1	0	0	0
Griffiths	James T	CF	1962-63	1	3	0	0	0	0	0	0	0	3	0	0	0
Griffiths	John	F	1970-71/1974-75	5	167/15	31	8/1	0	9/1	0	0	0	184/17	31	0	0
Griffiths	Joseph L	OL	1920-21/1923-24	4	50	3	0	0	0	0	0	0	50	3	0	0
Griffiths	Joseph R	CF	1931-32/1932-33	2	48	32	1	0	0	0	0	0	49	32	0	0
Groves	Arthur	IF	1939-40	1	0	0	0	0	0	0	0	0	0	0	9	0
Guy	Ronald	CF	1958-59/1959-60	2	9	2	3	2	0	0	0	0	12	4	0	0
Hacking	John	GK	1946-47	4	4	0	1	0	0	0	0	0	5	0	0	0
Haddington	Ray W	IR	1951-52	1	11	4	0	0	0	0	0	0	11	4	0	0
Haigh	George	CH	1938-39	1	2	0	0	0	0	0	0	0	2	0	0	0
Haigh	Kenneth J	FB	1934-35/1935-36	2	10	0	0	0	0	0	0	0	10	0	0	0
Hales	Herbert	OL	1934-35	1	16	0	5	0	0	0	1	0	22	0	0	0
Halford	Carl	M	1977-78/1978-79	2	65/9	5	3	0	3	0	0	0	71/9	5	0	0
Hall*	George W	GK	1939-40	1	0	0	0	0	0	0	0	0	0	0	8	0
Hall	Thomas	HB	1896-97/1906-07	9(2)	76	6	21	3	0	0	0	0	97	9	133	11
Halliday	Brian	OR	1958-59	1	1	0	0	0	0	0	0	0	1	0	0	0
Halligan	W	IR	1917-18	1	0	0	0	0	0	0	0	0	0	0	1	0
Hallworth	Ralph S	OR	1919-20	1	2	0	0	0	0	0	0	0	2	0	0	0
Hamilton	Charles McD	OR	1955-56	1	7	1	0	0	0	0	0	0	7	1	0	0
Hancock	Anthony E	F	1988-89	1	12/10	5	0	0	0	0	0	0	12/10	5	0	0
Hancock	Frederick	HB	1905-06	1	9	0	0	0	0	0	0	0	9	0	0	0
Hancock	Harry	CF	1904-05	1	0	0	0	0	0	0	0	0	0	0	12	4
Harding	William	FB	1899-00/1900-01	2	2	0	2	0	0	0	0	0	4	0	9	0
Hardman	Colin	F	1975-76/1976-77	2	6/3	1	0	0	0/1	0	0	0	6/4	1	0	0
Hardy	Harry	GK	1920-21/1925-26	6	207	0	7	0	0	0	0	0	214	0	0	0
Hardy	William	RH	1910-11	1	1	0	0	0	0	0	0	0	1	0	0	0
Haresnape		OR	1894-95/1895-96	2	0	0	1	0	0	0	0	0	1	0	22	8
Harker	Willie	HB	1936-37/1938-39	3	35	3	5	0	0	0	2	0	42	3	0	0
Harley	Albert G	M	1966-67/1968-69	3	77/3	11	3/1	1	3	0	0	0	83/4	12	0	0
Harman*	Charles	OL	1943-44	1	0	0	0	0	0	0	0	0	0	0	1	0
Harold	Michael L	FB	1964-65	1	4	0	0	0	0	0	0	0	4	0	0	0
Harries	Edward R	CH	1924-25	1	1	0	0	0	0	0	0	0	1	0	0	0
Harrison	Charlie	FB	1891-92	1	0	0	0	0	0	0	0	0	0	0	3	0
Harrison	James	OL	1942-43	1	0	0	0	0	0	0	0	0	0	0	4	0
Harrison	Thomas	IF	1914-15/1919-20	2	7	0	0	0	0	0	0	0	7	0	0	0
Hart	Nigel	D	1988-89/1989-90	2	38/1 .	2	1	0	2	0	2	0	43/1	2	0	0
Hart	Paul	D	1970-71/1972-73	3	87	5	5/1	0	7	0	0	0	99/1	5	0	0
Hartford	Richard Asa	M	1987-88/1988-89	2	42/3	0	4	0	2	0	1	0	49/3	0	0	0
Harthill	C	OL	1939-40	1	0	0	0	0	0	0	0	0	0	0	1	0
Hartle	Barry	D	1967-68/1969-70	3	88	1	7	0	2	0	0	0	97	1	0	0
Hartley	Thomas W	IL	1919-20	1	7	0	0	0	0	0	0	0	7	0	0	0
Harvey	Benjamin	HB	1893-94/1900-01	5	12	0	10	0	0	0	0	0	22	0	76	2
Haslam	Charles	LB	1945-46	1	0	0	0	0	0	0	0	0	0	0	2	0
Haslam	Fred G	OR	1925-26	1	31	0	1	0	0	0	0	0	32	0	0	0
Haslam*	Harry	RB	1940-41	1	0	0	0	0	0	0	0	0	0	0	1	0
Haughton	William	HB	1903-04/1904-05	2	0	0	1	0	0	0	0	0	1	0	1	0
Hawes		CH	1891-92	1	0	0	0	0	0	0	0	0	0	0	1	0
Haydock	William E	F/D	1965-66/1970-71	6	257/4	3	16	0	10	0	0	0	283/4	3	0	0
Hayes	Thomas William	GK	1927-28	1	16	0	2	0	0	0	0	0	18	0	0	0
Hayward*	Douglas S	IR	1944-45	1	0	0	0	0	0	0	0	0	0	0	1	0
Heald		IF	1892-93	1	0	0	0	0	0	0	0	0	0	0	8	1
Heath	Westby	FB	1919-20/1922-23	4	84	14	2	0	0	0	0	0	86	14	0	0
Hegarty	Richard	FB	1905-06	1	1	0	0	0	0	0	0	0	1	0	0	0
Hegarty	Thomas	FB	1905-06	1	2	2	1	1	0	0	0	0	3	3	0	0
Heginbotham	Brian	FB	1958-59/1959-60	2	11	0	0	0	0	0	0	0	11	0	0	0

Surname	First names	Pos	Seasons played First/Last	No	League App	Gls	FA Cup App	Gls	Lge Cup App	Gls	Divisional App	Gls	TOTAL App	Gls	Other App	Gls
Helliwell	Ernest	LH	1926-27/1930-31	5	83	3	6	0	0	0	0	0	89	3	0	0
Henderson	Frank	RH	1923-24	1	3	0	0	0	0	0	0	0	3	0	0	0
Henderson	Thomas W	M	1966-67	1	17/2	4	3	0	1	0	0	0	21/2	4	0	0
Hendrie	Paul	M	1984-85/1988-89	5	114/7	5	4	0	8/1	1	4/1	0	130/9	6	0	0
Henshaw	Tommy	OL	1894-95/1898-99	5	0	0	0	0	0	0	0	0	0	0	5	3
Henson	Philip M	M	1978-79/1979-80	2	65/2	13	4	0	4	1	0	0	73/2	14	0	0
Herd‡	Alexander	IR	1945-46/1951-52	6	111	35	8	6	0	0	0	0	119	41	1	0
Herd	David G	IF	1950-51/1953-54	3	15	6	0	0	0	0	0	0	15	6	0	0
Herod	Dennis J	GK	1953-54	1	33	0	4	0	0	0	0	0	37	0	0	0
Hewitt		CF	1893-94	1	0	0	5	4	0	0	0	0	5	4	16	7
Hewitt*		LB	1917-18	1	0	0	0	0	0	0	0	0	0	0	1	0
Heyes	Charles	GK	1891-92	1	0	0	0	0	0	0	0	0	0	0	1	0
Heyes	Herbert	IF	1894-95/1898-99	5	0	0	12	5	0	0	0	0	12	5	95	33
Heywood	James	RB	1903-04/1906-07	4	65	0	10	0	0	0	0	0	75	0	33	0
Hibbert	Henry C	CH	1908-09	1	1	0	0	0	0	0	0	0	1	0	0	0
Hiftle	Jacob E	IF	1911-12	1	4	1	0	0	0	0	0	0	4	1	0	0
Higson	TA	CF	1891-92/1895-96	2	0	0	0	0	0	0	0	0	0	0	2	1
Hill	S	FB	1904-05	1	0	0	0	0	0	0	0	0	0	0	1	0
Hill	Joseph	IR	1933-34/1937-38	5	133	63	10	4	0	0	11	4	154	71	0	0
Hill*	Maurice	IF	1944-45	1	0	0	0	0	0	0	0	0	0	0	21	2
Hindmarsh	James	LH	1910-11/1912-13	3	69	2	5	0	0	0	0	0	74	2	0	0
Hinks	Charles William	IF	1901-02	1	1	0	0	0	0	0	0	0	1	0	0	0
Hodder	Kenneth	CH	1951-52/1963-64	12	258	1	10	0	4	0	0	0	272	1	0	0
Hodgkinson	Derek	IF	1964-65/1965-66	2	46	9	6	2	1	0	0	0	53	11	0	0
Hodgkinson	James C	OR	1904-05/1908-09	4(2)	19	3	4	0	0	0	0	0	23	3	26	6
Hodgkiss	Jack	GK	1919-20	1	22	0	0	0	0	0	0	0	22	0	0	0
Hodkinson	Andrew J	M	1985-86/1987-88	3	114/4	18	5	1	7	0	5/1	0	131/5	19	0	0
Hoggart	Dennis J	OR	1964-65/1965-66	2	30	6	0	0	1	1	0	0	31	7	0	0
Holbrook	Ian	GK	1976-77	1	37	0	1	0	5	0	0	0	43	0	0	0
Holden	Alan	M	1966-67	1	1	0	0	0	0	0	0	0	1	0	0	0
Holden	William	IF	1956-57/1958-59	3	87	37	9	3	0	0	0	0	96	40	0	0
Holland	David W	IF	1959-60/1960-61	2	25	4	3	0	1	0	0	0	29	4	0	0
Hollingworth		OR	1904-05	1	0	0	1	0	0	0	0	0	1	0	0	0
Hollis*	Harry	LH	1939-40	1	0	0	0	0	0	0	0	0	0	0	1	0
Hollis	K Michael	F	1973-74/1975-76	3	106/6	33	4	0	5/1	0	0	0	115/7	33	0	0
Holmes	Carl S	M	1991-92	1	0	0	0	0	0	0	1	0	1	0	0	0
Holsgrove	John W	D	1975-76	1	9	0	1	0	2	0	0	0	12	0	0	0
Hooker	Evan	HB	1924-25/1928-29	5	36	0	0	0	0	0	0	0	36	0	0	0
Hooley	Samuel	OR	1931-32	1	18	1	0	0	0	0	0	0	18	1	0	0
Hope		IF	1891-92	1	0	0	0	0	0	0	0	0	0	0	1	0
Hope	Darren	F	1989-90	1	4	0	0	0	0	0	0	0	4	0	0	0
Hopkinson	Paul E	GK	1975-76/1976-77	2	39	0	1	0	0	0	0	0	40	0	0	0
Horrocks	J	OL	1908-09	1	32	5	2	0	0	0	0	0	34	5	0	0
Horsfall	Walter	GK	1930-31	1	8	0	0	0	0	0	0	0	8	0	0	0
Hosie	James	CH	1902-03	1	25	3	0	0	0	0	0	0	25	3	0	0
Houghton	Frederick	HB	1911-12/1914-15	4	21	0	0	0	0	0	0	0	21	0	0	0
Howard	Barry P	F	1977-78	1	12/1	1	0	0	0	0	0	0	12/1	1	0	0
Howard	Mark E	M	1987-88/1989-90	3	13/6	2	1	0	2/3	0	1/1	0	17/10	2	0	0
Howcroft		CH	1899-00	1	0	0	1	0	0	0	0	0	1	0	0	0
Howe‡	Fred	OL	1931-32/1941-42	5(2)	2	0	0	0	0	0	0	0	2	0	57	18
Hudson	Edward K	FB	1919-20	1	11	0	0	0	0	0	0	0	11	0	0	0
Hudspeth	Frank C	LB	1928-29/1929-30	2	14	2	0	0	0	0	0	0	14	2	0	0
Hughes	Charles	OL	1917-18/1918-19	2	0	0	0	0	0	0	0	0	0	0	32	7
Hughes	Herbert	CH	1902-03/1904-05	2	2	0	0	0	0	0	0	0	2	0	3	0
Hughes	John I	F	1975-76	1	11/1	3	0	0	0	0	0	0	11/1	3	0	0
Hulligan	John	CF	1900-01	1	1	1	0	0	0	0	0	0	1	1	0	0
Hullock	James	HB	1914-15	1	20	0	0	0	0	0	0	0	20	0	0	0
Hulme	T	GK	1898-99	1	0	0	0	0	0	0	0	0	0	0	3	0
Humphrey	Douglas	OL	1922-23/1923-24	2	30	2	2	0	0	0	0	0	32	2	0	0
Humpish	Albert E	IF	1932-33/1933-34	2	58	11	4	0	0	0	2	0	64	11	0	0
Hunt	Samuel W	CF	1937-38	1	11	2	0	0	0	0	0	0	11	2	0	0
Hunter	Robert	FB	1902-03	1	3	0	0	0	0	0	0	0	3	0	0	0
Hunter	Robert	CH	1926-27	1	7	0	0	0	0	0	0	0	7	0	0	0
Hutchinson	Robert	IL	1923-24	1	4	1	0	0	0	0	0	0	4	1	0	0
Huyton	James	CF	1919-20	1	2	1	0	0	0	0	0	0	2	1	0	0
Hyde‡	Eric W	IF	1942-43/1945-46	3	0	0	2	1	0	0	0	0	2	1	28	10
Hyde	Lincoln	OL	1913-14/1918-19	4	13	1	0	0	0	0	0	0	13	1	9	0
Ingham	Frederick R	F	1971-72/1972-73	2	12/7	1	0	0	0	0	0	0	12/7	1	0	0
Ingle	Stephen P	D	1972-73	1	29	0	3	0	5	0	0	0	37	0	0	0
Inglis	William	RH	1931-32	1	35	1	1	0	0	0	0	0	36	1	0	0
Ireland*	Harold W	CF	1944-45	1	0	0	0	0	0	0	0	0	0	0	1	1

Surname	First names	Pos	Seasons played First/Last	No	League App	Gls	FA Cup App	Gls	Lge Cup App	Gls	Divisional App	Gls	TOTAL App	Gls	Other App	Gls
Ironside	Ian	GK	1993-94	1	10/1	0	0	0	0	0	1	0	11/1	0	0	0
Jackson	Arnold	IF	1954-55/1958-59	5	153	48	9	4	0	0	0	0	162	52	0	0
Jackson	Harold	FB	1947-48	1	2	0	0	0	0	0	0	0	2	0	0	0
Jackson	Philip J	F	1976-77/1977-78	2	15/3	1	0	0	1	0	0	0	16/3	1	0	0
Jackson	William	FB	1937-38/1938-39	2	11	0	0	0	0	0	0	0	11	0	0	0
James‡	George C	IL	1942-43/1944-45	3	0	0	0	0	0	0	0	0	0	0	34	12
James	Martin	M	1992-93/*	2	13/18	0	0/1	0	2	0	0/2	0	15/21	0	0	0
James	Roland W	HB	1924-25/1927-28	4	33	3	1	0	0	0	0	0	34	3	0	0
Jarratt	RH	CF	1900-01	1	1	0	0	0	0	0	0	0	1	0	0	0
Jarvis	Joseph	RB	1954-55/1956-57	3	43	0	0	0	0	0	0	0	43	0	0	0
Jeffreys	Alec	CH	1901-02/1902-03	2	43	0	4	1	0	0	0	0	47	1	0	0
Jenkinson	Fred	FB	1931-32/1938-39	8	269	1	14	0	0	0	12	0	295	1	0	0
Jennings	Samuel	IF	1931-32	1	14	2	1	0	0	0	0	0	15	2	0	0
Jepson	William	HB	1891-92/1893-94	3	0	0	2	0	0	0	0	0	2	0	45	1
Jessop	William	CF	1946-47/1947-48	2	17	4	1	0	0	0	0	0	18	4	0	0
Jobson	John T	CH	1927-28/1931-32	5	171	7	10	0	0	0	0	0	181	7	0	0
Johnman	John	RB	1932-33	1	1	0	0	0	0	0	0	0	1	0	0	0
Johnson	Frank	GK	1914-15/1917-18	3	2	0	0	0	0	0	0	0	2	0	2	0
Johnson	Harold	HB	1930-31/1932-33	3	12	0	0	0	0	0	0	0	12	0	0	0
Johnson	Jack	OR	1940-41/1945-46	4	0	0	2	0	0	0	0	0	2	0	31	10
Johnson	Jeff	F	1976-77	1	6/2	0	0	0	0	0	0	0	6/2	0	0	0
Johnson	Joseph	IR	1925-26	1	7	0	0	0	0	0	0	0	7	0	0	0
Johnson*	T	CH	1940-41	1	0	0	0	0	0	0	0	0	0	0	1	0
Johnston	David D	FB	1963-64	1	26	0	0	0	1	0	0	0	27	0	0	0
Johnston	Harold	FB	1898-99/1899-00	2	0	0	7	0	0	0	0	0	7	0	42	1
Johnston	William Gifford	IF	1924-25/1928-29	5	79	27	2	0	0	0	0	0	81	27	0	0
Johnstone	H	LB	1918-19	1	0	0	0	0	0	0	0	0	0	0	3	0
Johnstone*	Joe	LH	1943-44	1	0	0	0	0	0	0	0	0	0	0	1	0
Jones		CF	1891-92	1	0	0	0	0	0	0	0	0	0	0	5	5
Jones	Alexander	D	1984-85	1	3	0	0	0	0	0	0	0	3	0	0	0
Jones*	Benjamin W	CF	1942-43	1	0	0	0	0	0	0	0	0	0	0	1	1
Jones	Charles	OL	1921-22/1922-23	2	48	9	1	0	0	0	0	0	49	9	0	0
Jones	Ernest Peter	D	1966-67/1967-68	2	51/3	3	1	0	1	0	0	0	53/3	3	0	0
Jones	Frederick S	CF	1925-26/1933-34	4(2)	24	11	0	0	0	0	0	0	24	11	0	0
Jones	Graham	D	1983-84	1	32/3	2	1	0	4	0	1	0	38/3	2	0	0
Jones*	Gwen T	LB	1940-41	1	0	0	0	0	0	0	0	0	0	0	5	0
Jones	Gwyn F	FB	1936-37/1937-38	2	30	0	1	0	0	0	0	0	31	0	0	0
Jones	Leonard	HB	1933-34/1939-40	7	202	1	13	0	0	0	11	0	226	1	1	0
Jones	P	IL	1916-17	1	0	0	0	0	0	0	0	0	0	0	1	0
Jones	Paul B	D	1989-90	1	25	0	0/2	0	1	0	3	0	29/2	0	0	0
Jones	Richard	LH	1923-24	1	6	0	0	0	0	0	0	0	6	0	0	0
Jones	Richard	OR	1944-45/1945-46	2	0	0	0	0	0	0	0	0	0	0	8	0
Jones*	Thomas G	LB	1944-45	1	0	0	0	0	0	0	0	0	0	0	2	0
Jones	Walter H	IF	1908-09	1	3	1	0	0	0	0	0	0	3	1	0	0
Jones*	William Lot	IR	1918-19	1	0	0	0	0	0	0	0	0	0	0	3	2
Kay	George	CH	1927-28	1	2	0	0	0	0	0	0	0	2	0	0	0
Kay	James	IR	1954-55/1955-56	2	9	3	2	0	0	0	0	0	11	3	0	0
Kaye	Albert	CF	1903-04	1	16	2	0	0	0	0	0	0	16	2	0	0
Kearslake	Joseph	OR	1921-22/1922-23	2	15	2	0	0	0	0	0	0	15	2	0	0
Keating	Reginald	OL	1930-31	1	5	0	0	0	0	0	0	0	5	0	0	0
Keelan	Kevin D	GK	1960-61	1	3	0	0	0	0	0	0	0	3	0	0	0
Keeley	John	GK	1993-94	1	10	0	0	0	0	0	3	0	13	0	0	0
Keenan*	William G	OL	1945-46	1	0	0	0	0	0	0	0	0	0	0	1	0
Kellock	William	IF	1915-16/1918-19	2	0	0	0	0	0	0	0	0	0	0	18	7
Kelly	Francis	OL	1909-10/1910-11	2	46	11	3	0	0	0	0	0	49	11	0	0
Kelly	George L	IF	1959-60	1	34	4	0	0	0	0	0	0	34	4	0	0
Kelly	Walter M	CF	1957-58/1959-60	3	47	12	0	0	0	0	0	0	47	12	0	0
Kennedy		OR	1896-97	1	0	0	0	0	0	0	0	0	0	0	18	2
Kennedy	Frank	IL	1937-38	1	6	1	0	0	0	0	0	0	6	1	0	0
Kennedy	Gordon M	RB	1953-54	1	20	1	0	0	0	0	0	0	20	1	0	0
Kennedy	James	CH	1909-10	1	18	1	2	0	0	0	0	0	20	1	0	0
Kennedy	William	IL	1906-07	1	18	2	0	0	0	0	0	0	18	2	0	0
Kenny	Frederick	LB	1948-49/1956-57	8	204	0	10	0	0	0	0	0	214	0	0	0
Kenyon	James	CF	1908-09/1918-19	6	21	5	3	0	0	0	0	0	24	5	59	16
Kerr	John	F	1983-84/1984-85	2	47	16	1	0	2	0	3	1	53	17	0	0
Kerr	Leonard	OL	1917-18	1	0	0	0	0	0	0	0	0	0	0	1	1
Kevan	Derek T	F	1966-67/1967-68	2	38/2	10	1	1	3	1	0	0	42/2	12	0	0
Keyes	Anthony J	M	1971-72/1973-74	3	7/1	0	0/1	0	0	0	0	0	7/2	0	0	0
Kilner	Andrew W	M	1990-91/1991-92	2	34/8	14	1/1	0	1	0	2/2	1	38/11	15	0	0
Kinnear*	David	CF	1945-46	1	0	0	0	0	0	0	0	0	0	0	1	0
Kinsella	Patrick G	M	1968-69	1	12/1	0	0	0	0	0	0	0	12/1	0	0	0

Surname	First names	Pos	Seasons played First/Last	No	League App	Gls	FA Cup App	Gls	Lge Cup App	Gls	Divisional App	Gls	TOTAL App	Gls	Other App	Gls
Kirby	Norman	OL	1927-28	1	1	0	0	0	0	0	0	0	1	0	0	0
Kirk	Harold	M	1973-74/1974-75	2	60/8	7	3	0	2	0	0	0	65/8	7	0	0
Kirkwood*	Samuel J	CH	1942-43	1	0	0	0	0	0	0	0	0	0	0	1	0
Kirton		OL	1895-96	1	0	0	0	0	0	0	0	0	0	0	3	0
Kitchen	George	GK	1897-98	1	0	0	0	0	0	0	0	0	0	0	8	0
Kitching*	N	CH	1940-41	1	0	0	0	0	0	0	0	0	0	0	1	0
Kite	Philip	GK	1992-93	1	5	0	0	0	0	0	0	0	5	0	0	0
Knowles	Darren T	M/D	1989-90/1992-93	4	51/12	0	0	0	2/4	0	14/1	0	67/17	0	0	0
Knowles	Frank	LH	1922-23	1	14	1	0	0	0	0	0	0	14	1	0	0
Knowles	Herbert	OL	1920-21	1	2	0	1	0	0	0	0	0	3	0	0	0
Lamb	Joseph	HB	1926-27	1	5	0	0	0	0	0	0	0	5	0	0	0
Lambourne	Albert	LH	1929-30/1932-33	4	61	10	3	0	0	0	0	0	64	10	0	0
Lancelotte*	Eric C	IF	1942-43	1	0	0	0	0	0	0	0	0	0	0	4	2
Langley		IL	1896-97	1	0	0	0	0	0	0	0	0	0	0	4	0
Law	William G	CF	1938-39	1	1	0	1	0	0	0	0	0	2	0	0	0
Lawler	Chris	D	1977-78	1	33/3	3	3	0	1	0	0	0	37/3	3	0	0
Lawrence	Norman J	CH	1941-42/1942-43	2	0	0	0	0	0	0	0	0	0	0	21	0
Lawrence	Oswald	CH	1942-43/1945-46	2	0	0	1	0	0	0	0	0	1	0	7	0
Lawson	David	GK	1978-79/1980-81	3	106	0	3	0	9	0	0	0	118	0	0	0
Lawther	Ian	F/D	1971-72/1975-76	5	158/6	29	7	1	12	4	0	0	177/6	34	0	0
Layton	Arthur	LB	1920-21/1922-23	3	59	0	2	0	0	0	0	0	61	0	0	0
Lea	Harold	GK	1958-59/1953-64	6	117	0	10	0	3	0	0	0	130	0	0	0
Lea	William	OL	1959-60	1	1	0	0	0	0	0	0	0	1	0	0	0
Leach	Thomas	CH	1936-37	1	16	4	0	0	0	0	0	0	16	4	0	0
Leckie	John T	GK	1933-34	1	5	0	0	0	0	0	0	0	5	0	0	0
Ledgard	Ian	M	1967-68/1968-69	2	4/4	0	0	0	0/1	1	0	0	4/5	1	0	0
Lee	Arthur	OL	1896-97/1898-99	3	0	0	11	1	0	0	0	0	11	1	60	10
Lee	F Stuart	F	1978-79/1979-80	2	49	21	2	2	7	2	0	0	58	25	0	0
Lee	Frank	M	1974-75	1	13	1	1	0	0	0	0	0	14	1	0	0
Lee	Jason B	F	1990-91	1	2	0	0	0	0	0	0	0	2	0	0	0
Lee	Joseph	GK	1896-97/1897-98	2	0	0	5	0	0	0	0	0	5	0	45	0
Lees	William Harry	OL	1906-07	1	13	1	2	0	0	0	0	0	15	1	0	0
Leicester	E	CF	1944-45	1	0	0	0	0	0	0	0	0	0	0	2	1
Leigh*	James J	OL	1943-44	1	0	0	0	0	0	0	0	0	0	0	1	0
Leigh	W	OL	1893-94/1895-96	3	0	0	7	0	0	0	0	0	7	0	68	17
Leigh	Mark B	M	1980-81/1983-84	3	6/5	1	0	0	0	0	0/1	0	6/6	1	0	0
Leighton	Leonard	IF	1940-41/1941-42	2	0	0	0	0	0	0	0	0	0	0	4	1
Lennard	David	M	1976-77	1	39	4	1	0	5	0	0	0	45	4	0	0
Leonard	Gary A	M	1988-89/1989-90	2	15/2	1	0	0	0	0	2	0	17/2	1	0	0
Leonard	Mark A	F	1984-85/1986-87	3	73	23	1	0	5	2	2	3	81	28	0	0
Lester	Abraham B	CF	1949-50	1	8	2	0	0	0	0	0	0	8	2	0	0
Lester	Hugh	OL	1917-18	1	0	0	0	0	0	0	0	0	0	0	3	1
Lester	Michael J	M	1975-76/1986-87	2(2)	19/1	1	0	0	4	1	0	0	23/1	2	0	0
Lever	James	FB	1894-95/1896-97	2	0	0	2	0	0	0	0	0	2	0	39	0
Levick	Oliver	CH	1926-27	1	5	0	1	0	0	0	0	0	6	0	0	0
Lewins*	Dennis Ronald	LB	1943-44/1944-45	2	0	0	0	0	0	0	0	0	0	0	38	0
Lewis	Daniel L	IR	1937-38	1	1	0	0	0	0	0	0	0	1	0	0	0
Liddell*	John	GK	1943-44	1	0	0	0	0	0	0	0	0	0	0	6	0
Lievesley*	Leslie	RH	1942-43/1944-45	3	0	0	0	0	0	0	0	0	0	0	63	1
Lillis	Mark A	M	1991-92	1	9/2	2	0	0	0	0	4	0	13/2	2	0	0
Limond	Andrew Thomas	HB	1899-00/1900-01	2	30	0	2	0	0	0	0	0	32	0	11	1
Lincoln	Andrew	IL	1929-30/1930-31	2	81	39	5	3	0	0	0	0	86	42	0	0
Liptrott	David A	M	1982-83	1	0/1	0	0	0	0	0	0	0	0/1	0	0	0
Lister	Herbert F	F	1966-67	1	16	11	0	0	0	0	0	0	16	11	0	0
Littlemore	R	GK	1942-43	1	0	0	0	0	0	0	0	0	0	0	3	0
Littler	Thomas	OL	1955-56	1	1	0	0	0	0	0	0	0	1	0	0	0
Lloyd	Brian W	GK	1967-68/1982-83	4(2)	123	1	3	0	7	0	0	0	133	1	0	0
Lloyd	Edward H	LB	1930-31/1932-33	3	67	0	1	0	0	0	0	0	68	0	0	0
Lloyd	Ernest	OL	1914-15	1	10	0	1	0	0	0	0	0	11	0	0	0
Lloyd	Norman W	M	1970-71/1974-75	2(2)	46/2	2	2	0	1	0	0	0	49/2	2	0	0
Loadwick	Derek	M	1976-77/1978-79	3	84	0	4	0	10	0	0	0	98	0	0	0
Lodge	Frank	CF	1946-47	1	1	0	0	0	0	0	0	0	1	0	0	0
Lodge	Paul	M	1984-85/1985-86	2	10/3	2	0	0	1	0	0	0	11/3	2	0	0
Logan	David	D	1988-89/1989-90	2	60	4	1	0	1	0	5	0	67	4	0	0
Lomas		GK	1898-99	1	0	0	2	0	0	0	0	0	2	0	13	0
Lomax	James	IF	1908-09/1911-12	4	72	17	7	5	0	0	0	0	79	22	0	0
Longstaff	G	OR	1901-02	1	5	2	0	0	0	0	0	0	5	2	0	0
Loram	Mark	M	1991-92	1	1/3	0	0	0	0	0	0	0	1/3	0	0	0
Lord	Frank	CF	1965-66/1966-67	2	27	18	2	0	1	0	0	0	30	18	0	0
Lovell	Alan	OL	1960-61	1	1	0	0	0	0	0	0	0	1	0	0	0
Lovell	Stephen J	F	1979-80	1	12	0	1	0	0	0	0	0	13	0	0	0

Surname	First names	Pos	Seasons played First/Last	No	League App	Gls	FA Cup App	Gls	Lge Cup App	Gls	Divisional App	Gls	TOTAL App	Gls	Other App	Gls
Lovery	James	IL	1936-37	1	0	0	0	0	0	0	1	0	1	0	0	0
Low	Gordon A	D	1968-69/1969-70	2	63/1	7	5	1	4	1	0	0	72/1	9	0	0
Lowis	Paul N	LH	1959-60	1	9	0	0	0	0	0	0	0	9	0	0	0
Lumberg	Albert	RB	1934-35	1	2	0	0	0	0	0	0	0	2	0	0	0
Lumby	Walter CW	HB	1937-38/1945-46	5	15	1	1	0	0	0	0	0	16	1	12	1
Lunn*	George	LB	1944-45	1	0	0	0	0	0	0	0	0	0	0	1	0
Lunn	Thomas H	GK	1913-14	1	2	0	0	0	0	0	0	0	2	0	0	0
Lythgoe	Alfred P	CF	1932-33/1938-39	5(2)	119	104	7	1	0	0	3	5	129	110	0	0
Lyons	Edward	FB	1940-41/1943-44	4	0	0	0	0	0	0	0	0	0	0	54	0
Madden	MG	CF	1901-02	1	23	4	3	2	0	0	0	0	26	6	0	0
Maddison	Ralph	OL	1948-49	1	5	0	1	0	0	0	0	0	6	0	0	0
Maden	James	IL	1917-18	1	0	0	0	0	0	0	0	0	0	0	1	0
Maguire	Peter	F	1990-91	1	0/2	0	0	0	0	0	0	0	0/2	0	0	0
Makin*	George W	OL	1944-45	1	0	0	0	0	0	0	0	0	0	0	1	0
Makin	James	IR	1909-10/1910-11	2	16	5	3	0	0	0	0	0	19	5	0	0
Malkin		HB	1891-92	1	0	0	0	0	0	0	0	0	0	0	1	0
Malley	Philip	D	1984-85	1	3	0	0	0	0	0	0	0	3	0	0	0
Malone	Patrick	GK	1902-03	1	1	0	0	0	0	0	0	0	1	0	0	0
Maloney	Sean	D	1979-80	1	0/1	0	0	0	0	0	0	0	0/1	0	0	0
Manley	George	RH	1917-18/1918-19	2	0	0	0	0	0	0	0	0	0	0	9	0
Mann	Robert	OL	1894-95/1898-99	4	0	0	2	0	0	0	0	0	2	0	64	14
Manson	Robert	IF	1905-06	1	19	8	2	3	0	0	0	0	21	11	0	0
Mantle	Joseph	CF	1936-37/1937-38	2	22	12	0	0	0	0	0	0	22	12	0	0
Marples	Christopher	GK	1986-87/1987-88	2	57	0	4	0	2	0	2	0	65	0	0	0
Marshall	Arthur G	IF	1901-02	1	11	2	0	0	0	0	0	0	11	2	0	0
Marshall	John	CF	1929-30	1	2	1	0	0	0	0	0	0	2	1	0	0
Marsland	Samuel	IL	1925-26	1	5	0	0	0	0	0	0	0	5	0	0	0
Marsland	William	IR	1926-27	1	1	0	0	0	0	0	0	0	1	0	0	0
Martin	Alfred	CF	1926-27	1	4	2	0	0	0	0	0	0	4	2	0	0
Martin	Harold	GK	1943-44/1944-45	2	0	0	0	0	0	0	0	0	0	0	32	0
Martin	William	CF	1908-09	1	11	3	1	0	0	0	0	0	12	3	0	0
Masefield	Paul	D	1992-93	1	7	0	0	0	2	0	0	0	9	0	0	0
Massey		CH	1897-98	1	0	0	0	0	0	0	0	0	0	0	2	0
Massey	Stephen	F	1974-75/1977-78	4	87/14	20	5	1	8	3	0	0	100/14	24	0	0
Mathieson	H	OL	1944-45	1	0	0	0	0	0	0	0	0	0	0	1	0
Matthews	Cyril H	OR	1930-31	1	34	10	2	0	0	0	0	0	36	10	0	0
Matthews	Michael	M	1988-89/1989-90	2	35	3	2	0	4	1	0	0	41	4	0	0
Matthews	Neil	F	1990-91/1992-93	3	27/16	15	0/1	0	1/1	0	1	0	29/18	15	0	0
Matthews*	Ronald	IL	1942-43	1	0	0	0	0	0	0	0	0	0	0	1	1
Matthews	Robert W	CH	1930-31	1	4	0	0	0	0	0	0	0	4	0	0	0
Matthewson	Trevor	D	1985-86/1986-87	2	79/1	0	2	0	3	0	3	0	87/1	0	0	0
Maudsley	Richard C	OL	1940-41/1941-42	2	0	0	0	0	0	0	0	0	0	0	9	0
Mawson	Joseph S	IF	1935-36	1	3	0	0	0	0	0	0	1	4	0	0	0
McAdam	Thomas	D	1986-87	1	5	1	0	0	2	1	0	0	7	2	0	0
McArdle	Peter	OL	1937-38	1	4	0	0	0	0	0	0	0	4	0	0	0
McBeth	George	M	1976-77/1977-78	2	51/5	3	1	0	5/1	0	0	0	57/6	3	0	0
McCaig	Robert AM	OR	1951-52	1	15	2	2	0	0	0	0	0	17	2	0	0
McCann	James	F	1975-76	1	4/1	0	0	0	0	0	0	0	4/1	0	0	0
McCombie	William	IR	1893-94/1894-95	2	0	0	6	4	0	0	0	0	6	4	24	7
McCord	Brian	M	1992-93	1	4/4	0	0/1	1	0	0	3	0	7/5	1	0	0
McCulloch	William D	RH	1943-44/1953-54	10	309	4	29	1	0	0	0	0	338	5	47	9
McCusker	James	GK	1959-60	1	2	0	0	0	0	0	0	0	2	0	0	0
McDonald		HB	1896-97	1	0	0	2	0	0	0	0	0	2	0	6	1
McDonald	Gary	F	1989-90	1	1	0	0	0	3	1	0	0	4	1	0	0
McDonnell	Charles	IL	1961-62/1963-64	3	84	32	2	0	3	0	0	0	89	32	0	0
McDonough	Francis JB	GK	1934-35/1939-40	5	132	0	8	0	0	0	9	0	149	0	12	0
McFetteridge		CF	1896-97	1	0	0	2	1	0	0	0	0	2	1	2	0
McGann	James L	GK	1929-30/1933-34	4	54	0	2	0	0	0	2	0	58	0	0	0
McGann	William TA	RB	1949-50/1950-51	2	14	0	2	0	0	0	0	0	16	0	0	0
McGowan	George	IL	1964-65	1	5	0	0	0	0	0	0	0	5	0	0	0
McGreevey	Brian E	OR	1956-57	1	1	0	0	0	0	0	0	0	1	0	0	0
McGuigan	James	OR	1949-50/1950-51	2	43	9	6	4	0	0	0	0	49	13	0	0
McInerney	Ian	M	1989-90/1990-91	2	37/5	8	2	0	2/1	1	5/1	0	46/7	9	0	0
McIntosh	Robert A	HB	1924-25	1	8	0	0	0	0	0	0	0	8	0	0	0
McIver	William	GK	1911-12/1912-13	2	68	0	6	0	0	0	0	0	74	0	0	0
McKay*	William	LH	1942-43/1944-45	2	0	0	0	0	0	0	0	0	0	0	9	2
McKecknie	James	RB	1922-23	1	8	0	0	0	0	0	0	0	8	0	0	0
McKenna	John	IL	1942-43	1	0	0	0	0	0	0	0	0	0	0	1	0
McKenzie	Dr George D	OL	1934-35	1	7	3	0	0	0	0	0	0	7	3	0	0
McKenzie	Ian E	D	1986-87/1988-89	3	51/8	0	1/1	0	3	0	2/1	0	57/10	0	0	0
McKiernan	Thomas	IR	1902-03	1	5	1	0	0	0	0	0	0	5	1	0	0

Surname	First names	Pos	Seasons played First/Last	No	League App	Gls	FA Cup App	Gls	Lge Cup App	Gls	Divisional App	Gls	TOTAL App	Gls	Other App	Gls
McLachlan	Peter	OL	1900-01/1904-05	5	46	11	3	0	0	0	0	0	49	11	1	1
McMillan	Sammy	M	1970-71/1971-72	2	74	29	3	2	3	0	0	0	80	31	0	0
McNab	James	D	1974-75/1975-76	2	30	1	0	0	1	0	0	0	31	1	0	0
McNaughton	William F	CF	1934-35/1935-36	2	50	32	3	1	0	0	4	2	57	35	0	0
McNeill	Alan A	M	1975-76/1976-77	2	69/2	1	2	0	5/1	0	0	0	76/3	1	0	0
McPhillips*	Lawrence	IL	1942-43	1	0	0	0	0	0	0	0	0	0	0	1	0
McRailt	William	CH	1913-14	1	1	0	0	0	0	0	0	0	1	0	0	0
Meads	Thomas	IF	1923-24/1926-27	4	117	21	3	0	0	0	0	0	120	21	0	0
Melville	David	HB	1909-10/1918-19	4(2)	73	2	4	0	0	0	0	0	77	2	1	0
Melvin	Martin	D	1986-87	1	0	0	0	0	0/1	0	0	0	0/1	0	0	0
Mercer	H	GK	1918-19	1	0	0	0	0	0	0	0	0	0	0	6	0
Merrifield		OR	1891-92	1	0	0	0	0	0	0	0	0	0	0	2	0
Metcalf‡	Arthur	IF	1917-18/1919-20	2	36	13	1	0	0	0	0	0	37	13	1	1
Middleton	Alfred	IL	1912-13	1	2	0	0	0	0	0	0	0	2	0	0	0
Middleton	George Norman	CF	1902-03	1	2	1	0	0	0	0	0	0	2	1	0	0
Middleton*	John	OL	1940-41/1941-42	2	0	0	0	0	0	0	0	0	0	0	4	3
Miller	David B	D	1991-92/*	3	72/6	1	5/2	0	5	0	12/2	0	94/10	1	0	0
Miller	W	OL	1916-17	1	0	0	0	0	0	0	0	0	0	0	2	0
Mills	Neil	D	1987-88	1	5/2	0	0	0	0	0	0	0	5/2	0	0	0
Milner	Michael	D	1968-69	1	41	0	3	0	3	0	0	0	47	0	0	0
Minshull	Owen	FB	1940-41/1941-42	2	0	0	0	0	0	0	0	0	0	0	4	0
Mitchell	Harold J	IL	1906-07/1907-08	2	26	2	0	0	0	0	0	0	26	2	0	0
Mitchell	Roy	M	1986-87	1	2/1	0	0	0	0	0	0	0	2/1	0	0	0
Mitchell	Thomas	OL	1924-25/1925-26	2	66	13	3	0	0	0	0	0	69	13	0	0
Mitton	F.Jack	CF	1915-16	1	0	0	0	0	0	0	0	0	0	0	4	3
Mitton	James	HB	1910-11/1920-21	9	88	6	2	0	0	0	0	0	90	6	44	0
Moir	Howard L	GK	1902-03	1	1	0	0	0	0	0	0	0	1	0	0	0
Moir	William	IF	1955-56/1957-58	3	70	26	3	0	0	0	0	0	73	26	0	0
Molloy	Peter	RH	1936-37	1	10	0	0	0	0	0	2	0	12	0	0	0
Molloy	William	OR	1927-28	1	9	0	0	0	0	0	0	0	9	0	0	0
Molyneux‡	James	GK	1906-07/1924-25	9(3)	97	0	5	0	0	0	0	0	102	0	65	0
Monks	John	LB	1946-47/1952-53	6	91	0	11	0	0	0	0	0	102	0	0	0
Moore*		LH	1940-41	1	0	0	0	0	0	0	0	0	0	0	2	0
Moore	Christian	M	1991-92	1	0/1	0	0	0	0	0	1	0	1/1	0	0	0
Moore	NC	LB	1909-10	1	2	0	0	0	0	0	0	0	2	0	0	0
Moores		CH	1893-94	1	0	0	0	0	0	0	0	0	0	0	1	0
Moores	J James	GK	1898-99/1900-01	3	28	0	4	0	0	0	0	0	32	0	35	0
Moran	Edward	IF	1951-52/1956-57	6	110	44	7	3	0	0	0	0	117	47	0	0
Morrin	Anthony J	M	1966-67/1976-77	4(2)	39/5	3	4	1	2	0	0	0	45/5	4	0	0
Morris	Ian G	M	1967-68	1	1/1	0	0	0	0	0	0	0	1/1	0	0	0
Morris‡	James	HB	1939-40/1948-49	8	61	3	8	2	0	0	0	0	69	5	26	0
Morrison*	Angus C	OL	1944-45	1	0	0	0	0	0	0	0	0	0	0	4	0
Morrison	Robert	LH	1922-23/1924-25	3	30	0	2	0	0	0	0	0	32	0	0	0
Morrison	William C	RB	1928-29	1	2	0	0	0	0	0	0	0	2	0	0	0
Morrow	S	GK	1898-99	1	0	0	0	0	0	0	0	0	0	0	1	0
Morton	Alan	F	1969-70	1	12/2	2	0	0	0	0	0	0	12/2	2	0	0
Morton	William P	OL	1925-26	1	3	0	0	0	0	0	0	0	3	0	0	0
Moseley*	William A	CH	1942-43	1	0	0	0	0	0	0	0	0	0	0	4	0
Moss		FB	1894-95	1	0	0	0	0	0	0	0	0	0	0	6	0
Moss	Ernest	F	1986-87	1	26	7	0	0	0	0	0	0	26	7	0	0
Mossman	David J	M	1985-86/1987-88	3(2)	37/2	6	2	0	3/1	1	2	0	44/3	7	0	0
Mountford	Robert W	F	1980-81	1	6/1	3	1	0	0	0	0	0	7/1	3	0	0
Muggleton	Carl D	GK	1989-90	1	4	0	0	0	0	0	0	0	4	0	0	0
Muirhead	Jack	FB	1891-92	1	0	0	0	0	0	0	0	0	0	0	13	1
Muir	John G	F	1991-92/1992-93	2	10/3	3	0	0	2/1	0	0	0	12/4	3	0	0
Mulhearn	Kenneth J	GK	1964-65/1967-68	4	100	0	12	0	5	0	0	0	117	0	0	0
Mulholland	James	F	1968-69/1969-70	2	28/4	5	1/1	0	1	0	0	0	30/5	5	0	0
Mulvaney	James	F	1970-71/1971-72	2	38/2	8	0/1	0	0	0	0	0	38/3	8	0	0
Mulvey	Edward PN	IF	1957-58/1959-60	3	26	5	0	0	0	0	0	0	26	5	0	0
Murdoch	William R	IF	1960-61/1961-62	2	58	17	5	0	3	0	0	0	66	17	0	0
Murphy	Michael	OR	1944-45	1	0	0	0	0	0	0	0	0	0	0	1	0
Murray	Bruce	F	1993-94	1	2/1	0	0	0	0	0	0	0	2/1	0	0	0
Murray	Robert L	RH	1952-53/1962-63	11	465	32	27	0	3	0	0	0	495	32	0	0
Mycock		FB	1895-96	1	0	0	0	0	0	0	0	0	0	0	1	0
Needham	Frederick R	CH	1942-43/1943-44	2	0	0	0	0	0	0	0	0	0	0	9	0
Neilson*	Richard	HB	1939-40/1940-41	2	0	0	0	0	0	0	0	0	0	0	24	1
Nelson	Alfred	IR	1931-32	1	19	6	0	0	0	0	0	0	19	6	0	0
Newbigging	Harry	IL	1920-21	1	15	1	0	0	0	0	0	0	15	1	0	0
Newman	Alfred	OR	1924-25	1	4	0	0	0	0	0	0	0	4	0	0	0
Newman	Arthur P	IL	1919-20/1920-21	2	4	0	0	0	0	0	0	0	4	0	0	0
Newman	Ernest	IL	1909-10	1	19	5	2	1	0	0	0	0	21	6	0	0

Surname	First names	Pos	Seasons played First/Last	No	League App	Gls	FA Cup App	Gls	Lge Cup App	Gls	Divisional App	Gls	TOTAL App	Gls	Other App	Gls
Newton	Frank	CF	1927-28/1930-31	4	94	86	7	7	0	0	0	0	101	93	0	0
Newton	Robert	F	1985-86	1	6	1	0	0	0	0	0	0	6	1	0	0
Newton	William	RH	1927-28/1940-41	5(2)	150	2	10	0	0	0	0	0	160	2	1	0
Newton	WA	FB	1916-17/1918-19	3	0	0	0	0	0	0	0	0	0	0	17	0
Nibloe	John A	IF	1964-65	1	22	4	1	1	1	0	0	0	24	5	0	0
Nixon	Ernest A	CH	1905-06	1	4	0	0	0	0	0	0	0	4	0	0	0
Nixon	J	OR	1909-10/1910-11	2	39	6	4	0	0	0	0	0	43	6	0	0
Noble	John	OL	1940-41/1946-47	3	1	0	0	0	0	0	0	0	1	0	2	0
Norris	Patrick	IF	1920-21	1	5	1	0	0	0	0	0	0	5	1	0	0
Norton	Joseph	OL	1911-12	1	8	1	1	1	0	0	0	0	9	2	0	0
Nuttall	Tommy	IF	1915-16/1918-19	4	0	0	0	0	0	0	0	0	0	0	44	9
O'Berg	Paul J	M	1984-85	1	2	0	1	0	0	0	0	0	3	0	0	0
O'Brien	Richard	OL	1911-12/1917-18	4	69	10	7	2	0	0	0	0	76	12	1	0
O'Kane	Joseph	IL	1921-22	1	16	12	1	0	0	0	0	0	17	12	0	0
Odenrode	Harold	OR	1926-27/1927-28	2	20	6	0	0	0	0	0	0	20	6	0	0
Oghani	George	F	1989-90	1	5/3	2	0	0	1/1	0	0	0	6/4	2	0	0
Ogley	Alan	GK	1967-68/1974-75	8	240	0	18	0	11	0	0	0	269	0	0	0
Oldham	G	LB	1939-40	1	0	0	0	0	0	0	0	0	0	0	2	0
Oldnall	William J	CF	1945-46	1	0	0	0	0	0	0	0	0	0	0	1	0
Oliver	Alan Joseph	OL	1950-51/1953-54	4	139	29	12	3	0	0	0	0	151	32	0	0
Ollerenshaw	F	GK	1918-19	1	0	0	0	0	0	0	0	0	0	0	19	0
Olynik	Peter	M	1974-75	1	4	0	0	0	0	0	0	0	4	0	0	0
Ormrod	Leslie	D	1969-70/1973-74	5	103/5	0	5	0	7	0	0	0	115/5	0	0	0
Owen	A Sidney	IL	1907-08	1	1	0	0	0	0	0	0	0	1	0	0	0
Owens	E	RB	1944-45	1	0	0	0	0	0	0	0	0	0	0	11	1
Owens	Patrick	LB	1938-39/1939-40	2	20	0	4	0	0	0	0	0	24	0	18	0
Oxley	Bernard	OR	1936-37/1937-38	2	68	10	2	0	0	0	0	0	70	10	0	0
Park*	James Brownlie	OL	1940-41	1	0	0	0	0	0	0	0	0	0	0	1	0
Park	Terry	M	1976-77/1982-83	7(2)	159/3	15	10	7	9	2	0	0	178/3	24	0	0
Park	Thomas	OL	1944-45	1	0	0	0	0	0	0	0	0	0	0	1	0
Parker	Stuart J	D	1983-84	1	0/1	0	0	0	0	0	1	0	1/1	0	0	0
Parker	William	IF	1899-00/1905-06	6	30	4	3	2	0	0	0	0	33	6	40	12
Parry	Colin	CH	1962-63/1967-68	6	132/1	0	10	0	5	0	0	0	147/1	0	0	0
Partridge	Brendan D	OL	1960-61/1961-62	2	31	6	0	0	1	0	0	0	32	6	0	0
Paskin	William John	F	1991-92	1	3/2	1	0	0	0	0	0	0	3/2	1	0	0
Pass	James E	IF	1903-04/1906-07	4	59	18	12	2	0	0	0	0	71	20	27	13
Paterson	Alexander	LH	1947-48/1952-53	6	160	7	11	0	0	0	0	0	171	7	0	0
Paterson	John	IL	1943-44	1	0	0	0	0	0	0	0	0	0	0	1	0
Patterson	John	CF	1899-00/1901-02	3	31	3	5	1	0	0	0	0	36	4	27	11
Payne	Mark RC	M	1988-89/1990-91	3	77/10	16	3/1	0	6	0	4	0	90/11	16	0	0
Peacock	Frank E	HB	1964-65	1	5	0	0	0	0	0	0	0	5	0	0	0
Pearson	Albert V	HB	1925-26/1928-29	4	69	6	3	1	0	0	0	0	72	7	0	0
Pemble	Albert	GK	1905-06	1	17	0	1	0	0	0	0	0	18	0	0	0
Pendlebury	Keith D	LH	1953-54	1	2	0	0	0	0	0	0	0	2	0	0	0
Pennington	John	GK	1928-29	1	6	0	0	0	0	0	0	0	6	0	0	0
Percival*	John	RH	1940-41/1941-42	2	0	0	0	0	0	0	0	0	0	0	41	4
Perrins	George	HB	1901-02/1904-05	2	29	0	3	0	0	0	0	0	32	0	1	0
Perry	G	OR	1891-92/1893-94	3	0	0	7	1	0	0	0	0	7	1	52	15
Phillips	Trevor	F	1981-82/1982-93	2	49/2	13	1	0	2	0	0	0	52/2	13	0	0
Phoenix	Peter P	OL	1964-65	1	19	1	6	0	0	0	0	0	25	1	0	0
Pick	William E	OL	1933-34	1	1	0	0	0	0	0	0	0	1	0	1	0
Pickering	Michael J	D	1987-88/1988-89	2	15/1	0	2	0	0	0	2	0	19/1	0	0	0
Pickford	Percy	HB	1899-00/1902-03	4	59	1	6	0	0	0	0	0	65	1	0	0
Pilkington	George	RH	1953-54/1955-56	3	77	4	5	0	0	0	0	0	82	4	0	0
Pimblett	Frank	F	1976-77	1	0/1	0	0	0	0	0	0	0	0/1	0	0	0
Pixton	Thomas	HB	1891-92	1	0	0	0	0	0	0	0	0	0	0	3	0
Platts	Laurence	GK	1952-53/1953-54	2	28	0	0	0	0	0	0	0	28	0	0	0
Pollitt	J	OL	1939-40	1	0	0	0	0	0	0	0	0	0	0	1	0
Pollock	William	OL	1935-36	1	7	0	0	0	0	0	0	1	0	8	0	0
Porteous	Trevor	HB	1956-57/1964-65	9	337	9	21	0	6	0	0	0	364	9	0	0
Porter	Thomas Chris	IF	1905-06/1908-09	4	66	23	2	0	0	0	0	0	68	23	0	0
Poskett	Malcolm	F	1985-86	1	8	1	0	0	0	0	0	0	8	1	0	0
Power	Michael D	F	1980-81/1985-86	6	67/4	16	2	0	0/1	0	3	0	72/5	16	0	0
Preece	Andrew	F	1991-92/1993-94	3	89/7	42	7	3	2/1	0	12/2	9	110/10	54	0	0
Prentis	John	D	1966-67/1967-68	2	16/3	0	3	0	0	0	0	0	19/3	0	0	0
Preston	Stephen	CF	1902-03	1	11	2	0	0	0	0	0	0	11	2	0	0
Price	Edward	GK	1909-10	2	34	0	3	0	0	0	0	0	37	0	0	0
Price	J Leonard	IF	1903-04/1904-05	2	11	1	2	2	0	0	0	0	13	3	8	1
Price	John	OL	1965-66/1975-76	10(2)	292/20	24	17/1	1	15	2	0	0	324/21	27	0	0
Pritchard	Thomas F	CF	1925-26	1	2	0	0	0	0	0	0	0	2	0	0	0
Proctor	Benjamin	OR	1913-14/1914-15	2	37	6	1	0	0	0	0	0	38	6	0	0

Surname	First names	Pos	Seasons played First/Last	No	League App	League Gls	FA Cup App	FA Cup Gls	Lge Cup App	Lge Cup Gls	Divisional App	Divisional Gls	TOTAL App	TOTAL Gls	Other App	Other Gls
Proudfoot	Peter	CH	1908-09/1912-13	3(2)	45	1	3	0	0	0	0	0	48	1	0	0
Prout	Richard	CF	1910-11/1912-13	3	59	19	3	0	0	0	0	0	62	19	0	0
Prudham	C Edward	F	1977-78/1979-80	3	80/7	22	3/1	2	4	0	0	0	87/8	24	0	0
Pugh		IF	1898-99	1	0	0	0	0	0	0	0	0	0	0	3	0
Purcell	George	IF	1922-23/1923-24	2	20	4	1	0	0	0	0	0	21	4	0	0
Quinn	James	F	1993-94	1	0/1	0	0	0	0	0	0	0	0/1	0	0	0
Quinn	Michael	F	1982-83/1983-84	2	62/1	39	2	0	5	2	0	0	69/1	41	0	0
Quirk	Albert C	IR	1944-45	1	0	0	0	0	0	0	0	0	0	0	1	0
Quixall	Albert	M	1966-67	1	13	0	0	0	1	0	0	0	14	0	0	0
Raby	Joseph	IL	1902-03/1903-04	2	52	12	3	1	0	0	0	0	55	13	0	0
Rainford	J	IL	1918-19	1	0	0	0	0	0	0	0	0	0	0	1	0
Raisbeck	Leslie	IF	1928-29/1931-32	2(2)	2	0	1	0	0	0	0	0	3	0	0	0
Ramage		FB	1891-92	1	0	0	0	0	0	0	0	0	0	0	2	0
Ramscar	Frederick	IL	1942-43	1	0	0	0	0	0	0	0	0	0	0	1	0
Ramsden	Charles W	OR	1927-28	1	21	9	0	0	0	0	0	0	21	9	0	0
Ratcliffe	Raymond	RH	1948-49	1	1	0	0	0	0	0	0	0	1	0	1	0
Rathbone	H	HB	1902-03	1	6	0	0	0	0	0	0	0	6	0	0	0
Rathbone	Matthew	OR	1930-31	1	2	0	0	0	0	0	0	0	2	0	0	0
Rawcliffe*	Frank	IL	1943-44	1	0	0	0	0	0	0	0	0	0	0	2	2
Rawlings*	James SD	OR	1945-46	1	0	0	0	0	0	0	0	0	0	0	1	0
Ray	Richard	FB	1903-04	1	34	0	2	0	0	0	0	0	36	0	0	0
Raynes	William	M	1984-85	1	2	0	0	0	0	0	1	0	3	0	0	0
Read	Thomas	GK	1926-27	1	11	0	0	0	0	0	0	0	11	0	0	0
Redfern	David	GK	1989-90/1992-93	4	48	0	1	0	2	0	2	0	53	0	0	0
Redfern	Fred	RB	1942-43/1947-48	6	36	0	6	0	0	0	0	0	42	0	103	1
Reece*	Thomas J	LH	1943-44	1	0	0	0	0	0	0	0	0	0	0	18	2
Reid	Frank J	OL	1949-50/1950-51	2	23	0	2	0	0	0	0	0	25	0	0	0
Reid	George H	IL	1924-25	1	11	3	0	0	0	0	0	0	11	3	0	0
Reid	James	OR	1958-59	1	11	2	0	0	0	0	0	0	11	2	0	0
Reid‡	John Douglas	HB	1936-37/1945-46	8	84	23	6	1	0	0	1	2	91	26	38	23
Reid	Joseph	FB	1920-21/1925-26	6	145	1	3	0	0	0	0	0	148	1	0	0
Renwick	Richard	D	1971-72	1	30	1	2	0	0	0	0	0	32	1	0	0
Reynolds	J	HB	1903-04	1	1	0	0	0	0	0	0	0	1	0	0	0
Rice	Arthur	IL	1936-37/1937-38	2	15	0	0	0	0	0	1	0	16	0	0	0
Rich‡	Leonard	OL	1939-40/1945-46	2	0	0	1	0	0	0	0	0	1	0	2	0
Richardson	R	IL	1942-43	1	0	0	0	0	0	0	0	0	0	0	1	0
Richardson	William	RB	1921-22/1925-26	5	159	0	6	0	0	0	0	0	165	0	0	0
Richardson	William	GK	1929-30/1930-31	2	41	0	0	0	0	0	0	0	41	0	0	0
Rickards	Charles J	IF	1945-46	1	0	0	0	0	0	0	0	0	0	0	36	16
Ricketts	Graham A	LH	1961-62/1963-64	3	119	6	2	0	2	0	0	0	123	6	0	0
Ridgway	Frederick	IF	1940-41/1944-45	4	0	0	0	0	0	0	0	0	0	0	21	3
Rigby		FB	1895-96	1	0	0	0	0	0	0	0	0	0	0	1	0
Rigby	E	OL	1918-19	1	0	0	0	0	0	0	0	0	0	0	3	0
Rigby‡	Walter	GK	1937-38/1945-46	6	11	0	0	0	0	0	0	0	11	0	54	0
Rigby	William	OR	1931-32	1	3	0	0	0	0	0	0	0	3	0	0	0
Ritchie	David M	F	1989-90	1	0/1	0	0	0	0	0	0	0	0/1	0	0	0
Ritchie	William S	CF	1958-59/1960-61	3	52	12	1	1	1	0	0	0	54	13	0	0
Roberts		OR	1891-92	1	0	0	0	0	0	0	0	0	0	0	1	0
Roberts	Thomas	OL	1964-65/1965-66	2	20	0	0	0	0	0	0	0	20	0	0	0
Roberts	Walter	OR	1905-06	1	3	0	0	0	0	0	0	0	3	0	0	0
Robertson		IL	1895-96	1	0	0	1	0	0	0	0	0	1	0	1	0
Robertson	Paul	D	1989-90/1990-91	2	7/3	0	0	0	3	0	3	0	13/3	0	0	0
Robinson	A	IF	1905-06/1906-07	2	20	3	0	0	0	0	0	0	20	3	0	0
Robinson	Charles	RH	1932-33/1935-36	4	115	11	10	0	0	0	9	0	134	11	0	0
Robinson	Leslie	M	1986-87/1987-88	2	67	3	4	0	2	0	4	0	77	3	0	0
Robinson‡	William	OL	1942-43/1949-50	2	9	2	0	0	0	0	0	0	9	2	2	0
Robson	Thomas	FB	1914-15/1922-23	9	93	0	1	0	0	0	0	0	94	0	69	0
Rodgers	Norman	CF	1911-12/1919-20	9	156	72	8	4	0	0	0	0	164	76	115	70
Rogan	L Michael	GK	1977-78/1980-81	4	73	0	6	0	5	0	0	0	84	0	0	0
Rooke	William	HB	1903-04	1	16	0	0	0	0	0	0	0	16	0	0	0
Rosbotham	Arthur	IF	1920-21/1921-22	2	21	2	0	0	0	0	0	0	21	2	0	0
Ross		LB	1891-92	1	0	0	0	0	0	0	0	0	0	0	1	0
Ross	Robert A	RB	1954-55	1	9	0	0	0	0	0	0	0	9	0	0	0
Rourke	James	CH	1911-12	1	12	0	3	0	0	0	0	0	15	0	0	0
Rowland	Leonard C	FB	1952-53/1956-57	5	61	0	3	0	0	0	0	0	64	0	0	0
Rowlands	John H	F	1969-70/1970-71	2	45/1	11	4	1	1	0	0	0	50/1	12	0	0
Russell	Malcolm	M	1972-73	1	11	0	0	0	5	2	0	0	16	2	0	0
Russell	Robert	CH	1911-12	1	27	0	1	0	0	0	0	0	28	0	0	0
Rutter	John T	D	1976-77/1985-86	10	400/2	9	16	0	29	0	4	0	449/2	9	0	0
Ryan	Darren	M	1992-93/*	2	29/7	6	1/1	0	2	1	5/1	0	37/9	7	0	0
Ryan	John G	M	1983-84	1	1/1	0	0	0	2	0	0	0	3/1	0	0	0

Surname	First names	Pos	Seasons played First/Last	No	League App	Gls	FA Cup App	Gls	Lge Cup App	Gls	Divisional App	Gls	TOTAL App	Gls	Other App	Gls
Ryden	Hugh	F	1963-64/1972-73	5(2)	150/11	24	5/1	0	6/2	1	0	0	161/14	25	0	0
Saer		GK	1899-00	1	0	0	0	0	0	0	0	0	0	0	2	0
Salmon	Michael B	GK	1983-84/1985-86	3	118	0	3	0	10	0	3	0	134	0	0	0
Sambrook	James M	IF	1923-24	1	17	4	2	1	0	0	0	0	19	5	0	0
Samuels	Leslie	IF	1957-58/1958-59	2	25	5	0	0	0	0	0	0	25	5	0	0
Sanaghan	Joseph	LB	1949-50/1950-51	2	52	0	5	0	0	0	0	0	57	0	0	0
Sanders*	Robert M	RB	1939-40	1	0	0	0	0	0	0	0	0	0	0	1	0
Sanderson	Frederick C	LH	1926-27	1	2	0	0	0	0	0	0	0	2	0	0	0
Sandiford	Ian R	CF	1964-65/1965-66	2	47	9	6	1	1	0	0	0	54	10	0	0
Sargeant	Charles	OL	1937-38/1938-39	2	49	19	5	6	0	0	0	0	54	25	0	0
Sawyers	Thomas	OR	1895-96	1	0	0	0	0	0	0	0	0	0	0	3	1
Scales*	George	GK	1942-43	1	0	0	0	0	0	0	0	0	0	0	5	0
Schofield	Gary P	M	1977-78	1	0/1	0	0	0	0	0	0	0	0/1	0	0	0
Schofield	Joseph	OR	1905-06	1	33	3	3	1	0	0	0	0	36	4	0	0
Scholes	John	IL	1943-44	1	0	0	0	0	0	0	0	0	0	0	1	0
Scotson	James	IF	1903-04	1	6	0	2	1	0	0	0	0	8	1	0	0
Scott	Alexander	OL	1934-35	5	11	6	1	0	0	0	1	0	13	6	19	3
Scott	Ian R	D	1987-88/1988-89	2	23/2	0	1	0	0/1	0	1/1	0	25/4	0	0	0
Scott	William J	RB	1935-36	1	11	0	1	0	0	0	0	0	12	0	0	0
Scullion	James P	OL	1927-28/1931-32	2(2)	33	10	0	0	0	0	0	0	33	10	0	0
Scurr	Thomas W	OL	1925-26/1927-28	3	61	10	3	2	0	0	0	0	64	12	0	0
Seabrook	Arthur	OR	1929-30	1	3	1	0	0	0	0	0	0	3	1	0	0
Seagrave	John W	CH	1939-40	1	0	0	0	0	0	0	0	0	0	0	2	0
Seale		HB	1899-1900	1	0	0	2	0	0	0	0	0	2	0	2	0
Seddon	Andrew J	D	1981-82/1982-83	2	3	0	0	0	0	0	0	0	3	0	0	0
Seddon	Harry	IF	1942-43/1943-44	2	0	0	0	0	0	0	0	0	0	0	12	1
Seddon	Ian W	M	1975-76/1978-79	2	5/3	0	0	0	0	0	0	0	5/3	0	0	0
Seemley	Ivor J	LB	1955-56/1956-57	2	81	0	2	0	0	0	0	0	83	0	0	0
Self*	Edward R	IF	1940-41	1	0	0	0	0	0	0	0	0	0	0	2	1
Sertori	Mark E	F	1986-87/1987-88	2	3/1	0	0	0	1	0	0	0	4/1	0	0	0
Settle	James	IL	1908-09	1	26	2	3	0	0	0	0	0	29	2	0	0
Shanks	Robert	FB	1931-32	1	13	1	0	0	0	0	0	0	13	1	0	0
Shannon	David L	F	1973-74	1	3/1	1	0	0	0	0	0	0	3/1	1	0	0
Sharpley	Herbert	HB	1900-01/1903-04	4	37	3	1	0	0	0	0	0	38	3	0	0
Shaw	Kenneth	OL	1941-42/1947-48	7	41	8	10	3	0	0	0	0	51	11	131	48
Shawcross	Francis David	LH	1965-66/1966-67	2	59/1	14	3	1	1	0	0	0	63/1	15	0	0
Shawcross	Kenneth	OR	1941-42/1944-45	2	0	0	0	0	0	0	0	0	0	0	8	2
Shelton	Walter	LH	1920-21	1	3	1	0	0	0	0	0	0	3	1	0	0
Shepherd	George	IF	1943-44	1	0	0	0	0	0	0	0	0	0	0	2	1
Shepherd	Wayne D	GK	1989-90	1	0	0	0	0	0	0	1	0	1	0	0	0
Sherlock	Stephen E	D	1979-80/1985-86	7	236/9	7	6	0	19/1	1	2	0	263/10	8	0	0
Sherwood	George W	IF	1938-39/1945-46	3	39	10	4	0	0	0	0	0	43	10	5	0
Siddall	Barry	GK	1989-90	1	21	0	2	0	4	0	2	0	29	0	0	0
Silto	N	CH	1917-18	1	0	0	0	0	0	0	0	0	0	0	3	1
Simmons	Harvey V	OR	1930-31	1	2	0	0	0	0	0	0	0	2	0	2	0
Simms	Ernest	CF	1923-24/1925-26	3	66	20	2	1	0	0	0	0	68	21	0	0
Simms	S	CF	1916-17	1	0	0	0	0	0	0	0	0	0	0	2	0
Simpson*	Jimmy	LH	1943-44	1	0	0	0	0	0	0	0	0	0	0	1	0
Simpson	Robert	LB	1917-18	1	0	0	0	0	0	0	0	0	0	0	1	0
Singleton	Bertram Harry	OL	1899-00/1900-01	2	1	0	0	0	0	0	0	0	1	0	3	2
Slack	Robert C	OR	1958-59	1	8	1	0	0	0	0	0	0	8	1	0	0
Smailes	James	OL	1936-37/1937-38	2	63	17	2	0	0	0	1	0	66	17	0	0
Smith	Charles A	GK	1960-61	1	6	0	0	0	0	0	0	0	6	0	0	0
Smith	David B	M	1973-74	1	7/1	0	0	0	0	0	0	0	7/1	0	0	0
Smith	Fred	OR	1931-32	1	16	1	1	1	0	0	0	0	17	2	0	0
Smith	Frederick	FB	1906-07/1908-09	3	27	0	0	0	0	0	0	0	27	0	0	0
Smith	Frederick	CF	1911-12/1918-19	3	48	19	1	0	0	0	0	0	49	19	1	0
Smith	G	IF	1891-92/1896-97	6	0	0	8	4	0	0	0	0	8	4	102	39
Smith	George Rowley	IF	1904-05/1906-07	2	1	1	0	0	0	0	0	0	1	1	1	0
Smith	Graham L	D	1974-75/1978-79	5	147/4	2	6	0	3	0	0	0	156/4	2	0	0
Smith	Harry	FB	1898-99	1	0	0	0	0	0	0	0	0	0	0	5	0
Smith	James AG	D	1969-70/1970-71	2	78	2	5	0	1	0	0	0	84	2	0	0
Smith	John R	CF	1931-32	1	1	1	0	0	0	0	0	0	1	1	0	0
Smith	Joseph	CF	1926-27/1928-29	3	70	61	3	2	0	0	0	0	73	63	0	0
Smith	Joseph Barry	CF	1958-59	1	17	4	3	0	0	0	0	0	20	4	0	0
Smith	Nigel G	D	1980-81/1985-86	6	118/5	1	2	1	7	0	2/1	0	129/6	2	0	0
Smith	Paul M	F	1985-86	1	7	5	0	0	2	1	0	0	9	6	0	0
Smith	Samuel	FB	1901-02	1	30	0	2	0	0	0	0	0	32	0	0	0
Smith	Wilfred	IF	1957-58/1959-60	3	6	1	0	0	0	0	0	0	6	1	0	0
Smith	William	IF	1900-01	1	25	2	2	0	0	0	0	0	27	2	0	0
Smith	William	CH	1934-35/1936-37	3	3	0	0	0	0	0	1	0	4	0	0	0

Surname	First names	Pos	Seasons played First/Last	No	League App	League Gls	FA Cup App	FA Cup Gls	Lge Cup App	Lge Cup Gls	Divisional App	Divisional Gls	TOTAL App	TOTAL Gls	Other App	Other Gls
Smith	William H	FB	1938-39/1939-40	2	34	0	4	0	0	0	0	0	38	0	0	0
Sowden	William	CF	1957-58	1	15	7	1	1	0	0	0	0	16	8	0	0
Spencer	Frank	CF	1942-43	1	0	0	0	0	0	0	0	0	0	0	1	0
Spencer	Jimmy	LH	1894-95/1895-96	2	0	0	2	0	0	0	0	0	2	0	49	4
Spratt	Thomas	M	1972-73/1973-74	2	65	6	4	1	9	1	0	0	78	8	0	0
Stafford	Andrew	M	1981-82	1	21/4	1	0	0	2	0	0	0	23/4	1	0	0
Stainsby	John	IF	1963-64	1	5	0	0	0	0	0	0	0	5	0	0	0
Stainwright	H	IF	1918-19	1	0	0	0	0	0	0	0	0	0	0	3	0
Stanger	John	OR	1934-35/1935-36	2	14	2	1	0	0	0	2	0	17	2	0	0
Staniforth	Ronald	RB	1946-47/1951-52	6	223	1	22	0	0	0	0	0	245	1	0	0
Stansfield	Harold	OR	1900-01/1903-04	3	88	11	3	3	0	0	0	0	91	14	0	0
Stapleton	John R	M	1988-89	1	1	0	0	0	0	0	0	0	1	0	0	0
Steele	Edward C	CH	1941-42/1945-46	3	0	0	0	0	0	0	0	0	0	0	42	1
Steele	Gilbert	CF	1921-22	1	15	4	0	0	0	0	0	0	15	4	0	0
Stentiford	George R	HB	1924-25/1925-26	2	43	0	2	0	0	0	0	0	45	0	0	0
Stevens	George Leo	CF	1936-37/1937-38	2	28	9	0	0	0	0	2	1	30	10	0	0
Stevens	Ian D	M	1986-87	1	1/1	0	0/1	0	0	0	0/1	0	1/3	0	0	0
Stevens	J	RB	1940-41	1	0	0	0	0	0	0	0	0	0	0	1	0
Stevens	John	CH	1932-33/1933-34	2	66	0	2	0	0	0	4	0	72	0	0	0
Stevenson	James	IF	1932-33/1944-45	5	97	38	7	2	0	0	6	3	110	43	1	0
Still	Robert Arthur	LH	1934-35/1938-39	5	155	2	15	1	0	0	5	0	175	3	0	0
Stock	Harry	IF	1938-39/1947-48	4	19	5	6	2	0	0	0	0	25	7	9	1
Stokes	Tom	IL	1906-07	1	1	0	0	0	0	0	0	0	1	0	0	0
Stokes	Wayne D	D	1986-87	1	17/1	1	1	0	0	0	2	0	20/1	1	0	0
Stringfellow	A	IL	1917-18	1	0	0	0	0	0	0	0	0	0	0	1	0
Stuart	Alex	IL	1942-43/1943-44	2	0	0	0	0	0	0	0	0	0	0	2	1
Stuart*	Douglas	OL	1943-44	1	0	0	0	0	0	0	0	0	0	0	1	0
Stuart	Edward A	D	1966-67/1967-68	2	77	1	4	0	0	0	0	0	81	1	0	0
Suart‡	Robert	HB	1903-04/1917-18	8(2)	109	9	10	0	0	0	0	0	119	9	55	5
Sullivan	Leslie G	OL	1939-40	1	0	0	0	0	0	0	0	0	0	0	5	0
Sullivan	William	OL	1935-36/1939-40	4	27	8	1	0	0	0	2	2	30	10	2	2
Summerbee	Michael G	M	1977-78/1979-80	3	86/1	6	6	1	7/1	0	0	0	99/2	7	0	0
Sumner	Alan	F	1978-79	1	3/2	0	0	0	0	0	0	0	3/2	0	0	0
Sunley	David	F	1979-80/1981-82	3	79/4	7	2/1	1	5	3	0	0	86/5	10	0	0
Sutcliffe	Peter D	M	1975-76/1983-84	3(2)	19/9	2	0/1	0	0	0	0	0	19/10	2	0	0
Sutherland		CF	1895-96	1	0	0	2	1	0	0	0	0	2	1	13	8
Swan	Christopher	IR	1923-24/1924-25	2	32	4	1	0	0	0	0	0	33	4	0	0
Swann	Andrew	CF	1901-02	1	14	4	0	0	0	0	0	0	14	4	0	0
Swannell	John	GK	1959-60	1	1	0	0	0	0	0	0	0	1	0	0	0
Sweeney*	Frederick J	IL	1942-43	1	0	0	0	0	0	0	0	0	0	0	1	0
Swift	Webster	CF	1931-32	1	3	1	0	0	0	0	0	0	3	1	0	0
Swindells	Herbert	CF	1942-43/1943-44	2	0	0	0	0	0	0	0	0	0	0	17	9
Swinscoe	Thomas W	CF	1947-48/1949-50	3	72	31	9	1	0	0	0	0	81	32	0	0
Sword	Thomas W	F/D	1979-80/1987-88	9(2)	242/3	52	6	0	16	3	3	0	267/3	55	0	0
Sykes	Norman AJ	CH	1965-66/1966-67	2	52	7	6	1	1	0	0	0	59	8	0	0
Tabram		IL	1943-44	1	0	0	0	0	0	0	0	0	0	0	7	1
Tagg*	Ernest	IF	1941-42	1	0	0	0	0	0	0	0	0	0	0	3	0
Talbot		RH	1891-92	1	0	0	0	0	0	0	0	0	0	0	1	0
Talbot*	Frank L	IF	1943-44	1	0	0	0	0	0	0	0	0	0	0	20	6
Tarbuck	F	LB	1921-22	1	1	0	0	0	0	0	0	0	1	0	0	0
Tattersall	Harold	RH	1912-13/1913-14	2	34	0	3	0	0	0	0	0	37	0	0	0
Taylor	Alan	GK	1970-71	1	5	0	0	0	1	0	0	0	6	0	0	0
Taylor	Harold W	HB	1933-34/1934-35	2	9	0	0	0	0	0	3	2	12	2	0	0
Taylor	Jacob	HB	1930-31/1935-36	6	80	10	4	2	0	0	6	0	90	12	0	0
Taylor	John L	GK	1975-76	1	1	0	0	0	0	0	0	0	1	0	0	0
Taylor	Joseph	IF	1936-37/1937-38	2	19	4	1	0	0	0	0	0	20	4	0	0
Taylor	Samuel	RH	1917-18	1	0	0	0	0	0	0	0	0	0	0	2	0
Taylor	Steven J	F	1983-84/1984-85	2	26	8	1	1	4	2	0	0	31	11	0	0
Taylor	Tom	OL	1940-41	1	0	0	0	0	0	0	0	0	0	0	8	1
Thomas	John W	OR	1954-55	1	6	0	0	0	0	0	0	0	6	0	0	0
Thompson	Alan W	D	1976-77/1978-79	3	93/1	17	6	0	9	1	0	0	108/1	18	0	0
Ttompson	E	RH	1917-18	1	0	0	0	0	0	0	0	0	0	0	1	0
Thompson	John E	CF	1920-21	1	6	2	0	0	0	0	0	0	6	2	0	0
Thompson*	Alex	IF	1943-44	1	0	0	0	0	0	0	0	0	0	0	1	0
Thomson	Robert Gillies	D	1967-68	1	16/1	0	0	0	0	0	0	0	16/1	0	0	0
Thorpe	Andrew	D	1977-78/1991-92	14(2)	484/5	3	14	0	32/1	0	18/1	2	548/7	5	0	0
Tidman	Oliver E	OL	1935-36	1	24	4	0	0	0	0	1	0	25	4	0	0
Tillotson	Maurice	FB	1964-65/1965-66	2	35	0	1	0	1	0	0	0	37	0	0	0
Titterington	William	IF	1934-35/1943-44	10	113	11	4	0	0	0	0	0	117	11	57	5
Todd	Lee	M/D	1990-91/*	4	96/9	0	9	2	6/1	0	22/1	0	133/11	2	0	0
Toman	Wilfred	CF	1903-04	1	5	1	0	0	0	0	0	0	5	1	0	0

Surname	First names	Pos	Seasons played First/Last	No	League App	Gls	FA Cup App	Gls	Lge Cup App	Gls	Divisional App	Gls	TOTAL App	Gls	Other App	Gls
Tomkinson	GE	IR	1902-03	1	3	1	1	0	0	0	0	0	4	1	0	0
Tompkinson	William V	OR	1928-29/1929-30	2	76	26	6	1	0	0	0	0	82	27	0	0
Toms	William	IF	1923-24	1	5	1	0	0	0	0	0	0	5	1	0	0
Topping*	Harry	RB	1941-42	1	0	0	0	0	0	0	0	0	0	0	17	0
Topping	Henry W	FB	1938-39/1945-46	7	3	0	1	0	0	0	0	0	4	0	82	0
Torbet	John	OL	1935-36	1	6	1	0	0	0	0	0	0	6	1	0	0
Toseland*	Ernest	OR	1939-40/1941-42	3	0	0	0	0	0	0	0	0	0	0	45	4
Townsend	Alfred H	OL	1928-29	1	7	0	0	0	0	0	0	0	7	0	0	0
Trentham*	Douglas H	OL	1945-46	1	0	0	0	0	0	0	0	0	0	0	4	1
Trevis	Derek	D	1973-74	1	33/2	2	1	0	2	1	0	0	36/2	3	0	0
Trotter		CH	1899-00	1	0	0	0	0	0	0	0	0	0	0	3	0
Trotter	George	OR	1911-12/1912-13	2	15	1	2	0	0	0	0	0	17	1	0	0
Turner		CH	1904-05	1	0	0	0	0	0	0	0	0	0	0	2	0
Turner	Cecil	LH	1928-29	1	1	0	0	0	0	0	0	0	1	0	0	0
Turner	John A	GK	1926-27/1927-28	2	38	0	0	0	0	0	0	0	38	0	0	0
Turner	Joseph	GK	1954-55/1956-57	3	79	0	1	0	0	0	0	0	80	0	0	0
Turner	Mark B	D	1975-76	1	8	0	1	0	0	0	0	0	9	0	0	0
Tutty	Paul	M	1970-71	1	1	0	0	0	0	0	0	0	1	0	0	0
Upton	William	RH	1891-92/1894-95	4	0	0	8	1	0	0	0	0	8	1	68	5
Urmston	Thomas	GK	1891-92/1895-96	2(2)	0	0	1	0	0	0	0	0	1	0	61	0
Urwin	Joseph S	CF	1934-35	1	6	2	5	1	0	0	0	0	11	3	0	0
Uzelac	Stephen	D	1979-80/1981-82	3	31	2	2	0	7	0	0	0	40	2	0	0
Vairy	Roy H	GK	1956-57	1	5	0	0	0	0	0	0	0	5	0	0	0
Vaughan	Ian	D	1981-82	1	2	1	1	0	0	0	0	0	3	1	0	0
Vennard	Walter	HB	1947-48	1	5	0	0	0	0	0	0	0	5	0	0	0
Vernon	John E	F	1974-75/1975-76	2	4/2	0	0	0	0	0	0	0	4/2	0	0	0
Vincent‡	Norman E	FB	1928-29/1941-42	7	132	20	7	2	0	0	4	1	143	23	2	0
Vose*	George	CH	1942-43	1	0	0	0	0	0	0	0	0	0	0	7	0
Wainwright	H James	LB	1895-96/1900-01	6	29	0	16	0	0	0	0	0	45	0	129	0
Waites	Sydney H	OR	1928-29	1	2	0	0	0	0	0	0	0	2	0	0	0
Walker	Gary	GK	1985-86/1986-87	2	29	0	1	0	2	0	4	0	36	0	0	0
Walker	Michael J	F	1970-71	1	1/1	0	0	0	0/1	0	0	0	1/2	0	0	0
Walker	Victor	HB	1946-47/1949-50	4	94	10	13	1	0	0	0	0	107	11	0	0
Walker	William	IF	1919-20	1	6	3	1	0	0	0	0	0	7	3	0	0
Walker	Willis	GK	1926-27	1	19	0	1	0	0	0	0	0	20	0	0	0
Wallace	Clive L	IF	1959-60	1	13	4	1	0	0	0	0	0	14	4	0	0
Wallace	Michael	M/D	1992-93/*	2	41/4	3	3/1	1	2	0	9/3	0	55/8	4	0	0
Wallwork	RT	OR	1902-03/1903-04	2	7	1	2	0	0	0	0	0	9	1	0	0
Wallwork	Jack	OR	1891-92	1	0	0	0	0	0	0	0	0	0	0	13	0
Walmsley	Albert	RH	1920-21/1922-23	3	80	3	2	0	0	0	0	0	82	3	0	0
Walsh	James Arthur	IR	1920-21/1921-22	2	38	5	2	0	0	0	0	0	40	5	0	0
Walton	William E	LB	1936-37	1	0	0	0	0	0	0	1	0	1	0	0	0
Ward	Denis	GK	1949-50/1952-53	4	52	0	2	0	0	0	0	0	54	0	0	0
Ward	Derek	OR	1961-62/1963-64	3	81	21	2	0	1	0	0	0	84	21	0	0
Ward	Michael H	IR	1948-49	1	1	0	0	0	0	0	0	0	1	0	0	0
Ward	Peter	M	1991-92/*	3	113/1	7	6	0	5	0	25	5	149/1	12	0	0
Ward	Ronald	IF	1953-54/1954-55	3	17	3	0	0	0	0	0	0	17	3	0	0
Wardrobe	Michael	F	1981-82/1982-83	2	19/8	2	0	0	2	0	0	0	21/8	2	0	0
Waring*	Jack	OL	1944-45	1	0	0	0	0	0	0	0	0	0	0	1	0
Warren	George	CF	1911-12	1	3	0	0	0	0	0	0	0	3	0	0	0
Wassall	John V	IF	1946-47/1947-48	2	19	2	1	0	0	0	0	0	20	2	0	0
Waterall	Albert	HB	1913-14/1925-26	13	290	35	10	1	0	0	0	0	300	36	97	9
Waterall	Tommy	OL	1915-16/1917-18	3	0	0	0	0	0	0	0	0	0	0	87	12
Waters	Arthur	FB	1904-05/1910-11	7	158	8	16	0	0	0	0	0	174	8	27	1
Watson	Frederick	IF	1940-41/1941-42	2	0	0	0	0	0	0	0	0	0	0	20	16
Watson	Harry	IR	1932-33	1	1	0	0	0	0	0	0	0	1	0	0	0
Watt	John	OR	1963-64/1964-65	2	55	4	5	0	2	0	0	0	62	4	0	0
Watters	John	OR	1944-45/1947-48	2	5	1	0	0	0	0	0	0	5	1	13	1
Weaver‡	Samuel	IL	1945-46/1946-47	2	2	0	0	0	0	0	0	0	2	0	23	6
Webb	William	LB	1957-58/1962-63	6	243	0	16	0	3	0	0	0	262	0	0	0
Webber	Keith	F	1971-72	1	36/4	7	2	0	2	0	0	0	40/4	7	0	0
Webster	William T	OL	1930-31/1931-32	2	73	17	3	1	0	0	0	0	76	18	0	0
Weigh	Raymond E	OL	1951-52/1953-54	3	75	29	3	2	0	0	0	0	78	31	0	0
Weir	Alex	LH	1909-10	1	1	0	0	0	0	0	0	0	1	0	0	0
Welsby	Arthur	CF	1934-35	1	4	2	4	0	0	0	0	0	8	2	0	0
West	George	IF	1921-22	1	3	0	0	0	0	0	0	0	3	0	0	0
West	Thomas	CF	1937-38/1938-39	2	3	1	0	0	0	0	0	0	3	1	0	0
Wharton	Arthur	GK	1901-02	1	6	0	0	0	0	0	0	0	6	0	0	0
Whatley*	William J	RB	1942-43	1	0	0	0	0	0	0	0	0	0	0	6	0
Wheatley*	Joseph	LH	1944-45	1	0	0	0	0	0	0	0	0	0	0	1	0
Wheeler	Paul	F	1991-92/1992-93	2	13/10	5	1	0	0/2	1	6/4	1	20/16	7	0	0

Surname	First names	Pos	Seasons played First/Last	No	League App	Gls	FA Cup App	Gls	Lge Cup App	Gls	Divisional App	Gls	TOTAL App	Gls	Other App	Gls
Whitcombe	George C	CH	1925-26	1	15	0	0	0	0	0	0	0	15	0	0	0
White	E Winston	M	1983-84	1	4	0	1	0	0	0	0	0	5	0	0	0
White	Fred	IL	1923-24/1924-25	2	9	1	0	0	0	0	0	0	9	1	0	0
White	Leonard R	CF	1964-65/1965-66	2	53	24	4	1	1	0	0	0	58	25	0	0
White	Thomas	OR	1906-07	1	32	1	2	0	0	0	0	0	34	1	0	0
Whitehead		OR	1893-94	1	0	0	0	0	0	0	0	0	0	0	6	2
Whitehouse	Benjamin	IF	1908-09/1910-11	3	75	21	8	4	0	0	0	0	83	25	0	0
Whitelaw	George	CF	1961-62/1962-63	2	52	18	1	0	1	0	0	0	54	18	0	0
Whitelaw	John	IF	1925-26/1927-28	2	20	5	1	0	0	0	0	0	21	5	0	0
Wilde	J	LH	1915-16	1	0	0	0	0	0	0	0	0	0	0	1	0
Wilks		IF	1897-98/1898-99	2	0	0	0	0	0	0	0	0	0	0	6	1
Wilkes	David A	D	1986-87	1	8	0	0	0	4	2	0	0	12	2	0	0
Wilkins	Leslie	IF	1933-34	1	3	1	0	0	0	0	0	0	3	1	0	0
Williams	Albert	CH	1903-04	1	6	1	0	0	0	0	0	0	6	1	0	0
Williams	Brett	D	1986-87	1	2	0	0	0	0	0	0	0	2	0	0	0
Williams	Frederick A	RB	1945-46	1	0	0	0	0	0	0	0	0	0	0	4	0
Williams	J	OL	1917-18	1	0	0	0	0	0	0	0	0	0	0	3	0
Williams	Leonard H	LB	1926-27	1	39	0	1	0	0	0	0	0	40	0	0	0
Williams	Oshor J	M	1979-80/1984-85	6	192/1	26	6	3	17	2	0	0	215/1	31	0	0
Williams	Paul A	F	1990-91/1993-94	2(2)	30/10	17	0	0	3	1	8	3	41/10	21	0	0
Williams	Paul RC	M/D	1989-90/1992-93	3	61/8	4	5	0	2	0	7/5	0	75/13	4	0	0
Williams	Thomas H	CF	1940-41	1	0	0	0	0	0	0	0	0	0	0	3	1
Williams	Thomas R	OR	1939-40/1941-42	2	0	0	0	0	0	0	0	0	0	0	2	0
Williams	William R	D	1985-86/*	9(2)	257/3	8	12	1	16	0	26	0	311/3	9	0	0
Willis	James A	D	1987-88	1	10	0	0	0	0	0	0	0	10	0	0	0
Wilmott	Gordon A	CH	1948-49/1958-59	11	205	1	14	0	0	0	0	0	219	1	0	0
Wilson		GK	1892-93	1	0	0	0	0	0	0	0	0	0	0	2	0
Wilson	Bev	D	1969-70/1973-74	5	59/2	1	2	0	3	0	0	0	64/2	1	0	0
Wilson*	Charles M	HB	1941-42/1944-45	3	0	0	0	0	0	0	0	0	0	0	28	0
Wilson	Charlie	HB	1895-96/1897-98	3	0	0	7	1	0	0	0	0	7	1	59	1
Wilson	David	LH	1916-17/1918-19	2	0	0	0	0	0	0	0	0	0	0	2	0
Wilson	Eugene	OR	1954-55/1961-62	8	223	42	14	4	2	1	0	0	239	47	0	0
Wilson	George W	FB	1934-35	1	2	0	0	0	0	0	2	0	4	0	0	0
Wilson	John T	HB	1922-23/1925-26	4	131	12	3	0	0	0	0	0	134	12	0	0
Wilson	Thomas	FB	1925-26	1	4	0	0	0	0	0	0	0	4	0	0	0
Wilson	Walter	HB	1908-09	1	6	0	0	0	0	0	0	0	6	0	0	0
Wilson	William	FB	1927-28/1929-30	3	109	1	8	0	0	0	0	0	117	1	0	0
Winstanley	L	LB	1939-40	1	0	0	0	0	0	0	0	0	0	0	1	0
Witterance		CF	1892-93	1	0	0	0	0	0	0	0	0	0	0	1	0
Wood	Norman A	IF	1913-14/1914-15	2	58	12	2	0	0	0	0	0	60	12	0	0
Woodcock	Arthur	IF	1939-40/1945-46	7	0	0	1	0	0	0	0	0	0	0	39	12
Woodcock	Wilfred	CF	1921-22/1923-24	3	75	23	2	2	0	0	0	0	77	25	0	0
Woodhouse		CF	1899-00	1	0	0	0	0	0	0	0	0	0	0	1	0
Woods	Harry	OL	1941-42	1	0	0	0	0	0	0	0	0	0	0	2	0
Woods	Maurice	D	1966-67/1967-68	2	85	2	5	0	4	0	0	0	94	2	0	0
Woodward	William	IL	1937-38	1	7	0	0	0	0	0	0	0	7	0	0	0
Worrall	A	CF	1897-98/1898-99	2	0	0	8	2	0	0	0	0	8	2	33	8
Worrall	Joseph	OL	1945-46	1	0	0	2	0	0	0	0	0	2	0	12	2
Worsley	Arthur	FB	1905-06/1906-07	2	7	0	0	0	0	0	0	0	7	0	0	0
Worsley*	Herbert	OR	1942-43/1944-45	3	0	0	0	0	0	0	0	0	0	0	65	18
Worth	Albert	OL	1907-08/1908-09	2	21	1	1	0	0	0	0	0	22	1	0	0
Worthington	Frank S	F	1987-88	1	18/1	6	2	0	0	0	0	0	20/1	6	0	0
Wright*	Frank	CF	1942-43	1	0	0	0	0	0	0	0	0	0	0	7	2
Wright	Isaac	FB	1891-92	1	0	0	0	0	0	0	0	0	0	0	17	1
Wright	Herbert M	IL	1953-54	1	1	0	0	0	0	0	0	0	1	0	0	0
Wright	Ralph	D	1971-72	1	19/2	0	2	0	1/1	0	0	0	22/3	0	0	0
Wroe	Mark	M	1984-85/1985-86	2	26/4	4	0	0	1	0	1	0	28/4	4	0	0
Wylde	Rodger J	F	1988-89	1	24/2	12	1	0	2	1	2	1	29/2	14	0	0
Wylie	John	RH	1962-63/1963-64	2	69	2	1	0	1	0	0	0	71	2	0	0
Yates		CH	1899-00	1	0	0	0	0	0	0	0	0	0	0	4	0
Yates	Stephen	D	1985-86	1	2	0	0	0	0	0	0	0	2	0	0	0
Young	Alexander	F	1968-69/1969-70	2	23	5	2	1	1	0	0	0	26	6	0	0
Young	David	CF	1921-22	1	2	0	0	0	0	0	0	0	2	0	0	0
Young	Eric R	M	1973-74	1	16	0	0	0	0	0	0	0	16	0	0	0
Young	Richard	CF	1965-66	1	27	5	1	0	1	0	0	0	29	5	0	0
Yuill	Jack G	OR	1907-08	1	1	0	0	0	0	0	0	0	1	0	1	0

Subscribers

1	Stockport County FC	60	Chris Thornhill
2	The Football Association	61	David Shasha
3	The Football League	62	Keith Brown
4	Peter Freeman	63	Daryl Richardson
5	Richard Harnwell	64	Phil Sheridan
6	Reva Freeman	65	Peter James Hayes
7	Simone Freeman	66	Harry Angel
8	Teresa Freeman	67	Shaun Hanley
9	Dr Anthony Freeman	68	David Matthews
10	Ives Crofts	69	Nigel Penn
11	Geoffrey Hawley	70	Mr I E Wilson
12	Arthur Woodcock	71	A J Fowler
13	Elizabeth Stevenson	72	Stephen Southart
14	David Woolley	73	John Horsfield
15	Sheila Paterson	74	Chris Johnson
16	Lesley Heath	75	Roy Smith
17	The Smith Family	76	Ray Drake
18	Barry Ridgway	77	Derek Hyde
19	Caroline Holland	78	Jabber Foulkes
20	Harry Beatson	79	Jonathan Hargreaves
21	Barry Roberts	80	Allan J Ward
22	Anthony J Haines	81	Kenneth Shaw
23	Carole A Perry	82	Mr Alexander Calvert
24	A A Chamley	83	Adrian Ainscough
25	Derek Longson	84	Alan Barlow
26	D M Shackley	85	John Torkington
27	Neil Lister	86	Marcus Heap
28	Andy Gosling	87	Graham Lloyd
29	Paul Kelly	88	Pam and Claire Braham
30	Dean K Williamson	89	David Waterhouse
31	Simon Hopes	90	The Late Bill Truman
32	Brian Jones	91	Sarah, Leslie & Katy Mitchell
33	Paul Greenhalgh	92	Sammy Brown
34	M A Pretty	93	Chris Hewitt
35	Peter Holland	94	John Jennison
36	Fred Garner	95	Jonny Stokkeland
37	Keith Baylis	96	David Booth
38	Mr E Leigh	97	John Henshaw
39	Kerri Dobbins	98	Alison Johnson
40	Alan Bell	99	Arthur Burrows
41	Peter Kitchen	100	Ian Watts
42	Roy Davies	101	Fingerpost Travel Club Charity Cricket Match
43	Andrew Molloy	102	Robb Dakin
44	John Powell	103	John Snellgrove
45	Tony Smith	104	Herbert Bennett
46	Brian Coyne	105	Peter Pickup
47	Bob Cole	106	Gareth A Evans
48	Michael David Flanagan	107	Gerry Taylor
49	Peter Snape MP	108	Lawrence G Cross
50	M Wharmby	109	John Canovan
51	Paul Stock	110	David Pickford
52	Stuart A Hill	111	Donald Noble
53	Kevin Ravenscroft	112	Andrew Bebbington
54	Keith Bailey	113	Mr T D Culshaw
55	Lee C Woodiwiss	114	Charles Ducker
56	Steve Murray	115	Merv Jones
57	Ian Cross	116	Mr Harry Kay
58	J A Williams	117	Mr I H Normanshire
59	Sambrook Family	118	Fred Lee